PHILIPP SPITTA

JOHANN SEBASTIAN BACH

HIS WORK AND INFLUENCE ON THE
MUSIC OF GERMANY, 1685-1750.

TRANSLATED FROM THE GERMAN BY
CLARA BELL
AND
J. A. FULLER-MAITLAND.

IN THREE VOLUMES
VOL. II

LONDON
NOVELLO & CO., LTD.

NEW YORK
DOVER PUBLICATIONS, INC.

Published in Canada by General Publishing Company, Ltd.,
30 Lesmill Road, Don Mills, Toronto, Ontario.

This Dover edition, first published in 1992, is an unabridged
republication (in three volumes) of the two-volume 1952 Dover
reprint of the Bell and Fuller–Maitland translation originally
published in three volumes by Novello & Company, Ltd., in
1889. The Bibliographical Note that appears in Volume I was
specially prepared for the Dover edition by Saul Novack.

Manufactured in the United States of America
Dover Publications, Inc., 31 East 2nd Street, Mineola, N.Y.
11501

Library of Congress Cataloging-in-Publication Data

Spitta, Philipp, 1841–1894.
    [Johann Sebastian Bach. English]
    Johann Sebastian Bach : his work and influence on the
music of Germany, 1685–1750 / Philipp Spitta ; translated
from the German by Clara Bell and J.A. Fuller-Maitland.
        p.   cm.
    Includes bibliographical references and indexes.
    ISBN 0-486-27412-8 (v. 1 : pbk.). — ISBN 0-486-27413-6
(v. 2 : pbk.). — ISBN 0-486-27414-4 (v. 3 : pbk.)
    1. Bach, Johann Sebastian, 1685–1750. 2. Bach, Johann
Sebastian, 1685–1750—Criticism and interpretation.
3. Composers—Germany—Biography. I. Title.
ML410.B1S713   1992
780'.92—dc20
[B]   92-25199
                                                 CIP
                                                 MN

CONTENTS.

BOOK IV.

CÖTHEN, 1717-1723.

BOOK V.

LEIPZIG, 1723-1734.

BOOK IV.

I.

ARRIVAL AT CÖTHEN.—DEATH OF BACH'S FIRST WIFE AND
JOURNEY TO HAMBURG IN 1720.—REINKEN.—BACH AND
HANDEL AS ORGAN-PLAYERS.

PRINCE LEOPOLD of Anhalt-Cöthen was born November 2, 1694; and, at the time when he invited Bach to his court, was at the end of his twenty-third or the beginning of his twenty-fourth year. He had entered into possession of his little dominions on the last day of the year 1715; and a few weeks later a marriage was solemnised between his sister and Prince Ernst August of Sax-Weimar, in the royal castle of Nienburg, on the Saale. This was the dower-house of his mother, Gisela Agnes, an active, energetic, and prudent woman, who had governed during Leopold's minority, and had given a careful education to the boy whom death had deprived of his father when he was ten years old. Leopold had been for some time at the "Ritter Akademie" at Berlin, to which at that time many young princes were attracted by its celebrity. Then, in October, 1710, he had set out on the usual grand tour—first to Holland and England, and then through Germany to Italy; and in the spring of 1713 he had returned, by Vienna, to Cöthen. His conspicuous musical tastes and talents had been promoted and cultivated, particularly during his stay in Italy. In Venice he was assiduous in visiting the opera-house. In Rome he attracted to himself the German composer Johann David Heinichen, and under his guidance he became familiar with the promised land of music.[1] The

---

[1] Gerber, N. L., II., col. 615, according to Hiller, Wöchentliche Nachrichten, I., p. 213. But Heinichen must have been in Rome first and afterwards in Venice. From a very slight sketch of his travels we gather that Prince Leopold was in Rome from March 2 till June 6, 1712, and then turned towards Vienna by Florence. Heinichen must have accompanied him part of the way, and have remained behind in Venice, where he composed two operas in 1713. The manuscript of the diary of his journey is in the Castle Library at Cöthen.

famous organ in Santa Maria Maggiore, at Trient—where
Handel had carried away his audience by his masterly playing a few years previously[2]—may have been played upon
before the music-loving Prince on Sundays, during the service.   He also showed an intelligent taste for pictures,
admired Michael Angelo's "Moses," and had a number of
masterpieces copied for him in the galleries of Rome.   He
had, indeed, a frank and independent nature, alive to every
impression; his information was general and sound; and,
at a later period, he laid the foundation of the library of the
castle at Cöthen.[3]

His open countenance—with a high brow and large clear
eyes, and its setting, contrary to the fashion of the time, of
long, naturally waving hair—has a most winning expression of
youthful freshness, and an unmistakable trace of his artistic
bent.   Of this Prince's deeds as a ruler there is little to be
told; but that little corresponds to the promise of the face.
The court was of the Reformed Church, as also was a large
part of the population.   His predecessor, Emanuel Leberecht,
had granted to the Lutherans the free and public exercise of
their religious observances, probably under the influence of
his wife, who was of that confession.   A Lutheran church
had been built in 1699; and, in 1711, Gisela Agnes
founded a Lutheran home and school for women and girls.
One of Leopold's first enactments was not merely to confirm, but to increase, the liberty granted by his father,
" because it was the greatest blessing when the subjects in
a country were protected in their freedom of conscience."
The results were visible in the happy and flourishing condition of the little capital and of the whole province.

The court was held on a small and modest scale; it had
never possessed a theatre, and the Reformed services did not
encourage music.   Bach had nothing to do with the organ
service in either of the three churches in the town.
Christian Ernst Rolle was Organist in the Lutheran church,

---

[2] Chrysander, Händel, I., p. 229.

[3] Joh. Christoph Krausen, Fortsetzung der Bertramischen Geschichte des
Hauses in Fürstenthums Anhalt, Part II., p. 672 (Halle, 1782).   Stenzel,
Handbuch der Anhaltischen Geschichte, p. 279 (Dessau, 1820).

and Joh. Jakob Müller held that post in the principal Reformed church until 1731.[4] He probably also undertook to serve the castle organ. It was the same here, no doubt, as at Arnstadt. Its small dimensions and compass would scarcely fit it for any use but that of playing chorales; and this amply sufficed for the requirements of the reformed service. The two manuals had together ten stops; the pedal had three.[5] Though, even in cases where Bach gives at full length the titles he bore at that time, he never calls himself "Hoforganist," it need not be inferred that he never played on this little instrument.

The strength of music there, however, lay in chamber music, and in this it is evident that the Prince himself took part. If we may judge from an inventory of the instruments in his private possession, he played not only the violin, but the viol-di-gamba and the clavier[6]; and he was also a very good bass singer. Bach himself said of him later, that he had not merely loved music, but had understood it. Under whom he studied is not known. Bach's predecessor as capellmeister was Augustin Reinhard Stricker, the same who in 1708, as chamber musician at Berlin, had composed the festival music for the marriage of the King with the Princess Sophie Louise of Mecklenburg.[7] At about this time Leopold must have been at the " Ritter Akademie " there, and the hypothesis is probably not unfounded that the connection he then formed with Stricker may have led to the composer's obtaining the

[4] Walther, *sub voce* "Rolle"; and the Cathedral Registers at Cöthen.

[5] I conclude from this that the present very dilapidated organ is the one which existed in Bach's time. From an inscription on the bellows, which have been renewed not long since, it would seem that they were constructed in 1733. It does not therefore follow that the organ itself is no older, for the bellows are often the part that first needs mending. It may very likely have been built at the time when the wing of the castle was finished in which the chapel stands. But, even if it were not so, no organ there could have been any larger than the present one, for there is not space for it. It would seem easier to believe that the chapel had no organ until 1733.

[6] This inventory, which his brother and successor, August Ludwig, entered under April 20, 1733, is in the ducal archives of Cöthen. See also Gerber, op. cit.

[7] Walther, Lexicon.

post of capellmeister at Cöthen. Afterwards in Italy, and later still by a renewal of his intercourse with his capellmeister, he sought to cultivate still farther his taste in music, and Stricker was in his service as early as 1714. However, to judge from all that we can learn concerning his labours as a composer, Stricker was more devoted to vocal than to instrumental music, and this no doubt is the reason of his having soon left Cöthen, for that place had but small vocal resources. Mattheson has preserved the memory of two young singers—two *Demoiselles de Monjou*—from Cöthen, who sang at Berlin in July, 1722, before the Queen of Prussia, and then retired to their native town. "The younger," we are told, "had a fine clear voice and great perfection in music." It is said they both went to Hamburg, and were there engaged in the opera.[8] There must also have been among the cantors and teachers in the town some good bass to be found, and probably also a tenor, but of any regular vocal band or trained chorus like that at Weimar we find not the smallest trace. If there had been, Bach would not have failed to avail himself of it in composing his birthday serenade for the Prince.

Among the members of the Prince's band we find the names of Johann Ludwig Rese, Martin Friedrich Marcus, Johann Friedrich Torlée, Bernhard Linike, the "Premier Kammer musicus," Josephus Spiess, and the "Viol-di-gambist," Christ. Ferdinand Abel. This cannot have constituted the whole of the band; still those here named were no doubt the most important members; at the same time the only one, even of these, who became more widely known, was Abel. He, like Sebastian Bach's brother Joh. Jakob, had in his youth followed Charles XII. into the field; he was already employed in Cöthen when Bach was invited thither and was still living there in 1737. Of his two gifted sons, Leopold August and Karl Friedrich, both born at Cöthen, the second, as is well known, attained European celebrity.[9]

---

[8] Mattheson, Crit. Mus., Vol. I., Part III., p. 85.

[9] From a document in the archives of Cöthen, preserved at Zerbst, entitled " Protocoll über die Fürstl Capell- und Trompeter-Gagen von 1717-18." Also Gerber, Lexicon, I., cols. 3 and 4.

A pupil of Bach's at this time was Johann Schneider, born near Coburg ; he played the organ, clavier, and violin, and entered the band at Weimar as violinist in 1726 ; in 1730 he went to Leipzig as Organist to the Church of St. Nikolaus.[10] He must no doubt have been employed in the band. Bach himself, as " Capellmeister and director of the Prince's chamber music," as he describes himself with his own hand, received a salary of 400 thalers a year: a good round sum at that period. And the terms of his appointment prove the high estimation in which the Prince held him, for it was dated, and the salary paid, from August 1, 1717, though Bach cannot have entered his service before the end of November. This, with a few other meagre notices, is all that is known to us concerning his official position in Cöthen. Time has effaced or overgrown almost every trace of his labours, as the grass has overgrown the castle-yard which the master must so often have crossed ; and his name has died out among the people of the place almost as completely as the sounds with which he once roused the echoes of the now empty and deserted halls.

It must not be supposed, indeed, that even at that time his efforts resulted in much outward display. They were quite private and unpretending, as were his surroundings, and barely extended beyond the limits of the castle concert-room. It was only by his journeys that Bach kept up any connection with the outer and wider world ; in his place of residence he had nothing to do with public life. Nevertheless, it was here that he passed the happiest years of his life ; here, for a time, he felt so far content that he was resigned to end his days in the peaceful little town. This seems quite incomprehensible so long as we conceive of Bach's artistic side as directed exclusively to sacred music ; then, indeed, his residence in Cöthen, where he was debarred from any occupation in the church, must appear to be lost time, and his own satisfaction in it as mere self-deception.

---

[10] Walther's article in the Lexicon shows again how little he interested himself in the biography of his great contemporary Bach. He does not even know that Bach was still in Cöthen in 1720, or does not think it worth mentioning.

But it all becomes natural and intelligible when we do not lose sight of the fact that instrumental music—that is to say, music for music's sake—was the aim and essence of his being: a fact I have endeavoured to insist on from the first. It must have been with a feeling of rapture that for once he found himself thrown back exclusively into this his native element, to drink from it fresh strength for new struggles towards the high ideal that remained hidden from his fellow-men. An essential feature of German art becomes more conspicuous in Bach at this period of his life than at any other: that meditative spirit which is never happy till it dwells within narrow bounds—the joy of occupation and the pleasure of a quiet and homelike circle of a few appreciative friends, whose sympathetic glance responds to the deepest feelings of the heart. From this German characteristic the quartet took its rise; and its very embodiment was the delicious chamber music of Sebastian Bach, which took form chiefly in Cöthen, and in the first rank of it was the Wohl-temperirte Clavier.[11] The musical performances that now took place in the castle, when and how often we know not, were of an intimate and thoughtful character, and always undertaken with a genuine zeal for art; the gifted young Prince threw himself into it, heart and soul; all the more so since he was as yet unmarried. He soon became aware of the treasure he had found in Bach, and showed it in the frankest manner. He could not bear to part with him—he took him on his travels, and loved him as a friend; and after his early death Bach always cherished his memory.

An act of homage, dating probably from the first year of his residence in Cöthen, was a serenade for the Prince's birthday. Having to rely on the modest musical resources of the place, he employed in it only one soprano and one bass, with an accompaniment of two flutes and one bassoon, besides the quartet of strings and harpsichord.[12] The writer

---

[11] The Well-tempered Clavier—*i.e.*, preludes and fugues to be played on a clavier tuned according to the system of "equal" temperament, by which system all keys are equally in tune, whereas in the unequal temperament, formerly in use in tuning claviers, many of the keys could not be employed. The work is better known in England by the title Forty-eight Preludes and Fugues.

[12] The autograph is in the Royal Library at Berlin.

of the congratulatory words is not named; if this was out
of modesty he had ample reason. At a later period, Bach
himself is known to have written certain texts for music,
and, knowing this, we cannot altogether avoid suspecting
that he may have written these words. Of course some
other dabbler in verse is quite as likely to have been the
criminal; for they are wretched, be the writer who he
may. But the music covers every deficiency; in it we
find a perfect reflection of Bach's spirit at this period. It fits
the tone of festive feeling in a merely general manner, and
within the limits of this idea disports itself freely, developing
all that charm of novel invention and elaborate artistic
structure of which Bach availed himself with such fascinating grace in his chamber music. There are seven
numbers in all: the soprano begins with a recitative and
aria in D major; the bass follows with an aria in B minor,
and all the music for this voice is pitched very high, showing
that it was written for a particular singer. He then goes
on to the graceful and dignified minuet in G major, the
soprano continues it in D major, and they presently combine
in A major, the bass singing the melody, as leading in the
dance. Then comes a duet in recitative, again an air for
soprano and one for bass, in D major and A major
respectively, and finally the closing piece, in two parts
and in the leading key, inscribed *Chorus*, by which it
is intended to distinguish the crowning finale, for the way
in which the parts are treated prohibits all notion of a
multiplicity of performers. A happy and self-contented
spirit smiles from it throughout. In later years the
composer thought it a pity to leave this noble music
wedded to its text, and made use of it for a Whitsuntide
cantata, as he also did of the music written for the
birthday of the Duke of Weissenfels.[13]

On May 9, 1718, the Prince set out to take the baths at
Carlsbad, which was at that time a favourite resort of all the
high personages of Germany, and took with him Bach and
six members of his band. Again, in 1720, Bach had to

---

[13] "Erhöhtes Fleisch und Blut": this autograph also is in the Royal Library
at Berlin.

accompany the Prince to Carlsbad;[14] an old tradition still survives of the way in which Bach was wont to occupy his more or less involuntary leisure on these journeys—to this I will return presently. He received another mark of favour in the autumn of the same year, when Maria Barbara gave birth to their seventh child—a boy—on November 15, and on the 17th, the Prince stood godfather to the infant, with his younger brother August Ludwig, his sister Elenore Wilhelmine—who had married into the house of Weimar—with Privy Councillor Von Zanthier, and the wife of Von Nostiz, Steward of the Household.[15]   From this it is very evident in what high favour Bach must have stood at court. The child held at the font with so many honours did not survive his first year; he was buried September 28, 1719. A pair of twins had already died in February and March, 1713, soon after their birth ; but four children lived to grow up as witnesses of a calm and happy family life. The firstborn was a daughter, Katharina Dorothea, born December 27, 1708; she remained unmarried. On November 22, 1710, followed Wilhelm Friedemann, his father's remarkable and gifted favourite ; then Karl Philipp Emanuel (March 8, 1714), who was the most distinguished of the family, though he was not, perhaps, the most talented. Finally, Johann Gottfried Bernhard, born May 11, 1715.[16] We shall have occasion to speak again of all these sons.

---

[14] The dates of these journeys are derived from the orders for special prayers on both occasions issued by the Chancellor of the Duchy, in the archives at Cöthen. It seems certain that during the time from 1718 to 1733 the Prince was at Carlsbad only on these two occasions, since this agrees with an old chronicle of Carlsbad, as I am obligingly informed by Dr. Hlawacek, of that town. The musicians were paid in advance, on May 6, their salaries for the month of June.

[15] Parish Register of the cathedral church of St. James: " 1718, the 17th of November, the Prince's Capellmeister, Herr Johann Sebastian Bach, and his wedded wife, Maria Barbara, had a son baptised in the castle chapel, born on the 15th ult., named Leopold Augustus."   The names of the sponsors follow.

[16] The Parish Registers give the names of all their sponsors, many of whom were distinguished by birth or office. Philipp Emanuel, in the Genealogy, gives his birthday as March 14; but I have adhered to the date in the Register, though I must confess it is hardly likely that he should be mistaken as to his own birthday.

As has been said, Bach did not give up his own journeys in pursuit of art, even in Cöthen; indeed, his personal need for them was perhaps greater there than in Weimar. Only a few weeks after quitting that town he accepted an invitation to the university town of Leipzig, in order to test the large new organ completed in the Church of St. Paul there, on November 4, 1716. The examination took place December 16, 1717, and was highly favourable to the builder, Johann Scheibe; Bach was greatly satisfied, not only with the quality and construction of the separate portions, but also with the general arrangement, which he declared to be among the completest in Germany. He conducted the examination by himself; only two competent witnesses accompanied him.[17]

In the autumn of 1719 he made another journey, which took him to Halle; this town, no doubt, was not the only goal of the excursion, but we hear of his being there from a circumstance connected with him. Handel had arrived in Germany in the spring, from England, to find singers for the newly founded operatic academy in London; on his return journey he remained for a short time with his family at Halle, and Bach sought him out, but was so unlucky as to find that Handel had that very day set out for England. Another attempt made by Bach, ten years later, to make a personal acquaintance with the only one of his contemporaries who was in any way his equal was just as unsuccessful. Inferences, unfavourable to Handel, have been drawn from these incidents, but there is no sufficient reason for supposing that he would have repelled Bach's courteous advances. We nowhere find any indication that he intentionally took himself out of Bach's reach by leaving Halle on the day of Bach's arrival there; while, on the other hand, it is difficult to overlook the fact that Bach, in this first attempt at a meeting, merely availed himself of an opportunity. Otherwise, as Handel had been in Germany since the previous

[17] This incident is recorded by Christoph Ernst Siculs in his Anderer Beylage zu dem Leipziger Jahr-Buche (Leipzig, 1718), p. 198; and it is to A. Dörffels that the praise is due of having first brought it to light. See Musikal. Wochenblatt (Leipzig: E. W. Fritzsch); Annual Series, I., p. 335.

March, he might have arranged a meeting somewhere or other.[18]

On the second occasion, in June, 1729, Bach, who was prevented by illness from travelling himself, sent his eldest son from Leipzig to Halle, with an invitation to Handel, who was staying there on his way from Italy. Handel regretted his inability to accept it, and it seems most probable that the time he had left was in fact too short. It may, however, be confidently denied that it is in any way very regrettable in the interests of art that these two men should thus have failed to meet ; it would have been interesting, no doubt; and a desire to hear them compete is said to have been very prevalent among the lovers of music in Leipzig.[19]   But the whole object of their meeting would have merged in this, and would have ended, very certainly, without any decision being arrived at on the vexed question as to which of the two should bear off the palm, seeing how totally different their natures were.   Any intercourse leading to reciprocal incitement, such as can only be developed from long acquaintance and contact, was out of the question, from the dissimilarity of their outward circumstances.   On the other hand, the judgment goes against Handel, without any bias being given by our appreciation of Bach's artistic greatness; for in 1719, when Handel spent eight months in Germany, he certainly might have found time for making a visit which might have originated with him more properly than with Bach, who was occupied with his official duties.   Added to this, he resided in Dresden and Halle, places where Bach's importance as an artist was fresh in the minds of living witnesses, and he must there have heard the most splendid reports of the great composer who was working in his immediate neighbourhood.   No facts have come to light that prove him to have taken any interest in Bach's works ; Bach, on the contrary, not only purposed more than once to make Handel's personal acquaintance, but bore emphatic witness to the value he

---

[18] I entirely agree in Chrysander's views as to this incident.   Händel, II., p. 18, note.

[19] Forkel, p. 47.

attributed to his works. Handel's music to Brock's text for a " Passion Music " is still extant in a manuscript of sixty leaves, of which the twenty-three first (exclusive of the last two staves) were copied by Bach's own hand, and the remainder by his wife. The parts of a very meritorious Concerto Grosso in seven movements, by Handel, also exist in Bach's handwriting.[20] The same is the case with a solo cantata by Handel, of which Bach even seems to have possessed the original autograph, for this and Bach's parts are now in the hands of the same owners.[21] It is with particular satisfaction that I am able to point out these indications of a magnanimous artist, free from all envy or prejudice. A few words will yet remain to be said as to their reciprocal relations as organists.

On May 27 of the following year Prince Leopold again went to Carlsbad ; he must have returned in July. When Bach entered his home, full of the happy prospect of seeing his family, he was met with the overwhelming news that on the 7th of the month his wife had been buried. He had left her in good health and spirits ; now a sudden death had snatched her away in the bloom of life, not yet thirty-six years old, without any news of it having reached her distant husband, who, indeed, had probably begun his return journey. When his son, Philipp Emanuel, thirty-three years after, compiled the notice of his father for the Necrology, though he treated many family events with the brevity of a chronicler, his mother's death and the circumstances connected with it dwelt so vividly in his memory that he

---

[20] Both these MSS. are in the Royal Library at Berlin. The name of the author is wanting to the last, of which Dr. Rust has arranged a score. Dr. Chrysander informs me that the work is unquestionably Handel's, since the motives of the concerto reappear in later works by him. It has indeed struck me that certain passages of the third number, a fugue, have a remarkable resemblance to the double canon treatment of the final chorus of the " Messiah." In the fifth movement, on the other hand, there are passages which recur almost precisely in the B flat minor Prelude in Part I. of the Wohltemperirte Clavier, bars 20-22.

[21] Messrs. Breitkopf and Härtel, of Leipzig. The cantata is entitled "Armida Abbandonata"; the parts written out by Bach at his Leipzig period are those for the first and second violins and continuo. Chrysander pronounces the autograph to be Handel's, and he is an unimpeachable authority.

reported it in detail. But we do not need his evidence to
believe in Sebastian's grief; it is easy to guess the feelings
that must have tortured his strong, deep nature as he stood
by the grave of the wife who had been his companion through
the years of his youthful endeavour, and of his first success,
only to be snatched from him when fortune was at its height.

We know too little of Maria Barbara Bach to attempt to
sketch her character. But, remembering the intelligent
nature of her father, and the happy, naïve temper of her
second son—who appears to have greatly resembled his
mother, while the father fancied he saw himself reproduced
in the eldest—we have grounds for picturing to ourselves
a calm and kindly nature, with enough musical gift to
sympathise keenly with her husband's labours; a wife who
enabled him to enjoy in his home that which was one of
his deepest needs, the family life of an honourable and
worthy citizen.

His terrible loss did not crush Bach's energy; he bore it
manfully. A journey to Hamburg, which he had planned
for the autumn, was not given up; still there is reason to
suppose that he put it off for several weeks. The cantata,
" Wer sich selbst erhöhet der soll erniedrigt werden,"[22] stands
as evidence of this. The text is taken from a cycle of poems
which was printed in 1720, by order of the government
secretary, Johann Friedrich Helbig, at Eisenach, for the use
of the band there.[23] In Cöthen itself, as no church music
was performed there, no such texts were procurable. When
Bach desired to compose a cantata he had to look elsewhere
for the poetic materials; and, again, the impulse to such a
work could only arise from journeys which took him to places

---

[22] B.-G., X., No. 47.

[23] "Auffmunterung | Zur | Andacht, | oder: | Musicalische | Texte, | über |
Die gewöhnlichen Sonn- und | Fest- Tags Evangelien durchs | gantze Jahr, |
Gott zu Ehren | auffgeführet | Von | Der Hoch-Fürstl. Capelle | zu Eisenach. |
[Incitements to Devotion, or Musical Texts on the Gospels in use for Sundays
and Holydays thoughout the whole year. Performed in God's honour by the
Prince's band at Eisenach.] Daselbst gedruckt und zu finden bey Johann |
Adolph *Boëtio*, 1720. | " A copy is in the library of the Count of Stolberg, at
Wernigerode. There is a notice of Helbig in Mattheson, Ehrenpforte, under
" Melchior Hofmann," p. 118.

where church music was cherished, and into the society of famous church composers. Thus he selected the text for the Seventeenth Sunday after Trinity out of this very indifferent poetry—which, however, came home to him as being that of a fellow-countryman—intending to visit Hamburg and to have his cantata performed there. It also seems highly probable that he set it to music during his excursion to Carlsbad; crushed, however, immediately after by the blow he had suffered, he was unable to carry out this project, and did not reach Hamburg till November.[24] Whether the cantata was then and there performed it is impossible to know; perhaps it was once, irrespective of Divine service. From beginning to end it is the expression of the most complete structural power, and it surpasses his earlier works more particularly by the scope and extent of the grand introductory chorus on the final words of the gospel for the day: "He that exalteth himself shall be abased, and he that humbleth himself shall be exalted." No chorale is introduced, but the whole, in agreement with the text, is made into a double fugue; still its second theme undergoes no independent development.

The great stride forward marked by this piece, when compared with Bach's earlier works for instruments and voices, is conspicuous, not merely in the bold, broad grasp of the parts and their stately, free movement, even where they are most intricate—not only in the grandeur of the proportions, but above all in the fact that the master was no longer satisfied with allowing the instruments to take part in the fugal treatment or to work out a particular motive, but, on the contrary, gave them a theme of their own, thus building up his palace of sound out of the material of three distinct ideas. Still, as the instrumental theme appears in homophonic harmony, the structure necessarily became something else than that of a triple fugue. When we hear the beginning of the movement, in G minor, common time, *allegro*, it is difficult to believe that a choral work can grow out of it; it is like the beginning of an Italian concerto, with its

---

[24] See Appendix A, No. 1.

stringed instruments, oboes and organ.   First comes a *tutti*
theme, to which is added the contrast of busy passages; the
dominant is led up to in the regular way, and the same
development is worked out upon it; then, at bar 45, we return
to the leading key.   But there the tenor takes us by surprise
with the entrance of the eight-bar theme, which rises and falls
through an octave; after which the counter-subject, nine
bars long, comes in, descends an octave and a half, and then
shoots up again with a swift, strong flight.   Meanwhile the
instruments continue to work out their *tutti* theme, *piano*, and
in the manner of an episode, but at last the main current
sweeps them up also, and bears them on.   After a cadence on
B flat there comes a shorter episodic interlude, derived from the
alternation of the chorus and the instruments; then, again,
a grand fugal movement, as at first; another interlude; again
a fugal passage; and, to form a *coda*, as it were, the whole
chorus takes up the instrumental subject of the beginning;
the whole forty-five bars are gone through with the entire body
of sound, so that the picture is grandly rounded off, and it
closes in dignified magnificence.   It is a composition born
of the most supreme command over all the forms of music,
great and small, and which at the same time affords the
most perfect solution conceivable of the problem as to the
amalgamation of instrumental and vocal music.   After
this introductory movement no increase of mere effect
could lie within Bach's view; he was content in this, as in
all similar cases, to let the cantata flow directly into the
symbolical and significant form of the simple chorale.
Intermediate between the two are two arias, connected by a
recitative.   The first, of which the moralising words were
most intractable to poetic treatment, is a most ingenious
trio for soprano, continuo and organ obbligato or solo violin,
and no less a masterpiece in its way.   The second is still
finer in polyphonic richness, and at the same time glows
with noble poetic feeling.

Telemann, who had always been capellmeister at Eisenach,
and still was so, also composed music to this text.[25]   The

---

[25] An ancient MS. in the Gotthold Library at Königsberg (Prussia), No.
250,862 of the catalogue.

Bible words themselves made the commencement with a double fugue obvious; it is a singular coincidence that he should have chosen the same key as Bach. In everything else the gulf between them, which was visible in their earlier works, yawns more widely than ever. Telemann works out his fugue of thirty-eight bars, common time (Bach's has two hundred and twenty-eight bars), shortly and dryly, and without warming to it at all; the instruments only strengthen the voice parts. Of the rest of the text he only composed the second aria and set the chorale; the air is not even cast in the Italian form, and has the simplest possible accompaniment.

Bach subsequently troubled himself no farther about Helbig's texts, which he had used merely for want of better, with one exception, and that again must have been because he had no choice ; for it is evident that in hurriedly arranging the cantata for the third Sunday in Advent of that same year, " Das ist je gewisslich wahr "—" This is certainly the truth "—he worked up earlier compositions in the first chorus (G major, common time); it is impossible to doubt that it is founded on what was originally a duet, particularly if we compare it with the almost identical style of the opening chorus in the second arrangement of the Whitsun-tide cantata, " Wer mich liebet "—" Whoso loves me." [26] In bars 52 and 53 of the first aria the bad adaptation to the text betrays him. We cannot expect to find any great merit in such hasty work, though it contains much that is pleasing —nay, beautiful. [27]

Johann Reinken was still living in Hamburg, and, in spite of his ninety-seven years, still officiated as Organist in the Church of St. Katharine with much energy and vigour. He was held in higher respect than any of his fellow officials in the city, not only by reason of his great age, but also on account of his distinction as an artist, of which I have already spoken in detail. To Bach, who as a youth had derived benefit in the most direct way from Reinken's art, it

---

[26] B.-G., XVIII., No. 74.

[27] I only know this cantata from the copy in the Royal Library at Berlin. The final chorale is absent; according to the text it should be " Christe, du Lamm Gottes."

must have been very delightful to present himself to the veteran master as a perfectly accomplished musician. What we learn of Reinken's character is not, on the whole, favourable; he was not only conscious of his own merit, but vain, and jealous of other artists. His predecessor in office had been Heinrich Scheidemann, so fine an organist that any one might have been regarded as somewhat rash who ventured to succeed him; so, at least, a great Dutch musician said, when he learnt that Reinken was to take his place. Reinken, hearing of this, sent him his arrangement of the chorale, " An Wasserflüssen Babylon," with this note: That in this he might see the image of the rash man. The Dutchman, finding that through this certainly very remarkable work he had made the acquaintance of a man who was his superior, came to Hamburg, heard Reinken, and when he met him kissed his hands in admiration.[28]

Mattheson, who in the matter of vanity could do something himself, indignantly observes that Reinken, in the title-page to his *Hortus Musicus*, styles himself, *Organi Hamburgensis ad Divæ Catharinæ Directorum celebratissimum*,[29] and in general he finds nothing good to say of him; but this was Reinken's own fault, for he would never forgive Mattheson for the fact that at one time it had been proposed to give him his (Reinken's) place.[30] Mattheson took his revenge by all sorts of petty hits in the " Beschütztes Orchestre"; and, in the brief obituary notice which he bestowed on him,[31] he even says: " As regards his social character, one and another of the clergy have at times been known to say that he was a constant admirer of the fair sex, and much addicted to the wine-cellar of the Council." Still, he cannot avoid admitting that he kept his organ at all times in beautiful order and in good tune, and that he

---

[28] Walther, Lexicon, *sub voce* " Scheidemann."

[29] Ehrenpforte, p. 293. But Mattheson, consciously or unconsciously, does not here speak the truth. Reinken, on the title-page of the *Hortus Musicus*, writes, " *Organi Hamburgensis ad D. Cathar. celebratissimi Director.*" Hence it is the organ, and not the organist, that he says is famous.

[30] Adlung, Anl. zur Mus. Gel., p. 183. Reinken's deputy and successor was Johann Heinrich Uthmöller (1720-1752).

[31] Crit. Mus., I., p. 255.

could play it in so exceptional and pure a style "that, in his time, he had no equal in the matters he was practised in"; adding, maliciously, that he was always talking of his organ, for it was really very fine in tone.

These observations are a necessary introduction to our comprehension, in all its significance, of Reinken's attitude towards Bach. At an appointed hour the magistrate of the town, and many other important personages, met .in St. Katharine's Church to hear the stranger perform. He played for more than two hours, to the admiration of every one; but his greatest triumph was won by an improvisation on "An Wasserflüssen Babylon," which he carried on for nearly half an hour in the broad, motett-like manner of the northern masters, with which we are already familiar. Reinken came up to him, having listened attentively throughout, and said : " I thought this art was dead; but I perceive that it still lives in you."[32] Irrespective of the high recognition it conveys, there is more in this than mere self-conceit ; but, in fact, Bach's mental culture had long since advanced far beyond that stage of organ chorale treatment. Still it is an evidence of his extraordinary mastery over the whole realm of form in music, that he could deliberately revert to it so promptly and so perfectly. He has not left us any written version of what he played, then and there, on the spur of the moment ; but it has been already remarked, when speaking of the organ chorale with double pedal, on this same melody, that it may have had some connection with the Hamburg journey. It is quite conceivable that he should have worked it up previously, and have laid it before Reinken as a specimen of imitative art in both subject and treatment; and then, still further to accommodate himself to Reinken's comprehension, have gone on following out his imagination in the way to which "the worthy organists of Hamburg were formerly accustomed in Sunday vespers." Possibly he added something to it, as he did, twenty-seven years later, to a theme set him by Friedrich the Great. At any rate, Reinken was so well satisfied that

---

[32] Mizler, Nekrolog., p. 165.

he invited Bach to visit him, and treated him with distinguished attention. Two years later he departed this life,
November 24, 1722, and was buried, by his own wish, in the
Church of St. Katharine, at Lübeck, where his kindred spirit,
Buxtehude, had already been resting for fifteen years. Reinken had seen, in its full and glorious bloom what Buxtehude
had only noted in its bud—the genius of the man who was
destined to reach the summit to which they had so successfully opened the way.

Bach was perfectly happy with the organ of St. Katharine's (Hamburg), with its four manuals and pedal. It is
interesting to learn that he was greatly in favour of good
reeds, and these he found in abundance.[33] The organ
also possessed a posaune, and a "principal" (*i.e.*, diapason)
of thirty-two feet which spoke clearly and quickly down
to C, and Bach subsequently asserted that he had never
heard another "principal" of such a size which had this
merit. The instrument was not new; it dated at least
from the sixteenth century, and had been renovated, in 1670,
by the organ-builder Besser, of Brunswick.[34] It preserved
a remnant of older taste in a mixture of ten ranks. But
this was not the only organ for which Hamburg was famous.
The instrument in the Church of St. James was still more
powerful as regards the number of stops, and had likewise four manuals and pedals; it was built, between 1688
and 1693, by the Hamburg organ-builder Arp Schnitker,[35]
who had given proof of his remarkable skill in other
churches in the city. Among this crowd of fine instruments Bach's affectionate longing for his own special province of music revived all the more strongly because, quite
unexpectedly, a prospect opened before him of finding a
suitable position in Hamburg. Heinrich Friese, the Organist

---

[33] Adlung, Mus. Mech., I.; p. 66, note. The specification is given in Niedt.
Mus. Handl., II., p. 176.

[34] H. Schmahl, Nachrichten über die Orgel der St. Catharinen-Kirche in Hamburg. Hamburg: Grüning, 1869, pp. 4-8.

[35] H. Schmahl, Bericht über die Orgel der St. Jacobi-Kirche. Hamburg, 1866.
Gerber, N. L., IV., col. 106. This organ had sixty sounding stops, and was
restored in 1865-66.

cf St. James's, had died, September 12, 1720; so short a time, therefore, before Bach had arrived there that it is probable that he had not heard of it till then. It is, at any rate, certain that the aim and end of his journey was not to seek this appointment, since he had prepared for the expedition in the summer by composing a cantata. However, as it had so happened, he offered himself. Not a little tempting must have been the circumstance that Erdmann Neumeister was chief preacher at this church; he could hardly have pictured to himself a more promising perspective for composing for the organ as well as cantatas, and for the practice of every branch of his art, than that which opened on him here.

Seven other candidates came forward besides himself, mostly unknown names; but a son of the excellent Vincentius Lübeck, and Wiedeburg, Capellmeister to the Count of Gera, were among the number. On November 21 the elders of the church, among whom was Neumeister, resolved on holding the examination on the 28th, and to select as experts, to aid in their decision, Joachim Gerstenbüttel, the cantor of the church, Reinken, and two other organists of the town, named Kniller and Preuss. Bach could not wait so long; his Prince required his return by November 23. Three of the other candidates, including Wiedeburg and Lübeck, had already retired, so that there were but four to submit to the tests, which consisted in the performance of two chorales—" O lux beata Trinitas," and " Helft mir Gott's Güte preisen "—with an extemporised fugue on a given theme. The election was not to be held till December 19. Bach had promised to announce, by letter from Cöthen, whether he chose to accept or decline the appointment; and that it should have come to this, without his being required to pass any examination, proves that he had been regarded as particularly eligible, and distinguished above the other candidates. Unfortunately, nothing is known as to the contents of his answer. So much as this alone is certain—he did not decline the post; the letter was publicly read to the committee, and then, by a majority of votes, they elected—Johann Joachim Heitmann. What he had ever done in his art is less well known than the fact that, on

January 6, 1721, he paid over to the treasury of the Church of St. James "the promised sum of four thousand marks current," in acknowledgment of having been elected. A transaction in view of this, by the church committee, had already been recorded with astonishing frankness, on November 21. They had come to the conclusion: "That, no doubt, many reasons might be found why the sale of the organist's appointment should not be made a custom, because it appertained to the service of God; therefore the choice should be free, and the capability of the candidate be considered rather than the money. But if, after the election, the elected person, of his free will, desired to show his gratitude, this should be favourably looked upon by the church."

Neumeister was extremely indignant at this proceeding, which he had not been able to prevent; he probably would rather have brought Bach into his church than any one. After the election, he would not wait till the nominee came, but left the room in a rage. What further·happened, and what the public opinion was of the choice made, we will let Mattheson tell, as he was intimately acquainted with all the details. "I remember," says he in 1728—"and, no doubt, many other people still remember likewise—that some years ago a great musician, who since then has, as he deserves, obtained an important appointment as cantor, appeared as organist in a certain town of some size, boldly performed on the largest and finest instruments, and attracted universal admiration by his skill. At the same time, among other inferior players, there offered himself the son of a well-to-do artisan, who could prelude with thalers better than he could with his fingers, and the office fell to him, as may easily be guessed, although almost every one was angry about it. It was nigh upon Christmastide, and an eloquent preacher, who had not consented to this simony, expounded very beautifully the gospel concerning the angelic music at the birth of Christ, which, very naturally, gave him the opportunity of expressing his opinions as to the recent event as regarded the rejected artist, and of ending his discourse with this noteworthy *epiphonema*. He believed quite certainly that if one of the angels of Bethlehem came from heaven, who played divinely, and desired to be organist to St. James's church, if he had no money he would have nothing to do but to fly away again." [36]

The homage to Bach's merits which Mattheson was obliged to pay—and, in this passage, does pay—was somewhat bitter to him, if we are not deceived by appearances. The only place in which he speaks of him with warm admiration is in the " Beschütztes Orchestre," written four years earlier.[37] If we collect out of all his numerous writings the few paragraphs which refer to Bach, we come to the conclusion that, though he never under-estimates him, he judges him narrowly; his heart is always cold towards him ; and we feel as though Bach must have been to him one of those distant and puzzling natures whom we are compelled by our intellects to admire, but who have no hold on our feelings. It is not safe to assume that Bach ignored and so offended a man who was no doubt eminent, though he had more reason for ignoring him than had Handel, who, from 1703 to 1706, had lived in constant intercourse with Mattheson, and who never again sought his acquaintance, though he often was in Germany afterwards, and passed through Hamburg. Mattheson had politely requested Bach to furnish him with the facts of his life for the " Ehrenpforte." He already enjoyed a considerable reputation as a writer on musical subjects ; and Bach must have seen that this request was a compliment, although he never acceded to it. But their natures were too dissimilar. It is perfectly evident that Bach did not think much of the Hamburg composer's music : he could copy out the works of Keiser and Telemann, but it is not known that he ever did the same with Mattheson's, though he formed the third of the trio ; and as a busy, practical musician, he had neither time nor inclination to form an estimate of his literary work.

---

[36] Mattheson, Der Musicalische Patriot (Hamburg, 1728), p. 316. Herr Schmahl, the present Organist of St. James's, has been so obliging as to write out for me all that refers to the matter in question in the archives of the church.

[37] See ante, Vol. I., p. 393.

Now Mattheson was very vain; he thought that artists ought
to flock to him to prove their devotion, to crave his counsel
and instruction; and such as did he mentioned at great
length in his books: "In August, 1720, an organist came
from Bremen and had himself taught composition by Mattheson, for which he paid highly"; "My Lord Carteret arrived
in Hamburg (November 8) from his embassy to Sweden,
and took such pleasure in our Mattheson's music, that he
once sat for two whole hours listening to him, without
stirring from the spot; and at last, in presence of the whole
assembly, he pronounced this judgment: 'Handel certainly
plays the clavier finely and skilfully, but he does not make
it sing with so much taste and expression.'" So the man
writes of himself.[38]   It sounds almost as if he were trying
to indemnify himself when we consider that this compliment
was paid him by the ambassador at the very time when
Bach happened to be in Hamburg.   If there had been anything to accrue to his fame in his meeting with Bach, he
certainly would not have forgotten it in his autobiography;
but he does not say a syllable about it.

The carping criticism which he published a few years after
of the cantata "Ich hatte viel Bekümmerniss," and which
is fully discussed in its place, can only be accounted for by
wounded vanity.   And when he praised Bach subsequently
it was always with an invidious distinction as to his execution or his clever settings.[39]   We learn that he already knew a
good deal of Bach's work in the year 1716, both of chamber
pieces and church music.   On the present occasion he had
no doubt heard and seen much that was new—perhaps
the criticised cantata and new organ pieces.   It is singular,
and again only explicable by his feelings towards Bach,
that, several years after, he betrays some such knowledge,
and, contrary to his usual boasting of information, tries to

---

[38] Ehrenpforte, p. 206.
[39] "The famous Bach, whom I have already mentioned honourably, and here
mention again especially for manual skill," &c., Volk. Capellm., p. 412; "The
artistic Bach, who was particularly happy in this department" (the construction
of fugues on a given theme), &c.; ibid., p. 369.

conceal it. In the second edition of the " General Bass-Schule " [40] he states that, in a test performance on the organ, the candidates had given to them the following theme—

to work out extempore, with this—

to be treated as the counter-subject. Now this is the theme of one of Bach's most magnificent organ fugues, and the counterpoint is also of his invention. Mattheson does not mention this, and only observes, in a note, that he knows very well with whom the idea originated, and who formerly had worked it out with great skill. He chose it because it was wiser in such cases to take something familiar, so that the examinee might get through with a better grace. Nevertheless, we are grateful to him for this notice. It tells us that this fugue of Bach's was known to a wide circle as early as in 1725. It leads us to suppose that the composer may have taken it with him in 1720, and to imagine the sensation made by its appearance in the circle of organists there—for the organist examined by Mattheson must have been a native of Hamburg, or of the neighbourhood. Finally, it tells us that the fugue in its present state must be a later remodelling, for the theme is now wonderfully improved by two small alterations. The prelude belonging to this work is strong evidence of its having been originally composed on purpose for the Hamburg journey. It is conspicuously different from the thematic treatment of the later Weimar period, reverting, indeed, to the imaginative style of the northern masters.[41]

Here, too, Bach seems to have wished to meet the Hamburg organists on their own most peculiar ground. Bursting torrents of ornament, imitative episodes, organ recitatives,

[40] Called also Exemplarische Organisten-Probe, Hamburg, 1731, p. 34.

[41] Prelude and fugue, B.-G., XV., p. 177. P. S. V., C. 2 (241), No. 4. In this a variant is also given, which, however, seems to me to be due to accident. No manuscript has as yet come to light containing the oldest form of the fugue.

the boldest modulations, and broad, resonant progressions
of chords—all are here in apparent disorder. And yet the
mature genius of Bach presides over it and informs it all.
The close answers exactly to the ornate commencement; the
polyphonic movement in bars 9 to 13 are precisely the
same as bars 25 to 30; the organ recitative—bars 14 to 24—
are balanced by the free harmonies of bars 31 to 40. Even
in the modulations, which almost beat Buxtehude in audacity, a plan is clearly traceable; they rise from *a*—bar 14—
by degrees through B minor, C minor, up to *d*, then to
E flat minor, of which the bass seizes the dominant, and
thence proceeds upwards by six chromatic steps; to correspond to this, the harmonic body subsequently descends from
d—bar 31—through C minor, B flat minor, A flat minor,
after which the six chromatic steps up from B begin in the
pedal. It is necessary to keep the outline of the prelude
resolutely in mind at first, in order not to be confused by the
swift runs, and deafened by the heavy masses of sound; but
presently we become accustomed to it, and not only recognise the purpose and method of the work, but feel it too;
while in similar pieces by Buxtehude, and particularly in
the interludes to his fugues in several parts, there is rarely
any plan at all. We are also struck by the wide difference
between this and earlier works by Bach, in which Buxtehude's influence could be seen; its remarkable peculiarities
can only be accounted for by referring it to some special
incident in Bach's history; and it seems most obvious to
suppose that this was the Hamburg journey.

The most beautiful contrast to this is offered by the
grand, calm modulations and strict four-part treatment of
the fugue, which is a long one, and which, on the other
hand, certainly bears some relationship to Reinken; hence
the hypothesis that it was composed in 1720 is further confirmed. The theme, particularly, has an unmistakable
resemblance with the fifth sonata of Reinken's *Hortus
Musicus*. It begins thus:—

We may unhesitatingly view this resemblance as an

intentional allusion, and therefore a certain homage to Reinken. A musician of the last century spoke of the G minor fugue as " the very best pedal piece by Herr Johann Sebastian Bach." I modify this verdict only so far as to say that no other fugue appears to stand above it. It is in view of such a production as this that we are justified in making what may seem an exaggerated assertion—namely, that there never was a fugue written by any other composer that could compare with one of Sebastian Bach's.[42] We have shown how highly Buxtehude's works of the same kind are to be esteemed, and it cannot be disputed that in a few clavier fugues Handel proved himself Bach's equal; but this soaring imagination, this lavish and inexhaustible variety of form— again, this crystal lucidity and modest naturalism, this lofty gravity and deep contentment which strikes awe into the hearer, and at the same time makes him shout with joy— all this is so unique in its combined effect, that every notion of a comparison with others appears preposterous. Once, and only once, has anything been produced in the whole realm of instrumental music which can be set by the side of these most perfect organ fugues by Bach—namely, Beethoven's symphonies.

The mention of Mattheson brings us once more to a comparison and contrast of Bach and Handel—this time, however, not as men, but as organists. That Bach had no equal in Germany in playing the organ was soon an admitted fact; friends and foes alike here bowed to the irresistible force of an unheard-of power of execution, and could hardly comprehend how he could twist his fingers and his feet so strangely and so nimbly, and spread them out to make the widest leaps without hitting a single false note, or displacing his body with violent swaying.[43] But from England, on the other hand, Handel's growing fame had reached Germany, not only as a composer of opera and oratorio, but as an unapproachable organ-player. So far as England was concerned, that was not saying too much, but other foreigners

---

[42] Forkel, p. 33.
[43] Scheibe, Kritischer Musikus. New ed., 1745, pp. 839, 875.

who had heard him there brought the same news; and
as he was a German, the comparison with Bach was
obvious, while Bach's cantatas, Passion Music, and masses
were scarcely appreciated in the contemporary world as
compared with Handel's music. The attempt made by his
Leipzig friends, in 1729, to bring about a meeting of
the two players miscarried, so opinions and assertions could
spread unchecked. Some came from England full of
Handel's praises, but saying nevertheless that there was but
one Bach in the world, and that no one could compare with
him; others, on the other hand, were of opinion that Handel
played more touchingly and gracefully, Bach with more art
and inspiration, and it was always the one then playing who
at the moment seemed the greatest.[44]

In one thing all were agreed: that if there was any one
who could depose Bach, it could be none but Handel; as,
however, the names of those who formed this judgment
have remained unknown, and we are no longer able
to determine how far they were competent, it may
be considered a happy accident that Mattheson heard
both the masters, and has recorded his opinion.[45] Soon
after the transactions of 1720, he writes that among the
younger composers he had met with no one who displayed
such skill in double fugues as Handel, whether in setting
them or in extemporising, as he had heard him do, with
great admiration, a hundred times.[46] A very laudatory
general opinion of Bach has been already quoted; and in a
remark written later they are set in direct comparison, as
follows: " Particularly, no one can easily surpass Handel
in organ-playing, unless it were Bach, of Leipzig; for which
reason these two are mentioned first, out of their alphabetical
order. I have heard them in the prime of their powers, and

---

[44] Scheibe, ibid., pp. 843, 875, note 15.

[45] Peter Kellner also heard them both play (F. W. Marpurg, Historisch-
Kritische Beyträge, I., p. 444. Berlin, 1754), but his verdict remains unknown.
Ph. Emanuel Bach, on the other hand, records his judgment, but only from
hearsay and suppositions, as to Handel's playing. See his letter to Eschenburg,
in Nohl, Musikerbriefe, ed. 2, p. XLIX. Leipzig: Duncker und Humblot, 1873.

[46] Crit. Mus., I., p. 326.

have often competed with the former, both in Hamburg and in Lübeck."[47] It is beyond a doubt that Mattheson was quite competent to pronounce judgment in such a case; he was a musician of incontestably sound training. But I regard it as equally beyond a doubt that in this instance his information is wholly worthless. Mattheson's recollection of Handel's organ-playing dated from the days of their youth, when they were much together—days which, as he grew older, he recalled with peculiar pleasure. The experience is universal that favourable judgments cherished in youth are apt to persist, in spite of our progressive development, even when the subject of our interest is never again within reach for the verification of the opinion; and this was the case here. Mattheson had never heard Handel play since 1706.[48] Even if he had, his decision might have remained the same, because Handel's proclivities as an artist were far more sympathetic than Bach's to Mattheson, who had grown up under the influence of the opera—more particularly of Keiser's opera—and who, while still young, had become indifferent to organ music.[49] And this sympathy did not cease to exist, in spite of Handel's distant behaviour; still, it is an error to assert that after 1720 Mattheson showed a warm interest in Bach.[50] I have already stated that this was not the case, and a collation of the passages from Mattheson's writings relating to Handel and Bach reveals his attitude very clearly. Finally, it is of some importance to note that vanity would prompt him to set Handel's importance as an organist as high as possible, for had he not competed with him in Hamburg and Lübeck? The notable mode of expression used in the sentence quoted— not free from partisanship, but only wavering — also had its origin in the want of lucidity and the indecision of the writer, whose inclination and judgment balanced on

---

[47] Vollk. Capellmeister (Hamburg), 1739, p. 479.

[48] Chrysander has shown that Handel was already in Italy in 1707. Händel, I., p. 139.

[49] This is very conspicuous in the " neu eröffnetes Orchestre."

[50] Compare Chrysander, Händel, III., pp. 211-213; his views throughout are opposed to mine.

opposite sides. All attempts to explain it away are vain; for
this purpose he is useless.

We may, however, accept his statements about Handel as
a player and composer of double fugues, for there is at any
rate something characteristic in it; but this brings us back
to deciding upon internal grounds, which is, in fact, what
we must do with the whole question. It must all rest on
this: to which of the two musicians organ music was of the
deepest vital significance. Handel, too, had derived his first
training from a German organist, and had been one himself,
for a while, in his youth; but he turned towards other aims,
ending at last by using the organ as a musical means, one
among others in the general mass of instruments he
employed, but merely as a support or to introduce external
embellishments. Bach started from the organ, and remained
faithful to it to the last day of his life. All his productions
in other departments—or, at any rate, all his sacred compositions—are merely an expansion and development of
his organ music; this was to him the basis of all creation,
the vivifying soul of every form he wrought out. Consequently in this he, of the two composers, must have been
capable of the greatest work—the greatest, not merely in
technical completeness, but also in the perfect adaptation of
its purport to the instrument. When once we are clear as
to this, the accounts handed down to us are equally clear,
and leave no doubt in our minds that Handel's organ-playing
was not, properly speaking, characterised by *style* in the
highest sense—was not that which is, as it were, conceived
and born of the nature of the instrument. It was more
touching and graceful than Bach's; but the proper function
of the organ is neither to touch nor to flatter the ear.
Handel adapted to the organ ideas drawn from the stores of
his vast musical wealth, which included all the art of his
time, just as he did to any other instrument. In this way
he evolved an exoteric meaning, intelligible to all, and hence
the popular effect. To him the organ was an instrument for
the concert-room, not for the church. It corresponds to this
conception that we have no compositions by Handel for the
organ alone, while it was precisely by these that Bach's

fame was to a great extent kept up till this century; but we have by Handel a considerable number of organ concertos with instrumental accompaniment, and adapted with brilliant effect to chamber music.

His fondness for the double fugue—an older, simpler and not very rich form, of which, however, the materials are easier to grasp, and which is therefore more generally intelligible, can also be referred to his exceptional attitude towards the organ ; and so no less may the improvisatory manner which was peculiar to his playing and to his clavier compositions, which came close to the limits of organ music; while the organ—which, both in character and application, is essentially a church instrument—must be handled with the utmost collectedness of mind and an absolute suppression of the mood of the moment. It is in the highest degree probable that Handel—whose technical skill was certainly supreme—with his grand flow of ideas, and his skill in availing himself of every quality of an instrument, produced unheard-of effects in his improvisations on the organ. But even the more fervid and captivating of these effects must have been very different from Bach's sublimer style. I must at least contravene what has been asserted by an otherwise thoughtful judge[51]—namely, that he was surpassed on this one point—taking it for granted that improvisation is to be criticised by its intrinsic musical worth, and not merely by its transient and immediate effect. At a time when so much importance was attached to extempore music, which indeed, as an exercise in thorough-bass, was part of the musical curriculum everywhere, it would have been most strange if the man whose whole being as an artist was wrapped up in the organ, and who had exhausted its powers in every direction, had not risen to a corresponding height in this point also. The express testimony of his sons and pupils as to his " admirable and learned manner of fanciful playing"—*i.e.*, improvising—as to the " novelty, singularity, expressiveness and beauty of his inspirations at the moment, and their perfect rendering," stands in evidence. " When he

---

[51] Chrysander, p. 213.

sat down to the organ, irrespective of Divine service, as he
was often requested to do by strangers, he would choose
some theme, and play it in every form of organ composition
in such a way that the matter remained the same, even
when he had played uninterruptedly for two hours or more.
First he would use the theme as introductory, and for a
fugue with full organ. Then he would show his skill in
varying the stops, in a trio, a quartet or what not, still on
the same theme. Then would follow a chorale, and with its
melody the first theme would again appear in three or four
different parts, and in the most various and intricate development. Finally, the close would consist of a fugue for full
organ, in which either a new arrangement of the original
theme was predominant, or it was combined with one or
two other subjects, according to its character." [52]

So far as concerns the other aspects of organ music the
author of the Necrology might with justice appeal to Bach's
existing compositions, which call into requisition the highest
technical means in order to express the profoundest ideal
meaning and "which he himself, as is well known, performed
to the utmost perfection," and so confirm his statement
that " Bach was the greatest organ-player that has as yet
been known."

II.

BACH'S CLAVIER MUSIC.—TOCCATAS.—HIS REFORM IN FINGER-
ING.—ADJUSTMENT OF PITCH.—INVENTION OF THE PIANO-
FORTE.—BACH AS A TEACHER.—THE CLAVIER-BÜCHLEIN.—
INVENTIONEN UND SINFONIEN.

WE must now investigate more closely the field in which
Bach had been especially invited to labour at Cöthen. At

[52] Kirnberger, Die wahren Grundsätze zum Gebrauch der Harmonie, p. 53,
note. Berlin und Königsberg, 1773. Mizler, p. 171. Forkel, p. 22. Forkel
observes that the method of organ improvisation attributed to Bach is precisely
that form of organ music which Reinken had supposed to have died out; and we
must assume that it was so, inasmuch as northern masters depended much upon
the stops, used independent themes in contrast to the lines of the chorale, were
fond of dissecting and remodelling the ideas of the fugue, and of extending and
enlarging upon it generally.

that time the harpsichord was the instrument nearest to the organ ; its soulless tone—which could only acquire a certain amount of expressiveness by the use of several keyboards—indicated the necessity for infusing an intrinsic animation by means of polyphony and rich harmonic treatment, of a steady and thoroughly progressive melodic development ; and, in addition to these—since it was defective in duration of sound—of increased rapidity of action. Henceforth he cultivated both these instruments with equal devotion, and endeavoured to extend the province of each in its style by reciprocal borrowing. Just as, on one hand, he adapted to the harpsichord the tied and *legato* mode of playing which the organ imperatively demands, so, on the other hand, he transferred to the organ so much of the florid execution of the clavier style as could be engrafted on its nature. Hence, though the organ, as was due to its superior importance, always had the precedence, his art was developed quite equally on both instruments ; and, in the very year which saw the end of his official work as organist, he was required to stand a triumphant comparison with one of the great French clavier-masters. Hitherto no particular attention has been directed to the clavier compositions of the Weimar period, with the express purpose of not confusing our general purview, which has been cast in other directions. We will now hastily sketch, in broad outlines, what has been neglected so far, and thus directly lead on to the consideration of the whole department of his clavier and other chamber music in Cöthen.

When speaking of the cantata " Nach dir, Herr, verlanget mich " (Vol. I., p. 433), it was said that the fugal thema of the first chorus had undergone further development in a toccata for the clavier in F sharp minor. This theme is, no doubt, a favourite subject of Bach's, and recurs frequently ; nevertheless, the identity—alike in the whole and in the details, in the feeling and in the expression—is so complete that we may regard the piece as a remodelling of the chorus quite as certainly as we detect in the beautiful organ fugue in A major the further development of the subjects of the overture to " Tritt auf die Glaubensbahn." That the

chorus is not the later and the toccata the earlier work is
proved by the greater musical completeness of the latter
piece, and, in the second place, by its superiority to the
three clavier toccatas previously mentioned, in D minor, G
minor and E minor (Vol. I., p. 433), from which, indeed, it
differs widely as to form. Like them, however, it is not
unique in its way, for Bach, following out his old principles,
wrought out at least two such pieces, thus giving us a right
to regard them as constituting a new species of toccata.[53]

The essential improvement that characterises it consists in
the introduction of a slow subject thoroughly worked out as
an organic element, and in reducing the two fugues formerly
included to one—if not in the strict sense of the word, at
any rate so far as the thematic material is concerned. The
ornate portions at the beginning remain, and have also
appropriated a certain space in the middle. The slow
subject follows immediately on the introductory runs; it is
worked out with great skill and feeling on the themes—

and :—

A half-close prepares us for the fugue, which in one place
runs to sixty-one bars, and in the other only to forty-seven.
The process is only apparently different in the two works;
in the toccata in F sharp minor an episode of one bar serves
for the development of a free interlude, which is, it cannot
be denied—like the second part of the clavier prelude in
A minor—somewhat digressive and fatiguing, in spite of
several modifications of the motive. In the C minor
toccata the composer is content with a few bars full of
brilliant passages, and then the fugue begins again; but
now, by the addition of a second subject, it becomes a
double fugue, while in the F sharp minor toccata he returns
to the theme of the *adagio*, and constructs on that a quite

---

[53] B.-G., III., pp. 311, 322. P. S. I., C. 4, Nos. 4 and 5; Vol. 210, pp. 10, 20.
See Appendix A, No. 2.

new fugue, distinct even in time. Why he should have done
this here is clear by a reference to his model—the cantata—
for there also the theme at first appears broad in style and
full of longing, and then, after a highly varied interlude, it
returns *agitato* and with intricate elaboration.

These two toccatas are superior to the former set, not
merely by the greater concentration of their form, but also by
the solidity and significance of their subject-matter; the
E minor toccata alone is worthy to be compared with them in
its peculiar dreamy and longing expression. The rather tame
interlude of the F sharp minor toccata renders it somewhat
inferior to its fellow, although, from its prevalent imaginative character, it does not seriously disturb the flow of
the piece. For, when the *adagio* comes in with its deep
accents, after the introductory passages, which seem to
have met fortuitously, as it were, it is as though spirits
innumerable were let loose—whispering, laughing, dancing
up and down—teasing or catching each other—gliding
calmly and smoothly on a translucent stream—wreathed
together into strange and shadowy forms; then suddenly
the phantoms have vanished, and the hours of existence
are passing as in every-day life, when the former turmoil
begins afresh—only now the memory of a deep grief pierces
through it unceasingly.

It is otherwise with the second toccata. After a stormy
beginning, the *adagio* sinks into grave meditation, from
which the fugue springs forth with a most original repetition
of the first phrase of the theme; this indeed is conspicuous
throughout the arrangement, and serves to determine its
general character. It is a proud and handsome youth,
swimming on the full tide of life, and never weary of the
delightful consciousness of strength. Compare with this,
again, the closing fugue of the E minor toccata, and marvel
at the master's inexhaustible creative wealth.

By the side of these two toccatas stands a three-part
fugue in A minor, which is prefaced by a short *arpeggiato*
introduction.[54] This is the longest clavier fugue that Bach

---

[54] B. G., III., p. 334.   P. S. I., C. 4, No. 2 ; Vol. 207, p. 36.   Andreas Bach
has a manuscript copy.

II.

left complete; it consists of a hundred and ninety-eight bars, 3-4 time; besides this, it moves in uninterrupted semiquavers, so that it may be called another "moto perpetuo," and placed by the side of Weber's well-known movement.

It is hard to decide which most to admire—the unbridled and incessant flow of fancy or the firm structure which connects the whole; or, again, the executive skill and endurance that it presupposes. The theme, consisting of six bars, appears only ten times; more than two-thirds of the composition are worked out episodically, from the material it affords, and the nearer we get to the end, the less do we hear the theme in a regular form—only three times, in fact, in the last hundred bars. The mighty rush of the initial portion gradually swells to a raving storm, which almost takes the hearer's breath away; but, of course, without an *accelerando*, only by an increment of internal effects. When we now learn that Bach was accustomed to take the *tempo* of his compositions very fast, a degree of execution is suggested compared to which the hardest tasks of any other composer are as child's play. Bach owed his own attainment of it not merely to his iron perseverance, but also to the formative force of genius, which taught him to find the means of giving an adequate clothing to the world of ideas that seethed within him.

At the beginning of the seventeenth century the musical world was very indifferent as to the mode of using and playing on keyed instruments. A musician who was conspicuous for this way of thinking, Michael Prætorius, despised all who even spoke of them in real earnest, declaring that if a musical note were produced clearly and agreeably to the ear, it was a matter of indifference how this was done, even if it had to be played with the nose.[55] At a later date, the advantage—indeed, the absolute necessity—of a regular scheme of fingering was better understood; but it was not till the beginning of the eighteenth century that a rational and methodical practice began to prevail. Up to that time the thumb was almost excluded from use, and the exercise

---

[55] Prætorius, Syntagma Musicum.

of the little finger very lame, to say the least. The reason for this lay in the conspicuous difference in length between these and the three middle fingers, which seemed to disable them from equal efficiency. Still, as it was necessary to attend to the slurring of the notes one into another, particularly on the organ, the middle fingers were slipped over or under each other; the thumb simply hung down. It is, indeed, beyond a doubt that the school of Sweelinck and his compeers—that is to say, all the northern composers, more or less—who did so much to improve rapidity of execution, also did much in the regulation of the principles of fingering.[56] At the same time, even these never used the thumb, excepting under necessity; for, when Sebastian Bach told his son Philipp Emanuel Bach that he, as a lad, had heard great men play who could only make up their minds to use this despised finger for very wide stretches, we cannot understand him as meaning any but the northern masters, and Böhm, who was so closely allied to them. To Bach himself the unnatural conditions of such a limitation were soon obvious; he began to turn the thumb to the same account as the other fingers, and he must at once have perceived that the whole art of playing had thereby undergone a complete revolution. While the useless hanging of the thumb had resulted in an outstretched position for the other fingers, the use of it, being so much shorter, naturally necessitated a curved position for the others. This curving at once excluded all rigidity; the fingers remained in an easy, elastic attitude, ready for extension or contraction at any moment, and they could now hit the keys rapidly and accurately as they hovered close over them. Thus, by diligent practice, the greatest possible equality of touch, strength and rapidity was acquired in both hands, and each was made quite independent of the other.[57]

---

[56] There have been hitherto hardly any direct authorities that are copious on this subject. C. F. Becker, in his work Hausmusik in Deutschland, p. 60, has given a few examples of fingering for scales and passages, dating from the seventeenth century, and Hilgenfeldt has repeated them (p. 173); and a complete and very valuable MS., of 1698, with clavier pieces, many of them very precisely fingered, is in my possession.

[57] Mizler, p. 171.

Practical insight and a talent for composition combined
to discover the surest and quickest road to these ends; every
finger must be made equally available for every purpose; and
Bach learned to perform trills and other embellishments with
the third and little finger just as evenly and roundly as with
the others. Nay, he even found it quite easy, meanwhile,
to play the melody lower down with the same hand. The
natural tendency of the thumb to bend towards the hollow
of the hand made it of admirable use in passing it under the
other fingers, or them over it. The scales—those most important of all the sequences of notes—were newly fingered
by Bach ; he established the rule that the thumb of the
right hand must fall immediately after the two semitones of
the scale in going up, and before them in coming down, and
vice versâ in the left hand.[58] To release the note, the tips of
the fingers were not so much lifted as withdrawn ; this was
necessary to give equality to the playing, because the passing of one of the middle fingers over the little finger or the
thumb could only be effected by drawing back the latter ;
and it also contributed to a *cantabile* effect, as well as to
clearness in executing rapid passages on the clavichord.
The result of all this was that Bach played with a scarcely
perceptible movement of his hands; his fingers hardly
seemed to touch the keys, and yet everything came out with
perfect clearness, and a pearly roundness and purity.[59] His
body, too, remained, perfectly quiescent, even during the
most difficult pedal passages on the organ or harpsichord ;
his pedal *technique* was as smooth and unforced as his
fingering.[60] His peculiar fertility of resource enabled him to
overcome incidental difficulties ; in keyboards placed one
above the other he preferred short keys, so as to be more
easily able to move from one to another, and he liked the
upper row to be somewhat shallower than the lower, because

---

[58] Kirnberger, Grundsätze, &c., p. 4, note 2. Compare Ph. Em. Bach, p. 18.
[59] Quantz, Versuch einer Anweisung die Flöte Traversiere zu spielen, third
edition, 1789, p. 232. Forkel, p. 12. Compare Ph. Em. Bach, p. 13. See
App. A., No. 3.
[60] Scheibe, p. 840.

he could slip down imperceptibly, without any change of finger.[61]

It was not Bach alone, however, of the musicians of that period who had hit upon the more extensive use of the thumb; the whole art of organ and clavier music, now so rapidly developing, cried out for the introduction of more ample methods of rendering. In France, François Couperin (1668-1733), Organist of the church of St. Gervais, opened the way to a more rational rule of fingering by his work, "L'Art de Toucher le Clavecin" (Paris, 1717). Johann Gottfried Walther, Bach's contemporary—and, at one time, his colleague in Weimar—has left us a few organ chorales, with marked fingering, in which the thumb is variously employed.[62] Heinichen, who has been already mentioned, invariably requires the employment of all five fingers for the performance of his directions for playing from figured bass.[63] Handel also brought the thumbs into constant play, as necessarily follows from the bent position of his fingers, as described by eye-witnesses,[64] by which they fell upon the notes almost by themselves.

Still the new method was not methodically worked out either by Couperin or by Walther. In the scales Couperin certainly prescribes starting with the thumb on the first note, but not the turning under of the thumb in the progress upwards ; he is very ready to employ the thumb in changes on the same note, and also in extensions, where he freely allows it to strike the black keys, but hardly ever in such a way as that it is passed under the middle finger, or the middle finger over it. Two solitary cases occur among the vast selection of examples and test-pieces in " L'Art de Toucher le Clavecin," in which the method is different; one of these is for the left hand, and it is remarkable that the left-hand thumb

---

[61] Adlung, Mus. Mech., II., p. 24.

[62] See the Königsberg autograph. There are arrangements of "Allein Gott in der Höh," "Wir glauben all an einen Gott," "Wo soll ich fliehen hin" (verse 3).

[63] J. D. Heinichen, Der General-Bass in der Composition, p. 522. Dresden, 1728.

[64] Chrysander, Händel, III., p. 218 ; from Burney.

seems to have been brought into frequent use at a much
earlier date, and here the passing over of the middle finger
is several times indicated. The other has the following
fingering [65]—

a decisive piece of evidence as to the want of practice in the
use of the thumb; by turning the thumb according to
Bach's rule—that is to say, on the _c″_—the passage runs of
itself. In the three organ chorales Walther only twice
crosses the middle finger over the thumb, and then in the
left hand; in other cases only the first finger. Of Handel's
method we know nothing exact; however, Mattheson
supplies this deficiency to a certain extent, since, as has
been said already, he thought he could compete with him
in clavier-playing, and he, in the most crucial instance—
namely, in the scales—does not know the method of turning
the thumb under, but in ascending he puts the middle finger
over the third in the old manner, in the right hand, and,
in descending, the middle finger over the first.[66] Philipp
Emanuel Bach, himself one of the most remarkable, if not
the most remarkable, of the clavier-players of the middle of
the eighteenth century, has laid down his views on the method
of teaching the clavier in an admirable and very thorough
work.[67] In the lesson on fingering, section 7, he speaks of its
extension and improvement by his father, "so that now
everything that is possible can be easily performed"; and
he there explains that his wish is to base his teaching on
the progressive development of his father's method.

It has been universally assumed that Emanuel Bach's
method is the same as his father's, not merely in fingering,
but in the other elements of instruction, although there is no
statement in the book which satisfactorily proves it. How-

---

[65] L'Art de Toucher le Clavecin, p. 66, lowest stave.   From the second book
of Pièces de Clavecin; in the new edition by J. Brahms, p. 121 (Denkmäler der
Tonkunst, IV.).

[66] Kleine Generalbasschule, p. 72.   Hamburg, 1735.

[67] Versuch über die wahre Art Clavier zu Spielen.

ever, two small pieces with the fingering marked throughout
in Sebastian Bach's own hand have come down to us, and
a comparison of these with the rules laid down by his son
proves that they differ widely. Philipp Emanuel prohibits
the passing of the middle finger over the first; Sebastian prescribes it in the fifth bar of the first piece and in bars 22 and
23 of the second, agreeing with Couperin, as is shown by
the example given above. Emanuel does not allow the third
finger to cross over the little finger; Sebastian requires it of
the left hand in bars 38 and 39 of the second piece. The practice of crossing under Emanuel limits to the thumb; Sebastian
makes the little finger pass under the third in bars 34 and 35 of
the same piece. Of the crossing of the little finger over the
thumb, which Emanuel also forbids, there is, as it happens,
no example in Sebastian's little pieces, but we find it in one
of Walther's chorales. Yet more: although Sebastian's rule
for using the thumb after the semitone intervals of the scale
is most distinctly authenticated,[68] he himself has not observed
it at the beginning of the first of these pieces, but has fingered
it in the old manner, and though in the third bar the left hand
advances, it is true, by a turn over the thumb it is only
with the first finger, in the old fashion. Thus, though his
fingering is distinguished from that of his predecessors and
contemporaries by the regular use of the thumb, it differs
from his son's method by certain peculiarities, some of which
are retained from the older method of playing, while others
were naturally derived from it; the origin of Sebastian
Bach's method is thus tolerably clear. It took into due consideration all the combinations which the use of the thumb
now rendered possible, but without abandoning the technical
accomplishment which the earlier method had afforded;
still, we may be permitted to suppose that Bach, who
always followed the path pointed out by Nature, avoided, as
far as possible, passing a smaller finger over a larger: for
instance, the first or the third over the middle finger.

This combination of methods gave him such an unlimited

---

[68] By Mizler, as well as by Kirnberger; he also was a pupil of Bach's, and in
the Mus. Bib., II., p. 115, he thus fingers certain scale passages.

command of means that it is easy to understand how it was that difficulties had ceased to exist for him. And, as though he had been destined in every respect to stand alone and at the summit of his art, he remained the only master of clavier-playing who acquired such stupendous technical facility. All who came before him, and all who succeeded him, worked with a much smaller supply of means; he stood on an eminence commanding two realms, and ruled that which lay before him as well as that he had left behind. His son even, who represents the actual starting-point of modern clavier-playing, greatly simplified his father's rules of fingering. He limited the crossing of the longest fingers to that of the middle finger over the third, and cultivated a more extensive use of the thumb. He did not, indeed, require such a wealth of resource for his far easier and more homophonic style of composition; and in art all that is superfluous is faulty. Then, with the introduction of the modern pianoforte, the door was finally closed on the old method of fingering, because the mechanism of hammers demands an elastic tap on the key from above, and prohibits the oblique blow which is given by crossing the middle fingers. Thus, even in these days, when we boast of a sovereign command of all the resources of clavier *technique*, Sebastian Bach's own mode of playing can only be restored to the extent to which it was carried out by his son, and is even now indispensable to enable us to perform Bach's compositions. It would be lost to us as a whole, even if we could be conversant with all its details; but the abnormal difficulty of his compositions is in great part grounded on this; for all that modern skill has gained on one side it has necessarily lost on another, from the very nature of the instrument. For this reason it cannot be denied that the modern *technique* is, after all, not superior to Bach's, or at any rate that he overcame many difficulties far more easily. What holds good for the clavier does so still more for the organ; indeed, Bach stamped the character of the organ on the clavier, without, however, detracting from its intrinsic value. But here, where there were no hindrances arising from the construction of the instrument, a further development of *technique* on the lines he had laid down would not be impossible ; and, so soon as this instrument attained somewhat more importance in our artistic life, the attempt was immediately made.

The utmost improvement of finger practice was indispensable to Bach, if for this reason only : that he was accustomed to play on claviers of equal temperament, and could therefore avail himself indifferently of all the twenty-four keys. The idea of establishing the equal temperament by a regular distribution of the ditonic comma—that is to say, by an adjustment of the difference resulting from twelve fifths, as compared with the twelve degrees included in the scale of an octave—had been already thought of at the beginning of the seventeenth century, and soon found universal acceptance. Many of the musicians already so frequently mentioned had made theoretical use of it—as Andreas Werkmeister (1644-1706) and Johann Georg Neidhardt (died 1740)—still the discovery can hardly have led to any practical application, since the differences of pitch were so minute as to be finally distinguishable by the ear alone. The methods of tempering which were evolved from the theory were at first singular enough. About the year 1739, the three following general rules still obtained : (1) The octave, the minor sixth and third must be absolutely pure ; (2) the major sixth and the fourth were to be somewhat enlarged ; (3) the fifth and major third were to be somewhat diminished.[69] How far this may have sounded well or ill may be approximately estimated when we remember that the determination of only the octave, fourth and fifth has any foundation in the nature of things ; all the intervals which have a more complicated relation to the keynote, like the major and minor sixths and the minor third, will bear, as is well known, greater deviations from their pure relation ; and how the major thirds can have been diminished is quite inconceivable, since the sum of three major thirds, even when purely tuned, does not equal an octave, which is what equal temperament demands.

---

[69] Mattheson, Vollkommener Capellmeister, p. 55.

It is very satisfactory to know that in this, too, Bach was in advance of his time, and had already made himself master of the method of tuning which is now universally followed. It is expressly stated that he took all the major thirds a little sharp—that is to say, slightly augmented—which is indispensable for the equalisation of the diesis.[70] But as it is impossible that he should have tuned from nothing but major thirds, he must have proceeded as we still do at the present day—that is to say, by four successive fifths, each slightly flattened, so that the last note forms a major third with the key-note, and, with the aid of the first fifth, a common chord on it. Of the various artifices which are used to facilitate the application of this method, he must have known, at any rate, that which consists in testing the deviation of the fifth by striking it, together with its octave, the fourth below the key-note, and taking the fifth up again from thence.[71] That he evolved all this by his own study and reflection, and not from reading theoretical treatises, would be very certain, even if we had not the testimony of his contemporaries;[72] and he carried out his method with such rapidity and certainty that it never took him more than a quarter of an hour to tune a harpsichord or a clavichord.[73]

---

[70] F. W. Marpurg, Versuch über die Musikalische Temperatur, p. 213. Berlin, 1776. "Herr Kirnberger himself has often told me and others how, during the time when he enjoyed the instruction of the celebrated Joh. Sebastian Bach, he would intrust to him the tuning of his clavier, and expressly enjoined him to make all the major thirds sharp."

[71] Emanuel Bach speaks of this, as well as of the tuning of the fifth downwards and the testing of the third, in section 14 of the introduction to the Versuch über die wahre Art, &c.; and he could scarcely have had any inclination to deviate from his father's practice in the matter of temperament.

[72] Mattheson was a sworn enemy to certain folks who insisted on making music a branch of mathematical science, and in this he was one with Bach. In Mizler's autobiography in the Ehrenpforte he adds, on p. 231, à propos to Mizler's intercourse with Bach, this observation: "Bach very certainly would no more have brought forward this mathematical basis of composition than the present writer [Mattheson]; that I will warrant." And what he says as to composition naturally holds good for the other branches of art: "Our late friend Bach never entered into deep theoretical considerations about music, and was all the more efficient in performance." Necrology, p. 173.

[73] Forkel, p. 17.

We soon shall see the splendid use in creative work which he made of the newly opened realm of tone, now for the first time accessible. But he did not allow himself to be led away into excursive modulations ; this was quite opposed to his style. It was only under special circumstances that he now and then showed how keenly alive his ear was to the inner connection of keys, and how admirably he could avail himself of enharmonic transitions when he chose. An instance occurs in the prelude, previously mentioned, to the Hamburg fugue in G minor ; another in the Chromatic Fantasia, as it is called, to which we shall return later.

I cannot decide, in view of the slender evidence, whether a piece called "Das kleine harmonische Labyrinth"— "The Little Labyrinth of Harmony"—is by Bach or not; it consists of an entrance full of enharmonic wandering, leading up, as to a central goal, to a little fugue, which is worked out, and then has its exit through similar mazy paths, returning to daylight in the key of C major. It was Heinichen—Prince Leopold's companion in Italy—who first clearly displayed, and practically applied, the sequence and connection of the twenty-four keys. We know of no similar attempt from Bach's hand; the soaring independence of his genius was averse to every merely mechanical device.[74]

We have designated the tone of the harpsichord as soulless, and, so far, similar to that of the organ. At the same time it cannot have remained unnoticed by a delicate ear that it responded more kindly under the hands of one player than those of another; hence it is not altogether unreasonable to speak of a subjective mode of treatment, even of the harpsichord. The possibility of such a treatment depends partly on the indefinable peculiarities of touch, and then on the yet more indescribable art of calling forth in the hearer those responsive emotions which are indispensable to the appreciation of the artistic idea; a power which clavier music demands with peculiar insistence. We have reason

---

[74] Heinichen (Gen. Bass, p. 837, Dresden 1728); and even before this in the title work published in 1711. The test piece, pp. 885-895, is wrongly assigned to Bach in a MS. in the Royal Library at Berlin (press-mark p. 295). The "kleine harmonische Labyrinth" is also to be found there.

to suppose that Bach must have possessed this power.
That he had a peculiar charm of touch is a matter
of course, with his new modes of playing; and that his
playing, even on the harpsichord, which he always furnished
with quills himself, must have been, in a certain way, inspired. His son Philipp Emanuel points out that the only
way to attain this is the diligent cultivation of the clavichord,[75] and this was precisely Sebastian's favourite instrument. Even though it had not much strength, the tone was
wonderfully capable of light and shade, and comparatively
persistent. It was possible to play *cantabile* on it, and this
cantabile style was regarded by Bach as the foundation of all
clavier-playing. In view of these indisputable facts, the
opinion we find expressed here and there, that, in the performances of his clavier pieces, Bach gave no light and shade of
expression, and that the introduction of such a rendering
is a presumptuous modern innovation, must fall to the
ground as an unfounded hypothesis.

Nowhere can we see more strikingly than here how a
great genius can contain within itself the aim and end of a
long process of historical development, and foresee it across
the lapse even of centuries. The ideal instrument which
floated in the mind of Bach for the performance of his
Inventions and *Sinfonias,* of his suites and clavier fugues, was
not altogether the clavichord; the ideas brought down by
him from the sublime heights of the organ were too ponderous, and weighed too heavily on its delicate frame. But
it was not the organ either. From the organ, no doubt,
emanated that craving for more abundant alternations of
feeling which sought its satisfaction in chamber-music, just
as the endeavour after definition of feeling gave rise to the
main idea of the church cantata as proceeding from the
organ chorale. Its solemn, calm and rapt solitude blos-
somed out into blooming beauty and the living speech of
man. The harpsichord could not here satisfy him; no

---

[75] Ph. Em. Bach, op. cit., section 17: "By constant playing on the harpsichord we get into the way of playing with one sort of tone, and the different
varieties of tone which can be brought out even by an ordinarily good clavichord-
player are entirely lost."

instrument but one which should combine the volume of tone of the organ with the expressive quality of the clavichord, in due proportion, could be capable of reproducing the image which dwelt in the master's imagination when he composed for the clavier. Every one sees at once that the modern pianoforte is in fact just such an instrument. Nothing can be more perverse than to wish to have the old clavichord restored in order to play Bach's clavier pieces— or even the harpsichord, which, indeed, was of the very smallest importance in Bach's musical practice; this might do for Kuhnau, for Couperin, and Marchand; Bach's grander creations demand a flowing robe of sound, an inspired mien and expressive motions.

If, in recent times, more and more attention has been paid to Bach's clavier works, one reason for this, among others, and by no means the least, is that we have felt that at last the means were not altogether inadequate to the purpose. Of course this is not said with reference to executive embellishment; but, indeed, the danger in this direction is not imminent; the fabric of these compositions is so compact, the progression of the parts so melodious throughout, that any arbitrary insertion of heterogeneous details is all but impossible, after a little studious attention to their organic structure. Where a phrase is intended to be conspicuous, the composer has taken care that it shall become so of itself. The echo-like contrasts of *forte* and *piano*, which are indicated by the character of the harpsichord, with its several keyboards, are almost always marked, and where they are not they are easily recognisable—they invariably refer each to a complete phrase. Whatever more than this depends on the performer will infallibly be clear to him when once he has accustomed himself to follow, in his own mind, the vocal phrasing, so to speak, of the separate parts, and their symphonic combined effect. He will then breathe life into the emotions they embody, in due proportion as they swell and fall, and give more or less fulness of tone in sympathy with their agreement or antagonism to the fundamental harmony at the moment. Then will he become aware of that melody which pervades the inner parts of the

harmonic progression of every piece by Bach. He will ride
on its wings, whether it roars with the force of a storm, or,
again, whispers like the breath of May—intangible, invisible,
and yet all-pervading. Bach's clavier compositions are a
heritage into which it has been left to this generation to
enter in the fullest extent—an inestimable legacy to a
period when the spring of musical inspiration no longer
flows with its former abundance—an immovable rock in the
midst of the troubled waters of passionate aberrations, and
a solemn warning to all who still have ears to hear never to
neglect the dignity of art.

The master lived to see the early youth of the pianoforte,
and aided it by severe criticism. Gottfried Silbermann, of
Freiburg, somewhere between 1740 and 1750 constructed two
claviers with hammer action, probably after the invention
of Cristofori, the Florentine. Bach played on one of these,
praised the tone highly, and found fault only with the heavy
touch and the feebleness of the upper notes. Deeply as
Silbermann felt this criticism, he nevertheless was willing to
bow to it; he worked for years at the improvement of his
hammer action, and at last earned Bach's unqualified
praise.[76] It is not likely that Bach ever became himself the
possessor of such an instrument, for, if he had, his pupil
Agricola, through whom we hear of the affair, would have
mentioned it. And the reason is very clear: the hammer
mechanism did not accommodate itself readily enough to all
the appliances of Bach's method of fingering. Still, his
satisfaction at Silbermann's instrument shows very clearly
whither his clavier music tended.

To remedy at least one main defect in the harpsichord—
namely, its brief resonance—in the year 1740 (or thereabout)
he devised a "Lauten-clavicymbel" (Lute-harpsichord),
which was constructed by the organ-builder Zacharias
Hildebrand, under his direction; the greater duration of
tone was produced by gut strings, of which it had two to
each note, and these were supplemented by a set of metal
strings giving a four-foot tone. When the ringing tone of

---

[76] Adlung, Mus. Mech., II., p. 139.

these was checked by a damper of cloth the instrument sounded much like a real lute, while without this it had more of the gloomy character of the theorbo. In size it was shorter than the ordinary harpsichord.[77] The thorough comprehension of the construction of instruments which Bach here displays, and the experience he had already proved in the department of organ-building, together with his skill in tuning and his perfection of ingenuity in fingering, are the outcome of his technical talent. His superb nature stands firm on the true foundations of all art—an inexhaustible depth of imagination; while his thorough technical knowledge includes even the humblest mechanical means of casting the precious material in the noblest forms. We need only remember the talents of Joh. Michael and Joh. Nikolaus Bach respectively to verify once more the statement that in Sebastian all the capacity of his family converged.[78] An admirable musical connoisseur of the last century exclaims that "the immortal Joh. Seb. Bach combined all the great and different talents of a hundred other musicians."[79]

Nor was it only that all the ways and means of artistic production and utterance were at his command; he was besides a distinguished teacher of music. Of all the great German composers, Bach is the only one round whom are grouped any great number of disciples—men, too, who do not owe their chief glory to their master. Irrespective of his sons, Ziegler, Agricola, Altnikol, Ernst Bach, Homilius, Kirnberger, Goldberg, Müthel, Kittel, Transchel, Vogler and, above all, Joh. Ludwig Krebs were musicians of undoubted merit, and some of them of great eminence. Though no one of them opened out new paths in composition, the reason of this lay partly in the isolated supremacy

---

[77] Adlung, Mus. Mech., II., p. 139.

[78] Bitter, in his book on J. Seb. Bach, I. (p. 141), states that the composer constructed a musical clock for the castle at Cöthen, which still exists in the Castle of Nienburg, on the Saale. Herr Albert, the minister there, was good enough to examine this clock at my request; it bears on a disc in the interior the words "*Johann Zacharias Fischer Fecit. a. Halle.*"

[79] Marpurg, Lo. Cit., p. 234.

of their master himself; it was hard to make any approach to that, and creative power is a thing that can neither be imparted nor acquired. The strong point of Bach's pupils lay in their executive art, to which industry and good guidance are the chief aids. That Bach could so well cultivate these is due in the first place to the moral worth of his character, which prompted him to place his own acquirements with self-denying liberality at the service of his fellow-men. "Dem höchsten Gott allein zu Ehren, Dem Nächsten draus sich zu belehren," was what he wrote (see Vol. I., p. 598) on the title-page of the precious "Little Organ Book," and he acted up to his motto. It both commands our reverence and quickens our heart to see this man, whose Titanic imagination could at one moment lift its hand to grasp a sublime ideal, sitting down, the next hour, among his scholars, the sons of organists and cantors of the most modest pretensions, explaining patiently the mechanical use of the fingers, generously helping a blunderer by writing out a special exercise, and urging them on to higher aims with all the earnestness of a teacher, by performing the examples he had set them. Thus he began in Mühlhausen, and thus he continued forty years later, when declining into old age. The native Bach spirit, the great German ideal, penetrated him throughout in all its depth and modesty.

Besides this, even his teaching promoted his own progress. No doubt one reason why most of the great masters have proved more or less unfitted for teaching is to be sought in their lack of patience in explaining clearly to others the things they have drunk in, as it were, instinctively; but there is, more certainly, another—namely, that they are all merely carrying forward and completing a process already begun, and that therefore they fail in that living experience which gives an interest even in the simplest elements. In the province of the organ this was Bach's attitude also. But in clavier music he had not only entered into the inheritance of his predecessors; he had brought to it so much from the stock of organ music that it acquired a perfectly new aspect, and in the same way he had so completely transformed its vehicle of expression—namely, the *technique* of fingering—by his intelligent and ingenious novelty of method that it was radically different. Here he felt himself the creator of the art from its most elementary principles; here he had tried and tested the best methods of training by his own indefatigable labours ; and from the nature of things that method of instruction took its rise in and from the clavier. It was one more instance of the truth long since uttered by Socrates: that every one can ·be eloquent on a subject he understands. And how could this eloquence fail of convincing effect, when his pupils saw to what results Bach's methods had brought him ? how in him the most exact knowledge and the utmost executive power were combined ? Then a third aspect of his gift for teaching lay in this : that he could, when needful, interrupt himself, set aside the clear logic of the intellect in favour of the flight of genius, and by a perfect revelation of his own powers show his pupils the goal which, under his guidance, they had begun to approach. Thus he refreshed and invigorated their courage ; and though on one hand he required the severest application, he at the same time had hours in store for them which, by their own admission, were among the happiest in their lives.[80]

We have some information, too, as to his course of instruction. In the first instance he only gave exercises in touch, in fingering and in the equal and independent action of every finger of both hands. To this he kept the pupil for at least a month, but would sweeten the bitter dose by giving him graceful little pieces, in each of which some special technical difficulty was dealt with. Even embellishments and *maniers,* as they were called, had to be practised persistently in both hands from the very first. When a certain proficiency had been attained in these elements he went on at once to the root of the matter in difficult compositions, by preference in his own. Before the pupil began to study one, he played it to him, thus rousing his zeal and a desire not to fail of a

---

[80] So says Heinrich Gerber, Lexicon, I. col. 492.

happy result.[81]   He set the highest value on industry, and
set himself up as an example to them in this alone.   " I
have to be diligent," he would say, " and any one who is
equally so will get on equally well."   He never seemed to
be aware of his wonderful gifts.

A happy circumstance has also enabled us to overhear, as
it were, a whole practical course of teaching by Bach, so far
at least as it is worked out by purely mechanical exercises
rounded off into complete musical pieces.   When his eldest
son was nine years old, finding he had great musical gifts,
his father began to cultivate them.   On January 22, 1720,
he projected the " Clavier-Büchlein" (Little Clavier-Book) for
Wilhelm Friedemann Bach,[82] in which, beginning with the
simplest elements, he introduced, by degrees, compositions
of progressive difficulty, and here and there even let the boy
himself write some.   On the first page the keys and the
principal ornaments are explained.[83]   Then follows the little
piece before mentioned as having the fingering marked.   It
is called *Applicatio*, and headed with the pious words, *In
nomine Jesu*.   Here scale passages and ornaments are combined with a special view (as is shown in bars 2, 6 and 8)
to the practice of the shake with the third and little fingers
of the right hand.   The second piece (a *preamble* of eighteen
bars in C major) is for the practice of embellishments in the
left hand, with a perfectly equal semiquaver movement for
the right in precise alternation with the left.[84]   Then comes
—and this is highly significant in its bearing on Bach's
attitude towards clavier music—the three-part chorale
" Wer nur den lieben Gott lässt walten," lavishly embellished in both hands.   It is, in an improved form, the same
subject as he had some years previously arranged for church
purposes by the addition of a prelude, interlude and postlude.[85]
Since that time he had given up the use of such elaborate

---

[81] " My late father had a happy way of putting his pupils to the proof. With
him his scholars had to go at once to his by no means easy pieces." Ph. Em.
Bach, I., p. 10.—Forkel, pp. 38 and 45.

[82] See ante, Vol. I., note 21, p. 12.   The size is a small oblong quarto.

[83] The little diagram arranged for this purpose is to be found, B.-G. III., p. 14.

[84] P. S. I., C. 9, No. 16, I. (Vol. 200, p. 3).

[85] See ante, Vol. I., p. 313, note 135.

accompaniments to congregational singing, and had arrived at the conclusion that they were only serviceable for purposes of practice on the clavier; and to perform this smoothly and roundly demands a skill far beyond that of a beginner.

The fourth lesson consists of a somewhat longer prelude in D minor, a calm movement in quavers closing with a cadence in semiquavers for both hands alternately.[86] Bars 9 and 13 each have a slurred passage lasting into the next bar. But as a true *legato* could only be produced on the clavichord by increased pressure, involving added intensity of tone, the slur indicates at the same time a shading in the force of tone; this is all the clearer because it does not cover a complete phrase, but is lost in the following bar; thus the passage began *forte*, then *diminuendo*, down to *piano*—a practical hint as to Bach's attention to expressive execution.

The fifth place is occupied by another three-part chorale, "Jesu meine Freude," coloured and ornamented like the former one; but it is not written out to the end.[87]

Two easy allemandes follow as a pleasing change, both in G minor; but the second of these is also only a fragment. Then follow three preludes, in F major and G minor—this one has the fingering marked—and F major again.[88] The two first again aim at rapidity, and a smooth execution of semiquavers and quavers, to which it is evident that Bach gave much attention; but the third is already of that category of more difficult pieces to which the pupil was ere long introduced. The polyphony which governs all the parts, and which is so essentially Bach's, combined as it is with an equally characteristic variety in the musical ideas, presupposes a by no means contemptible independence and rapidity of finger. The polyphony, however, is restricted to three parts, and these are used at first with caution; but, in spite of this, they demand smooth handling and some stretching and grasping power in the hands.

---

[86] P. S. I., C. 9, No. 16, V. (Vol. 200, p. 7).

[87] The fragment occurs in P. S. V., C. 5 (Vol 244), after the variants.

[88] P. S. I., C. 9, No. 16, VIII., XI., IX. (Vol. 200, pp. 9, 10, 11). More exactly the two first are called *preambles;* however, there is no perceptible difference between this and a prelude.

Corresponding to the three preludes are an equal number
of minuets—in G major, G minor, G major[89]—in which the
study of polyphonic treatment is carried farther ; in the
third, too, a rhythmical figure is introduced, of the greatest
utility in practising clearness of touch.

This is, as it were, a stage reached ; the next exercise
represents a higher level of study. It consists of eleven preludes, which recur later in a more or less altered shape in
the Wohltemperirte Clavier. The order in which they stand
shows that their purpose was the attainment, in due sequence,
first, of increased rapidity, and then of a sustained and equal
execution, going on to a cantabile and polyphonic style of
playing. The keys follow thus: C major, C minor, D minor,
D major, E minor (this is for left-hand practice only), then E
major, F major, C sharp major, C sharp minor, E sharp minor,
F minor. The preludes are not all finished to the end, but we
shall of course consider them again with reference to the
relation they bear to the pieces collectively of the Wohltemperirte Clavier, as well as with regard to their intrinsic merit.
After them we come, for the first time, on a composition not
by Bach—an allemande in C major, by J. C. Richter.[90] The
courante which follows it may be by the same composer.

Then, among a number of trifles and fragments, we may
distinguish a prelude in D major and a three-part fugue in
C major.[91] In the fugue, among other technical aims, it is
easy to perceive a special adaptation to the exercise of the
third and little fingers of the right hand ; however, for this
prelude there is a general demand on the true Bach mode
of playing. What had before been an end is now merely
a means ; the student is one step nearer to perfection.
This is confirmed by the rest of the little work, which is
filled almost exclusively by the Inventionen und Sinfonien,
the first of the three great master-works for the clavier
which owe their existence to the Cöthen period.   There

---

[89] P. S. I., C. 13, No. 11, I., II., III. (Vol. 216, pp. 30 and 31).

[90] Probably the same who was afterwards Court Organist in Dresden, Joh.
Christoph Richter. See Gerber, N. L. III., col. 855. Nothing further is known
as to any acquaintance between him and Bach.

[91] P. S. I., C. 9, No. 16, IV., and No. 9 (Vol. 200, pp. 6 and 24).

remain only two little suites, of which one in three parts
(A major) is not, it is true, in Sebastian Bach's handwriting; it may nevertheless be of his composition; the
other, in four parts (G minor), is by G. H. Stölzel, Capellmeister of Gotha. Bach amused himself by adding to
its minuet a trio, which is as delightful as it is learned.[92]
All the original compositions here mentioned not only perfectly fulfil their instructive purpose, but are masterly productions when viewed as works of art—a varied and fragrant
wreath, in which roses, lilies and perfumed stocks have
their place, as well as wilder growths—each in their degree,
but each with its own peculiar charm. The forms are at
first quite simple, but with the advance of technical acquire-
ment they become gradually broader till the fugue is reached.
We are not now speaking of the peculiar structure of the
Inventionen und Sinfonien; that of the latter approaches
very nearly to the four-part construction of the fine prelude
in D major.

There are still many more pieces written by Bach
especially for technical practice, though most of them were
no doubt dispersed and lost among his pupils. Very admirable
is a little prelude in C minor, which runs whispering on in
harp-like tones from one set of harmonies to another, and
yet lets the mystical romanticism of Bach's genius pierce
through it all.[93] We find even fugues, both with and without preludes, which, like the former one, probably served as
pieces for testing the progress of the pupil, three-part fugues
of really enjoyable perfection as to form and purport, and
conceived with that concentration of structure which does
not allow of a single superfluous note, nor say a word too
much—the distinguishing mark, in short, of all the fugues
written at Cöthen or later. The preludes are as artistic as
they are profound, particularly that grave and melancholy
one in D minor, in which we might fancy we had found an

---

[92] P. S. I., C. 9, No. 16, X. (Vol. 200, p. 81).

[93] P. S. I., C. 9, No. 16, III. (Vol. 200, p. 4). Also for others, see II., VI.,
VII. and XII.

organ piece, if Bach had not with his own hand added to it a fugue unmistakably written for the clavier.[94]

Our study of Bach's qualities of *technique* and as a teacher has led us back again to his work as a composer. His nature is a grand homogeneous whole ; all his various characteristics reacted on each other—interpenetrated each other—to compose an indivisible unity. Just as every exercise he wrote is a true work of art, so, on the other hand, every independent composition is full of technical instruction. He never wrote a clavier piece which did not serve as a healthy gymnastic for the fingers ; but, on the other hand, he never composed anything which fulfilled no other end than that of an exercise. It is precisely in one of his profoundest masterpieces that he addresses himself directly to " the young who desire to learn." Their advancement and culture in the comprehension of art were to him objects of the warmest interest, and inspired him to creative effort. The way in which, by patient waiting and diligence, he gradually educated his pupils to be his public is a brilliant example for every artist who cherishes the natural desire to make a way for his ideas. But he was far from all affectation —from all delight in unintelligent admiration. Instrumental music, more than any other art, demands a certain understanding, and claims a higher degree of musical culture in those who would deserve her favours ; her votaries must be specially trained in her service, or she turns her blessings to a curse—a mere futile and demoralising means of luxury. This Bach knew very well; even his zeal as a teacher was at bottom merely an emanation from that true art which gives dignity to humanity, and makes no distinction between the good and the beautiful.

---

[94] Four fugues with two preludes are published in P. S. I., C. 9, Nos. 4, 5, 8 (Vol. 200, 11, Vol. 212, p. 3). See Griepenkerl's preface to the volume. In it there are also two other fugues, in D minor and A minor, Nos. 12 and 6 (Vol. 212, p. 5 ; Vol. 200, p. 33), which, however, do not fit with the two other preludes. No data as their origin and purpose are forthcoming, but their internal character indicates beyond a doubt that they were not written later than the others. They are by no means inferior: the A minor fugue has a strongly marked organ type.

When, at the beginning of 1723, he revised the Inventionen und Sinfonien, and wrought them into the form of an independent volume, he gave it the following title: "An honest guide by which the lovers of the clavier, but particularly those who desire to learn, are shown a plain way, not only (firstly) to learn to play neatly in two parts, but also, in further progress (secondly), to play correctly and well in three obbligato parts; and, at the same time, not only to acquire good ideas, but also to work them out themselves, and, finally, to acquire a *cantabile* style of playing, and, at the same time, to gain a strong predilection for and foretaste of composition."[95]   Here, once more, we have the whole confession of faith of the musical instructor: "A Guide": here the instructional purpose is most clearly indicated—"an honest guide"—for true art can be served by no hollow mockery.   "The lovers of the clavier"—that is, the clavichord, the foundation of all Bach's teaching, on which alone a *cantabile* or flowing and expressive mode of execution is indeed possible—"particularly those who desire to learn": the persevering youth, whose sympathetic intelligence must be won, for the future is theirs.   Pieces, first in two and then in three parts *obbligato*, are given, and the development of polyphonic playing is the highest goal; in these, again, purity, accuracy and grace are required.   The musical idea contained in the piece was intended to ripen the imagination of the learner and encourage him to produce both improvised pieces (*inventiones*) and more artistic works, duly arranged and worked out (*composition*).   Finally, in the carrying out the ideas, he was to study the organism of a grand composition.

How far it was from Bach's views that a clavier pupil need only be trained in mere finger-work—in *riding* the

---

[95] " Auffrichtige Anleitung, Wormit denen Liebhabern des *Clavires*, besonders aber denen Lehrbegierigen, eine deutliche Art gezeiget wird, nicht alleine (1) mit 2 Stimmen reine spielen zu lernen, sondern auch bey weiterer *progressen* (2) mit dreyen *obligaten Partien* richtig und wohl zu verfahren, anbey auch zugleich gute *inventiones* nicht alleine zu bekommen, sondern auch selbige wohl durchzuführen, am allermeisten aber eine *cantable* Art im Spielen zu erlangen, und darneben einen starcken Vorschmack von der *Composition* zu überkommen." B.-G., III., Preface.

clavier, as he used to call it—how thoroughly, on the contrary, he guided the player at the same time through the intricacies of construction and the feeling of the piece he was playing, is here made very plain; nay, that he knew, too, how to incite him to living and original production by arousing his own formative faculty. The plan of the programme seems at first sight somewhat confused; still it is not very difficult to disentangle the different ideas that seem to cross each other. He wished, in the first place, to produce an exercise-book for the clavier-player; but, with the mechanical practice, he proposed also to cultivate the pupil's artistic powers generally, both on the side of impromptu invention—which was so essential for the use of the figured bass, then thought very important — and on that of serious composition. Having formerly been a first-class scholar in St. Michael's School, at Lüneburg, he had not so far forgotten the terminology of rhetoric as not to know that *collocatio* (order) and *elocutio* (expression) are indispensable to *inventio* (invention); and thus, immediately after his observations on good inventions, we find order or arrangement discussed, and a *cantabile* handling; otherwise, certain other sections might have seemed more nearly connected with it. The ancient rules of rhetoric come in again in another place, when he teaches that in two-part pieces purity of execution is essential, but in three-part pieces correct and finished playing—not meaning, of course, that purity is less requisite in three parts, or correctness and finish in two. It is perfectly clear that these words stand for the *emendatum* (correct), *perspicuum* (pure—*i.e.*, clean and neat) and *ornatum* (finished—*i.e.*, winning or graceful) of the old rhetoricians, the three chief requisites of a good image or statement.[96]

It is extremely interesting to observe that, in spite of his musical occupations at Lüneburg, Bach cannot have been a

---

[96] Compare Mattheson, Grosse General-Bass Schule, p. 8 (Hamburg, 1731). " For there were then already wise folks who were not satisfied that the figured bass should be carried out *correctly* (*recht*)—that is to say, without mistakes—but demanded that it should also be *good*—that is, artistic and elegant. Hence it is not without reason that we contrast right (or correct) and good (or beautiful)."

very bad Latin scholar, since twenty years after he still had a present memory of these matters, and could apply his knowledge so aptly and correctly.   But what is more important still is the direct parallel he institutes between music and human speech.   This he could not possibly have done if he had not felt that the art of music was a perfectly evolved language of emotion—that the progression of each part in his polyphonic pieces was like the utterance of a distinct personage—that the composer was indeed in some sort a dramatic poet.   It would seem that he often applied this comparison himself in order to disclose to his pupils the inner life and purport of his music.[97]   What a performance it must have been that was inspired by this idea needs to be no further enlarged upon.   And it is now quite clear what the association of ideas must have been that led him to call the two-part pieces *inventions,* when the name *preamble,* which he had applied to them in Friedemann's book, did not satisfy him. Indeed, the true prelude style is certainly not recognisable in these strict and simple compositions, with the exception, perhaps, of two of them ; still the name *inventions* is not particularly happy either ; the pieces are too far from mere inventions, too carefully worked out, and, in contrast with the *sinfonias* which follow them (this was the new name so happily bestowed on what had been first called "fantasias," and are now more generally known as "inventions in three parts."), can at most be accepted as pictures more lightly projected and more directly invented.[98]

If we now consider this work—which more than any other displays an instructive aim—from the side of its artistic

---

[97] Since Forkel, p. 24, says quite the same thing as we have here derived from our analysis of Bach's words, I have no doubt that his statement is founded on a direct communication from Friedemann or Ph. Em. Bach.   Birnbaum also states it distinctly in Scheibe, Critischer Musikus, p. 997.

[98] It is not probable that Bach was the first to use the name "invention" for a piece of music.   See App. A, No. 7.   In Breitkopf's list for Easter, 1763, wc find, on page 73 : " Bach, Joh. Seb., Capellm. und Musik-Director zu Leipzig, XXII. *Inventiones* vors Clavier: Leipzig, fol. *a,* 1 thl., 12 gr." This established the interesting fact that a printed edition of the Inventionen existed so early as 1763.   Only the number is puzzling ; it is perhaps a misprint for XXX., which would include the sinfonias.

value, it is a striking illustration of the fact that Bach's fertility and inspiration grew in direct proportion as he more distinctly formulated his educational purpose. In extent alone is it inferior to the two parts of the Wohltemperirte Clavier and the Kunst der Fuge, in its more modest dimensions and the limitations imposed by the fewer means employed, but certainly in no other respect. Nay, in one way it is superior to them and to all Bach's later clavier music— namely, in its perfect novelty of form. The master had good reason to seek for a suitable name for these pieces, for there was nothing like them in all the clavier music of the time. It is not merely the treatment of the polyphony, which pursues its two or three parts without an instant's interruption, and nevertheless reveals the harmony throughout with absolute distinctness and fulness, never diminishing in interest by monotony of changes, never wearying us by repetition : more than all this is the whole development of each tone-picture—the sovereign independence with which all the forms of music are applied—the canon, the fugue, free imitation, double and triple counterpoint, episodic working-out, inversions of the theme—all combining and following each other in pieces of very moderate extent, without anywhere obtruding themselves on our notice; these are what render the Inventionen und Sinfonien unique in the whole body of clavier music. A slight leaning towards the Italian music of the time is certainly discernible, and somewhat more decidedly in the sinfonias than in the inventions. Still these lovely blossoms have sprung principally from Bach's own organ and clavier pieces: a quintessence, as it were, of all he had accomplished. And yet we can perceive the efforts he has made to ripen his work, for, besides the fifteen inventions in two parts and the sinfonias in three, there are among the works he has left more pieces in the same style, which prove that he only gave his more earnest labour to what seemed to him best or most suitable for the work out of the abundance he could produce.

He seems to have struggled longest after the ideal form of the inventions. A two-part fugue in C minor is, as it were, the butterfly half-escaped from the chrysalis ; it is, properly speaking, a fugue only to the end of the sixth bar, and afterwards more and more of an " invention " in its freedom of theme and episode. Another aspect of the process of evolution is discoverable in three small pieces in D minor, E major and E minor, of which the first especially shows already in a high degree that bewitching play of inversion and double counterpoint which is equally characteristic of the inventions and the sinfonias. But they all three have that verse or song form in two divisions, which Bach with one exception excluded from the collection that forms the book, because it disturbed the flow of polyphonic development. He has perfectly attained his aim in another piece in C minor, only it is difficult to decide whether it should be designated *fantasia* or *invention*.[99] If the rest could be regarded merely as studies this is a *paralipomenon*, which, from its completeness of form, is worthy to be called either. The case is the same with two two-part and two three-part compositions which, however, he thought worthy to grace another work ; these are the preludes in C sharp major, F sharp major and A major in the first part of the Wohltemperirte Clavier, and that in B flat minor in the second. It is certainly doubtful whether the last piece can have been written so soon as this ; still, there are in the second part several pieces which can be proved to be of early date. In the case of the other three their early origin is certain, since the date of the first part of the Wohltemperirte Clavier is well ascertained. That Bach should here have given the name of prelude to what he elsewhere calls a sinfonia shows, again, how unique was the style here unfolded. We have already seen three names applied to one and the same kind of piece. Another three-part piece must, on the contrary, be regarded as a study—we might say, indeed, is a study—for the first sinfonia in C major, and it is in the same key. This also is entitled a prelude.[100]

---

[99] P. S. I., C. 7, No. 2 ; No. 1, III., V., VI. (all in Vol. 201) ; C. 9, No. 10 (Vol. 212, p. 2).

[100] P. S. V., C. 8, No. 7 (Vol. 247). Here it is placed among organ works, and appears indeed to have been used for that instrument. Its connection with the sinfonia will be apparent to any careful examiner.

Bach, it is evident, was no less doubtful as to the order of the thirty pieces than as to their designation. This is interesting to observe, because we can detect that it was always ultimately decided on instructive grounds. The work exists in three distinct autographs. In Friedemann Bach's Little Clavier Book the inventions are separated from the sinfonias, but the principle of the arrangement is the same in each, since, so far as the number and keys of the pieces allow, they proceed first upwards and then downwards.[101] A second autograph copy, which also seems to have been written in Cöthen, gives the pieces in the same order; but the sinfonia in the same key is placed immediately after each invention. The third copy, on the contrary, is arranged on the principle of using the keys only in the ascending order of the scale; here all the inventions are given first, and then the sinfonias in the same order.[102] At the present day we should rather attempt to group such a collection of clavier pieces with reference to a pleasing contrast in their various characters, but such an idea seems never to have occurred to Bach; indeed, there was no need for it, for each is so different from every other that, in whatever order they may be played, the effect of contrast will necessarily be produced.

The scheme of the inventions is, for the most part, that they are divided into three sections, and have a remote resemblance to the form of the Italian aria. The first part is generally obviously disjoined from the rest by a decided cadence on the dominant or supermediant (*i.e.*, the relative major, if the piece be in the minor); it comes in again in a more or less shortened form at the close. The sixth invention alone is in the two-part "song-form," with repeats; but here, too, at the end of the second section,

---

[101] Thus: C major, D minor, E minor, F major, G major, A minor, B minor, B flat major, A major, G minor, F minor, E major, E sharp major, D major, C minor. But there are only twelve bars written of the D major sinfonia, and that in C minor is wholly wanting.

[102] The second autograph is a little book in oblong quarto in the Royal Library at Berlin. The writing is not quite that of the Leipzig period, but sharper and more pointed; still, it is essentially different from Bach's writing when he was at Weimar. The B.-G. edition is founded on the third autograph.

the first is practically introduced again, constituting a regular sonata movement in miniature. The first and seventh inventions are in three sections, but without being in cyclic form. Even in this contracted sphere an astonishing variety of conception is displayed.

The first invention grows from this germ —

and is treated in imitation; at the third bar there begins a moderately long episode on the inverted subject, which, in the course of the piece, is set in opposition to the subject in direct motion, giving rise to playful alternations of each. Of all fifteen this one has the most reserved and dispassionate character, and even the theme is somewhat conventional, only revealing its importance by degrees.

The second, in C minor, is quite different. A passionate and eager phrase comes rushing in, followed by its exact facsimile and companion, and the two figures pursue one another, first one and then the other taking the lead. It is a canon on the octave; at first the upper being followed by the lower part, at the distance of two bars, until bar 10 is reached, when they change places; the lower part leads, now followed by the upper one, bar for bar, in exact imitation; then, after a short digression, the first order of parts is resumed until the last bar.

No. 3, in D major, is of a merry character, and consists of free imitation; it is followed and eclipsed by the gloom of No. 4, which is treated now in direct, now in inverse motion, in D minor.

No. 5, E flat major, which sets off at once in two parts, is in double counterpoint on the octave throughout, modulating through B flat major, C minor, and F minor, and then, by means of episodical extensions, back to the original key. It is a piece full of grace and dignity.

The one in E major (No. 6) is full of roguish fun, and also begins in two parts; a prominent part is taken by the double counterpoint, and the formation of episodes on the chief theme.

No. 7, in E minor, shows an affinity in form with No. 1; but its expression is different; it is suppliant and mournful; still, in spite of its disturbed character, has extraordinary melodic beauty.

In contrast to this, the next one, in F major (No. 8), is full of a happy and innocent contentment. It begins in canon, and after the twelfth bar it becomes freer, and most lovely little episodes are developed.

The companion piece in the corresponding minor key (No. 9, F minor), which is similar in form to No. 5, but richer in episodic formations, again is full of impassioned strains of sadness, which rise to a great intensity of effect in bars 21 to 26.

No. 10, in G major, begins like a fugue, but without any of the fetters of that form; it flits to and fro—now in imitation, and now in episodic extension. There is a piece of quite wanton fun at the *reprise*, when the upper part takes upon itself the double duty of a theme and response (*dux* and *comes*).

The piece which follows has a character of tormented restlessness. A chromatic counter-subject of two bars long, attached from the outset to the chief theme, evolves, by means of inversion in the fourth bar, an episode of the most painful and insistent kind, which reappears in alternation with the original counterpoint at bar 14. The phrases consist of six bars, but at the last two recurrences it is only five bars and a half long, and these two are merged directly in one another without any cadences to give a moment's rest (see bars 12, 13, and 18); each beat of the bar is more restless than the last.

A feeling of honest German fun is given by No. 12, in A major, which corresponds in form to Nos. 5 and 9.

The two next inventions, in A minor and B flat major, both have somewhat the character of preludes, because the subjects and the workings-out alike move almost exclusively in harmonic passages; the second betrays a close relationship to the prelude of the B flat partita in the first portion of the Clavierübung. The three-fold division is, however, preserved in this case. In the B flat invention the first subject comes in in canon at its repetition (bar 16, in the middle), and in this place it has a bold, soaring character, while in the former it was dreamy and rather melancholy.

The last invention comes in gravely, yet not without a certain dignified grace ; in its fugal working-out it alternates with episodical interludes, founded on the counterpoint to the theme. It is remarkable that the theme does not come in alone, but is supported by short notes in harmony in the bass. In no other of the inventions is this the case ; but it always happens so in the sinfonias (or inventions in three parts), and I believe that these have had a reactive influence on this invention. The form of the Sinfonias in their barest outlines is founded on that of the Italian instrumental trio, as settled by Corelli and diligently cultivated by Albinoni, Vivaldi, and many others ; it had also become widely known throughout Germany.

We have already seen how Bach could make the Italian forms serve his purpose. He was the more likely to go on assimilating these forms since, in Cöthen, chamber-music demanded his chief energies. It was a favourite mode of construction in the fugal movements of these trios—which were generally written for two violins, string bass, and figured bass—that the theme should not be given out quite alone, but supported by a figured bass, played by a fourth performer—some particular accompanist—with proper harmonies. Subsequently the figured bass was drawn into the fabric of the fugue, and the accompanying harmonies had to follow and support the other parts, so as to fill up any gaps left by the instruments in the harmonies. It is plain that Bach got this manner of treatment from the trio form. But that this influence was purely external is shown by the fact that absolutely nothing remains of the supporting bass but a slight remnant in those few bars at the beginning; and even this appears, not as the groundwork of a set of accompanying chords, but as a free and independent part, and it soon establishes its full and individual right to a share in the polyphonic working-out. For this reason a further comparison would be out of place ; the Bach clavier trios (or inventions in three parts) are so thoroughly original that we cannot but doubt whether he thought at all of the Italian instrumental trio, and whether he did not rather think of his own works of that kind, to which we shall presently draw the reader's attention. The style which pervades these last has at least a general similarity to the sinfonias, although the treatment is much broader and bolder. The original source of both sets of works, however, is the organ. The polyphony is chiefly fugal, and but seldom (Nos. 2, 5, 15) canonic, although there is no actual fugue or canon in the set. It is difficult to say anything more on the general characteristics of the form of the sinfonias. With the greatest freedom, and yet with a marvellous order and arrangement, every device of thematic and episodic polyphony is employed; each piece is a microcosm of art—a vessel of richly cut crystal filled with the purest and most precious essence. The effect of these is heightened if the (two-part) invention corresponding in number to each is played before it. For it cannot be doubted that the composer conceived each pair at the same time; in Nos. 15, 12, and 6 the themes agree, although not perhaps note for note, yet in their chief features. No less do the emotional characteristics of each correspond, and even in respect of form certain connections can be seen.

The one in C major has the same brilliantly polished, reserved, and dispassionate nature as the invention in the same key, and the theme is treated in the same masterly manner, whether in its direct or inverted form :—

The C minor invention, with its feverish restlessness, is followed by a sinfonia full of the deepest yearning, which, however, is interrupted throughout by quicker passages; the imitations are in canon form, as in the invention, but are thrown into the background in the second half by episodic developments of the loveliest kind.

The one in D major exhibits the same cheerful character in three parts that its forerunner did in two, and adds to it some tender prattling. We might call this sinfonia, above

all, a golden fruit in a silver shell. What a charming theme
is this—

which, when it is taken up by the second part in A major,
is met by this as second subject, which pleasantly accompanies it—

while both parts are surmounted with this lovely and expressive phrase :—

And now it proceeds in triple and double counterpoint with
delicious animation, and between whiles little episodes peep
out roguishly and vanish again; there is something to
be said of nearly every bar. By this means of performing
each pair together the player will be able to appreciate in
every number the inner connection between the invention
and its companion sinfonia ; how that which was fore-
shadowed there is brought out with firmer strokes; what
was there abrupt and stiff becomes gentler in contour ; what
was trivial becomes deepened ; what was restless and
capricious becomes calm and firm ; and sometimes, too,
how anxious complaint is intensified into the deepest woe
and the most acute suffering.

Particular mention must be made of the caressing sweetness—almost in the style of Mozart—of the sinfonia in E flat,
coming after the haughty grace of the invention—a piece
which is also distinguished above all the others in its form,
the upper parts being in free canon, while the bass repeats
the same figure in each bar.

Then comes the touching lament of the E minor sinfonia,
which, however full of character, is yet in contrast to the
pathos of the invention, and of an organic beauty such as
Bach alone could create.

II.

Allied to its invention, both in feeling and in contrast, is the sinfonia in G minor (No. 7), but in this a lovely melody, with broad and sustained notes, is continuously heard above the lower parts in a way that could hardly be deemed possible in a piece of such polyphonic character; it also has the character of an aria.

How splendid is the intensifying of emotion in coming from the invention to the sinfonia in A minor, the theme of which, with its working-out by passages in thirds and sixths, bears a distinct resemblance to the beautiful organ fugue in A major!

The theme of the B minor sinfonia is strictly evolved from that of the invention—at first in canon, but then treated in a more episodical way, as in No. 2; but, in the meantime, impetuous passages in demi-semiquavers rush up and down, overtake, and cross each other in contrary motion, which, by the way, must have been a difficult task for the fingers on the clavichord, which never possessed two manuals.

Finally, the sinfonia in F minor (No. 9) is positively steeped in anguish and pain; but to compensate for this abnormal emotion the form is as strict and concentrated as possible; or, to speak more accurately, the feeling first acquires its intensity by means of the form, and the form achieves its astounding concentration by means of the feeling, so that the two factors are indissolubly heightened in effect, in and through one another. The piece consists of three themes in triple counterpoint, neither of them inferior to the others in force of expression; and, though they are externally in contrast to each other, they nevertheless all reflect the same particular emotion :—

At first only the first and second themes appear together, but then all three come in together nine different times in four permutations, and various though nearly related keys. As a relief to these there are five interludes, of which the first is in free form, but the others are built episodically upon the first theme ; direct and inverse motion and augmentation unite to give a most complex effect. Of the workings-out of the themes, sometimes two follow closely on one another, without an interlude between them, sometimes one stands alone ; but this is always in accordance with a fixed plan, as the interludes correspond closely with each other. The following scheme may serve to exhibit the wonderful arrangement of the phrases; the Arabic numerals stand for the number of times that the workings-out occur consecutively, and the Roman for the different interludes—

2. I. 1. II. 2. III. 1. IV. 2. V. 2.

(the curved strokes indicate the connection between the different parts of the piece). The first interlude alone (bars 5 and 6) stands by itself and without any corresponding part afterwards ; it releases the ear for a moment from the strain caused by the first bars, and lets it become acquainted with the themes themselves. In the development of the piece the greatest possible daring is shown in the way of bold leaps of intervals, discords resolved by skips, and false relations. But we must not suppose that this originated in a forced and artificial correctness. Bach shows in the sinfonias how he can combine the most elaborate art with the most exquisite loveliness of effect. It was no caprice of pedantry that gave rise to the sinfonia in F minor; on the contrary, it bears the impress of true imaginative work. This will be the ultimate feeling about the piece if, instead of being repelled by the disjointed impression produced perhaps on most people on a first acquaintance with it, we pay due attention to the course of the separate parts, and in playing the piece try and give to each its full effect as a living individual. Then perhaps it will strike the sensitive hearer with awe that such a deep abyss of woe could open in the human breast but he will enjoy the comforting

thought that the moral force of the will can by perfection of
form triumphantly bridge over even such depths as these.
Kirnberger, Sebastian Bach's theoretical pupil, regarded the
F minor sinfonia as an experiment which was bold even to
obscurity, and quoted it as a proof of Bach's having
infringed the rule which forbids the unprepared entrance of
the fourth in the bass—the so-called chord of the six-four.[103]
The passages where Bach took this liberty (bars 4, 14, 19,
27, and 32) sound indeed strange, and at first unsatisfactory; they are justified by his general view of the nature of
part-writing, which, according to him, took its rise no longer
from the polyphonic system, but the harmonic.   More will
be said on this subject in another place.

III.

BACH AS A VIOLINIST.—THE SUITE AND THE SONATA.—WORKS FOR VIOLIN, VIOLONCELLO, FLUTE, ETC.

BACH's first musical impressions arose from his hearing his
father's violin-playing.   His own first public post was that
of violinist in Weimar.   He afterwards held this position
in the Duke's band for nine years, and in course of time was
promoted to be concertmeister.   In his later years, too, he
did not neglect his string-playing, and in instrumental
pieces in several parts he preferred to play the viola, since
he enjoyed, as it were, surveying the harmonies on both
sides from the middle position; besides, good viola-players,
and such as satisfied his requirements, were seldom to be
met with.[104]   It is not indeed necessary for a concertmeister
to be an extraordinary performer—a thorough musician with
moderate technical qualities, if they are genuine and sound,

---

[103] Kunst des Reinen Satzes, II., 2, p. 39, ff.   All the six possible permutations of the three themes are given here, the second and sixth of which are not
employed by Bach in the sinfonia.

[104] Forkel, p. 45.   Quantz, Versuch einer Anweisung, &c., p. 207.

will often be much more useful in this place[105]—and considering that no contemporary, not even his son Philipp Emanuel,
mentions Bach's violin-playing, and that he devoted his chief
energies to the organ and clavier, we shall hardly be wrong
in supposing that he was not possessed of any extraordinary
facility on the violin. But it is not intended to give the
impression of his having been an insignificant player. He
was not the only one of the great musicians of Germany in
whom the defects possibly arising from an insufficient technical method have been made up for by the individuality
and magnificence of their creative genius. Thus, the pianoforte playing of C. M. von Weber lacked much in neatness
and equality, and nevertheless it had in it a soaring flight
and a magic charm which enraptured those who heard him.
Nay, even Handel's violin-playing, although he laid less
stress upon it after his residence in Hamburg, was
sufficiently full of fire and importance to induce great performers to come to learn of him.[106] Bach's familiarity with
stringed instruments extended so far that he even undertook
to make changes in their shape and build to suit his purposes ; while in Cöthen he invented an instrument, something between a tenor and a violoncello, which was held like
a violin, and had five strings tuned to the notes C, G, *d, a*,
and *e'* ; he called it *viola pomposa*, and wrote a suite for it ; he
also had it used in Leipzig for the easier performance of his
difficult and rapid basses.[107] But from a consideration of his
compositions for strings, and especially those for violins
alone, it follows that his knowledge of this branch of art
must have been enormous. Granted that he may not have
been able to execute these himself quite perfectly—and
yet he must also have been a good violoncellist, for he wrote

---

[105] Quantz, p. 179 : " But there is no absolute necessity that he (*i.e.*, the
leader of the music) should possess the skill to execute passages of peculiar
difficulty ; this can well be left to those who try to distinguish themselves only
by playing to please, of whom there are plenty to be met with."

[106] Chrysander, Händel, I., p. 228.

[107] Compare on this App. A, No. 4. A composition for flute and *viola pomposa* without bass, by Telemann, is to be found in his Getreuen Musikmeister
(Hamburg, 1728, pp. 77 and 84).

similar solo compositions for that instrument—at all events, only one who had the most thorough experience of the capabilities of the instrument and their utmost limits could produce such works. And such experience is not to be attained by theoretical speculation, but only by practical exercise.

It is easy to see, from the individuality of Bach's violin compositions, from the number of parts employed, from certain types of figures, and from the interweaving of one or even two more instruments *obbligato*, that their peculiar style did not, at all events, take its rise solely in the nature of the instrument. The overpowering influence of the organ style, which relentlessly overmastered all that came within its reach, is even here too evident to be overlooked. With special regard to the employment of double stopping, it must be added that Corelli had already raised it to an important place in the art by his violin sonatas with harpsichord accompaniment, and had even attempted to employ fugal treatment, as far as it could be conveniently adapted to the instrument; and that the Germans, who at the end of the seventeenth century were in other respects far inferior to the Italian violinists in execution and inventive faculty, had cultivated this very branch of *technique*—viz., playing in more than one part at a time—with especial energy, which is very significant, as showing how it was their nature to strive after harmonic richness much more than after clearness of melody. Nikolaus Bruhns, Buxtehude's talented pupil, who was mentioned before as an eminent violinist, attained such a proficiency in double stopping that it seemed as if three or four violins were being played together; and then he would sometimes sit down in front of the organ with his violin, and with his feet add a pedal-part to the full harmonies he elicited from the strings.[108]   In the case of that native of Celle, Nikolaus Strungk—of whom we have spoken before (Vol. I., p. 201), and to whom Corelli, after hearing him play, was forced to cry in amazement, " I am called *Arcangelo*, but you must be called *Arcidiavolo*"

---

[108] Mattheson, Ehrenpforte, p. 26.

—the chief feature of his performance was probably the playing in several parts, since he, as well as Bruhns, was an organ and clavier player.[109] The secretary of the elector of Mainz, Johann Jakob Walther (born 1650), who was also a violinist, gives no little attention to this particular branch of *technique* in his "*Hortulus Chelicus*," published in 1694, and especially alludes to it in the title.[110] So that in adopting this form Bach was aiding and furthering a tendency which was particularly German; but he wedded to it all that had been acquired by the Italian feeling for form, and improved this by means of his incomparably greater power of construction.

He wrote a book containing six compositions in several movements, without any accompaniment, for the violin, and a similar one for the violoncello (or the viola pomposa). I do not know whether he had any predecessor in the isolated treatment of a stringed instrument, but I should be inclined to doubt it, because the Italians, who were the general exemplars in matters of this kind, in defiance of all art, put a cantabile and one-part style of playing in the foremost place, whereby the music must have lost half the intended effect through being deprived of the supporting harmonies.[111] All that can be said with certainty as to the date of these compositions is that it cannot be later

---

[109] Gerber, Lex. II., col. 604. Strungk tuned his violin in such a way as to facilitate the performance of passages in harmony.

[110] "*Hortulus Chelicus.* Das ist Wohl-gepflanzter *Violin*ischer Lust-Garten Darin—auch durch Berührung zuweilen zwey, drey, vier Seithen, auff der Violin die lieblichiste Harmonie erwiesen wird."—"Garden of the Lyre. That is, the well-stocked pleasure-garden of violin practice, in which is shown how to produce the loveliest harmony on the violin by occasionally touching two, three, or four strings."

[111] A remark of Mattheson's in Critica Musica may be here quoted, I. (1722), p. 224, i.: "I was lately shown a *Suonata per Violino solo del Sigr: M. M.*, which, to say nothing of the key being in F minor, demands such long fingers that I know no one who could easily execute the passages ('*praestanda praesti*ren'). And yet I cannot blame such a work if its object is intended for showing his own exceptional advantage in the way of long fingers, or else for an exercise, rather than for everybody's execution for them to boast of." The violin solo sonatas by Telemann and Pisendel were certainly all composed later than Bach's.

than the Cöthen period. The six violin solos consist of three sonatas and three suites; and if at the present day we are accustomed to speak and write of Bach's six violin sonatas, it is an inaccuracy for which Bach is not to blame.[112]   The difference of the two generally is clearly definable, since the suite consists principally of dance-forms, which are mostly introduced by a prelude.

The suite-form, by which a new laurel branch was added to the immortal crown of Bach's fame—for he it was who brought it to its highest perfection—stretches back its roots into the sixteenth century.   Its development I believe to be easily discernible in general, although in the details much is obscure.[113]   It was in dance-music that the song-tunes from which they took their rise were first transferred to the imitating instruments, and then were independently enlarged and extended, the song-form being retained.   It followed naturally, from this, that people wanted to hear such dance-music on other festive occasions, so that, as its popularity increased, the composers turned their attention to this kind of composition.   Wandering musicians carried the most popular of these from place to place and from country to country.   About the year 1600, the Italian *paduanas* and *gagliardas*, or *romanescas*, became very widely known; and how charmingly they lent themselves to instrumental treatment is seen in the five-part pieces in this form which Johann Moller (the court organist at Darmstadt) published in the years 1610 and 1611. Besides these, much attention was given to the forms of the *volta*, the *passamezzo*, the *balletts*, and the *intradas*, which last were called "Aufzüge," or "processions," by the German composers, and indicated a particular kind of solemn music which preceded a more intricate dance. The ring-dance (*branle*) and *courante* came from France, unless, indeed, the last was originally Italian.   The only

---

[112] P. S. III., C. 4 (vol. 228).—B. G. xxvii., 1., *Vide* App. A, No. 4.

[113] I must own that my opinions are founded on very incomplete materials. Any one who knows the state of musical history with regard to the seventeenth century will pardon this.

German dance which figures here is the *allemande*, showing, as it would seem by its name, that there were no different varieties of dance in Germany. But to make up for this the Germans showed their individuality in the working-up of the foreign forms ; thus, in 1604, Johann Ghro, of Dresden, published thirty paduanas and gaillards, and announced in the preface that they were "set in the German manner."[114] No general name could be given to such collections of dances, seeing that they were not yet arranged according to any comprehensive principle. The only arrangement was that the paduana was followed by the gagliarda, because of the contrast between their rhythms (the first being in common time and the second in triple time).

At this stage came the Thirty Years' War, which, although it brought the most fearful misery upon Germany, nevertheless appears to have forwarded the development of the *suite* in that country. The idea of choosing out from among the dance-forms of civilised Europe the most original and adaptable, and uniting them in an artistic whole, received a certain impulse in the unhappy state of Europe, which had driven Italians, Spaniards, Frenchmen, Swedes, Danes, and Poles to jostle one another in the busy ferment of warfare for a series of years. When affairs became settled again, efforts were plainly made to arrive at a higher form of art. To this end it was, before all, needful for the clavier composers to step in and preserve the adaptable musical essence of the dance-tunes by transferring them from the province of the unruly guilds of German town musicians to the quieter, purer atmosphere of domestic music. All evidence goes to prove that the invention of the clavier suite must be sought for in the school of Sweelinck. That it was German is plainly seen from the order of the pieces, which had by this time become firmly settled, and in which the allemande held the first place, followed by the courante ;

---

114 Compare Carl Israël, Die Musikalischen Schätze der Gymnasialbibliothek und der Peterskirche zu Frankfurt a. M. (Frankfurt. a. M., 1872, p. 41).

for the finale two new dance-forms were employed — the
Spanish *sarabande* and the English *gigue*, either both
together or singly. The Germans continued to work up
foreign materials "in a German style," and to associate
them with their own forms, as they had done at the beginning of the century. At the same time dance-music
naturally did not decrease among the town pipers, but was
carefully cherished by them, though more or less disjoined
from its original practical purpose. It was very likely that
for "table-music" or other festive occasions several contrasted dance-tunes would be played one after another.
Whether from this circumstance a sort of customary and
regular order arose—as we saw in the case of the juxtaposition of paduanas and gagliardas—is at present uncertain. At all events, the town pipers had a common name
for such collections of dances, which name was appropriated
by the composers of the clavier suites ; its general meaning
was that of a complete whole consisting of many parts, and
thence it came to be applied to clavier variations. This
name is *partie,* or, in Italian, *partita.*[115]

In the sets of variations, as in the sets of dances called by
this name, the same key was generally adhered to in all the
sections, which shows that their origin was that of mere external juxtaposition. The form invented by the German clavier
masters was now adopted in the Italian chamber sonatas
of Corelli and his followers. But the different technical
requirements of the violin, and the nature of the Italians,
who gave the greatest attention to melodic beauty,
threatened to obliterate the characteristics of the separate
types until they could no longer be recognised. Even the
German nature, with its predilections for harmonic elaboration, could not entirely counteract this. Then the French,
who loved strongly marked rhythms, adopted these sets of
dances. French orchestral music had long been familiar

---

[115] The Lustige Cotala (compare Vol. I., p. 20, note 36) says, at p. 181 :
"One asked us if we had by us any *sonatas,* or any other things set for *instru-
menta.* I said, Yes, and opened my portfolio and took out several pieces and
parthies." On Kuhnau's *parties* see p. 237, note 79 ; on the *partie* as a variation see Vol. I., p. 127.

to the court bands and guilds of town pipers,[116] and its influence had extended to clavier music as well. It was no less a man than Pachelbel who was first infected by it, and who transferred the French overture to the clavier (see Vol. I., p. 124). But this was not enough; the French must lay their hands even on the clavier dances. But the order of the parts was already so firmly fixed that they could not venture to alter it. The component sections even among them were still the *allemande*, the *courante*, the *sarabande*, and the *gigue;* but they introduced them by an overture, and added dances of their own at the end, such as the *gavotte*, the *minuet*, the *rigaudon*, the *passepied*, the *bourrée*, and the *chaconne*, which was properly Italian, inserting it before the gigue, or else in substitution for it; but in all these they had recourse to the most pronounced rhythm. And as this is the most important element in any dance, it was only natural that they should give these compositions the names by which they became known. The form returned to Germany under the name of "suite," there to attain its fullest perfection under Sebastian Bach, who had been preceded by George Böhm, and whose contemporary Handel treated it in a few important compositions. Bach ultimately rejected the French titles; he restored the name *partie* in one of his chief clavier works, as well as in the three so-called suites for violin solo. The suite—the oldest form of instrumental music in many movements—is a German production, in the perfecting of which all the then important nations of Europe took a more or less active part.

It is more difficult to define the limits of the sonata, the history of which is contemporary with that of the suite. It does not entirely dispense with dance forms, but never consists of them alone. What was understood by the sonatas of Giov. Gabrieli at the beginning of the seventeenth century—how this form influenced Sebastian Bach's

---

[116] Compare Vol. I., p. 201. The oboe, or the "French Schalmey," was quite a common instrument among the town pipers in the last decade of the seventeenth century, as appears from "*Battalus*, der vorwitzge Musikant." Freyburg, 1691, pp. 63, 64. Compare, also, the catalogue on Vol. I., p. 169.

cantatas, how sometimes it keeps to its original unity of
movement, and again sometimes is extended to two movements—has been shown before (see Vol. I., p. 124). When,
in the second half of the century, chamber music and solo
violin-playing made such gigantic strides in Italy, Corelli
adopted the form in two movements, and by freely combining two such pairs of movements, made up a whole constituting a three-part *sonata da chiesa* (church sonata), which
he transferred from chamber music back to sacred music, and
in its new form it was accompanied on the organ. When it
was not intended for church performance dances might be
inserted ; and this was done sometimes in the manner of a
suite, with an allemande at the beginning, and more
frequently by concluding with a gigue. The chief principle,
then, of the sonata consisted in the alternation of slow,
broadly treated movements with quick and generally fugal
ones ; they must also contrast with each other in rhythm,
and, if dance-forms were introduced, they had to be adapted
to this rule. As in the suite, so also here, the normal number of movements is four. But, inasmuch as the second slow
movement was by preference in another key, the sonata
resembled the concerto, of which the influence was also felt
in the construction of the several movements, especially the
last. Thus the Gabrieli sonata assisted in forming a new
type of art without being absorbed into it ; indeed, even in the
latter half of the seventeenth century, the secular sonata
for full instrumental band was still retained and kept up
by the town pipers, who used to play it as a beautiful
piece of music in the manner of a motett[117] at their performances of "table music" and on other suitable occasions.[118]
These two types are thus quite distinct from Corelli's church
and chamber sonatas. While in course of time the suite

---

[117] So runs the well-known definition in M. Prætorius. Syntagma Musicum,
III., 2.

[118] The " Lustige Cotala " (p. 44) says, in an account of a " table music " at
a wedding : " We then played a *sonata*, in which there was a *fuga ;* he himself
played the viola." Battalus (Loc. Cit., p. 63) says : " Then the musicians began
to make music. They played a sonata with two trumpets, two hautbois, and a
bassoon, which sounded very well."

was left entirely to the clavier, the reverse was the case with the chamber sonata, in so far that, having been properly a violin composition, it remained so for a time; however, as we have seen (Vol. I., p. 237), it was transferred to the clavier by Kuhnau. No direct step is perceptible from this stage to the modern sonata form; but the polyphonic nature of the allegro movement, which no longer appealed to the spirit of the time, had to be replaced by another kind of treatment. It was another Italian—Domenico Scarlatti—who detected this; he wrote clavier sonatas, of which each movement was in song form, homophonic, and decorated with new and tasteful passages. The three-movement form of the concerto was already adopted, and this opened the way by which the modern sonata could reach its final perfection, coming down by way of Philipp Emanuel Bach and Haydn to Beethoven.

Sebastian Bach's three sonatas for violin solo display the form in its strictest and purest development. All are in four movements. But, inasmuch as the second slow movement is in another though nearly allied key, while the rest keep to the original key, the fundamental scheme is still in three movements; the first adagio unites with the following allegro to form one section, and in the majority of cases leads directly into it by means of a cadenza on the chord of the dominant. The difference of the modern sonata consists only in the style of the several movements: in other respects the conditions are similar. In both, the first part is followed by a second in thorough contrast to it, and the last movement is an attempt to resolve into itself the different meanings of the other two; thus, by a psychological process, as it were, it serves as a bond between them. In both, the greatest musical importance is given to the first allegro movement, while the finale is of lighter calibre as regards both substance and form. The introductory adagio is not considered indispensably necessary in the later sonata; but in the most important branch of the genus, the orchestral symphony, it is almost always retained, although in a shortened form. Still, even here the introductory adagio is in its scheme very different from the middle one, retaining throughout the nature of a prelude; while the second adagio enters as a piece of music in strict form. This fundamental rule is indeed not always adhered to in the master's other works in sonata-form; it is enough that it appears generally in such a way as to leave no doubt as to this method of treatment being intentional.

In spite of their being written for an instrument which, in comparison with the organ and clavier, and considering the direction in which the composer's chief power and importance lay, is confined within the narrowest limits, these sonatas have something very great about them. By the extension of the chords produced by double stopping, and the skilful employment of the open strings, an almost inconceivable fulness of tone is produced; the sharply defined rhythms, the bold and often almost violent execution made necessary by the polyphonic treatment, and especially the fire and force of the fugal allegro movements, give to the sonatas more perhaps than to any other of Bach's instrumental works a certain demoniacal character. The type of the first movement is settled by Corelli in his violin sonatas (Op. 5); it is broad and melodious, but a free and fantastic character is imparted to it by the introduction of many ornamental figures of various types. This character is rendered even more conspicuous in Bach by the form which his polyphonic treatment takes; because, for practical reasons the progression of the subsidiary parts frequently can only be indicated, and has to be filled up by the hearer. In the beautiful and impassioned introductory adagio of the first sonata, in G minor, the melody first appears in the middle part; the upper part meanwhile is progressing in single notes and phrases, and seems to vanish away; it is then lightly touched in the course of the melody, and so brought to sight again; but it is there all along for him who can hear it. From bar 14, where the melodic phrases of the opening are repeated in C minor, the upper part plays the principal *rôle;* the middle part is not on that account inactive, but often displays remarkable independence. The same method is of course pursued with the lower part; the melody has often to be interrupted for a moment in

order to play a short bass note, and often the bass is
vaguely heard through the ornamental figures. It is quite
an exception when the treatment is in more than three
parts, allowing of course for the single four-part chords
occasionally thrown in for the sake of fulness. In the
case of fugues, it is a matter of course that the counterpoint can only be very simple—mere chords often having to
suffice for the accompaniment of the theme—and in spite
of the more animated time, much can only be indicated.
Passages of runs and arpeggios in one part, are introduced
in Corelli's manner to rest and prepare the mind for the
polyphony that is to follow. For the rest we may be
sure that the master of the fugue himself would be as
careful as possible to satisfy the strictest requirements ;
we find not only free fugatos, but genuine and thoroughly
worked-out fugues, displaying the most marvellous wealth
of combination and invention. At present the best known
fugue is the one in the first sonata ; Mattheson, in
two of his writings, draws attention to that in the second
sonata (A minor), as being a model in its kind ; which
circumstance is of importance when we remember what his
feeling was towards Bach. He says:[119] " The length of the
theme in a fugue is, in some measure, left to the taste of the
composer, but, as a general rule, it may be said that the
earlier and the closer the response follows the theme the
better will the fugue sound. Frequently the most excellent
working-out is found in a fugue on the fewest notes. Who
would ever think that these eight short notes—

could be fruitful enough to give rise naturally to a counterpoint of more than a whole sheet of music without any considerable extension ? And yet this has been done, as is plainly

[119] Kern melodischer Wissenschaft, Hamburg, 1737, p. 147.—Vollkomm
Capellmeister, p. 369. Mattheson's citations are incorrect in both place⸗
chiefly so in the first, where he writes the theme in 3-4 time; the sharp before
d″ is lacking in ·he second piece.

to be seen, by the great Bach, of Leipzig, who was particularly happy in this kind of composition; and more than that, it is treated directly and in inversion."

But the fugue in the third sonata in C minor must be allowed to surpass these two in grandeur and importance; the only obstacle which prevents its attaining a wide-spread popularity is its enormous difficulty. It will presently be shown that this difficulty may probably be explained by the history of its composition. The third movement of the G minor sonata consists of a charmingly conceived *Siciliano* in B flat major, with marvellous polyphonic working-out, but the tender character of this dance-form is injured by the strength and harshness of tone necessarily resulting from the employment of several parts; this is one of the cases in which the alien character of the style is very prominent. The corresponding movement of the A minor sonata is in C major and in song-form, with two sections; a broad and expressive melody comes in supported by short, staccato notes in the lowest part, while the middle part takes a small share in the development of the melody. The sonata in C major has, in this place, a largo in F major of quite as expressive a character, which is not separated from the other movements by any pause. In all three the treatment of the last movement is identical. The form is in two sections, and in only one musical part; it flies along in almost incessant semi-quavers; the type is exactly that of the last movement of a concerto, which has been before described (Vol. I., p. 409).

Bach's standpoint at the time of his writing these sonatas is plainly shown by the circumstance that all three reappear either in parts or in their entirety, in the form of clavier or organ pieces. The whole of the middle one is arranged as a clavier sonata, and transposed for this from A minor to D minor.[120] Although it does not exist in Bach's handwriting, the wonderful genius displayed in the arrangement leaves no room for doubting that it is from the composer's own hand. In its clavier form it is so much richer in treatment that at times the original appears

---

[120] P. S. I., C. 3, No. 3 (Vol. 213, p. 24).

a mere sketch beside it; the natural way in which the
polyphonic richness is brought out shows what was the
proper birthplace of Bach's violin compositions of this kind.
At the same time it is quite certain that the sonata was
originally written for the violin; this is shown not only by
many details, but also by the selection of D minor as the
key, whereby a great deal is brought into depths of pitch
which we are not accustomed to in Bach; this transposition
was necessary in order to avoid too great extension in the
compass of the parts. The fugue of the G minor sonata
exists in an arrangement for the organ; that it, too, was
first intended for the violin is shown by the nature of the
theme.[121] Its connection with the original is here not so
close, and in two places there is an extension of about one
bar; the arrangement must have been made very soon after
its composition, for a copy exists which was made in the
year 1725. A more complicated method has been taken
with regard to the C major sonata. A clavier arrangement
of the first movement was made by Bach, and its lower
pitch (G major) shows again that the violin form is the
older.[122] In this, more than any other place, it is clear that
the composer's imagination clung to the clavier style,
even in the original conception. Here there appears no
melody with fanciful figures suitable to the violin, but that
sort of soft progression of slowly changing harmonies which
owes its origin neither to the nature of the violin nor to any
Italian influence; indeed its source is very evident. Even
with the most perfect performance the intention of the composer can never be realised on the violin; the execution of
chords of three or four notes has inevitably a violent and
harsh effect, which contradicts the character of the movement. When played on the clavier in that enriched form
which the composer himself gave it, it is discovered to be
one of the most marvellous productions of Bach's genius;
one of those preludes which is pervaded by a single
rhythm throughout, and in which the harmonies softly melt

---

[121] B.-G. XV., p. 149, transposed into D minor.—P. S. V., C. 3, No. 4
(Vol. 242). Compare Appendix A., No. 4.

[122] P. S. I., C. 3, Appendix pp. 1 and 2 (not in English edition of Peters).

II.

into one another like cloud shapes, while from beneath their magic veil comes a long-drawn and yearning melody. All that the heart feels, and that the tongue vainly endeavours to utter, is here revealed at once, and yet remains remote and unapproachable. No human being since has ever created such tones!

Nothing remains of the other sonata movements arranged for the clavier. Did any such arrangement exist? As to the fugue this question may safely be answered in the negative. I take it to be rather a transcription of an organ piece. Its theme consists of the first line of the chorale tune "Komm, heiliger Geist, Herre Gott," an unheard-of procedure in a violin sonata. The contrapuntal artifice is so complicated for a solo violin that it demands impossibilities from the player, and skilled players have assured me that at times the method of writing is as contrary to what is playable as if the composer had never set eyes upon a violin at all.

Special attention must be drawn to the fact that Mattheson, in his "grosse Generalbasschule," gives a description of an organ fugue on the same theme, which agrees almost entirely with Bach's treatment. He gives the theme as follows—

and remarks "(1) that it is the beginning of a chorale; (2) that in the response not the least artifice is attempted; (3) that the fugal counter-subject might be chromatic, and that the fugue might therefore be treated in augmentation since it is too simple without such treatment; (4) that the chief subject allows of being turned both ways; (5) that direct and inverse motion could be united and harmonised together; (6) also that there are many other neat combinations which might be made into the subject and the response by bringing them into closer contact," &c. He then (p. 38) gives his own views as to the right way of treating the work.[123]

---

[123] The theme is also quoted in the Vollkomm.-Capellmeister, p. 363.

Now in Bach's violin fugue there occurs at the very beginning the chromatic countersubject which he requires; and we
here find that complicated stretto which he speaks of under
No. 6, with the entrances now after the first, and now after
the fourth note of the theme (compare bars 93 ff and
109 ff); here, too, is the inversion (bars 201 ff), and of
course there is plentiful employment of double counterpoint.
Those of Mattheson's precepts which Bach fails to comply
with are either unnecessary for the free and irrepressible
swing of the fugue (such as the inversion of the theme,
retaining the exact semitones), or else tasteless (such as the
combination of the direct and inverse motions of the theme);
such a combination could only be pleasing if one part
entered after the other. But, in fact, Bach worked in a
richer material than Mattheson could elaborate. Thus he
adds to the chromatic countersubject a second counter-
subject—

(compare for example bars 135-136 and the episodical
extension in the bars that follow; also bars 293-294 and bars
107-108); possibly these are included in Mattheson's "&c."
Now it certainly cannot be said that the whole treatment as
devised by Mattheson, and actually executed by Bach, was
altogether an obvious one—only the introduction of the
chromatic countersubject was not unusual, but occurs
several times in works of this period [124]—so that Mattheson
must have been familiar with Bach's fugue, though certainly
not in its present form. It would be very easy to point
to the Hamburg journey as the time when Mattheson
became acquainted with it, but Bach would hardly have
taken his violin solos with him, if indeed they were written
at this time, but rather his organ pieces only, and possibly
some vocal compositions. Mattheson for the first time
betrays his acquaintance with the violin sonatas in the year
1737, but he had already set the fugue theme quoted above

---

[124] For example, in a fugue by Pachelbel on a theme nearly similar to this
one in Commer. Musica Sacra I., p. 156, and also in Sebastian Bach's Organ
Canzone.

as an exercise at a trial of organists on October 8, 1727. It may be remembered that in the same passage of the "grosse Generalbasschule," the theme and countersubject of Bach's great G minor fugue had been quoted, which the author had once employed for a similar purpose (see p. 23). Apparently there was a chorale fugue by Bach on the hymn "Komm, heiliger Geist, Herre Gott," which he had performed in Hamburg in 1720, and which he then made free use of for the violin fugue. Little as it profits a man to deck himself in borrowed plumes, yet it was not an unheard-of trait in Mattheson, since he could not prevail upon himself to name Bach as the composer of the G minor fugue. Many of his remarks sound as if he wanted to justify himself in his own eyes—for instance, when he calls the fugue theme "easy," and insists that it is borrowed from a chorale, and when he suggests the introduction of the chromatic countersubject with the remark that without it the fugue would be too simple. And yet here it is, in its place.

Among Bach's chief works I place the three sets of compositions for the clavier known by the name of the French Suites, the English Suites, and the six Partitas. We may go farther, and extend the observation, with some inconsiderable limitations, to the three other violin solos, and all the compositions for solo violoncello, with which we shall have more to do subsequently. But we must remark in passing that in them Bach only adheres quite slightly to the Italian form, but keeps very closely to that of the clavier suite as it had been developed first by the Germans, then by the French, and lastly by himself. There is a greater adaptation of style in these than in the sonatas. What was gained from the French was the careful marking of the rhythm, which was almost unrecognisable among the Italians, although it is the most essential feature of dance-music. Corelli's Sarabandes are often nothing more than slow Sicilianos, and sometimes are divested of every characteristic, even the three-time. His Gavottes lack the important feature of beginning with the second half of the bar of common time, and once he even begins with a short note before the bar. In the Allemandes no rhythmic type whatever can be recognised; a dignified movement and a polyphonic style seem to be considered sufficient; the dignity is often sacrificed in an Allegro or Presto. The old courante, according to its etymology, indicated among the Italians a piece full of flying, running passages, but the Germans and French gave it a grave, sustained, and impassioned character. But the Italian type had shown itself too prolific in art, and too firmly settled, and in particular had exercised too important an influence upon the last movement of the concerto (see Vol. I., p. 409), to be easily driven from its position ; thus there existed side by side two utterly different types. It would be well to distinguish once for all between the *corrente* and the *courante*.

From the attempt to smooth away all peculiarities of rhythm, there grew up among the Italians an inclination to confuse the characteristic divisions of the suite with those of the sonata and the concerto. The French, on the other hand, not only gave important assistance to the development of the suite form, by giving definiteness and prominence to the contrasts of rhythm, but they also made an important advance by the suppleness and pliability of their passages, and by the elegance and richness of their adornments. Since this was willingly acknowledged by every one, they wished to be taken as the universal models of suite compositions. But, happily, the musical world was not so blinded by this as to set aside the service, at least as important to this form of music, rendered by the Germans, and Mattheson says, quite justly and with happy preciseness: "The French indeed wrote, or rather pretended to write, Courantes and Allemandes for the clavier, and indeed they made very free with these particular forms ; but he who will compare without prejudice their bald, thin, and empty jingling with a well-written, *nerveuse*, German courante with its distributed polyphony, will see how little truth there is in their pretensions."[125] He might have said yet more; for the French not only did nothing towards the combination of the dances to a com-

---

[125] Neu eröffnetes Orchestre, S. 187.

plete whole, but rather checked the growth of the best type of arrangement. Marchand, in a suite in D minor, introduces after a prelude, first an allemande, two courantes, a sarabande, and a gigue, and then a chaconne in four "couplets," a gavotte and a minuet. The true idea of concluding with a gigue is either misunderstood or ignored. Couperin's sets of pieces are scarcely to be called suites at all; the second set of his *Pièces de Clavecin* (D minor) contains allemande, two courantes, sarabande; then a free interlude in D major; a gavotte, minuet, *les Canaries* (a kind of gigue) with a variation, a passepied and trio, a rigaudon and trio—eleven independent pieces varying between major and minor—a rondeau, and then for the close a piece in the style of a gigue but very freely written. The fifth set (A major) consists of an allemande, two courantes, a sarabande, a gigue, and six rondos, intermingled with pieces in free style. In spite of this he never entirely quits the ground of the suite, for he keeps to the same key throughout, even when he does not begin with the usual pieces. But it is clear that he never felt the necessity of welding together the various constituent parts to one perfect whole of many members. Why he failed is seen in the titles that Couperin bestowed on his clavier pieces, in which he either followed or introduced a custom that was general, though I have previously found it only in the case of Gaspard de Roux. He tries to make them represent definite personifications, or a connected series of actions, or even of public events. Thus, titles such as these occur: The Sublime, The Majestic, Industry, Shyness, Gloom, Danger; and still more individual names in the rondos and free pieces, such as The Florentine Lady, The Sailor of Provence, the Gossip, Nanette, Manon, Mimi; and in one case a piece called "The Fair Pilgrims" is in three sections, of which the first represents the pilgrimage (treated of course in a thoroughly French and frivolous manner), the second a petition for alms, and the third gratitude for it.[126] Another piece in three sections is called *les Bacchanales*, and

---

[126] Couperin's Werke, edited by J. Brahms. Vol. I. Bergedof, near Hamburg, 1871, p. 55. f., from whence the examples quoted above are taken.

is divided into *Enjouements bachiques, Tendresses bachiques,* and *Fureurs bachiques.* Pictures from nature are of rare occurrence, and it is always the idea of motion that is represented, as clouds, bees, or a floating veil. The chief point of interest is nearly always outside the pieces, as it were, and music is a mere accessory; briefly it is a refined kind of ballet music, and is like the orchestral dance tunes in Lully's operas transcribed for the clavier. This corresponds, as we saw in another case (Vol. I., p. 246), to the theatrical nature of the French, but restrains and destroys the activity of free musical genius. We must, however, consider that every day the French either saw or performed in the theatres the other orchestral types of dances, if not actually the allemande, and so got to connect them in their minds with certain definite ideas and representations. In Germany the case was different; in the courts it is true that they aped the French ballet music, but the people were, happily, not affected by this, and so could enter into the purely musical value of the dance-form without any disturbing connections with the stage.

It had become usual among the German suite-composers before Bach to work out the courante on the lines of the allemande. This custom exactly corresponds with the fugue form of two or three sections, so much in favour with the northern organ masters, in which the same theme is worked out in a variety of ways. This has been fully gone into in speaking of Buxtehude's organ works, and the analogy with the suite form was then pointed out. (See Vol. I., pp. 264 and 275.) The contrasts of rhythm between the allemande and the courante, and between the courante and the gigue, are precisely the same as those between the three sections of Buxtehude's great E minor fugue. It is clear that, with the exception of Froberger, it must have been chiefly the northern masters who improved and enlarged the suite in the second half of the seventeenth century, for they have stamped it with a lasting impression of their own specific individuality. All through Reinken's *Hortus Musicus* the courantes are nothing more than modifications of the allemandes which precede them, and the sarabandes, and

even the gigues, show a plain connection with the allemandes. Walther says of the allemande: "In a musical
partie (*i.e.*, suite) it is, as it were, the proposition, from
which flow forth the other movements, for instance the
courante, the sarabande, and the gigue, like the constituent
parts of it (*partes*)."[127] Handel, too, followed this method in
all essential particulars. The suites of the second and third
collections of his clavier works especially show a connection
between the allemande and the courante; it is found, too, in
the first collection, and in particular in the E minor suite,
where it goes farther and is carried on into the gigue.[128]

From these circumstances, as well as from productions
like Buxtehude's suites on the chorale "Auf meinen lieben
Gott,"[129] it is evident that the Germans first sought for
the unity by which the different sections might be combined,
in the use and treatment of variations. They must soon have
become aware, however, that by this means the characteristic
types of the dance-forms were too severely weighted, and so
for the most part they contented themselves with treating
the courante alone as a variation. But when once the rule
was given up this custom might easily be abrogated.
Sebastian Bach saw that unity could be attained by a
scheme of internal treatment alone, since the four fundamental types had been arranged in so happy an order that
each contrasted with, and made up for, the deficiencies of the
others. He, therefore, adhered steadily to these four types,
and the few exceptions he allowed himself only prove the
rule. It is not difficult to recognise even in the suite that
far-reaching principle in art: that of the triple form. The
allemande and the courante are closely connected even when
their subject-matter is not the same. The allemande has
always a medium character, being neither fast nor slow,
neither solemn nor impassioned; it is, as Mattheson says,
"the picture of a contented and satisfied mind, delighting in
order and repose."[130] It is always in common time: it con-

---

[127] Lexicon, p. 28.
[128] German Handel Society's Edition, Vol. II. Peters, Vol. IV., A and B.
[129] See my edition of Buxtehude's Organ Works, Vol. II., sect. ii., No. 33.
[130] Vollkomm.-Capellmeister, p. 232, s. 128

sists of two sections, tolerably equal as to length, of from
eight to sixteen bars each on an average, and has this
peculiarity, that it begins with either one or three short
notes before the bar (Böhm in one case begins with seven,
Bach with four, semiquavers). The harmonies are broad,
and by preference in broken chords, and the upper part has
various figures. This character is not decided enough to
produce the effect of contrast; but it gains in intensity in
the courante which follows it, which, even when not treated
in the Italian manner, gives the effect of animation by means
of its triple rhythm. Besides the notes before the bar at
the beginning and the similar length of the sections—
which it has in common with the allemande—its typical
characteristics consist in certain disturbing syncopations of
accent produced by the mixture of triple and double
rhythm; for the 6-4 time runs into the 3-2 time, and *vice
versâ* (according to rule at the end of each section).
According to Mattheson the courante expresses " Hope,"
but this is saying too much, for a definite emotion of that
kind is not to be attained by instrumental music; still the
view has some foundation.[131] Thus the allemande prepares
the way for the courante, and both form one whole, just as
the introductory adagio and the fugue do in the sonata.

Then the sarabande fills the same place in the suite as
the second adagio in the sonata, or the slow movement
in the modern form of the sonata. Its movement is quiet
and solemn, suggesting Spanish haughtiness, and its tone
is grave and calm. It is in triple time, and begins, as a
rule, with a whole bar. The accent falls by preference on
the·second beat, which is so prolonged as to include either
half or the whole of the last beat. Its length was originally
limited to two sections of eight bars each. This number
was seldom exceeded in the first section, even in later times,
but the second section was extended to twelve, sixteen,
or even more bars, and sometimes even a third section is
added.

Lastly, the concluding gigue corresponds entirely to the

---

[131] Vollkomm.-Capellmeister, p. 231, s. 123.

last movement of the sonata and concerto—in place of which it was frequently employed—its quick running and capering form, which is inconsistent with thoughtful intensity, forms a vivid contrast to the allemande and the courante as well as the sarabande. The more grave impressions produced by the movements that have gone before are gathered up into a cheerful and animated form, and the hearer goes away with a sensation of pleasant excitement. The rhythm of the gigue is chosen from the most animated kinds of triple time—12-8 (or common time in triplets), 6-8, and 3-8 times are of the most frequent occurrence, but 6-4, 9-8, 9-16, 12-16, and 24-16 are also found. It is of course in two sections, and its length, which cannot be well compared by numbering the bars because of the various *tempi*, is proportional to the rest of the dances. The Italian and the German modes of treatment have not, it is true, resulted in a complete division into two different types—as in the case of the courante—but yet its structure has become modified. In the former treatment it is essentially homophonous, accompanied in chords by a figured bass and other instruments, but in the latter it is developed polyphonally even to a genuine fugue. This is fresh evidence that the northern masters had a hand in the formation of the Suite. Just as in their organ fugues in several movements, the last was in 12-8 or 6-8 time, so here they write the concluding piece of the suite in 12-8 or 6-8 time. They were the first to follow the method of thematic working out with any great powers of invention, and it is to them that we owe the plan of the second section of the fugal gigue—which has been a type and model since the end of the seventeenth century—namely, the treatment of the theme of the first part in inversion in the second.[132] It is evident that by this means, without detracting from the cheerfulness of the concluding movement, a balance was struck between that and the gravity and importance of the other movements, and the suite form was consolidated, and made worthier to receive and utilise material from wherever it might come.

---

[132] Thus it is, for instance, throughout Reinken's *Hortus Musicus.*

In Bach's clavier compositions the fugal gigue with the
inversion in the second part is the only form employed,
whereas Handel nearly always treats his in the Italian
manner ; where he does not, he supports the entry of the
theme with harmonies, and in only one instance—in the
F minor suite in the first collection of his clavier works—
does he make use of an inversion in the second section.
The French did nothing worthy of mention towards the
development of the gigue.

The form was now complete in itself, and when new
numbers were introduced—as they were sure to be from the
multiplicity of unemployed and piquant French dance types—
a suitable place was found for them between the sarabande
and the gigue. Since the first section of the suite was
composed of the allemande and the courante together,
something might be inserted before the gigue without
disturbing the balance ; nay, the greater the importance
given to the gigue by the use of polyphony, the more would
the need be felt of some light, short, bright intermezzo, in
contrast to the measured gravity of the allemande, the
passionate eagerness of the courante, and the calm dignity
of the sarabande. So it became customary to insert one, or
even two or three such pieces, according to circumstances ;
the forms of the *gavotte*, the *passepied*, and the *bourrée* were
found ready to the composer's hands, and they ultimately
gave rise to the scherzo and minuet of the modern
symphony.[133] Whether the impulse to do this came
first from the French or the Germans must be specially
inquired into.

In the suites of Dieupart and Grigny, which Bach copied
out for himself, and which seem to date from the year 1700,
a gavotte and a minuet are found inserted between each
sarabande and gigue (Vol. I., p. 202). And in Germany, Johann
Krieger published, in the year 1697, six *Parties* " consisting

---

[133] These inserted pieces are well called " intermezzi " by G. Nottebohm,
who has written a series of well-considered articles on the nature of the
suite in the " Wiener Monatsschrift für Theater und Musik " ; Vol. for 1855,
pp. 408-412, 457-461 ; Vol. for 1857, pp. 288-292, 341-345, 391-396. He has also
pointed out the reciprocal internal relations of the other movements.

of Allemandes, Courantes, Sarabandes, *Doubles* (*i.e.*, Variations on a dance-tune), and Gigues, besides interspersed Bourrées, Minuets, and Gavottes." In every case the French were misled by their theatrical proclivities. When once the admission of such an intermezzo was decided upon, it could be more freely used, and just as in Beethoven's later and latest works the scherzo often comes before the adagio, so in Bach the sarabande is several times preceded by a gavotte and a passepied, or the like.

If we now compare the form of the suite with that of the sonata in respect of their general value, we find that the comparison is not, as we should expect, so greatly in favour of the latter, but that they must be considered as of equal value. In the sonata, the inner connection is so close that an element of contrast has to be brought in by the introduction of a movement in another key; and the very existence of this form depends on the adequate treatment of this contrast. The sonata proceeds with the inexorable precision of a causal nexus; its very essence is emotion or *Pathos*. The suite has no internal self-contradiction to overcome; it presents, on the level ground of one unchanging key, a concordant and reasonably differing variety; its spirit is that of repose or *Ethos*. The love for the sonata form, which increased from Bach's time onwards, corresponds to the love for subjective and impassioned expression, and to the decided leaning towards poetry, which appears more prominently from this time forth in German instrumental music; while in the suite a simpler and more purely musical view of the art is taken. Accordingly the materials of the sonata were invented by individual composers, while those of the suites had their rise in the natural forces of nationalities. The suite, in spite of the multiplicity of its movements, is simple when compared to the sonata; it is a single stone cut with many facets, and the sonata is a ring composed of many stones. Thus the movements of the suite could never give rise to such expansions as those of the sonata; a development corresponding to that of the sonata into the symphony was quite impossible. But the introduction of the minuet or

scherzo in the same key as the first and last movements, shows that even the sonata, when the number
of movements was increased beyond three, could not
transgress the law of the suite, since it was that of all
instrumental music. The relations of the movements in
both forms are based on the catholic and inherent laws
of art. But the more purely musical the character of
the piece, the more freely can the question of the propriety
of different kinds of forms and of details be decided by
feeling. So that if it is difficult to prove the necessary
connection of the movements in a sonata, in each particular
case, the difficulty is much greater in the case of the suite.
Nevertheless, the demands of art are always valid, and
the reason why the diligent study of the masterpieces of
this class has so great an influence in the formation of
musical taste is because it leads, as scarcely any other
means can, to the appreciation of the finer and more
delicate degrees of proportion and feeling between the
sections and the whole.

It still remains for us to glance at the suites for violin
and violoncello[134] in detail. The three *Parties* correspond
nearly in character to the three sonatas, with which they
were united in one work by the composer. He seems to
employ the contrast between the two forms as a structural
plan, for each sonata is followed by a suite. All three
are remarkably irregular in their formation. In the B
minor suite each movement has a variation which follows
it like its shadow. It is very probable that the addition
of variations in the suite was an after effect, resulting from
the attempt to work up the dance-forms that followed the
allemande as variations on it. At all events this method
occurs at a very early period; for instance, in an excellent
suite in F♯ minor by Christian Ritter (Kammerorganist
at Dresden from 1683-1688,[135] subsequently Capellmeister
in Sweden), in which the sarabande is followed by two

---

[134] B.-G., XXVII., 1.

[135] Fürstenan, Zur Geschichte der Musik am Hofe zu Dresden, I., pp. 267
and 299.

variations; in a *Partie* by Johann Ernst Pestel (b. 1659),
where the treatment is the same; and in the violin suites
in Walther's *Hortus chelicus* (for instance, Nos. 20 and 23),
where each dance is followed by a variation, as in Bach.
When employed in moderation there was nothing to
complain of in a method which impressed the import of
a piece more plainly on the hearer, and gave it in certain
ways a more emphatic resonance; only the fundamental
relations of the parts must not be disturbed by it, and
the number of permissible variations must never exceed
two.[136]   Bach in almost every case contented himself with
one.   Since in the B minor suite he wished to avail
himself of variations in all the sections, he could hardly
use the gigue as the concluding movement, as it is
ill adapted for variations.   In its stead he chose the
Bourrée, a dance-form of light, pleasant, and somewhat
reckless character (in common time, beginning with the
last beat of the bar, moderately quick, and smooth in
its style), which, however, has here an air of uncouth
jollity, only coming back to its proper character in the
Double.   For the rest, it is wonderful how sharply defined,
in spite of the limited means, are the individualities of the
types; the most difficult task was in the case of the allemande, which combines richness of harmony and polyphony
with varied figures in the upper part.   The courante in
the French and German style is contrasted with one in the
Italian style which follows it, as a variation, rushing by in a
wild and irresistible manner.   After this, the sarabande
comes in heavily and proudly in three and four part harmony.

The second suite, in D minor, has the customary four
movements.   In the quick time of the gigue no fugal style
can be expected of course from the single instrument; it is
throughout in one part, but produces the effect of harmonic

---

[136] Joh. Jak. Walther begins his *Scherzo da Violino solo* which appeared in 1676
with a regular suite in four movements, in which the allemande has no fewer than
six variations, while the courante has only one, and the sarabande and gigue
none at all.   Since, however, the courante, the sarabande, and the gigue are
all formed on the same subject as the allemande, it is strictly nothing but a
continuous series of variations.

fulness by the way in which the passages are written. This
is followed by a chaconne. It is longer than all the rest
of the suite put together, and must not be considered as
the last movement of it, but as an appended piece ; the
suite proper concludes with the gigue. The French were
fond of introducing chaconnes, but in a somewhat different
form from that now known to us. They were accustomed to
treat both the chaconne and the passacaglio in clavier music
with a much greater freedom. Either no ground theme at
all was taken, but a number of phrases of four bars long
and in the same rhythm in 3-4 time were put together,
in which case the artifice consisted in making them grow
more animated and louder (as is done in a chaconne in
Muffat's *Apparatus musico-organisticus*) ; or a subject of four
bars with a *reprise* was taken and repeated without
alteration after each of a number of independent phrases,
or *couplets*. Couperin and Marchand usually followed this
method, and Muffat, in the work just mentioned gives a
passacaglio constructed on this scheme. The form was
closely allied to that of the rondo, and even the essential
triple rhythm was not always adhered to by Couperin ; the
only characteristic that is retained is the somewhat grave
and solemn style. Bach so far adopted this rondo form that
in several cases, and with great effect, especially in the middle
and at the end he returns to the eight bars of the opening
and introduces new ideas between the repetition of them,
but in general he remains true to the fundamental working-
out of the chief theme in the old and thoughtful way. In all
cases his manner of treatment corresponds exactly with the
definition given above of the passacaglio (Vol. I., p. 279); a
free handling of the theme was necessary inasmuch as it
had to be played solo on a violin. An analysis of the whole
will not be unacceptable, since the notes of the themes are
often dispersed through different octaves in the whirl of
the figurations, so that their connection is not always easy
to recognise. The first and principal theme is as follows—

it is once gone through, and then comes (bar 17):—

In the manner of a rondo, but in a new dress, the first theme returns once; and the second, which soon is wrapped up in smooth semiquaver figures, recurs twice. The third, from bar 49 onwards, comes in, but never in a simple form; without the ornaments it would be approximately in this shape—

in which it must be noticed that the skips of thirds are afterwards enlarged into tenths or inverted into sixths. This is gone through four times, then, at bar 81, the second returns, still with new figures, and resulting in its second section in a new modification of the first; [137] this in its turn prepares for a fourth subject, which comes in with bar 97—

and is carried on to bar 121; then, to conclude, all four themes come in, combined with marvellous genius, the third being in this form—

alternating during four bars with rushing demi-semiquavers and semiquavers; the first then recurs in a broad and heavy style, as at the beginning; and lastly the second and fourth together for four bars, so that the former lies in the

---

[137] The meaning of this passage (bars 89—97) is not doubtful, but we do not get a clear idea of the first theme. It is, however, quite in accordance with rule that after so long a silence it should reappear once more. Mendelssohn and Schumann were of the same opinion, as appears from their arrangements.

upper part, and the latter in the form it took in bar 113, in
the lowest part.   In gavottes, minuets, bourrées, and in
chaconnes, contrasting trios were in great favour; such an
one now makes its appearance in D major with a modification of the third theme, which must be reckoned as a fifth
subject on account of its independent treatment :—

In bars 133—209 it becomes larger and freer, and at last is
varied once only, the ground rhythm being retained; then
the minor mode recurs, and all five themes are gone through
again in it : the third until bar 229, the fifth (in the form
adopted in bar 161) combined with the second until bar 237,
the fourth until bar 241, and again the third until 249 ; and
at last this production, so prodigious of its kind, is crowned
by the first theme in its original form.   The hearer must
regard this chaconne as some phenomenon of the elements,
which transports and enraptures him with its indescribable
majesty, and at the same time bewilders and confuses him.
The overpowering wealth of forms pouring from a few
and scarcely noticeable sources displays not only the most
perfect knowledge of the *technique* of the violin, but also the
most absolute mastery over an imagination the like of
which no composer was ever endowed with.   Consider that
all this was written for a single violin !   And what scenes
this small instrument opens to our view !   From the grave
majesty of the opening, through the anxious restlessness of
the second theme to the demi-semiquavers which rush up
and down like very demons, and which are veiled by the weird
form of the third subject—from those tremulous arpeggios
that hang almost motionless, like veiling clouds above a
gloomy ravine, till a strong wind drives and rolls them
together and scourges them down among the tree tops,
which groan and toss as they whirl their leaves into the
air—to the devotional beauty of the movement in D major
where the evening sun sets in the peaceful valley.   The
spirit of the master urges the instrument to incredible
utterance ; at the end of the major section it sounds like

an organ, and sometimes a whole band of violins might seem to be playing. This chaconne is a triumph of spirit over matter such as even he never repeated in a more brilliant manner. There have been many attempts in later days to melt down the precious material for other instruments. Little as this is to be blamed on æsthetic considerations—for Bach himself led the way with his own additional arrangements[138]—yet it is certain that it needs a master hand to do it with success, and it was no contemptible task for two of the greatest musicians of modern times, Mendelssohn and Schumann, to make an adequate pianoforte accompaniment to the chaconne. The wonderful result shows how profound and fruitful is the original theme. And yet Schumann, who is known to have arranged accompaniments for all six violin solos in this way, not only intensified the general musical import, but also shed a clearer light on the chaconne form by following it out phrase for phrase in the most exact way. The fear that by this means an incoherent effect might be produced is as unfounded as it would be were it a whole suite; for it is the principle of the suite which animates the organism of this chaconne. In both there are movements and groups of movements of different characters in juxtaposition which must be all in the same key; in spite of all changes of emotion and all their passionate character, one ruling feature is evident to every one, the undisturbed unity of repose. And so the union of the chaconne with the suite had at last a still deeper issue; the amalgamation of two equally complete forms to a more perfect whole, so as to give the greatest possible importance and value to the idea which permeates them both.

At the beginning of the third partie, in E major, there stands a wonderfully fresh prelude moving in incessant semiquavers, now in runs, and now in arpeggios. It was not unusual to begin the clavier suites with a prelude. That

---

[138] Thereby confuting his pupil Kirnberger's remarkable assertion that no other part could be added to the violin and violoncello solo without harmonic faults. (Kunst des reinen Satzes, I., p. 176.)

there is here a transference of style is proved by the
composer himself, for he subsequently arranged the movement for organ obbligato and orchestra (transposing it into
D major), and used it as an instrumental introduction to a
cantata written for the election of senators in 1731.[139]   The
prelude is followed neither by an allemande, a courante, nor
a gigue; all these forms are lacking in this suite. Bach has
for once given the reins to his love for contrast as he has
done nowhere else, excepting in his suites for orchestra,
where he had historical precedent for it.   Thus, there comes
next a *loure* in 6-4 time, moderato—a kind of gigue, but slower
and graver.[140]   Then comes a gavotte in rondo form, with its
rollicking merriment, a genuine piece of fun in the style
of the older Bachs.   Two minuets about fill the place
of the sarabande, the first fine and solemn, the second
tender and delightful—a charming little pair.   Between these
and the concluding gigue is inserted a bourrée.   This last
partie has perhaps the same meaning with regard to the
whole collection of the six solos as the gigue has in the
single suite ; its bright cheerfulness almost takes away the
impression produced by the solemn greatness of the others ;
but the connection of the different emotions is brought
about by the concluding allegro of the C major sonata.

In the six compositions for violoncello alone[141] a general
character may also be perceived, which is distinct from that
of the works for the violin in proportion to the difference of
the instruments in readiness of expression.   The passionate
and penetrating energy, the inner fire and warmth which
often grew to be painful in its intensity, is here softened
down to a quieter beauty and a generally serene grandeur,
as was to be expected from the deeper pitch and the fuller
tone of the instrument.   In the same ratio (four to two) in
which the minor keys preponderated in the other case, do

---

[139] B.-G. V., 1, No. 29.   The whole suite is also extant in an arrangement for
clavier (Royal Library in Berlin), and the autograph is still existing.

[140] Mattheson (Vollkomm.-Capellmeister, p. 228, § 102) says that the loures
had a proud and inflated style ; but Bach's loures, at all events, are the very
opposite to this.

[141] P., S. IV., C. 1 (vol. 238a).   B.-G. XXVII., 1.

the major keys preponderate here; while there one-half
consisted of sonatas, here there are only suites; and while
there all the suites differed in form from one another, here
they all agree entirely. Each begins with a grand prelude,
boldly constructed out of broad arpeggios and weighty
passages, and in the fifth suite Bach introduced in their
place a complete overture in the French style, in which the
adagio, with its long pedal points on C and G, has an
imposing and glowing character. Then follow, according
to rule, the allemande, courante and sarabande, and before
the concluding gigue in each case there are two intermezzos
which consist in the first two suites (in G major and D
minor) of minuets, in the third and fourth (in C major and
E flat major) of bourrées, and in the last two (C minor and
D major) of gavottes. The uniformity of design in all the
suites shows, too, that the last suite is conceived of as one
whole with all the rest, and hence we may include it without
further remark among the violoncello solos, although it was
written for the *viola pomposa* invented by Bach. The great
extent of tone opened up by this instrument may have been
one reason for the remarkable and quite unique beauty of the
work, and it is to be most deeply deplored that, with this
viola has vanished the possibility of ever hearing this suite
which was destined for it in its original form.[142] Since Bach
himself devised the instrument, he must have played it
himself, and this suite upon it: we can the more easily
imagine this, since we are told he was a skilful player
on the tenor. I, not being a proficient, cannot judge of the
technical difficulties of the work, as compared with the violin
solos, but they seem to be very considerable. At all events,
for the violoncello he possessed a friend in the gamba-
player Abel, who could be at hand to give his advice on
technical points, and for whom the suites were probably
written. Their value is much more than this, however; the
decisive character of the dance-forms places them almost

---

[142] In the Peters' edition, superintended by Fr. Grützmacher, and unfortunately
much disfigured by many arbitrary additions, it is arranged for violoncello and
transposed into D major, whereby much is of course lost.

above the violin suites, and they show just as much inexhaustible fulness of invention. In a single case—in the
C major suite—the courante is evolved from the allemande ;
this is the exception, before alluded to, to the general statement made on page 85, as to the rule of contrast in the movements. The majestic structure of the C minor courante,
which is built on a subject rising gradually from the depths
at intervals of a bar, and in the second part sinking down
again in a scale passage of equal length, should be noticed as
a remarkable point.

The way in which Bach treated the violin and violoncello
as solitary instruments was of course entirely altered as soon
as, by the introduction of another and a supporting instrument,
the duty of elucidating the harmonies no longer fell to their
share; for indeed, although treated with the most masterly
skill, they could never be entirely free from a certain feeling
of constraint. The most usual combinations were those
of one, two, or even three stringed instruments with the
clavier, the first called a solo and the last trio, which was
not quite a consistent name, inasmuch as in the trio the
string bass when it was added only strengthened the bass
of the harpsichord, while in the solo an accompanying
harpsichord bass is taken for granted. The task of the
accompanist was of only secondary importance ; he had only
to put in the background before which the other parts were
to move, and so his part was not written out in full, but the
harmonies indicated by numerals over the bass part were
sufficient, and had to be turned into a complete fabric of
harmony without gaps or mistakes, on the spur of the
moment. Bach followed this custom, although not without
modifying it to suit his own views. An inserted part in
mere progression of chords, and without intrinsic importance,
was little in accordance with his artistic soul, which always
strove after organic unity. The *Basso continuo*, from the
beginning of the seventeenth century, when an Italian,
Ludovico Viadana, first employed it in vocal works for one or
more voices, until Bach's period, had exercised an universal
influence in all branches of the art—since there was scarcely
one worth mentioning that is altogether without it ; with

its assistance all the component parts of the music could be grasped with freedom and certainty, a result which, without its aid, could scarcely have been obtained at all, and certainly not in so wonderfully short a time. But the chief object was now either to free itself entirely from this support, or else to cause it to strike root and become alive, so that the branches might embrace and grow together into one organism. The whole development of art was directed towards the latter course. Bach transferred the polyphonic style of the clavier into this sphere of art also, and thus his mode of writing for instruments supported by the harpsichord though less strange than that of the solo compositions just mentioned, is not exclusively formed on the inherent nature of those instruments, but upon the character of Bach's polyphony, which had already attained its full growth and took its rise from the organ.

It is of importance to make as clear as possible Bach's fundamental principles with regard to the performance of accompaniments, for this, the highest attainment in the art of that time, has now quite died out, and yet an essential part of the possibility of making Bach's works accessible in our time rests on its due reawakening. Before all else—we are speaking now only of chamber music—two different cases must be clearly distinguished. Disregarding the custom of the time, Bach in his most important works treats the clavier as an obbligato instrument. These works are almost entirely in strict trio form, really in three-part writing, in which the clavier takes two parts, and a violin, viol da gamba or flute the third; there is one largo in quartet form in which the clavier takes three parts. The background of harmony is almost entirely dispensed with. Only when, at the opening of a movement, or of a new working out in a movement, the theme is first given out by the chief instrument over a supporting bass, full chords must be struck in order to give especial distinctness and emphasis. Bach, who was generally most particular about writing out his works with the figured bass, and indeed had the more reason to be so the more his practice departed, as is here the case, from custom—clears up all doubts in this respect by his own hand-

writing. Besides there are a few scattered passages, in which
the part for the chief instrument is written over a simple
harpsichord bass and nothing more, where light supplementary chords should be inserted; this is indicated by
figures or else by a written direction and may be regarded
as an exception. In general, however, any completion of
the harmony would not only be superfluous by reason of
the wonderfully animated and perfected three-part writing,
but would also be impossible to insert without ruining the
beauty of the outlines. Whenever a part is added for fulness,
not counting one separate full chord as such, it is done in a
perfectly organic way, and is indicated not only in the part
for the clavier, but in that for the violin. Whenever a
movement is not in three parts only, from the first note to
the last, it is to be ascribed to the freedom of chamber-
music style, and to the dry, ineffective tone of the
harpsichord. This was Bach's ideal; we see it plainly in
the six great organ sonatas for two manuals and pedals,
which remain to be noticed later on, and which agree in
form with most of the chamber trios ; we have already seen
it in the three-part clavier sinfonias which we spoke of as
unique in their kind, and the accompanied violin sonata is
also idealised by Bach in such a manner as to admit of no
comparison with any, even the best, of his contemporaries.[143]

But compositions are not lacking in which, according
to universal custom, the harpsichord has to accompany
from a figured bass. Even at the end of the seventeenth century a three-part accompaniment was often considered sufficient, but in the following period the four-part
accompaniment became universal, and, if desired, the parts
might be doubled to help out the poverty of the harpsichord.[144] That Bach also was fond of accompanying with
full parts we know for certain from several of his scholars.
This of course means not a continuous treatment in four or
more parts, but an accompaniment varied in fulness accord-

---

[143] See Appendix A, No. 5.

[144] Heinichen Der Generalbass in der Composition. Dresden, 1728, pp. 131
and 132.

ing to the circumstances, since it is the part of a good
accompanist to accommodate himself at every moment to
the form and expression of the particular work.[145]   Johann
Christian Kittel, one of the last of Bach's scholars (b. 1732),
gives an interesting account of how he used to go to the
rehearsals of a cantata under the master's direction in
Leipzig.   "One of his most proficient pupils had to accompany on the harpsichord.   It may be imagined that he
could not venture on playing too meagre an accompaniment from the figured bass.   Notwithstanding, he had
always to be prepared to find Bach's hands and fingers
suddenly coming in under his own, and without troubling
him any farther, the accompaniment completed with masses
of harmony, which amazed him even more than the unexpected proximity of his strict master."[146]   Here the talent
for improvisations, which Bach possessed in so remarkable a
degree (see p. 27), fourd its right place.   But it had most
opportunity for its display in a solo.   " Whoever," says his
Leipzig friend, Mizler, " wants to hear true delicacy in
figured bass playing, and what is called really good accompanying, need only trouble himself to hear our Capellmeister
Bach, for he accompanies a given figured bass in such
a manner for a solo, that one would think it was a concerto,
and that the melody he is making with his right hand had
been composed before."[147]   It must not, however, be understood from this, as will be shown in another place, that
Bach always accompanied in polyphony *ex tempore*.   In
a minuet in a sonata in C major for the flute,[148] Bach's
own accompaniment is extant, fully written out, and really
makes an independent piece of itself.   It is, in accordance
with the tender character of the minuet, chiefly in three

---

[145] Quantz, Versuch einer Auweisung, &c., p. 223 : " The general rule as to a
figured bass is to play always in four parts.   If you want to accompany really
well, however, it often has a better effect not to keep too strictly to this."

[146] Johann Christian Kittel.   Der angehende praktische Organist.   Section 3.
Erfurt, 1808, p. 33.

[147] Musikalische Bibliothek, Pt. IV.   Leipzig, 1738, p. 48.   This is confirmed
to Heinichen.   Op. cit. p. 547 f.

[148] P., S. III. C. 6, No. 4. (vol. 235).

parts. The upper part goes smoothly on in graceful quavers, always emphasising the chief progressions of the melody, and now soaring above it and now going below with great freedom. We must imagine that Bach, when accompanying, often gave the reins to his talent for improvisation, and adorned the accompaniment in a wonderfully charming way, with freely inverted counter-melodies. We cannot but lament that this charm was utterly and irrecoverably lost when the master died; and yet, if he had considered this kind of accompaniment essential to the full effect, he would assuredly have fixed it in all his works by an obbligato clavier part. But he allowed them to be spread among the people by his pupils with only a figured bass, so that he must have supposed that he had indicated all that a discerning player would need, and we may hope that an accompaniment of quite simple form would not be contrary to his intentions.

The fuller the writing, the less room was there left for free improvisation. It must be plain from the art with which Bach treated three-part writing, and the pleasure he took in it, that nothing was left to be desired in the way of fulness, even in the trio with figured bass. And, by a happy circumstance, an irrefragable testimony offers itself to this point. A trio for two flutes and harpsichord was afterwards changed by the composer into a sonata for the viol da gamba with obbligato accompaniment for the clavier.[149] The autograph of both is in existence. In the first shape the bass part is carefully figured, but in the second there is not the least sign of any figuring. This shows that in the first case the accompaniment cannot possibly have been very independent, and that its aim was not so much to produce fulness of harmony as to amalgamate the differing qualities of tone. If the harpsichord was entrusted with the bass alone, a certain medium must be interposed between its dry short tone and the liquid fulness of that of the flute or, in other cases, the flexible and pathetic tones of the violin ; this was not necessary when the harpsichord took

---

[149] B.-G. IX., pp. 175 ff, and 260 ff.

parts and thus came into the same register as the other instrument. The accompaniment in four parts is arranged by one of the master's best pupils, Johann Philipp Kirnberger, who did the same thing in a trio-sonata of Bach's, and declared plainly that it was by Bach's desire.[150] This style of accompaniment always follows the progression of the parts that are written down, doubling them with the addition of a fourth part, or it repeats their harmonies in another position, but in accordance with the rule that the hands should not be too widely separated in accompanying;[151] there is nowhere a trace of any arbitrary or independent additions. Bach himself may often have proceeded differently. He sometimes would exercise his harmonic genius, when a trio was put before him, in extemporising a real fourth part in addition to the other three; and what he did with the works of others he may well have done with his own.

But these were probably the effects of a happy fancy, or of a joyful sense of power, just as he would play off a complete trio or quartet from nothing but the mere bass part, or read an unknown work from the separate parts placed side by side.[152] As a rule the simple supporting four-part accompaniment remained in vogue. The character of the harpsichord tone prevented the outlines of the principal parts from being entangled or obliterated. To this purpose the modern pianoforte is much less adapted, and demands double care and discretion.

Now in concertos and orchestral suites the accompaniment throughout follows the harmonic changes of the parts which

---

[150] Namely, to the one in the "Musikalischen Opfer" for flute, violin, and clavier, in P., S. III., C. 8, No. 3 (vol. 219). The accompaniment to the third movement is also quoted by Kirnberger in his "Grundsätzen des Generalbasses," who says of it: "Lastly, as an overwhelming testimony for the necessity of knowledge as to the different kinds of figured basses, I have added (fig. LI.) an example from a trio by John Sebastian Bach, which although it is only a trio must notwithstanding be accompanied in four parts; and this may serve to confute the common opinion, as also may the case of trios, sonatas, &c., for a 'concerto' part with bass; likewise cantatas that are only accompanied on the clavier should not be accompanied in four parts."

[151] Quantz. op. cit., p. 233.

[152] Forkel, pp. 16 and 17.

are written out, so that it is of necessity simple.   Passing and non-essential notes are generally omitted, and the accompaniment is played in the middle range of notes, so that the accompanist's only task is to represent just the germ from which the harmony springs.   In fugal passages it used to be the custom in time past, when counterpoint was very much simpler, to indicate whatever part had the theme in written notes above the figured bass, and there still exist two fugues for clavier by Bach himself, which, with the help of figuring, are written on a single stave, but then they are of a very simple construction as compared with his others.[153]

In other cases in fugues he used to express all that he wanted in the accompaniment by means of figures, with such wonderful clearness that even at the present day any musician moderately skilled in the rules of playing from figured bass could, without much trouble, produce a good and flowing accompaniment from it ; and at that time an accompanist who was accustomed to Bach's style of writing could easily perform the task without a mistake. His mode of writing was indeed, in many points, exceptional, and adapted to his own style ; he required his pupils to learn to read it aright, just as they would the ordinary notation.   His system was such as to exclude all doubt as to the proper harmonies to be added in the case of those sustained basses which so often occur in his works ; he always wrote out the figures representing the desired chord, reckoning upwards from the first bass-note of the group, whether it were a dissonance or not ; the harmony was sustained until the next figure, or until it was clear that it

---

[153] P., S. I., C. 4, Nos. 7 and 8 (apparently not in English edition).   In the royal library at Berlin there is a book with the title, *Praeludia et Fugen | del signor | Johann Sebastian | Bach | Possessor | A. W. Langloz | Anno 1763. |* It contains 62 preludes and fugues, in every case on a single stave with figuring. There is no single fugue theme which can be recognised as like anything of Bach's elsewhere, and the composition is so poor that I do not believe it to be by him.   Possibly they were pieces for practising figured bass playing, collected by a pupil of Bach's, and transcribed by the said Langloz.   As to this old manner of writing out fugues in the figured bass part, compare Niedt. Musikal-Handleitung, I., Hamburg, 1710, sheet *E.*

had to be resolved into a triad.[154]   In the case of Bach's
concertos for clavier and orchestra it is worth remarking
that the figured bass accompaniment is to be played on a
second harpsichord, so that the first may come out prominently as the solo instrument.[155]   In the vocal chamber
music, in the ritornels of the airs sung to the harpsichord
alone, a special demand is made on the accompanist, for a
whole phrase has to be treated melodically and perfectly
finished off.   In a general way the material can be borrowed
from the vocal melody which follows or precedes; but sometimes this melody lies in the bass part itself, and in such
cases the task is to produce in the upper parts a correct and
flowing counterpoint.

It follows from all this that Bach, in the obbligato
treatment of the clavier in free accompaniment, left out
nothing whatever except in a few quite distinct cases;
that in performing an accompaniment from figured bass
he delighted in indulging his talent for improvisation and
playing in this way against a solo instrument or voice,
except in the case of trios or pieces of rich texture; and that
wherever he wrote a mere figured bass a correct accompaniment in four parts was all that he required.   In his
writing in three or more parts, his harmonies do not stand
in need of any amplification, and the harpsichord is only
brought in for the sake of blending the differences in qualities
of tone.   But its importance is in no way lessened by
this.   Although almost withdrawn from sight, it exercises a
powerful influence in settling the artistic form, since the
solo instruments are assimilated to it and not contrasted
with it.   It is the hidden root by which nourishment is
supplied to the tree.   This root, however, derived its
nourishment from the organ.   This accounts for the somewhat *foreign* effect which strikes us even in this chamber
music, for a peculiar quality, which was common to the
organ and the harpsichord, is lacking in the piano, our

---

[154] Kirnberger, op. cit., p. 87.

[155] W. Rust was the first to remark this, in B.-G. IX., p. xvii.   Compare B.-G.
VII., p. xv.

modern substitute; a certain amount of habit, however, overcomes this feeling. The place of the harpsichord, thus influenced by the organ, in chamber music is exactly the same as that of the organ itself in church music, and all that was said about the place of that instrument in accompanying applies here equally well and unconditionally.

We have already shown, in an earlier part of the work, that the style of Bach's church music, with all its individualities, resulted from organ music. In order to keep this point always in view, it is necessary to bear in mind continually the power which this instrument possesses of governing and uniting different heterogeneous elements, and the fact that by its aid alone could true church music be produced. An important, though obvious, testimony to this is that although, under Italian influence, an attempt was made to introduce harpsichords into the churches, yet Bach invariably used the organ for accompanying from figured bass. Remove the organ, and the soul has gone: only a machine remains. Distinct evidence that this was Bach's view is provided by five movements from his church cantatas, arranged by himself for the organ alone, three of which are in three parts, and two in four parts; in the cantatas, where they are set for voices and instruments over a figured bass, these have an accompaniment in figured bass, while, as organ pieces, they are quite independent of it.[156] Of course the nature of the accompaniment was changed to suit the character of the instrument, the strict four-parts were more strongly insisted on, and the full chords used on the harpsichord were excluded, because the effect could be produced by stops. But that the organ

---

[156] The organ chorales "Ach bleib bei uns, Herr Jesu Christ," "Meine Seele erhebet den Herren," "Wachet auf, ruft uns die Stimme," (B.-G. xxv., 2, Part II. P., S. V., C. 6 (Vol. 245), No. 2, and C. 7 (Vol. 246), Nos. 42 and 57, were published with three others, arranged by the composer himself, by G. Schübler at Zell; they are taken from the cantatas " Bleib bei uns, denn es Abend werden" (B.-G., I., No. 6. P. Vol. 1015), "Meine Seele erhebet den Herren " (B.-G., I., No. 10. P. Vol. 1278), and " Wachet auf, ruft uns die Stimme " (Winterfeld, Evang. Kischeng, III. Supplement p. 172).

took so important a part as to be entrusted with the special
and essential part of every piece, and that, consequently,
all Bach's church music, in the form in which it has come
down to us, consists of mere sketches, is by no means proved.
It was enough for the organ to define the general expression;
as an instrument participating in the effect, it was quite
in a secondary position, the chief parts alone being written
down in notes.[157]

Of the sonatas for violin with clavier obbligato six were
again united by Bach into a whole set. The year of their
composition cannot be ascertained with any certainty, but
there is a very credible tradition to the effect that they were
written at Cöthen.[158] So, probably, were three sonatas for
viol da gamba and clavier, and three for flute and clavier.
A comparison of these three collective works shows with
wonderful clearness how much attention Bach paid to
the nature of the instruments; for although he did not
directly form these works from the idea of a violin, a gamba,
or a flute, yet, putting aside for a moment the general style
which all these works have in common, the character of
each of these instruments really is reflected in a clear and
distinct manner in the compositions designed for them.
The violin sonatas are throughout pervaded with that feeling
of manly vigour which, although capable of the most
various shades of expression, is the true characteristic of the
violin. To this feature, which they have in common, must
be added agreement in form; this, with the single exception
of the last sonata, is the four-part structure with which we
are already acquainted. The description of the several
forms given us in the solo sonatas is here insufficient; it
was not for nothing that Bach transferred the violin sonata
to a sphere especially his own. In parts he enlarged the
structure of the separate movements to such bold proportions
that he seems to bridge over a whole century, and approaches
nearly to the fully perfected forms of the Beethoven sonata.

---

[157] See Appendix A, No. 6.

[158] Forkel, p. 57, asserts it quite decisively, so that it must have emanated
from Bach's son.

The chief advance is the employment of the Italian aria-form and the genius with which it is united with the fugal style of chamber music ; by this means the triple form is seen as distinctly or even more distinctly than in the Beethoven sonata form, and the proportion of the sections to each other is the same, so that the third repeats the first, and the second works up for the most part the material thus supplied ; the only difference consists in the fact that the modern sonata is built on the song or dance form in two sections (Lied-form), while the older is developed from the fugue, and accordingly in the former homophony, and in the latter polyphony with its auxiliaries predominates. It has already been said that the contrasting relations of the movements of the older sonata, if the first adagio is regarded as an introductory movement, are not very different from those of the modern sonata. In these, and for the most part in Bach, the first allegro dispenses with the strict and typical organism in three sections ; in the last allegro he was accustomed to employ the dance-form in two sections, which was in general use at the time, combining the fugal form with it in no less remarkable a way. That he did not go on from this point to the perfect Beethoven form in three sections was because the development of his style was too much fettered by the form in two sections. In the extended and amplified form, afterwards employed by Philipp Emanuel Bach, and generally, too, in the clavier sonatas of Haydn and Mozart, it had been long known to him, as is shown by the Invention in E major ; the solo movement for harpsichord in E minor from the last violin sonata, is also a perfect model of this type. As a rule no new instrumental forms were created after Bach's time ; those which occur are only modifications of those existing before, and worked out by Bach ; and all the varieties which they took in the following century put together do not nearly amount to the number of the forms which he alone brought to perfection.

The six violin sonatas are in B minor, A major, E major, C minor, F minor, and G major,[159] and in spite of their

---

[159] B.-G., IX., pp. 69-172, P., S. III., C. 5 (Vols. 232 and 233).

general unity of design show a marvellous variety. The first opens with an adagio in 6-4 time, of which both the mélody and the harmony are equally broad and beautiful. Notwithstanding its introductory character, its form is complete, for, in the first place, a distinct bass subject and a fluctuating quaver figure are retained through the whole piece, and, secondly, the phrase which appears in the dominant in bars 13 to 20 recurs in the tonic in bars 24 to 31, after which in the last passages reference is made to the beginning of the movement, so that the two chief divisions have two subdivisions each, which correspond in an inverted order :—

(A B̂ b a).

This is followed by a bold fugal allegro in aria form with three sections ; in the second section (bars 41-101) Bach displays his wonderful power—which he got from the northern school—of episodical development, which is applied to the theme that was strictly worked out in the first section ; the third is an unaltered repetition of the first. At the beginning of these fugal sections the theme is never brought in without a supporting bass ; this license came from the Italian chamber music style, and first occurs in Bach in the clavier sinfonias. Now comes the second, the real adagio, which is here, however, an andante in D major, a piece of wondrous beauty, wrought as if with wreaths of flowers, and an organism as perfect in construction as any even of Beethoven's adagios ; attention should be paid to the fine artistic feeling with which the tender and expressive subsidiary theme appears in the sub-dominant after the return of the chief subject (bars 22 ff.). The finale is a movement in two sections with repeats, in fugal form, but of such a kind that the theme is always brought in with two-part counterpoint ; its character is martial and defiant ; observe, besides the splendid theme, the sudden change to the dominant at the close of the first section, and the bold introduction of the chord of the sixth of C major just before the end.

The second sonata, now the best known of all the six,

begins with a movement in 6-8 time, very tenderly developed from a theme of one bar in length, and afterwards
(from the eighth bar) combined with a whispering subject in
semiquavers. In marked contrast is the splendid *Allegro
assai* in 3-4 time which follows. The form is the same
as that of the first movement of the B minor sonata, the last
section being an exact repetition of the first, while the second
is different in structure; for in bars 30—33 a new subject is
introduced which alternates with the chief theme, so that
a working-out in the style of the concerto before described
is the result; finally the new subject generates broad violin
arpeggios, while the harpsichord works out the chief theme
episodically, supported by a splendid pedal point of nineteen
bars, and then the third section is brought in. As to the
well known canon in F sharp minor, with its deep thought-
fulness and melodic beauty, it need only be said that its two
chief sections correspond to one another in a reversed form,
like those of the first movement of the B minor sonata:
the first period, consisting of four phrases, leads into C sharp
minor and begins anew from that key, but by the insertion
of a middle section and by repeating the second phrase it
returns to F sharp minor; for the end the expressive and
melancholy notes of the opening are heard again like
the echo of a vanished past, and the way is prepared by a
half close for the last Presto. This is in two sections, and
fugal, but the second section prefers to work out a theme of
its own, and never takes up the first theme until the end,
when it is brought in in playful strettos.

In the first movement of the third sonata the violin
wanders freely and melodiously over a subject in the accompaniment, worked out in the usual way; the second agrees
in form with the corresponding movement of the A major
sonata, except that the repetition of the third division is
abridged. The third movement is an adagio in C sharp
minor full of the most touching expression. It is a chaconne
of which the bass subject is repeated fifteen times, and
besides this Bach has worked out an independent theme in
the upper parts; it is in the same form as the canon in F
sharp minor, but of grander dimensions. The last move-

ment is in three sections instead of two, and the second is, as before, in concerto form, and each part is repeated.

At the outset of the fourth sonata, instead of a largo, we meet with a Siciliano full of grief and lamentation, the beginning of which is almost identical with that of the celebrated air in B minor from the Matthew-Passion, " Erbarme dich, mein Gott "—" Have mercy upon me, O God." An unusually bold and important allegro snatches us from this melancholy mood ; it is the richest and broadest movement of the kind in the whole set of sonatas. This great wealth of ideas resolves itself into four sections, a comprehensive epilogue (bars 89—109) being added on after the third (bars 55—89), which does not consist of mere repetition, but is treated with great freedom, and affords more opportunity than the second section (bars 34—55) for interesting developments of episodes. The adagio, in E flat major, goes by in a lovely restful way, calm and gentle as a summer evening ; the violin has the melody, accompanied by simple triplets, and now and again breaks off to listen, as it were, to the echo of its tones, and the parts are first united in a full stream of emotion quite at the end. An allegro in two sections, full of Bach's delight in his work, forms the final movement ; in this also the second section has a characteristic fugal treatment.

The fifth sonata is introduced by a largo, the only one in which four real parts are employed. Besides being especially distinguished by this fact, it is also one of the most powerful pieces in the collection, and of Bach's chamber music altogether. The three-part clavier part is so independent that almost the whole of it might be played alone ; the violin has now passages of broken arpeggios, and now an apparently unending flow of broadly treated melody in 3-2 time. And the violin is far from bringing a foreign element into the organism ; it rather raises it to a higher level ; it does not cripple the effects but gives them a loftier and more general tendency—as if carrying out in music some eternal law of nature. Its hundred and eight bars fall naturally into four sharply defined sections, the first of which closes in the relative major (bar 37) ; the second, extended by imitation and by episodes, gets into C minor (bar 59) ; the

third refers back at this point to the first section, still in
this key, but only by way of reminding us of it; it then
diverges again, and only gets back to the original key at
bar 88; in the fourth section there is a real repetition,
which combines the beginning and end of the first section
together in a concentrated form. The theme on which
the clavier part is exclusively formed—

occurs again, hardly altered, in an eight-part motett, "Komm,
Jesu, komm, gieb Trost mir Müden, Das Ziel ist nah, die Kraft
ist klein,"[160] and the sentiment of the two works is very
similar. The movement is imbued with a desire, not agitated,
but of inexpressible intensity, for redemption and peace, and
spreads its wings at last with such a mighty span that
it seems as though it would throw off every earthly tie.
Some passages (such as bar 90 ff) sank deep into the
sensitive mind of Schumann, there to put forth new
blossoms—like the andante of his quartet for piano
and strings. The allegro movements follow in inverted
order, the one in two sections being the second movement, and that in three the fourth; between them there
is an adagio in C minor, formed on the same plan as
those dreamy clavier preludes whose development is only
harmonic; the violin has two-part harmony in slow quaver
movement, which derives a greater fulness from arpeggio
semiquavers, alternating between both hands in the accompaniment.[161]

The last sonata as has been said, differs essentially in its
general plan. First of all there are five movements, three
slow movements being as it were enclosed by two in quick
time, the first allegro being repeated at the end. There is
no second example of such an extension of form in Bach's

---

[160] Motetten, von Johann Sebastian Bach, Leipzig. Breitkopf und Härtel,
No. 4.

[161] Bach subsequently replaced these by groups of demi-semiquavers; the
earliest form is given in B.-G. IX., p. 250 f.

works, and it is doubly surprising in a composition which
was designed to be united into one work with five others,
all agreeing among themselves in form.   It can hardly have
been on artistic grounds that such an irregularity is found in
this particular place.   I am inclined rather to ascribe it to
some personal motive arising from some incident in his life,
for the investigation of which no means are, however, at
hand.   For the rest the form is ruled by the highest artistic
intelligence; the third movement, judging by its importance,
is to be regarded as the germ of the organism; it is *Cantabile,
ma un poco Adagio,* and around it the two other adagio
movements in E minor and B minor, and outside them again
the allegros complete the harmony of the grouping.   They
are written with a creative power all his own, and with
evident inspiration.   In the first movement, which is in
three sections, passages of demi-semiquavers glide busily
and unceasingly up and down, enticing or mocking cries are
heard here and there; it is as though we were looking at a
merry, busy throng of people.   The grave second movement,
largo, as well as the fourth, *adagio,* with its passionate
longing, are wisely made quite short, so as not to crowd too
closely upon the heart of the whole work.   This is a fully
developed and extended piece in 6-8 time and in three
sections, remarkable for a singularly bridal feeling: it is
marked by a sweet fragrance and a breath of lovely yearning
such as are seldom found in Bach.   The lengthy superscription—which Bach was wont to disdain as a rule—is
remarkable; and there is developed in the two upper parts
a kind of loving intercourse, a dialogue as from mouth to
mouth, carried on above a bass which has nothing to do
but to support the harmony.   All these are quite at variance
with the style of Bach's trios in other places; and what is
just as unique is that all three parts do not conclude at the
same time: the clavier melody ceases twelve bars before the
end, while the violin repeats the whole of the opening phrase
of the melody, supported by the bass.   For justification of
the epithet " bridal " it may serve to refer to certain arias in
Bach's wedding music, particularly the one in A major which
was afterwards rearranged for the Whitsuntide cantata,

" O ewiges Feuer, o Ursprung der Leibe," [162] and also to the
aria in G major from the cantata, " Dem Gerechten muss das
Licht immer weider aufgehen." [163] It need hardly be said that
I have no idea of drawing conclusions from the creation of
this adagio as to events in Bach's life which may have given
rise to it.   But circumstances of a personal and intimate kind
certainly influenced him ; this is clear from the fact that in
later life, dissatisfied with the whole form of the sonata, he
altered its shape twice, the last time quite in the decline of
life, and that neither of these alterations pleased him ; and
it is well known that any especially subjective productions
become more and more difficult to alter as life goes on.   I,
at least, cannot see that these alterations—in the first two
dance-forms designed for a clavier Partita are inserted,
while in the second, against all precedent, a sonata movement in two sections for harpsichord alone is made the
third movement, and followed by two entirely new concluding movements—have in any way improved the form,
beautiful as the three last mentioned movements are in
themselves.   The central point, the G major adagio, is
omitted in both cases, perhaps because its personal element
no longer pleased the mighty spirit of its creator as time
went on ; but the whole structure was endangered by its
removal. [164]

The viol da gamba was an instrument with five strings
or even more, somewhat like Bach's *viola pomposa* in
compass, the lowest string giving D and the highest *a ;* but
it differed essentially from that in being tuned by fourths
and thirds, and also in being held between the knees,
like the violoncello.   It afforded a great variety in the
production of tone, but its fundamental character was
tender and expressive rather than full and vigorous.   Thus

---

[162] B.-G. VII., p. 146 ff.   P., vol. 129.

[163] B.-G. XIII., I., p. 34 ff.

[164] As to the relations of the different attempted recensions, the last of which
is given in the Bach Society's edition, compare the careful discussion by W. Rust
in the preface to Vol. IX., p. XX f.   The differences in the first recension are
there given in an appendix, p. 252 ff.

Bach could rearrange a trio originally written for two flutes and bass, for viol da gamba, with harpsichord obbligato, without destroying its dominant character.[165]   This sonata in four movements in G major is the loveliest, the purest idyl conceivable.   In the romantic andante alone (in E minor) is there a gentle yet awful whispering and fluttering, as of leaves softly moved at night, and a ghostlike murmur runs over the still depths (represented in a marvellous manner by an *e* sustained for four bars on the viol da gamba).   With this exception all is happy, bright with sunshine in a blue sky.   In the last movement, a fugue of that mingled strength and grace that is so typical of Bach, there are introduced, between the separate groups in the working-out, light and charmingly worked episodes on the Corelli model, after each of which the unexpected and yet natural entry of the theme has a delightful effect.   This sonata was not united with the two others into a collective work by the composer, who, as it appears, did not intend to do so, since the very carefully written autographs of two of them still exist.

The second sonata (in D major) is somewhat inferior to the others in merit and, moreover, is not free from a certain stiffness in the first allegro.[166]

The third, on the contrary (in G minor), is a work of the highest beauty and the most striking originality.[167]   It has only three movements, like a concerto, and the concerto form has had a very important share in the construction of the allegros.   The first allegro begins, indeed, in the manner of a sonata, but the long and prolific theme attains a freer development.   No fugal working-out in the dominant follows, but a repetition, more richly ornamented, in the tonic, and then episodical work until the end of the first section (bar 25).   Part of the principal subject fugally treated and answered, serves to bring in the second sec-

---

[165] B.-G. IX., p. 175 ff (in its older form at p. 260 ff).   P., S. IV., C. 2, No. 1 (vol. 239).

[166] B.-G. IX., p. 189 ff.   P., S. IV. C. 2 (vol. 239), No. 2.

[167] B.-G. IX., p. 203 ff.   P., S. IV. C. 2 (vol. 239), No. 3.

tion, and soon is followed by a new tributary of half a bar in length :—

We must notice, too, the passage of four bars which comes in at bar 53—

this, with the chief subject, constitutes the whole material from which the movement is developed, quite in the style of a concerto. After this there is no need of a third section : the movement goes its restless way, unceasingly renewing itself from within. If we are forced to marvel at the absolutely inexhaustible wealth of fancy in almost every new work of Bach's, this especially shows how Bach's style, in spite of its polyphonic nature, was capable of assuming a characteristic picturesqueness of the most marked kind. Here we have a composition in Magyar style : a rushing as of wild and fiery steeds across an open space; the impetuous tributary themes sound like strokes of a whip ; now the figures fall confusedly into the discord of the diminished seventh, resolved by means of a bright shake in the upper part; and now they unite in the chief subject in heavy unison—an effect so seldom found in this master— beneath its tread the very earth groans. The irresistible swing which keeps up the movement and action by new and un- expected impulses is almost the same as that which we admire in Weber's overtures. How much Bach himself was carried away by it is seen both in the frequent unisons in bar 64, where the chief theme suddenly appears in three parts on the clavier, the harmony thus becoming fourfold ; and then the magnificent end (from bar 95 onwards), where the whole array of notes rushes tumultuously from one diminished seventh to another. In this movement no use is made of the tender character of the viol da gamba, but only of its wide compass and its flexibility. A lovely

adagio in B flat major (3-2 time) satisfies our desire for
melody with a devotional and earnest strain, of which the
beginning is a clear foreshadowing of Beethoven. In the
last allegro there seems to be an inexhaustible fund of the
loveliest melodies : the most extraordinary number of subjects
is produced out of materials already given out, in the manner
which we now call the art of thematic working. We have
all along used the expression "episodical formation" to
distinguish the imitative working-out of an unaltered theme
from the alterations incident upon "thematic development."
Except at the beginning the concerto form governs the
whole. The theme—

is twice worked out in all the parts, and closes in B flat
major. From the first bar is evolved a softly pulsating
figure for the harpsichord bass, above which the viol da
gamba gives out a new and expressive melody, while the
right hand has broken chords in semiquavers, and then
changes place with the viol da gamba in F major. After the
chief theme has been once again brought in, this accompanying semiquaver figure is episodically extended, and
a new and no less charming melody appears (bars 37—55).
Then comes a thematic and episodical working-out of the
chief theme, and the first tributary theme is brought in,
in D minor; with this is contrasted a third subject, and
these two engage in a pleasing contention (bars 69—79). In
the cadence of this phrase there comes in a fourth working-
out of the chief theme in C minor, which leads back into
G minor; and at bar 90 a fourth tributary is brought in on
the viol da gamba, accompanied in the same manner as was
the first ; reappearing subsequently, after a fifth working-out
of the chief theme on the clavier, at the end of the movement. Thus on the stem of the theme one flower replaces
another in a way which is marvellous in itself, and not only
for the time when it was written. Even in Beethoven's day,
when, in accordance with the altered style of instrumental
music, episodical work was much more employed than

thematic, it would be hard to find anything of this kind more masterly or richer in invention. Bach held as absolute a sway over the art of episodical treatment as over that of thematic treatment ; and while his predecessors often preferred the former method, both alike found favour with him, and were used to complete and raise each other.

The Sonatas for the flute are influenced by the form of the concerto both in outline and in details, and in some points correspond exactly with it. They are all in three movements, and the E flat major sonata is a concerto from the first to the last bar.[168] In the first movement the form is somewhat timidly handled ; this sonata may have been one of the first attempts to construct a trio on this entirely new plan.   The middle movement—a Siciliano—and the final allegro are quite perfect, the soft and pleasing nature of the whole expression agreeing admirably with the character of the flute. This was the emotional character that lent the works of Philipp Emanuel Bach and his successors their peculiar stamp.   Joseph Haydn's clavier sonatas had their root in this expression, and it remained in force to Mozart's time ; indeed it is the distinguishing characteristic of the period. The height and depth, the sublimity and strength of Sebastian Bach's music were beyond the apprehension of the next generation ; still they could drink of the living fount in such a degree as was suited to their capacities and needs.   The connection between Bach and Haydn is not indeed self-evident, but it nevertheless exists, and is proved by other works besides the E flat major sonata ; the same feeling equally pervades a sonata in G minor, which in its present form is intended for violin and harpsichord, but which was certainly meant by the composer for the flute ; Bach wrote it at the same time as the E flat major sonata, and the construction is identical even in the smallest particulars.[169]   And among his later

---

[168] B.-G. IX., p. 22 ff.   P., S. III. C. 6 (vols. 234—235), No. 2.

[169] B.-G. IX., p. 274 ff.   That the sonata cannot be considered spurious as long as the authenticity of the E flat major sonata is undoubted is shown by W. Rust on p. xxv. of the same volume.   Besides this, in the adagio there is an unmistakable resemblance to the largo of the concerto for two violins.

works the resemblance to the works of Haydn—I am speaking only of his clavier music—is very prominent in the great organ prelude with which the third part of the Clavierübung begins,[170] a sufficient evidence that this element of feeling was deeply rooted in Bach's inmost nature.

In the flute sonata in A major,[171] the first movement, which unfortunately is incomplete, is quite on the lines of a concerto, not, of course, that the clavier and flute have each a theme belonging to themselves alone, which they contrast with one another; here, as in the E flat sonata, it is only the general musical principle that Bach has assimilated. The fresh and important finale, this time the crowning point of the work, is in three sections; of these the middle one falls into two groups, in F sharp minor (bars 53—118) and E major (bars 118—209), in each of which the chief theme is combined with a new subject in a masterly way: a more ingenious and striking way of coming back to the theme than that employed in bars 160—166 could hardly be imagined.

By far the best of the three, however, is the sonata in B minor; the magnificent freedom and beauty of its form, its depth and overpowering intensity of expression, raise it to the position of the best sonata for the flute that has ever existed. There is none of equal merit in the works of any great master of a later time; and so perfectly does it correspond to the character of the instrument, which indeed is soft and pleasing, but of only moderate capabilities of expression as compared to the violin and instruments of that class, that it reaches the highest level of Bach's style, with its calm surface and its depths of passionate intensity ever craving for expression. The first movement is in three sections and of the broadest proportions; but the composer has here departed entirely from his customary method of treating the first and middle sections. Neither a fugal entrance with episodical or concerto-like working-out, nor a concerto form from the beginning, could fit an imaginative

[170] B.-G. III., p. 173 ff. P., S. V., C. 3 (vol. 242), No. 1.

[171] B.-G. IX., p. 245 ff and 32 ff. P., S. III., C. 6 (vols. 234—235), No. 3.

work which was to flow on in unchecked expression of a single and deeply felt emotion like a grand elegy. So the master begins by forming one section from two subjects smoothly worked out side by side. They are not themes, but two melodies of imperishable beauty: the first is carried on for twenty bars in the most lovely way, supported by a soft rocking accompaniment; the second closes in the same key and then goes into D major. The process of development consists of this whole section being repeated, first in F sharp minor and then again in B minor for the close; but between the two last groups is brought in a passage formed of parts of the first and second melodies worked together (bars 61—77) so as to emphasise the return to the principal key. No one who has not seen and heard the work can form any idea of the genius with which Bach varies the theme. The development is carried on bar by bar, but is constantly altered in some way—ornamented more richly or made longer, especially by means of beautiful imitations in canon, which are, as it were, imperceptibly generated from it by a natural power; a special charm is given by reversing the order of several single phrases. This incomparably beautiful piece is closed by a wonderful little coda formed of phrases from the first melody (bars 111—117). The fact that the form is built upon the Italian aria betrays itself by one feature at the opening; the manner in which the melody begins in a kind of tentative way, breaking off after two bars to begin again at the fourth bar, is the same as that so frequently employed by Bach in the sacred arias,[172] The second movement in D major, *largo e dolce*, is simply in two sections with repeats, and is in all respects worthy of what goes before it; in particular the painful yet sweet expression in the last bar but one, where the flute rises in long syncopated notes on the chord of the diminished seventh, must appeal to every heart. The presto begins with a passionate and beautiful three-part fugue, but soon a pause comes on

---

[172] It has been already noticed (Vol. I., p. 26) that the beginning of this melody is identical with a fugal theme from one of Bernhard Bach's orchestral suites.

the dominant and, in accordance with the requirements of the concerto form, a gigue in Italian style (12-16 time) is introduced, which is quite new and yet familiar, since it is evolved most beautifully in Buxtehude's manner from the fugal theme.

All of Bach's independent chamber trios with clavier obbligato which exist have now been enumerated, except one, which is in neither sonata nor concerto form, but has a certain resemblance to that of the suites. This composition for violin and clavier in A major, is not a true suite in the strictest sense, and it is only designated as a "Trio." For, although it adheres to unity of key, and consists chiefly of dances, it is abnormal both in the number and order of the dances. It comprises seven sections worked out at some length, of which the last is an independent allegro in common time, while the first is a free fantasia.[173] The work stands by itself among Bach's works, an exceptional production such as a master who has perfect command over all forms might allow himself; because it has a certain affinity with the independent style of the orchestral suite. The attempt was crowned with success; the pieces with their masterly forms, though they nowhere attain grandeur, are models of graceful and delicate workmanship; fresh, bright music, the full expression of a vigorous and healthy mind.

Solo sonatas with harpsichord accompaniment were less to Bach's taste, as they were not as yet a thoroughly developed form of art. Only four of the kind are known, besides one fugue by itself. One in E minor is for violin and harpsichord; a prelude of running or *arpeggiato* semiquavers is followed by a lovely adagio, an allemande, and a gigue in the Italian style, on the old Corelli pattern. The great fugue in G minor is intended for the same instruments; such compositions may have served as preparations for the fugues in the sonatas for violin solo.[174] The other three sonatas are for flute and clavier. The one in C major has rather an old-fashioned aspect, the fourth (and last)

[173] B.-G. IX., p. 43 ff.   P., S. III., C. 7 (vols. 234—236), No. 1.

[174] P., S. III., C. 7 (vols. 234—236), Nos. 2 and 3.

movement consisting of a couple of minuets, to the first of which Bach has written out the accompaniment in full. The others, in E minor and major respectively, are in regular form, but their allegros are for the most part in two sections, and of course no such rich display of variety is possible as in the sonata with harpsichord obbligato. Still, they are full of interest and beauty.[175]

There are also very few examples of the trio for two instruments and figured bass. It has already been said that the sonata for viol da gamba in G major originated in a trio of this kind for flutes. A sonata in the same key for flute, violin, and bass is a gem of polished and concise form, full of delightful beauty.[176] Another sonata for two violins and bass, in C major, is not quite equal to this in merit; a gigue serves as the last movement, otherwise the forms are regular.[177]

The principle of concerto-like form which plays so important a part in Bach's creations had hitherto been applied by him only to works which were not actually concertos in external construction. In fact, he only availed himself of the principle to turn it to account for his own purposes (Comp. Vol. I., p. 408 et seq.); he can hardly have written any true concertos before the Cöthen period. In order to understand this point historically and fully, we must remember a licence of which the composers of that time availed themselves to a considerable extent in writing concertos. According to rule a tutti subject and a solo subject were placed side by side, and the solo instrument and the tutti instruments vied with each other in producing the greatest amount of material from their respective subjects. The principal key and those nearest to it were the fields

---

[175] P., S. III., C. 6 (vols. 234—236), Nos. 4, 5, and 6.

[176] B.-G. IX., p. 221 ff. P., S. III., C. 8 (vol. 237), No. 2. The autograph parts, which were written in the Leipzig period, are in the possession of Herr J. Rietz, Capellmeister at Dresden.

[177] B.-G. IX., p. 231 ff. P., S. III., C. 8 (vol. 237), No. 1. The resolution of the figured bass given in this and other pieces in the edition of Peters by Fr. Hermann is clever and very good musically, but it might be wished that he had kept more closely to the original figuring.

on which these contests were alternately displayed; when
the disputants returned to their original position the combat
was over. According to the quality of tone of the contrasting
instruments the one theme was heavy and firm, and the
other light and pliable. But there were also cases in which
one chief subject was considered sufficient. Then it was
given out by the tutti and taken up and worked out by the
solo instrument. When strictly carried out this plan gave
the work a rather poor effect, but when the composer
possessed the power of inventing and devising episodes, he
might take a phrase of the tutti subject, and by making new
matter out of it for the solo instrument, give the form a
particular charm. The feeling of dramatic contest between
two individualities was, however, much weakened by this
method; the form more strictly belonged to the realm of pure
music. But it was just this which chiefly interested Bach:
the purely musical duality, its contrasts, its combinative
fertility, and the impulse given to episodic development by
its antagonisms. Thus, even in the concerto-like sonatas
for the flute, he made the themes alternate between the
clavier and the flute on purely musical grounds. And thus
it happens, too, in his concertos, that the tutti passage
comprises all the material for the solo subjects. The
effectiveness of this departure from the rule of formation
depends on the way in which the instruments are treated.
This is especially the case with the violin concertos. Here,
where the solo violin is set against the string band completed
by the harpsichord, the contrast of the two bodies of sound is
of course natural and obvious. The class of work had a
great interest for Bach, as will be easily understood, after his
thorough study of the structure of Vivaldi's concertos. We
possess three concertos in their original shape, and three
only in a later remodelled form for clavier with instrumental
accompaniment; out of the three original ones two have
been treated in the same way.[178] These rearrangements
were made in Leipzig, to judge from the nature of the

---

[178] P., S. III, C. 1, 2, and 3 (vol. 229, 230, &c.). Compare the dissertation by
W. Rust, in B.-G. XVII., p. xiii ff, and B.-G. XXI., 1; p. xiii, f.

autographs; we have no direct evidence that the originals
are of the Cöthen time, but we conclude this to be the case
from a series of other instrumental concertos to which these,
with their far simpler construction, form the natural stepping-
stones; it is also probable from the official post held by Bach
at Cöthen. Notwithstanding the lack of sterling compositions for violin with orchestra, these concertos have hitherto
not achieved the wide popularity which is due to their high
musical worth; the reason is partly to be found in the comparative neglect of the simple and generally intelligible
cantilena style—since the animated harpsichord style, which
had taken possession of the concerto-form, prefers passages
and figurations; and a second reason is, that the form has
become strange to us. We can, of course, get over these
peculiarities, and particularly the second, for the older concerto form is more comprehensible than the new, which
has more or less become merged in the modern sonata
form. In fact, the charm of the episodical working-out is
not less in Bach than in the best concerto composers of
Beethoven's time. In this respect the first movement of
the E major concerto is especially remarkable, with the
working-out of the subject—

which Bach cast in the three-section form that we have seen
so much of in the violin sonatas with harpsichord. In the
second movement we have one of those free adaptations of
well-known forms which Bach alone knew how to treat. It
is a chaconne, such as had been already employed in the E
major violin sonata; but the bass theme not only wanders
freely through different keys, but is also extended and cut up
into portions of a bar long; it often ceases altogether, but
then a few notes revive the conviction that, in spite of all,
it is the central point on which the whole piece turns.
The middle movement of the A minor concerto has what is
seldom found with such definiteness in the adagios, a heavy
tutti subject contrasted with a light figure for the solo instrument; the organism is built on the interchange of these,
without becoming a strict violin *cantilena*. The D minor

concerto[179] is without doubt the finest of the set, and is held in due esteem by the musical world of the present day. Two solo violins are here employed, but it is not in any way a double concerto, for the two violins play not so much against one another, as both together against the whole band. Each is treated with the independence that is a matter of course in Bach's style. In the middle movement, a very pearl of noble and expressive melody, the orchestra is used only as an accompaniment, as was usual in the adagios of concertos.

The free and purely musical concerto form, however, achieved its perfect and untrammelled development in a collection of six concertos which was completed in March, 1721. The occasion was a very special one. Several years before Bach had met, possibly at Carlsbad, a Prussian Prince who was a lover of art, and who delighted in his playing; he had desired Bach to send him some compositions for his private band.[180] This was Christian Ludwig, Margraf of Brandenburg (b. May 14, 1677), the youngest son of the great Elector by his second wife. A sister of his was second wife of Duke Ernest Ludwig of Saxe Meiningen, with whose court Bach had been connected apparently ever since he had been to Weimar. The Margraf, who was at this time provost of the cathedral at Halberstadt and unmarried, lived alternately at Berlin and on his estates at Malchow; he was especially devoted to music, over and above the ordinary aristocratic amateur dabbling in science and art, and he spent a great part of his income on music.[181] In the spring of 1721 he was living in Berlin, and thither Bach must have sent these six concertos which he had finished as the execution of his honourable commission on the 24th of March. The French dedication in which he mentions the

---

[179] P., vol. 231.

[180] Bach himself specifies the space of time which had elapsed since this— "*une couple d'années.*" If we take this quite literally, as is hardly necessary, we get the year 1719, but no journey of Duke Leopold to Carlsbad is known of in that year.

[181] Amounting sometimes to 48,945 thalers, but this was not always sufficient for him.

occasion which gave rise to the composition may have been written by some courtier at Cöthen. He himself was evidently not skilled enough in French to trust to his own knowledge in such a case, and the mistaken fashion of the time, when nothing but French was spoken or written at the German Courts, was in vogue here. How the offering was received by the Margraf is not known. His band was not lacking in members capable of executing these difficult works in a fit manner; we know the name of one of his private musicians, Emmerling, and that he was distinguished as a composer and performer on the clavier and viol da gamba.[181] After the Margraf's death, which took place at Malchow, September 3, 1734, Bach's precious manuscript experienced the risk of being carelessly sold off among a lot of other instrumental concertos at a ridiculously low price, but a happy fate has preserved it to us. These works exhibit the highest point of development that the older form of the concerto could attain.[182]

Bach calls them *Concerts avec plusieurs instruments*. According to the custom of the time, this means the so-called *Concerti Grossi*, in which, instead of one single instrument, several (generally three) play against the tutti. But to this category belong only the second, fourth, and fifth concertos; the common feature which unites them to a single unity is rather the concerto-like form which is here developed to the greatest musical freedom. Bach had for a long time been on the track of this ideal. The reader will remember the great instrumental introductions

---

[181] Walther, Lexicon.

[182] The few facts I have been able to give concerning Margraf Christian Ludwig are the results of my researches in the royal domestic archives at Berlin. The musical property, which was considerable, was catalogued and valued. Compared with concertos by Vivaldi, Venturini, Valentini, Brescianello, &c., Bach's work was not thought worthy the honour of a special mention by name, and so it must have been in one of the two following lots, " 77 concertes by different masters, and for various instruments, at 4 ggr. (altogether) 12 thlr. 20 ggr."; and " 100 concertos by different masters for various instruments. No 3, 3 16 thlr." As to the subsequent fate of the autograph, see B.-G. XIX., Preface. These concertos are also published with a facsimile of the dedication in P. S., VI., Nos. 1-6 (Vol. 261-266).

to the Weimar cantatas " Uns ist ein Kind geboren,"
" Gleichwie der Regen," and " Der Himmel lacht " (Vol. I.,
pp. 487, 492, and 541).   But it is not only the separate
movements, but the whole form of many parts, that he
set in so definite a manner on its ideal musical basis.
Throughout his concertos the disposition into three movements is employed, which had indeed been elevated into
a canon of art by Vivaldi's delicate instinct; but the
Concerto grosso was not always confined to this : ere long
four movements or more were introduced, giving a resemblance to the sonata, and even dance-forms were intermingled.   But the three-movement form was amply sufficient
for the materials which were to be displayed in the concerto :
for the grave and exciting strife between the bold and active
solo instruments and the strong and mighty tutti; for the
broad *cantilena,* with its ingenious and beautiful ornamentation; and for the joyful triumphant bravura close which
carries all before it.   For this reason the three-movement
form has remained in general use for instrumental concertos
until the present day.   The orchestration of Bach's concertos
is very strong, and in particular the wind instruments
appear in greater force, though they were already employed
in the chamber concerto.   Such an application of them as
we find here had, it is true, never been dreamed of by
any one before; like the stringed instruments they were
altogether brought under subjection to that polyphony of
Bach's by which everything was quickened and compelled
to his will.   Let us now consider the concertos separately.

First concerto, in F major.   Instruments : the string
quartet, strengthened in the bass by the *Violone grosso*
(the double-bass), and in the first violin part by the *Violino
piccolo* (a bright-toned and smaller violin tuned a fourth
higher), two horns, two oboes, bassoon, and harpsichord
of course as the accompaniment (*Basso continuo*).   The
usual relations between solo and tutti are disregarded in
this concerto, and there are no special subjects for each
respectively.   The material for the first movement is given
out by all the instruments together in bars 1-13.   They then
divide into three groups—horns, wood, and strings—and

work out this material in the style of a concerto. The
first bar—

is now raised to the rank of a tutti subject, and is used to
mark the beginning of each new section; the rest of the
phrase serves for the contrasting solo subject. When
distributed on the instruments, this antagonism is no longer
prominent, the working-out obeys the laws of free writing,
but so that the concerto style is preserved between the three
groups, which are united together at the climaxes to a
magnificent body of sound in ten parts. The divisions are
very clear and intelligible, as they are in all well written
movements in the concerto style; they are as follows, the
" exposition," or first few bars being reckoned in : A, bars
1-13 (F major); B, 13-27 (F major); C, 27-43 (D minor);
D, 43-52 (C major); E, 52-57 (G minor); F, 57-72 (F major);
G, 72-84 (F major). The reciprocal relations of the divisions
are of especial interest; the first two in the principal key
return at the close in inverted order, enclosing the others in
the middle, so that they correspond as follows :

A B C D E F G

Thus the form is cyclic, in the same way as that of the
violin sonata in G major, and the cantata " Gottes Zeit "
(see Vol. I., p. 456), except that in the latter case it extends
over the whole work. Exactly the same disposition is found
again in the third movement, where bars 1-17 correspond
to the closing bars 108-124, and bars 17-40 to bars 84-108,
while the working-out is enclosed in the middle. And
again these two divisions of similar form and fresh and
exuberant character enclose, in the adagio (D minor, 3-4
time), the true kernel of the whole. The adagio is one of
the most impassioned songs of woe ever written. The melody
gives expression to a piercing grief, often rising to a shrill
cry ; the oboe begins it in an apparently objectless way on
the dominant, and then the high violin and the gloomy bass
take it up one after another, after which it is carried on in

close canon on the oboe and violin; while below, the quavers of the accompanying instruments keep on in a calm and mournful manner. The finale, as bold and full of genius as the opening, breaks in upon this movement, as that of Beethoven's Eroica Symphony does upon its funeral march; the unsatisfied cries of woe suddenly cease: only a soft sob is heard in the empty air. Appended to the concerto are a Minuet diversified by a Polacca and two trios. These are fine music and a work of genius, but have nothing to do with the true concerto. Dance-forms were much in favour, as has been said, even in orchestral concerto, although they were in entire opposition to the ideal of the form. This is the only instance of Bach having made a concession to the taste of the time; and as the dances can be separated from the rest of the work, if desired, they hardly impair its beauty.

Second concerto, in F major. Instruments: trumpet, flute, oboe, violin, and the string band as tutti. It is thus a true *Concerto grosso*, excepting that the *concertino—i.e.*, the group of solo instruments which is contrasted with the tutti—here consists of four, all of high register: namely, one string and three wind; so that a departure is made in every way from the custom which decrees that the concertino shall consist of two violins and a violoncello. The plan of the first movement is a model of clearness and simplicity, but an indescribable wealth of episodical invention and the most delicate combination sparkles and gushes forth from all sides. The andante (in D minor) consists of a quartet of flute, oboe, violin, and violoncello, with harpsichord; the finale, *allegro assai*, is a fugue in the concertino parts supported by the bass and accompanied by the tutti in a modest and masterly manner. On account of its crystal, clear, and transparent organism, this concerto is a greater favourite than the closer fabric of the first; the feeling, moreover, is throughout of a kind easily entered into. The marvellously beautiful andante is only soft and tenderly simple, while the first and last movements rush and riot with all the freshness and vigour of youth. Truly, even if Bach could not avail himself of the full colours used by later musicians, yet his instrumental music is steeped in the true spirit of German romance.

This first movement: how it goes past like a troop of youthful knights with gleaming eyes and waving crests! One begins a joyful song which echoes through the tree-tops in the forest ; a second and a third take it up, and their comrades chime in in chorus ; now the song loses itself in the distance : it gets fainter and fainter : anon it is heard for an instant, and then wafted away by the wind and drowned by the fluttering of the leaves.

" Fainter and fainter still, upon the air
The music dies away—but where ? ah, where ? "

And this is evolved from the simple concerto form !

Third concerto, in G major.   Instruments : three violins, three violas, three violoncellos, violin and harpsichord.   The first movement is similar in its development to that of the first concerto, but is superior, from the art and charm with which it is treated.   The violins, violas, and violoncellos play in three groups, sometimes treated polyphonally among themselves, sometimes not, and frequently combined in unison.   What is made out of these subjects—

 and

is astounding—in fact, the whole movement is built on them. It is throughout instinct with life and genius.   One passage (from bar 78 onwards) is as fine as anything in the whole realm of German instrumental music ; the chief subject is given out in the second violin part, the first violin then starts an entirely new subject which next appears on the second violin, drawing in more and more instruments, and is at last taken up by the third violin and the third viola, and given out weightily on their G string; this is the signal for a flood of sound to be set free from all sides, in the swirl of which all polyphony is drowned for several bars.   There is no adagio in regular form.   Two long-held chords alone release the imagination for a moment, and then begins the concluding movement, a true concerto finale in 12-8 time.

Fourth concerto, in G major.   Instruments : violin, two flutes, and the strings as tutti.   It is a *Concerto grosso* in the manner of No. 2.[183]   The first movement, allegro in 3-8 time, is of a very pleasing character.   The material is given out in bars 1-83, for the most part by the concertino, the tutti only interrupting it now and then.   Here again we meet with the "cyclic" arrangement, showing that this still was the master's ideal of form.   The " exposition " (A) is followed in bars 83-157 by a working-out (B) going into the relative minors ; then there is a further working-out (C) up to bar 235, after which (B) returns with some alterations and extensions until bar 345, when (A) is brought back for the close.   The adagio in E minor, which is entirely taken up with alternations between the tutti and the concertino, is a beautiful and grave piece, in a mournful measure, like music for a funeral procession.   The last movement consists of a fugue— *presto* and in common time—which is grand in every respect.   It is 244 bars long, and for animation, for importance of subjects, for wealth of invention, for easy mastery over the most complicated technical points, for brilliancy and grace it is in the very first rank of Bach's works of this kind.

Fifth concerto, in D major.   Instruments : flute, violin, harpsichord and the ordinary tutti.   It is not a strict clavier concerto with accompaniment, but the clavier combines with the violin and flute to form a contrasting group with the tutti ; in this a second harpsichord for accompanying only was probably introduced, in accordance with Bach's usual practice, even in concertos for the clavier only.   In this way this work belongs properly to the class of *Concerti grossi*, or at least it is derived from them.   But that the clavier must have taken the lion's share in this combination is obvious from its character, and this is more easy to understand when we consider the great subjective importance of the place held by the harpsichord in this class of Bach's chamber compositions.   Two subjects for tutti and solo respectively are given out in perfectly developed form, and engage in the most

---

[183] W. Rust, in the B.-G. edition, is wrong in calling it a violin concerto.   The word *ripieni* in the title applies only to the violins, since there are no *flauti ripieni*.   Besides this, the intention is clear from the work itself.   Dehn, in the Peters edition, gives it the right title.

charming alternations.   One fragment of the tutti in particular—

is worked out with the loveliest combinations.   In the
middle there is evolved a new subject in F sharp minor of a
quiet and calm character—

it sets out in its course over the gently moving waves of
harmony, and loses itself as on an immeasurable ocean,
guided only.by a rhythm on one note, until the wind swells
the sails and brings us to the wished-for destination (bars
71-101).   Before the last tutti there is a great clavier solo,
which demands, as does also the other clavier part, a finger
dexterity which no one except Bach could have possessed at
that time.   A lovely and tender *affettuoso* in B minor stands
for the middle movement.   The general character of the
concerto is not so much deep or grand as cheerful, delicate,
and refined.   The last movement is of the same character.
It is in the form which was noticed first in the violin sonatas
with harpsichord obbligato—for instance, in the second
movement of the sonatas in A major.   The structure is in
three sections, after the pattern of the Italian aria ; the first,
which is completely repeated for the third, is fugal, and the
second introduces a subsidiary theme and combines it with
the chief subject.   This subsidiary, however, is here derived
from the chief theme and is of exceptional melodic charm ;
in the harmonic treatment a false relation which constantly
recurs and quickly vanishes again is very remarkable.

Sixth concerto, in B flat major.   Instruments : two violas,
two viol da gambas, violoncello, and violin, with harpsichord.
There are two subjects for tutti and solo respectively (bars
1-17 and 17-25), but only in idea, not specified by particular
instruments.   That for tutti consists of a canon for the two
violas at the distance of a quaver,[184] while the other instru-

---

[184] Kirnberger, in his " Kunst der reinen Satzes," II. 2, p. 57, quotes it as
a model.

ments have a simple harmonic accompaniment of quavers, so that the result is a movement similar to the church sonatas of Gabrieli and Bach. In the solo subject this phrase—

is taken up in all parts in an animated manner. The whole movement has a strangely mysterious character, such as Bach alone could give it, and doubly strange when we consider the original object of a concerto. The theme of the adagio (E flat major, 3-2 time) is a lovely melody, given out by the two violas alone over the basses. For a long time they keep the theme to themselves, treating it fugally, until at last it is taken up by the basses with beautiful effect. The final close is, curiously enough, in G minor. This movement is unusually noble and grand in character. The last movement, a concerto finale in 12-8 time, is powerful, without abandoning the fundamental character of the first movement, and it requires very good viola-players. While retaining the general character of the Italian gigue, it is in three sections, and yet altogether concerto-like in treatment.

From a production of the highest genius and mastery in art, as these six Brandenburg concertos must be called, one glance may not unfitly be directed to corresponding works by Bach's contemporaries. The *Concerto grosso* rapidly came into favour at the beginning of the eighteenth century, and the best musicians tried experiments in it. But they only followed the pattern of Vivaldi's style to a limited extent, and there was another style, as has been said, which originated with Corelli's sonatas. These composers retained the four-move-ment form in the recognised order : an adagio, a fugue in the same key, an adagio in an allied key, and a finale ; but they did not forget that the form admitted of more movements, and did not exclude dance types. But at the same time this imitation and dependence on a previous style exercised a powerful influence on the shaping of the separate movements. The dialogue between solo and tutti remained only an external alteration of different bodies of sound on the same material, and was scarcely more than a contrast, phrase by phrase, between strong and weak tones ; in the clavier and organ music this was represented by the different manuals—in the fugal movements of the French over- tures by the contrast of the whole orchestra with the trio of oboes and bassoon.   Thus in their essential nature these works were not concertos at all, but orchestral sonatas. Telemann liked this form, but did not devote himself exclu- sively to it ; the man who did the greatest things with it was Handel.   Handel's *Concerti grossi* cannot be compared with Bach's, since they have scarcely anything in common but the name.   It might have been said that there was nothing in common, if he had wholly avoided the form of Vivaldi's con- certos in them.   Where he uses it, however, he is always the great artist ; but the fact is plain that his genius was unsuited to this class of composition.[185]   In the broad adagios, in the fugues, and in the simple dances of the Corelli sonata he found the impulses which most certainly set in motion the purely musical side of his nature.   In accordance with his aim, which was to produce something brilliant and showy, he gave this form larger proportions and filled it with meaning. A precisely similiar case is that of Handel's organ concertos, the mention of which is suggested by the fifth of the Branden- burg concertos.   In these, too, the form and order of the movements are influenced in the most striking way by the sonata.   But with him the organ is only a more powerful clavier, and of true organ style there is as good as none.   But here, more than in the *Concerti grossi*, we meet with the real form of the concerto movements, because it was suggested so plainly by the independent and complete nature of the clavier or the organ.[186]   As far as the form had been developed by the Italians, especially by Vivaldi, so far Handel wielded it with mastery ; but he in no degree furthered its true growth.

---

[185] For instance, in the C major concerto (Handel Society's edition, XXI., p. 63), which, excepting in the last gavotte, has quite the Vivaldi form ; and in the second movement of the great G major concerto (same ed., XXX., No. 1).

[186] Handel Society, XXVIII.   Compare particularly concertos 1, 2, 4, and 6 from Op. 4 ; from Op. 7, concertos 3 and 6.

It is a significant fact of his musical nature that no single instrumental form of the many that were being developed at the time received any furtherance of growth from him. He appropriated what had been done in this way up to the time of his own work, and his incomparable wealth of ideas enabled him easily to surpass even the important works of other composers. When he lighted upon anything of this kind which was, comparatively speaking, formed, he was successful in producing instrumental works of lasting worth. Irrespective of the undeveloped condition of the Corelli sonatas as regards the arrangement and connection of the movements, Handel's *Concerti grossi*, so far as they depend upon those, are important enough to take a lasting place of honour in German instrumental music; and we do not wish to see the time when works like the concertos in E minor, A minor, and G minor shall have lost their effect,[187] for they contain at least separate sections of a solid and concise kind. But for the form of the concerto the Italians had scarcely done more than prepare the skeleton; the best was yet to be done, and chiefly by means of the art of treating episodes. Like the Italians, Handel possessed but little of this art, and that explains the unsatisfied feeling left more or less by all his movements in concerto style. Nothing is developed : all is ready made from the beginning, and only awaits the moment when it shall be displayed.[188]   Other German composers, such as Telemann, or the Kammer-musicus at Dresden, Dismas Zelenka, produced works of this class which were more conformable to rules, though not so rich in ideas. These, however, after all, are too inferior in talent to Bach to be allowed to share in the fame of having brought the concerto form to its highest point of development.

The Brandenburg concertos form a class by themselves in German orchestral music, since they must be reckoned as such. As among mountains the highest points seem close to one another, and the ravine that lies between them, and that will take many toilsome hours to traverse, is almost

---

[187] Handel Society, XXX., No. 3, 4, 6.

[188] Compare the intelligent and clever dissertation on Handel as an inst mental composer in Chrysander's Handel, III., p. 174 ff

indistinguishable at a distance, so these seem nearly allied to the modern symphony, and yet no direct way lies between them. They stand upon another and a much narrower foundation, upon which only a gigantic creative power could raise such a structure. The orchestral music proper of the period was not the *Concerto grosso*, then hardly invented, but the orchestral suite. This form, together with the clavier suite which had sprung from its root in the seventeenth century, practically reached its completion and end in the first half of the eighteenth century. So rational a unity as that presented by the clavier suite was out of the question in the orchestral suite, on account of the surroundings among which it grew. Whether there was ever any half-established custom with regard to the arrangement of the dances is for the present uncertain, but it is clear that the most eminent employers of this form recognised no such rule, and that the separate component parts are always grouped quite in an arbitrary way. But this lack of definite form was only the reverse side of an important advantage—namely, that the orchestral suite had sprung directly from the life of the German people. The freshly flowing fount of popular melody of the older centuries sprang forth from the ruins of the Thirty Years' War and divided into two streams : the sacred song or hymn, which was soon appropriated to the use of the organ, and the instrumental dance, which fell to the care of the town pipers. It matters not that so many other nations, especially the French, should have contributed some of their tunes and style. On the contrary, by this means the German spirit was kindled into that activity so peculiarly its own, which absorbs and amalgamates foreign elements to be part of its own strength ; this, as has been said before, was an advantage won directly from the turmoil of war. The French at all events contributed largely to the more delicate bringing out of rhythm in German dance music, and not only that, but we owe to them the first orchestral form of a secular character—namely, the so-called French overture. But they had hardly any share in the artistic development and elevation of this overture and of the dance types. Nor did they attempt to form an artistic whole from these elements. Even the Italians were far superior to them in these respects: there are overtures by Antonio Lotti, in the French style, such as no true Frenchman could have written in so excellent a way, to say nothing of Handel with his Italian education.

But the Germans formed a suitable set of dance pieces into a purely musical collective whole, prefixing to them a French overture. This is evident from the remarkable circumstance that the name "Suite" was not used for the analogous orchestral form, as it surely would have been had the French done as much for it as for the dance series for the clavier. But no general and collective name exists for it. With that modesty which is so characteristic of the true German musician, and which confines itself to the matter in hand, careless about outward appearance, the composers either indicated the separate component parts in the title of such a work, or were content to abbreviate it in this way, "Ouverture, &c.," then giving a list of the instruments employed. But the separate dances contained in any particular set were called by the town pipers "Parties" ("Partheyen") and we only do justice to the Germans in calling the class of music henceforth by the German name of "Orchester-partien."

If any one was destined to bring forth something extraordinary in this class, it was assuredly Sebastian Bach. In order to prove this it is sufficient simply to look back to his ancestors. His father, uncle, and grandfather had followed exclusively the calling of town pipers. How could this tendency of German art-life fail to find its completion in the musician who was to comprise in himself all the abilities which his family had developed for a hundred years? If the number of his "Orchester-partien" is not large—since the whole form was not earnest or prolific enough for this to be the case, and the clavier suite had absorbed a good part of his creative impulse in this direction—yet their very existence goes to show how thoroughly national was Bach's individuality. Let no one, as we have said before,[189] think

---

[189] See Vol. I., p. 162.

lightly of the importance of the place held in music by the town pipers of the seventeenth century. Granted that there were no little roughness and disorderliness among them; the *Volkssänger* (people's singers) of the sixteenth century were also rough and disorderly in their way. Nevertheless their songs handed down a genuine element of the old German spirit, and became a model of its expression; and so it was with the instrumental dance of the later period. Add to this that the Bach family made the most strenuous efforts to keep as clear as possible from the vulgarity of their companions. The great composer truly had no reason to be ashamed of coming into this part of the inheritance of his ancestors. And in fact he had taken possession of it with joy, with full intent to apply all the wealth of his powers to this ideal of national art. His four *Orchester-partien* are altogether works of a master hand, and in this respect of equal excellence. The keys are C major, B minor, and (twice) D major.[190] They all begin with a French overture worked out at some length. First, there is a *grave*, which is repeated and followed by a fugue leading back into the *grave*, and also repeated. The typical character, consisting of the contrast between broad beauty and eager impetus, is plainly recognisable, but is marvellously refined, so that we hear no opera music, but the most delicate chamber music, especially in the overture in B minor.

After that, in the C major partie, comes a courante, a gavotte, a *Forlane* (a Venetian dance in 6-4 time, resembling a gigue), a minuet, a bourrée, and a passepied. All the pieces except the courante and the forlane are double, so as to bring out in each the favourite contrast between the strong and the tender, and make each complete in itself. The name "trio," now universally known, came from this custom, for the tender subject was played by only three instruments, or was in only three parts ; but soon the number of parts was not restricted, although the general character of the music remained the same. Here only the

---

[190] Three of these are published in P. S., VI., Nos. 7, 8, 9 (Vols. 267-269). See Appendix A, 9.

bourrée and the passepied have trios in the strictest sense ;
the last-named dance is repeated in a different setting for
its own trio, in a wonderfully ingenious manner, all the
violins and tenors playing the melody in the inner part,
while the oboes have a rocking motion above it in quavers.
The trio of the gavotte is properly only in three parts, but
the united violins and tenors give out at intervals, and
without finishing it, a soft passage in the style of a fanfare—
a fancy which Bach had introduced before on the horns, in
the first movement of the first Brandenburg concerto.   The
trio of the minuet, on the other hand, is played by the
strings alone ; it goes by with an elastic step, and a sweet
and caressing character.

   In the B minor partie the overture is followed by a rondo,
a sarabande, a bourrée, a polonaise, a minuet, and a little
piece in free style in 2-4 time, entitled " Tändelei "
(*Badinerie*) ; the bourrée has a trio, and the polonaise a
variation.   This partie, in which there is only a flute in
addition to the string quartet, has throughout a distinguished
and debonair character peculiar to itself ; it thus stands
in a certain contrast to the other, without ever entirely
casting off the popular feeling.   The rondo form, which
we meet with here for the first time in Bach's works, seems
to have been imported from France ; in it a short phrase,
generally of eight bars, alternates with an arbitrary number of
somewhat longer interludes.   The rondo in question is freely
constructed on this plan, but the chief theme is heard even in
the interludes ; it is a real pearl of musical invention, and
steeped in Bach's peculiar melancholy.   In the sarabande
the ear is occupied with following an interesting canon
between the upper part and the bass; the first bourrée has a
delightful burlesque working-out of a basso ostinato—

the variation on the lovely polonaise keeps the melody in the
bass from beginning to end, while the flute has a figure above
it, supported by chords on the harpsichord.   With this
should be compared the beautiful and effective polonaise in
G major, from Handel's E minor concerto, the whole of

which throws a very clear light on the different character of the two masters, even in this class of composition.[191] The *Badinerie* at the close represents indeed no clearly defined dance type, but completely retains the form of two sections. The introduction of such pieces was taken, as its name implies, from the French. Even real dances were given names *à la Couperin;* thus once Bernhard Bach calls a bourrée "*les plaisirs,*" and another time a piece of like form "*la joye;*" but even this composer introduced pieces that entirely departed from the dance form. On the other hand, I know an orchesterpartie by Telemann, in which all the pieces are in dance rhythm, but no single one has any name. Thus, as we see, the greatest liberty prevailed. A general title for such free dance forms was "*Air,*" which was not especially used for simple or *cantabile* pieces.[192]

One of the parties in D major concludes in the same way as that in B minor. The finale is here called *Réjouissance* and has a bold and vigorous motion in triple time. The other numbers are, after the overture : Bourrée 1 and 2, Gavotte, Minuet 1 and 2. The component parts of the other D major partie are : Air, Gavotte 1 and 2, Bourrée and Gigue in the Italian style. Besides having the same key they are both more strongly orchestrated; for, besides the string quartet, three trumpets, three and two oboes respectively, and drums are employed. The last-mentioned partie is a favourite in our time and is often performed, but the others are no less worthy. It is to be hoped that in time all the orchestral works of Bach will take their proper place in our public performances, as soon as the material hindrances are removed which have hitherto stood in the way of the performance of a great part of them. Before all else the restoration of the old trumpet, so rich in animation, compass, and expression, is indispensable. The instrument which is now substituted for it can either not perform what is required of it at all, or else by its piercing tones distorts

---

[191] Handel Society, XXX., p. 40.

[192] Comp. Vol. I., p. 576. Dismas Zelenka also gives complicated and various forms under this name.

the delicate proportions of Bach's outlines in such a way that only a caricature is the result.

It was pointed out earlier in this work[193] that Bernhard Bach, Sebastian's cousin, had done remarkable things as a composer of orchester-partien. In this composer, too, the influences of the family of town pipers from which he sprung are very clearly to be seen. He has a right to be considered as the foremost in this branch of art after Sebastian Bach. Ludwig Bach, of Meiningen, is only known to posterity by a single partie, but in this there are traces of that old style which are all the more remarkable when we consider his leaning towards softness and Italian charm of sound. At all events, all the orchester-partien by other composers with which I am acquainted are far inferior to the productions of the Bachs. Handel, so far as I know, made no attempt in this class of composition.

We have called Handel's the more universal talent as contrasted with Bach's; and justly, so far as his relation to the culture of nations and his effect upon it are concerned. He was educated in Germany, travelled in Italy, studied French music, and lived in England. He succeeded, as no other of our great masters have ever done, in setting in vibration those cords. of the human heart, which are independent alike of nationality and of time, and more or less the same all over the world. But if we look at the musical material presented in the whole body of his work we see that he left a considerable part of the elements with which the musical atmosphere of the time was filled entirely unused. It was not he, but Bach, who was universal in amalgamating all the musical forms of the national culture of the time. The course of our investigations justifies us in saying that there was no single musical form existing all through the seventeenth century or in the beginning of the eighteenth that was not brought to lasting perfection either by Bach alone or by Bach and Handel together. At the close of the narrative of the Weimar period I drew attention to the vast wealth of forms worked upon by Bach. Add to these the Chamber

---

[193] See Vol. I., p. 26.

Sonata, the Suite, and the "Orchester-partie" with the French overture, and we have before us all that Germany, Italy, and France can offer us in the sphere of pure music. If the verdict that Handel was broader and Bach more profound is to remain in force, it must not be understood to mean that Bach restricted himself to one or to a few branches of art. The very essence of music is depth, and the more this is the case, the richer will its outcome be. To Handel the poetic aspect of the art was the chief object, and this, by means of sung words, is universally intelligible; Bach devoted himself to what was purely musical. Without question many a true German characteristic found noble and worthy expression in Handel also—for instance, his predisposition to devote himself to what was foreign in order to absorb it into his own personality, while purifying and completing it; consider, too, his fearlessness, his perseverance, his right-mindedness, and high morality! On these grounds he is and he remains German; but in his whole nature rather than in a specially musical way, for he neglected the most characteristic German art of his time—namely, that of the organ, with the chorale as its central point. It is the very fact that in Bach this was the true focus in which every ray of light was concentrated, from thence to radiate with new effects, which renders him in the most emphatic sense a national musician. The activity which permeated all the art elements of the time was not due to his personality alone, but to that music which was at the time the fullest and purest expression of the German nature, and of which he was merely the most famous representative. On this foundation he constructed the church cantata in Weimar, and from it he evolved there—and with still more energy at Cöthen—every musical form which is now universally accepted, and imbued it with nobler substance. But this was not enough. These newly created musical entities showed their vitality by twining round each other, sending out shoots hither and thither, and meeting again, from opposite poles as it were, to unite once more and become the parents of newer and greater forms. Bach's development, when we once recognise the motive power of it,

grows and blossoms like a flower; it is as though we saw
into nature's mighty workshop :—

> Each to the whole its influence gives,
> Each in the other works and lives!
> Like heavenly angels upward, downward soaring,
> And fragrant odours from their vials pouring,
> All joy, all bliss abounding,
> The earth with heavenly life surrounding,
> And all the Eternal's praise resounding!

Yea, verily! for it is not that Bach's creations reproduce
—more purely perhaps than those of any other German
master—the inmost soul of music; no, it is that his very
being, his moral essence, and the breath of his life were
music music in that deepest sense in which it is conceived
in Goethe's "Faust" as a reverberation of the sempiternal
harmony of the Macrocosm.   That effect which is produced
alike by an absorbed contemplation of nature and by the
enjoyment of any truly great music—the strengthening of
our moral tone combined with the purest pleasure—is also to
be found in the apparently simple and undisturbed current of
the great man's life.   Hitherto it has lain dormant: would
that it might wake to bring gladness and exaltation to his
country!

IV.

BACH'S SECOND MARRIAGE.—CHANGE OF POST.—THE FRENCH
SUITES.—THE WOHLTEMPERIRTE CLAVIER.

KNOWING the views of life that prevailed in the Bach
family, it is hardly necessary to say that Sebastian did
not live long in the state of widowhood to which he had
been brought by the death of his first wife.   His father,
under similar circumstances and at a far more advanced
age, had remarried at the end of only seven months.   Though
the son could not, like him, console himself at the end of so
short a time for such a bitter loss, he nevertheless was
making preparations for a second marriage at the end of the
year 1721.   He had long been known among the ducal band
at Weissenfels; in 1714 he had chosen one of its members—
a chamber musician—to be godfather to his son Philipp

Emanuel. In the youngest daughter of the Court trumpeter, Johann Caspar Wülken, he found the woman who could reconstitute the household which had been so suddenly broken up. Anna Magdalena Wülken was at that time twenty-one years old; the wedding took place on the 3rd of December, 1721, in Bach's house. This was in obedience to the commands of Prince Leopold, who felt a personal interest in the important step his friend was taking; all the more so because, just eight days later, his own marriage was to be solemnised with Frederike Henriette, a princess of Anhalt-Bernburg, aged nineteen.[194]

His young wife was to the master a source of deep and permanent happiness. She was extremely musical and took a part in her husband's labours, which extended far beyond a mere enjoyment of them. She was endowed with a fine soprano voice, and assisted in the performance of Sebastian's compositions—not, it is true, in public, but all the more zealously in the family circle—and she was the centre of the little domestic band which Bach was beginning to gather round him, formed of his nearest relations. He writes feelingly of this on October 28, 1730, to his friend Georg Erdmann : " They are one and all [his children] born musicians, and I can assure you that I can already form a concert, both vocal and instrumental, of my own family, particularly as my present wife sings a very clear soprano and my eldest daughter joins in bravely." Anna Magdalena was skilful, too, with the pen, and not seldom, when her household work was done, she would help her too busy husband in copying his own or other music. In this way she assisted with her beautiful handwriting in copying out the solo sonatas for violin and violoncello, and a manuscript copy of Handel's music to Brocke's text on the Passion is in great part executed by her. Her notation is rather less

---

[194] Gerber, Lexicon, I., col. 76. Register of the Cathedral of Cöthen. It would seem that Anna Magdalena was not born at Weissenfels, since the register does not mention her. Even before her marriage she was Court singer at Cöthen and betrothed to Sebastian Bach as early as September, 1721. As such she stood sponsor with him to a child of Christian Halen, cellar clerk to the Prince. Baptismal register of the Cathedral of Cöthen.

light than Sebastian's and differs from it in the form of the
C clef, the naturals, and the sharps, and in a few other trifles,
but it is very flowing and free, without a trace of feminine
ineptitude, as also is the alphabetical hand, which also differs
from her husband's in certain particulars; still the whole
effect both of notes and letters is often so like Bach's as to be
difficult to distinguish.   But she was not satisfied with this:
she was her husband's diligent pupil in clavier-playing, and
even in playing from figured bass.

Two music-books, kept in common by the husband and
wife, display very touchingly their intimate and tender
relations.[195]   They are full of the most miscellaneous
matters; the older of the two is in small oblong quarto
and is modestly bound in dull green boards with back
and corners of brown leather.   On the inside of the board
is written, not very regularly, in Gothic letters, " Clavier
Büchlein | vor | Anna Magdalena Bachin | ANNO 1722."
Then follows the letter B on a fresh line as if something was to have been added; and then, in Bach's
hand:

"Anti Calvinismus und⎫
Christen Schule *item* ⎬ von *D*. Pfeifern."[196]
Anti Melancholicus ⎭

Thus, this little book must have been begun immediately
after their marriage.   The words written under the title
are a playful, but perfectly serious indication of the purpose
of the work, which was to oppose that dry Calvinistic
doctrine, inimical to all art, which reigned supreme in
Cöthen, and to counteract all the sorrows and bitter
experiences of life—the " School of the Christian "—all
gloomy thoughts and dismal moods.   How could the
fountain of music, either in the church or in home-life,
be better described?   *Dominus* Pfeiffer was a theological

---

[195] Both in the Royal Library at Berlin.

[196] More correctly " Ante Calvinismus," either a slip of the pen or perhaps
only indecipherable.   Dr. F. L. Hollmann, in Lübeck, soon after the appearance of this first volume, suggested to me that it was the Leipzig professor
Dr. August Pfeiffer who was probably meant by these words, and the
accuracy of this view was subsequently confirmed by the list of Bach's Theological Library. See Vol. III., Appendix B., VI.

writer of the seventeenth century. Bach had his works—
Evangelische Christen Schule, *Anti-Calvinismus*, and *Anti-Melancholicus*—on his own bookshelves, and the Clavier-büchlein was to be, to a certain extent, their musical reflection. Its contents were for the most part worked out in the French suites, to which we shall come presently. Besides these it contains an ornate chorale in three parts, " Jesus, mein Zuversicht,"[197] a fragment of a fantasia for the organ—perhaps Anna Magdalena wished learn to play the organ too—an air with the beginning of some variations on it, and a minuet.[198]

The second and larger book has a green binding stamped with gold, and gilt edges, and has a more imposing appearance ; it is tied with a band of brown silk fastened to the upper cover. In the middle of the cover there is stamped in gold—

A. M. B.

1725.

It belongs, therefore, to the Leipzig period, and must have been a gift from her husband. Besides two clavier partitas (those in A minor and E minor of the first part of the " Clavierübung "), two of the French suites, the C major prelude of the Wohltemperirte Clavier, and the air for the Goldberg variations published in Part IV. of the Clavier-übung, it chiefly contains little pieces written out by Anna Magdalena herself — polonaises, minuets, marches, and such like—which are not indeed all by Sebastian himself ; for one minuet (page 70) bears the express statement " *fait par Mons. Böhm.*" However, we come upon various vocal pieces : first, the beautiful hymn by Paul Gerhard " Gieb dich zufrieden und sei stille in dem Gotte deines Lebens "—" Be still, my soul, and rest contented in the hand of God thy Maker." It must have been a favourite with Bach, for it is to be found three times in succession, and with two quite new melodies in F major and E minor (or G minor). With regard to the last, Bach is stated to be the

---

[197] P. S., V., Appendix No. 2.
[198] P. S., I., C. 13. No. 11, I.

composer of it, and a special importance is very justly
attached to this melody, for it is one of the most impressive
sacred airs in existence, and any one who hears it under conditions worthy of it, in Bach's own four-part setting, will
carry away an impression which he will not forget so long as
he lives.[199]   Towards the end of the book Bach has written
another beautiful composition of his own on the hymn by
B. Crasselius " Dir, Dir Jehovah will ich singen;[200] before and
after this are the hymns " Schaffs mit mir, Gott, nach deinem
Willen " and " Wie wohl ist mir o Freund der Seelen."[201]

Besides these compositions, which stand halfway between
the congregational hymn and more secular music, there are
a few true arias written for Anna Magdalena's voice.   The
first place must be awarded to the lovely piece " Schlummert
ein, ihr matten Augen, fallet sanft und selig zu," with the
recitative belonging to it, taken out of the sacred cantata
" Ich habe genug, ich habe den Heiland," and transposed
to suit the singer from E flat major to G major.[202]   A second
and more song-like aria in E flat major, " Gedenke doch,
mein Geist, zurücke ans Grab und an den Glockenschlag "—
" Consider, oh, my soul, remember the grave and ponder on
the end "—is a warning to prepare for death ; this likewise
is a composition by Sebastian in Anna Magdalena's handwriting.   This is followed by the chorale " O Ewigkeit, du
Donnerwort "—" Eternity, oh word of might "—not, it is
true, in the same key, but evidently connected with the
former in the mind of the transcriber.   A third aria, similar
to these, in F minor, " Warum betrübst du dich und beugest
dich zur Erden, mein sehr geplagter Geist "—" Wherefore
art thou so sad, and why so crushed and broken, oh, much
tormented soul "—treats of submission to the will of God.
The interest she evidently took in these compositions shows

---

[199] Published by L. Erk, Johann Sebastian Bach's mehrstimmige Choralgesänge und geistliche Arien. I., 43, 44; II., 208. Leipzig : Peters.

[200] L. Erk, ibid., I., 19 and 20.

[201] L. Erk, ibid., I., 111, has given the air of the first of these. Both were
well-known hymns, and are to be found in Schmelli's collection.

[202] B.-G., XX., 1, No. 82. The accompaniment is not written down, since
Bach would have transposed it at sight from the score of the cantata.

how near the young wife's sympathies must have been to the grand world of ideas, with its " dim religious light," in which her husband had his being.

Two other songs are of a more familiar character. The " Edifying reflections of a Smoker" show us Bach in the comfortable attitude of a citizen and *house-father*, as the Germans say ; still, even here, his reflections take a sober hue :—

> So oft ich meine Tabakspfeife,
> Mit gutem Knaster angefüllt,
> Zur Lust und Zeitvertreib ergreife,
> So giebt sie mir ein Trauerbild,
> Und füget diese Lehre bei,
> Dass ich derselben ähnlich sei.

> Whenever in an hour of leisure,
> With Knaster good my pipe I fill,
> And sit and smoke for rest or pleasure,
> Sad pictures rise without my will.
> Watching the clouds of smoke float by,
> I think how like this pipe am I.

This comparison of the fragile clay pipe and its fleeting fire, so soon burnt out, with the brevity of human existence, is carried through five stanzas. The song occurs twice, once in D minor and then transposed for a soprano into G minor; Anna Magdalena desired to sing it and has transcribed it herself. The second song having a da capo form is still more a true aria. The text—

> Bist du bei mir, geh ich mit Freuden
> Zum Sterben und zu meiner Ruh.
> Ach wie vergnügt wär so meine Ende,
> Es drückten deine schönen Hände
> Mir die getreuen Augen zu.

> Be thou but near, and I, contented
> Will go to Death, which is my rest.
> How sweet were then that deep reposing
> If thy soft hand mine eyes were closing
> On thee, their dearest and their best !—

is evidently supposed to be addressed by a husband to a beloved wife, and has a peculiarly delicate and tender sentiment bordering on hyperbole and still perfectly true in feeling. Bach has given it a setting full of fervour and

of purity (E flat major, 3-4 time).   This also is intended for
a soprano, and Anna Magdalena herself has it written out ;
but a few resolutions of discords have been added subsequently
by her husband, if I am not mistaken.   This receptivity and
sympathy with the moods of a man's mind marks a tender
and childlike devotion in the wife.[203]   The musical portion
of the book extends to the chorale " O Ewigkeit, du Donnerwort," on page 121, where the paging ceases.   Then, after a
blank page, come some wedding verses; of course they can
only refer to Anna Magdalena.   That they should find their
place here after the lapse of several years is a striking proof
of a happy married life :—

> Ihr Diener, werthe Jungfer Braut,
> Viel Glücks zur heutgen Freude!
> Wer sie in ihrem Kränzchen schaut
> Und schönen Hochzeit-Kleide,
> Dem lacht das Herz vor lauter Lust
> Bei ihrem Wohlergehen ;
> Was Wunder, wenn mir Mund und Brust
> Vor Freuden übergehen.

> Your servant, sweetest maiden bride :
> Joy be with you this morning!
> To see you in your flowery crown
> And wedding-day adorning
> Would fill with joy the sternest soul.
> What wonder, as I meet you,
> That my fond heart and loving lips
> O'erflow with song to greet you ?

On the other side of the leaf we come upon rules for
figured bass playing, which are continued over four pages.
The first and smaller portion, in which the major and minor
scales and major and minor triads are explained, Anna
Magdalena wrote out from a sketch or precis by Sebastian ;
all that follows, and which contains serious instructions for
playing from a figured bass, has been inserted by Bach's

---

[203] This aria begins on p. 75 and goes on to p. 78, the copyist probably
turned over two leaves by mistake.   On the vacant pages 76 and 77 the air for
the Goldberg variations was subsequently written.   With regard to the spurious-
ness of the song attributed to Bach, which is certainly to be found in this book,
see App. A, No. 10.

own hand, and in a note at the end he says that the sequel must be taught by word of mouth. I shall take a future opportunity of returning to these rules for thorough bass.

In the course of twenty-eight years of married life, Anna Magdalena brought him thirteen children, six sons and seven daughters: thus, by his two wives, Bach had in all twenty children. A portrait of her in oils, twenty-five inches high by twenty-three wide and painted by Cristofori, was afterwards in the possession of her stepson Philipp Emanuel.[204] In their rank of life it was an unusual distinction to have a portrait taken, and she must have had it done by Sebastian's desire: a fresh proof of the affection and high estimation on which the married life of this pair of artists was founded—a model to all.

When, in 1707, Bach was married for the first time, he had had the agreeable surprise of a legacy from his uncle, Tobias Lämmerhirt, of Erfurt, then lately deceased.[205] It was a strange coincidence that, a few months before his second marriage, that uncle's widow also died without surviving heirs, and by her will part of her fortune fell to him. Sebastian had been on excellent terms with his aunt and had made her godmother to one of his elder children. He now had the opportunity of proving that his regard for her endured even beyond the grave, for a lawsuit was immediately begun as to the property she had left. Tobias Lämmerhirt, not long before his death, had made a will to the effect that in the event of his decease legacies of various amounts were to be paid first to the children of his brothers and sisters, and to his godparents and half-brothers and sisters. The remainder was to go to his wife as residuary legatee, but with this proviso: that, if she remained a widow, at her death half the fortune was to revert to his nearest relations. The widow paid the legacies, and on October 8, 1720, made a will on her own part, in which she treated her husband's fortune as being her own inheritance and property, from which, at her death, she alienated a whole catalogue of legacies,

---

[204] Gerber, Lexicon, II., App., p. 60; it is now unfortunately lost.
[205] See ante, Vol. I., p. 339.

and then divided the remainder among ten legatees,
five of whom, in agreement with her husband's will, were
his nearest relations and five her own. The will was read
September 26, 1721 ; and at first the distribution was agreed
to, the legacies were deducted, and the residue divided into
ten equal parts. It was not till after this that the idea
occurred to some of Tobias Lämmerhirt's relations that his
will might be interpreted to their greater advantage. They
demanded for their share, first, half of the whole fortune left
by Tobias Lämmerhirt, and they calculated that it should
amount to 5,507 thl., 6 gr. Out of the other half, the
legacies left by the widow should then be paid and the
residue divided into ten portions. A petition to this effect
was filed January 24, 1722, in the names of the five relations who preferred the claim—namely, Joh. Christoph Bach,
of Ohrdruf, Joh. Jakob Bach, Joh. Sebastian Bach, Maria
Salome Wiegand—born Bach—and Anna Christine Zimmermann—born Lämmerhirt—the daughter of a brother of
Tobias Lämmerhirt. But practically it emanated only from
the two last-named petitioners, who, to give the claim more
weight, had taken for granted the consent of the brothers
Bach in this proceeding.

The carelessness with which they had gone to work
may be understood when we remember that Christoph
Bach had been already dead ever since February 22, 1721 ;
at the same time they had given the attorney who had
drawn up the document such insufficient information that
he allowed Jakob Bach, of Stockholm, to answer for the
consent of his brother Sebastian, of Cöthen; though it
might also be inferred from this that they, knowing his
magnanimous nature, simply dared not mention the transaction to him at all. In point of fact, it was only through a
third person that it came to Sebastian's knowledge. He at
once sent the following letter to the Council of Erfurt :—

MOST NOBLE, PRUDENT AND VERY LEARNED, MOST JUDICIOUS
    GENTLEMEN, AND, MORE PARTICULARLY, MOST WORSHIPFUL
    PATRONI,
            It is already known to your worships how that I and my
brother, Joh. Jacob Bach (at present in the service of the King of
Sweden), are co-heirs under the will of the late Lemmerhirt. Because

whereas I learn by hearsay that the other co-heirs are minded to bring a lawsuit with regard to this will, and whereas I and my absent brother have not been served with a notice, since I am not minded to dispute the Lemmerhirt will by law, but am quite satisfied with what is thereby given and allotted to me and my brother, I desire by this letter to renounce on my own part, and *sub cautione rati nomine* on my brother's part, all part in any such lawsuit, and to have it ratified by the usual form of protest. I have, therefore, esteemed it necessary humbly to lay this letter before your Worships, with due submission, and to beg you favourably to receive this my protest and renunciation, and that of my brother, and to restore whatever is to come to us out of the money, both that which has already been paid in and that which yet remains, for which great favour I beg humbly to thank you, and remain

Your Worships'
Most devoted servant,
JOH. SEB. BACH,
Capellmeister to the Prince of Anhalt-Cöthen.

CÖTHEN, *March* 15, Ao. 1722.

(Addressed to) The most noble, prudent, learned, and judicious Gentlemen, the Provosts, Burgomasters, *Syndic*, and other members of the Council, more particularly to my most gracious masters and patrons in Erffurth.[206]

After this emphatic declaration, no steps could be taken to initiate the proceedings, and no documents exist which have any bearing on the matter. To hinder the unfilial conduct of his relations, Sebastian came forward at once in the name of his brother Jakob, whose opinion he was sure would be identical with his own. Joh. Jakob Bach, after quitting his quiet home, in 1704,[207] had been a brave follower of Charles XII. of Sweden through all his wild campaigns, had taken part in the battle of Pultawa, and had followed his royal leader as far as Bender, in Turkey. There he had remained on duty till 1713, and then obtained leave to retire in peace to Stockholm as Court Musician there. But first he had gone from Bender to Constantinople, and had there studied playing the flute under Pierre Gabriel Buffardin (afterwards Chamber Musician at Dresden and teacher of the famous Quantz), who happened to be there in

---

[206] This letter, and the documents on which the petition was based, are in the town archives of Erfurt, Part IV., No. 116. I owe my knowledge of this letter to Herr Ludwig Meinardus, of Hamburg.

[207] See Vol. L, p. 235.

the suite of the French Ambassador, and who afterwards related the circumstances to Sebastian Bach.[208] Whether he then passed through Germany to Sweden and took that opportunity of visiting his relations in Thuringia we have no means of knowing. It can be proved that he received his salary from the privy purse of the Court of Stockholm from 1713 till 1721 inclusive. He must have died in 1722, hardly more than forty years old, and probably much broken by the terrible fatigues of the Russian campaign. Thus he probably never even heard of the circumstances under which Sebastian had answered for him, while Sebastian had to mourn the loss of this the last of his brothers, not long after the death of Joh. Christoph, who had formerly been his teacher, and of another highly esteemed relative.[209]

Thus, between joy and sorrow, more than four years were passed at Cöthen; but that which lay at the foundation of Bach's happiness there remained unchanged. The eager and intelligent interest the Prince took in his art had enabled him entirely to forget how narrow was the musical circle within which he moved there, its exclusive limitation to chamber-music, and the absence of all development in the direction of sacred composition. Since, however, it was for this that Bach must have felt himself especially fitted, nothing was needed but some external impulse to make him aware that his genius would not permit him to set up his tent for the rest of his life in this spot, however delightful he might feel it. This impetus was given by the Prince's marriage. His wife had no love of music, and she absorbed her husband's whole attention, all the more because she was delicate and needed every care. The Prince's interest in music seemed falling off, and it now suddenly became clear to Bach that it was no part of his work in life to make his transcendent gifts subservient to one single dilettante prince.

---

[208] According to the Genealogy and Fürstenau, II., p. 95.

[209] Johann Jakob left no children ; I cannot even find out whether he ever married. In the private accounts of the Court of Sweden he figures as "Johann Jakob Back." The salary, for various obvious reasons, was not then paid with great punctuality, so that " Back " almost every year had to prefer a petition to the crown for arrears of pay. This occurred for the last time in 1723, and the payment was probably made to his relations in Germany.

In the letter to Erdmann, before quoted,[210] he states this in plain terms. "From my youth up," he writes, "my fate has been known to you until the last change which took me to Cöthen. There lives a gracious Prince who both loves and understands music, and with him I purposed to spend the closing term of my life. However, as it fell out, the above-mentioned *Serenissimus* married a Princess of Berenburg, and as then it began to appear as though the said Prince's musical inclination was growing somewhat lukewarm, and at the same time the new Princess seemed to despise my art, it was the will of God that I should be called to be *Director Musices* here, and Cantor in the Thomas Schule. Still, at first it did not perfectly suit me to become Cantor from having been Capellmeister, for which reason my resolution was delayed for a quarter of a year; however, this position was described to me as so favourable that at last, particularly as my sons seemed to incline to study here, I ventured in the name of the Highest and betook myself to Leipzig, passed my examination, and then undertook the move to Leipzig."

It is clear, however, that the temporary cooling of the Prince's interest in music was in fact only the external impetus to a step for which the necessity lay in the general conditions of Bach's artistic nature; and we see this in the fact that his decision remained unaltered, although that "music-hating" personage, the Princess Friederike Henriette, died so early as April 4, 1723, and it was not till May that he pledged himself in Leipzig to take the place of Cantor to the school of St. Thomas. Meanwhile the obsequies of the deceased Princess took place in Cöthen without any musical adjuncts.[211] The Prince married for the second time, June 2, 1725, Charlotte Frederike Wilhelmine, a Princess of Nassau Siegen.

Though Bach had to quit the spot where his patron resided,

---

[210] See ante, p. 144.

[211] The funeral sermon preached on the occasion was published in folio, with all the poems in praise and lamentation of the deceased Princess, in 1724. Among them there is no funeral cantata or text for music of any kind to which Bach could have composed. The castle library at Cöthen possesses a copy of these memorials, which is graced with an engraved portrait of the Princess.

he continued to be his honorary Capellmeister.[212]   In this
capacity he composed for November 30, 1726, in honour of
the first birthday of the second Princess after her marriage,
a congratulatory cantata for which the Leipzig "occasional"
poet Christian Friedrich Henrici—or Picander, as he
was wont to style himself—composed the words.[213]   It
begins with a chorus, "Steigt freudig in die Luft zu den
erhabnen Höhen "—" Rejoice and soar aloft to distant
heights ethereal" (D major, 3-4 time); this is followed by
four recitatives, alternating with three graceful airs, of
which the second is much the most interesting, not unintentionally perhaps, since it is written for a bass voice,
and Prince Leopold himself was a good bass singer.   The
finale consists of a cheerful homophonic chorus in a gavotte
rhythm, and little recitative subjects are introduced ; its
beginning, it may be observed incidentally, is almost identical
with the theme of Beethoven's Choral Fantasia.   This
pleasing, though not very important, work was afterwards
adapted, with the text somewhat altered, to another birthday ode, and finally it was remodelled into a cantata for
the first Sunday in Advent, where the recitatives are eliminated and chorale arrangements inserted in their place.[214]

Not long after, this beloved patron ended his short life,
November 19, 1728,[215] and Bach had to contribute to
the funeral solemnity.   This he did by composing a
grand mourning ode (Trauer Musik) which he himself conducted at Cöthen in 1729, probably early in the year.   The
musical performers he took with him from Leipzig (he had
most likely done the same for the birthday cantata); in
Cöthen itself nothing of the kind could have been got up.

---

[212] So says the genealogy. This connection must still have existed in the
year 1735.

[213] They are printed in " Picander's | Ernst-Schertzhafft | und | Satyrische |
Gedichte | Mit Kupffern. | Leipzig, | in *Commission* zu haben bey Boetio. | Anno
1727," p. 14.

[214] It is given in this form, B.-G., VII., No. 36. See the preface and appendix
to that volume.

[215] Not November 17, as is stated in J. Ch. Krause's History of the House
of Anhalt.

The text was again by Picander.[216] It consists of four parts, and is intended for a double choir. The music was still in existence in 1819 ; it then vanished leaving no trace, perhaps for ever, and we have nothing to indemnify us for this loss but the enthusiastic praise of its last possessor;[217] there can be no doubt that the master would have put forth his whole strength in it. Thus death broke the tie which distance could not sever.

It must have been with a heavy and sorrowful heart that Bach moved to Cöthen;[218] but what Cöthen could give him was now a thing of the past. More than five years almost exclusively devoted to instrumental chamber music had invigorated his genius from the purest and freshest fountain of musical art, and he now could aim directly at that sublime goal which he was born to reach.

He had turned the time to good account. We have tried to glance over the vast mass of chamber compositions which were written—some certainly and some probably—in Cöthen. Still there are wanting to the complete picture the two works which, with the Inventions and Sinfonias, represent the highest summit of his clavier compositions at that period; these are the French Suites and the "Wohltemperirte Clavier."

The French Suites are, as has been said, contained for the most part in Anna Magdalena's first book, and almost fill it.[219] The name "French" was given to them later, without the master's concurrence, on account of the meagre form of their component sections, which, even in external dimensions, adhere as closely as possible to the dance type on which they are founded. In this respect they offer a conspicuous contrast to the broad symphonic forms of the

---

[216] "Picander's | bis anhero herausgegebene | Ernst-Scherzhafte | und | Satyrische | Gedichte, | auf das neue übersehen, | und in einer bessern Wahl und Ordnung | an das Licht gestellet. | Vierte Auflage." | Part I., p. 328. Leipzig, 1748.

[217] This was Forkel, who died 1818. He mentions it on p. 36.

[218] Mizler, Nekrology, p. 166.

[219] P. S., I., C. 7 (Vol. 202). B.-G., XIII., 2, pp. 89-127. See Appendix A, No. 11.

later partitas and the "English" Suites, as they are called.
Beyond this there is no idea of imitating or carrying out
any specially French characteristics; none such are to be
discerned anywhere in Bach, nor could they be possible
except in his very earliest work.[220]   It would be more
natural to detect a certain affinity with the Suites of Georg
Böhm, who, no doubt, for his part, was strongly influenced
by French art; but this affinity even is only one of feeling.
The arrangement of the French Suites is always that which
has already been fully described—Allemande, Courante, Saraband, Giga, are the essential sections; between the last two
pieces intermezzi are introduced.   Not one of them has a
prelude; there would seem to have been one originally to
the fourth, which was afterwards cut out for the sake of
uniformity.[221]   The whole work does not give the impression
of being a collection made or determined by accident; on
the contrary, it is arranged with artistic intelligence—a whole
cast in one mould.   As in the Inventions and the Sinfonias,
we here too find a considerable number of " Paralipomena "
which prove the care with which the master selected the
best.   No less than three complete suites exist besides
these, and identical with them as to the character of the
details and the whole arrangement.   They are in A minor,
E flat major, and E minor, and are so admirable that only
something of very superior beauty could have a right to
displace them.[222]

It was careful consideration which gave the first place
in the French Suites to three in minor keys (D minor,
C minor, B minor) and the last to three in major keys

---

[220] Compare Vol I., pp. 202 and 210.

[221] It is to be found in the Royal Library at Berlin, in a MS. copy, press
mark P. 289.

[222] P. S., I., C. 3 (Vol. 214), Nos. 6, 7, and 8. Besides these there are a Prelude,
Saraband, and Giga in F minor (P. S., I., C. 9, Vol. 212, No. 17); and in MS.
Allemande and Giga in C minor; Prelude, Fugue, Saraband, and Giga in C
minor. This last work seems to hesitate between the clavier and the violin,
and perhaps, as it lies before us now, it is only an arrangement of a violin piece.
Ph. Em. Bach is our authority for its genuineness. In other manuscripts in
the Royal Library at Berlin are to be found the beginnings of the subjects in
the thematic catalogue, p. 84, No. 2. The two first-named pieces are in the
same Library, but in a more modern MS.

(E flat major, G major, E major). But even the minor Suites are of a pensive and elegiac character rather than profound or grave, and the giga at the close gives a sense of vigorous and elastic reaction. The giga of the D minor Suite is exceptional in form; it is in common time, and strides on heavily and steadily almost like the *grave* movement of a French overture. A most delightful feeling pervades the three last Suites—a happy mood of joy and blessing; a sentiment of content that the world is so fair and that men may rejoice in its beauty; a radiance as of spring sunshine and an atmosphere as of the scent of violets prevail throughout. Truly, indeed, *Antimelancholicus.* The separate numbers are each more beautiful than the other in their indescribable and constantly varying charm. It would be in vain to try to say anything of each in particular. The forms are of the very simplest. Schumann once observed [223] there were some things in the world of which nothing can be said— for instance, of the C minor Symphony with fugue by Mozart, and a few things by Beethoven: if we add of many things by Bach, particularly of the French Suites, this still remains quite within Schumann's meaning. And that this very work had quite captivated a spirit so nearly akin to that of Bach himself he unintentionally proved by the resemblance which exists in one of his string quartets to the gavotte in the E major Suite.[224]

Many independent examples have already shown us the transcendent mastery which Bach had achieved in the fugue, chiefly on the organ, but also on the clavier. It must have occurred to him often to collect a number of compositions of this type, and arrange them in a single work. He accomplished this in the year 1722, and gave the work the following title: "Das wohl temperirte Clavier oder *Praeludia* und *Fugen* durch alle *Tone* und *Semitonia* so wohl *tertiam majorem* oder *Ut Re Mi* anlangend, als auch *tertiam minorem* oder *Re Mi Fa* betreffend. Zum Nutzen und Gebrauch der Lehrbegierigen *Musical*ischen Jugend als auch derer in

---

[223] Gesammelte Schriften, I., p. 198 (of 1st Ed.).
[224] The *Quasi Trio* in the finale to the Quartet in A major, Op. 41, No. 3.

diesem *Studio* schon *habil* seyenden besondern *Z*eit Vertreib
aufgesetzet und verfertiget von *Johann Sebastian Bach p. t.*
Hochfürstl. Anhalt. Cöthenischen *Capell*-Meistern und *Direc-
tore* derer Cammer-*Musiquen. Anno* 1722." ("The well-
tempered Clavier, or preludes and fugues in all the tones
and semitones, both with the major third or 'Ut, Re, Mi,'
and with the minor third, or 'Re, Mi, Fa.' For the use and
practice of young musicians who desire to learn, as well as
for those who are already skilled in this study, by way of
amusement; made and composed by Johann Sebastian Bach,
Capellmeister to the Grand Duke of Anhalt-Cöthen and
Director of his chamber-music. In the year 1722.") Thus the
instructive purpose is here distinctly set forth, and it was
this certainly which prompted the principle on which the
order of the collection was based—a course, namely, through
all the twenty-four keys, major and minor, a few of which
at that time were never used at all; so that it was Bach
who, by his new principles of fingering and his method of
tuning the clavier, first made them accessible.[225]   Even in
this the instructional aim stands out in all its simplicity,
since Bach has not arranged the twenty-four keys according
to the rule of their relationship, as Heinichen had laid it
down ten years previously in his Musikalische Zirkel,
but in simple chromatic order.   And this direct simplicity
is equally characteristic of the separate compositions: they
are bereft of all superficial embellishment; the severest
solidity and chastest treatment, purposeful to the very last
note, is the stamp of them all.

By far the larger number of them, at any rate, were
written by Bach during the Cöthen period; probably all
under the same impulse, and quickly one after the other.   A
trustworthy tradition informs us that this was in a place and
under circumstances when he was deprived of all musical
occupation—nay, even of any instrument whatever; he strove
to preserve himself against depression and tedium by such

---

[225] Heinichen, in his Generalbasslehre, p. 511, § 17, says, "Nowadays we
play but rarely B major and A flat major, and pieces are never set in F sharp
major or C sharp major." This was published in 1728.

an exercise as this.[226]   This very possibly occurred during
that journey on which he had to accompany the Prince.
Still this work is not cast in a single mould like the French
Suites or the Inventions and Sinfonias ; in the first place,
some of the fugues, though but a few, bear clear traces
of an earlier origin; also they are not all of them duly
thought out and connected with their preludes.   The older
handling most conspicuously betrays itself in the fugue in A
minor, first by the pedal note which enters at the end—a
license which we have already noticed in different places,
and which was altogether abjured by the composer in
riper years.   Besides, from this pedal note it is clear
that the fugue was originally written for the harpischord.
Thus, it is in opposition to the intention of the whole
collection, which is properly intended to be performed on
the clavichord.   When we consider the position given to the
clavichord by Bach, this is almost self-evident in a work like
the Wohltemperirte Clavier : it is shown, however, by bars
15 and 16 of the E flat minor fugue, where each time the
upper part is not continued up from c''' flat to d''' flat, because
this last note was lacking in most clavichords ; and, moreover,
by bar 30 of the A minor fugue, where on account of the
limited compass the regular imitation in the right hand is
altered.[227]   In like manner the bass does not go below C,
except in the case of some unimportant doubling of octaves,
though the harpischord had a larger compass both ways,
which Bach employed without hesitation.[228]   But, moreover,
the A minor fugue is an evident imitation of one of
Buxtehude's organ fugues in the same key.[229]   This deserves
special description.

First there comes a working-out *in motu recto* till bar 14,

---

[226] Gerber, Lexicon, I., col. 80.   The tradition is trustworthy for this reason—
that the lexicographer would have heard it from his father Heinrich Gerber,
who was Bach's pupil in Leipzig soon after 1722.

[227] In the second part of the Wohltemperirte Clavier no d''' flat occurs
with the single exception of the A flat major prelude.

[228] Compare in the overture in the partite in D major (Clavierübung, Part I.,
No. 4), bars 68–70 and 90–91 of the fugue, and for the three-stroke octave many
passages in the Goldberg variations.

[229] Comp. Vol. I., p. 276.

then *in motu contrario* till bar 27 ; then a stretto *in motu recto* till bar 48, stretto *in motu contrario* till bar 64 ; at this point there follows a stretto in two parts *in motu recto*, and in two others *in motu contrario*, then another such stretto between the alto and bass parts in F major, and finally from bar 76 the theme is brought in in inverted motion, the response a note higher in direct motion, and a stretto in direct motion from bar 80, and then a close on a pedal point. The playing about between direct and inverted motion is exactly the same in Buxtehude's fugue, only that he extended the structure, in his own way, by change of rhythm and episodical treatment, adding a coda rich in ornamental passages. Bach retains externally a greater concentration, but his whole plan appears to have been thought out collectively and coolly rather than conceived directly in the imagination. The fugue is somewhat scholastic, is lacking in emotional development, and has no climaxes. One chief reason is that the theme is not adapted for such extended strettos, which move chiefly in intervals of sixths and thirds, and so sound only like harmonies supporting the theme, while they display much harmonic ·and polyphonic development ; the rhythm is also tedious. The inversion of the theme is even less happy. The characteristic skip of the seventh from F to G sharp is inverted, and in the inversion seems not like a necessary sequence of the melody, but like an unmelodic arbitrary transposition of the theme into the higher octaves, since the ear demands at each repetition of the passage to be carried up a semitone higher. The tonality is also uncertain, the theme wandering from minor to major and from major to minor. One glance at the fugue in B flat minor in the second part of the Wohltemperirte Clavier, which is quite similar in scheme, is all that is necessary in order to see how the mature master dealt with materials of this kind. We can hardly be wrong in assigning the A minor fugue to the years 1707 or 1708. The G sharp minor fugue, too, is more or less clearly recognisable as a work of his youth. The theme strikes us as somewhat stiff, when contrasted with the incomparable elasticity of other subjects by Bach ; the counterpoint in chords, which is of frequent occurrence here, is well enough in Buxtehude, Buttstedt, and other composers of the older generation, but we do not expect it in Bach, any more than we do the repetition of one and the same phrase in a higher octave.   In its manner of treatment certain similarities with a fugue in A minor before mentioned[230] are apparent, which is of the same date as this, but much more graceful and charming.[231]

With reference to the Preludes, Robert Schumann—who in certain respects was the most competent judge of Bach's work in recent times—was of opinion that many of them had no original connection with the Fugues.[232]   In fact we already know that Bach cultivated the prelude as an independent form;[233] and it can moreover be proved, not only that all the preludes of both parts of the Wohltemperirte Clavier had been collected into an independent whole by Bach himself, even without the fugues—which is certain from the state of an autograph copy to be fully described elsewhere—but also that several of those belonging to the first part were originally conceived of as independent compositions.   For instance, in Friedemann Bach's Little Clavier Book, which was begun in 1720, we find in an isolated form the eleven preludes in C major, C minor, D minor, D major, E minor, E major, F major, C sharp major, C sharp minor, E flat minor, and F minor.   There is not, on the face of it, the smallest ground for assuming that these were less independent pieces than the other preludes in this volume, but their distinct origin is all the more surely proved by the fact that several of them are used in the Wohltemperirte Clavier as subjects of a more extensive elaboration.   This can be demonstrated as regards the preludes in C major, C minor,

---

[230] Compare Vol. I., p. 432.

[231] The opinion that several youthful works are contained in the first part of the Wohltemperirte Clavier is given by Forkel (p. 55), who, I believe, derived much general information from Bach's sons.   I cannot approve of his judgment in particular points : especially he is in evident error when he takes the fugues in C major and F minor for early works.   Those in F major, G major, and G minor seem to me not to belong to the most important in the collection, but I can find no indication of their being of a different date from the most important of the set.

[232] Gesammelte Schriften, II., p. 102.

[233] See Vol. I., p. 432.

D minor and E minor.[234]   Nor is it difficult to perceive that
the feeling frequently does not altogether harmonise with that
of the fugue, particularly in the case of the C major prelude ;
and the insignificant A minor prelude is not in its place as
leading to the fugue that follows, a stately piece of workmanship, attired in all the panoply of its race.

Nevertheless the Wohltemperirte Clavier, as a whole,
remains a masterpiece among Bach's instrumental works.
All of it that does not stand on the very highest eminence is
important enough to hold its place worthily ; otherwise the
master who criticised himself so severely and so constantly would certainly have cast it out ; he would have been
in no difficulty to find a substitute.   That he himself set a
high value on the work is proved by the three copies extant in
his own handwriting (possibly, indeed, a fourth)—an unusual
number for a work of such extent.   However, he hardly can
have thought of publishing it, though Mattheson challenged
"the famous Herr Bach, of Leipzig, who is a great Master
of Fugue," in print, to do something of the kind.[235]   This
profoundly conceived and original music could have no success with the ordinary class of clavier-playing amateurs, and
Mattheson described the organists of the time as ignorant
folks, ready enough to take lucrative places, but who would do
nothing and learn nothing "but what they might pick up by
chance."   Bach used the work as material for the practice
and improvement of his advanced pupils,[236] and at a later
period composed, as a fellow work to this, twenty-four more
preludes and fugues, which we shall discuss in their proper
place.   They are usually included in the work now under
consideration under the general title of the "Well-tempered
Clavier," though this name was originally given by Bach to
the older series only.[237]

---

[234] The C major prelude is given in the supplement (No. 5) to this work in the
form in which it exists in Friedemann Bach's Little Book. See also App. A, No. 12.

[235] Vollkommener Capellmeister, p. 441, § 66.

[236] Gerber, Lexicon, I., col. 492.

[237] Of the different editions I will here name only that of the B.-G., XIV.,
edited by Franz Kroll. In the introduction to it there is a very careful enumera-
tion of the various MSS. and printed editions. With reference to an autograph copy, hitherto unknown, see App. A, No. 13.

In considering the general æsthetic aspect of this work, what is most striking is the wonderful variety in the character of the twenty-four fugues, each of which is entirely different from all the rest. This is equally true even of the least important; and the endeavour after variety was probably the reason why Bach selected characteristic pieces from among the works of his earlier time. The preludes are no less various, though most of them are kept in one and the same form—that, namely, to which Bach was accustomed to adhere in his independent preludes; the whole subject is worked out from an animated phrase that sometimes becomes definite enough to be called a theme, but often is only distinct in rhythm, or wanders on dreamily from one harmony to another. A model of this form of composition, of which we have already pointed out several examples, is the famous C major prelude, a piece of indescribable fascination, in which a grand and beatific melody seems to float past, like the song of an angel heard in the silence of night through the murmur of trees, groves, and waters. The fugue belonging to it is worked up, and not without good reason, to the highest pitch of finish and intricacy; it was to hold its high position with fitting dignity. A marvellous art is displayed in the various strettos on the fifth, octave, third, seventh, and fourth, which are brought in by turns at the third, fifth, and seventh quavers, for the most part in double counterpoint; in the direct and inverted motions of the counter-subject, and its treatment with counterpoint at the twelfth.[238] It is no light task even for the player. The theme of the fugue begins on the second quaver of the bar, and it must be noted that the fervid and culminating force which is characteristic of Bach is here strongly marked; for it is not till nearly a bar later that we feel the strongest accent, though all that has gone before has tended towards it with peculiar yearning. It is an internal *crescendo*, to which, in playing it, the master would also have given as much expression as possible. By far the greater number of his clavier fugues are constructed

---

[238] Compare Kirnberger, Kunst des reinen Satzes, II., 2, p. 192 f.

in the same or a similar way. Of the forty-eight numbers
of the two parts of the Wohltemperirte Clavier, eighteen
begin after the first quaver (or semiquaver, as it may
be), seven after the first crotchet, and three after the
first crotchet and a half. Indeed, in most of Bach's other
clavier fugues—for instance, in those in E minor, F sharp
minor, and C minor—the same is observable. In the whole
two parts of the Wohltemperirte Clavier only fourteen
themes begin with the bar, and only six at the half bar.

In the organ fugues the conditions are somewhat different:
here the entrance of the theme with the bars predominates;
still, instances to the contrary are to be found, particularly
in early works, where they are not unfrequent; and here it is
all the more perceptible, because the organ is incapable of
accent, and therefore the feeling of the true rhythmical
value can only be given gradually, and by other means.
Bach had to submit to the natural conditions of the instrument, and subsequently restricted his use of these modes
of utterance, full of internal emotion and unrest, to the more
sympathetic clavier; but on this instrument he still further
developed this rhythmical extension, of which the F sharp
minor fugue in the second part of the Wohltemperirte
Clavier is an admirable example.[239] The C minor prelude
has the same general plan, still, irrespective of the key, it is
both sadder and more intricate; the motive does not consist
merely in a broken chord, but has besides something of a
melodic character—nay, towards the close a vehement
passion betrays itself. Even its indescribably graceful and
charming fugue, which has something peculiarly piquant in
the bold use of false relations in the harmony, is not devoid
of pensive passages.[240]

We have already studied the C sharp major prelude as
the finished sketch for the invention in two parts; this with
the fifth, ninth, and twelfth are in one category. This,
however, refers only to its first and shortest form, which was
subsequently extended to nearly forty bars. It may be
remembered that Bach had originally called the Inventions

---

[239] See Vol. I., p. 253.
[240] Marpurg gives an analysis of it. Kritische Briefe, I., p. 218.

" Preambles." In this, as in those, both hands are employed alternately in working out a complete melodic phrase, and an extremely graceful composition is evolved, sporting gaily up and down. The fine fugue, which carries out and intensifies the happy and vigorous sentiment of this prelude, is based on a bold theme which only the mind of a genius could have devised.

The C sharp minor prelude is more akin to a type of work which we have already had occasion to notice in the compositions of the later Weimar period; it is founded on a real theme worked out in imitation.[241] The triple fugue in five parts, which follows it, suits admirably with this noble and deeply pathetic movement; it is one of the grandest creations in the whole realm of clavier music. The main theme, consisting of four notes, massive as if hewn out of granite, is associated, after the thirty-fifth bar, with another in a smooth flow in quavers, and finally, in bar 49, with a more energetic and insistant one ; and then, for sixteen bars more, it expands into a composition of such vast breadth and sublimity, of such stupendous—almost overwhelming— harmonic power, that Bach himself has created but few to equal it. It is as though we were drifting rapidly over a wide ocean; wave rises over wave crested with foam, as far as the eye can reach, and the brooding heavens bend solemnly over the mighty scene—the surging forces of nature and helpless, devoted humanity.

The preludes in D major and D minor are wrought out on ornate motives in semiquavers, and they are almost exclusively in two parts or homophonic. The first is graceful and playful, the second restless and yearning. The D major fugue has a very distinctive character; it seems to march in defiantly, and then stride on proudly with a somewhat rigid dignity. A not inconsiderable space is taken up by some highly interesting episodical figures, which are rendered necessary by the peculiar structure and the brevity of the theme ; after bar 17 it never appears again, and it is precisely here that the composition attains its

---

241 See Vol. I., p. 590.

greatest brilliancy from the contrasts suggested by the theme: sudden bursts and pathetic grandeur developed side by side. The D minor fugue is remarkable for its artistic inversions and strettos, and the extraordinary economy it displays in the use of musical material; the expression is bitter and capricious, as the composer's humour could be at times.[242]

A very peculiar composition lies before us in the E flat major prelude. It is broadly, artistically, and firmly constructed, in four parts on two themes; but they are first carried through independently, one after the other, in a free and, as it were, explanatory manner—the *agitato* theme first, to bar 10, then the calmer one in crotchets and minims as far as bar 25. The strong contrast between the two phrases reminds us at once of the toccata form as Bach was wont to begin it; indeed, we are already acquainted with a similar instance of explanatory treatment.[243] What was attempted rather than achieved in the last movement of the D minor toccata is here carried out with perfect mastery in every respect. The feeling is most noble, deep, and purposeful. All this, of course, tells to the disadvantage of the fugue that follows it, which, notwithstanding its grace and sweetness, is too light when compared with the prelude, which, properly speaking, ought only to lead up to it and prepare us for it. The two pieces cannot possibly have been originally designed at the same time; Bach must have wished to make use of the lovely toccata movement in this work, and as it was too ponderous as a true prelude, he inverted the order for once, and intentionally supplemented it with a very short fugue in three parts, and not above half as long.

The prelude in E flat minor is one of those which bears the clearest stamp of genius. From this germ—

which is applied in various ways—first in the right hand and

[242] This fugue is exhaustively analysed by S. W. Dehn, Analysen dreier Fugen aus Joh. Seb. Bach Wohltemperirten Clavier und einer Doppel-fuge A. M. Bononcini's, pp. 1—7. Leipzig: C. F. Peters, 1858.

[243] See Vol. I., p. 437.

then in the left, now dismembered, now lost in figurations, while this rhythm ♩♪♪♩ follows it all through in ponderous chords—is developed a piece unique among Bach's works. The triumph achieved here by episodical art is all the greater because we are quite unconscious of it under the spell-bound feeling which envelopes us, heavy and oppressive as a sultry stormy evening, when not a breath is stirring and lurid lightning flickers along the horizon. From bar 29 the sentiment is sad as death, and the change to the major at the close is awful. The three-part fugue suits this to perfection : a real *ricercar* again, and the only piece of the first part in which he has availed himself of the enlargement of the theme (bar 62 ff). Art is here raised to such a pitch that, after all the strettos and inversions that we are already familiar with have been applied, from the sixty-second bar the theme is carried on in augmentation as well as in the ordinary form, both at once, and in direct as well as inverted motion ; and from bar 77 in all the three parts. This closely compacted fabric of parts leaves an impression of nervous excitation, of anxious and passionate seeking, and at the same time we still hear the passages of the upper part in bars 15 and 16, and 48 to 52 : the same form as we find again in the contrapuntal violin part to the chorale " Ich ruf zu dir, Herr Jesu Christ, ich bitt, erhör mein Klagen" which forms the finale of the cantata " Barmherziges Herze der ewigen Liebe "[244]—"All-merciful heart of the love everlasting." This fugue made so deep an impression on Ludwig Krebs that he attempted to compose an imitation of it.[245]

We have in E major a bright and charming prelude worked out on a motive of six quavers, and the fugue is still more delightful, with its theme that sets out with an audacious leap and then proceeds so deliberately. To do anything like full justice to Bach's incredible flow of invention we must study other fugues of this period, in which it is conspicuous in the endless variety of the themes; they are so many pictures which once known and understood can never be forgotten.

[244] See Vol. I., p. 546.
[245] In A minor. In MS. in my possession.

The E minor prelude, as we now have it, is the working-
out of a little piece which was written for Friedemann Bach,
and, as it would seem, to exercise the left hand; semiquavers roll up and down, while the right hand strikes short
chords. With that mastery which was his alone, Bach has
devised an independent melody for the bass. It is evident
that the ideal form he had in his mind was the adagio
movement of the Italian Violin Sonata, of which he has
left us such admirable specimens in his own Sonatas.
From bar 23 the bass motive is subjected (in a quicker
tempo) to a farther elaboration in both hands, and it rises by
degrees from two parts to four. This most original prelude
is followed by an equally remarkable fugue, the only one in
two parts in the whole work. A liberty quite unheard of for
a two-part fugue is the use of unison which occurs twice,
bars 19 and 38 : a license which we do not expect to meet with
in Bach's work, and least of all here. There are, however, a
few places from which we learn that the master did not
scorn even these means when he required a particular effect.
We have already noticed one, in the cantata "Bereitet die
Wege," where, in the first recitative, the voices and instrumental bass twice concur in ascending and descending passages in unison, as an illustration of the union of the Christian with his Redeemer.[246] Another example is in the wild
first movement of the Sonata in G minor for viol di gamba;
a third occurs in the little G minor " Preamble " in Friedemann Bach's Little Book, the fifth bar from the end,[247] and a
fourth in the *Burlesca* of the A minor partita in the first part
of the Clavier Uebung, bar 16 of the second section.[248] And
in the E minor fugue under discussion the object is unmistakably a peculiar effect. On both occasions the parts do
not coalesce in their natural course, but one breaks in
assertively and wilfully on the quiet flow of the other. This
character of wilful caprice, indeed of pugnacity, is stamped
on the whole fugue, and is still farther confirmed by the

---

[246] See ante, p. 558. Note 277.
[247] P. S., 1, C. 9, No. 16, XI.
[248] B.-G., III., p. 78.—P. S., 1, C. 5, III.

pertinacious assertiveness of the semiquavers that force
their way through the maze of sounds.

The prelude and fugue in F major are pleasing and
sweet, but have no conspicuous peculiarities of form. The
following pair, on the contrary, in F minor, are deep and
passionate ; the prelude is fine, founded almost throughout
on this motive—

and the theme alone—

sufficiently proves that the Fugue is worked out on the
broadest lines.

The prelude in F sharp major again is a two-part composition, and, with its happy sportive fugue, it forms an
indescribably delightful whole. That in F sharp minor
starts from a motive in rolling semiquavers one bar in
length, which is then developed with the most wonderful
imaginativeness ; the form is crisp and round, the sentiment
sad and weird. This truly Bach-like counterpoint—

is used in contrast to the long-winded fugal theme in
3-4 time, and in the progress of·the fugue it increases in
intensity, particularly from bar 35 onwards, by coming
out in doubled thirds and sixths. This is the kind of
counterpoint Kirnberger means when he says :[249] " When the
cantus floridus (where more than one note is opposed to
one) is the composer's intention, Bach adopts at once
a definite phrase to which he adheres throughout the
piece." In this wide sense the statement is certainly not
accurate ; on the contrary, it is precisely in the invention
of constantly new counterpoint that Bach is so great and
inexhaustible. Kirnberger, however, as may be seen by

---

[249] Gedanken über die verschiedenen Lehrarten in der Composition, p. 8.
Berlin, 1782.

the context, had something quite different in his mind—
namely, the skill with which Bach was wont to work out
his counterpoint from the first counter-subject, for it was by
this means that he attained in great measure that admirable
homogeneity and characteristic purpose which give to each
of his fugues a distinct individuality, while most of his
predecessors and contemporaries were satisfied with using
contrapuntal treatment in a perfectly arbitrary manner, just
as they would have worked out an episode in an organ
chorale.

The gay and jovial prelude in G major is followed by
a very fresh and merry fugue full of positive audacity,
particularly in the inversion of the theme. The violin
adagio seems again to have suggested the form of the
G minor prelude—a melody composed of long-held notes
and varied figures lies above a series of interesting harmonies;
presently they change parts, the bass takes up the melody
for a time and then joins the upper part. The sentiment
is grave and deep, and it continues the same in the fugue,
which is marked by great moderation.

The lively prelude in A flat major owes its origin entirely
to this motive :—

In the fugue, besides the brevity of the theme, we are
struck by its hardly moving out of the principal key,
while the melody is insignificant; hence its progress is
worked out very quietly and inconspicuously.

The G sharp minor prelude is· a really inspired composition of the most subtle construction. I have already
spoken of its fugue.

The A major prelude is of the same type as the three-
part sinfonias, and worthy to stand side by side with those
glorious works of art. The theme of its fugue is a grand
invention, which with its first note seems to knock at a
door and then, after a pause of three quavers, to walk
quietly in; presently greater vigour is introduced by the
counterpoint in semiquavers. The merits of the A minor

fugue and its relations to its prelude have been already discussed.

In B flat major we have a fiery prelude in demisemiquavers now rocking softly and now storming up and down, followed by a fugue of a soothing and peculiarly sweet character, reminding us in many ways of the beautiful D major sinfonia.   The unusual equality of the phrases contributes to give it its character.

The B flat minor prelude is of a deeply melancholy cast of beauty ; Bach works it out with consummate genius from this germ :—

In bars 20 to 22 the resemblance is very remarkable to the fifth movement of Handel's *Concerto grosso* in F minor, of which Bach copied out the parts.[250]   A grand fugue follows it, remarkable for its massive theme, mighty harmonies, and skilful strettos.   The two last preludes and fugues once more vividly illustrate at the close the spirit of contrast which prevails throughout the twenty-four pairs of pieces which constitute the work.   The B major prelude starts up before us from this motive—

in the most perfect order and freedom ; its bright, fresh feeling revives the soul,,and it flows on for nineteen bars, polished and smooth down to the most insignificant detail, a perfect gem of chamber-music.

The B minor prelude on the other hand—the only one of the whole first set which is in two sections with a repeat— is a duet in imitation above a bass in unflagging quavers, and is equally masterly even in the minutest details, but still apparently too compact and self-contained for a prelude. Apparently—and so long as the fugue is left out of the question.   While the fugue which belongs to the B major

<hr />

[250] See ante p. 11.

prelude goes on its way contentedly, *debonnair*, and without
pause, this one—

proceeds slowly, sighing, saddened, and pain stricken ; its
feeling is akin to that of the F minor sinfonia, only here
the suffering is so intensified as to be almost unendurable.[251]   And we must beware of regarding the piercing
bitterness of the effect in this fugue as a mere result
of contrapuntal skill.   From this point of view indeed
it is in no way remarkable, and even if it were, Bach has
proved again and again that he could preserve a sweet and
pleasing character even with the greatest intricacy of construction.   No, it was his purpose to produce a picture of
human misery, to give it full utterance here, in his favourite
key, and at the close of this glorious work in which all his
deepest sympathies with human feeling had found expression.
For to live is to suffer.   This is the idea—persistent as an
organ point—which asserts itself through all the manifold,
motley, and endless variety in this work, gradually built up
by the master's unresting industry, and which asserts itself
once more in its closing chords.

There is another reflection which again forces itself upon
us as we close the Wohltemperirte Clavier.   How little can
a composer who finished one of his most important instrumental works, conceived and produced as a grand whole,
with such a crown of thorns, have counted on the sympathy
of the great music-loving public !   Still, that which the god
prompted his deep heart to utter, that he spoke without
reservation or calculation ; he appealed only to a restricted
circle of docile pupils and intelligent friends.   But their
sympathy, on which he could no doubt fully rely, did not

---

[251] Kirnberger has analysed its harmonic structure, Die wahren Grundsätze
zum Gebrauch der Harmonie, p. 55.   I avail myself of this opportunity of
alluding to Carl van Bruyk's Technische und aesthetische Analysen des
Wohltemperirten Clavier.   Leipzig: Breitkopf und Härtel, 1867.   Though I
cannot agree with all the views expressed in it, the work contains many
charming observations and is written with a real inspiration of love for the
subject.

betray him into pouring out his feelings in capricious imagery; he must always refine and purify them to be the soul of the severest possible forms. It is impossible to speak with too high praise of this supreme artistic morality.

It is very difficult to say anything that will convey a general idea of the character of these fugues. Their forms are so complete within their narrow limits that what distinguishes them could only be made clear by a thorough technical analysis of each, or of most of them, and that, it is evident, is impossible here. And—in spite of their strong individuality—their character as a whole is even more inaccessible to verbal description than that of the other instrumental works, by reason of the lofty idealisation which the feeling they express derives from the severity of the form which expresses it. There is a legend which tells us of a city of marvels that lies sunk beneath the sea; the sound of bells comes up from the depths, and when the surface is calm, houses and streets are visible through the clear water, with all the stir and turmoil of busy, eager human life—but it is infinitely far down, and every attempt to clutch the vision only troubles the waters and distorts the picture. We feel the same thing as we listen to this music. All that stirred the soul of the composer—love and hatred, joy and sorrow, with their fortuitous and transient impulses—lie deep below the surface: faintly, remotely, we hear their echoes, and as we gaze through the crystal flood of sound we see the living soul within, and perceive that it suffered or was gay even like ourselves, only what it was that stirred it we may not see. But each of us can recognise with kindred feelings the experience of his own life: every one of all the human hearts which, for the last century and a half, has duly studied and absorbed this work; and this it is which has made it, to our own day, a perennial source of joy and of spiritual refreshment and strength. Indeed, what has already been said of Bach's clavier works in general is especially true of this—that he wrote them for an ideal instrument, which it was left to our own time to realise. A movement so pervaded with profound melancholy as the C sharp minor prelude and its fugue, through which the spirit of God seems to rush with sublime terrors, could find no adequate interpretation on the clavi-chord.   So that it is to us in fact that all the glories which filled the master's fancy have been first revealed ; we hear more clearly the sweet bells from the deep, and stand more nearly face to face with the forms that people it.   But the work will long survive our generation : it will stand as long as the foundations of the art endure on which Bach built. It finds a fitting place at the end of this section, for it reflects at parting the whole of the Cöthen period of Bach's life, with its peace and contemplation, its deep and solemn self-collectedness.

BOOK V.

LEIPZIG, 1723—1734.

BOOK V.

I.

BACH'S APPOINTMENT AND INSTALLATION AS CANTOR AT LEIPZIG.

THE post of Cantor to the town-school of St. Thomas at Leipzig was not a brilliant one; but those who were familiar with its conditions knew that it had certain valuable advantages. Kuhnau died June 5, 1722, and a month later the Council had had a choice among six candidates. For the most part these were men who from their own knowledge were aware of what the Cantor of the Thomasschule[1] had to expect. Fasch, Rolle, and Telemann were conspicuous among them. Johann Friedrich Fasch, Capellmeister to the Prince of Anhalt-Zerbst, had been at the Thomasschule from 1701 to 1707, and had enjoyed Kuhnau's instruction. As a student of law he got up a musical society among the Leipzig students, and with them provided a part of the church music in the University church of St. Paul, in 1710. After this he led a life of vicissitude, and he had only been a few weeks in his place at Zerbst when one of his Leipzig patrons, the Hofrath Lange, suggested to him that he should become a candidate for the vacant place of Cantor.[2]

Christian Friedrich Rolle we have already met with in the course of Bach's history; it was with him and Kuhnau that he had tested the organ of the Church of the Blessed Virgin at Halle in 1716; at that time Rolle had already

---

[1] So called in German; the designation is retained here for convenience and brevity.

[2] Records of the University of Leipzig; and Gerber, n. d., II., col. 9.

been for a year at Quedlinburg; he was now musical director
in Magdeburg.[3]   Telemann, finally, who had gone from
Eisenach to Frankfort am Main, and from thence, in 1721,
to Hamburg as musical director and Cantor, had formerly
first shown his great musical powers at Leipzig; he had
gone thither in 1701, intending to study jurisprudence and
to suppress all his musical proclivities.   But his talent was
discovered, and he was immediately engaged to produce a
composition once a fortnight for the Church of St. Thomas,
where Kuhnau had lately been made Cantor.   He also
formed a *Collegium Musicum*, a Musical Union of students,
which rapidly rose to importance, and during the first ten
years of the eighteenth century was a power in the musical
life of Leipzig.   He soon found occupation as a dramatic
composer, and wrote a number of operas for the Leipzig
Theatre, for some of which he also wrote the text, and
even appeared in them himself.   When at last he obtained
the place of Organist to the New Church (August 8, 1704)
the Council hastened to instal him (August 18).   " He
was a very good composer—he was to give his services at
the Thomasschule on occasion—he was not only to play
on the organ, but to direct all the music—but he must
refrain from theatres and give up acting."[4]   In the same
year he was invited to Sorau, as Capellmeister, and thence-
forth Germany rang with his fame.   Hence, when the point
under discussion was the selection of a new Cantor for the
Thomasschule, he was preferred above all the other candidates, and some days after, when he had passed the
customary tests, his appointment was definitely settled by
the Council.   The only difficulty raised was the obligation
under which the Cantor lay to teach some other branch of
knowledge in the school ; to this Telemann would not consent.   The Council, however, declared their willingness to
make other arrangements in this respect, and prepared to

---

[3] See Vol. I., p. 520.   In the documents preserved in the archives at
Magdeburg he is called Johann Christian Rolle, but there is no doubt as to
their identity.

[4] Acts of the Leipzig Council.   Telemann's Autobiography in Mattheson's
Grosse General Basschule, p. 173.   Ehrenpf., p. 238.

instal the famous musician in his office, when he returned to Hamburg and wrote from thence that he could not accept it.

The Council, much provoked, proceeded to a new election. Meanwhile, Georg Friedrich Kauffmann, of Merseburg,[5] and after him Christoph Graupner, Capellmeister of Darmstadt, had come forward as candidates, and the town was represented by Georg Balthasar Schott, the highly-esteemed Organist of the New Church. The decision fell on Graupner, for whom Kauffmann voluntarily made way. Even Graupner might regard himself as an old Leipziger, so far as that he owed most of his musical and general culture to a nine years' discipline at the Thomasschule. From being a prize scholar under Kuhnau, in clavier playing and composition, he had become a master who, as a composer for the clavier, may rank as one of the best of his time.[6] In his application for the post of Cantor he had been strongly recommended by his old friend Heinichen, the Capellmeister at Dresden. Graupner came to Leipzig, and seems to have passed his tests and presented his testimonials; but, when all had proceeded so far, the Landgrave of Hesse Darmstadt refused to part with him. As the transaction had been conducted privately, Graupner was able to retire more honourably than Telemann.

Besides Graupner, and as it would seem rather later—at any rate, not till the end of the year 1722—Bach came forward[7] to offer himself. It is not probable that he should only now have heard for the first time of the vacant post; his late appearance must have had other causes. He was, in fact, in a critical position. Prince Leopold's failing interest in music, his own anxiety for the higher education of his sons, the feeling that in the service of the Court only one side of his artistic genius could thrive and labour—all this made a further residence in Cöthen seem undesirable. On the other hand, he no doubt did not undervalue the comfort-

---

[5] See Vol. I., p. 118.

[6] Mattheson, Ehrenpf., p. 410.

[7] Documents of the Leipzig Council. The appointment, dated Dec. 21, says that several had become candidates—namely, Capellmeister Graupner, of Darmstadt, and Bach, of Cöthen.

able and honourable position, free from all petty anxiety, which the Prince's favour secured to him. In Leipzig a wider circle of labour awaited him; he would be standing midway in a broader and fuller stream of public life, but "from a Capellmeister to become a Cantor" was not at all to the mind of a man who was both proud and famous. Even after he had actually put out his hand to gather the inheritance of Kuhnau, for fully three months he doubted whether he should not do better to withdraw. But certain persons whose counsel he asked urged it so strongly that at last he took the decisive step. He went to Leipzig at the beginning of February, 1723; on the 7th, being the Sunday called *Estomihi* (Sunday next before Lent), he performed as his test piece the cantata on " Jesus nahm zu sich die Zwölfe "—" Jesus called the Twelve unto Him."[8]

His appointment did not immediately follow; the Council were still in treaty with Graupner, who, three weeks previously, had passed his tests, and besides him Kauffmann and Schott were still candidates. However, when Graupner had retired, no long consideration was needed to discern the worthiest of the three remaining competitors. Bach had been acquainted with Kuhnau; he knew Leipzig and Leipzig knew him. He had already been invited thither in 1717 to inspect the great organ in St. Paul's Church, and the Council knew that it was strengthening itself by such a selection. They reflected that he was a distinguished clavier-player, a man for whose sake even Telemann might be forgotten, the equal of Graupner, and one who was famous enough to attract even the students to take part in his musical performances, which in the then state of affairs was highly desirable. Besides this, Bach seemed to be willing to fulfil the Cantor's duties in every branch, and in this he was distinguished from the other candidates; he was willing even to undertake the general instruction required of him. This consisted in giving five Latin lessons weekly to the third and fourth classes; in these the course included written exercises,

---

[8] So says a note on a copy of this cantata, which, though not an autograph, was revised and completed by Bach. It is in the Royal Library at Berlin. See also ante, p. 157.

grammar, the *Colloquia Corderii*,[9] and an explanation of Luther's Latin Catechism.[10] At first Bach would seem to have resisted the demand that he should be Latin teacher as well,[11] or else, from the refusal of all the other candidates it was taken for granted in his case. However, when the Council met for final decision on the 22nd of April, Burgomaster Lange was in a position to state that Bach had expressly pledged himself both to hold his official classes and to give private lessons in the Latin tongue. He cannot have been ignorant that in Telemann's case a dispensation from these duties had been contemplated, and this relief would undoubtedly have been at once granted to him also, since the gentlemen of the Council declared of their own accord that if he could not accomplish all the instruction required in Latin no objection would be raised to paying a deputy to do it for him. Bach, however, felt equal to performing his own duties, and no doubt regarded it also as a point of honour to be in no respect behind his predecessors; after such a man as Kuhnau this was saying something, but we have already had occasion to observe that Bach from his schooldays had been a sound Latin scholar. Still it must no doubt have seemed to him a strange experience to stand in front of the third class of boys with the Latin Grammar in his hand, a church cantata, perhaps—who knows?—running in his head. Beyond instructing his own children, perhaps, such teaching had never been any part of his duties. Indeed, he soon felt the task a burthen, and paid his colleague, Magister Pezold, the sum of fifty thalers per annum to relieve him of the greater part of his teaching; after this he held the class only when Pezold was ill or otherwise prevented, and then he would dictate an exercise to the boys for them to *elaborate* (construe and parse).[12]

---

[9] *Maturini Corderii Colloquia Scholastica, pietati, literarum doctrinis, decoro puerili, omni muneri, ac sermoni præcipue scholastico, utiliter concinnata.* 3rd ed. Leipzig, 1595.

[10] Acts of the Leipzig Council concerning the " Schuel zu S. Thomas."

[11] " All three "—namely Bach, Hauffmann and Schott—" will not be able to teach (Latin) as well." Document dated April 9.

[12] This condition of affairs was reported to the Consistory by Superintendent Deyling, Feb. 24, 1724.

About a fortnight after the transaction above mentioned, Bach, who had appeared in person before the Council, received an official intimation that he was considered the best of the candidates, and had been unanimously elected; the office was therefore conferred upon him on the same conditions as those on which his predecessors had held it. He then had to sign a contract deed which had been prepared for Telemann the year before (and which, twenty-seven years after was used again for his successor); this contained the customary stipulations, as to leading a respectable and sober life, to fidelity and diligence in the performance of his official duties, and to due and proper respect and obedience to the worshipful Council; it pledged him, among other conditions, not to make the church music too long nor too operatic, to instruct the boys not only in singing but—for the avoidance of expense—in instrumental music also, to treat them with humanity; not to send any incapable singers to join the chorus of the New Church, which was exempt from his supervision, not to make any journeys without permission from the Burgomaster, nor to accept any office in the University without the consent of the Council.[13] And even after all this the appointment was not an accomplished fact. Its confirmation was needed by the Consistory of Leipzig, a superior municipal body, composed partly of ecclesiastics and partly of laymen.[14] When the Council desired to appoint to any post in the town churches or schools, the candidate had to present himself before the Consistory, which then put him through a sort of examination on its own account, with the object of ascertaining the religious principles of the examinee. If the result was satisfactory his appointment was forthwith confirmed by the Consistory. Bach was presented, on May 8, by Deyling, Superintendent and Consistorial Assessor, and his examiner was the Consistorial Assessor Dr. Schmid. The two assessors then

---

[13] See App. B, VI.

[14] Sicul gives a list of the names of the members of the Consistory for 1724, with the dates of their election; Leipziger Jahrbuch, Vol. iii, p. 358. It had at that time six Assessors—the Doctors Wagner, Lange, Schmid, Packbusch, Deyling, and Mascov. The director, since 1709, was Dr. Johann Franz Born.

testified that Herr Johann Sebastian Bach had answered the questions put to him in such wise that he might be permitted to assume the post of Cantor in the Thomasschule.[15] On the 13th he was confirmed in his appointment by the Consistory; he had to subscribe the *concordia* formula,[16] and be sworn.

On Monday, May 31, his formal installation at last took place.[17] At nine in the morning two deputies from the Council—namely, one Lehmann, who was at that time superintendent of the school, and who held the civic office of "Baumeister,"[18] and Menser, the chief town clerk—proceeded to the Thomasschule, where they were received at the door by the Rector (or warden) Joh. Heinrich Ernesti, and conducted to the hall appointed for the examination of the deed. Here they were met by the licentiate Weisse, preacher at the Church of St. Thomas, who appeared as the representative of Superintendent Deyling, and as the ambassador from the Consistory. The six other masters of the school now joined them, with their new colleague—namely, Licentiate Christian Ludovici, the sub-warden (Conrector), Magister Carl Friedrich Pezold, Master of the third class; Christoph Schmied, of the fourth; Johann Döhnert, of the fifth; Johann Breunigke, of the sixth; and Christian Ditmann, of the seventh.[19]

They took their seats, the pastor and the two reporters of the Council in one row, and opposite to them the school

---

[15] "Du. Jo. Sebastianus Bach ad quaestiones a me propositas ita respondit, ut eundem ad officium Cantoratus in Schola Thomana admitti posse censeam.
"D. Jo. SCHMIDIUS.
"Consentit. D. SALOMON DEYLING."
Act of the Leipzig Consistory.

[16] The "concordia formula" is an abridgement of the contents of the Concordienbuch, a kind of religious statute book, in which are embodied the tenets and doctrines of the Reformed Church.

[17] The official documents date it on June 1. Deyling, in a letter written a month later, says May 31; and this is certainly right, since it fell in 1723 on a Monday, and Bach would begin his school work after conducting the services of the previous day.

[18] This answered rather to the Roman Aedile, and does not mean an architect; Baumeister Lehmann was a lawyer. See Sicul, Leipziger Jahrbuch, Vol. IV., p. 764.

[19] From E.E. Hochw. Raths | der Stadt Leipzig | Ordnung | Der Schule | Zu S. THOMAE | Gedruckt bey Immanuel Tietzen, 1723, p. 11.

officials according to their rank. The choir first sang a
piece of music at the door, and then all the scholars came
in. The town clerk made a speech bearing on the installation, and the pastor then pronounced the fact of installation,
adding the customary admonitions and injunctions. Bach
replied in a few words, he was congratulated on his new
appointment, and the ceremony concluded with another
musical performance.

It was plainly shown on this occasion that in the Consistory the Council had a thorn in the flesh, for the superior
court fettered its liberty and independence in various ways.
Up to this time it had never been the custom for the
Consistory to interfere in this direct manner with the
installation of a school official. The deputies of the Council
declared then and there that it was an infringement of their
rights, that the superintendent and pastor when present at
such a ceremony had no more share in it than to congratulate the new officer. It was owing only to the
moderation of Weisse's conduct that matters did not come
to an outbreak between him and the irate councilmen in
the presence of the whole assembly. The Council immediately proceeded to draw up a formal protest, however,
and the Consistory appealed against it to the regulations
of the canon law of the electorate of Saxony.[20]

Bach had an official residence in the left wing of the
school buildings; this had probably been the Cantor's
dwelling from time immemorial, for Kuhnau, at any
rate, had inhabited it before him.[21] The building at that
time had only two storeys, and was much too small for
its purpose. At the beginning of 1731 it was added to,
and an additional storey was built, and meanwhile Bach
had a temporary residence assigned to him, from the
spring of 1731 till the New Year of 1732, probably,
in the house of Dr. Cristoph Dondorff, who from 1730

---

[20] See Appendix B, III., of the German for the entire document.
[21] Das jetzt lebende und florirende Leipzig; Leipzig, bey Joh. *Theodori
Boetii* seel. Kindern, 1723. " Joh. Sebastian Bach, *Director Music*, und
Cantor, am Thomas Kirchofe auf der Thomas-Schule." We know that Kuhnau
lived here, from a note as to his interment in the Leipzig Register.

had owned the Mill of St. Thomas,[22] and who was a friend
of the Bach family.[23] St. Thomas' Mill stood outside the
city walls, which ran round the back of the schoolhouse,
where the Schlobach estate now lies, on the farther side
of the Promenade. It may be mentioned, as characteristic
of the conditions of life at that time, that the rent paid
by the Council for this house, which Bach occupied for
nearly a year, was sixty thalers. His residence, as Cantor,
was meanwhile somewhat altered ; a room on the first floor
was lost in consequence of the rebuilding, and Bach had
another instead on the third floor. It would seem that the
dwelling was made on the whole more commodious. Bach
never quitted it again till his death ; and after him it was,
with very little alteration, the residence of all the Cantors
of the school down to the time of Moritz Hauptmann. The
view of the open place near the church, to which the school
buildings turn their front, and the houses which enclose two
sides of it, must be much the same now as they were then;
only the great stone fountain, which at that time graced the
middle of the quadrangle, has now disappeared.[24]

II.

THE THOMASSCHULE—DUTIES OF THE CANTOR—STATE OF MUSIC IN LEIPZIG.

LEIPZIG, at the time of which we are speaking, had three
public schools : those of St. Thomas and St. Nicholas,
and the Orphanage. The first of these was by far the
oldest, dating from the thirteenth century as a foundation
school under the Augustine monks (or Austin Friars). It
had not become a town school until four years after the
introduction of the reformed doctrines into Leipzig, when,

---

[22] According to the Ward-book of the town, preserved there in the Lower
Court of Justice.

[23] He was godfather to a son of Bach's, born in 1732.

[24] A view of this quadrangle, engraved on copper, is prefixed to the school
regulations printed in 1723. But the Thomasschule, in the autumn of 1877,
quitted this venerable and memorable home for a new building outside the
town.

in the year 1543 the Council took possession of the Monastery of St. Thomas and all its dependencies. The Monastery had had an *Alumneum*, or foundation school, in which a number of boys were maintained for the proper performance of the choral portions of the Liturgy and other parts of Divine worship. As a Protestant establishment the school was soon considerably extended. At first it had four classes and the same number of masters. When the St. Nicholas school (founded in 1511) could no longer contain the pupils that resorted to it, the Council decided that, at any rate till further orders, little boys should be admitted to the Thomas-schule. Their instruction was at first carried on by monitors called *Locates*, but under-masters were afterwards substituted for these. The school now consisted of seven classes, of which the three lowest, particularly, were for a long time very much crowded. The foundation school was kept up, and the number of scholarships had been gradually increased by a succession of endowments. For a time there were thirty-two, these increased to fifty-four, and at last, by the munificence of Privy Councillor Born, to fifty-five.[25]

The principal aim and end of the multiplication of the scholarships was the cultivation of church music. Formerly most of the Leipzig churches, and among them those of St. Thomas and St. Nicholas, had been under the management of the Augustine choir brethren; the Reformation clung to a close alliance between Church and school, and the foundation scholars of the Thomasschule were the means most obviously at hand for the musical requirements of the Protestant service. It is well known how urgently Luther has insisted on the use of music, and how he relied upon it greatly for securing the extension of the reformed doctrines.

Thus the Cantor of such an institution was a personage of much importance, doubly so since he also was required to take a share in the general course of instruction. This, in fact, was sufficiently recognised by the position he took

---

[25] Various documents referring to the school are preserved among the Archives of Leipzig. Stallbaum, Die Thomasschule zu Leipzig. Leipzig, 1839. See, too, his work, Ueber den innern Zusammenhang musikalischer Bildung, &c. Leipzig: Fritzsche, 1842.

among his colleagues. He ranked third in order,[26] and, while the other teachers had to give four hours of lessons daily, he, like the Rector, had only to give three. This moderate requirement which, as time went on, was even farther reduced, was the reason why at last eight masters were needed for seven classes. The hours of work were from seven to ten in the morning, and from twelve to three in the afternoon. Before the issue of the school regulations of 1634, the Cantor had daily to give a lesson in Latin grammar from seven to eight—Luther's Latin Catechism was used only on Saturday—in music from twelve to one; and from one to two Latin syntax with the third class. In accordance with those regulations, the hours of singing lessons were somewhat increased; those of the Latin lessons were considerably diminished, quite irrespective of the usual division into three lessons daily. Instruction in singing was now given on Monday, Tuesday, and Wednesday, at nine and at twelve; on Friday at twelve only. It comprised all the classes at once; that is to say, the four upper and original classes, to which alone the foundation boys belonged. On Thursday, at seven in the morning, the Cantor had to take the boys to church, and then was free for the rest of the day; on Saturday, at the same hour, he had to expound the Latin catechism to the third and fourth classes; on other days he had to give one Latin lesson to the third class. This plan of lessons was still kept up with remarkable regularity till the time of Bach's arrival, and for a time was carried on by him with undiminished regularity, excepting that he went to early church with the boys on Friday morning, and so had Thursday entirely free. The Cantor gave instructions in singing only to the four upper classes, his few lessons in

---

[26] In the Act of election one of the members of the Council designates the Cantor as *Collega Quartus*. This is an inaccurate statement, and can only have referred to the instruction in Latin (or what not) in which the Cantor did in fact rank below the third master; but in order of rank he came next to the *Conrector*, and he next to the *Rector*. (See Ordnung der Schule zu S. *Thomas*, 1723.) But when this mentions, besides the Rector, eight other masters, this certainly does not refer to Kuhnau's time. From the Acts of 1717 we learn that there were only seven masters besides the Rector, just as in Bach's time; there was no Quartus above the two Bachelors.

Latin to the third alone, the *Tertius*, as he was called,
being their master in other things. He, with the Rector,
the Conrector, and the Cantor, formed the circle of the
four upper masters (*superiores*), who held themselves aloof
from the others, the *Baccalaureus funerum, Baccalaureus
nosocomii* and the first and second *collaborators* (under
masters), or, as they were called after 1723, the *Quartus,
Quintus, Sextus*, and *Septimus*. The four upper masters,
including the Cantor, were also required to inspect the
foundation boys, and took this duty in weekly rotation.
They had them to live entirely with them, and to comply
with the regulations of the schoolhouse, which required
them to rise at five in the morning (at six in winter); to
dine at ten; sup at five in the afternoon; and go to bed
at eight.[27]

These were the Cantor's duties in the school itself. With
regard to the public, further duties arose from the position
he took as director of certain church choirs which were
formed of the foundation scholars. The two most important churches of the town were those of St. Thomas
and St. Nicholas. But in 1699 the church of the
Franciscan friars had been repaired and restored to use,
under the name of the New Church, and after Telemann's
appointment in 1704 had had music of its own. After
this, in 1711, the services, which for a while had entirely
ceased in St. Peter's church, had also been revived, so
that from that time the scholars of the Thomasschule had
had to supply the music every Sunday in four churches, and
on high festivals in the church of the Hospital of St. John.[28]
Thus they were divided into four choirs. The beginners
and weaker singers were assigned to St. Peter's, where only
chorales were sung; this choir probably also served the church
of St. John, as its festival and that of St. Peter would not

---

[27] Acts of the Council relating to the School of St. Thomas. Under
Gesner's wardenship these arrangements were somewhat modified. See
Gesetze der Schule zu S. Thomae, 1733.

[28] For this they received a special gratuity, at first consisting of food and
cakes, but afterwards of 13 thlrs. 3 gr., a year. Accounts of the Hospital are
preserved in the Town Hall at Leipzig.

interfere with each other.[29]   The rest of the singers were
pretty equally distributed; still the service in the New
Church was comparatively the easiest, since there the
scholars had only to sing motetts and chorales under the
direction of the choir Prefect; while on holy days, and
during the great Fair times other church music of a concerted
character was performed, and not by the boys.[30]   Since
Telemann's time the director of this had always been the
organist then in office, and the function of the Cantor of the
school extended no further than the selection of the hymns,
and perhaps of the motetts which were to be sung.[31]

He had nothing to do with the churches of St. Peter and
St. John, but the music in St. Thomas' and St. Nicholas'
was under his direction.   On ordinary Sundays a cantata
and a motett were performed in only one of the churches,
each in turn; the first choir sang the cantata under
the leading of the Cantor.   But on the first two days of
each of the great festivals, and at the New Year, Epiphany,
Ascension Day, and Trinity Sunday, and on the festival of
the Annunciation, concerted music was performed twice a
day, and in both churches at once, the plan being that
the first choir sang at St. Thomas' in the afternoon the same
cantata that it had performed in the morning at St. Nicholas',
and on the next holy day following sang at St. Thomas' in
the morning and St. Nicholas' in the afternoon: the second
choir taking the reverse order.   This second choir sang
under the conduct of its Prefect.[32]   The rehearsals of the
Sunday music took place in the church regularly on
Saturday after two o'clock vespers, and lasted till four
o'clock.

The direction and performance of music for wedding
festivals and funeral processions were also regarded as part
of the Cantor's official church duties, as being in direct

---

[29] Bach observes in a tabulated list of the four choirs which he drew up:
" And this last choir must also serve the *Petri Kirche*."   Documents of the
" Schuel zu St. Thomas," Vol. IV.

[30] See Appendix B, VII.   Sicul, *Neo-Annalium Lipsinesium Continuatio*, II.,
2nd Ed., 1719, p. 508.

[31] See Appendix B, VII.   [32] Sicul, ibid., 568.

connection with the divine services. If the funeral procession was of a grand and solemn character, the whole school—or at least the larger half of it, *i.e.*, the three first classes and the fifth—accompanied the body, and were accustomed first to sing a motett at the door where the deceased lay. While the bier was being carried to the churchyard, the boys marching in front of it sang a simple chorale, and only performed part-music on specially grand occasions. The Cantor had at all times to accompany the funeral train, and to decide on what should be sung, and as a rule he led the motett himself. The fact that the Cantor not unfrequently escaped this task, and left his musical duties to the choir Prefect, gives us a clear insight into various official utterances; for instance, Bach was specially enjoined in the deed he signed at all times to accompany his scholars in funeral processions as often as possible. As regarded wedding services, the use of music on such occasions was also very various, depending on the position and wishes of the persons chiefly concerned. In all cases the arrangement of the music lay with the Cantor, even when he himself took no part in it and it consisted merely of chorale singing. He had a representative in the Prefect of each choir, who could relieve him in many ways, not merely of the labour of leading, but also of the rehearsals. This custom prevailed so early as in the seventeenth century. After the school regulations of 1634 had instituted two hours of singing lesson for each of the first three days of the week, the Rector, Conrector, and Tertius petitioned the Council that the Cantor should be relieved of the singing lesson at twelve o'clock, and give a Latin lesson instead, since this singing lesson was very inconvenient to him by reason of his dinner hour, and he therefore but seldom presided at it; nor indeed was it needful that he should, as the boys could and did sing without him. The old order of instruction was, however, adhered to, and, as we have seen, it still continued in Bach's time. But so, to be sure, did the lax practice of the Cantor, which, in fact, gave rise to a complaint on the part of the Rector, Joh. Aug. Ernesti, that Bach held but one hour's singing class, whereas he ought to have held two, and that consequently the boys had not enough practice in music. But it was in the nature of things that an opportunity for the development of a certain independence should be afforded to the Prefects, for, irrespective of the fact that a school choir was not unfrequently required at weddings and festivities by personages connected with the school to sing during the banquet, the scholars also had to perform their perambulations at fixed seasons of the year with processional singing, and in both cases they had to rely upon themselves for the conduct of the singing.

The processions took place at Michaelmas and the New Year, and on St. Martin's and St. Gregory's Days (the 11th of November and 12th of March, N.S.).[33] On these occasions likewise the boys who could sing were divided into four choirs, each with a Prefect of its own, and apparently each of these had one of the four quarters of the city assigned to it as the scene of its performances. For instance, in 1718 the four choirs were thus distributed; the first included three basses, three tenors, two altos, and three trebles; the second, two voices for each part; the third, two basses, two tenors, two altos, and three trebles; the fourth, two basses, three tenors, two altos, and three trebles, and each choir had besides one or two torch-bearers. The Cantor's duty was restricted to selecting and composing the choirs, to determining generally what should be sung during the perambulations, and to superintending from time to time the rehearsals held for the purpose; all else was the Prefects' affair. The Prefects of the first two choirs especially held an important position.[34] They had to lead the motetts on Sundays and

[33] According to the report of the school visitation held in the year 1717. In the school regulations for 1723 a payment is mentioned for music performed in the summer ("Music-Gelde so im Sommer colligiret wird.") When and how these summer processions took place I am not able to say.

[34] It must be supposed that the four church choirs were somewhat differently constituted to those which were selected for the processional singing. These, indeed, cannot at all times have been equally strong. At the New Year only thirty-two foundation scholars sang, eight in each choir, an arrangement which had evidently survived from the time when there had been only thirty-two scholarships. This also explains the case when in the acts and school regulations here and there mention is made of the eight *concentores*.

festivals, and start the hymns in church; the Prefect of the second had to conduct the cantata on those festivals when the Cantor was not in the church, while the Prefect of the first could distinguish himself in his duties of leading the vocal music at wedding feasts and similar occasions, in taking his choir on its Michaelmas perambulation, and in representing the Cantor as conductor of the cantata, when he was prevented attending.[35]

If to all this we add that the Cantor was director of the music in the two other town churches, and required to inspect their organs and to superintend the town musicians —both singers and players—who had to bear a part in the church music, all his official duties have been enumerated. It cannot be said that they were oppressively heavy. Besides five lessons in Latin—from which, as we have seen, Bach soon released himself—he had to give seven singing lessons weekly; but of these he commonly left the afternoon practice to the Prefects. There was no lack of holidays at the Thomasschule. At each of the Fair times—*i.e.*, at Easter, Michaelmas, and the New Year—there was a week of whole holidays, and a second week when the afternoons were free. In the dog-days there were four weeks of half-holidays. Morning lessons were pretermitted on Saints' days, on the occasion of funeral orations in the university church, and on the quarterly academical speech days. A whole holiday was given in honour of the fête or name days of the four upper masters. Eight days were to be given up to the rehearsals for the processional singing at the New Year, St. Martin's, and St. Gregory's, but so arranged that morning lessons should be attended on Monday, Tuesday, Wednesday, and Saturday, and that "no one should sleep through them"— so runs the school regulation. So in point of fact not less than four weeks were given up to preparing for the New

---

[35] All these details are derived from original documents, of which a considerable number are preserved in the Archives of the ancient town of Leipzig. It has not been thought necessary to trouble the English reader with the press-marks and references in detail. The duty of starting the hymn properly belonged to the Cantor, but common custom had deputed it to the Prefects and the practice continued, like many others, in spite of the rules laid down by the school regulations of 1723.

Year's singing. In 1733 the Rector made an attempt to
restrict the preparation for St. Gregory's Day to six or eight
afternoons, for St. Martin's Day to four, and for the New
Year to twelve or at most fourteen. While these rehearsals
were going on all the Cantor's afternoon lessons were
omitted. Even his church duties did not continue the whole
year through. All through Lent no concerted church-music
was performed excepting on the festival of the Annunciation,
and the same was the case on the three last Sundays in
Advent.[36] Excepting on these occasions the Cantor had
to conduct one cantata every Sunday. It was only on high
festivals that he was very much occupied, particularly at the
time of the three holy seasons, when he had to provide two
sacred pieces for two holy days in each, and to give two
performances of each on both days, but the second Prefect
relieved him of one.

As has been already shown, the Cantor had a residence
given him free of rent; the rest of his income amounted to
about 700 thlrs.,[37] though, from its nature, it could not
be exactly estimated. The fixed salary as paid by the
Town Council was only 100 gülden (=87 thalrs. 12 ggr.),
and 13 thlrs. 3 ggr. in money for wood and lights. Besides,
the Cantor received—at any rate, in Bach's time—1 thlr.
16 ggr. on the Berger foundation and a similar sum on that
of Frau Berger and that of Adlershelm, with 5 ggr. yearly
from the Meyer foundation; he also had a variable sum
(3 thlrs. and 18 ggr., 2 thlrs. 1 ggr., 10 ggr. 6 pf., and so on)
forming a share in certain bequests to the school; and, finally,
in kind, 16 bushels of corn, 2 cords of firelogs, and from the
Church revenues two measures of wine at Easter, Whitsuntide and Christmas. Everything beyond this came from
incidental fees. These, of course, were derived chiefly from
the school money. Twice a week eight of the scholars went

---

[36] Leipziger Kirchen Staat, Das ist Deutlicher Unterricht vom Gottes
Dienst in Leipzig, wie es bey solchem so wohl an hohen und andern Festen,
als auch an denen Sonntagen ingleichen die gantze Woche über gehalten
wird," &c. Leipzig, 1710, p. 32. (This work is to be found at Halle in the
Ponickau Library.)

[37] As we learn from Bach's statement in his letter to Erdmann.

round the town with boxes to collect small donations from a
certain number of benefactors to the school—the "*runners'
money*," as it was called. Out of this 6 pfennigs were
deducted weekly as school payment for each scholar, and
this was divided among the four upper masters.[38] The
very small sum is accounted for by the principle observed in
the Thomasschule of bringing up by preference the children
of parents without means. Out of the money collected at
the Michaelmas and the New Year perambulations, after
one thaler was deducted for the Rector, the Cantor received
one-eleventh, one-eleventh more was taken for the Conrector,
and sixteen thirty-thirds for the singers; the Cantor then
took one quarter of the residue. The money collected in
the summer was divided in like manner. Out of what was
obtained on St. Gregory's Day the Rector first had one-tenth
to give an entertainment to the four upper masters, and out
of the residue the Cantor took one-third. Funeral money
was another source of income; if the whole school accompanied the procession, and if a motett was sung outside the
house of mourning, the Cantor received 1 thaler 15 ggr.;
without a motett he had 15 ggr.; for the larger half of the
school he took 1 thlr., for the smaller half 4 ggr., for a quarter
of the school 6 pf. The Cantor received 2 thlrs. for a
wedding service. An income which consisted mainly of
fees had of course its unsatisfactory side. It could never be
calculated on with certainty beforehand, and was dependent
on all sorts of accidents—nay, literally on wind and weather;
for, as Bach writes to Erdmann, "when the air of Leipzig is
wholesome there are fewer funerals," and consequently a
perceptible diminution in the Cantor's receipts. On this
theory the comfort of the Cantor would naturally increase
with the mortality of his neighbours. Many, indeed, strove
to deprive the Cantor of his dues by evading the prescriptions

---

[38] This was the custom under the wardenship of Rector Joh. Heinrich Ernesti
even after the school regulations of 1723 had decided that school money should
only be deducted for the foundation scholars at the rate of 12 pfennigs each
weekly. The state of affairs generally above described as existing at the time
of Bach's election is not in accordance with the rules laid down by the Council.
They by no means corresponded on every point.

of the law and breaking through ancient usages. Kuhnau had had to complain to the Council that many distinguished couples chose to be united without any music and singing, or even away in the country; that in those Sunday and weekday hours when formerly only solemn and profitable weddings had ever been permitted, now everybody was allowed to be married ; that many deceased persons even were quietly buried with only the smaller half of the school, and without music because they were ashamed of making this public, so that new compositions were hardly ever ordered for such occasions, even of him. However, it is very evident—in spite of many differences of opinion, both now and formerly—that there was a strong sense of the undignified attitude of an institution which allowed an important school and church official to derive his means of subsistence in groschen and pfennigs, which moreover were partly obtained by the agency of begging scholars. Rector Gesner was of opinion that " in the increasing conceit of youth it was much to be desired, since it would cut off the roots of many evil temptations, that the payment of the teachers should no longer be subtracted from the runners' money." Joh. Hein. Ernesti took the distribution of the funeral money into his own hands merely to avoid the complaints, vexation, and dissatisfaction which at all times had arisen on account of this money ; but in doing so he found much to put up with, and was presently traduced before the Council and the whole town as a most iniquitous man. But, in spite of everything, so much as this remains certain—the income of the Cantor allowed a man such as Bach, even with his numerous family, to live comfortably in the fashion of a simple artisan. We have evidence of this in his well-managed finances and the well furnished and fitted house he left behind him at his death.

With regard to its official conditions and labours, the post of Cantor to the Thomasschule may also be considered to have been a satisfactory one. Merely glancing at the surface of things, some dark shadows are certainly to be seen in the bright picture. From the beginning of the eighteenth century the school had been falling into frightful decay.

Part of the blame was due to the organisation. In com-
pliance with the conditions of the foundations round which
it had grown up, it was to be on one hand a nursery and
academy for church music, and on the other a *schola pauperum*.
A thorough and uniform intellectual training, with strict
and incessant supervision of the scholars, had become almost
impossible in the course of the many and various employ-
ments which arose from their musical vocation. And yet,
among children of the humbler classes, particularly those of
that generation, these were doubly needful; but for a long
time men really fit for their position had been wanting
among the masters. When Bach became Cantor he found
in the Rector of the school an old man who had held his office
for nearly forty years. Johann Heinrich Ernesti, born in
1652, was the son of a village minister of Saxony, and had
studied theology and philosophy in Leipzig ; in 1680 he was
appointed Sunday preacher at the church of St. Nicholas
and Conrector at the Thomasschule; in 1684 he became
Rector there, and in 1691 *Professor Poeseos* in the University
of Leipzig.[89] Though a learned man enough, he does not
seem to have been fitted to be at the head of a public school
of this kind ; he could keep neither masters nor scholars well
in hand. The college of masters lived in disunion and
jealousy, and but meagrely discharged their duties ; the
scholars fell into undisciplined and slovenly habits. All the
year round the school was a centre of disease, which took
the deeper root because the accommodation was to the last
degree limited—but for this, to be sure, the Rector was not
to blame.

Before the extension of the school buildings in 1731, the
second and third classes on one side, and the fifth, sixth,
and seventh classes on the other, were all held at once,
and in the same hall, by their respective masters.[40] The
result was that the number of scholars was rapidly diminishing. No doubt there were always plenty of applicants for
scholarships, since these provided a maintenance almost

---

[89] Sicul, Leipziger Jahrbuch, Vol. IV., p. 920, and Neue Zeitungen von
Gelehrten Sachen. Leipzig, 1729, p. 791.
[40] See Appendix B, VII.

free of cost and, besides this, a not inconsiderable income. Boys were attracted even from remote places to the foundation of the Thomasschule just as they were also to the richly endowed convent of St. Michael, at Lüneburg. But beyond this the better classes began to keep aloof from a place of such evil repute. This is very clearly proved by the class lists of the lowest classes. In Ernesti's early time they had often numbered one hundred and twenty scholars; in 1717 they show altogether no more than fifty-three. Those who did not send their children to the school of St. Nicholas preferred to send them to one of the many private schools, or kept a tutor—which was not too extravagant, for the price of private lessons in Leipzig at that time was not more than from twelve to eighteen pfennigs. The lowest classes of the Thomasschule were frequented only by boys of the very worst character, who wanted to make a profit of singing at funerals, and had to be kept by the masters from running barefoot after them, and who were not at all above begging about the town.[41] The Council could at length no longer shut their eyes to this wretched state of things, and determined on a visitation of the school and a revision of its statutes. For a while, however, it was content with good intentions; the Superintendent of the school appointed by the Council, Dr. Baudiss, warned them in 1709 that the school was in the direst need of the long-planned visitation, both as regarded the masters and the scholars. It was evident that the authorities were afraid to meddle, and let matters go on in their wild way.

At last, in 1717, the reform was begun apparently in real earnest; the visitation was carried out, and each master was required to write a report on the condition of the school, and to state his wishes as to any improvements. Here much that was far from pleasant came to light. The venerable Ernesti himself was obliged to confess: "On this opportunity I cannot conceal to what an extent a very sad state of things has hitherto obtained in the *Classes inferiores*, which, indeed, have almost ceased to exist. Also I cannot do otherwise

---

[41] According to a sketch penned probably by Gesner.

than write, with deep regret, of the condition at this time of the *Superiores*, and particularly of the *Chorus musicus*, that there is more of evil to be guarded against than of good to be hoped for." Then a few more years slipped away ; in 1721 a project was drawn up for a new school code, and in 1722 it was made public. In point of fact, little or no improvement was to be gained from it : Ernesti withstood to the utmost every kind of change. So far as it bore upon the distribution of the school and choir funds and other money matters, he read it as an insult to his old age, and an abridgement of his emoluments ; and in this he was seconded by the Cantor. It then seemed only reasonable not to hurt the old man's feelings, so the old state of things was allowed to continue, or rather, to grow worse and worse, till his death, October 16, 1729. On November 11 of the same year all the foundation scholars were cited to appear before the Council and earnestly admonished as to the unseemly irregularity of their lives and insubordination to the masters. On August 30, 1730, the Superintendent of the school, Dr. Stiglitz, the Counsellor of Appeal, reported a disagreement among the " Herren Praeceptoren," and that, because all and each did not duly fulfil his official duties, a falling-off in discipline, and disorders in the lives and conduct of the scholars were only too rife. The school, he said, was " fast going to ruin, and had almost run wild." Soon after this the number of scholars in the lower classes was so small that it was proposed to close them altogether.

Of course all these circumstances reacted on the character of the choirs. We could not, in any case, speak very favourably of their efforts in the seventeenth and eighteenth centuries. The bold statement with which J. A. Hiller opens his Anweisung zum Musikalisch richtigen Gesange (1774) — " Every one sings, and the greater number sing badly"—was an even more pointed truth fifty or a hundred years previously. At that time there was nowhere in Germany any true art of singing, much less could it have found a refuge in the school choirs. No available material for a good choir could have been found among uneducated boys' and immature men's voices, even if more

favourable conditions of general culture and higher views of
art had prevailed than those which, in the prospectus of
studies, considered that, next to the glory of God, the first
aim and end of the singing classes was the promotion of the
scholars' digestion.[42]   The universal and secular institution
of professional singing had, no doubt, done much to cherish
a feeling for music, and to preserve the connection between
the people and that branch of art ; but there is no doubt, too,
that the custom had done at least as much to hinder the
development of singing as an art.   Those long, slow perambulations, almost always in the most inclement seasons,
during which the scholars either sang from house to house
for hours in the cold foggy air, or else scampered in breath-
less haste up and down long flights of stairs, so as to sing
before the door of each separate inhabitant, were absolute
ruin to the voices.   Kuhnau spoke from an experience of
many years when he stated, in 1717, that the best singers,
and particularly the trebles, if they were not taken proper
care of in all these funerals, weddings, and perambulations,
lost their voices long before they had reached a moderate
proficiency in the art of using them.[43]   Now we must
remember, too, that these singers were untrained youths
who wasted all the money they earned by singing in
prohibited pleasures, and were often enfeebled and miserable from disease.   It cannot have been a very pleasing
task to work with such materials.

There was another thing which, before 1710, had brought
the choir of the Thomasschule completely to ruin.   Leipzig
was in dangerous proximity to Dresden and Weissenfels, two
courts much addicted to opera music.   In the prevailing
influx of foreigners it seemed to be a timely and promising
undertaking when, in 1693, Nikolaus Strungk opened an

---

[42] The *hora Cantoris* was always from twelve to one, thus immediately after
dinner (see Ungewitter, Die Entwickelung des Gesangunterrichtes in den
Gymnasien seit die Reformationszeit, Königsberg, in Pr. 1872, p. 11).   This, to
be sure, was not the case in the Thomasschule, since the dinner hour was
ten.   But even so refined a mind as Gesner's could go so far as to propose that
the dinner hour should be eleven, in order that the singing lesson might follow
it, as this was the healthiest form of exercise after eating.

[43] See Appendix B, VII.

opera-house of his own in the Brühl, in which at Fair time
"certain operas were performed." The Leipzig opera it is
true had not existed any longer than that at Hamburg,
and had certainly always stood far behind it, because
it was only open at certain short seasons of the year.
It was closed in 1729, and the opera-house pulled down.
Still, it had lasted long enough to produce a marked
influence for some few decades on the musical life of the
place. In the licence for its opening the Elector expressed
a hope that the Leipzig opera might contribute to the
advancement of art, and at the same time prove a sort of
preliminary school for the Dresden opera, meaning with
regard to the instrumentalists, since he could not use the
German vocalists among his Italians.[44] In the first place,
it is certain that the opera for a long period ruined the native
musical tendencies of Leipzig. The man who, perhaps unconsciously, dealt them the first decisive blow was Telemann;
and it is a singular coincidence that, after Kuhnau's death,
the Council exerted itself greatly to place him at the head of
an institution he had done so much to damage. It has been
mentioned that Telemann, while a student in Leipzig,
developed great talents as a poet, composer, and director
of opera. In 1704 he was appointed to the post of organist
and director of the music in the New Church. The church
choir was usually composed of scholars from St. Thomas';
and, as the Cantor of the school had been completely
ignored in the question, Kuhnau took offence, and not
without reason.

The direct connection between opera and sacred music
which thus took form in the person of Telemann at once
exerted its baleful influence. Formerly the St. Thomas'
choir had derived a by no means contemptible amount of
support from students with musical tastes and good voices,
some of whom had belonged to the school and still clung to
its traditions. Even when the opera was opened, and the
students who could sing joined it for amusement and profit,

---

[44] Geschichte des Theaters in Leipzig. Von dessen ersten Spuren bis auf
die neueste Zeit. Leipzig, 1818.

the custom survived among them of joining the choir in the Sunday and festival performances. But since one of themselves had written the operas for them, had formed a musical society among them, and was now directing the church music, they attached themselves to him, and left Kuhnau in the lurch.[45] The performances in the New Church found a rapidly increasing popularity; not only was a lively and operatic style of music to be heard there, but a fresh and excellent method of execution. The musical union which had originated these performances soon assumed important dimensions, and for twenty years or more it was the most important musical institution of Leipzig. Its directors were the organists of the New Church, and so it naturally followed that they were always closely connected. Among Telemann's successors, Melchior Hoffmann (1705 to 1715) seems to have presided over it at its most brilliant period. It often numbered as many as sixty members, who met twice a week, on Wednesdays and Fridays, from eight till ten in the evening, for general practice. Their performances, which only took place on grand occasions, or at Fair time, were always regarded as public events. The union kept up its connection with the opera through its directors, who also trod in Telemann's footsteps in composing for the Leipzig stage. The circle was in truth a jolly one; during the day they made music in pleasant society, and at night serenaded in the streets; besides, at the regular practisings, which were held in a coffee-house in the market place, and from which listeners were not excluded, there was a general cheerfulness which was in strong contrast to the school practisings. The hope which the Elector had expressed as to the Leipzig opera was to a great extent fulfilled by the Musical Union of the town. On various occasions when the ruling heads of Saxony and other provinces came to Leipzig they had to perform before them, and their best members found engagements in the bands of the Elector and other princes. Thus Pisendel and Blochwitz went to Dresden, Böhm to

---

[45] See Appendix B, VII.

Darmstadt, and the singers Bendler and Petzhold to Wolfenbüttel and Hamburgh. Others, who had previously been opera singers, when they came to Leipzig, joined the Union. But, on the whole, vocal music was less well represented than instrumental, as was very usual at that time.

For the performances in the New Church the vocal parts were allotted to single voices ; Stölzel, who belonged to the Union between 1707 and 1710, has handed down to us the names of the four singers at that time. The bass was Langmasius, afterwards Kammerrath at Eisenach ; the tenor was Helbig, afterwards secretary to the Government at Eisenach, and a writer of cantata texts ;[46] the treble was Markgraf, who, at a later period was Conrector in Augsburg ; and, as alto, Stölzel thinks he remembers a certain Krone, who died at Weimar as private musician to the Duke. Hoffmann himself was an excellent musician, who endeavoured to extend the circle of musical knowledge ; in 1710, he is said to have made a tour of two years' duration in the interests of art, and to have visited England ; in the meantime his place was taken in the musical union by Pisendel, a famous violinist.[47] Hoffmann's successor was Johann Gottfried Vogler, "a lively composer and good violinist," as Telemann says. A certain " liveliness " appears to have characterised his life as well as his music ; he ran into debt, and in 1719, at the time of the Michaelmas fair, he secretly vanished from the town.[48] The affair attracted much notice, and he seems to have been caught and brought back, for he received his salary up to the first quarter of the next year, inclusive ; but that for the second quarter was withheld because he had made away with some instruments belonging to the church, and had not yet restored them. At the third quarter his place was taken by Georg Balthasar Schott, who is already known to us as a competitor with Bach for the post of Cantor to the Thomasschule.

---

[46] See p. 12.

[47] Mattheson, Grosse Gen. Basschule, p. 173. Ehrenpf., p. 117. Sicul, op. cit., p. 414. Gerber, L., I., col. 656.

[48] " *Continuation* derer Leipzigischen Jahrbücher von *Anno*, 1714, bis. 1728." MS. in fol. in the town Library at Leipzig ; Pressmark, Vol. 18.

So long as the musical union of students and the opera gave the tone to the music of Leipzig, the Cantor fell on evil days. The lack of sympathisers and assistants was all the more keenly felt, because it was always most conspicuous on festivals and at Fair times, when he was in greatest need of reinforcement, and wanted to appear in a favourable light before strangers ; for it was difficult to see what he could do with a wild mob of dirty schoolboys who had shouted themselves hoarse in the streets, and a few very mediocre town musicians. Pieces of a high class could no longer be sung at all ; if he ever attempted them the performance was such a miserable result that he could only feel himself shamed before the audience. Formerly the Town Council had lent some assistance to the formation of the choir. In the time of Johann Schelle they had always four or five more foundation scholars to be maintained in the school than the revenues allowed, and as there were ample means for the purpose, this bounty benefited the music. But when Schelle died, and his wife was allowed to provide the food for the scholars, the Council, to assist her, removed these supernumeraries, and she had fewer to provide for, with the same money. Kuhnau was indefatigable in his exertions to restore the former state of things, or, at any rate, some substitute for it ; he represented that an increase of the musical resources of the school had never been more necessary, and the Superintendent supported his statement, but without any result worth mentioning. He could not even obtain that two trebles should be assigned to sing church music only and released from all other vocal duties. Since they then could have no share in the funeral and "runners'" money, some compensation would be indispensable, and the Council would not vote an equivalent. They granted a permission to release two boys each year from the New Year's perambulations, which were the most injurious, and they were to have in compensation four gülden a year for the two.[49] This was the end of it. Obviously the interest in supporting the

---

[49] Accounts of the churches of St. Thomas and St. Nicholas.

music of St. Thomas and St. Nicholas was waning when so
much better could be heard in the New Church.

After Vogler had withdrawn, Kuhnau made a last attempt
to recover the lost ground. He represented that the tendencies of the " *Operists* " in the New Church were destroying all feeling for true church music among the citizens;
that the organ was belaboured first by one and then by
another pair of " unwashed hands," since the director of the
music either could not play or, after the manner of the
" Operists," was constantly away. It would be better that
a really permanent organist should be appointed, and that
the direction of the music should be given to the Cantor of
St. Thomas'. Then every Sunday music could be properly
performed in the three churches alternately, just as now was
done in two; and when, on festivals, cantatas were to be
given in all three churches, as heretofore, the Cantor could
very well give these also, since he would then have at his
command a large number of students, and could distribute
them among the churches according to his judgment. The
students must have a gratuity in order that they might be
ready and willing in the matter, and a student might also be
appointed as organist in the New Church. If, however, the
Council would not consent to all this, some means must at
least be thought of to attach those young men who quitted
the school for the University to the choir of St. Thomas.[50]
But again Kuhnau wrote in vain. Schott was appointed
organist and director of the music, and all went on in the
old way. Kuhnau once more made a timid attempt at
opposition in 1722, when he made difficulties as to
lending the scholars for the Passion Music in the New
Church, but he was ruthlessly called to order by the Council.

To put a climax to the confusion the St. Thomas' boys
caught the opera fever. This was, indeed, not to be wondered
at when they had the temptation perpetually before their
eyes. As soon as they had attained a certain proficiency in
singing and music in the school, they pined to escape from
its narrow bounds and find themselves at liberty, dreamed of

---

[50] See Appendix B, VII.

artists' laurels and ceased to be of any use where they were.
If they then could make acquaintance with any operatic
impresario, the most advanced among them could obtain
engagements; they straightway demanded to be released
from their school indentures, and if this were not granted
they ran away, returning with some opera troupe at Fair
time, and exciting the envy of their former schoolmates by
their appearance on the boards and at the New Church. A
treble named Pechuel had gone, by permission of the
Council, from time to time to Weissenfels to perform in the
opera; in the course of time he wished to extend these
excursions and to take a leading part at Naumburg. The
Council forbade this, and then the young genius broke his
bonds and ran away; two years later a bass named Pezold[51]
followed his example. A respectable citizen of Leipzig had
aided and abetted them both, and it is not hard to see on
which side the sympathy of the public was. When Kuhnau
died the music of the Thomasschule was at the lowest
possible ebb, and the twelve months of interregnum which
followed before another Cantor was appointed certainly did
nothing to mend matters.

It is impossible that Bach should not have been exactly
informed of all these circumstances, as he was intimately
acquainted with Kuhnau, and had been in Leipzig several
times. As has been said, he doubted for a long time
whether he should do wisely in becoming Kuhnau's
successor, and in more than one respect these doubts were
well founded. Did Leipzig then offer him some special
temptation as a musician, some opening and incitement to
profitable effort in his art? It is difficult to answer this
question in the affirmative. There were no remarkable
musicians there at the time; the only one, besides Kuhnau,
who had done anything important in his own branch
of art was Daniel Vetter,[52] who had died two years before,

---

[51] Probably the same who afterwards distinguished himself in the Musical
Union.

[52] "Herr Vetter, our able Organist here." See the report on the Organist
of St. Paul's church in Die andere Beylage zu dem Leipziger Jahrbuche,
1718, p. 198.

as Organist to the church of St. Nicholas. This absence of fellow artists would certainly have been no great grief to Bach, a man of such vigorous productivity and such emphatic independence, if only he had had at his command some means and resources worthy of him, to enable him to do himself justice. Leipzig was a populous town, a centre of resort, and stirred by various interests; but a focus of art, such as Dresden, Vienna, Munich, or even Hamburg, it certainly was not. It was, no doubt, to some extent musical, but that was common to all Germany. No special effort on the part of the better class of citizens to develop anything truly artistic is at that time discernable; it was not till Bach was growing old, and it was too late, so far as he was concerned, that a different spirit began to show itself. It was only among the student class that any love and taste for music were manifested. Kuhnau might, indeed, have succeeded in attaching the Academic youth to himself if he had been less hesitating and less conservative; even side by side with Telemann's flourishing musical union it might have been accomplished, if only he had known how to grasp the matter; but he did not. He saw Fasch—who for many years was his pupil—founding a second Musical Union among the students, which established itself as securely in the University Church as Telemann's had done in the New Church.[53]   The new organ, which was finished in the autumn of 1716, was entrusted to a very diligent musician in the person of Gottlieb Görner. It cannot now be ascertained whether the Musical Union directed by Görner was that founded by Fasch, or whether, indeed, that society survived to his time; we only know for certain that Görner was at the head of such a Collegium musicum when Bach was appointed Cantor.[54]

Görner, who was born in 1697, had been made organist of St. Nikolaus after Vetter's death. When, in the autumn of 1729, old Christian Gräbner died, he succeeded him as organist to St. Thomas'. He was thus, to a certain extent,

---

[53] See the document by Bach, given presently in the account of his quarrel with the University.

[54] Das jetzt lebende und florirende Leipzig, 1723, 8, p. 59.

under Bach's direction; but it did not at all meet Görner's views to give way to the greater man; on the contrary, he boldly put himself forward as his rival. When, in the winter of 1727-8, there was a public mourning, he asked permission to continue, notwithstanding, his musical gatherings. For—said he—in his Union the students coming from the school brought to perfection any skill they might have acquired there, and were enabled to make themselves heard at the performances at the Fair times, and thus found their way to places as cantors and organists.[55] Thus when the scholars left Bach's hands they received the finishing polish from Görner! His audacious pretensions are all the more singular, because he seems to have been in fact but a very mediocre musician. A contemporary Leipzig musician, Johann Adolf Scheibe, in the year 1737, recorded a very bitter opinion of him, which may, no doubt, have been influenced by personal feeling, but cannot, on the whole, be very far from the truth: "He has been engaged in music for many years, and it might be supposed that experience would have brought him into the right way; but nothing can be more disorderly than his music. The real meaning of the different modes of writing according to their distribution (of parts) is wholly unknown to him. Rules are things he must daily dispense with, for he knows them not. He can never set a pure line (of music), and the grossest blunders grace—or disgrace—every bar. In a word he can depict disorder in his music to perfection." Then, as to his character: "He is so completely possessed by conceit and rudeness that through the first he does not know himself, and through the second asserts his pre-eminence among a large number of his equals." On a subsequent occasion Scheibe still further embitters this verdict and adds: "Nor would he be even what he is if a certain man had not done everything for him. And the result he has shown is that on a certain occasion when he could and ought to have proved himself grateful, he was anything rather than grateful,

---

[55] "Ephoralarchiv," at Leipzig: "Trauer Feiern beim Absterben der Sächsischen Fürsten," Vol. I.

but repaid the kindness that had been done him by a piece of treacherous spite."[56] Who is meant by this benefactor does not appear; but it throws a significant light on the state of affairs in Leipzig that such a man as Görner should have played his part by the side of Bach for a whole generation. And at the University Church he had planted his foot so firmly that Bach could not succeed in getting him removed in spite of his own powerful name and influence.

We will now contemplate Bach's position in all its aspects. This time, more than ever before, he had taken a step into the unknown; he had made the venture—to use his own words—in the name of the Most High. The craving and need of his artist soul to live once more under circumstances where there was work worth doing to be done for music seemed likely to find some satisfaction in Leipzig. The downward step from Capellmeister to Cantor—for so it was deemed at that time—was made easier to him by the high position the Cantor of St. Thomas' held among musicians. Seth Calvisius, Hermann Schein, Tobias Michael, Sebastian Knüpffer, Johann Schelle, and Johann Kuhnau, who had held the appointment in succession during one hundred and twenty-five years, had all been distinguished—some of them highly distinguished— practical musicians and learned men. To continue the series was an honour, and Bach felt it as such. Besides, the post gave him some tangible advantages, and it would seem that it was this which turned the balance. The place was endowed and the duties were light; at the same time this did not mean that for their complete fulfilment a man of merit and of mettle was not required; but there was no overwhelming load of official work; Bach would have time enough for his own occupations. Finally, he would now be enabled to give his sons a superior education without too great a pecuniary sacrifice. How near his heart this matter lay is shown by a little circumstance. On December 22, 1723, when he had been about six months in Leipzig,

---

[56] Johann Adolf Scheibe, Critischer Musikus, New Ed., Leipzig, 1745, p. 60. Görner's name is not mentioned, nor that of the place; but there is ample evidence that he and Leipzig are meant. The passage was written in 1737.

he applied to the university to have his son, Wilhelm
Friedemann, then thirteeen years old, entered on the
register as a future student (academic citizen), although
it was not till April 5, 1729, that he actually became a
member of the University.[57] Such an early nomination was
not unheard-of; it even sometimes happened that a matri-
culation at the University was a christening gift from a
godfather. Bach appears to have given it to his favourite
son as a Christmas-box. If against these advantages he
could not but weigh the dark side of the appointment, he
no doubt hoped that the great fame he enjoyed and the
influence of his strong individuality would bring the choir
into better condition, and that by degrees he might get
the management of all the musical concerns and under-
takings of Leipzig into his own hands. However great the
talents of his predecessors, in celebrity he beyond a question
stood far above them; the name of Bach was famous far
and near—the great player, who came from a Prince's court,
and was the friend of Princes. Indeed, he not only continued to hold the honorary post of Capell-meister at Cöthen,
but in the very year of his removal to Leipzig the same
honour was conferred on him by the Court of Weissenfels.[58]

III.

BACH'S OFFICIAL DUTIES AS CANTOR, HIS DISPUTE WITH
THE TOWN COUNCIL, AND ENDEAVOURS TO IMPROVE THE
CONDITION OF THE MUSIC.—HIS LETTER TO ERDMANN.—
GESNER'S APPOINTMENT AS RECTOR OF THE SCHOOL.

THE direction of the music in the University Church was
not inseparable from the office of Cantor to St. Thomas';
it was, however, customary, and had been from time
immemorial allowed by the Council, that he should have
the charge of it. So long as the University Church was

[57] " Bach, Wilhelm Friedemann, *Vinario-Thuringensis*," under the heading
of *Depositi, nondum inscripti*, of December 22, 1723.

[58] Walther, Lexicon, p. 64. Among the deeds of appointment of the Weissen
fels court from 1712 to 1745, which are preserved among the State Archives at
Dresden, all those belonging to 1723 are wanting, including, of course, that of Bach.

opened only on the three great festivals, on the festival of
the Reformation, and for the quarterly speeches, no severe
tax was thus laid on the Cantor. But since 1710 a regular
Sunday service had been performed there, and consequently
the post of the director of the music became very important.
Kuhnau had been able to secure it for himself, though, in
the first instance, Fasch had attempted to establish there a
musical union that should be independent of the Cantor.
By great efforts and sacrifices Kuhnau had succeeded in
exploding this scheme ; he declared himself fully prepared to
fulfil these new duties without any emolument, and this was
a consideration[59] to which the University was keenly alive.
After Kuhnau's death Görner for a time took his place as
director of the music at the University Church. Bach's
accurate comprehension of the position is shown by the fact
that he made it his first business to get this function out of
Görner's hands. Unless he could create for himself a strong
following among the University students, there could be no
prospect of his moulding the musical affairs of the town
according to his own views. His appointment was confirmed to him on the 13th of May. The first church cantata
he composed as Cantor of St. Thomas' he conducted on the
30th of May, the first Sunday after Trinity, before he took
his place in the school, thus, as it were, inaugurating his
musical labours as Cantor. He had already begun his
duties as Musical Director to the University a fortnight
earlier, on Whit Sunday—at any rate, he had supplied them
with a composition of his own.[60] But Görner knew very
well what the upshot must be, and had determined to save
as much for himself as possible. On the four great festivals
and the quarterly speeches he knew he must retire into the
background ; the Cantor's claims were too strongly supported
by ancient rights of custom ; but it was different with regard
to the regular Sundays and the other church holidays. It
appears that Görner had set it very clearly before the
University that, with all his duties in the churches of St.

---

[59] See Appendix B, VII.

[60] See Bach's detailed statement as to his quarrel with the University,
towards the end of it.

Thomas and St. Nicholas, the Cantor could not always provide with due punctuality for the performance of the service
in St. Paul's, which began when the others were only about
half over. At any rate, Görner still continued to officiate in
the New service, as it was called, as Musical Director to the
University.

In the third place there were the extraordinary University
high days to be considered. With regard to these Bach
took his stand on the ground that they had been customary
long before the arrangement was made for the New service,
and that the Cantor had always presided over them; that,
consequently, they constituted part of his duties, and he
proceeded to act on this basis. On Monday, August 4,
1723, the birthday of Duke Friedrich II., of Sax-Gotha—a
prince who had specially distinguished himself in promoting
the cause of learning and of the church—was solemnly
kept; a Bachelor of Philosophy, named Georg Grosch,[61]
delivered a discourse, *De meritis Serenissimi Friderici in rem
litterariam et veram pietatem;* which was followed by a Latin
ode composed and conducted by Bach—"an admirable piece
of music," says the Leipzig chronicler; ."so that this
solemnity was concluded to everybody's satisfaction by
about eleven o'clock in the morning."[62] Heinrich Nikolaus
Gerber, who in 1724 went to the Leipzig University, at a
later date told his son that he had heard many concerts
at that time under Bach's direction.[63] As any music but
church music is out of the question, and as Bach did not
direct any Union of his own, this can only mean academic
performances.[64]

Meanwhile Bach's vigorous self-assertion from the very
first, by no means settled the matter at once. Görner
evidently was a favourite with those who gave the cue

---

[61] Grosch was a native of Gotha, and in 1724 became the Prince's tutor:
he subsequently held various livings in that province. (Archives of Gotha.)

[62] Vogel; Continuation Derer Leipzigischen Jahrbücher.

[63] Gerber, L., I., col. 491.

[64] In the *ACTA LIPSIENSIUM ACADEMICA*, Leipzig, 1723, p. 514,
Bach is called "*Cantor* and *Collegii Musici Director.*" Possibly *Collegii* is a
slip of the pen or a misprint for *chori;* at any rate, it is quite certain that the
St. Thomas' choir is what is meant.

to the University, and he also received an *honorarium* out
of the fund set aside for the Cantor's services. At last,
Bach, who knew very well how to reckon, and was particularly precise in money matters, thought this beyond
a joke. After swallowing the affront for two years with
as good a grace as he might, he resolved that, even if he
could not take the whole direction out of the hands of Görner,
who was tough to deal with, he could at any rate secure his
income. He, therefore, addressed a petition to the King-
Elector at Dresden, by which he thought he should obtain
full security for his interests, all the more as he was in
favour at court : —

MOST SERENE,
MOST POTENT KING AND ELECTOR,
MOST GRACIOUS SOVEREIGN,
May your Royal Majesty and Most Serene Highness graciously
permit me to represent, with the humblest submission, with regard to
the Directorship of the Music for the Old and New services of the
church in the Worshipful University of Leipzig, that, together with the
salary and usual fees, they had always been associated and joined with
the place of Cantor at St. Thomas', even during the lifetime of my
predecessor ; that after his death, and while the post was vacant, they
were given to the Organist of St. Nicholas, Görner ; and that, on my
assuming my office, the direction of the so-called Old service was
restored to me again, but the payment was withheld and assigned, with
the direction of the New service, to the above-mentioned organist of St.
Nicholas ; and, although I have sued duly to the Worshipful University,
and made application that the former regulations may be restored, I have
nevertheless not been able to obtain anything more than that I should
have half of the salary, which formerly amounted to twelve gülden.

Nevertheless and notwithstanding, Most Gracious King and Elector,
the Worshipful University expressly required and assumed that I
should appoint and direct the music for the Old service, and I have
hitherto fulfilled this function ; and the salary which has been given to
the director of the New service did not formerly belong to it but
properly to the Old services ; and at the same time the New were
connected with the Old ; and, if I were not to dispute the right of
directing the New service with the organist of St. Nicholas, still
the retention of the salary which formerly and at all times—nay, even
before the new cultus was instituted—belonged to the Cantor, is extremely painful and prejudicial to me : and church patrons are not
wont to dispose otherwise of what it assigned and fixed as the regular
payment of a church servant, either withholding it altogether, or
reducing it, while I have already for more than two years been forced

to fulfil my duties concerning the above-mentioned Old service for nothing. Now, if my humble suit and petition may find favour with your Royal Majesty and Most Serene Highness, you will graciously communicate it to the Worshipful University, to the end that they may restore the former state of things, and assign to me, with the direction of the Old service that also of the New, and more particularly the full salary of the Old service and the enjoyment of the fees accruing from both. And for such Royal and gracious favour,

I shall ever remain,

Your Royal Majesty's and Serene Highness's

Most humble and obedient

LEIPZIG, *Sept.* 14, 1725.　　　　JOHANN SEBASTIAN BACH.

Addressed to the Most Serene and Most Potent Prince and Lord— The Lord Friedrich Augustus, King of Poland (Here follow all his Titles) my Most Gracious King, Elector, and Sovereign.[65]

Bach was not deceived in his presumption. On the 17th of September a requisition was forwarded from the Ministry at Dresden to the University to relieve the petitioner or to adduce their reasons to the contrary. The expedition brought to bear on the matter was so great that there seems not even to have been time to read Bach's petition; in the references to his statement of grievances there are inaccuracies by which the circumstances are placed in a false light.[66]

The University attempted to justify itself in every particular, and caused Bach to be informed that they had forwarded their version of the case. Bach, however, had reason to suppose that in this statement the affair had not been truly represented, and to forefend an unfavourable decision he wrote a second time to the king:—

THE MOST SERENE,

MOST POTENT KING AND ELECTOR,

MOST GRACIOUS SOVEREIGN,

After that your Royal Majesty had most graciously been pleased to issue your orders in the matter of the request preferred by me on the one part, and by the University of this town on the other part

The said University submitted the required very humble report, and duly notified me of its departure; and I, on the other hand, for my further need, deem it necessary to observe that if my most humble petition may find favour with your Royal Majesty and Serene Highness you will communicate to me a copy of the said report, and be

---

[65] This letter is in the Archives at Dresden, and was obligingly copied for me by Herr Moritz Fürstenau.

[66] This and the following documents are in the Archives at Leipzig.

graciously pleased to wait, and defer your Sovereign determination till I again have made the necessary representations; and I will not fail to hasten with them as much as possible, and for the whole of my life remain with the deepest submission,

Your Royal Majesty's and Serene Highness's
Most obedient and humble

LEIPZIG, *Nov.* 3, 1725.   JOHANN SEBASTIAN BACH.

[Addressed as before.] [67]

This petition was granted. He then preferred a thorough refutation of the justification drawn up by the University. The document is extremely interesting, for it displays, as no other does, Bach's keen and business-like intelligence and incisive mode of expressing himself:—

MOST SERENE AND MOST POTENT
KING AND ELECTOR,
MOST GRACIOUS SOVEREIGN,

I beg to acknowledge, with the humblest thanks, your Royal Majesty's and Serene Highness's favour in graciously condescending to allow to be communicated to me the copy of that document in which the University of this place objected to my accusation brought against it, as concerning the direction of the music in the Old and New services in the Church of St. Paul, and the salary belonging to the former of the two, which has hitherto been withheld. Although I am of opinion that the University will at once indemnify me, as is proper, and grant my well-founded suit without further formality, it must yet be examined how they make various excuses, and give themselves the trouble to make themselves out innocent, that is to say :—

(I.) That I had stated without reason that the direction of the music for the Old and New services was necessarily connected with the office of Cantor to St. Thomas'—nay, that the University in giving the above-mentioned Direction was *in libertate naturali*, whereby, however, they cannot contest with me the direction of the Old divine service, nor can they deny that on account of the fulfilment of those duties, they paid me an *honorarium*. Moreover,

(II.) That my representations that I had hitherto had to do my duty for nothing surprised them all the more, since it was clear from the *Rationes Rectorales*, that at all the Quarterly *Orationes*, and at the three great Festivals, as well as the *Festum Reformationis Lutheri* a special and profitable *honorarium* of 13 thlrs. 10 gr. was paid me, and that I have hitherto received it. Also

(III.) That I have hitherto not generally presided in person at the Quarterly *Orationes*, but, as the register shows, have allowed the Prefects to direct the singing of the motetts. Likewise

---

[67] This letter is autograph throughout. The seal seems to be the rose with a crown. See Vol. I., p. 39, note 76.

(IV.) That, in consequence of his Sunday and holy day duties, the Cantor of St. Thomas' is quite unable to undertake at the same time the direction of the music in the University Church without prejudice to it, and confusion; since he would also have, at very nearly the same hour, to direct the music in the churches of St. Thomas and St. Nicholas. Especially

(V.) It is very expressly stated that a new *honorarium*, of 12 fl. was newly granted to my predecessor on account of the direction of the music for the new service. Moreover

(VI.) That so many difficulties were made on the part of the Council with reference to the St. Thomas' scholars and the town musicians that the University availed itself of the services of its students, and was forced to consider of the selection of another individual who might in his own person preside unhindered over the direction of the music, and who could better maintain that good understanding with those students who refused to assist the Cantor without additional payment. To which it was added

(VII.) That during the long vacancy of the office after the death of the former Cantor, the University had given over the direction of the music for the New service to Johann Gottlieb Görner, and assigned to him the new salary devoted to it of 12 fl., so that this salary had nothing to do with the former direction of the Old service, but was a new institution.

But, Most Gracious King, Elector, and Sovereign, these objections brought forward by the University are not founded on fact, and are quite easy to refute. For, in the first place—

(I.) As to the connection of the New Service with the Old, I did not say that the connection was a necessary one, only that the direction of the latter had formerly been combined with that of the former, and it was not for me to inquire as to the power and liberty of joining or separating them; that can be settled in the proper place: On the contrary, I admit that the direction of the Old service, according to previous custom (as set forth) in the very humble report would be granted and vouchsafed to me. But, if this were so, the Direction of the music at the solemn *Acts*, ceremonies of the universities, of conferring Doctors' degrees, and others, which take place in St. Paul's church, with the fees accruing from them, ought not to be withheld from me, because all this, at any rate as regards the music, was in direct connection with the Old service, according to custom before the New service was instituted. In the next place

(II.) It surprises me not a little how the University can refer to a profitable *honorarium* of 13 thlrs. 10 gr., which I ought to have received from them, and deny and contradict that I have hitherto performed the work for nothing, since the *honorarium* is something apart from the salary, which is 12 fl., and this gratuity does not include the salary; how too, my complaint can have been regarded as concerning not the *honorarium* but the ordinary salary of 12 fl. attached to the Old service, which, however, has hitherto been withheld from me—nay, since it can be proved from the *Rationes Rectorales* put forward by the University itself, that this honorarium, which ought to have amounted to 13 thlrs. 10 gr., has not once been paid in full, but that each quarter the two beadles, as they could depose on oath, have paid to me instead of the 20 gr. 6 pf., as set down in the *Rationes Rectorales*, no more than 16 gr. 6 pf.; and at the three high festivals, as also on the *Festum Reformationis Lutheri*, each time instead of 2 thlrs. 12 gr. no more than one thaler. Thus, instead of 13 thlrs. 12 gr. altogether, only 6 thlrs. 18 grs. in the year; also my predecessors, Schelle and Kuhnau (witness the attestations of their widows *sub lit.* A and B), received a no larger sum for the quarterly and festival music, and consequently never gave receipts for any larger sum, and yet in the extract from this *Rationes Rectorales* a much higher *quantum* is set down. That

(III.) I have frequently not attended the quarterly *Orationes*, and that the register of October 25, 1725, proves this, is of no importance; for, from the month and the date, it appears that the entry was made in the register after I had previously complained against the University, while before that time nothing had been registered against me; thus my absence did not happen more than once or twice, and then, indeed, of *impedimenta legitima*, since I was travelling on necessity, and, in particular, several times had business in Dresden; moreover, the Prefects are appointed under the Cantor to the before-mentioned quarterly music, so that my predecessors, Schelle and Kuhnau, never conducted these in person, but the singing of the motetts was arranged and directed by the Prefects.

(IV.) Neither can it have any foundation when the University urges that the attendances for the music in the two churches are not compatible for one person; for certainly the instance which might be given of Görner, the Organist of St. Nicholas' Church in this town, is far more striking, since it was even less compatible for him to direct the music in both churches in his own person, because the Organist had not only in the same way to be at one and the same time at the Church of St. Nicholas and in that of St. Paul, to attend to the music before and after the sermon, but also had to play the organ even to the very last hymn, while on the other hand the Cantor, after having performed his music, can go out, and need not stay for the hymns at the close of divine service; and the late Kuhnau in his time did both quite well, without prejudice and confusion, and in the church, where no formal music is ordered, common music can be directed perfectly well by the *Vicarii* and *Præfecti*.

(V.) As to what particularly regards the 12 fl. under discussion, the University can never again assert with reason that they began giving it to my predecessor as an independent gratuity on account of the direction of the music in the New service. The state of the case is rather that the

12 fl. having been from time immemorial the salary for the arrangement of the music in the Old service, my predecessor, in order to avoid other consequences disadvantageous to himself which might be feared from the division of the director's duties, directed the music in the New service for nothing, and never demanded a penny for it, and thus never before enjoyed the said new gratuity of 12 fl. Nay, not only by Kuhnau but also by Schelle, and even before that, before anybody had ever thought of the New services, a receipt was always given for these 12 fl. And, as the widows of Schelle and Kuhnau, in their attestations, *sub lit.* A and B, distinctly state, the 12 fl. were always the regular salary for the arranging of the music in the Old service. The University cannot escape making public the above-mentioned receipts. Therefore

(VI.) The salary connected with the music of the Old service cannot be tampered with, notwithstanding that the ordering of the New service was not well received by the students, and they would not assist the Cantor for nothing. Now, while this can be neither proved nor gainsaid, and it is well known that students who are lovers of music are always ready and willing to assist, I, for my part, have never had any unpleasantness with the students; they are wont to assist me in both vocal and instrumental music without hesitation, and to this hour gratis and without payment. Moreover

(VII.) If the *directorium* of the music in the New service at that time and as far as regards Görner himself was to remain *in statu quo;* if, besides, no one had any doubt that a new salary could be granted on account of such new arrangements; then the salary of 12 fl. hitherto assigned to him was in no respect a new institution, nor assigned to the direction as anything new, but this was withdrawn from the *directorium* of the music in the Old service and not received by Görner until subsequently, during the vacancy of the post of Cantor at St. Thomas'; and when Görner had the new direction assigned to him it was granted to that new direction.

All the foregoing had even before been proved, nay, it is all a matter of notoriety to those who hitherto have had to do with the music in both churches, and by their deposition it could be still further confirmed and made public. In fact, I feel compelled here and now to adduce this particular circumstance : that two years since, when I took occasion to speak of the direction to the then *Rector Magnificus Junius* and he wanted to demonstrate the contrary to me out of a written account-book, which probably was a *Liber Rationum Rectoralium*, it must needs happen that on the page he opened appeared written the account, and my eyes fell on the plain words, " To Schelle, *pro Directorio Musices*, 12 fl., *Salarium;* " and this entry was then and there shown and pointed out by me to the *Rector Magnificus Junius*.

Finally, the University have already granted and offered me the half of the payment of these 12 fl. through *D. Ludovicus*, who during last summer administered the rectoral affairs, and they certainly would not have done this had they not been convinced that the matter rests on sound foundations. Hence this alteration seems to me all the harder, when they choose to ignore all salary whatever, and to deprive me of it altogether. Afterwards, too, I expressly mentioned this offer, in my very humble memorial, but the University, in their counter-statement, pass over this point, and have answered nothing to it. Thus, in fact, by their silence the ground of my pretension and the justice of my case are established afresh and, as they themselves have been con‧vinced, are tacitly acknowledged.

Since the University, according to their own confession, offer me, for the *Quartal-Orationes*, 3 thlrs. 10 gr. per annum, and for the three high festivals and the Reformation Festival, a peculiar *honorarium* of 10 thlrs. per annum, thus making in all 13 thlrs, 10 gr. by reason of the custom already referred to; and as I, from the time when I entered into my duties under the University at Whitsuntide, 1723, until the end of 1725, which makes 2¾ years, ought altogether to have received 36 thlrs. 18 grs. 6 pf., and have not received so much, but only 11 thlrs., in payment for many festival performances, and 7 thlrs. 13 grs. 6 pf. for eleven *Quartal-Orationes*, in all 18 thlrs. 13 gr. 6 pf.; I thus have to require 18 thlrs. 5 gr., the regular salary of 12 fl. for 2¾ years—*i.e.*, 33 fl. remaining owing. They, the University, since they are willing to agree as to the salary, and since they have already offered to give me the half of it, cannot *eo ipso* regard my request as unjust and unfounded, but must admit it; also, since they in their humble report pass this over in silence, and thus once more tacitly admit the facts to me, and moreover, have not been able to adduce the smallest thing of any importance—when my most submissive prayer is presented to your Royal Majesty and Electoral Serenity, be graciously pleased immediately to command the University that they not only acquiesce in the previous order of things, and henceforth confer upon me the full payment, consisting of 12 fl., for the old service, together with the fees of the *Promotiones Doctorales* and other solemn occasions formerly attached to it, but also that they shall hand over to me the arrears of *honorarium* amounting to 18 thlrs. 5 gr. and the regular salary already owing, amounting to 33 fl. and moreover, allow me all expenses incurred by me in this business, or else, inasmuch as the University may not be convinced by what has hitherto been adduced, that it shall be made to publish the receipts given by Schelle and Kuhnau, both as regards the special *honorarium* as well as the regular salary. This great favour I will recognise with humblest thanks all my life, and remain,

Your Royal Majesty's and Electoral Serenity's

Most humble and obedient,

Leipzig, *Dec.* 31, *Anno.* 1725.   JOHANN SEBASTIAN BACH.

[Addressed with the full title as given above.][68]

---

[68] Without seal. The transcript of this document, preserved among the deeds of the University, is only signed by Bach.

This was followed up by a document dated from Dresden Jan. 21, 1726, not very definite in tone, still apparently deciding in Bach's favour on the whole; the presentation of this document to the University did not take place, strange to say, before May 23. Whether during these four months attempts were made to bring about a friendly compromise can only be conjecture; even as regards the settlement of the money question, which became more and more prominent, we can come to no more definite conclusion. From a comparison of various intimations, culled here and there during the following years, we are led to infer that Görner remained at the head of the "New service." In the solemnities of the University, sometimes one and sometimes the other of the rivals seems to have been called in, but more frequently Bach. On August 3, 1725, he had composed, to order, a "*Dramma per musica*" in honour of the name day of Professor August Freidrich Müller ("Der zufriedengestellte Aeolus"—"Aeolus satisfied"), and after this, so soon as December 11 of the following year, he wrote another cantata, in honour of the promotion of *Magister* Gottlieb Korte to be Professor extraordinary; again, on May 12, 1727, for the birthday of King Friedrich August, who happened just then to be in Leipzig, another *Drama musicum*, which was performed under his direction by the prizemen of the University; then the music for the mourning celebration held in the University Church, October 17, of the same year, in memory of Queen Christiane Eberhardine, who died September 5. Görner, on the other hand, was commissioned to compose the Latin Ode which was sung in the University Church on that same Royal birthday. For the two-hundreth anniversary of the introduction of evangelical doctrine into Saxony, which was celebrated in the University on August 25, 1739, Görner also composed the music to a Latin Ode, of which the first portion was performed before and the second after the sermon.[69] On the first of these occasions we find him styled quite plainly *Director Chori Musici*

---

[69] Gretschel, Kirchliche Zustände Leipzigs vor und währund der Reformation, p. 293.

Academici, of the New service in the *Pauline.*[70]   A
report of the year 1736, in fact, names him alone as the
Musical Director of the Academy, and adds that on grand
occasions solemn music was performed by the students and
other musicians, under his direction.[71]   Still, this need not
refer to academical performances, since the Musical Union
was wont to hold independent festival concerts; thus, for
instance, in that very year, 1736, Görner's Union gave a
cantata in honour of the King's birthday with words by
Joh. Joachim Schwabe.   And it is very precisely pointed
out, in the year 1728, that St. Paul's church had a special
musical director, Herr Joh. Gottlieb Görner for ordinary
Sunday and holy day music, but that on other festivals
and for the quarterly speeches the Cantor of St. Thomas'
filled his place, as from time immemorial.[72]

Finally, Bach may very well have been content with the
issue of his efforts.   He had, at any rate, gained an established
position among the music-loving youth of the University;
and this was still farther secured when, in 1729, Schott
went to Gotha as Cantor, and the direction of the famous
old Musical Union founded by Telemann, fell into his
hands.   So far as the general condition of things at that
time can be said to have allowed it, a good and favourable
time for public musical performances would seem now to
have dawned upon him.   He performed regularly once a
week with his Union; in the summer season from four to
six on Wednesday afternoons, in the Zimmermann Garden, in
Windmühlengasse (Wind Mill Street); in winter from eight
to ten on Friday evenings, in the Zimmermann Coffee-house,
in the Katharinenstrasse—the corner house of the Böttcher
Gässchen, now No. 7.   During Fair times they played twice
a week, on Wednesdays and Fridays.   Under his direction
the Union distinguished itself by several festival concerts.
On December 8, 1733, he produced a *Dramma per Musica*
for the Queen's birthday, "Tönet ihr Pauken, erschallet

---

[70] Sicul, (Christoph Ernst) *ANNALIVM | LIPSIENSIVM | MAXIME
ACADEMICORVM | SECTIO* XXIX. | &c., Leipzig, 1728. 8.

[71] Das jetzt lebende und florirende Leipzig, p. 32.

[72] *ANTONII WEIZII* Verbessertes Leipzig, 1728, p 12.

Trompeten"—"Sound ye drums, peal forth ye trumpets"; in
January, 1734, another work of the same character, "Blast
Lärmen, ihr Feinde, verstärket die Macht," for the coronation
festival of August III., both, of course, of his own composition; and the old Weimar Cantata "Was mir behagt
ist nur die muntre Jagd" had to serve again for the King's
birthday, with different words.[73] And what was more, the
Union ceased to perform in the New Church, and so was at
liberty to do so in Bach's church music. The organist who
had been appointed in Schott's stead, Carl Gotthelf Gerlach,
was a protégé of Bach's, and had obtained the place by his
recommendation,[74] so he had to submit when his patron
deprived him of the assistance of the Union; but at the same
time—whether from a sense of propriety, or from their old
preference for the musical performances in the New Church
—the Council supported him with, relatively speaking,
abundant means for forming a small choir of his own for
the needs of the service there. In later years Gerlach was
promoted to be the director of Telemann's Musical Union,
Bach himself retiring from the post. It is not known precisely when this took place, it is only certain that it was
after 1736. However, the good old days never returned for
the New Church; the Union seems even to have stood
more completely aloof from it, as it lost its first importance
and was passed from hand to hand. The focus of musical
art in Leipzig had centred elsewhere by the year 1740.[75]

Bach of course took the management of the church music
at St. Thomas' and St. Nicholas' vigorously in hand from
the first. It is highly characteristic of him that he should
have regarded his position as Cantor less as being that of
a teacher in a public school—which is what it certainly was,
first and foremost—than as a civic and official Conductorship,
with the additional duty of giving certain lessons. His
predecessors in office had been simply entitled Cantors; if the
words *Director Musices* were added, they referred only to the

---

[73] See Vol. I., p. 567.

[74] Gerlach had four rivals, but he was "praised by Herr Bach."

[75] See Appendix A., No. 14.

University church.[76] Bach subscribes and describes himself
almost always, and from the first, as *Director Musices*, or
Chori Musici and *Cantor*, or even *Director Musices* alone ;[77]
and it is the exception, in speaking of singing rehearsals
in the school itself, when he calls himself only *Cantor*.
Even his pupils give him the title.[78] In a Leipzig
address book of 1723[79] he is thus designated; he evidently
chose to assert his position as being an essentially
musical and independent official, and would do so with all
the more determination in proportion as the petty officials
persisted in giving him the simple title of Cantor. This is
very characteristic of the determined temper which supported
him through many conflicts, for his outward conduct bespoke
the inner man. The protestant church music had always
depended on the school, and had become what it was
through its instrumentality. It certainly was not mere
caprice or arrogance which led Bach to regard his connection
with the school as a secondary consideration. Bach's music
is no doubt true church music, characterised by a style of
its own; but it is impossible not to perceive that it also
contains the germ of an independent branch of concert music,
and in the course of Bach's own labours this is now and
then very prominent. He was conscious of this peculiarity
in his art, and his determined insistance on his position as
musical director, and not as a school and church employé,
clearly proves this.

The Town Council had received him with due respect, but
in order to raise the standard of church music as he, on his

---

[76] Johann Schelle " was in 1677 Cantor at the Thomasschule, with which
the University entrusted to him the *Directorium Chori Musici* in St. Paul's
Church." MS. addition in G. M. Telemann's copy of Mattheson's Ehrenpforte,
in the Royal Library at Berlin. In the Leipzig register the entry of Kuhnau's
death styles him " *Director Musices* bey der Löbl. Universitaet und *Cantor* bey
der Schulen zu *St. Thomæ*."

[77] As in his memorial as to " well appointed church music " of the year
1730, although this almost exclusively concerns the St. Thomas' scholars.

[78] Heinrich Nickolaus Gerber always wrote in his copies of the French and
English Suites " *Joh. Seb. Bach*. H. (ochfürstlich) A. (nhalt) C. (öthenischer)
*Capell*meister, *Dir. (ector) Ch. (ori) M. (usici) L. (ipsiensis) et* (sometimes " auch ")
Cant. (or) S. (ancti) T. (homæ) S. (cholæ) Lips. (iensis)."

[79] Das ietzt lebende und florirende Leipzig, 1723, p. 78.

part, deemed fitting, he had dipped more deeply into their
money-bags than they approved. Bach's immediate superior
in the church services was the Superintendent of the Diocese
of Leipzig, at that time Dr. Salomo Deyling. He took
pleasure and interest in the district under his official juris-
diction, and enjoyed a well-deserved esteem far beyond its
limits. He was a man of extensive learning, strong
character, and undoubted administrative capacity. He was
born, the son of poor parents, in 1677, at Weida in Voigtland,
and by indefatigable energy had worked up to becoming a
student at Wittenberg; in 1703 he qualified in the philo-
sophical faculty, and two years later became Archdeacon of
Plauen; by 1708 he was Superintendent at Pegau, and in
1716 General Superintendent at Eisleben. Meanwhile he
had obtained the degree of licentiate in theology, and in
1710 had been made *Dr. Theol.* This was followed by his
call to Leipzig as minister of the Church of St. Nicholas and
Superintendent of the Diocese, in 1720. He entered on
these offices in 1721, and at the same time was made
Professor extraordinary of the University, which subsequently
resulted in his being Professor in ordinary;[80] he was also
Assessor to the Consistory. His abundant labours in all these
relations ended only with his death, which took place in
1755.[81] The most interesting question to us, is what
attitude he took up as regards church music. He had ample
opportunity for expressing his views on the subject, for the
number of his published writings is considerable. They
treat of philosophy, philology, mathematics, and antiquities,
but principally of theological matters, alike exegetical, dogmatic, historical, and practical. The greater part of his
Latin dissertations is contained in his *Observationes Sacræ*,
which were published in three parts, each containing fifty

---

[80] "Professor extraordinary," is used to denote those who had no fixed post
in the university; in this case he became regular professor.

[81] Sicul. Leip. Jahr. Gesch., 1721, p. 227.—Adelung Fortsetzung zu Jöchers
Gelehrten Lexicon, Leipzig, 1787, V. II., p. 684. A portrait in oil of Deyling
hangs in the choir of St. Thomas' Church, and a copperplate from it is to be found
in Geographischer Schau-platz Aller vier Theile der Welt, von Christian
Ehrhardt Hoffmann. V. II. (Town Library, Leipzig.)

essays, at Leipzig, 1708, 1711, and 1715 ; in these he displays great learning and a strictly conservative, high-Lutheran tendency.

Of all the 150 dissertations, one only deals with things musical. It is entitled *Hymni a Christianis decantandi* (V. III., No. XLIV., p. 336 to 346). But even this is almost entirely of a theological and antiquarian character. What the Greeks understood by a hymn, how many kinds of song the Jews distinguished, on what occasions the Greeks used singing, how far the early Christians may have imitated them in this and how far not ; all this and much more is amply and learnedly discussed, with a final reference to two passages in the Epistles to the Ephesians and to the Colossians. It is not till the last paragraph that he mentions that among the heathen certain persons were appointed as superintendents to lead public singing on the occasions of great festivals and he closes the treatise with this practical application :[82]

" Therefore, since profane men, strangers ·to the true worship of God, used to institute societies of singers of hymns and pæans for the purpose of singing to the praise and glory of false gods publicly in temples and other places of resort, and even used to sing to their praise in their very feasts, how much more ought Christians to be 'singers of hymns and pæans' to the true God ? How much more does it beseem them to celebrate God's goodness and glory in 'psalms and hymns and spiritual songs,' both in their feasts and in their temples, both in public and private ? "

This is all Deyling could find to say in his *Observationes Sacræ* to indicate his attitude towards church music, but it is enough. The parallel drawn between the hymn and pæan singers on one hand, and the choirs in protestant churches on the other, is an obvious one, and when he

---

[82] " Cum igitur profanus hominum coetus, et a vero Dei cultu peralienus, in commentitiorum numinum honorem, et ad laudes eorum decantandas, publica quondam Ὑμνῳδῶν et Παιανιστῶν in Templis, aliisque conventibus instituerint Collegia, ac inter ipsas epulas consueverint ὑμνολογεῖν ; quanto magis Christianos decet esse Hymnologos et Paeanistas veri Dei ? Quanto hos magis decit ψαλμοῖς καὶ ὕμνοις, καὶ ᾠδαῖς πνευματικαῖς Dei beneficia et laudes in conviviis, ac Templis, publice privatimque celebrare ? "

speaks of convivial singing he evidently has in his mind
the prevailing custom of having the choir of boys to sing
at festivities, particularly at wedding banquets. We must
remember, too, that this was written at a time when the
question of part-music being introduced into the church
service was under eager dispute, and especially as to whether,
and how far, it was suitable for independent choirs. Thus
Deyling considered church music, as represented by Bach,
to be desirable. From the meagreness of his treatment of the
whole subject it may be doubted whether he took any
intelligent or sympathetic interest in music. However, all
that was needed was that he should give Bach full liberty
to act. All that has been said as to a re-organisation of
the services in which Bach and Deyling co-operated rests
on unfounded assumptions and baseless opinions.[83] A confusion between the words of the church music and the
hymns sung by the congregation could not occur if the
Cantor did but understand his duty, since the congregational
hymns to be sung on holy days were fixed once for all, and
the choice of the hymns for ordinary Sundays was one of the
traditional duties of the Cantor. Any lack of connection
between the cantata and the Epistle and Gospel for the day
was hardly possible either, because the texts to which the
cantatas were composed for each Sunday and holy day were
usually written to suit their ecclesiastical significance and
the contents of the portions of Scripture appointed for the
day. Any alteration in the musical arrangements of the
form of worship would have been an infringement of Bach's
official rights, since, on his induction, the Council had
expressly enjoined him not to allow any innovations in
the services; they were, and remained throughout Bach's

---

[83] Rochlitz, Sebastian Bach's Grosse Passionsmusik nach dem Evangelisten
Johannes, Vol. IV., 3rd ed., Leipzig, 1868, p. 271. Part of it is printed as a
preface to the B.-G., IV., p. 13—15. It will be seen from ch. IV. of this section
that the picture given by Rochlitz of the services before and during Bach's time
is in part perfectly inaccurate. Rochlitz says that at the beginning of each
week Bach sent several, usually three, texts of cantatas suitable for the
following Sunday to the Superintendent, who made a selection. I can find
nothing to confirm this statement, but it is not impossible that Rochlitz, who
himself was a foundation scholar at St. Thomas', followed a credible tradition.

life, the same as in Kuhnau's time. They afforded abundant opportunity for the use of music ; indeed, Bach did not even usually avail himself of them to the full. Certainly he had to submit the text he chose for his composition to the censorship of the Superintendent. It can hardly be said that they co-operated in the matter ; it was rather a check on the composer's liberty, which he much resented, for Bach always evaded every kind of surveillance, and liked to feel himself perfectly independent in his own sphere of work.

A circumstance which occurred—at a later period, it is true, but which may find a fitting place here—serves to prove this statement. On Good Friday, 1739, Bach had announced the programme of a " Passion Music," by the plan, then customary, of sending round printed copies of the text. The Council must needs once more assert its superiority at a wrong time ; one of their subordinates was commissioned to announce, verbally, to the Cantor that the Passion Music must be postponed till a regular permission had been granted by the superior authorities. Bach, however, was refractory. He had proceeded on this occasion just as he had done on all others, and, as regarded the text, there was nothing reprehensible in that, since the work had already been performed several times. And besides, he did not care whether the performance took place or not, for he had nothing but the trouble of it and no profits. He would explain to the " Herr Superintendent that the Council had forbidden it." The Council and Consistory were often at loggerheads, and the fray resulting from this must have been an additional incentive to Bach to act, as far as possible, on his own account.[84]

The congregational hymns were subject to the censorship of the church authorities, as well as the texts of the Cantatas. A certain series of hymns was sanctioned once for all ; within these limits the Cantor was free to choose, but he might not go beyond them. It is possible that Bach

---

[84] As a parallel case we find that on April 4, 1722, Kuhnau had received a reproof from the Burgomasters, because he had asked permission of the Consistory and not of the Council with regard to a " Passion Music " in St. Thomas'.

may at some time have made the attempt, and that it was reported to the Consistory. On February 16, 1730, a warning reached the Superintendent that he should take heed lest hymns not hitherto in use should be sung without the concurrence of the authorities, as had recently been done.[85] When we see what a subtle and profound feeling Bach shows in the selection of those chorales, for instance, which are introduced as Madrigal texts into the Passion according to St. Matthew, it is quite credible that he should be very ready to avail himself of the Cantor's right to select the congregational hymns, in order to produce the greatest and most symbolical variety of effect in the different musical portions of the church services. And even if he had not been a determined man who would not yield an inch in the department which belonged to him, it would still be intelligible that he should allow no one to interfere in the arrangement of the hymns. However, an attempt to do so was made ere long. *Magister* Gaudlitz, the sub-dean of St. Nicholas, began in 1727 to select the hymns for the Vesper sermons given by him—at first with the knowledge of the Superintendent and the Cantor's consent. After he had done this about a year, our master would no longer submit to his interference; he chose to ignore the sub-deacon's decision, and made the choir sing the hymns he himself selected. Gaudlitz reported him to the Consistory, who, somewhat over-hastily, sent a notice to the Cantor, through the Superintendent, to the effect that for the future he was to have the hymns sung which the preacher had selected. Bach now thought it time to appeal to the Council, and he wrote as follows :—

Magnifici,

MOST NOBLY-BORN, MOST NOBLE, POWERFUL, HIGH, AND LEARNED AND MOST WISE,

MOST HONOURABLE LORDS AND PATRONS,

Will your *Magnifici*, well-born and noble lordships condescend to remember how I was admonished by your *Magnifici*, well-born and noble lordships on the occasion of my being called to the Cantorate of the School of St. Thomas in this place, of which I was always to

---

[85] I have not been able to discover the document which is given by Bitter, II., p. 86, and must therefore refer to him.

perform the traditional usages in the public divine service, duly in all respects, and not to introduce any innovations; and how, under the same contract, you were pleased to assure me of your high protection? Among these usages and customs was also the right of ordering the hymns before and after the sermons, which right was left entirely to me and to my predecessors in the Cantorate; provided that the hymns chosen be in conformity with the gospels and the use of the Dresden hymn-book regulated by these, and as may seem suitable according to time and circumstances; and certainly, as the worthy *Ministerium* can well attest, no contradiction to this has ever arisen.[86] But, to the contrary of this, the *Sub-diaconus* of St. Nicholas Church, Herr *Magister* Gottlieb Gaudlitz, has attempted to introduce an innovation, and instead of the hymns hitherto ordered in accordance with church customs, has ordered other hymns; and when I scrupled to yield to this because of serious consequences which might result, he brought an accusation against me before the worshipful *Consistorium* and obtained an injunction against me, by the contents of which I, for the future, am to let those hymns be sung which shall be commanded by the preachers. But it seemed to me not proper, without the knowledge of your *Magnifici*, well-born, and noble lordships, the patrons of the churches in this place, to carry this into effect; and all the less so because hitherto the arrangement of the hymns by the Cantor had for so long a time remained undisturbed, the afore-mentioned Herr *Magister* Gaudlitz having himself allowed in the document presented to the most worshipful *Consistorium*, of which a copy is subjoined, that when once or twice he had been allowed to do it, my consent as Cantor had been required. In addition to which, when the hymns which had to be sung as part of the church music were of inordinate length, the service would be prolonged, and thus all kinds of irregularities would have to be provided for, putting aside the fact that not one of the officiating clergy, with the exception of Herr *Magister* Gaudlitz, as *Sub-diaconus*, seeks to introduce this innovation. Thus, I esteem it necessary most submissively to bring before your *Magnifici*, well-born, and noble lordships the humble prayer that you will most graciously protect me in the use and ordering of these hymns, as has hitherto been usual. And with life-long devotion,
I remain,
Your *Magnifici*, well-born, and noble lordships'
Most obedient,
JOHANN SEBASTIAN BACH.[87]
Leipzig, September 20, 1728.

---

[86] " As I appoint the hymns for all three churches ": Kuhnau, Memorial of December 4, 1704, see Appendix B., VII.

[87] Council deeds " Schuel zu *St. Thomas*. Vol. IV., Stift, VIII., B., 2." Fol. 410. Only the signature of Bach's memorial is autograph.

Thus the Council once more found itself in conflict with the Consistory, but how the affair terminated among them is not known.

Under the circumstances, all that Bach proposed and hoped to do for the improvement of the music in the principal churches in the direction which he had always pursued in art, involved nothing less than the training of singers and players alike to a higher pitch of executive power, and the education of their feeling for art by keeping them engaged on fine and important works. And indeed this was inevitably the case, since he himself composed for them as much as possible; it was quite in accordance with his own wish, and, as we shall see, he at once began to develop this side of his genius, and during a long series of years was incessantly productive. With regard to the improvement and extension of his choir, he had made a great step quite at the beginning of his official life by establishing a connection with the students. He knew very well that without them little could be done, still he was wholly dependent on their free-will for whatever support they contributed to his Sunday performances; the foundation scholars, who were bound to sing, still formed the main body of the choir. They were not required to sing only; since by his deed of installation Bach was pledged to instruct them diligently, not only in vocal but also in instrumental music. As things then stood this was highly necessary, for the performance of the instrumental accompaniments by the corps of musicians kept up by the Town Council was neither efficient nor strong enough by itself to fulfil his requirements. It consisted of only seven members—four "Stadtpfeiffer," and three "Kunstgeiger," who, with a single exception, belonged to the class of "doubtful characters."[88] There was indeed no lack of instrumentalists, and of good ones, in Leipzig,[89] but their assistance would

---

[88] During the first twelve years of Bach's official life their names were— Gottfried Reiche, Christian Rother, Joh. Cornelius Gentzmar, Joh. Caspar Gleditsch, "Stadtpfeiffer." The "Kunstgeiger" were Heinrich Christian Bezer, Christian Ernst Meyer, Joh. Gottfried Kornagel. Accounts of the churches in the Archives of the Foundation Library, Leipzig.

[89] "*Dunkeln Ehrenmänner.*" A party of five musicians performed, under Schott, in the New Church. See the accounts from 1725 to 1729.

cost money, while the scholars had to fiddle for nothing. We must picture to ourselves Bach's plan of instruction in clavier, violin, and organ-playing, as consisting very much in attaching to himself any scholar he found qualified, and endeavouring to urge him forward by his example and by opportune instruction. Many young men, whose names we shall meet with again, sought instruction at the Thomas-schule, less in general knowledge than in music; and these became Bach's pupils in the strictest sense of the word, both in playing and in composition, and quitted the school, not as good general scholars, but as accomplished artists.

However, the singing choir was the first musical object which the scholars had to keep in view. What kind of training it was that Bach put them through to this end is a very interesting question, but one not easy to answer. A number of testimonials in Bach's own hand have come down to us—reports written after the examinations of the singers. They refer for the most part to such youths as had applied for admission to the foundation of the Thomas-schule. In the summer of 1729 a certain Gottlieb Michael Wünzer was candidate for a scholarship. Ernesti, the Rector, gave him a testimonial for Latin, and under this Bach wrote :—

The above-named Wünzer has a rather weak voice, and still but a poor method, still he may—if he is diligent in private practice—be available in time.

JOH : SEBAST : BACH.

Leipzig, *Jun* 3, 1729.   Cantor.[90]

On another occasion he writes :—

This present Erdmann Gottwald Pezold of Auerbach, *ætatis* 14, has a fine voice and tolerable proficiency. Witness my own hand,[91]

JOH : SEB : BACH.

---

[90] Obig benandter Wünzer hat eine etwas schwache Stimme und noch Wenige *profectus* dörffte aber wohl (so ein *privat exercitium* fleissig getrieben würde) mit der zeit zu gebrauchen seyn.

[91] Vorzeiger dieses Erdmann Gottwald Pezold von Auerbach, *ætatis* 14 Jahr, hat eine feine Stimme und ziemliche *Profectus*. So hiermit eigenhändig attestiret wird

von
JOH : SEB : BACH.

And again :—

This present Johann Christoph Schmied of Bendeleben, in Thuringia, *ætatis* 19, has a fine tenor voice and reads well at sight.[92]

JOH: SEB: BACH.
Director Musices.

Or :—

Carolus Heinrich Scharff, *ætatis* 14, has a tolerable alto voice and a moderate proficiency in music.[93]

J. S. BACH.
Cantor.

A number of similar testimonials will presently be given on another occasion, since they do not contribute any new information as to the present question. Here, however, I may adduce another piece of evidence of a later date, though, it is true, it does not deal with the entrance of any member of the Thomasschule. In 1740 a new office of *Collaborator* in the Thomasschule was to be instituted. Since the new master was to be charged with the duty of grounding the boys in the elements of music, the candidates were sent to Bach to be examined. He reported the result of this examination in these words :—

By command of their Excellencies the Vice-Chancellors, the three competing persons have been with me and I found them as follows :—

(I.) Herr *Magister* Röder renounced the examination, having altered his determination and taken the place of Steward in a noble family in Merseburg.

(II.) Herr *Magister* Irmler has a fine method of singing, but he is somewhat wanting in accuracy of ear.

(III.) Herr Wildenhayn plays a little on the clavier, but in singing he is not skilled, by his own confession.

LEIPZIG, *Jan.* 18, 1740. JOH: SEB: BACH.[94]

---

[92] Vorzeiger Dieses Johann Christoph Schmied von Bendeleben aus Thüringen, *ætatis* 19 Jahr, hat eine feine Tenor Stimme und singt vom Blat fertig.

[93] Carolus Henrich Scharff, *ætatis* 14 Jahr, hat eine ziemliche Alt Stimme, und mittelmässige *Profectus in Musicis.*

[94] Irmler got the place.

Auf Ihro *Excellence* des Herrn *Vice-Cancellarii* hohe *Ordre* sind die drey *competenten* bey mir gewesen, und habe Sie folgender massen befunden :

(I.) Der Herr *M.* Röder hat die *probe depreciret*, weiln er seine *resolution* geändert und eine Hoffmeister Stelle bey einer Adelichen *Familie* in Merseburg angetreten.

(II.) Der Herr *M.* Irmler hat eine gar feine Singart ; nur fehlet es ihm in etwas am *judicio aurium.*

(III.) Der Herr Wildenhayn spielet etwas auf dem Clavier, aber zum Singen ist er eigenem Geständniss nach, nicht geschickt.

LEIPZIG, 18 *Januar,* 1740. JOH: SEB: BACH.

Brief and general as these documents are, we learn from them to what aspect of vocal art Bach principally directed his attention. The word *profectus*, which was much used at that time in the sense of proficiency or productive power, may certainly include everything that can be required of a singer ; but it here bears a more limited meaning, if we remember that the first consideration was a serviceable choir singer, and then weigh what is said of one and another of the candidates. Bach required of his singers, in the first place, accuracy of pitch and time, a pure intonation, fertility of resource, and also, if possible, a pleasing quality of voice—" er hat eine feine Stimme." In all this it is the musician that speaks, and not the singing master ; there is no allusion even to the cultivation, utterance, equality of register, or any other vocal technicality. It would be absurd to suppose that Bach was insufficiently acquainted with all these matters ; besides, it must be remembered that his second wife was a well-trained and accomplished singer. It by no means follows from his silence that he left them out of consideration in the education of his singers, but we may venture to assert that he thought it no part of his task to make accomplished vocalists of the scholars who could sing in at all the same way as he trained Krebs, Ernst Bach, his own sons, and others, to be distinguished players and composers. There was not time for this in seven hours of singing a week, especially when forty pupils took part in them, as was the case when the choirs were complete. He would have had to take the best of them under his private tuition, and before he could do this he must have acquired a more thorough knowledge of the art of singing than he actually possessed, since we know nothing of his having had any practical experience of it since the days of his boyhood.

Bach was, before and above everything, a composer for the organ, as the whole course of his development shows us ; all his writing for other instruments has something about it that suggests the organ, and his vocal compositions might be designated as the last and utmost embodiment of the true Bach organ style. Nor does the admission of this view necessarily imply any reproach; not even if we insist on regarding the subject exclusively from the most purely musical and artistic point of view. As long as instrumental music has existed it has been on terms of mutual inter-change with vocal music, and they have borrowed reciprocally. But to Bach, as we have already seen, the organ was imbued with a peculiar, more essentially ideal, character, which gives a higher justification to much that might otherwise seem faulty in style in his vocal music. At any rate, he required of the singers something different in itself, as adapted to the views he held of church music, from what was expected by the musical world he lived in. He required less, in so far that he attached less importance to all that characterises skilled singing as such, all that must be made as prominent as possible where the human voice is the principal element in the piece; but, on the other hand, he required more, inas-much as in his compositions he often put before the singers technical difficulties in the music which could not have been suggested by an imagination working with the single idea of writing for the voice. It is self-evident that in such music as this the distinction between the demands on a chorus singer and soloist is far less than in Handel's oratorios. A scholar who was thoroughly trained in singing Bach's choral music might soon be qualified to perform an aria, since its effect would depend far less on him alone than is the case with the singer of an opera or oratorio air. Certainly the feeling of Bach's arias could not have found that flow of passionate utterance when sung by youths and boys which they are capable of when the finest singers regard their due rendering as one of their noblest tasks. But we may rest convinced that Bach himself would not have endured a mere mechanical reading of them. Johann Friedrich Agricola, Bach's pupil from 1738 to 1741,[95] says it is indispensable that a singer should learn elocution, or at least acquire, by the verbal instructions of a good speaker or by accurate observation of his mode of delivery, what sort of sound of the voice is requisite for the due expression of certain

[95] Gerber, L. I., col. 17. Burney's Diary. Rolle, Neue Wahrnehmngen, &c. Berlin, 1784, p. 93.

emotions or figures of speech, and that he should also
diligently practise himself in reading or declaiming, according to these rules, emotional passages from the works of good
orators and poets.[96]　And we know that Bach himself was
fond of illustrating the proper method of musical performance
by the rules of rhetoric.　" He so perfectly understood the
resemblance which the performance of a musical piece has
in common with rhetorical art that he was listened to with
the utmost satisfaction and pleasure when he discoursed of
the similarity and agreement between them ; but we also
wonder at the skilful use he made of this in his works."　So
writes his friend *Magister* Birnbaum.[97]

Though these were the principles which Bach regarded as
the foundation of his vocal training, it by no means follows
that he should have been successful in practically carrying
them out.　For this, two things were necessary : a real talent
for teaching youth on his part, and musical talent on that of
his pupils.　It seems to be a contradiction to what was said
in a former chapter,[98] as to Bach's great gift for teaching,
when the younger Ernesti (who was Rector of the Thomasschule after 1734) states that he could maintain no discipline
among the choir boys, and that after Bach's death it was
stated in the Council that " Herr Bach was indeed great as
a musician, but not as a schoolmaster."　But it is one thing
to guide one single teachable and reverently disposed pupil,
and quite another to quell an unintelligent and unruly mob
of boys.　Bach was peculiarly fitted for the former task by his
gifted, sympathetic, and essentially wise and humane nature ;
but in the latter case his artist's irritability hindered him,
and this was all the boys could see, who were incapable of
understanding his greatness.　In this respect the man in
Leipzig in no whit differed from the youth at Arnstadt ; and
we shall presently see that the musical qualifications of the
scholars received but a meagre share of his attention.　Bach
frequently visited Dresden from Leipzig, heard there the

---

[96] Tosi, Anleitung zur Singkunst.　Mit Erläuterungen und Zusätzen von
Joh. Friedrich Agricola.　Berlin, 1757, p. 139.
[97] See Scheibe, Critischer Musikus.　Leipzig, 1475, p. 997.　Birnbaum's
statements refer to the year 1739.　See ante, p. 56.　　[98] Ante, p. 47.

beautiful performances of the Italian singers, and the admirable playing of the Court Band, and was himself a much admired personage both among his fellow artists and in court circles. It was but human nature that under these circumstances he should often fulfil his proper duties with his foundation boys and town musicians in a grudging spirit; and work done without any heart in it is but rarely successful.

The fact thus indicated did not become publicly evident, however, till after the lapse of a few years. At first the charm of novelty, the natural desire to justify the expectations formed of him by those who were most intimately concerned, and, above all, the delight of being able at last to perform and compose church music to his heart's content, would easily have outweighed many disagreeables and disadvantages; at any rate, we have no information which stands in the way of this assumption. The first traces of a misunderstanding became visible in 1729. At Easter in that year nine foundation boys had finished their studies and quitted the school. They had been useful musicians and among them indeed there was one of distinguished talent, Wilhelm Friedemann, Bach's eldest son. On this occasion it came to light that the Council, who were still as negligent in all that concerned the school choir as they had been in Kuhnau's time, had for a long time ceased to pay the requisite attention to the question whether the new foundation scholars who were admitted had any musical gifts. The choir in consequence had fallen into such a wretched condition that some very decisive steps had to be taken, if the music were to be carried on at all in the way that had become traditional. Nor was it only Bach who represented in the strongest terms that the vacant places must be filled up by boys of musical qualifications; even the old Rector Ernesti requested it, and Dr. Stiglitz, the Inspector of schools, who had to transmit their demands to the Council, supported them by a petition, couched in the most emphatic terms, dated May 18. He also forwarded, as supplementary, a report drawn up and written by Bach as to the new candidates and their capabilities, as well as on the indispensable constituents of the different church choirs. This is as follows:—

The boys, who under the present vacancies in the school of St. Thomas, desire to be received into it as *Alumni* are the following:—

I. Such as have musical qualifications, and, firstly, *trebles*.

1. Christoph Friedrich Meissner, of Weissenfels, *ætatis* 13, has a good voice and a fine method.
2. Johann Tobias Krebs, of Buttstädt, *ætatis* 13, has a good strong voice and a fine method.
3. Samuel Kittler, of Bellgern, *ætatis* 13, has a tolerably strong voice and a very pretty method.
4. Johann Heinrich Hillmeyer, of Gehrings Walde, *ætatis* 13, has a strong voice and a fine method.
5. Johann August Landvoigt, of Gaschwitz, *ætatis* 13, has a passable voice; his method is tolerable.
6. Johann Andreas Köpping, of Grossboden, *ætatis* 14; his voice is tolerably strong and his method moderate.
7. Johann Gottlob Krause, of Grossdeuben, *ætatis* 14; has rather a weak voice and very mediocre method.
8. Johann Georg Leg, of Leipzig, *ætatis* 13; his voice is rather weak and method indifferent.

Alti.

9. Johann Gottfried Neucke, of Grima, *ætatis* 14, has a strong voice and tolerably fine method.
10. Gottfried Christoph Hoffmann, of Nebra, *ætatis* 16, has a fairly good alto voice, but his method is rather faulty.

II. Those who did not offer themselves as musicians:—

1. Johann Tobias Dieze.
2. Gottlob Michael Wintzer.[99]
3. Johann David Bauer.
4. The son of Johanna Margaretha Pfeil.
5. Gottlob Ernst *Hausius*.
6. Friedrich Wilhelm, the son of Wilhelm Ludwig.
7. Johann Gottlieb Zeymer.
8. Johann Gottfried Berger.
9. Johann Gottfried Eschner.
10. *Salomon* Gottfried Greülich.
11. Michael Heinrich Kittler, of Prettin.

> Joh: Sebast: Bach,
> *Direct: Musices,*
> u. *Cantor* at S. Thomae.

Then, as supplementary to the former list, we have:—

Gottwald Pezold, of Aurich, *ætatis* 14, has a fine voice and tolerable method.[100]

---

[99] Evidently the same who, on the 3rd of June, obtained a somewhat warmer testimonial.

[100] No doubt the same to whom Bach had already given a separate testimonial.

Johann Christoph Schmid, of Bendeleben, *ætatis* 19, has a tolerably strong tenor voice and sings very prettily.

And, finally, we have the following supplement :—

In the Church of St. Nikolaus, there are belonging to the first choir :	Of St. Thomas, to the second choir :	In the New Church, to the third choir :
3 Trebles.	3 Trebles.	3 Trebles.
3 Alti.	3 Alti.	3 Alti.
3 Tenors.	3 Tenors.	3 Tenors.
3 Basses.	3 Basses.	3 Basses.
	To the fourth choir :	
	2 Soprani.	
	2 Alti.	
	2 Tenors.	
	2 Basses.	

And this last choir must serve the Church of St. Peter as well.

Nevertheless, this representation was only half attended to by the Council. On May 24, it granted, it is true, five scholarships to the musical boys named as Meissner, Krebs, Kittler, Hillmeyer, and Neucke ; on the other hand three were given to those who " did not offer themselves as musicians " (Dieze, Zeymer, and Berger), and the last scholarship was given to a candidate named Feller, who is not mentioned by Bach, and who, therefore, had evidently not even come before him. Soon after this there must again have been a vacancy, for on June 3 Wintzer was admitted. Pezold and Schmid, who had both been recommended by Bach, were passed over; Krause, who is probably the lad named by Bach as No. 7 of list 1, was not admitted till October of the following year.

In the Holy week of 1729, Bach had for the first time conducted a performance of his Passion Music according to St. Matthew. From this we see that this work had made so little impression on the gentlemen of the Town Council of Leipzig, that they did not even accede to the request of the composer so far as to choose the nine musical scholars out of the candidates for the scholarships. After so signal a proof of their ignorance of his value, it seems almost surprising that Bach should not at once have sought to resign his office ; and it certainly is not strange that for a time he was thoroughly disgusted with it. It happened just at the same time that he undertook the direction of the Musical Union formed by Telemann, and might there hope to find rather more love of music and intelligent sympathy. It may be that this prospect may have inspired him with courage for the future. But so far as his functions as Cantor were concerned, the Musical Union was a source of fresh vexation. Kuhnau had, before this, vainly striven to obtain that a sufficient stipend might be allotted to prove an inducement to the students to co-operate regularly and in considerable numbers with the choir of St. Thomas. As we shall see from a memorial drawn up by Bach (given below), the only result up to this time had been that a few donations, and those very insufficient, had been made to the students who had assisted; and in Bach's time these had become more and more meagre, till at length they entirely ceased. The Council no doubt thought them now unnecessary, since from Bach's position at the head of the Union the students would join the choir without payment. Their conduct really bears the aspect of dishonesty, and yet it was simply the result of mental narrowness; for, when the church music became obviously worse, they were very indignant with the Cantor.

On October 16, 1729, the Rector, Joh. Heinrich Ernesti, died;[101] the place remained vacant for many months, and then, on June 8, 1730, the elders (*Väter*—fathers) of the town agreed in inviting Johann Matthias Gesner to fill it, since the choice of a native of the town would have " caused jealousy." One member of the Council expressed a wish that they might "fare better in this appointment than in that of the Cantor." The neglect of his duties which the Council thought it had observed of late had already given occasion to his receiving various warnings and admonitions, but the gentlemen must have discovered to their amazement that they did not produce the expected effect. The offended and defiant artist roundly refused to give any explanation, and this must have happened several times, for one of

---

[101] Neue Zeitungen von Gelehrten Sachen. Leipzig, 1729, p. 791.

the Council declared point blank that the Cantor was "incorrigible." This occurred at a meeting of the Council on August 2, 1730, on the discussion of a question as to the restoration of the school buildings. As has been said, Bach, at his installation, had received permission to employ a substitute, as far as might be necessary, in giving general instruction. This substitute had hitherto been found in the person of the *Tertius*, afterwards Conrector, *Magister* Pezold, but he had failed to give satisfaction in this, and indeed in his work generally, and a proposal was therefore made to employ as Bach's substitute, instead of Pezold, a younger master, *Magister* Abraham Krügel. It would have been the most obvious course to restore to Bach the duty of giving the lessons; but the strong feeling against him now came to light. He had not conducted himself as he should—for instance, he had sent a member of the choir into the country without any previous intimation to the municipal authorities; he had gone on a journey himself without asking leave; he did nothing; he did not attend to the singing classes, not to mention other accusations. The meeting proposed to put him down to one of the lowest classes, where he could either give the elementary instruction himself or, as they would not withdraw the permission originally given, put a deputy to do so for him. But this motion was not passed, and it was resolved instead "to sequestrate the Cantor's income," besides addressing to him an admonition and appealing to his conscience. The accusation that the Cantor "did nothing" is really startling when we learn that, within the few weeks previous, on the occasion of the Jubilee of the Augsburg Confession, the 25th, 26th, and 27th of June, Bach had produced and conducted three grand cantatas; that, besides such a monumental work as the Passion according to St. Matthew, during the seven years that he had been Cantor he had composed a series of cantatas which, to any other musician, would have represented the labours of half a lifetime. But this sort of work counted for nothing with the Council; what they required was that the Cantor should hold his classes regularly, and should not neglect his duties as an instructor in so independent a fashion.

There can be no doubt that Bach had taken things easily as regarded the singing lessons, and it was a neglect of duty which we shall not attempt to screen or defend; still, there were so many and such important circumstances to excuse it that they might almost constitute a justification. It has been already said that the afternoon practising had always been left entirely to the management of the Prefect since the time of Tobias Michael. Thus, when Bach in the same way only gave one singing lesson in the morning of Monday, Tuesday, and Wednesday—and it would seem that he was certainly accustomed to do so much as this—he was only following the established custom.[102] Up to this time hardly any one had found anything to say against this; nay, Michael's colleagues had even opined that the Cantor's presence at the afternoon singing was quite unnecessary. Even if we go farther, and suppose that Bach had been irregular in giving the three morning lessons, we must remember above all the inefficient state of the choir, and that the Council did not even think it necessary to do what lay in their power to improve it and meet the difficulty which Bach experienced in dealing in the right way with this half-wild troop of boys. Nor must we forget that the state of affairs in the Thomasschule was constantly most unsatisfactory, and that the picture given of it above continued to be true during the first seven years of Bach's official life. The careful re-organisation of the institution had been a merely superficial labour; regulations can have no value if no one is concerned to carry them out, and this was the case here. Bach must soon have perceived that in this state of entire demoralisation, this war of each against all carried on by the body of teachers, and

---

[102] From an act of the Council referring to the school. At the end of this document we find certain "remarks" as to the regulations of the school from the pen of the younger Ernesti, in which he speaks of a proportionally small preparation for the processional singing at the three seasons being limited to certain afternoons. Finally he says, "It must be considered whether these practisings could not be transferred to the hours after the lesson (*Lection*), from three till six o'clock. In this way the singing lesson which the Cantor has to give from twelve till one would not be lost, but, on the contrary, more strictly kept up, for at present he gives only one hour's lesson, whereas he ought to give two, and thus the boys do not have enough practice in music." This was written about 1736.

the confusion which resulted from the constant disputes as to their authority between the Council and the Consistory—in which he was especially involved—the only safe course was to look neither to the right hand nor to the left, but to act as independently as possible. To this course his natural disposition inclined him, and he no doubt indulged it all the more since, in point of fact, the post of school Cantor was a singularly independent position. The Rector was little accustomed to trouble himself about the singing lessons, of which Bach's duties as a teacher principally consisted. Since it was one of the chief tasks of the scholars to perform the church services, the Cantor was, in their eyes, almost as important a personage as the Rector himself. In the time of the elder Ernesti, candidates offered themselves to Bach in the first instance quite as often as to the Rector himself; that is to say, they applied to him in person and were examined in music, and he then procured their admission.[103] No doubt that pleased the old Rector best which gave him the least possible trouble, and it is plain that Bach always remained on excellent terms with him, since he asked his wife and daughter to stand sponsors to the two children born to him in 1724 and 1728. Such a position, which really forced him into independence, might easily lead to his occasionally kicking at those limitations which necessarily existed, particularly when they were fixed by an authority before which Bach, as an artist, could not bow, however great his respect for it in other ways. Added to all this, as a factor of special significance, we must count the deep mortification which must have filled the master's mind when he found the best he could do so absolutely unintelligible to his superiors in office.

In short, he was to be called to order. Documents exist which show that the mere order to withhold his emoluments was not the end of the matter. His actual salary and the fees could hardly be interfered with; but there were endowments, holiday money, and other revenues to be distributed,

---

[103] On May 18, 1729, Dr. Stiglitz writes to the Council that the new applicants for the scholarships had either addressed themselves in writing, and with the recommendation of some witness, to the Rector or Conrector, or else had been introduced merely by the nomination of " Cantor Bach."

and these afforded opportunities for aggrieving those who were out of favour. The fees that had accrued to the Rector during the time that elapsed between Ernesti's death and Gesner's appointment were to be divided into three equal parts by order of the Council—for the widow, the Conrector, and the *Tertius*, since the two last had to fill the place of the Rector in the school. As against this, Dr. Stiglitz, the Superintendent of the school, represented in a statement made September 23, 1730, that the Conrector had had much more trouble than the *Tertius*, since he had had to take the Rector's place in other matters besides the lessons, and that the Cantor had also had to take his turn in the duties every three weeks instead of every four. That, therefore, it was fit and proper that more should be given to the Conrector than to the *Tertius*, and that something should also be allotted to the Cantor. The sum in question amounted to 271 thlrs. 7 ggr. 3 pf., and the Council decided as follows on November 6, 1730: the widow was to have forty-one thlrs., the Conrector 130 thlrs. 7 ggr. 3 pf., and the *Tertius* 100 thlrs.; Bach getting nothing.

A similar case had already occurred during the course of the year, before the noble determination to curtail the Cantor's finances had been formally recorded, though an ill feeling already prevailed against him in the Council. A certain citizen, named Philippi, had bequeathed to the Thomasschule a sum of money of which the interest, amounting to twenty thlrs. yearly, was to be subdivided in such wise that twelve thlrs. were given to twelve poor scholars, one thlr. each to the Rector, Conrector, *Tertius*, and first bachelor, sixteen ggr. to each of the collaborators, and two thlrs. to the scholar who made the memorial speech of the year. Under this distribution there was a residue of sixteen ggr., and the question arose as to whether it should not be given to the Cantor or to the other bachelor, neither of whom were mentioned. The Council decided, December 3, 1729, in favour of the other bachelor. Bach was the only member of the college sent empty away.

When, twenty-four years previously, Bach had had to answer before the Consistory of Arnstadt for a dereliction of duty, similar to that he was now accused of, he avoided any farther verbal discussion by promising to clear himself in writing.[104]   He now at first would not be drawn into any discussion whatever with the Leipzig Council, but he subsequently was compelled to change his views, and he drew up a memorial, which we may regard partly as a formal declaration in writing and farther development of what he had said by word of mouth in the previous year to the school Superintendent, and partly as an outline of that officer's report to the Council:—

A short, but indispensable sketch of what constitutes well-appointed church music, with a few impartial reflections on its present state of decay.

For well-appointed church music, vocalists and instrumentalists are requisite. In this town the vocalists consist of the foundation scholars of St. Thomas, and these are of four classes : trebles, altos, tenors, and basses.

If the choir are to perform church pieces properly and as is fitting, the vocalists must again be divided into two classes : *concertists* and *ripienists* (soloists and choristers).   The concertists are usually four, but sometimes five, six, seven, up to eight, according to the requirements of the case and if the music is *per choros.*

The ripienists must be at least eight, two to each part.

The instrumentalists are of various sorts—as violinists, oboeists, flautists, trumpeters, and drummers. N.B.—Among the violinists are reckoned those who play the viola, violoncello, and violin.

The number of the foundation scholars of St. Thomas is fifty-five. These fifty-five are divided into four choirs, for the four churches in which they partly perform music (musiciren),[105] partly sing motetts, and partly chorales.   In three of the churches, *i.e.*—St. Thomas, St. Nicholas, and the New Church—all the scholars must understand music, and the residue go to St. Peter's; those, that is to say, who do not understand music, but can only sing a chorale at need.

To each of those musical choirs there must belong, at least, three trebles, three alti, three tenors, and as many basses, so that if one is unable to sing—which often happens, and particularly at this time of year, as can be proved by the recipes sent from the school of medicine to the dispensary—a motett may be sung with, at least, two voices to each part.[106]   (N.B.—How much better it would be if the *Coetus* were

---

[104] See Vol. I., p. 326.

[105] The word " Musiciren " in the common parlance of Bach's time, when applied to church music, never meant anything but the performance of part music with obbligato instrumental accompaniments.

[106] The Scholars were very fond of declaring they were ill, often for a month, or even a quarter, or a half-year ; they threw the medicine out of the window and revelled in the strengthening food allowed in case of sickness. Niclas, in Eyring's *Biographia Academica Gottingensis*, Vol. III., p. 52.

so arranged that four singers could be available for each part, each choir thus consisting of sixteen persons.)

From this it appears that the number of those who must understand music is thirty-five persons.

The instrumental music consists of the following parts :—

Two or even three	Violino 1°.
Two or three	Violino 2ᵈᵒ.
Two	Viola 1°.
Two	Viola 2ᵈᵒ.
Two	Violoncello.
One	Double bass.
Two or three, according to need ...	Oboes.
One or two	Bassoons.
Three	Trumpets.
One	Drum.

In all eighteen persons, at least, for the instruments. N.B.—Added to this since church music is also written for flutes (*i.e.*—they are either *à bec* or *Traversieri*, held sideways), at least two personsare needed for that; altogether, then, twenty instrumentalists. The number of persons appointed for church music is eight, four town pipers, three town violinists, and one assistant. Diffidence, however, forbids my speaking truly of their quality and musical knowledge; however, it ought to be considered that they are partly inefficient and partly not in such good practice as they should be. This is the list of them :—

Herr Reiche [107]	plays	first trumpet.
Herr Genssmar	,,	second trumpet.
Vacant	,,	third trumpet.
,,	,,	drum.
Herr Rother	,,	first violin.
Herr Beyer	,,	second violin.
Vacant	,,	viola.
,,	,,	violoncello.
,,	,,	double bass.
Herr Gleditsch	,,	first oboe.
Herr Kornagel	,,	second oboe.
Vacant	,,	third oboe or taille.
The assistant	,,	the bassoon.

---

[107] Reiche was the only prominent musician of the whole of this worthy society, but when Bach wrote the above he was already 64 years old. A volume of 24 *Quatricina* for a cornet and 3 trumpets, published by him in 1696, exists in the Royal Library at Berlin. He died in 1734, unmarried, in the Stadtpfeiffer Gasschen, whither he was carried home struck by apoplexy and lay there from Oct. 6 till he died (Register at Leipzig), and his funeral was followed by the larger half of the school. Gerber, Lexicon II., col. 258, says he was born at Weissenfels, Feb. 5, 1667; according to the register he was 68 years of age.

Thus the most important instruments for supporting the parts, and the most indispensable in themselves, are wanting, to wit:

Two first violins,	Two violoncellos,
Two second violins,	One double bass,
Two to play the viola,	Two flutes.

The deficiency here shown has hitherto had to be made good partly by the University students, but chiefly by the scholars. The students used to be very willing to do this, in the hope that in time they might derive some advantage from it, or perhaps receive a stipend or honorarium (as was formerly customary). But as this has not been the result, but, on the contrary, the little chance perquisites[108] which formerly fell to the *chorus musicus* have been in succession altogether withdrawn, the readiness of the students has likewise disappeared, for who will labour in vain, or give his service for nothing? Moreover, it must be remembered that, as the second violins generally, and the viola, violoncello, and double bass at all times, have been played by students (for lack of more efficient performers), it is easy to estimate what has thus been lost to the vocal choir; this refers only to Sunday music. But if I come to speak of the music for festivals, when music must be provided for both the principal churches at the same time, the lack of necessary performers will at once be still more striking, since then I have to give up such scholars as can play this or that instrument, and I am obliged to do altogether without their assistance.

Besides this it must not pass unnoticed that through the admissions hitherto granted to so many boys unskilled and ignorant in music the music has necessarily dwindled and fallen into decay. For it is easy to understand that a boy who knows nothing about music, who cannot even sing a second, can have no natural musical gifts, and consequently can never be of any use in music. And even those who bring some elementary knowledge to school with them, still are not of use so soon as is requisite and desirable. For time will not allow of their being duly trained for a year, or till they are skilled enough to be of use, but as soon as they are admitted they are placed in the choirs; and they ought to be at least sure of time and tune to be of any use in the service. Now, as every year some of those who have done something in music leave the school and their places are filled by others, many of whom are not immediately available, and most of them never of any use at all, it is easy to see that the choirs must by degrees diminish, and it is indeed notorious that the gentlemen, my predecessors Schell and Kuhnau, were obliged to have recourse to the assistance of

---

[108] These perquisites, "*Beneficia*," must have been derived from small savings, the residue of endowments, &c. No special funds were applied to the purpose or they must have been mentioned in the school and church accounts. In Kuhnau's time 50 gülden a year = 43 thlr. 18 ggr., were paid for church music out of the revenues of the church of St. Nicholas; Bach cannot refer to this sum for it was always regularly paid.

the students when they desired to perform complete and well-sounding music; which they were so far warranted in doing that several vocalists, a bass, a tenor, and an alto, as also instrumentalists, particularly two contra-bassists were favoured with salaries from a certain noble and learned councillor, and thereby were induced to strengthen the church music. Thus, since the present *status musices* is quite different to what it used to be formerly—the art being much advanced and taste marvellously changed, so that the old fashioned kind of music no longer sounds well in our ears, and competent assistance is thus rendered all the more necessary—such performers ought to be selected and appointed as may be able to satisfy the present musical taste and to undertake the new kinds of music, and at the same time be qualified to give satisfaction to the composer by their rendering of his work; and yet the few perquisites have been altogether withheld from the choir, though they ought to have been increased rather than diminished. And this, moreover, is passing strange, since it is expected of German musicians that they should be capable of performing extempore every kind of music, whether Italian or French, English or Polish, like some of those *virtuosi* before whom it may be placed and who have studied it for a long time beforehand, or even know it almost by heart, and who besides have such high salaries that their pains and diligence are well rewarded; but all this is not duly considered, and these (before spoken of) are left to take care of themselves, so that in the need of working for their bread many can never think of attaining proficiency, much less of distinguishing themselves. To give one instance of this statement we need only go to Dresden and see how the musicians are paid there by the king; it necessarily follows that all care as to maintenance is taken from these musicians; they are relieved of anxiety, and as, moreover, each person has to play but one instrument, it must be admirable and delightful to hear.

The conclusion is easy to arrive at: that in ceasing to receive the perquisites I am deprived of the power of getting the music into a better condition. Finally, I find myself compelled to depend on the number of the present scholars, to teach each one the methods of music, and then to leave it to more mature consideration whether under these circumstances the music can be carried on any longer, and whether its many and increasing deficiencies may be remedied.

It is, however, desirable to divide the whole into three classes. The really efficient boys are the following :—

1. Pezold, Lange, Stoll; *Prefecti* Frick, Krause, Kittler, Pohlreüter, Stein, Burckhard, Siegler, Nitzer, Reichhard, Krebs *major* and *minor*, Schöneman, Heder, and Dietel.

The motett singers, who must farther improve themselves in order to be efficient in the course of time for part-singing, [109] are the following :—

---

[109] Bach uses the word part-singing (figural music) in a restricted sense, which does not include the motett.

2. Jänigke, Ludewig *major* and *minor*, Meissner, Neücke *major* and *minor*, Hillmeyer, Steidel, Hesse, Haupt, Suppius, Segnitz, Thieme, Keller, Röder, Ossan, Berger, Lösch, Hauptmann, and Sachse.

Those of the last class are not musicians at all, and are named:

3. Bauer, Gross, Eberhard, Braune, Seyman, Tietze,[110] Hebenstreit, Wintzer, Osser, Leppert, Haussius, Feller, Crell, Zeymer, Guffer, Eichel, and Zwicker.

Total: seventeen available, twenty not yet available, and seventeen useless.

Leipzig, August 23, 1730.   JOH: SEB: BACH.
                                        Director Musices.

Certainly this document is not couched in very dutiful, much less very submissive, language. We need only compare it with Kuhnau's memorial which contains representations to the same effect, to understand how new and strange such a mode of address must have seemed to the Town Council, and it may be easily supposed that Bach's demeanour was not likely to dispose them to take steps to remedy the abuses he had pointed out. They simply let the memorial fall through with a certain expression of opinion. After the sitting of August 2, the Burgomasters called Bach before them to communicate to him the admonition that has been mentioned, and at the same time asked him whether he would be disposed to give the general lessons again in the place of *Magister* Pezold. Whether this interview took place before or after August 25, the date of Bach's memorial, at any rate the subject of it also came under discussion. When, on August 25, Dr. Born again presided at a meeting of the Council to which he reported his conversation with Bach, it is most probable that he already had Bach's document in his hands, or, at any rate, he knew perfectly well that it was on its way, and what its contents were. What he proposed, however, was only as follows: That the Cantor had shown very little inclination to resume the school work in question, and it was therefore advisable to entrust the teaching to *Magister* Krugel. The Council agreed unanimously and the whole affair was dropped.

Nor was Bach's application reconsidered later, or at any rate not in a sense favourable to him. This is quite evident

---

[110] Identical, no doubt, with Joh. Tobias Dieze named above.

from his letter to Erdmann; and the account books of the
Council place it beyond a doubt that, up to the year 1746, no
real addition was made to the funds devoted to keeping up
the music in the churches of St. Thomas and St. Nicholas.
But if any one would fain try to infer from these unsatisfactory and discreditable proceedings that the town authorities
felt a certain longing to make their mere material superiority
felt by the genius that was striving to escape into light and
air, that they intentionally oppressed him and so tried indirectly to hinder him in the full development of his artistic
faculties, it would be altogether an error of judgment. The
Council were for the time very wroth with Bach, and, in this
frame of mind, allowed themselves to be carried away and to
pass an odious measure—carried out, however, for only a short
time, and they kept the purse strings tight whenever they
thought outlay unnecessary; but they never deliberately
hindered the progress of the music under Bach's direction.
Indeed, when the authorities closed the year's accounts they
could prove by figures that considerably more had been voted
and paid for musical requirements in the last few years than
in the previous years. A complete restoration of the great
organ in St. Thomas', costing 390 thalers, had been effected
in 1720 and 1721; in 1724 and 1725 a thorough renovation
of the "very dilapidated and injured" organ of St. Nicholas
was effected at a cost of 600 thalers. In 1725 forty thalers
were again expended in repairing the organ of St. Thomas,
and two years later fifteen thalers more, and in 1735, when
Bach's relations with the Council were at the highest strain, a
sum of fifty thalers was voted for making the *Rückpositiv*
of the same organ an independent and separable instrument. In 1729, two new and "fine" violins, a "similar"
viola and a violoncello were bought for church use at a cost of
thirty-six thalers, and in the same year Bach was enabled to
purchase the *Florilegium Portense* by Bodenschatz, at the price
of twelve thalers,[111] for the use of the St. Thomas scholars

---

[111] In 1736 another copy of this collection of motetts was acquired for the
special use of the church of St. Nicholas; this cost ten thalers, and another in
the following year for St. Thomas' at the price of eight thalers. It would thus
seem that one copy was insufficient.

in church music. This outlay to us seems but small, even at
the higher value of money at that time. But it was not so
when compared with the usual average of expenditure in
matters musical, though, on the other hand, it was not
large in proportion to what such a musician as Bach was
justified in expecting. The fault of the Council lay in their
ignorance of what a genius and power they possessed in
him, and that double and treble the opportunities and
materials they afforded would not have sufficed for his full
and free development.

After this last experiment it may well be supposed that
Bach was deeply embittered against his superiors in authority,
and he seriously considered the question of quitting Leipzig.
If at this moment any advantageous prospect had offered
itself he very certainly would have followed it up, and his
official existence as Cantor of St. Thomas would have closed
at the end of his seven years' tenure, with small credit to
the town of Leipzig. But this was not the case, otherwise
it would not have occurred to Bach to apply to Erdmann,
the friend of his youth, who had meanwhile been appointed
the agent in Dantzig for the Emperor of Russia, to procure
him an appointment there. What could Bach want to be at
in Dantzig? It will be seen that it was but a clutch in the
empty air. However, we owe to this idea the most interesting letter that exists in the master's hand :—

EXCELLENT AND RESPECTED SIR,

      Your Excellency will forgive an old and faithful servant for
taking the liberty of troubling you with this letter. Nearly four years
have now elapsed since your Excellency did me the pleasure of kindly
answering my last sent to you;[112] though, as I remember, you were
graciously pleased to desire that I should give you some news of my
vicissitudes in life, and I hereby proceed to obey you. From my youth
up my history has been well-known to you, until the change which led
me to Cöthen as Capellmeister. There lived there a gracious Prince,
who both loved and understood music, and I thought there to spend my
life and end my days. As it turned out, however, his Serene Highness
married a Princess of Berenburg, and then it appeared as though the
musical dispositions of the said Prince had grown somewhat lukewarm,

---

[112] Erdmann had come from Dantzig in 1725 to Sax Gotha, his native place,
to arrange some matters of business; but, as we gather from this letter, he
had not seen Bach on this occasion.

while at the same time the new Princess served as an amusement to
him, and it pleased God that I should be called to be Director Musices
and Cantor to the Thomasschule in this place.   At first it did not
altogether please me to become a Cantor from having been a Capellmeister, and for this reason I deferred my decision for a quarter of a
year; however, the position was described to me in such favourable
terms that finally (and especially as my sons seemed inclined to study
here) I ventured upon it, in the Name of the Most High; I came to
Leipzig, passed my examination, and then made the move.   And here,
by God's pleasure, I remain to this day.   But now, since I find (I.) that
this appointment is by no means so advantageous as it was described to
me ; (II.) that many fees incidental to it are now stopped ; (III.) that
the town is very dear to live in ; (IV.) and that the authorities are very
strange folks, with small love for music, so that I live under almost
constant vexation, jealousy, and persecution, I feel compelled to seek,
with God's assistance, my fortune elsewhere.   If your Excellency
should know of, or be able to find, a suitable appointment in your town
for your old and faithful servant, I humbly crave you to give me the
benefit of your favourable recommendation.   Nothing shall be wanting on
my part to give satisfaction (and justify) your favourable recommendation and intercession, and to use my best diligence.   My present position secures me about 700 thlrs., and when there are rather more deaths
than usual the fees increase in proportion ; but it is a healthy air, so
it happens, on the contrary—as in the past year—that I lost above 100
thalers of the usual funeral fees.   In Thuringia I can do more with
400 thalers than here with twice as many hundred, by reason of the
excessive cost of living.   I must now make some small mention of my
domestic circumstances.   I am now married. for the second time, and
my first wife died in Cöthen.   Of my first marriage, three sons and a
daughter are living, which your Excellency saw in Weimar, as you may
be graciously pleased to remember.   Of my second marriage, one son
and two daughters are living.   My eldest is *Studiosus Juris*, the other
two are one in the first and the other in the second class, and my eldest
daughter is still unmarried.   The children of my second marriage are
still little, the eldest, a boy, being six years old.   They are all born
musicians, and I can assure you that I can already form a concert,
both vocal and instrumental, of my own family, particularly as my
present wife sings a very clear soprano, and my eldest daughter joins
in bravely.   I should almost overstep the bounds of politeness by
troubling your Excellency any further, so I hasten to conclude with
most devoted respects, and remain your Excellency's life long and most
obedient and humble servant,

LEIPZIG, *October* 28, 1730.[113]   JOH: SEBAST: BACH.

---

[113] The history of this letter is given in the Preface ; the address is wanting.
Since quoting certain passages of this letter on p. 147, a friend has put me in
possession of a photograph copy of the whole document.

This letter had not the hoped for result; Bach remained in Leipzig, and, as we may safely conclude, not altogether unwillingly in the end. If the conditions of his life had been really unendurable, a man of such energetic character would never have rested till he had set himself free; and, enjoying such fame as he did, it certainly could have been a matter of no great difficulty. Though Bach dwells with some insistance on the high price of the necessaries of life in Leipzig, and complains of the insufficiency and uncertainty of his income—and the eloquence with which he alludes, in his memorial to the Council, to the financial advantages of the musicians in Dresden is highly significant—some immediate pressure of circumstances and his general sense of discomfort evidently made him take too black a view. We may counterbalance these complaints merely by the facts that at Bach's death his private concerns were left in good order, that his household was established on a comfortable footing, and that he even left a small sum of money. When Kuhnau even could say that, with his fixed salary, a musician like himself—who was always receiving visits from his fellow artists, who often had to treat the students who sang with the choir, and had besides a large household to keep up— could not make much show in the world, how much more must this have been the case with Bach, whose family was so much larger and whose house no musician on his travels ever passed by? That he should, under these circumstances, have laid anything by, speaks volumes.

Then he speaks of suffering from the jealousy of his fellow artists, we think at once of Görner. But where could such a man as Bach have gone without finding others jealous of him? The musical resources of the place were no doubt meagre, but this he must have known from the first, and in some respects they had actually increased and improved. And, finally, if the attitude of the authorities was not very encouraging—nay, at times, oppressive and offensive—Bach himself must have seen that the matters at issue were not of so crucial a nature as to lead to the question " To be, or not to be?" So by degrees the black clouds rolled over and the sky cleared again, and an occurrence which took place

in that same year must have had a considerable influence
over his affairs, an event which may be said to have led to
the happiest period of Bach's life in Leipzig.

In September, Johann Matthias Gesner, the newly elected
Rector of the Thomasschule, came to take up his appointment.   Gesner was born in 1691, at Roth, near Nuremberg,
he had studied at Jena, and in 1715 he became Conrecter of
the Academy at Weimar.[114]   Here he remained till 1729,
and for seven years had been Principal of the Ducal Library.
He then was placed at the head of the Academy at Anspach,
but at the end of a year he gave up his appointment in order
to go to Leipzig.   Here he only remained till 1734; he had
pledged himself not to hold a professorship in the University
at the same time as his office as Rector (or Warden) of the
school.   But as this had always been the custom with the
former Rectors, Gesner's position was much injured by this
condition of remaining outside the pale of the University,
and besides this, his distinguished abilities qualified him
for the highest academical honours.   In 1734 he therefore
obeyed a call to the University of Göttingen, where he died,
in 1761, after many years of brilliant and successful labours.[115]
All that Gesner did for classical learning in Germany—how
he revived the study of Greek, and was the first to contemplate the works of the ancients from a higher standpoint
as to their purport and form, giving them life and value in
the mental training of his pupils—is familiar to every student
of philology.   But even more important to the purpose of
the present work was the talent he immediately displayed as
a master of schoolboys.   In him the Council had found the
very man they needed, if the regulations drawn up for the
resuscitation of the institution were to be anything but a
dead letter.   Under Gesner's mastership a new period
dawned on the fallen fortunes of the school.   Together with
a vast store of practical learning he possessed in an eminent

---

[114] Vol. I., p. 390.
[115] *J. Aug. Ernesti* narratio de Jo. Matthia Gesnero ad Davidem Ruhnkenium.
Addita opusculis oratoriis, 1762, p. 306.   H. Sauppe, Johann Matthias Gesner,
Weimar, 1856.

degree the power of governing; resolute firmness was combined in his character with humanity and gentleness; in his conduct to the Council he was uniformly polite, but decided. It was inevitable that he should soon win their high esteem and complete confidence; indeed, he was from the first treated by the authorities with a distinction which proves that they were not so absolutely devoid of all sense of intellectual superiority as we might perhaps infer from Bach's experience. We may here quote a fact recorded by his successor, Johann August Ernesti. Gesner, whose health was feeble, and who during his residence in Leipzig had two severe illnesses, at first had a residence assigned to him at some distance from the school, which was being rebuilt; and to relieve him of the inconvenience of the daily walk to the schools he was always carried thither in a chair, and back again to his house when lessons were over, at the cost of the Council. He was also so far relieved of the exercise of his functions as to be released from the duty of inspecting the school, which the Rector usually was required to do in weekly rotation with the three upper masters, and which was now undertaken by the *Quartus*, *Magister* Winkler.

Gesner introduced a better mutual understanding among his colleagues, and set them an admirable example in the fulfilment of his duties. He secured the affection of his scholars by his new and intelligent methods of instruction, by his unwearying interest in their progress and welfare, and by the determination with which he enforced discipline and morality. He carried out the new regulations with exactitude, endeavouring to amplify and emphasise certain provisions and to modify the existing condition of things in harmony with their purport. Thus, for instance, under the existing system the Latin prayers, morning and evening, were replaced by German prayers; Gesner, who attached the greatest importance to the practice of speaking Latin, proposed that the Latin services should be restored, because otherwise "rudeness—*i.e.*, want of culture—and ignorance would once more get the upper hand." Again, in 1733, by his suggestion, rules in German, and in conformity with the new school regulations, were printed for the scholars.[116] One, who was a pupil at the Thomasschule under Gesner, describes his person and proceedings in the following pleasing manner:—"In discipline he guided himself very precisely by the laws of the school, at that time just revised; he was cautious in punishing, and in order to avoid undue severity would let a few days pass after the delinquency was committed. Then in the evening, after prayers, and when the motett was sung, he would come among the scholars, call up the criminal, point out with impressive gravity the impropriety and sinfulness of his fault, and then pronounce, besides the admonition, his verdict as to the punishment. This way of delivering judgment had a wonderful effect; all the more because he was universally respected. Every week all the scholars, even the outside day-boys, had to give in their diaries, and when they were returned to them they found ample evidence that nothing had escaped him. Ernesti also did this at first, but only, as before, with the foundation boys, and it was soon altogether given up, as Ernesti commonly forgot to give the diaries back. Gesner was in other respects very affable and affectionate in his intercourse with the boys, and would look in upon them even during the singing lessons, with which the Rectors did not usually trouble themselves, and would listen with pleasure to the practising of a piece of church music. If he found any boy at work in his room at anything which, though not part of his school task, was useful in itself—for instance, if he were writing from a copy—he did not fall upon him with a storm of indignation, but, if he saw a real talent for caligraphy, would recommend him to further study and practice, because, said he, the state had need of every variety of talent and skill. And to all he would preach, when opportunity offered, 'Always do something that is of some definite

---

[116] E. E. Hochweisen Raths der Stadt Leipzig Gesetze der Schule zu S. Thomae. Leipzig, druckts Bernhard Christoph Breitkopf, 1733, pp. 4, 39.

use, and which you can turn to account in your calling in life.' "[117]

Bach and Gesner had already known each other in Weimar; the acquaintance was now renewed and soon grew to be a hearty friendship between the two colleagues. Our authority has just told us how much interest Gesner took in Bach's musical efforts, how much he enjoyed his performances, even visiting him in lesson hours. He exerted himself also in other ways to give the music in the school a helping hand so far as lay in his power, and when, in 1732, Bach wished to acquire a MS. collection of motetts and responses for the choir of St. Thomas, he himself applied to the Council for the necessary sum, which was readily voted. He had a strong feeling for music and could do full justice to Bach's greatness; years after he had not forgotten the overwhelming impression made on him by that grand musician. We find eloquent witness to this in the note which he makes in his edition, published in 1738, of the *Institutiones Oratoriæ* of Marcus Fabius Quinctilianus to a passage (I., 12, 3) where Quinctilian is speaking of the capacity possessed by man of comprehending and doing several things at once; adducing as an example a player on the lyre, who can at the same time utter both words and tones and besides play on the instrument and mark time with his foot. To which Gesner remarks, "All these, my Fabius, you would deem very trivial could you but rise from the dead and see Bach (whom I mention because not long ago he was my colleague in the Thomasschule at Leipzig) ; how he with both hands, and using all his fingers, plays on a key board which seems to consist of many lyres in one, and may be called the instrument of instruments, of which the innumerable pipes are made to sound by means of bellows ; and how he, going one way with his hands, and another way with the

---

[117] Historia Scholarum Lipsiensium collecta a Joh. Frid. Köhlero, pastore Tauchensi, 1776 seqq., p. 160. MS. preserved in the Royal Public Library at Berlin. The author adds, " These remarks are from the words of a scholar of Gesner, who spoke often, and always with enthusiasm, of his master's great qualities."

utmost celerity with his feet, elicits by his unaided skill many of the most various passages, which, however, uniting produce as it were hosts of harmonious sounds ; I say, could you only see him, how he achieves what a number of your lyre-players and six hundred flute-players could never achieve, not as one who may sing to the lyre, and so perform his part, but by presiding over thirty or forty performers all at once, recalling this one by a nod, another by a stamp of the foot, another with a warning finger, keeping time and tune ; and while high tones are given out by some, deep tones by others, and notes between them by others, this one man, standing alone in the midst of the loud sounds, having the hardest task of all, can discern at every moment if any one goes astray, and can keep all the musicians in order, restore any waverer to certainty and prevent him from going wrong; rhythm is in his every limb, he takes in all the harmonies by his subtle ear, as it were uttering all the different parts through the medium of his own mouth. Great admirer as I am of antiquity in other respects, I yet deem this Bach of mine, and whosoever there may chance to be that resembles him, to comprise in himself many Orpheuses and twenty Arions."[118]

With such feelings of admiration and liking as Gesner had for Bach he must have made it his concern to lighten, as far as possible, his colleague's sense of discomfort, and also to bring him into pleasanter relations with the Council. And we can see that he actually attempted both, from two memorials which he addressed to the Council and which—as the petitioner was Gesner—were no doubt successful. Although Bach had been for the most part represented by a deputy in giving the Latin lessons, he was not altogether released from them, and at any rate had to hold himself in readiness in case of need. Gesner now proposed that the Council should entrust the Cantor with the general supervision of the school during week days, which he had hitherto undertaken only on Fridays, since it was a function which most naturally allied

---

[118] The first person to draw attention to this passage in Gesner's commentary was Constantin Bellermann in the *Parnassus Musarum*, p. 41 (see Vol. I., p. 801) ; it was subsequently pointed out again by Joh. Adam Hiller.

itself with his other duties. In exchange for this, and for a few hours more of singing lessons, he was to be exonerated altogether from general teaching of any kind. This suggestion was probably made by Gesner on the occasion of *Magister* Pezold's death, May 30, 1731, since on the arrival of a new functionary it was easy to modify the position of affairs; in the beginning of 1732 Joh. August Ernesti was appointed Conrector. While the place was vacant the Conrector's fees amounted to a sum of 120 gülden 10 ggr. 5 pf., of which Pezold's heirs received forty gülden, and Gesner begged the Council to divide the remainder equally among the Rector, Cantor, *Tertius*, and *Quartus*. Bach had not indeed ever given lessons in the place of the Conrector, but the Inspector's work had of course come round in more frequent rotation. Hence Gesner wrote: "The duties of teaching, it is true, have occasioned no trouble to Herr Bach. Still he hopes, this time, to have his equal share in the division, because on the last occasion (when Ernesti died) he was altogether passed over." So here we may suppose the great "sequestration" question was brought to a final issue.

Bach, however, was not so easy to conciliate. The same obstinacy which supported him in the pursuit of his aims characterised any antipathy he had once conceived. When, in 1733, he dedicated to the King and Elector the two first sections of his B minor Mass he frankly says, in the letter which accompanied it, that his object in this dedication was to obtain some court appointment. In his present position he had no doubt suffered from one and another unmerited insult and occasionally from a diminution in his fees;[119] all this he would then be relieved from. But although the appointment he desired was not for the present accorded to him, no farther serious differences arose between Bach and the Council. They had learnt to know each other and henceforth sought to accommodate matters. Bach's position in Leipzig could never be more favourable than it

[119] "Accidentien," which commonly means fees, in this letter had no doubt a more general meaning, including all moneys accruing from exceptional sources. The fees for funerals and weddings, and the Cantor's share of the money collected in the processional singing, were secured to him by law.

was now. He had the command of the most famous Musical
Society in the town, of which he could also avail himself
for the church services, and some excellent pupils, as Johann
Ludwig Krebs, the son of his old Weimar pupil Tobias
Krebs ; and his own three eldest sons—who already deserved
to be considered important, or at any rate highly promising
artists—were of efficient use in his work. The organist of
the New Church was a musician devoted to his service, and
at St. Nicholas' he procured the appointment, in 1730, of a
former pupil, Johann Schneider, who before that had been
Kammermusicus in Weimar.[120]

It is a sufficient proof of Bach's consequence and influence
that two of his former pupils should be among the candidates
for the vacant post of organist. Johann Caspar Vogler, an
admirable musician and court organist at Weimar, competed
with Schneider, but the decision arrived at was that Vogler
misled the people by playing too fast, so Schneider was preferred. He was at the same time a good violin player and
could be of use to Bach in other ways on various occasions.
He held his post for years after Bach's death.[121] And now,
last and best of all, he had the advantage of Gesner's friendship, and the support of his authority, which was favourable
to music. That this was in fact a source of happiness to him
we may take as a matter of course, though there is no direct
evidence of it. An altered version of the cantata composed
in 1726, for the birthday of the Princess of Anhalt-Cöthen,
may probably be attributed to Gesner, though no proof can
be adduced ; but we may regard as evidence of their hearty
co-operation the solemn ceremonial with which the enlarged
and improved school buildings were opened on June 5, 1732.
In the Latin speech made by Gesner on this occasion he did
not fail to mention, with a few words of warm approval, the
care given to music in the institution, and Bach conducted a

---

[120] Walther gives 1729 as the date of Schneider's appointment. But this
is an error; the place was no doubt vacant in 1729 but it was not given to
Schneider before August 1, 1730.

[121] In 1766 Schneider applied for an assistant which was granted, as we learn
from documents concerning the organists of the church of St. Nicholas.

cantata of which the words were written by his colleague
Winkler. The music to these verses—and very bad they
are—is not known to exist.[122]

IV.

THE PLAN AND ARRANGEMENT OF THE CHURCH SERVICES
IN LEIPZIG.—MUSIC USED IN IT; THE ORGANS AND
BACH'S TREATMENT OF ACCOMPANIMENTS.—DIFFICULTIES
OF PITCH AND TUNE.

THE arrangement of the Lutheran service throughout
Electoral Saxony was regulated by an act issued by
Duke Heinrich, in 1540. This decree aimed not merely at
establishing a uniform order of divine worship throughout
the Duchy of Saxony and its dependencies at that time, but
also at laying down a line of limitation within which different
parishes and congregations might regulate their respective
services according to their needs and wishes. This was in
accordance with Luther's own views, as expressly stated in
his treatise on the German Mass and the ordering of divine
service (Wittenberg, 1526), to the effect that each one should,
in all Christian freedom and in accordance with his own
pleasure, use only such customs of those he laid down "how,
when, where, and so long as circumstances suited and permitted." And this was actually continued even after
the church ordinances of the Elector August, in 1580,
had expressly introduced a greater uniformity in the
divine services in the different towns and villages of his
dominions. Thus there were certain usages in the church
services at Leipzig which gave them a quite peculiar
character. The Lutheran form of worship was a modification of the Roman Catholic Mass. In many towns and
districts this was more rapidly and completely abandoned;

[122] They are given in App. B., x., 4, of the German edition of this work. In
the invitation circular, sent out the day before, Gesner expresses a wish that
the scholars may be "*juvenes ad humanitatem, quæ litteris censetur et musice,
probe instituti atque exculti.*"

in Leipzig, for a long time—indeed even during Bach's residence there—it retained a close resemblance to it. This was visible partly in the external ceremonial and usage, as, for instance, in the use of a little bell at the consecration of the bread and wine at the Lord's Supper, in the retention of ceremonial robes for the officiating ministers and surplices for the singing boys, and partly in the continued use of the original form of certain portions of the Catholic ritual, and, as connected with this, of a more extended use of Latin. These traditions prevailed very extensively even in the more accessory details of religious life. The bequests which, even so late as Bach's time, were not unfrequently made to the school foundation for the public performance of certain chorales on the anniversary of the testator's death, plainly indicate a Roman origin.[123] Latin hymns and responses were sung even in the processional singing, as well as German hymns and songs, and there was no lack of timid souls who would gladly have seen the great resemblance of the Protestant services at Leipzig with that of the Roman church radically altered. Indeed, in 1702, the Council thought it ought to take the matter in hand, and on February 13 addressed a petition to the King-Elector, to request that devout and approved hymns, prayers, and texts in German might be for the future introduced in all the churches of Saxony. At the time of the Reformation matters had been otherwise. The authorities had been anxious not to cause a collision between the clergy and the simpler folks and new converts by any too rapid and conspicuous changes in the church ceremonial; they had hoped, indeed, to attract greater numbers to the Lutheran evangelical church by this moderation, but the pressing danger now was that many persons, not seeing any very great difference in the services, might be misled into a wrong interpretation of the Lutheran doctrines.

---

[123] To give a single instance, from November 19, 1736, the chorale " O Jesu Christ mein's Lebens Licht," was to be sung every year in the New Church in memory of Dame Anna Elisabeth Seeber, who bequeathed, in consideration, fifteen thalers a year for distribution. See the account book of the New Church for that year.

"Spiritual songs" in German were far better adapted to
rouse feelings of devotion than the old Latin responses and
versicles, which were, for the most part, not understood
by the people. However, the petition was not adequately
supported. The townspeople of Leipzig knew full well that
these forms of divine service were made interesting by
their peculiarity, and even the clerical body were of
opinion that the Latin hymns still pleased some people,
and particularly strangers. It had, therefore, but small
results; only, with regard to the school perambulations, it
was determined—but not before 1711—that instead of the
response "Sint lumbi vestri circumcincti" (Luke xiii. 35),
certain German hymns should be sung referring to the Day
of Judgment—namely, "Es ist gewisslich an der Zeit,"
"Wachet auf, ruft uns die Stimme," and "O Ewigkeit du
Donnerwort."

An exact comprehension of the order of divine service in
the churches of St. Nicholas and St. Thomas is of the
greatest importance to an estimate of Bach's church music,
for it is only perfectly intelligible when regarded in all its
bearings and relations to the nature and scheme of
these services. We have a note in Bach's own hand of the
order of the service on the first Sunday in Advent when he
was in Leipzig, in 1714.[124] As it is interesting on this
account it may find a place here, although it will be seen
from what follows that it is not altogether exact and complete:—

The order of divine service in Leipzig on the first Sunday in Advent,
in the morning: 1. The Prelude. 2. Motett. 3. Prelude to the *Kyrie*,
which is accompanied throughout. 4. Intoning at the altar. 5. The
Epistle read. 6. The Litany sung. 7. Prelude to the chorale. 8. The
Gospel read. 9. The Prelude to the principal music. 10. The Creed
sung. 11. The sermon. 12. After the sermon a few verses of a hymn
are commonly sung. 13. *Verba institutionis*. 14. Preludes and chorales
alternately until the celebration of the Communion.

The services were different on ordinary Sundays, on Holy
Days, and in Passion week. We will begin with ordinary
Sundays. The series of services, during which the houses

---

[124] See Vol. I., p. 519.

were closed all day and all public transactions were prohibited, began at 5.30 in the morning with matins in the
church of St. Nicholas. There was a special choral
institute attached to this church, under its own Cantor,
besides the choir from St. Thomas', and this was supported
by a municipal stipend. It consisted of students and was
governed by strict regulations of its own.[125] At the same
time the Cantor of St. Thomas exercised a certain supervision, since the musical property was entrusted to his
care.[126] The choir sung the Psalm " *Venite, exultemus
Domino*," then a Psalm, a *Responsorium;* afterwards one
of them read the Gospel for the day from the desk in
Latin, followed by another who read it in German. Then
came the *Te Deum*, started by the organist, and played and
sung verse by verse antiphonally between him and the choir.
The service ended with " *Da pacem*," or some other versicle
adapted to the season, and last of all " *Benedicamus
Domino*."

Morning service began precisely at seven in both churches.
An organ prelude introduced a motett suited to the Gospel
for the day, and usually sung in Latin. In Lent, or in
times of general mourning, when the organ was not played,
the motett was omitted, and the service began with the
Song of Zacharias " *Benedictus Dominus* " (Luke i. 68), and
" *Vivo ego*."[127] It was not till then that the Introit was
performed, with which, according to Duke Heinrich's *Diary*,
the service was said to begin; after that the Kyrie. This was
sung alternately in Latin and German in the two churches;
when it was in German the version beginning " Kyrie Gott
Vater in Ewigkeit " was used. Sometimes the Kyrie was

---

[125] These rules were drawn up in 1767, when the institute probably came
into existence. They were re-written in 1678 by Gottfried Vopelius, well
known as the compiler of the New Leipzig Hymn Book of 1682, and Cantor
at the time to St. Nicholas. The MS. exists in the library of the church.
The Cantor in Bach's time was *Magister* Johann Hieronymus Homilius.

[126] In 1767, when the hymn for Palm Sunday, " *Gloria, laus et honor tibi*,"
was to be sung, Doles, the Cantor, confessed that he had lost the music.

[127] The disuse of the organ in Lent was so far limited in the year 1780, that
from that time the Communion hymns at least might be sung with an organ
accompaniment; see the accounts of the Church of St. Nicholas, from Candlemas to Crucis, 1780.

in a concerted form, probably during the fasts—that is to say, on the first Sunday in Advent, which agrees with Bach's statement quoted above ; since on the last three Sundays in Advent, during Lent, and on the Ember days no concerted music was used. Another day on which the Kyrie was given in a concerted form will presently be mentioned in enumerating the festivals. Next the Lord's Prayer was said by the minister, kneeling at the altar, and the sacramental cup was placed on the altar by the sacristan ; one of the deacons intoned the "*Gloria in excelsis*," to which either the choir responded with "*Et in terra pax hominibus*," or the congregation sang the hymn "Allein Gott in der Höh"— "To God alone on high." Then followed the blessing in Latin, "*Dominus vobiscum*," with the answer of the choir, "*Et cum spiritu tuo*." The Collect was now read, likewise in Latin—that is to say, sung to the proper tone; and after the chanting of the Epistle for the day from the reading-desk—in Advent and Lent the Litany was sung in such a way as that the congregation not only repeated the responses, but joined in the petitions—the Litany was chanted in St. Thomas' by four boys specially appointed and called "*Altarists*," the choir responding.[128] Then came a congregational hymn suited to the Gospel, while on other Sundays the congregational hymn followed immediately after the Epistle, and the Litany was omitted. The Gospel was then intoned from the desk, and after it the minister whose weekly turn it was intoned the "*Credo*" before the altar, and on the three last Sundays in Advent and in Lent, as also on the Festivals of the Apostles, the whole of the Nicene Creed was sung in Latin by the choir. On other Sundays the prelude to the principal piece of music came immediately after the minister's intoning, and then the music itself.[129] When it was ended the Creed was sung in

---

[128] This is shown by the regulations of the Leipzig Consistory of Jan. 31, 1810, which abrogates the former custom. In the Ephoral Archives at Leipzig.

[129] In Bach's list of the order we find under No. 8, after the words "the Gospel read," the following addition scratched through—"and *Credo* intoned." Hence Bach must, by mistake at first, have noted down the order of the service as it was told him for the first Sunday in Advent.

German by the whole congregation. (Wir glauben all' an einen Gott.) As has been said, on ordinary Sundays part-singing was performed in the two principal churches alternately. Thus when it was not performed the German Creed was sung immediately after the intoning of the *Credo* in Latin.[130] Then came the sermon on the Gospel, which was once more interrupted before the Gospel itself was read by the congregational hymn, " Herr Jesu Christ dich zu uns wend." The sermon lasted an hour, from eight till nine, since the whole service was throughout adapted to an exact division of time, and to keep it strictly to these limits a sand hour-glass was used.[131] After the sermon the general confession was recited with the usual church prayers, and after the customary ascription of praise from the pulpit, and the Lord's Prayer, the blessing of St. Paul, " The peace of God which passeth all understanding," &c., closed the service. While the preacher was descending from the pulpit a few verses were sung of some suitable hymn.

The Communion celebration formed the principal part of the service. It is not quite clear whether on ordinary Sundays it was preceded by the introductory words of Luther's para-phrase of the Lord's Prayer and the admonition which follows; it may however be considered probable from Duke Heinrich's decree. During the communion German hymns appropriate to the service were sung; but before these, even on ordinary Sundays and holidays, another harmonised composition was sung, as we learn from the list made by Bach and from a note written on the second portion of the *continuo* part for his Trinity Cantata " Höchst erwünschtes Freudenfest "—" Feast of joy so long desired." The end of the whole service— without a final collect as it would seem—consisted in the bene-diction " God be gracious and merciful unto us and give us His blessing." The length of the Morning service varied with

---

[130] It was thus the custom took its rise which Rochlitz speaks of (Für Freunde der Tonkunst, S. 4, 2nd ed., note to p. 278) as a hardly credible monstrosity : that the Latin *Credo* was sung in a " lively " manner just before the German creed.

[131] " 12. ggr. for repairing the sand-clock on the organ." Account of St. Thomas, 1739-1740, p. 62.

the number of communicants; often it was not over till eleven o'clock, thus lasting four hours. This of itself accounts for its beginning so early, and the consequence was that, in winter, the music before the sermon was for the most part performed by candlelight.[132]

Mid-day service, which began at about a quarter before noon, was very simple in character. It consisted of a sermon with two congregational hymns to precede and one to follow it. The choir were not employed in it.

At about a quarter past one Vespers began with a motett, followed by a congregational hymn. One of the deacons intoned a psalm from the desk, the Lord's Prayer, and a collect. Then came another hymn and the sermon, which treated of the epistle, or in Advent of the Catechism, and in Lent of the history of the Passion. After the sermon the *Magnificat* was sung in German to the four-part melody by Joh. Hermann Schein,[133] and, after a collect recited at the altar and the Blessing, the service concluded with the hymn " Nun danket alle Gott."

As regarded the Holy days, three great Festivals were specially celebrated, each being honoured with a particularly full performance of the service for three days running. Matins in St. Nicholas' remained unchanged, excepting that they began at five instead of at half-past. Morning service and Vespers were begun on each day by a hymn sung by the choir; these hymns were: at Christmas, *Puer natus in Bethlehem*; at Easter, "Heut triumphiret Gottes Sohn"; at Whitsuntide, *Spiritus sancti gratia*. After this, at Morning service, came the organ prelude and motett. The collect, which preceded the epistle, seems to have had reference to some introductory verse from the Bible, appropriate to the day.[134] After the hymn that followed the sermon the complete Latin pre-

---

[132] When part-music was performed the Cantor and the Conrector had to provide the lighting for the organ choir. The Cantor received for this purpose eleven thlrs. fifteen ggr. per annum out of the revenues of St. Thomas, and for St. Nicholas', where the choir was much smaller, seven thlrs. twenty-one ggr.

[133] See Vopelius, Neu Leipziger Gesangbuch, p. 440.

[134] This I infer from Vopelius, who has verses appropriate to every festival in his hymn book.

fation was sung as introductory to the Communion, and then
the Sanctus was sung in parts; besides which during the
Communion either a motett or a concerted piece was performed.   The whole service closed with a festal hymn sung
by the congregation after the Benediction.

At Vespers the collect before the sermon was omitted, and
after the sermon the *Magnificat* was sung in Latin and in
parts.   Church cantatas were performed at Morning service
and at Vespers in both churches on the first two days of each
festival; at Vespers one took the place of the omitted offer-
tory collect.   Still only two cantatas were performed on each
day, since the one which had been sung in the morning in one
church served for the other in the afternoon, and *vice versa*.
The church of which the Superintendent for the time being
was the minister—in Bach's time therefore that of St.
Nicholas—had the precedence—that is to say, the first and
best choir sang there in the morning of the first Holy day
under Bach's own direction, while the *principal music*, as it
was called, was performed in the morning of the second day
at St. Thomas'; on the third day music was given in only
one of the churches.[185]

The festivals on which this double performance was given
were Christmas, Easter, and Whitsuntide, also at the New
Year, Epiphany, Ascension, and Trinity, and the Annunciation of the Blessed Virgin.   The hymns specially appointed
were, for the New Year and Epiphany, *Puer natus in
Bethlehem;* for Ascension, "Heut triumphiret Gottes Sohn";
for Trinity, "*Spiritus sancti gratia*," the same as at
Christmas, Easter, and Whitsuntide.   At the New Year
and Epiphany the mid-day sermon was preached in only
one of the churches.

---

[185] See, "Texte zur Leipziger Kirchen-*Music*, auff die heiligen Oster-Feyertage,
ingleichen auff Jubilate, Cantate, und das Fest der Himmelfarth Christi, *Anno*
1711.   LEIPZIG, gedruckt bey Jmmanuel Tietzen," und "Texte zur Leipziger
Kirchen-*Music*, Auf die Heiligen Weyhnachts-Feyertage, und den Sonntag
darauf, 1720.   Ingleichen auf das Fest Der Beschneidung Christi, den drauf
folgenden Sonntag, Das Fest der Offenbahrung, und den Sonntag darauf, des
1721 sten Jahres.   Leipzig, gedruckt bey Jmmanuel Tietzen." These are both
to be found in the Library of the Historical Society (Verein für die Geschichte]
at Leipzig.

Of the three festivals in honour of the Virgin, the Purification and the Annunciation had a specially ecclesiastical character; on the first, both morning and afternoon service were begun and ended alike with the hymn *Ex legis observantia*. The Festival of the Annunciation was held on March 25; but if this date fell on Maunday Thursday, Good Friday, or Easter Day, it was kept on Palm Sunday, and, in spite of its being in Lent, part-singing and the organ were allowed.

The Reformation Festival was kept only as a half-holiday and always on October 31; but if this fell on a Saturday or a Monday it was celebrated on the previous or the following Sunday.[136] The Morning service began with an organ piece and a motett; the Kyrie, which followed the Introit, was set in a concerted form. The Epistle—II. Thess. ii. 3-8—was intoned, and then for the Gospel, Rev. xiv. 6-8, was read. After the sermon the choir sang the *Te Deum* to the accompaniment of trumpets and drums, and, as a close to the service, the congregation sang "Nun danket alle Gott." The services for St. John's and St. Michael's days were essentially the same. All these festivals had this in common, that a festal hymn was sung in the middle of the sermon; apparently the collect before the Epistle was on all of these days founded on a suitable text, and that for the Reformation Festival seems to have been the Latin one *pro pace*, "for peace."[137]

The order of service for Passion week had this feature in common with the whole of Lent, that neither the organ nor concerted music were employed. This rule was not without exceptions, and it has already been said that it was broken through if the Annunciation fell on or was transferred to Palm Sunday. When Palm Sunday was celebrated as such the order of service was as follows: An organ

---

[136] Gerber, Historie der Kirchen-*CEREMONIEN* in Sachsen. Dresden und Leipzig, 1732, V. 4, p. 227.

[137] At least it was so in the year 1755, when, moreover, the order of the Reformation Day services underwent several changes. Compare also Schöberlein, Schatz des liturgischen Chor-und Gemeindegesangs, Part I., Göttingen, Vandenhoeck und Ruprecht, 1865, p. 487.

prelude led at once into the *Kyrie*. After the intonation of
the *Gloria*, the hymn "Allein Gott in der Höh sei Ehr"
was sung by the congregation. Instead of the Gospel, the
Archdeacon chanted the history of the Passion, in German,
according to St. Matthew, before the high altar, with the
assistance of a choir of scholars. This was followed by the
motett, *Ecce quomodo moritur justus*, by Gallus.[188]   The
celebration itself was not preceded by the whole of the
Præfation, but as an introduction to the Lord's prayer,
the so-called *praefatio orationis dominicae*[189] was read, as it
seems, in Latin, and this was usual also on the preceding
Sundays from the third Sunday in Lent onwards. Then a
motett was again sung, and hymns on the Passion or the
Communion, by the congregation. At the early service,
which began at about half-past five,[140] it may be noticed that
the choristers sang the hymn *Gloria, laus et honor tibi
sit, Rex Christe*. Also that on Maunday Thursday the
service began with an organ prelude. The passage from
Phil. ii. 8, *Humiliavit semet ipsum*, was sung as an
Introit after the Epistle, the hymn *Crux fidelis inter omnes*,
and, during the Communion, the Motett, *Jesus Christus
Dominus noster*. The same Introit was sung on Good Friday,
but the organ was altogether silent. For the Epistle and
Gospel, Psalm xxii. and Isaiah liii. were used inter-
changeably year and year about. Instead of the chanted
passage from the Gospel, however, the Passion according
to St. John was sung, as that according to St. Matthew
had been on Palm Sunday. The accounts of the Passion
in St. Mark and St. Luke were taken no cognisance of in
the Liturgy. This part of the service was followed, not by
the motett *Ecce quomodo*, but by the congregational hymn
"O Traurigkeit! o Herzeleid!" The celebration was again

---

[188] Vopelius, p. 263 ff. Johann Adam Hiller, in the preface to his Vier-
stimmige lateinische und deutsche Chorgesänge—"Four-part choral hymns
in Latin and German "—(Part I., Leipzig, 1791), says that this motett was
always sung in churches on fast-days.

[189] On this see Schöberlein, loc. cit., p. 371 and 373.

[140] The authorities give the time as half-past six, but this must be a mistake,
for the Morning service began at seven o'clock, and the early service must have
been celebrated on Palm Sunday at the same time as on other Sundays.

preceded by the *Praefatio orationis dominicae,* but no motett was sung in the course of it, only hymns on the Communion and the Passion were sung by the congregation. Until the year 1721 no performances of the Passion were known in Leipzig excepting in the chorale form. The influence of operatic music had gradually become so strong that it had at last penetrated even into Passion week. At the date just mentioned, the modern " madrigal " or polyphonic style of Passion music, consisting wholly of part-writing, first found a place in the vesper service for Good Friday. Kuhnau, who so often bewailed the destructive influence of the opera on church music, was obliged to yield, nay, even to compose a work in this style himself. This still exists, though only in the sketch, and will be described more fully farther on. The new performances of Passion music took place in the Churches of St. Nicholas and St. Thomas in alternate years. The Thomaskirche was chosen first, perhaps because it had more suitable accommodation for musical performances on a large scale.[141] This arrangement remained in vogue for nearly half a century until the old performances in a chorale style were entirely abolished by an order from the Consistory on March 20, 1766. The deacons were for the most part unmusical, the performances sounded ill and had not tended to edification.

From 1766 onwards Passion music in the madrigal style was employed also in the Morning service, being one and the same in the two churches, but so arranged that in one year the performance took place in the Thomaskirche on Palm Sunday, and in the Nikolai-Kirche on Good Friday, while next year the order was reversed. In time these performances disappeared altogether from the service. The vesper service on Good Friday was performed in the following order: It began with a motett, after which the congregation sang the hymn " Da Jesus an dem Kreuze stund." Then came the Passion music. The sermon

---

[141] That this was the case is seen from Bach being obliged to arrange for the first performance of his Passion music in St. Nicholas'. Rathsarchiv "*Acta die Kirchen-Musik.*"

which followed was always on the subject of Christ's
entombment—that is to say, before 1721, up to which time
the Good Friday vesper service was held only in the Thomaskirche. There is no doubt that this was the subject, as a
rule, even after that date, although it would have involved
an anomaly if the Passion music, like both of those by
Bach, were in two parts. In such a case, the first
part would have come before, and the second after the
sermon, and so the continuity in the idea of the service
would have been destroyed. After the sermon, the motett
Ecce quomodo was again sung. The congregation once
more sang the hymn " O Traurigkeit! o Herzeleid!" A
collect and the blessing were chanted, and for the close
the hymn " Nun danket alle Gott " was sung.[142]

Something still remains to be said with regard to the order
of service in the University church on Sundays and Fast-
days. Its course was considerably simpler. The Morning
service began at nine o'clock with an organ prelude and the
congregational hymn "Allein Gott in der Höh sei Ehr."
Then followed another hymn proper to the day, then the
creed, and after that the sermon, by one of the University
professors of theology, upon the Gospel. After the sermon
another hymn was sung, which concluded the music. In
Kuhnau's time music was only performed on the high
festivals and during mass. After Bach and Görner took
part in the direction it became more frequent ; but whether
it took place every Sunday, or, if not, what other arrangement was made, we cannot say. After the music the service
was brought simply to a conclusion by the blessing "Gott
sei uns gnädig"—"God be merciful to us"—spoken by the
preacher. In the afternoon a short vesper service was performed, lasting from a quarter-past three till four, and consisting only of a hymn, a sermon by one of the "candidates,"
and the closing hymn " Ach bleib bei uns Herr Jesu Christ."
A vesper service for Good Friday, with organ and sacred
music (probably a sort of Passion music), was begun in

---

[142] Documents with regard to the arrangement of public service for Palm
Sunday and Good Friday, &c., 1766. Ephoralarchiv at Leipzig.

1728.[143] This improvement was gradually achieved by Görner. Of the number of week-day services we need only mention those held in the Thomaskirche. In the church of St. Nicholas the liturgy was in the charge of the choristers, and in the University church there were no week-day services. The days on which the choir was employed in St. Thomas' were Tuesday, Thursday, Friday, and Saturday. On Tuesday, at a quarter-past six, there was a sermon, preceded by a hymn. The choir sang several Latin psalms, the canticle of Zacharias, a German psalm, and at the end the *Benedicamus Domino*. On Thursday, at the same time, there was a sermon and the communion; the service was identical with that of Tuesday, except that the creed was sung before the sermon. On Friday, the usual day of penitence, there was a full service at half-past one, when the Litany was sung. On Saturday, at two o'clock, a confessional service was held especially for those who were to receive the Sacrament on the Sunday. The Thomas-schule choir began with a vocal work (whether it were a motett, hymn, or psalm cannot be said); after a sermon on repentance, the *Magnificat*, a collect, and the blessing were chanted. While the private confessions were being heard, the chief practice of the music for Sunday took place in the organ loft. No composition by Bach can have been performed at these week-day services; at most there was only a possibility of it on Saturday. The mention of these services is, however, not unimportant, because they serve to complete the picture of the church life of which Bach's sacred music is an integral part. By this means alone, however, the picture cannot be presented in all its details. To do this it would be necessary to give an account of the services in the New Church and St. Peter's Church, with which Bach stood in some relation, if only a slight one, as well as those in St. John's and St. George's Churches.

---

[143] Antonius Weizius, Verbessertes Leipzig. Leipzig, 1728, p. 12. In the Paulinerkirche, "This year, 1728, the first Good Friday vesper sermon was delivered, on which occasion the organ was used to accompany German hymns, and other instruments were combined with it." These last words evidently indicate some sacred music of a concerted kind, since no hymn but the *Te Deum* was ever accompanied with instruments as well as the organ.

Their mere mention must here suffice; it will be readily imagined that there was an unusual variety of religious exercises at Leipzig. And this multiplicity of services had not been handed down from past times of different manners, so that they were kept up only out of respect; it was the last generation who, in 1699, had restored the service in the New Church, and in 1711 that in the Peterskirche, and who had changed the service in the University Church, which had hitherto been only occasionally held, into a regular service, to the delight of the whole town.[144] Thus it is beyond all doubt that at this time there was a very active devotional life, and that Bach was right in looking forward to a great effect in this place from any important sacred work.

The order of service, which was strictly prescribed in every detail, regulated even the share to be taken in it by the people. In the majority of cases not only were the places where the congregation were to join in prescribed, but the particular hymns to be used. In the ordinary Sunday services, as was said before, the hymns "Allein Gott in der Höh," "Wir glauben all," "Herr Jesu Christ dich zu uns wend," "Nun danket alle Gott," and "Ach bleib bei uns Herr Jesu Christ" had their own place assigned to them, while for the hymn before the Gospel, and that after the sermon, a choice, although always a limited one, was given. For festivals the specifications were more exact. Between the Epistle and the Gospel the following hymns were sung in the morning: at Christmas, "Gelobet seist du, Jesu Christ"; at Easter, "Christ lag in Todesbanden"; and at Whitsuntide, "Komm heiliger Geist, Herre Gott." After the exordium of the sermon: at Christmas, "Ein Kindelein so löbelich"; at Easter, "Christ ist erstanden"; and at Whitsuntide, "Nun bitten wir den heilgen Geist." For the evening service, after the anthem, the following were sung: for Christmas, "Vom Himmel hoch da komm ich her," "Vom Himmel kam der Engel Schaar," or Lobt Gott, ihr Christen allzugleich"; for Easter, "Christ

---

[144] Kuhnau begins one of his petitions to the Council with a statement that "the whole town had rejoiced at the new service being held regularly in the Church of St. Paul."

lag in Todesbanden"; for Whitsuntide, "Komm heiliger Geist, Herre Gott." For the New Year the Christmas hymns were repeated in the same places, and the New Year Hymns were sung also; the Christmas hymns were also used for the feasts of the Epiphany and the Purification of the Virgin, but besides them the hymn "Was fürcht'st du, Feind Herodes, sehr" was sung at the former, and "Mit Fried und Freud ich fahr dahin" at the latter, but only for the Evening service. For the Annunciation it was ordered that the hymn before the Gospel should be "Herr Christ, der einig Gott's Sohn," and that half-way through the sermon "Nun freut euch lieben Christen g'mein." The same hymn was sung on Ascension Day, before the Gospel. The one between the sections of the sermon being "Christ fuhr gen Himmel." On Trinity Sunday, before the Gospel, "Gott der Vater wohn uns bei" was sung, and on St. John's Day in the same place "Christ unser Herr zum Jordan kam." On Michaelmas Day, the hymn "Herr Gott dich loben alle wir" was indispensable. The festival of the Reformation was characterised by the hymn before the Gospel, "O Herre Gott dein göttlich Wort," and the sermon hymn "Erhalt uns Herr bei deinem Wort," besides the fact, which has been already mentioned, that the *Te Deum* was followed by the hymn "Nun danket alle Gott." For Palm Sunday, as ushering in the Passion Week, the hymn before the Gospel was "Aus tiefer Noth schrei ich zu dir," and for Maunday Thursday it was "Jesus Christus unser Heiland." On Good Friday, in the Morning service, the Passion music was preceded by the hymn "Da Jesus an dem Kreuze stund," and followed by "O Traurigkeit! o Herzeleid!" The hymn "O Lamm Gottes unschuldig" being sung between the sermon and the Communion. The hymns for the Evening service, which in the form used in Bach's time has a special interest for us, have already been described in connection with the general features of that service.[145]

---

[145] The following sources have been used, besides those already mentioned in the above description of the order of the Leipzig services: "Leipziger Kirchen-Staat, &c., Leipzig, 1710. Neo-Annalium Lipsiensium Continuatio II, &c., C. E. Sicul," 2nd edition, 1719, p. 565 ff. Bruno Brückner, Betrachtungen über die Agende der evangelisch-lutherischen Kirche. I. Leipzig, Edelmann. 1864. 4.

There was no general hymn-book in use in the Leipzig
churches, nor was there any great necessity for one. The
hymn-book of Vopelius was in use, but seems chiefly to
have been used only for general purposes of reference.[146]
Gesner wished every scholar to be in possession of a Dresden
hymn-book and always to bring it into church; this was to
be looked after by the Cantor and the Conrector, as the
inspectors of their conduct in church.[147] This must have
been the "Neuauffgelegte Dressdnische Gesang-Buch, Oder
Gottgeheiligte Kirchen- und Hauss-Andachten"—"The
newly-compiled Dresden Hymn-book, or Sacred Devotions
for public and private use"; it was provided with tunes and
appeared in a quarto form at Dresden and Leipzig in the
year 1707.[148] In the Church of St. George's Orphanage,
the hymn-book printed by Johann Montag in Halle was
used.[149] A hymn book expressly for Leipzig use was published in octavo by C. G. Hofman in 1747; the arrangement
was copied from that of Vopelius, but the tunes were
omitted. This handy volume, however, appears not to
have been much to the taste of the Leipzig church-goers,
for, five year afterwards, Hofman had his hymn-book brought
out in quarto. Bach himself made use of the rich
collection of hymns made by Paul Wagner, and published
after his death by Magister Johann Günther, Deacon of
St. Nicholas, in the year 1697, at Leipzig, in eight
octavo volumes under the title of "Andächtiger Seelen
geistliches Brand- und Gantz-Opfer"—"The whole spiritual
burnt-offering of devout souls."[150]

The custom, which was becoming more and more general,
of accompanying the congregational singing throughout on

---

[146] A copy of this was procured in 1722 for the scholars in the Neue Kirche;
vide the accounts of the Neue Kirche from Candlemas, 1722 to 1723, p. 34.

[147] See ante p. 232.

[148] The first edition appeared in 1694. In 1741, a Dresden hymn-book
was published in octavo.

[149] Apparently "Glaübiger Christen Himmel-aufsteigende Hertzens- und
Seelen-Music," a Halle hymn-book in octavo, of which the fifth edition
appeared in 1710. Sicul, loc. cit., p. 572, says, that as all were accustomed
to one hymn-book the practice arose of inscribing only the numbers of the
hymns on black boards.

[150] See the inventory of Bach's effects given in Appendix B., XIV.

the organ, had not yet come into use at Leipzig. In times of national mourning, on days of penitence and fasting, the partial or entire cessation of the organ had the effect of intensifying the gloom of the services. Even on festal and ordinary Sundays the "sermon" hymn at least was always sung without accompaniment.[151] The variety thus produced gave greater richness and colour to the services. The same object is apparent in the combination of the organ and the choir singing. In the early service in the Nikolai-Kirche, the choristers sang the *Te Deum* in such a manner that they alternated with the organ at every verse. From this it may be gathered that, as a rule, the choral dialogue between the priest and the choir was without accompaniment. But on this point practical considerations had due weight and no universal rule prevailed in any of the churches. For instance, in the Litany the organ was constantly employed in the churches of Saxony in order to prevent the choir falling from the original pitch.[152] In part-music the *a cappella* style was falling more and more into disuse. In 1717 Mattheson said, with regard to his quarrel with Buttstedt: "Where are the vocalists who used to sing without instruments, even without a bass, whether of clavier or organ? (the trios which occur in the middle of the piece are differently constituted). Where are the singers, I ask, who can sing a whole aria without accompaniment and can keep in tune? My opponent probably preferred the ordinary style, for I know no example of such singers elsewhere."[153] And in agreement with this is what we learn from Bach's pupil Kirnberger, whose testimony as to the Leipzig order of services is of especial importance. "Performances of church-music, even when sung in four, eight, or more parts without instruments, were always accompanied

---

[151] For the feast of the Reformation in the years 1755 and 1757, this custom was broken through. Vide "*ACTA* die Feyer des Reformations-Festes betr. *Superintendur* Leipzig, 1755."

[152] Gerber, Historie der Kirchen-Ceremonien, p. 230.—Ephoralarchiv at Leipzig.—Scheibe (Critischer Musikus, p. 421) speaks of an arrangement whereby, in the responses, the priest sings alone and the choir with organ accompaniment.

[153] Mattheson, Das beschützte Orchestre. Hamburg, 1717, p. 83.

on the organ, which served to support and to keep up the pitch of the voices; or, at least, the manual was employed when a performance of music for the Passion or some other occasion was sung below in the church, for which double basses were used according to the number of the singers. Another arrangement was to accompany each voice part with trumpets and cornets,[154] but never without due reference to the employment of at least one organ manual."[155] The custom of combining instruments with the voices in the motett became usual at the beginning of the seventeenth century, when the pure form of the motett began to degenerate and to borrow from other forms.[156] Although in this way it approached very near to the usual form of concerted music, yet there was this essential difference, that the accompanying instruments were never allowed to play obbligato;[157] an exception was occasionally allowed in the case of the instrumental bass. So thoroughly did this kind of accompaniment become understood as essentially part of the idea of the motett, in the eighteenth century, that choral music with organ accompaniment used to be called simply "mere vocal music" (blosse Vocalmusik), or "A cappella-Musik."[158] Mattheson's statement probably goes too far, but is not very exact. The Thomasschule scholars, who never practised without the support of a string-bass, took with them, whenever they had to sing out of doors beyond their usual circuit of streets, a Regal belonging to the school.[159] That the

---

[154] "In former times the music was usually accompanied with cornets and trumpets, and this was particularly the case in motetts." Ruetz, Widerlegte Vorurtheile von der Beschaffenheit der heutigen Kirchenmusik. Lübeck, 1752, p. 27.

[155] Kirnberger, Grundsätze des Generalbasses. Berlin, 1781, p. 64.

[156] Compare Vol. I., p. 55.

[157] Scheibe, Critischer Musikus, p. 182.

[158] Ch. G. Thomas, of Leipzig, in the programme of a church concert arranged by him on the 19th of May, 1790, in Berlin, calls the fifth number "Den 149 Psalm, für zwey Chöre, blosse Vokalmusik," but adds afterwards that the organ was to accompany. Zelter calls the opening chorus of Bach's Cantata "Sehet welch eine Liebe" (B.-G., XVI., No. 64, P. No. 1652), "a capella gearbeitet"—written in the a capella style; see his catalogue of the Amalien-bibliothek in the Joachimsthal Gymnasium in Berlin.

[159] Vide App. B. VII. B., under 1 and 2.

custom of accompanying the motetts with cornets and trombones, which was such a favourite one in the seventeenth century, had not yet been given up in Leipzig, is shown not only by different original compositions by Bach, but also by accompaniments to a Mass by Palestrina written with his own hand for cornets, trombones, and organ. An attentive consideration of the order of the services shows that it was the general rule here to accompany the motetts on the organ. On Good Friday morning, when the organ was entirely silent, the motett was also excluded, both before the sermon and in the Communion service; and in the evening when, on account of the Passion music the organ had to be used again, the motett was also there; and the same plan was followed on Palm Sunday and Maunday Thursday.[160] On ordinary Sundays the motett was preceded by a prelude on the organ, which would have been quite senseless if the motett itself were unaccompanied. On festivals the prelude came between the hymn and the motett, so that the former must have been without accompaniments and the latter with it. In all this the motive is clearly to employ the musical means which were usual in the service in alternation and contrast, and so to make even this a kind of work of art. It must be remembered, too, that it was usual to strengthen the voice parts with stringed instruments playing the same notes.[161]

The organs of the two principal churches, which, it is true, Bach in his capacity of Cantor was not required to play upon, answered only to the most limited expectations, for they were old and worn out. There were two in the Thomaskirche. The larger had been put there in the year 1525, having previously been in the Marienkirche of the Monks of St. Anthony at Eiche, not far from Leipzig. It was twice repaired in the seventeenth century, and in 1670 was also enlarged. In the year 1721, however, it was again renovated, as has been already said. The work, which consisted not only of a thorough improvement but also of the addition of

---

[160] Sicul, op. cit., p. 569, says, in general terms that when the organ was not played the motett was also omitted.

[161] Vide Vol. I., p. 61.

400 new pipes and the mixture stops,[162] was done under the direction of Johann Scheibe, the cleverest Leipzig organ builder of the time, who moreover was highly appreciated by no less strict a judge than Bach himself.[163] Although, during the time of Bach's holding office, the organ builders, David Apitzsch and Zacharias Hildebrand were still employed to keep the organ in repair, it was Scheibe who had charge of the principal improvements which were necessary during this period.　The first of these was in 1730, and consisted in making the *Rückpositiv* separate from and independent of the *Hauptwerk* and providing it with a keyboard of its own.[164]　The second was in the summer of 1747 when the organ had got so much out of order that it was hardly possible to use it at all.　Bach and Görner together superintended the repairs, the cost of which was estimated at 200 thalers, and pronounced that Scheibe had done them all suitably and well.[165]　The specification of the organ was as follows:—

Oberwerk.			Brustwerk.		
1. Principal	- - - - -	16 ft.	1. Grobgedackt	- - -	8 ft.
2. Principal	- - - - -	8 „	2. Principal	- - - -	4 „
3. Quintatön (dble. diap.)		16 „	3. Nachthorn	- - - -	4 „
4. Octave	- - - - -	4 „	4. Nasat	- - - - -	3 „
5. Quinte	- - - - -	3 „	5. Gemshorn	- - - -	2 „
6. Superoctave	- - -	2 „	6. Cymbel	- - - - -	2 ranks
7. Spiel-Pfeife	- - - -	8 „	7. Sesquialtera		
8. Sesquialtera	- -	doubled	8. Regal	- - - - -	8 ft.
9. Mixture of 6, 8 to 10 ranks.			9. Geigenregal	- - -	4 „

Rückpositiv.					
1. Principal	- - - -	8 ft.	8. Mixtur	- - - - -	4 ranks
2. Quintatön	- - - -	8 „	9. Sesquialtera[166]		
3. Leiblich Gedackt	-	8 „	10. Spitzflöte	- - - -	4 ft.
4. Klein Gedackt	- -	4 „	11. Schallflöte	- - - -	1 „
5. Querflöte (Fto. traverso)		4 „	12. Krummhorn (Cremona)		16 „
6. Violine	- - - - -	2 „	13. Trompete	- - - -	8 „
7. Rauschquinte	-	doubled			

[162] Accounts of the Thomaskirche from Candlemas 1721 to Candlemas 1722.

[163] A detailed account of various of Scheibe's ingenious inventions in the mechanism of organ building is to be found in the Leipzig " Neue Zeitung von gelehrten Sachen," XVIII., p. 833 f.　Scheibe died September 3, 1748.

[164] Vide App. A., No. 15.

[165] Accounts of the Thomaskirche for 1747-1748, p. 52.　According to this Bach and Görner were the makers of the contract, which still exists and is given in App. B., VIII.　　　[166] On this stop see App. A., No. 15.

Pedals.

1. Sub-bass of metal - 16 ft.
2. Posaune - - - 16 ft.
3. Trompete - - - 8 „ of metal pipes tinned
4. Schalmei - - - 4 „ over.
5. Cornet - - - - 3 „

The organ stood close to the west wall of the church. In 1773 it was first moved into a better position and brought farther forward, by which process the Rückpositiv got shifted out of its proper place. The organ loft in which the choir stood had a different form in Bach's time to that which it has now. It was very much smaller, and besides that the seats for the Thomasschule scholars were in it. Hiller turned them out and put the trumpeter and the drummer in instead.[167] But even with this arrangement the space was not sufficient after a time, and so, in the year 1802, at the instance of the Cantor Müller the organ loft was altogether rebuilt, being heightened and provided with an ornamental railing to the balustrade. Another enlargement was made in the year 1823. The smaller of the two organs in the Thomaskirche was the older, having been built in 1489. When the larger organ was put into the church the smaller one was just beside it by the west wall. But it did not stay there long. In 1638 the gallery which still exists was built over the raised choir, and the small organ was placed in it, so that it stood opposite the large one. At Easter, 1639, after being repaired, it was played in this place for the first time, and it stood there until Bach's time.[168] In 1727 it was once more put in order by Zacharias Hildebrand;[169] but it was of very little use, and in 1740 Scheibe had to take it quite away. Such parts of it as were still available he used in building the organ in St. John's church, which he constructed in 1742-1744, to the entire satisfaction of the overseers Bach and Hildebrand.[170] This is the specification of the small organ:

[167] Manuscript note by the Rector Rost on p. 35 of the school regulations of 1723, in the copy kept in the Thomasschule library.

[168] Vogel, Leipziger Chronicke, loc. cit., and his *Annales*, p. 562.

[169] Accounts of the Thomaskirche, 1727-1728, p. 41.

[170] Accounts of the Johanniskirche from 1740-1744. Agricola, quoted in Adlung's Mus. Mechan., p. 251.

Oberwerk.

1. Principal - - - - 8 ft.	5. Rauschquinte, 3 and 2 feet.[171]
2. Gedackt - - - - - 8 „	6. Mixtur, of 4, 5, 6, 8 and 10
3. Quintatön - - - - 8 „	ranks.
4. Octave - - - - - 4 „	7. Cymbel 2 ranks.

Brustwerk.

1. Trichter-Regal 8 ft.
2. Sifflöte - - - 1 „
3. Spitzflöte - - 2 „

Rückpositiv.

1. Principal - - - - 4 ft.	5. Octave - - - - - 2 ft.
2. Lieblich Gedackt - 8 „	6. Sesquialtera - - doubled
3. Hohlflöte - - - - 4 „	7. Dulciana - - - - 8 ft.
4. Nasat - - - - - 3 „	8. Trompete - - - - 8 „

Pedal.

1. Sub-bass of wood 16 ft.
2. Fagott - - - 16 „
3. Trompete - - 8 „[172]

The organ was only used on the high festivals. It was not unusual, where there were two organs, to employ them for double chorus motetts or arias, in such a manner as that each choir had its own organ accompaniment, in which case it was necessary to separate the two choirs by a wider space than usual. In Wismar at the beginning of the 18th century, Keimann's hymn, set to a melody by Hammer-schmidt, "Freuet euch, ihr Christen alle,"[173] was sung in this way at Christmas. The introductory Hallelujah was given out by the whole choir with accompaniment of cornets and trombones. Then the beginning of each verse was sung by a single voice supported by one organ, and answered by one of the full choirs accompanied on the other organ, to the words, "Freude, Freude über Freude," all joining

---

[171] *I.e.*, a Quinte of 3 feet and an Octave of 2 feet.

[172] When Scheibe broke up the organ several stops were taken away—namely, the Dulciana in the Rückpositiv organ and the Fagott and Sub-bass on the Pedal. Several ranks were also removed from the Mixture and Sesquialtera. The Lieblich Gedackt is now named "Grobgedackt," and the Trichter Regal "Ranquet." Rathsacten, book IX., *A.* 2, Vol. I., fol. 96.

[173] It is given by Winterfeld, in his Evang. Kirchenges. II., Musical examples, p. 102 ff.

together in the final Hallelujah.[174] The distance, by no means an inconsiderable one, between the two organs, in the Thomaskirche, rendered it indeed a matter of difficulty to keep the choirs exactly together. Everything, however, was done to overcome the difficulty, and if ever any confusion occurred it would be compensated for by the devotional effect which would be produced by the floods of sound streaming together from different parts of the church. For the celebration of the Reformation Festival in 1717, in the University Church, Kuhnau performed a festival work for three choirs, which were stationed in three different places in the church: one was put in the space in front of the newly built organ, and the other two in roomy pews by the side of the organ, and apparently behind the pulpit, where two loud sets of organ pipes were placed, and also instrumentalists.[175] In former times in the University church the very strange custom obtained of placing the singers at a great distance from the organ; that being behind the pulpit, the position of the choir was opposite, close to the church wall by the altar. Notwithstanding this, music had been performed successfully, although Kuhnau and Vetter rejoiced at the new arrangement, because it would be easier to avoid those differences between the choir and the organ which we have alluded to.[176]

---

[174] Ruetz, Widerlegte Vorurtheile, &c., p. 86 f.—Ruetz says that the full choir came in each time with the words " Freuet euch mit grossem Schalle." It is self-evident that this is a slip either of the pen or the memory, since the refrain does not begin with these words. Whether what he calls the single voice ought not to be really three, as is prescribed in the original, must be left undecided.

[175] Sicul. Die andere Beylage zu dem Leipziger Jahrbuche auf 1718, p. 73. In the year 1716 again Kuhnau had a Latin Ode set for three choirs performed in the same place; see Sicul, Beylage zu des Leipziger Jahrbuchs Dritten Probe, 1717, p. 11 ; compare p. 20.

[176] Archives of Leipzig University. Ch. G. Thomas, himself a Leipzig Musician, arranged, in 1790, a concert of compositions for three and four choirs in the garrison church at Berlin; the first choir was in the gallery opposite. the organ, the second in the organ loft, the third on the right, and the fourth on the left, in the middle of the gallery. In his account he states positively that the music went well together in spite of the distance. (Sammelband der königl. Bibliothek zu Berlin, Abtheilung *Bibliotheca Dicziana*. Quarto 2900.)

The Nikolaikirche contained an organ dating from the year 1597-1598. The last repairs before Bach's time had been done in 1692. It then consisted of the following stops:—

Oberwerk.

1.	Principal - - - 8 ft.	8.	Grobgedackt - - 8 ft.
2.	Sesquialtera - - 1⅗ „	9.	Quintatön - - - 16 „
3.	Mixtur - - - - 3 ranks	10.	Nasat - - - - 3 „
4.	Superoctave - - 2 ft.	11.	Waldflöte - - - 2 „
5.	Quinte - - - - 3 „	12.	Fagott - - - - 16 „
6.	Octave - - - - 4 „	13.	Trompete - - - 8 „
7.	Gemshorn - - - 8 „		

Brustwerk.

1.	Schalmei - - - 4 ft.	5.	Octave - - - - 2 ft.
2.	Principal - - - 4 „	6.	Sesquialtera - - 1⅗ „
3.	Mixtur - - - - 3 ranks	7.	Quintatön - - - 8 „
4.	Quinte - - - - 3 ft.		

Rückpositiv.

1.	Principal - - - 4 ft.	6.	Quintatön - - - 4 ft.
2.	Gedackt - - - - 8 „	7.	Octave - - - - 2 „
3.	Viola da Gamba - 4 „	8.	Sesquialtera - -·· 1⅗ „
4.	Gemshorn - - - 4 „	9.	Mixtur - - - - 4 ranks
5.	Quinte - - - - 3 „	10.	Bombart - - - 8 ft.

Pedal.

1.	Cornet - - - - 2 ft.	4.	Octave - - - - 4 ft.
2.	Schalmei - - - 4 „	5.	Gedackter Subbass 16 „
3.	Trompete - - - 8 „	6.	Posaune - - - - 16 „ [177]

In 1725 the organ was renewed by Scheibe. The improvements were very thorough and cost 600 thalers.[178] It is unfortunately impossible to know what alterations were made with respect to the disposition of the stops. In this state it remained till the year of Bach's death, when it was again repaired by *Zacharias Hildebrand*.

In both the Thomaskirche and the Nikolaikirche the organs were tuned to " chorus " pitch. This was then the usual pitch in Leipzig as well as in other places. The organ in the New Church was in the same pitch.[179]

---

[177] Vogel, Leipziger Chronicke, p. 97.

[178] Accounts of the Nikolaikirche from Candlemas 1724—1725, p. 49, and for 1725—1726, p. 53. The contract was concluded on Dec. 11, 1724, and the whole work finished on Dec. 22, 1725.

[179] See App. A., No. 16.

In contrast to these old organs, which were of only moderate capacity, and liable to get out of order frequently, there had been in the University church since Nov. 4, 1716, an organ which fulfilled the highest expectations, and which Bach must have chiefly employed when he played for his own pleasure or before other people. On this account it is of particular interest to become acquainted with its constitution.

Hauptwerk.

1.	Great Principal (of pure tin) - - - 16 ft.	8.	Quinte - - - - 3 ft.
2.	Great Quintatön - 16 „	9.	Quint-Nasat - - 3 „
3.	Small Principal - 8 „	10.	Octavina - - - 2 „
4.	Schalmei - - - 8 „	11.	Waldflöte - - - 2 „
5.	*Flûte allemande* - - 8 „	12.	Great Mixtur - - 5 & 6 ranks
6.	Gemshorn - - - - 8 „	13.	*Cornetti* - - - - 3 ranks
7.	Octave - - - - 4 „	14.	Zink (cornet) - - 2 „

Brustwerk.

1.	Principal, of pure tin (in front) - - - 8 ft.	5.	Rohrflöte - - - 4 ft.
		6.	Octave - - - - 2 „
2.	*Viola di Gamba natu- relle*[180]	7.	Nasat - - - - 3 „
		8.	*Sedecima* - - - 1 „
3.	Grobgedackt with a wide mouthpiece - 8 ft.	9.	Schweizer Pfeife - 1 „
		10.	Largo - - - - [181]
4.	Octave - - - - - 4 „	11.	Mixtur - - - - 3 ranks
		12.	Helle Cymbel - - 2 „

Unter-Clavier.

1.	Lieblich Gedackt - 8 ft.	7.	Viola - - - - 2 ft.
2.	Quintatön - - - - 8 „	8.	*Vigesima nona* - - 1½ „
3.	*Flûte douce* - - - - 4 „	9.	Weitpfeife - - - 1 „
4.	*Quinta Decima* - - 4 „	10.	Mixtur - - - - 3 ranks
5.	*Decima nona* - - - 3 „	11.	Helle Cymbel - - 2 „
6.	Hohlflöte - - - - 2 „	12.	Sertin - - - - 8 ft.[182]

Pedal.

Six stops, which by a new and special invention were brought into connection with the great bellows of the manuals :—

---

[180] Scheibe distinguishes between the real and the so-called Viola di gamba; the former had a narrower mouthpiece. In 1722 he turned a so-called Viola di Gamba in the organ in the New Church into a real one, with great success.

[181] The number of feet is not given.

[182] What kind of stop this may have been, or whether it may not be a mistake or misprint for Serpent, I cannot say.

1.	Great Principal of pure tin (in front) - - - - 16 ft.	4.	Octave - - 4 ft.
		5.	Quinte - - 3 „
2.	Great Quintatön - - - 16 „	6.	Mixtur - - 5 & 6 ranks
3.	Octave - - - - - - 8 „		

These stops on the small Brust-Pedal bellows :—

7.	Great (clear) Quintenbass (in front) - - - - - 6 ft.	9.	Nachthorn- 4 ft.
		10.	Octave - - 2 „
8.	Jubal - - - - - - - 8 „ [183]		

And these on the great bellows on both sides :—

11.	Great Principal of pure tin (in front) - - - 16 ft.	14.	Trompete - 8 ft.
		15.	Hohlflöte - 1 „
12.	Sub-bass - - - - - - 16 „	16.	Mixtur - 4 ranks
13.	Posaune - - - - - - 16 „		

Extra Stops (Couplers, &c.).

Ventils
- to the Hauptwerk
- to the Brustwerk
- to the Side Basses
- to the Brust and Manual[184]
- to the Stern
- to the Hinterwerk

A Bell to call the blower.[185]

As has been before mentioned,[186] the honourable task of trying this organ after its completion, which must have been superintended by Vetter, was entrusted to Bach. Just at that time he had come from Weimar and had taken up his abode in Cöthen. He laid his opinion before the University, which we subjoin :—[187]

"Since at the desire of his excellency Herr Dr. Rechenberg, at present chief Rector of the honourable Academy at Leipzig, I was charged with the examination of the organ in the Pauliner Kirche, which has been partly renewed and partly repaired; I have fulfilled the task according to my power, have remarked any defects, and have prepared the following statement with regard to the whole work :—

---

[183] An octave stop. See Adlung, *Musica mechanica*, p. 107.

[184] *Sic.* The meaning must be that there was a Ventil between the Pedal and Manual of the Brustwerk.

[185] Sammlung einiger Nachrichten von berühmten Orgel Wercken in Teutschland mit vieler Mühe aufgesetzt von einem Liebhaber der Musik. Bresslau, 1757, 4, p. 54.

[186] See ante, p. 9.

[187] Archive of the Leipzig University "*ACTA*. Den Orgel- und andern Bau, ingl. Verschreibung der Capellen, Verlosung der Stühle und was dem mehr anhängig, in der Pauliner Kirche betr. *De aͦ.* 1710. *Volum.* III."

Repert. $\frac{\text{II.}}{\text{III.}}$ No. 5. Litt. B. Sect. II., Fol. 63—64.

1. Touching the whole structure, it cannot be disguised that it is in a very contracted space, so that it is a matter of difficulty to get at such parts of it as may at any time require to be repaired; this must be Herr Scheibe's excuse, because he was not the original maker of the organ, but found the case ready-made to his hand, and had to adapt himself to it as best he could; besides that the extra space which he required in order to make the structure more commodious was not granted to him.

2. The ordinary constituent parts of an organ, as the wind trunks, the bellows, the pipes, the sounding boards, and the other parts, have been repaired with great skill, and it need only be remarked that the wind must be caused to come more equally so that the unequal blows of the wind may be avoided; the sound boards ought to have been encased in frames to avoid all noises of wind in bad weather, but Herr Scheibe according to a method of his own, made them with panels, assuring us at the same time that the effect would be the same as that produced elsewhere by frames, and in consequence of this explanation it was let pass.

3. The parts included both in the description and in all the contracts are right both in quality and quantity, with the exception of two reed stops—namely, the Schallmey, 4 ft., and the Cornet, 2 ft.—which may have been omitted by an order from the honourable College, but in their stead a 2 ft. Octave has been introduced into the Brustwerk, and a 2 ft. Hohlflöte into the Hinterwerk.

4. The defects which still remain, such as inequality of intonation, must and can be done away with immediately by the organ builder; in particular, the lowest pipes in the Posaune and the bass Trompete should not speak so roughly and harshly, but should begin with and retain a pure and firm tone; besides this the other pipes which are unequal in tone, must be carefully corrected and equalised, which by means of frequent and thorough tuning of the whole instrument, and also in better weather than there has been of late, it will be quite easy to do.

5. The management of the organ ought indeed to be somewhat easier, and the keys ought not to have so great a fall, but this indeed cannot be otherwise, because of the excessive narrowness of the structure, so that it must perforce be left; yet notwithstanding it is still possible to play in such a manner that there need be no fear of coming to a sudden stop.

6. As the organ builder had to make a new wind trunk to the Brustwerk over and above what had been contracted for, and as the old wind trunk which was to have been used instead of a new one possessed in the first place a *Fundament Brete* (*Qy.* a fixed board supporting the wind trunk?) in itself incorrect and objectionable; and secondly, as the manual had the short compass peculiar to the old style so that there was no possibility of adding the keys which were requisite in order to bring the three manuals to an equality, had the old one been

employed a *deformité* would have been caused ; it was, therefore, highly necessary to substitute a new one for it, so as to avoid the defects which were dreaded by the maker, and to preserve a satisfactory conformity. I consider, therefore, that the organ maker is entitled to the value of those parts which have been renewed over and above the terms of the contract, and that he ought to be indemnified.

Seeing that the organ builder has requested me to represent to the honourable College that, as certain parts were not allowed him, as, for instance, the ornamental woodwork, the gilding, and the other ornamentation which Herr Vetter had to superintend, these and whatever else may be necessary may be allowed for in payment, and that he be not held liable for them, since it is not the custom elsewhere to hold the builder liable for such things—and had it been the custom he would have made better terms—he begs humbly that he may be brought into no extra expenses on this account.

And finally it must not be left unmentioned (1) that the window behind the organ should be protected as far as to the top of the organ on the inside by a small wall, or a strong iron plate, so as to prevent any possible damage by weather; and (2) that it is customary, and in this case most necessary, for the organ builder to give a guarantee for one year at least to repair thoroughly any defects that may arise, which he moreover is perfectly willing to undertake to do, if his requests with regard to his expenses over and above the contract be granted speedily and completely.

This then is all that I have found necessary to remark upon in my examination of the organ, and recommending myself in all possible services to his most noble excellency, Herr D. Rechenberg, and to all the honourable College,

I remain,

Your most humble and devoted servant,

Joh: Seb: Bach.

Hochfürstlich Anhalt Cöthenische Capell Meister."[188]

Leipzig, Dec. 17, 1717.

When Scheibe undertook the work in 1710, Kuhnau and Vetter had no great opinion of his skill, but took note of him as an honest, cheap, and industrious workman; thus it was all the more praiseworthy that his completed work should come so well through a trial of so thorough and practical a kind. The organist who had the charge and care of the great instrument after Görner's departure was Johann Christoph Thiele, a man of whose artistic attainments nothing is known beyond this fact.

---

[188] Throughout in Bach's own hand. The address is wanting.

With the preludes and postludes which were then usual, the organ became an independent constituent part of the service. The technical expression for all such "voluntaries," as we should now call them, was "preludes," without regard to the place in the service when the organ was played by itself. From this it is evident that the postlude at the close of the service was not customary in all churches. Its use was not so much practical or liturgical as general and artistic, whereas the prelude was chiefly and expressly intended to prepare the congregation for the hymns which they were to sing, and especially in the case of a less known melody to make them acquainted with it. With the advancing development of the art of the organ, and with the growth of the chorale preludes into independent and organically shaped compositions, the custom of playing a concluding voluntary, in which the organist could exercise his talent at will in free fantasias or fugues, became more and more general. In none of our sources of information is anything said with regard to "playing-out" in the Leipzig churches. From this it does not follow that it was not the custom; indeed it may be inferred from the remarks of Johann Adolph Scheibe, that it was usual here.[189] With regard to the preludes, properly so-called, it was an universal rule to introduce the longest and most elaborate before the congregational hymn sung between the Epistle and the Gospel, and before the Communion hymns.[190] Here, again, the object was a practical one, for there was a greater freedom in the choice of these hymns, so that sometimes hymns with less known tunes were sung, whereas the other congregational hymns were always more or less the same. These preludes were, of course, formed upon the melody of the hymn that was to follow. The organ prelude which, as a rule, preceded

---

[189] He was born in Leipzig and worked for some time in his native town. Critischer Musikus, p. 428. On the other hand, Petri, in his "Anleitung zur Praktischen Musik," Leipzig, 1782, p. 297, says that the playing of a concluding voluntary only became "customary in several towns" at the end of the eighteenth century.

[190] Petri, op. cit., p. 299. Türk, von den wichtigsten Pflichten eines Organisten. Halle, 1787. P. 121 f.

any concerted church music, had a character of its own. Its practical purpose was to enable the instrumentalists to tune without disturbing the devotions of the congregation. For this reason the organist was not allowed to play in a strict style, but had to keep to a free fantasia style, and also to remain chiefly and for the longest time in those keys which corresponded to the tuning notes of the various instruments.   When the instruments were tuned the conductor gave a sign for the organist to stop playing; in addition to this, his prelude had to prepare the way for the composition that was to follow, and also to have a kind of finish and roundness of its own.   Thus the organist had no easy task if he was minded to make his prelude according to the rules.   This, however, was by no means the case, owing to the roughness and carelessness of so many of the performances of church music, and on most occasions all that was heard was a confused and ugly medley of sound.[191]

During the music itself the organist had to play the *basso continuo* from a figured bass part, above which, in the case of recitatives, the vocal part was sometimes indicated.[192] The organ in this case took the part which in chamber music was taken by the harpsichord.[193]   Since concerted music in churches had come into general use, this accompaniment became one of the regular duties of the organist, and that Bach viewed the matter in this light is clear from his report of the circumstance of his dispute with the University, in which he says that the organist had not only to accompany the music before and after the sermon, but also to play all the hymns until the very last.   Occasionally, and in an

---

[191] Voigt, Gespräch von der Musik zwischen einem Organisten und Adjuvanten, p. 92 f.   Adlung, p. 731.   Orders from the Council for preventing the disorder and confusion of this prelude are given by Petri, p. 176 ff., and Türk, p. 136 ff.

[192] Voigt, loc. cit., p. 27, says, however, that no cantor would take the trouble to write out the voice part; but it occurs in Bach occasionally, for instance, in the cantata "Christus der ist mein Leben," B.-G., XXII., No. 95.   See also App. A., No. 17.

[193] In Voigt, op. cit., p. 107, the Assistant says "I thought that it must be much harder to play in church than in a musical college, and that the mistakes would be much more noticed on the organ than on a harpsichord."

exceptional way, he may have handed over to some one else the task of accompanying from the figured bass, especially when Görner was officiating, since his discourses satisfied him but little. His manner of accompanying has been already spoken of at length.[194] It would be sufficient only to allude to it here, were it not that a document hitherto unknown has lately been discovered which places the circumstances in a still clearer light, and the importance of the subject justifies our returning to it. Heinrich Nikolaus Gerber must have learnt the art of playing from figured bass from Bach, and have practised it on the violin sonatas of Albinoni; subsequently he handed down to his son (the author of the Lexicon) the method of accompanying which he had learnt from studying these sonatas with Bach. The son informs us that an especial feature was that no one part was ever more prominent than the other, and that this accompaniment was of itself so beautiful, that no solo part could have added anything to the pleasure which it gave him. A specimen of an accompaniment of this kind by the elder Gerber still exists; it is throughout written by himself, and contains autograph corrections by Bach.[195] The corrections are comparatively few in number, so that the teacher was apparently satisfied with the work; still, having Bach's alterations, we are sure that this is such an accompaniment to a solo as he liked and approved.

Its state, however, proves that Gerber's work was unsatisfactory and forced, and that Bach's famous method was certainly not polyphonic. The term "polyphonic," it is

---

[194] See ante, p. 102.

[195] I obtained this in the Spring of 1876 from the musical collection of Musikdirector Rühl of Frankfurt a. M. who had died shortly before. Rühl had got the MS. from the bequest of Hofrath André, and he from that of the younger Gerber. A note by the younger Gerber on the MS. runs thus: " Made by Heinrich Nic. Gerber, and corrected by Sebastian Bach." The solo part and the figures of the bass are wanting, as is also all information as to the work of Albinoni from which the sonata is taken. It is, however, the sixth of Albinoni's *Trattenimenti Armonici per Camera divisi in dodici Sonate. Opera sesta,* and thus can be completely restored; it is given as Musical supplement I. to this work. A copy of the *Trattenimenti,* printed by Walsh in London, was bought some time ago at my instance for the Royal Library in Berlin, by Herr Dr. Espagne.

true, is capable of extension; but, when applied to Bach, a thematic and independent treatment of the parts is understood. Gerber's accompaniment, however, has no imitative use of motives, whether taken from the solo parts or freely invented. It is simple—a flowing movement in several parts, in which we never for a moment lose the feeling that the motive power is external to itself. It is only in so far as an unconstrained progression of harmonies which never encounters any obstacle must of itself have a certain melodic effect that we can speak of melody at all in this accompaniment, and this exactly suits the definition of a good accompaniment given by the younger Telemann: "a good flowing song (ein guter Gesang), *i.e.*, a well-proportioned and pleasing succession of sounds."[196] Four out of the small number of Bach's corrections owe their existence to the desire for such "pleasing sequence" (Nos. 1, 2, 9, and 10). Besides this we may observe that Bach even allows his pupil to pay no regard to the simple harmonies suggested by Albinoni, partly in order to make the harmonic motion more connected and flowing, and partly to make it more interesting. Accordingly we find a very independent treatment, only it has no melodic character, as we might suppose from the words of the younger Gerber; the limits which divide homophony and polyphony, or, which here is the same thing, the chief from the tributary subject, have been defined with the most accurate taste. Only a passing allusion can here be made to other instructive features in this accompaniment: to the constancy of the four-part writing, which corresponds exactly to the definition which Kirnberger gives of the characteristics of Bach's accompaniments; to the way in which in the second and third movements the themes which begin without accompaniment are strengthened by the other parts in unison—a method of treatment to be explained in the same way as the separate full chords in the three-part sonatas for violin and clavier.[197] Now that we are in a position to determine the exact mean-

---

[196] Georg Michael Telemann, Unterricht im Generalbass-Spielen. Hamburg, 1773, p. 17.

[197] See ante, p. 102.

ing of Gerber's words, we can judge of the precise import of Mizler's statement, that Bach used to accompany any given solo with figured bass in such a manner that it sounded like a concerto, and as if the melody which he made in the right hand had been written down before-hand. Mizler himself in another place gives a key to the right understanding of these words; but hitherto there has been no such certain example from which we might learn the practical application of it. In an account of Werckmeister's method of playing from figured bass, he deduces from it the general statement that, for a pleasing treatment of harmonies in accompanying, something more must be necessary than merely avoiding fifths and octaves. This "something more," says Mizler, is melody; and by melody he understands such a variety in the succession of notes that they could be sung with ease and would be pleasant to listen to. But since in the best melodies we notice the fewest leaps, it follows that the figured bass player must make no unusual leaps if he wishes to preserve intact the melodic element.[198] Apparently his description of Bach's method of accompanying tends the same way as what we already know from Heinrich Nickolaus Gerber's MS., namely, to a smooth combination of harmonies, the result of which is the production of a kind of melody in the upper part. The fact of Bach's scholar laying such stress upon this individuality is quite explained if we consider how irregular and tasteless the generality of accompaniments on a figured bass was at that time. Löhlein, a well-known teacher of music in the eighteenth century, tells us that soloists, even violoncellists, did not care to be accompanied on the clavier, but preferred a childish accompaniment on a viola, or even a violin; so that the bass part obtruded itself above the melody, and the effect was like a man standing on his head.[199] And even in the case of an accompaniment on the clavier or on the organ, many players

---

[198] Musikalische Bibliothek, Pt. II. Leipzig, 1737, p. 52.
[199] Georg Simon Löhlein, Clavierschule, &c., 4th edition. Leipzig, 1785, p. 114.

were quite content to take the chords just as they happened to suit the fingers, without respect to their position or connection.

Still, what has been said above must not lead us into supposing that Bach altogether forbade his pupil on the organ the use of all figured bass accompaniment that was adorned by imitations. Even if no great weight be laid on the fact that Kuhnau, Heinichen, Mattheson, Schröter and other authorities of that time valued an imitative treatment confined within proper limits, and considered it the highest art of the accompanist, there are still other evidences to prove that in special cases Bach sometimes used polyphony in accompanying, and even if it were not so, we have the right to conclude it from what we know of his musical nature in general. Gerber's work, then, confirms the difference, which we have before pointed out, that a distinction exists between what Bach allowed in this respect and what he required. With regard to the last, no doubt can any longer be entertained now that we possess Kirnberger's accompaniment to a trio by Bach, and that of Gerber to a solo sonata by Albinoni. It will not diminish the knowledge and power of the composition last mentioned if we allow that such an accompaniment could not have been put to an original composition by Bach, and that he would have required a very different sort of accompaniment for a work of his own. Every competent artist derives his standard from what he considers beautiful and fitting—namely, his own works. If the polyphonic enrichment of a solo composition by means of a figured bass accompaniment had seemed to Bach desirable on all occasions, he would have insisted on his pupils employing that method in this case also, where a work of an exclusively educational purpose was concerned. This is all the more certain, because the simple breadth of harmonic structure in Albinoni's sonata was particularly well adapted for the reception of elaborate detail, and, however much regard he may have had to the simple style of the whole work, some traces of polyphony must have been noticeable. Thus, when Bach's figured bass player went beyond what was required of him, he did it on his own responsibility. If some clever piece of ingenuity attempted here and there succeeded, he produced a feeling of pleasant surprise in the ear of the connoisseur, but if he failed he ruined the whole, and drew down upon him the wrath of the conductor. Löhlein says in one place, "The artistic or adorned style of accompaniment, that namely, in which the right hand plays some sort of melody with ornamented *agrémens* and imitations, is for those who have got beyond simple things; it demands great care and knowledge of composition. Herr Mattheson has given many examples of it in his Organistenprobe. Since, however, this kind of pretty decoration was found to spoil more than it improved, it has happily gone out of fashion."[200] This opinion meets the question very fairly ; the adorned accompaniment was entirely a thing of musical fashion, as were also the *agrémens* and *manieren* of the clavier player, or the *fioriture* of the singer. It is the same view of the question that Adlung brings forward when, after speaking of the accents, mordents, trills, &c., which a player from a figured bass had at his command, he adds : "But the best *Manier* is melody."[201] Like all fashions, this also serves as one of the characteristics of the time.

Bach worked in a period of wide-spread and abundant musical creativeness. The fit presentment of a musical composition depends on the performance, which cannot possibly take place without the admixture of a certain subjective element, and this element generally took the form of arbitrary ornamentation of the written melodic phrases, even going so far as to distort their very shape by alterations. The composer submitted to this arrangement because the disfigurement his ideas might suffer was atoned for by the individual vitality with which a composition might be performed by a player capable of taking an independently creative share in the work. It is certain that Bach neither would nor could hold entirely aloof from this, an universal feature of the time in which he lived. But

---

[200] Löhlein, loc. cit. p. 76.
[201] Adlung, Anleitung zu der musikalischen Gelährtheit, p. 653.

in proportion to the individuality of an artist will be the
care with which he will guard against the introduction of
any foreign element into his creations. Of all the great
musicians who appeared in this period, Bach is, without
doubt, the most subjective, and stands the most apart from
all others. He deserves the complaint made by Johann
Adolph Scheibe, that " he indicated with actual notes all
manieren, all the small ornaments, and everything that is
understood by the word *method* in playing,"[202] so that he
effectually closed the door upon any approach to individuality on the part of the performers. What Scheibe says of
Bach's vocal and instrumental works holds good also of his
figured bass parts, which he used, unless hindered by
circumstances, to figure in the most elaborate way. His
minute care extended even to the ritornels and short
ritornel-like passages, in which, as a general rule, the
accompanist was left to follow his own instinct as to what
was most suitable. Thus, in the terzet in the cantata "Aus
tiefer Noth schrei ich zu dir,"[203] he shows with the greatest
exactness, by means of figuring, the counterpoint to be played
in the right hand to the chief subject of the ritornel, which
lies in the bass part. His pupil Agricola had a better
appreciation of the case ; he approved the exactitude which
Scheibe blames, for he holds it to be no fault in a composer
if, in order to obviate disfigurement, he expresses his ideas
with the greatest possible clearness.[204] Bach's careful forethought is fully accounted for when we read the laments of
earnest musicians over certain vain and trivial organists
who, in contrast to those who never add more than is
absolutely requisite, take every opportunity of " shaking out
their sackfull of ornaments all at once, in fanciful tricks
and runs, and, when the singer has to execute a passage,
think it necessary to vie with the singer in ornamentation."[205] It is no less plain why the school of Bach always
insists on using the polyphonic, or, indeed, any adorned style

---

[202] Scheibe, Critischer Musikus, p. 62.

[20] B.-G., VII., p. 296 ff.   P. 1694.

[204] In the addenda to Tosi's Anleitung zur Singkunst, p. 74.

[205] Kuhnau, Der *Musicali*sche Qvack-Salber, 1700, p. 20 ff.

of accompaniment, as little as possible, and only as an exception,[206] as Philipp Emanuel does, often discarding it entirely. Kirnberger held that as the accompanist from a figured bass had only to add the harmonies, he ought to refrain from all ornaments which were not essential, and always aim at simplicity.[207] Johann Samuel Petri, a friend and pupil of Friedemann Bach, who made a special study of the art of accompanying under this master, forbids the organ-player to introduce shakes, or to play any melody with the right hand; he requires him to keep to the chords intended by the composer, and lays it down as a general principle that the organ accompaniment serves only to fill up the harmony and to strengthen the bass.[208] The same thing is said by Christian Carl Rolle, the intimate friend of Bach's sons and pupils.[209] But other musicians too, besides those of Bach's own circle, shared this opinion, and expressed it in the most decisive way. Johann Adolph Scheibe, with his well-known acuteness of æsthetic judgment, condemns the polyphonic accompaniment of a solo as contrary to good taste, and destructive to the composer's intentions.[210]

The question of the manner of accompanying also includes the way of employing the sound-material offered by the organ. In this respect there were firmly-fixed traditions. The bass was as a rule played by the left hand alone, while the right took the complementary harmonies. When an organ with several manuals was used, the left hand usually played on an independent manual with powerful stops. The pedal generally played the bass also, and then the left hand· could

---

[206] Versuch über die wahre Art das Clavier zu spielen. Pt. II., pp. 219 f and 241.

[207] In Sulzer's Allgemeine Theorie der schönen Künste, Second edition, Pt. I., p. 194. On Kirnberger's share in this work, see Gerber's Lexicon IV., co . 304 f.

[208] Anleitung zur praktischen Musik, p. 169 ff. Petri tells of his connection with Friedemann Bach in this very work, which is one of the best educational works on music of the eighteenth century, pp. 101, 269 (see also 268) and 285.

[209] Neue Wahrnehmungen zur Aufnahme und weitern Ausbreitung der Musik. Berlin, 1784, p. 49.

[210] Critischer Musikus, p. 416.

help to bring out the inner parts.[211] When the bass was strongly orchestrated it was considered sufficient to mark only the essential points in the harmonic progressions by short notes on the pedals.[212] In such cases, however, it was not unusual to leave the bass out altogether in order to avoid confusion, since it was generally taken by other instruments.[213] In the case of slightly instrumented works, some composers only used this accompaniment in the ritornels.[214] For accompanying arias and recitatives the eight-foot Gedackt was generally used alone, and from this circumstance got the name "Musikgedackt."[215] In the case of "recitativo secco," even when the bass notes were directed to be held, the chords on the organ, which used to be played *arpeggio* as on the harpsichord, were, as a rule, not held long, in order to give due prominence to the words sung.[216] Petri, however, holds that when there is a very soft stopped-flute, the chords may be held in the tenor register and that then each change of the harmony is to be indicated by a short pedal note. In order to give support to the singer, the organist was sometimes to hold out the bass note alone, and take off the rest of the chord quite short. Greater freedom was permitted in the case of accompanied recitative; he might either play both the chord and the bass together, or the latter alone, as it seemed good to him.[217]

---

[211] Adlung, p. 657. "At one time much attention was paid to divided playing, that is, when some of the inner parts were played by the left hand. It is also quite possible, if the notes can be given out on the pedals, for both hands to remain on one manual. But in the case of rapid basses, this arrangement fails, because such are best played on two manuals." Petri, p. 170.

[212] Rolle, p. 51. "The management of the pedals is attended with unusual difficulties, such as that of always knowing which are the right notes to play and which may be left out with impunity for the sake of rapidity." Schröter, Deutliche Anweisung zum General-Bass, Halberstadt, 1772, p. 188, § 348. Türk, p. 153. The same holds good, as a rule, for the double-bass also; see Quantz, Versuch, &c., p. 221, §. 7.

[213] Türk, p. 156.   [214] Petri, p. 170.

[215] Scheibe, Critischer Musikus, p. 415. Adlung, p. 386. Rolle, p. 50. Compare Gerber, Historie der Kirchen-Ceremonien, p. 280.

[216] (Voigt), Gespräch, &c., p. 29. Petri, p. 171, compare p. 311. Türk, p. 162 ff.

[217] Schröter, p. 186, § 344. Türk, p. 174.

It should be noticed that the staccato style of playing, now universally considered unsuited to the nature of the organ, was not considered so by the musicians of that time. The formation of fugue themes from reiterated notes, and the repetition of full chords served, in the opinion of organ masters of the Northern school, to produce a peculiarly charming effect—Christoph Gottlieb Schröter of Nordhausen, one of the most perfect organists of his time, always played staccato. By this method, indeed, he provoked the opposition of the scholars of Bach, who followed the example of their master in considering the *sostenuto* style as the finer,[218] and to their influence is to be ascribed the fact that the other style of playing gradually died out. But it was only for independent organ pieces that they insisted so definitely on the sostenuto style. For accompanying, the "lifted" style remained in use even within the circle of Bach's scholars. Kittel, who during a period of fifteen years' activity as a teacher spread Bach's systems among the organists of Thuringia, inculcated this method, and persons are still living who heard one of his best pupils, Michael Gotthardt Fischer of Erfurt, accompany the Church cantatas in this manner: he followed the harmonic course of the movement with short chords in the right hand while he played the bass *legato*, and with considerable power.[219] This agrees with Petri's direction, that the organist is to accompany in as short a style as possible and to withdraw the fingers from the keys directly after striking the chord.[220] From this it must on no account be concluded that Bach always accompanied in this way and in no other. As the style of his compositions was more *sostenuto* than that of Kittel's and Petri's time, he distinctly requires in the majority of cases a *legato* accompaniment, and what he directs to be accompanied in a "melodic" manner can generally be performed correctly in no other way. It must be remembered, however, that he was equally at home in

---

[218] Gerber, Lex. II., col. 455.

[219] It was heard by Herr Professor Edward Grell of Berlin, who was so kind as to narrate the circumstance to me by word of mouth.

[220] Petri, p. 170.

the other style, and employed it upon occasion; examples
are offered in the A major aria in the cantata "Freue dich,
erlöste Schaar," and the G major aria in the cantata "Am
Abend aber desselbigen Sabbaths."[221]   In general all customs
of this kind depend more or less upon the circumstances of
the time.   The original manuscripts of Bach's Matthew
Passion, and his cantatas "Was frag ich nach der Welt,"
"In allen meinen Thaten," shows that he also permitted
the organist to employ short chords in *recitativo secco.*   It
appears, too, that in passages where the instrumentation is
lighter, some of the double-basses must have been left out.
In the bass aria of the fifth part of the Christmas Oratorio,
one of the strengthening bass instruments is silent throughout.[222]   In the B minor aria of the cantata "Wir danken dir
Gott," the whole body of the basses scarcely take any part
except in the ritornels.[223]   We may notice something of the
same kind in a passage from the first chorus of the cantata
" Höchst erwünschtes Freudenfest."   Here, in addition to
the organ bass, string basses and bassoons are employed,
and, according to the orchestral parts, have to play throughout
without intermission.   In the score, however, at bar 86 in
the bass line, there is this direction : *Organo solo*, and again
at bar 97, *Bassoni e Violoni.*   The chorus is cast in the form
of the French overture ; this passage corresponds to the
stereotyped trio passages which are of a softer character,
and in the real overtures are given to the two oboes and
bassoon, and which are contrasted with the pompous and
complete effect of the full orchestra.   In order to make the
contrast really effective, Bach makes the bass of the orchestra
cease, and the organ play alone.   He must have deemed it
sufficient to inform the instrumentalists of his intentions by
word of mouth at the rehearsal.   We know, moreover, that
he considered the Gedackt as peculiarly adapted for purposes
of accompanying, from what he himself says in the specification of the repairs for the Mühlhäusen organ.[224]   We may

---

[221] B.-G., V.,[1] p. 352 ff.   B.-G., X., p. 72 ff.   P. Vol. 1017, 2144.
[222] B.-G., V.,[2] p. XVI.   [223] B.-G., V.,[1] p. 307 ff.   P. 1289.
[224] Vide Vol. I., p. 356.

therefore conclude with certainty that in similar passages he frequently dispensed with a part of the instrumental basses, and, especially in arias, employed the whole of them only for the ritornels ; that the *recitativo secco* was usually accompanied in a short style by his direction, and that, as a rule, the Gedackt was used for recitatives and arias.   We cannot, however, venture to deduce a rule which shall hold good for all cases, but must rather conclude that Bach, disregarding the practice of others, kept himself perfectly free in all matters of art; thus, in accordance with the character of the piece he would alternate short chords with *sostenuto* in recitatives, or the Gedackt with some other stop of especial fitness for accompaniment, and in other ways deviate from what was generally accepted, to the advantage of the particular instance.   Such deviations were the result of his nature, the time, and the subject.

Schröter and Petri lay down the law that in accompanying church music no use whatever must be made of reeds or mixtures.[225]   By this they only mean to lay stress upon the fact that the organ ought never to drown the voices and instruments.   Besides this, the task of the organ was not only to support and hold together the whole body of sound, but also to give it unity of colour.   In a certain sense it occupied, with regard to the other instruments, a position similar to that taken in the modern orchestra by the string quartet.   Just as the wind instruments group themselves round this as a centre, so all the instruments grouped themselves round the organ.   The relations were different however in this way, that the organ remained always in the background, its effect being merely that of power, and that on this background the other instruments were seen, not so much as solo instruments, but rather as choric groups.   One of these groups was the quartet of strings, another the oboes and bassoon, a third the cornet and trombones, and a fourth the trumpets (or sometimes horns)

---

[225] Schröter p. 187 ff, where precise directions are given as to the management of the stops in the different parts of a cantata, and also as to the various characteristics of such parts. Petri, p. 169.

and the drums. The flutes occupied a less independent place in Bach's orchestra, but in the seventeenth century they formed a group by themselves. Any individualisation of separate instruments such as is exhibited in the orchestra of Haydn was by this means excluded; the effects were produced rather by means of the juxtaposition and contrast of the great masses of sound, a method which perfectly corresponded to the character of the fundamental instrument, the organ. The sense of style in Bach's church music results partly from his having left these relations of the groups one to another, which had become fixed in the seventeenth century, unaltered both in outline and detail. In this, as in other respects, he had stronger sympathy with a bygone time than his contemporaries, who were more sensitively alive to the approaching development of concert music, and to whom, for that very reason, these traditional requirements were antipathetic; in their church cantatas we hardly ever entirely lose the feeling of a deep artistic anomaly. Besides this, to return to the comparison between the organ and the string quartet, an essential difference lies in the relation of the two bodies of sound to the voices. In a combination of voices with instruments, the natural condition is that the former rule and the latter serve; so that the former fix the character of the piece while the latter only give support and adornment. Now the vocal music of the sixteenth century had attained greatness, notwithstanding that each part was often sung by a single voice. These insignificant choruses had remained, with few exceptions, in universal use throughout the seventeenth century, and far on into the eighteenth, while on the other hand the treatment of the instruments continued steadily to increase in fulness and variety of colour; so that in Bach's time even what we should call an orchestra of weak strength outnumbered the singers by more than a third. In the Neue Kirche under Gerlach there were only four singers to ten instrumentalists.[226] Bach himself, in the memorial of August 23, 1730, fixed the number of singers at twelve

---

[226] Vide App. A., No. 14.

and that of the instrumentalists, besides the organist, at eighteen—in the ratio, therefore, of two to three, so the vocal parts certainly did not preponderate; thus the natural proportion was exactly reversed in consequence of an individual development. Handel and Bach, the two culminating centres of music at that time, sought, each in his own way, to rectify this state of things. The choir with which Handel performed his oratorios in England was indeed numerically smaller than the orchestra, but it consisted of singers of much greater technical ability than those of the German church choirs, and consequently the tone was much fuller; besides, Handel made a much more limited use of the organ. The characteristic feature of giving the vocal parts more importance than the instruments is very prominent with him, and pervades his music so strongly that, in the performances of his oratorios within a few years of his death, it was settled in England that the voices were to outnumber the orchestra. In Germany the change did not come so soon. In the festival performance of the Messiah, got up by Johann Adam Hiller in the Domkirche of Berlin, on May 19, 1786, the old proportions were adhered to; there were 118 vocalists, and 186 instrumentalists.[227]

This change, which was gradual in Germany, is to be ascribed to the influence of England. But it was only suited to the oratorio proper, not to German, or, which is the same thing here, to Bach's church music. In the case of most of Handel's oratorios, although the chorus is seldom or never to be regarded as representing persons in the drama, yet, for the proper understanding of the artistic idea in its entirety, the consciousness that it is constituted of human voices is of the greatest importance. In Bach the

[227] Hiller. Account of the performance of Handel's Messiah in the Domkirche in Berlin, on May 19, 1786, 4. The orchestra, strengthened by Hiller by the addition of flutes, oboes, bassoons, horns, and trombones, consisted of thirty-eight first, and thirty-nine second violins, eighteen violas, twenty-three violoncellos, fifteen double-basses, ten bassoons, twelve oboes, twelve flutes, eight horns, six trumpets, two trombones, drums, organ, and harpsichord. The choir, which comprised all the singers of the schools of Berlin and Potsdam, and all the opera singers, male and female, numbered thirty-seven sopranos, twenty-four altos, twenty-six tenors, and thirty-one basses.

use of the voice is of a much more abstract character; it is regarded rather as an instrument having the property of uttering words and sentences with and on the notes it gives forth. Handel's oratorio style tended towards laying a stronger and more decisive emphasis on the vocal factor, while Bach's chorus admits of strengthening additions only within narrowly-defined limits, and, from the first, never bore an indirect ratio to the instruments. For the practical side of German music, it has been a fatal error, although easily accounted for by historical fact, to reckon the oratorio as a branch of church music on the one hand, and on the other to regard church music from the point of view of the oratorio. This is one of the principal causes of the hybrid state of the German oratorio in the latter half of the eighteenth century; outward circumstances, it is true, contributed to this result, but so deeply imbued were the German composers with this amalgamation that, even after the practice of performing oratorios in the concert room had become usual, its influence long remained evident.

In Bach's church music the ruling or dominant factor is not the chorus or the voices—if there be any such factor, it can only be said to be the organ; or, to put it more decisively, the body of sound used in performing Bach's church music is regarded as a vast organ of which the stops are more refined and flexible and have the individuality of speech. Still, this organ is not to be conceived of as a dead mechanical instrument, but as the conveyer and the symbol of the devotional sentiment of the church, which is what it had indeed become in the course of the seventeenth century, and by the aid of Bach himself. While assigning it this place in his church music, he succeeded in effacing, so far as he was concerned, the disproportion which existed between vocal and instrumental music, and in combining them to form a third power higher than either; he could do it only in this manner in his position and sphere. Handel and Bach, the fundamental sources of whose genius were in part the same, had arrived at directly opposite results in this as in many other problems in art. This is obvious from a study of their works even without regard to comparison or analogy. It is, however, always interesting to have evidence that Bach was conscious of the individuality of his work. In the latter half of the century, as the influence of the Protestant church decreased, the spiritual meaning of Bach's church music became less understood. Kirnberger watched with anger the gradual and increasing disuse of the organ in church music, while a secular and theatrical style was demanded on all sides which lowered this whole branch of art. In his opposition to these tendencies he was joined by the school of Bach and many other musicians, who devoted themselves to the music of the better times that had gone by. Rolle, whom we have frequently mentioned, has formularised and handed down to posterity the verdict of these men. He says: " In theatrical performances, in serious operas, and particularly in operettas, and also in concert rooms where solo cantatas, great dramatic vocal pieces, and so forth are performed, we are accustomed to distinguish the voices in concerted pieces in the plainest manner possible, as they are not checked, obscured, and disturbed by any organ or other powerful accompaniment. We are misled by this into demanding the like delicacy of sensuous pleasure even in church music. Many practical musicians, however, judge quite differently. They say we must never mistake the right and true form of church music. We must treat that splendid instrument, the organ, rather as the ruling power than as passive or as a mere accompaniment, and this more especially in choruses, even though the ornamental details of both vocalists and instrumentalists may thereby be lost. We indeed desire good and beautiful melodies, which each separate part can and must have, but above all we require noble, complete, and splendid harmony."[228]

---

[228] Rolle, Neue Wahrnehmungen zur Aufnahm und weiteren Ausstreitung der Musik. Berlin, 1784. This book was severely criticised and soon forgotten. The style and arrangement are no doubt confused, but the work is notwithstanding full of practical observations and useful facts. The author, who was Cantor at the Jerusalem and New Church at Berlin, was a son of Christian F. Rolle (mentioned in Vol. I., p. 520), and familiar with Bach's school of music. The passage here quoted expressly refers to Bach's pupils, for the heading in

The vocal part of the church music was performed by boys and men. In Thuringia and other districts of central Germany the church choirs were strengthened by so-called "Adjuvanten," or assistants—*i.e.*, amateurs from the neighbourhood, who voluntarily took part in the performances. In Leipzig this custom seems not to have obtained to the same extent; we find it once mentioned that in Kuhnau's time an "advocate in law" had frequently accompanied the church music on the organ. The *Collegia Musica*, under the direction of Schott, Bach, and Görner, consisted almost exclusively of students, who certainly must have taken part in the church music. The solos for soprano and alto were given, as a rule, to the boys of the Thomasschule choir. In the case of pieces composed by Bach himself, their performance was no easy task, for in his arias, as is well known, great demands are generally made on flexibility of voice, and the art of taking breath; a boy's voice rarely lasts long enough for him to acquire a thorough technical education. His singers are said, indeed, often to have complained of the difficulty of this music.[229]

Still, it may be pointed out that a certain skill in technique was at that time more common than at present; it was in the air, so to speak, so that it would be more easily acquired. During all that period the Italian art of song was in full bloom and was known and admired throughout Germany. Little as the German school-choirs were capable of turning this art to account in its entirety, yet a certain superficial brilliancy found its way among them, and with some degree of success. To this, for example, is to be ascribed the study of the shake, which was enforced with great gravity and zeal in the school singing lessons. Wolfgang Caspar Printz, Cantor of Sorau, in his Gesangschule which appeared so early as 1678,[230] gives

---

the table of contents mentions Agricola, Graun, Hasse, Kirnberger, &c., and some of those who are related to the families of Bach and Rolle, as being "famous musicians, as distinguished in church music as in theatrical music."

[229] Forkel, p. 36.

[230] *Musica modulatoria vocalis*, oder manierliche und zierliche Sing-Kunst, 1678. He calls the shake "Tremolo," while he gives the name Trillo or Trilletto to the tremolo proper, which he also treats of (p. 57 f).

instructions as to the shake, and the same was done one hundred years later by Petri, who, like Printz, was a school Cantor,[231] and by Hiller, one of Bach's successors in the Thomasschule.[232] Both direct the study of the shake to be begun early and to be diligently practised every day. It is clear, from Bach's compositions, that he demanded and expected from his singers facility in executing shakes. The German style of vocalisation at this period was a mixture of roughness and over-refinement, which a great musician such as Bach could only make available for his ideal by merging it in the style of instrumental art, which then was at an incomparably higher grade of development. In these days even, a boy's voice seems to us to be utterly inadequate to the task of giving expression to the abundance of feeling contained in the arias of Bach; their depth and passion seem to demand before all else, and as an indispensable condition, a high degree of maturity of artistic feeling. Since it was impossible for Bach to reckon upon this condition being fulfilled,[233] the conclusion is unavoidable that it was not his intention to bring this feature of passionate depth prominently forward. Indeed, throughout his music the subjective emotions are rather suggested than fully developed; and this is the true explanation of the phenomenon that Bach's music has begun to be so deeply felt since Beethoven's time, for during this period men's feelings have been particularly open to such emotions. In Bach's own time an aria of his composition was, as it were, a lake frozen over; the boy's voice glided over the surface, careless as to the depths which lay below. Moreover, the suppression of all personal feeling was required by the very nature of church music; nor is this true only in the case of the soprano and alto voices, but for Bach's music as a whole; it is the deepest law of its individuality. Boys' voices were at least capable of

---

[231] Loc. cit., p. 203.

[232] Anweisung zum musikalische- richtigen Gesange, Leipzig, 1774. p. 38.

[233] " The more refined and expressive kind of singing is not to be expected of choir boys." Forkel in his admirable dissertation on Church music. (Allgemeine Geschichte der Musik, Vol. II., p. 37.)

fulfilling the requirements of this law. We cannot, however, venture to assert that the performance of the solos was as yet always assigned to boys alone, for the art of falsetto singing by men was still diligently cultivated. This art, the practice of which has now so completely disappeared[234] that even the rudiments of its *technique* seem to have become a secret, was quite an ordinary thing in Bach's time at Leipzig. In the musical societies, where cantatas were performed every year with the full number of parts, men alone were the performers; the names of the students to whom the four-part singing was generally entrusted, under Hoffmann's direction, have been given. And later, Gerlach had only four students at his disposal for the concerted music in the Neue Kirche; and the choristers of the Nikolai Kirche, when they had to sing in four-parts, must have been capable of doing it by themselves. By means of the falsetto a tenor voice was changed into a soprano and a bass into an alto. It is expressly stated that this style of vocalisation was employed not alone in choruses, but also with a particular effect in arias, and that a falsetto soprano could sing up to the astounding height of e''' and f'''.[235]

In speaking of customs in singing, the way of performing the recitative must not be forgotten. The singers of the present day are accustomed to deliver Bach's recitatives as they are written, and this they do with a view of giving them a solemn character, distinct from anything theatrical. It is a question, however, whether our present practice has not come to be directly opposite to that of the earlier time. The free alteration of separate notes and intervals in phrases of recitative was seldom if ever employed in theatrical recitative in Bach's time; it occurred more frequently in chamber music, but almost constantly in church recitative.[236] The reason was that the rule at that

---

[234] [In Germany, at least. Tr.]

[235] Kuhnau, Der *Musicali*sche Qvack-Salber, p. 336: "When he played the clavier, and let his alto falsetto be heard (his proper voice was a bass) in some favourite arias, the girl was quite captivated." Petri, p. 205 f, gives full directions as to the cultivation of the falsetto.

[236] Tosi-Agricola, p. 150 ff.

time universally followed was to treat church recitative
in a melodious rather than in a declamatory manner,[237]
whereas in opera it was to be exactly the reverse. These
alterations, however, serve for the most part the purpose
of increasing the melodious flow of the phrases. As to
the cases in which they are to be introduced as a regular
practice, we are given exact directions by Telemann and
Agricola. Telemann, in the preface to a collection of his
own cantatas which appeared in 1725, illustrates these
uses by examples.[238] On the one hand, they refer to the
downward skip of a fourth, especially common in final
cadences. ˙Phrases like these —

according to him, should always be sung thus:—

On the other hand, they treat of the employment of the so-
called accent—*i.e.*, *appoggiatura*, or prefatory note, consisting
of the next note above or below the principal one. To
make this clear, Telemann gives a recitative from one of the
cantatas which occur in the work, both in the usual notation
and according to the actual performance :—

---

[237] Scheibe, Critischer Musikus, p. 163.

[238] Georg Philipp Telemann, " Harmonischer GOttes-Dienst, oder geistliche
CANTATEN zum allgemeinen Gebrauche, &c." Service of Harmony, or
sacred cantatas for general use, which are intended for the furtherance of devotion, as well private and in the house as public in the church, on the ordinary
Epistles for Sundays and Holy Days throughout the year, &c. Folio. The
preface is dated " Hamburg den 19. *Decembr*, 1725."

uns nicht mehr so scharf, wie vor - mals, dräut! Ja se - gen - vol - le

Zeit,   da un- ser Heil sich ein - ge - fun-den! Zu diesem hal - te dich, mit

wah -rer Zu -ver - sicht,   und lass dir sol - che nicht bis an dein En - de

rau - ben,   so raubt dir gleich-falls nichts den Schatz der Se - lig - keit.

He remarks farther that it matters not though the accent should sometimes come in collision with the harmony, and that a phrase like this:—

must, notwithstanding, be sung in this way:—

The list of "*Manieren*" which are illustrated in the longer examples, does not, as Telemann himself says, exhaust all those that are possible, but comprises only the most usual of their kind. Agricola gives a certain number of these as well, but adds several others, particularly in an ornamental style. In order to understand Bach's position with regard to the vocal treatment of recitative, it is necessary to consider two points with regard to it. First, that of all church composers he undoubtedly is the one who strove most earnestly after melodiousness in his recitative; and, on the other hand, that he would be most unwilling to give undue license to the arbitrary caprice of the performer. The first consideration must have led him to regard a free use of these ornaments as desirable, and the second to express them with the greatest possible precision by written notes. Viewed in this two-fold aspect, Bach's recitatives give the result which we should expect. The skip of the fourth in the cadence is always intended to be performed as Telemann directs, but it is always fully written out. Where it is found written in the ordinary manner, it must be sung in strict accordance with the notes. One of these cases—which are of the greatest rarity—is found in the second part of the Matthew Passion, where Jesus says: "Hereafter shall ye see the Son of Man sitting on the right hand of power, and coming in the clouds of Heaven."[239] In this case the harmony of the accompanying violins shows plainly that at the close of the phrase the notes to be sung must be *b* twice and not *é b*. If the interval is to be sung in a florid manner, Bach writes it down as such. This florid treatment was accomplished by filling up the interval with the notes that lay between, by which means *mordents*, shakes, and similar ornament might be introduced.[240] In the Christmas Oratorio, when the crafty Herod sends the message to the wise men from the east, commanding them to seek diligently for the young child, the phrase which Bach here gives at the close of his speech would under ordinary circumstances have been written thus:—

that   I   may come and wor-ship Him al - so.
dass ich auch kom - me und es   an - be - te.

---

[239] B.-G., IV., p. 159, bar 1. Novello's edition, p. 102, lines 2 and 3.
[240] Agricola, loc. cit., p. 151 f.

In order to give expression to Herod's malignant scorn, Bach
wished to signify that the skip of a fourth was to be
slurred over; accordingly, he writes it completely out :—[241]

dass ich auch kom - me und es an - be - te.

The introduction of the accent or appoggiatura, which, as a
rule, was only employed to precede an emphasised note, was
possible in upward or downward direction. When it was used
in a descending passage it was permitted in the interval of a
third or a second. When only one emphasised note follows
the skip of a third, as occurs at the end of the longer example
of Telemann, Bach very frequently writes out the notes as
they are to be sung when they deviate from the rule. It
should be remarked, by the way, that he does not disdain the
use of the accent after the skip of a third, even on a note
which has no emphasis. Passages like the following :—

zu dem wer-de ich ein-ge-hen

or this—

so kann mich nichts von Je - su schei - den.

and many others exhibit this clearly. When two notes
follow, the first of which is emphasised, as in bars 4—5
of Telemann's example, Bach not unfrequently writes in
the notes to be sung; *e.g.*, in the cantata "Barmherziges
Herze":—

ver - bess - re dei - ne Män - gel.

[241] B.-G., V.,² p. 236, bar 9 ff. Novello's edition. Another example occurs in
the Cantata "Brich dem Hungrigen dein Brod," B.-G., VII., p. 335. P. 1295.
[242] B.-G., XVI., p. 15, bar 7 f ("Nun komm der Heiden Heiland"). P. No. 1668.
[243] B.-G., VII., p. 44, bars 3 and 4 ("Der Himmel lacht," &c.) P. 1695.
A passage where this accent is wanting in the original score, but is written
out in the autograph *part*, occurs in a duet B.-G., VII., p. 79, bar 3.
[244] Kirchengesänge von Johann Sebastian Bach. Berlin, Trautwein & Co.,
III., p. 19, bar 10.—See also B.-G., V.¹, p. 30, bar 1.—II., p. 27, bar 10.

When the voice descends only by a second, and one emphasised note follows, the accent may also be introduced; it occurs too in Bach several times written out, as in the cantata "Komm du süsse Todesstunde":—

zu mei - ner See - len Qual

If two or more notes follow (Telemann, bars 1—2), the first, supposing it to be emphasised, would be raised one note higher, exactly as Bach has written it in the "Himmelfahrt" Oratorio:—

245

der da hei - sset der Öl - berg

If, however, the second note has the emphasis it takes the accent, and thus gives rise to a melodic sequence, as in Telemann, bars 2—3 and 6; I have found no certain example to prove that Bach wrote this out in notes. With regard to its use in ascending passages, the accent when introduced *extempore* seems only to have been employed in the case of the interval of a second. A particularly expressive phrase resulted when two notes followed this interval, of which the first was emphasised (Telemann, 5—6 and 6—7); hence this kind of accent is found very frequently written out in Bach. See the passage from the Matthew Passion:—

Ich bin un -schuldig an dem Blut die - ses Ge - rech-ten, se - het ihr zu.

I am innocent of the blood of this just person; see ye to it. The notes referred to have been altered in the English

version to suit the words.[246]   Or at this from the Christmas
Oratorio:—[247]

So, too, when only one emphasised note follows, as in the
cantata "Was Gott thut, das ist wohlgethan":—[248]

When two notes followed, and the second was emphasised,
the accent might be introduced as is done by Bach in one
passage in the Matthew Passion:—

Finally, in the case of an ascending second followed by one
emphasised note, the accent may be formed by taking the note
below the emphasised one as the prefatory note. (Telemann,
bars 3—4.)   Accordingly in the cantata "Gott fähret auf
mit Jauchzen":—

---

[246] B.-G., IV., p. 200, bar 8. Novello's edition, p. 131, bottom line.
[247] B.-G., V.,[2] p. 246, bars 12—13. Novello's edition, p. 160.
[248] B.-G., XXII., p. 241, bars 7—8. Compare bars 10 and 11. P. 1669.

Taking these details into consideration, it seems safe to conclude that since Bach in general preferred to write out all the ornaments he wished used, and, as has been shown, wrote them out so very often in the recitatives, he must mean that they were not to be introduced in all the other places where they might perhaps be deemed suitable. I fear, however, that this summary method of proceeding would hardly fulfil his intention. Agricola, on whose works we have just been founding our opinion as to Bach's custom of writing out these embellishments, adds, after he has mentioned this as his custom, that we must at the same time be careful to distinguish between the places where supplementary notes are essential and those where they are only accidental and non-essential, and that a passage which is beautiful may have the possibility of becoming by many degrees more beautiful. When Bach wrote out an ornament in any passage, he regarded it as essential to that passage. We can see this from the fact that very often he supported the ornament by the harmony of the accompaniment, while the general custom was to leave the accents, which must always be dissonances, quite free. Proofs of this are afforded by the last two examples. It cannot be denied that the ornament thus ceases to be a mere ornament ; many passages lose their recitative character, and the tendency towards the arioso, which is the general characteristic of Bach's recitatives, is made still more prominent. Still, he can hardly have abandoned the general custom so completely that he would not leave to a trustworthy singer the task of improving upon an already beautiful work, as Agricola would say, by using even the simplest and most ordinary means of adornment. Scheibe's statement that Bach wrote down in actual notes " all " the *Manieren* and " all " the little ornaments, gives us most valuable information as to one of Bach's fundamental rules ; but it would scarcely be right to take it literally and apply it to each individual case. Besides, it must be remembered that in the case of a singer not pleasing Bach by his performance, he could always correct him by word of mouth, and we have already shown in one case quoted above how he availed himself of this resource in his relations with his musicians.[249]

To me it seems undeniable that very many passages in Bach's recitatives become more flexible, more expressive, and altogether correspond better to their inner meaning and nature by the use of the accent; so that it may be assumed that Bach himself conceived them as forming part of his idea. In such cases, indeed, the final decision must be left to taste. Before following taste, however, it must be considered in every case whether positive grounds cannot be found for singing the passage as it is written, and not unfrequently will such grounds appear. In the St. John Passion, when Peter denies Jesus, Bach sets the words the first time thus:—

I　am　not.

and the second time thus:—

I　am not.

To introduce the accent in the second of these passages would be to destroy the composer's idea, since the growing excitement with which it ought to be sung is plain to every one.[250] Bach was very fond of this kind of psychological refinement; the example given above from the Matthew Passion, where, after an ascending second, the first and emphasised note of the two which follow is raised, corresponds to a passage that has gone before, in which the accent is also written out.[251] In both it is Pilate who speaks, the first time is a doubtful query, "Why, what evil hath He done?" And the second time distinctly deprecating the deed: "See ye to it." The identity of his feeling and opinion is expressed by the phrase being of similar construction in both cases. When the same cadence is repeated

[249] Compare also Rust's preface to B.G., XXII., p. xxi.

[250] B.-G., XII., p. 29, bars 14—15, and p. 33, bar 7. Novello's edition, p. 30, line 2 and 3; p. 36, line 3.

[251] B.-G., IV., p. 192, bar 13. Novello's edition, p. 125, bottom line.

twice with a short interval between, having an accent in one case and not in the other, we must assume that there is at least a reason for it. On this account it is right to sing the following passage from the Christmas Oratorio :—

and sweet-est ten - der - ness will take me. Now, as my

Bridegroom, I re - ceive Him, And all my heart's de - vo - tion give Him.

exactly as the notes stand, and without raising the last note but one.

All this, however, as has been said, is only true of accents, the simplest and commonest of the embellishments of recitative. The rarer and more elegant adornments Bach always—and this may be definitely affirmed—wrote out in notes ; among these would be included the practice, usual in the case of several repetitions of the same note, of adorning one of the most emphatic of these with a mordent or something of the kind.[252] Passages in which Bach gave in to this custom in his own way, are for instance :—

253

for bu - ri - al will pre - pare,

tr 254

Lord Je - sus, my re -pose,

When all thy con - flicts o'er.

Also all prolonged *fioriture*, like this :

Die Freu - - - - - - - de wird zur Traurig-keit

6   5

[252] Agricola in Tosi, p. 155 f.

[253] Matthew Passion, B.-G., IV., p. 29, bars 9—10. Novello's edition, p. 23, line 3.

[254] "Cantate Ich hatte viel Bekümmerniss." B.-G., V.,[1] p. 30, bars 1 and 2, p. 31, bars 6—7. Novello's edition, "My Spirit was in heaviness," p. 28, lines 1 and 4.

and especially long florid passages [*Melismata*] at the close, which were very common in church-recitative.[255]　These are all in the same category, as well as the two celebrated *Melismata* on the words "And he went out and wept bitterly," in the St. Matthew and St. John Passions.

What has been said of Bach's recitatives is true also of his arias. Free deviations from the written notes were customary at that time in arias also, and even to a greater extent in certain passages. They consisted partly of little embellishments of the melody by accents, mordents, and the like, partly of prolongation of the cadences, and partly of actual varying of the passages of the melody. This last method most commonly occurred in the third part of the aria. Its object was to prevent the hearer feeling wearied by a repetition note for note, or if the musician thoroughly felt his work, to heighten the effect of the first part and so to bring the sentiment of the piece to a higher pitch of passionate emotion. Of such variations there were again three kinds : to a passage of few notes more could be added, a passage of more notes could be simplified into fewer, or a certain number of notes could be exchanged for as many others.[256]　In Bach, this last method could only be employed in the case of a true *da capo* aria, the first part of which comes to a full close in the principal key. This form is, however, by no means the rule in Bach's arias. He, who made it his first object to develop the materials at his command out of themselves, and to combine them one with another, could not long be contented with the cut and dried pattern of the *da capo* aria. Its form therefore appears in his case in manifold modifications, of which the most important consists in making the first part close in the

---

[255] Tosi-Agricola, p. 151.

[256] Agricola loc. cit. p. 235. In instrumental music the adagio movement especially used often to be played in this way. Examples are in Quantz, Versuch einer Anweisung die Flöte traversiere zu spielen. Tab. XVII.-XIX., and in Witting's edition of Corelli's Violin Sonatas. Wolfenbüttel, Holle. Two examples of varied arias, although of a somewhat later period, are given in Hiller's Anweisung zum musikalisch zierlichen Gesange. Leipzig, 1780. p. 135 ff.

dominant or some other nearly related key, so that the third part is not an exact repetition of the first but for its close contains another sequence of modulation; and besides this it very often happens that another aspect is given to the first part by new phrases and combinations. Thus, the tendency which led to the third part of the aria being altered and varied is by him intensified and endowed with meaning; not only is this part altered by means of outward adornment, but its inner nature is altogether changed. But in the case of a true *da capo*, we must remember Emanuel Bach's statement, that it was always understood that the accompaniment might be varied by simple alterations of the inner parts.[257] The polyphonic form of Bach's arias, the importance of each individual note of the melody, and the wealth of harmony allow, in most cases, of no alterations worthy the name. If a rudimentary knowledge of the rules of composition was always necessary for the proper execution of such variations, here it would surely be quite indispensable; but among the Thomasschule boys there can very seldom have been any who were capable of satisfying this demand. It is scarcely credible that Bach should have allowed his singers to do just what they liked with these profound and strictly-written compositions. With regard to the cadences the case may have been rather different. The adornment of these was confined, in the older periods of the art, to a shake on the second of the three notes which form the cadence proper. Subsequently a little ornament was introduced on the note before the shake, without however exceeding the proper length of the bar. It afterwards was carried farther, the last bar was sung more slowly, and at length began to be adorned with all manner of runs, skips, and other possible figures. This way of executing the cadence must have arisen between the years 1710 and 1716, and was in Bach's time in general use.[258] We can get a clear idea of it from a place where Bach, following his usual plan, has written it out; as, for example,

---

[257] Versuch über die wahre Art das Clavier zu spielen. Part II., p. 1.
[258] Agricola, loc. cit., p. 195 f.

at the close of the second part of the first bass aria in the cantata "Freue dich, erlöste Schaar."[259] Where this has not been done Bach often gives the voice part such expressive passages at the close that there is not much room left for the exercise of the singer's fancy. That he permitted however a certain slackening of the time and a sparing introduction of ornaments appears very plainly from the numerous passages where all the accompanying instruments leave off before the final bars, with the exception of the figured bass, which goes on alone to the end. This cannot possibly have any other object than to give the voice opportunity and space for unrestricted and arbitrary movement. Finally, with regard to the small ornamentations in the course of the melody, the fundamental rule still holds good that Bach wrote them out whenever he considered them essential to the furtherance of the desired expression. In other cases he allowed his singers more or less liberty, since in the rehearsal he always had the power of directing them by word of mouth as he wished. That he relied upon this power, but also that in many places he did not consider it a matter of great importance whether an ornament was introduced or not, appears very clearly from a comparison of the instrumental ritornels with the voice part; frequently the one part exhibits ornaments which are wanting in the others, and this not only when one comes in after the other, but even when they are together. Whether any agreement can be restored between them, and if so, in what cases, can in our time be decided by taste alone.

These considerations extend also to the rendering of the choruses. It may appear strange that there can be any question of arbitrary ornamentation in them at least. But it is a fact that the so-called "Manieren" were introduced also into choral singing, and Petri even gives directions, as we learn, for extemporising inner parts in a four-part chorus."[260] This phenomenon is explained by the small constitution of the choirs and the slight difference that there was between solo and chorus singers. The singers

---

[259] B.-G., V.,[1] p. 347. P. 1017.   [260] Petri, loc. cit., p. 211 f.

were, indeed, divided into concertists and ripienists (*i.e.,* nearly the same as into soloists and chorus); there was no impassable distinction between them, however, but the former, besides taking the solos, sang the *tutti* movements as well, and thus constituted the proper nucleus of the chorus, the ripienists joining in to strengthen it. It is, nevertheless, a fact that the free introduction of " Manieren " often resulted in wild and inharmonious confusion, for which reason true musicians would have nothing to do with them. The only exception was when one part led off a theme adorned with " Manieren "; then the part that imitated it had to sing it in the same way, without the adornments being expressly specified ; for the composer must have imagined his theme the second time to be the same as the first.[261] Whoever considers Bach's choruses knows that they are not wanting in all kinds of adornments, whether written out in full or only implied by the context. That these last had to be really and completely executed is, after all that has been said above, just as certain as that the singers were not permitted, as a rule, to introduce ornaments of their own invention.

The instruments added by Bach to complete and enrich the body of sound which before consisted simply of the organ and the voices, can only have been provided for in part from the town musicians. The rest must have been filled up by the scholars who could play. It was so both before and after his time, until Hiller succeeded in forming the entire orchestra from among the Thomasschule boys.[262] The limit thus set on the material, a limit regulated at that time solely by chance, must have proved a great hindrance to Bach in bringing out his works, had he treated the orchestra and chorus in the modern style. The older style of orchestral treatment had, it is true, defects of its own of a different kind. All wood wind instruments have a tendency to rise in pitch after playing some time. The strings can accommodate themselves to this, but not so the organ. Moreover, in the older style of treatment the wind

---

[261] Petri, p. 210.   [262] Gerber, N.L. II., col. 674.

was much more constantly kept in activity, and consequently the instruments got out of tune much sooner.
Attempts were made in different ways to overcome this
inconvenience. Johann Scheibe invented mechanism by
which, by means of greater or less weight on the bellows,
the pitch of the organ could be made higher or lower, and
he attached it first to a small organ made in 1731, which
had 12 manual stops, 2 manuals, and a 16-foot Fagott stop
on the pedals.[263] It appears, however, that his invention did
not meet with great success, since there was a simpler
means by which the same object could be obtained ; several
of ach kind of wood wind instrument were kept in readiness,
so that when one got out of tune by overblowing, another
could be taken up.[264] The " chorus pitch," to which organs
were generally tuned at that time, brought a difficulty
with it, since most of the other instruments were tuned to
the ordinary or so-called "high chamber pitch." This
difficulty was usually overcome by transposing the organ
part. If, however, it fell out that the only available wind
instruments were those which were tuned to the "low
chamber pitch," which was a semitone below the ordinary
chamber pitch,[265] and that no transposed parts had been
prepared for them, the strings were obliged to tune afresh.
In Kuhnau's time the flutes and oboes which were used for
the church music in Leipzig were of this pitch ; and in
Bach's cantata for Trinity Sunday, " Höchst erwünschtes
Freudenfest," which dates from the beginning of his Leipzig
period, they also occur. There can be no doubt that it
was to prevent the continual retuning of the strings, which
was detrimental alike to tone and purity of pitch, that
Kuhnau often employed violins tuned to " chorus pitch "
when no wood wind instruments were taking part. The
trumpets stood as a rule in " chorus pitch," but were
capable of being lowered to " chamber pitch " by an additional piece put on to the mouthpiece, so that the same

---

[263] Leipziger Neue Zeitung von gelehrten Sachen. XVIII. 833 f.
[264] Petri, loc. cit., p. 183.
[265] Adlung. Anl. zur Music Gel., p. 387.

instrument could be used for D major and C major according to " chamber pitch."[266]   And, lastly, the constant use of the whole group of trombones made it very often necessary to employ several players to relieve one another, because the bass trombone, in particular, when used, as was customary, to strengthen the bass part of the chorus, demanded an expenditure of physical strength for which a single player was incompetent.   The treble trombone, when used in this way, was even more trying ; this certainly was one reason for its being supplanted by the cornet, which is less fatiguing.[267]

The mode of conducting church music demands our special consideration, since in this respect, too, customs have much changed since the time of which we are speaking.   They differed, moreover, among themselves, even in Bach's time.   Johann Bähr, who was in his time Concertmeister at Weissenfels, says that one man conducts with the foot, another with the head, a third with the hand, some with both hands, some again take a roll of paper, and others a stick.   Every ordinary director will know how to regulate his method according to place, time, and persons ; whoever would give rules for general acceptation deserves to be laughed at.   " Mind your own business, and let another man conduct as he likes, and do you conduct as you like ; so there is no wrong done to any one."[268]   All the styles mentioned by him have this in common with the modern practice that throughout the piece the time is visibly marked by a person who leads or conducts the rest.   Pictorial representations, dating from the first decade of·the last century, which represent bands of musicians with conductors, make the matter quite clear.   In a collection of engravings published before 1725, by Joh. Christoph Weigel, in Nuremberg, in which are depicted different kinds of musicians playing, there is a figure of a music-director who stands with a roll of music in each hand, directing a four-part

---

[266] See Appendix A., No. 17.
[267] Petri, loc. cit., p. 184.
[268] Joh. Bähr's Musikalische Discurse.   Nürnberg, 1719, p. 171 ff.

motett, *Laudate Dominum,* from a score in front of him;
beneath may be read these words:

> Ich bin, der dirigirt bey denen Music-Chören,
> Zwar still, was mich betrifft, doch mach ich alles laut,
> Erheb ich nur den Arm, so lässet sich bald hören,
> Was unsern Leib ergötzt, und auch die Seel erbaut.
> Mein Amt wird ewiglich, dort einsten auch, verbleiben,
> Wann Himmel, Erd und Meer in pures Nichts verstäuben.

> 'Tis I who lead and guide the tuneful choirs here;
> Silent myself, I cause the music I control.
> I do but raise my arm, and lo, at once ye hear
> Tones that enchant your sense and edify your soul.
> My sway survives the grave, and shall create delight
> When sky and earth and sea are sunk in endless night.

In other representations, the conductor, armed with his
roll of music, stands near the organist and the bass
player, at the organ, or separated from the organist and
the trumpeters in the front of the organ loft, in the
midst of the singers and fiddlers, who are grouped around
him.[269]   But the director was not always so "silent himself."
Many cantors made use of a violin in conducting, so as to
come to the rescue of the singers if necessary.[270]   From
the thirtieth year of the century onward the practice
became different.   It ceased to be the fashion for the
conductor to stand and beat time all through the piece, and
in time it became more and more usual to conduct from
a harpsichord, that is, now to mark the time with the hand,
and now to play the piece with the others, according as it
was necessary, so that order was preserved, not merely by
mute signs, but by audible musical influence.   In very large
performances alone, with a great number of executants, the
older method remained in vogue, because it was indis-

---

[269] In the plates in "Der Durch das herrlich-angelegte Paradis-Gärtlein
Erquickten Seele Geist-volle Jubel Freude bestehend In einem Kern auf allerley
Anliegen und Zeiten angerichtete Lieder. Nürnberg, 1724." Also in "Altes
und Neues aus dem Lieder-Schatze, Welcher von GOtt der einigen Evangelischen Kirchen reichlich geschencket," &c., published by *M.* Herrmann
Joachim Hahn. Dresden, 1720, and also in Walther's Lexicon. Leipzig,
1732.

[270] (Voigt), Gespräch von der Musik, p. 36. Compare Petri, loc. cit., p. 172.

pensable. Besides this, the quiet unobtrusive style of conducting came to be a famous characteristic of musical performances in Germany, which compare very favourably in this respect with those in France, where they beat the time audibly with a large stick, and yet says Rousseau: "The opera in Paris is the only theatre in Europe where they beat the time without keeping it; in all other places they keep time without beating it." The practice of conducting from the harpsichord was widely imitated, because Hasse employed this method in Dresden with such happy effect that the opera performances there rose under his direction to a perfection very rarely surpassed. Rousseau has handed down to us a sketch of the disposition of the band under Hasse's direction.[271] From this we see what was indeed implied by the nature of the case, that the Capellmeister at his instrument did not undertake the task of playing the figured bass as well. For this a special *Clavecin d'accompagnement* was placed on the left side parallel with the front of the stage, while the Capellmeister and his clavier occupied the middle of the orchestra.

But the employment of the harpsichord as an instrument for direction had not been unknown even in earlier times. At Torgau a spinet (an instrument of the same genus as the harpsichord) was used in the Easter performances of 1660,[272] and in Leipzig there was in Kuhnau's time a harpsichord in the organ loft in both the Thomaskirche and Nikolaikirche, which he sometimes used; he preferred indeed to use the Italian lute, for he considered the penetrating tone of that instrument especially suitable for keeping the music together. When Bach entered on his duties he had the harpsichord in the Thomaskirche, which had become useless, set in order forthwith, and got the Council to expend the sum of six thalers a year upon keeping it regularly tuned, but it was out of use again in the year

---

[271] In his *Dictionnaire de Musique, Planche G., Fig.* I., reprinted by Fürstenau, Zur Geschichte der Musik und des Theaters am Hofe zu Dresden. II., p. 291.

[272] Taubert, Die Pflege der Musik in Torgau. Torgau, 1868, p. 18, note 3.

1733, till Easter, 1734, and also from Michaelmas, 1743.[273] In the Nikolaikirche, the organ loft of which was smaller, he used the harpsichord which was there, as it appears with a still longer interval during which it was not used ; he first had it put in order for Good Friday, 1724, when he had a performance of the Passion Music in that church, and after that traces of its use begin to appear in the year 1732 and continue till 1750.[274] From the New Year, 1731, until the same date in 1733, Bach's son Philipp Emanuel, who entered at the university of Leipzig on Oct. 1, 1731, took charge of the tuning of the harpsichord in the Thomaskirche. With reference to this an opinion of his on the cembalo as an instrument for direction will be especially interesting. " The Clavier," he says,[275] " to which our practice entrusts the direction of the music, is of all instruments the best fitted to keep, not the basses alone, but also all the musicians, in the necessary equality of time ; for even the best musician may find it difficult to preserve this equality, even though he may generally have his powers under control, or he may flag through fatigue. This being the case with one, the precaution is all the more necessary when many musicians are together, and the more so that by this means an excellent substitute is provided for the beating of the time, which is in our day only usual in the case of performances on a large scale. The notes of the clavier, which stands in the middle, surrounded by the musicians, are clearly heard by all. For I myself know that even performances on a large scale, where the performers are far apart, and in which many very moderate musicians take part voluntarily, can be kept in order simply by the tone of the harpsichord. If the first violinist stands, as he should, near the harpsichord, it is difficult for any confusion to ensue. In vocal arias, in which the measure is arbitrarily varied, or in which all the parts (of the accompaniment) sound together, and the voice part alone has long notes or triplets in which a very clear beat is

---

[273] Accounts of the Thomaskirche.
[274] Accounts of the Nikolaikirche.
[275] Versuch über die wahre Art das Clavier zu spielen. Part I., p. 5 f, note.

required, on account of the divided time, the singers' task is greatly facilitated by this method of conducting. The bass will find it easiest to keep up the equality of time when his part is least burthened with difficult embellished passages; and this often gives rise to the circumstance that a piece is begun with more vigour than it ends with. If, however, anybody begins to hurry or to drag the time, he can be corrected in the plainest possible way by means of the clavier; while the other instruments have enough to do with their own parts because of the number of passages and syncopations; and especially the parts which are in *Tempo rubato*, by this means get the necessary emphatic up-beat of the bar marked for them. Lastly, by this method—since the musicians are not hindered by the noise of the clavier from perceiving the slightest *nuances* of time — the pace can be slightly lessened, as is often necessary; and the musicians who stand behind or near the clavier have the beat of the bar given out in the most evident and consequently the most emphatic way before their eyes by both hands at once." Here we have a comprehensive statement of the advantages offered to a conductor by the harpsichord, from one well versed in the matter, and at the same time it is an open testimony that Bach availed himself of this method. For the words " our practice entrusts the direction to the clavier " can only have this meaning: that the person who directs the music, that is, the conductor, does so from the harpsichord and by its help. If we take the beautiful and lively description of Bach's conducting given by Gesner, who, by the way, represents him as sitting at the harpsichord, we shall get a clear and correct idea of him. Consistent with this picture is what Emanuel Bach and Agricola say when they are praising Sebastian Bach's facility in conducting: " In conducting he was very accurate, and in time, which he generally took at a very lively pace, he was always sure:"[276] for the use of the harpsichord did not by any means exclude an occasional beating of the time; the object of the instrument was only

---

[276] Mizler's Necrology, p. 171.

to keep the thing going, and quickly and imperceptibly to restore any defaulters to the right way.

Of course, for the most part the score was used in conducting, but sometimes, if this was for any reason impracticable, a simple conductor's part was used. The form of this part explains very clearly the task of the director. It has two staves, the lower for the bass and the upper for marking the points where the conductor's support was necessary. Generally the upper part alone is written, and in fugal movements the entrances of the parts are generally expressed by means of the clefs corresponding to the parts, generally in the bass stave, but sometimes in the upper one too. Besides this everything is given which is needful for information concerning the disposition of the work and the materials used in it; whether a particular movement is executed by an instrument or a singer, and by which, and whether for several voices or for all; whether they sing with or without instruments; when the ritornels come in, and so forth. Kuhnau, in leading the performance of his Passion according to St. Mark, used such a *"Directorium sive Quasi-Partitura"*; and such a director's part, which seems to have been used also for a figured bass part, to his cantata " Welt ade, ich bin dein müde," is still in existence.[277]

The method of using the clavier as an instrument for direction proved itself so good that it remained in vogue down to our century, for instance, in the performances of the Berlin Singakademie. It was also employed in purely instrumental works, and Haydn conducted his symphonies at Salomon's concerts in London from a harpsichord.[278] But at that time, besides the harpsichord director, there was a special conductor as time-beater. In the performance of Haydn's *Creation*, which took place at Vienna, in 1808, Kreuzer sat at the harpsichord, and Salieri conducted the whole.[279] In the year 1815, when Beethoven's *Christus* was

---

[277] In the Stadtbibliothek in Leipzig.

[278] Pohl, Mozart and Haydn in London. Second part, Vienna, Gerold. 1867, p. 119.

[279] Gerber, N.L. II., col. 557.

given at the same place, Wranitzky conducted, and Umlauf was at the clavier.[280] In the Berlin Singakademie, Zelter in his later years let one of his pupils, Rungenhagen or Grell, play the harpsichord, while he himself only beat time.[281] Here the clavier player had also to accompany the *recitativo secco* from the figured bass, which in Bach's performances was the duty of the organist. The harpsichord as an independent instrument crept gradually into church music, but yet the school of Bach used it only to strengthen the tone in such recitatives and arias as the composer had intended to be performed without organ accompaniment. Emanuel Bach at least recommends this practice; but Rolle, on the other hand, considers that such a strengthening of tone in the church is more or less an illusion, and that the constant new-quilling and tuning which were necessary in the winter months made the use of the harpsichord in the church difficult and expensive.[282] This, perhaps, was the reason why Bach gradually gave up its use in his later years. From 1730 onwards, he used instead the independent and practicable Rückpositiv organ in the Thomaskirche, and with greater convenience, as he could play the figured bass himself without being obliged to turn the organist out of his seat.[283] How he used to manage when the performers were so numerous as to require him to beat time throughout—whether in such cases he made some other persons, for example, his sons Friedemann or Emanuel, play the clavier, or whether he left it out and managed the whole thing by his beat alone, cannot be certainly known. If the first alternative seems to be probable, from internal con-

---

[280] Nottebohm, Beethoveniana, p. 37.

[281] From the verbal description given us by Herr Professor Grell.

[282] Rolle, loc. cit., p. 56. " The introduction of the harpsichord into church music has been strongly advised [alluding to the statement of Emanuel Bach given in Vol. I., p. 831]. Since, however, the sound rises in theatrical music, while in churches, on the contrary, the sound must come down from the organ loft, the introduction of the harpsichord would give no particularly emphatic support [E. Bach, loc. cit., had said that even in the loudest music, in the opera, and even in the open air, the harpsichord can be heard, if it be put on a raised place]."

[283] See Appendix A., No. 18.

siderations, the last is more likely when we remember that
he could dispense with the clavier altogether for a whole
year; thus he must, by his independent conducting, have
developed great energy, certainty, and clearness, as indeed is
expressly testified by Emanuel Bach and Agricola. What
can be said as to the position of the performers has been for
the most part given above in Emanuel Bach's words. We
must, however, remark that the instrumental basses—or at
least some of them, since, to ensure precision and time,
a good many were employed—always used to be placed
near the conductor, sometimes behind him as he sat at the
harpsichord, so as to be able, in cases of necessity, to play
with him from the score. Besides, the trumpets and drums
were always put rather at a distance from the rest, so as
not to drown the voices.[284]   A favourite place for them was
close to the organ, right and left of the organist.[285]

V.

KUHNAU.—THE CHURCH CANTATA.—TEXTS BY NEUMEISTER
AND PICANDER.—COMPARISON OF THEIR MERITS.—BACH'S
CHURCH CANTATAS.—THE " MAGNIFICAT."

KUHNAU, during the whole period of his being Cantor of
the Thomasschule, waged an unequal, and, as far as he
was concerned, an altogether unsuccessful warfare with the
opera and all connected with it. In all his complaints one
thought is uppermost: namely, that if he only had at his
command a sufficient number of performers to take part in
the church performances he would be able entirely to nullify

---

[284] Scheibe, Critischer Musikus, p. 713 ff.

[285] See the plate in the collection of songs by Hahn mentioned above, and
also in Hiller's description of the performance of the *Messiah* in 1786, the
appended ground-plan of the places of the performers. Compare the ground plan
of the Dresden orchestra where two platforms were built for the trumpets and
drums on the right and left sides; and lastly, Petri, p. 188. Hiller's ground
plan is very interesting, both historically and musically, even though it is of
little use for our purpose, since Bach did not dispose his great numbers of
performers in the ordinary way, and in Handel's oratorios the harpsichord
played quite a different part.

the pernicious influence of the theatre, and to promote the triumph of a more earnest musical feeling in Leipzig. He was mistaken : the fact that his influence on the public musical taste constantly diminished was only partly due to outward circumstances; the blame was equally due to his own character and that of his musical talents. In a time when the old and the new are striving together for the mastery, he alone is a successful leader of the public taste who is capable of understanding and recognising the rights of both. The power that was struggling for expression in the opera forms was unintelligible to Kuhnau and foreign to his whole nature. He had more than once attempted to enter the domain of dramatic music as a composer. In earlier life he himself translated a libretto on the story of Orpheus from the French and set it to music; it is not known with what degree of success.[286] But another opera of his, which must have been written very late in life, made a distinct *fiasco*.[287] It was his weakness not to perceive that the most versatile cannot do everything; otherwise he might have avoided giving such practical proof that his aversion to the opera was the result of his failure. Kuhnau was a master in the sphere of clavier music, and many considered him equally great in church music. There is no question that he showed abilities in this branch of art, which raised him above his contemporaries. He was better versed in the technicalities of vocal writing than most other German composers of the time. His five-part motett for Holy Thursday, *Tristis est anima mea usque ad mortem*,[288] may be reckoned among the more prominent works of the kind; if it is not of equal merit with the motetts of Joh. Christoph and Joh. Ludwig Bach

---

[286] "The foolish fellow now got upon the subject of the opera of 'Orpheus,' which I had formerly translated from the French into German poetry, and likewise composed the music." Kuhnau, Der *Musicali*sche Qvack-Salber, p. 456, compare p. 458 ff.

[287] Scheibe, Critischer Musikus, p. 879, note: "But notwithstanding his (Kuhnau's) great merit, we know well how badly he succeeded when he undertook to set an operetta to music, and put it on the stage."

[288] It exists in the separate parts in the library cf the Leipzig Singakademie and is numbered 362.

even in technical qualities, it has a breadth of conception which betrays the study of the classical Italian models. A chamber cantata, *Spirate clemente, o zephyri amici*,[289] also shows that Kuhnau endeavoured to form himself on the style of the Italians. There exist seventeen church cantatas, written at different periods of his life.[290]

Scheibe, who considers Kuhnau, Keiser, Telemann, and Handel the greatest German composers of the century, says: Kuhnau " is now and then carried away by the flood of harmonic ideas ; hence, he is often dull and devoid of the requisite poetic beauties and ornaments of expression, and consequently here and there he becomes too prosaic. That he was aware of this himself, however, and that sometimes he succeeded in writing deep and poetic music, is shown by his things for clavier, and by his last sacred works, especially his Passion oratorio, which he finished a few years before his death.   In these works we see how clearly he understood the employment and laws of rhythm. We see too, that he was always careful to make his sacred works melodious and flowing, and in many cases really affecting, though he was not so happy in his dramatic work."[291] These words prove—what is plain from the works themselves—that by degrees Kuhnau tried even in his church music to make his style similar to that which prevailed in opera.   The statement that he was " carried away by the flood of harmonic ideas " is not to be taken so much in the positive sense, *i.e.*, that Kuhnau immersed himself to too great an extent in polyphonic obscurity, as in the negative sense: namely, that he did not always give due consideration to the importance of melody and of variety of rhythm.   In his earlier works, *e.g.*, a cantata "Christ lag in Todesbanden," dating from the seventeenth century, he keeps entirely to the style of the so-called " older " church

---

[289] In the Royal Library in Berlin.

[290] Ten are in the Royal Library in Berlin, and seven in the Town Library in Leipzig.   Among the latter is a Christmas cantata " O heilge Zeit, wo Himmel, Erd und Luft," which however is certainly not by Kuhnau, but is the work of a younger master.

[291] Critischer Musikus, p. 764.

cantatas, of which illustrative examples by Buxtehude were
considered in an early part of the present work. His style
never radically altered from this, even in later life; though
he adapted himself to the operatic style in many ways, he
still composed to words by Neumeister, or in Neumeister's
manner, so that a compromise was the result.[292] This is
quite clearly seen in the recitatives. Bach's recitatives have
always a strongly marked melodious character, but this style
was invented by him, and founded on the dramatic recitative
of his time. Kuhnau's recitative still retains the arioso form
of the older church cantatas, varied, however, with the new-
fashioned recitative phrases. Of the aria form in three
sections he has left several excellent examples; one duet for
alto and bass, in the cantata for Ascension, " Ihr Himmel
jubilirt von oben," the polyphonic writing of which is very
flowing and ingeniously developed, must be allowed to be a
masterpiece. But Kuhnau felt himself much more at home
in the old simple form of hymn, with its short and pleasing
staves of melody and time-honoured ritornels.

Of the choruses, it can only be said that here and there
they show attempts at a broader and more artistic development, but generally in a tentative manner; as a rule,
they alternate between homophonic vocal movements and
meaningless interludes, or between little solo portions and
tutti movements. In the construction of the chorale, again,
there is nothing more than an attempt at development.
There is no free contrapuntal movement of the parts, and we
have to content ourselves with a few meagre imitations, as, for
instance, in the final chorus of the cantata "Christ lag in
Todesbanden" or at the beginning of the cantata "Wie schön
leucht't uns der Morgenstern." When the orchestra joins in
with the chorale in figurations, it is very far from being
employed in an independent way; in the Christmas cantata
"Vom Himmel hoch" the chorus sings this chorale in the

---

[292] Neumeister's cantata "Uns ist ein Kind geboren" (see Vol. I., p. 486)
was not performed in Leipzig till Christmas, 1720, but the words of church music
even in the year 1711, are completely in Neumeister's style.   For example
Kuhnau's cantata " Und ob die Feinde Tag und Nacht" is written on a poem
in this form.

simplest style of homophony, and the instruments support it, only the first and second violins having ascending and descending semiquaver passages quite in the style of the final chorus of Bach's early work, "Uns ist ein Kind geboren." The chorale "Gelobet seist du, Jesu Christ," in the cantata "Nicht nur allein am frühen Morgen," is treated in a similar way, but with the addition of a bass. Everything he writes is clever and in a flowing style, and hence the effect is pleasing; agreeable and even pathetic passages are frequently to be met with; but depth of feeling and grandeur of form are wholly wanting. Kuhnau must rank with the group of writers of the older church cantatas, because he had nothing in him to say which could not perfectly well be said in the forms of those cantatas; and this is equally true of the introductory instrumental symphonies, though his independent instrumental music was very admirable. His Passion according to St. Mark, composed for Holy Week of 1721, to which Scheibe gives especial praise, exists only as a sketch.[293] It can, however, be very plainly discerned, even here, that the prevailing characteristics of Kuhnau's church music have left their mark perhaps more strongly than ever, and that the composer endeavoured to assimilate the more emotional style of operatic music "by poetic beauties and ornaments of expression," *i.e.*, by the invention of such turns and phrases as had a certain innate dramatic value. His inmost nature, nevertheless, remained absolutely unchanged even in this. Kuhnau did not understand the world, nor did the world understand him; it was time that they should take leave of one another.

The position in which Bach found himself with regard to theatrical music was quite different. He had mastered the principles of all its forms, and had turned them to account for his own art. However unlike operatic music his compositions may seem, he was by no means devoid of an inner sympathy with that style, but rather held that it was

---

[293] "*Directorium sive Quasi-Partitura Passionis ex Evangelista Marco.*" A copy made by Burgmeister, in 1729, is in the Royal Library at Königsberg in Prussia, Department "Gotthold's Library."

a just demand of the time that respect should be had to it even in church music. The condition of music, as he clearly explained to the Council in his memorial on the improvement of church music, was quite different from what it had formerly been; the art had made considerable progress, taste had altered in a remarkable manner, the old-fashioned style of music in which Kuhnau was still writing had ceased to have any charm for the ears of his contemporaries. The interest which he took in the Dresden operatic performances, for instance, is well known, and a number of secular works in dramatic form by him still exist. So far as we know, however, he never wrote an actual opera. For although he may not perhaps have agreed with the opinion of Gottsched, who about this time gave out in Leipzig that the opera was the most preposterous absurdity that had ever been invented by the human mind,[294] it is yet conceivable that the glitter and glamour of this branch of art, which only serves for the entertainment of an hour, must have been antagonistic to his earnest, true, and deep artistic nature. Whenever he conceived the wish to go to Dresden he would say to his favourite son, "Friedemann, shall we go to Dresden again and hear their beautiful little songs?"[295] If the actual words of the expression have been handed down correctly, Bach's relation to the opera is characterised in them with striking brevity. Scheibe says, incidentally: "There are some great geniuses, who use the word 'song' (Lied) as a term of abuse; when they want to speak of a piece of music which is not sufficiently pompous and intricate for them, they call it a 'Lied.'"[296] Since a pompous and intricate style is just what Scheibe accuses Bach of,[297] it is more than probable that the words we have quoted were intended for Bach. The simple construction of the operatic forms seemed to him quite inadequate for the realisation of his art-ideal, and in this sense he may often have spoken disparagingly of them. But when employed by a Hasse and interpreted by a Faustina he could yet think them "beautiful,"

---

[294] Gottsched, Versuch einer Critischen Dichtkunst. Leipzig, 1730, p. 604.
[295] Forkel, p. 48.
[296] Critischer Musikus, p. 583.   [297] Idem. p. 62.

and he knew just as well as his critic did that without
operatic music he would not have been what he was.[298]

Bach's historical position in art can only be fully understood by regarding him not as opposed to this music, but as
accepting all he could from it.   The opera in Germany
was incapable as yet of becoming a living musical drama,
nor could such a change be effected at that time by
the hand of a German alone.   Under freer, broader conditions, such as were offered in England, it became the
oratorio under Handel, while in Germany it was developed
into Bach's church music.   In England the result was
attained by combination with the forms of Italian sacred
music, and in Germany by the complete purification
which it acquired by means of the national art of the
organ.   The history of the development of German opera
can be clearly traced.   After it had risen, by about 1700, to
be a considerable musical power, it sank rapidly from its
height, and in the next thirty years it had almost ceased
to exist, until it was revivified in the latter half of the
century by an impetus proceeding chiefly from France,
and shown in the operettas of Hiller and Weisse.   In
Leipzig itself, it was all over with German opera by
the year 1729.   What came to replace it was Bach's
music.   This contained what Kuhnau had vainly striven
after: namely, the spirit of the time, in so far as it
could find fitting musical expression in operatic forms,
and at the same time the genuine church style.   Whether
Bach did anything consciously and directly to extinguish the
flickering flame of the opera at Leipzig is not known.   But
that his art tendencies speedily became predominant there
cannot, under existing circumstances, be any doubt.   It has
been generally accepted and stated as a matter of fact,
that Bach's church music was not understood, and soon
forgotten, and that the mighty works of his creative genius
failed to meet with due appreciation.   I believe that too much
stress is laid on certain expressions of disapproval, on some

---

[298] Idem., p. 591. Note.—"If we in Germany insist on bringing about
the total banishment of operettas from the stage, we may be quite sure that
w : shall never again see a Hasse, a Graun, a Telemann, a Handel, or a Bach."

measures taken by the magistracy which are not properly understood, and on the partially insufficient means which Bach had at his command.[299] With regard to the last point, it may well be asked whether Handel was always so much better off for his oratorios, or Beethoven for his symphonies; and whether an eminent genius ought not to be capable of doing wonders with small means ? The high respect in which Bach's name and music remained throughout the century at Leipzig, the extensive influence which he exercised upon the music of Northern and Central Germany, and the fact that many of his sacred vocal compositions found their way into Saxony and Thuringia, may serve to show that we are justified in concluding that his work in Leipzig made its mark.

There had never been any good writer of words for cantatas in Leipzig. In 1716 Gottfried Tilgner had collected five annual series of Neumeister's poems, by permission of the author, and published them under the title of " Five-fold church devotions."[300] These poems, which had hitherto been disseminated privately, were now brought within the reach of every one, and had such a sale that a new edition was demanded in the following year. Tilgner, a young literary man, lodged in the house of *Magister* Pezold, a colleague of Kuhnau, whom we have frequently mentioned.[301] Kuhnau had undoubtedly set many texts by Neumeister, and besides he was very capable of writing texts himself on Neumeister's pattern. Bach, however, had no such skill in verse making; therefore he was at once obliged to look about for a poet, and he chose Franck in preference to Neumeister.

But he had not to wait long before he found in Leipzig

---

[299] Bierey, the well-known Music Director at Breslau, made the acquaintance, as he told Julius Rietz, of an old church servant in Leipzig, who had been employed in Bach's time. He fully agreed with Bierey in his admiration of the master, as far as concerned his power as an organ or clavier player, and his opinion of the cantatas was thus expressed : "Ah! but you should have heard them !" It is not known, however, whether this opinion was shared by the general public.

[300] See Vol. I., p. 474.

[301] Sicul, Die andere Beilage zu dem Leipziger Jahr-Buche, for the year 1718, p. 187 ff. This gifted and industrious man was driven by melancholy and overwork to commit suicide in 1717.

itself an adequately skilled and always willing collaborator. Christian Friedrich Henrici, born at Stolpe in 1700, had studied at Wittenberg, and had lately settled in Leipzig, where he was living for the present in poor circumstances chiefly by writing "occasional" verses. In two of his poems he petitioned the King-Elector to grant him free board; and in 1727 dedicated to him, through Count Flemming, a cantata for his *fête* day on August 3, beginning "Ihr Häuser des Himmels, ihr scheinenden Lichter."[302] In the same year he obtained a situation in the Post-office, and in the Leipzig Directory of 1736 he figures as *Ober-Post-commissarius*.[303] In 1743 we again come across his name as a tax-gatherer and exciseman, and in this capacity he died in 1764. The higher officers of the churches and schools received a certain annual sum as compensation for the general tax on liquors; this was a special favour.[304] To this circumstance a small document in Bach's own writing owes its origin; it is a receipt given to the tax-gatherer at Easter, 1743, for a compensation for three casks of beer.[305] But the intercourse of the two men was not simply on matters of business; it had been for a long time of a friendly and artistic character. Among the sponsors to one of Bach's children, born in 1737, was the wife of Henrici, who had then been working for more than twelve

---

[302] State archives of Dresden.

[303] Das jetzt lebende und florirende Leipzig, 1736, p. 14.

[304] "Fruuntur nostri privilegio potus a collectis cerevisiae exemti." (They enjoy a privilege of having liquors exempted from taxation.) Kuhnau, Jura circa musicos ecclesiasticos. Leipzig, 1688. 4, Cap. VI., § 1.

[305] "Having duly received from Herr Christian Friedrich Henrici, appointed exciseman of the district, from *Quasimodogeniti* (*i.e.*, first Sunday after Easter), 1742, until same date 1743, by his Majesty the King of Poland and Serene Elector of Saxony, according the Electoral decree of November 9, 1646, for three casks, each at forty ggr. making altogether five thlrs.

Five Thalers

for the two taxes in money and kind, I hereby acknowledge the receipt of the same most thankfully. Season of *Quasimodogeniti*, 1743, at Leipzig.

"*Joh. Sebast: Bach.*"

And beneath are the autograph signatures of Deyling and a certain Johann Andreas Vater. The impression of Bach's seal represents a rose surmounted by a crown. This document, in October, 1870, formed part of a collection of autographs in the possession of the late General-consul Clauss of Leipzig.

years in collaboration with Bach. Henrici began his literary career in 1722, as a satirist; in this respect we may call him a disciple of Christian Günther, though, as he is not to be compared to the last-named poet in talent, his mean style and bad taste are all the more repulsive. He was incapable alike of Günther's free and picturesque imagery, and of his audacious licence. When his satirical poems created ill feeling he was frightened, and declared that he had only the best intentions in writing such productions, but that the unfortunate results had spoilt the fun, and the threats of the evil-disposed had deprived him of all his pleasure in it. He now only wrote poems from time to time to please his patrons and friends, but he does not deny that he used "a sharpened pen." In the year 1724 he turned his hand to sacred poetry. He thought it incumbent upon him to give a public explanation of this sudden change. "He imagined that many people would laugh to see him assuming a devotional attitude. He wished to guard, however, against the imputation of having been quite unmindful of heavenly things, and considered it only right to offer to his Creator the fresh fruits of his youth, and not the worn out remains of his old age. Let not anyone blame him for making poetry his chief employment and troubling himself little or nothing about other branches of learning. If necessary he could produce credible testimony to his academic diligence. Besides, verse-making was easy to him, and took him very little time. Why should he not then employ this natural gift and turn it to account for his living?" The work to which these and other remarks served as preface was entitled: "Collection of profitable thoughts for and upon the ordinary Sundays and holidays"; he uses here the pseudonym of Picander, which he adopts from this time. The work consists of meditations in rhyme, mostly in Alexandrines, to which a set of verses to the melody of some church hymn is usually appended. They did not at first appear in a collected form; for a year the poet was in the habit, on Saturdays and Sundays after vespers, when other people were enjoying themselves in unseemly dissipation, of putting into rhyme his thoughts on the Gospel, and of bringing them out week by week on a half-folio sheet. To this custom he adhered; the first piece was written for the first Sunday in Advent, 1724, and the second and last for the same day in 1725.[306]

Considering that he had now made ample atonement for his sins, and that his reputation was firmly re-established, he once more threw himself into the arms of the secular muse. In 1726 there appeared, written by him, three German plays: "Der akademische Schlendrian," "Der Erz-Saüfer," and "Die Weiberprobe," "designed for amusement and instruction." They are low, repulsive farces,[307] but the tone which pervades them was his natural element, and he owns that it would be pleasanter and easier to him to sing four bridal songs than to grind out even one dirge. His chief object in writing these things was not attained, however: that of gaining enough to live on. He therefore brought out in the year 1727 a new collection, consisting of "Grave, gay, and satirical poems," and dedicated them "To fortune who will surely yet be kind to him, and grant him something more." Fortune was kind, and he got his situation in the Post-office. In 1728 there followed a collection of texts for cantatas in Neumeister's style.[308] This was the only collection of the kind which he brought out, and he subsequently incorporated it with his "Grave, gay, and satiric poems," to which four more parts were gradually added.[309] Henrici considered himself an original genius

---

[306] The title of the first part runs thus, differing slightly from that of the complete edition: "Sammlung | Erbaulicher Gedancken, | Bey und über die gewöhnlichen | Sonn- und Festtags- | Evangelien, | Mit | Poetischer Feder entworffen | Von | Picandern. | Leipzig, | Gedruckt bey Immanuel Tietzen." | 8. The Preface, which is wanting in the complete edition, is dated November 30, 1724. In the complete edition it is replaced by a short notice to the "kind reader" dated First Sunday in Advent, 1725; it is dedicated to Count Sporck. A copy is in the Royal Library at Berlin.

[307] On these and their connection with Weise's plays, compare Gervinus, Geschichte der deutschen Dichtung. Three Vols. (5th Ed.) p. 600 f.

[308] "Cantaten | Auf die Sonn- | und | Fest-Tage | durch | das gantze Jahr, | verfertiget | durch | Picandern. | Leipzig, 1728." The preface is dated June 24, 1728. A copy is in the Royal Public Library in Dresden, *Lit. Germ. rec. B.* 1126.

[309] The second in 1729, the third in 1732, the fourth in 1737, and the fifth in 1751. The series of cantatas is reprinted in the third part.

and a pioneer of public taste. He "foresaw," he says in the preface to the Sammlung erbaulicher Gedanken, "that imitators of his style would speedily arise; he wished them better success than he himself had met with. For his part, he would rather try an unbeaten track than follow in the footprints of another." And then he goes on alluding to the strong influence of English literature, which was then beginning to make itself felt: "Everybody at Leipzig wishes to be critics, patriots, and moralists, without having tested their powers, and it can only be regretted that the world-famous name of Leipzig should be used as a vain shelter for such unworthy productions. Nothing is more praiseworthy than the foresight with which the authorities have suppressed wretched trash of this kind, and these measures will go far to free Leipzig from the present polluted condition of its literature; Leipzig, so renowned even in foreign lands for good and refined taste. Well may such abortive productions hide their heads at last for very shame of their imperfection." He himself shines most in his satirical writings. They exhibit a certain keenness of perception, and a knowledge of human nature unusual in one so young, and they are very skilfully rhymed.[310] His giving up this line of work so soon is a sign that his satires were not so much the spontaneous production of his mind as imitations of others, suggested by outward circumstances. In the Epithalamia, the most numerous of his poems, a few pretty ideas are entirely overpowered by the dulness of the rest, while the plain-spoken improprieties are all the more odious from the weakness of the whole tone of the work. In spite of this, the fact remains that for a whole generation his poems enjoyed great popularity; they reached four editions before the year 1748, and no doubt they reflect with considerable truth the poetic taste of Leipzig at the time.

In his sacred poems, Picander shows even less original talent than in the satires and the secular occasional verses.

---

[310] The best specimens are to be found in the first edition of the first part of Ernst-, scherzhaffte und satyrische Gedichte, p. 477—566.

This branch of his art was utterly foreign to his nature, and probably he never would have attempted to write poems for cantatas had not Bach been in want of a versifier, and had it not been important to him, striving as he was for the mere necessaries of life, to be brought into connection with the celebrated composer. It is clearly perceptible too that Bach fashioned him for his own purpose. Many indications point to the fact of Bach having employed him in the beginning of 1724, or perhaps even for the Council-election of 1723. The first sacred poem by Picander to which he is known to have composed the music—the Michaelmas cantata "Es erhub sich ein Streit," was written in 1725. The "Sammlung erbaulicher Gedanken," begun in the previous year, afforded no opportunities whatever to the composer; but in this cantata Neumeister's form of poetry is used with success, at least in the recitatives, though the texts of the arias betray the hand of a beginner. As Picander had previously written words for several occasional cantatas, he cannot have found it hard to acquire the knack of getting the right form in the sacred cantatas. Many turns of expression show the influence of Neumeister, and especially in one particular, that he tries to give his diction an ecclesiastical tone by a free admixture of Scriptural expressions, and of allusions—often extremely far-fetched—to Biblical events. In the year 1725 he wrote for the first time a Passion poem, taking Brocke for his model. From this time the intercourse between Bach and himself became closer. Picander was himself not without musical talent and knowledge, and in this respect he had one advantage over Neumeister, to whom indeed he was not inferior in his easy use of language. In his secular poems the allusions to musical matters are of frequent occurrence, and they go into such detail that we may conclude that he not only took a lively interest in it, but practised it also himself.[311] In one place he even gives two very pretty dances as a musical

---

[311] Compare "Das Orgel-Werck der Liebe," written in 1723, in "Ernst-scherzhaffte und satyrische Gedichte," 1727, p. 303 ff., and "Die Vortrefflichkeit der Music," written 1728, in the collected edition of 1748, Vol. II., p. 662. ff. and the same, p. 621 f.

appendix,[312] and from a poem of the year 1730 we learn that he was a member of a musical society—which must have been the one conducted by Bach.[313]

In the preface to the year-book of cantatas written in 1728-1729, Picander says: "To the glory of God, and actuated by the requests of many good friends, and by much devotion on my own part, I resolved to compose the present cantatas. I undertook the design the more readily, because I flatter myself that the lack of poetic charm may be compensated for by the loveliness of the music of our incomparable Kapellmeister Bach, and that these songs may be sung in the chief churches of our pious Leipzig." This cycle of poems was thus directly intended for Bach, and it seems to owe its origin to an unexpected wish expressed by him, since it does not correspond with the ecclesiastical year, but begins with St. John's Day, ending with the fourth Sunday after Trinity. For Good Friday, 1726, Picander wrote the text of the St. Matthew Passion, this time, however, not imitating Brocke's plan, but keeping the Bible words unchanged. Here again Bach's influence is easily perceptible, and it may be also traced in the circumstance that Picander seems to have borrowed some of his ideas, at least, from Franck. It is impossible to give any positive evidence of this, since Franck's skill in cantata writing was never anything but moderate. Still, a comparison of certain portions of the German text will seem sufficient proof to the reader who cares to search into the matter, and as Bach certainly loved Franck's work for the sake of his fervent and rapturous sentiment, it can only have been he who referred Picander to Franck's works.

After 1729 Picander published only a very few sacred poems, but it must not be supposed that he ceased writing them altogether. We may indeed feel certain of the contrary, for a lasting intercourse remained between him and Bach, and he was the only person in Leipzig who could undertake tasks of this kind with adequate skill. If we are not to

---

[312] Poems of 1727, p. 540.
[313] Collected edition, Vol. II., p. 819 ff.

regard Picander as the author of most of the other cantatas
which Bach wrote in Leipzig, it is inexplicable that Bach
should never have set to music a single one (so far, at least,
as we know at present) out of the numerous collections
of cantatas which appeared at that time, and which must
have been accessible to him.[314] After what has been said,
Picander's omission of these cantatas from his collected
works is easily explained; he put no value on these manufactured compositions, which were put together hastily and
to please his friend. Franck wrote out of a true poetic inspiration; Neumeister as an active theologian and preacher;
while Henrici did not feel himself impelled to writing
sacred poems by any genuine or hearty interest in such
things. His impulse came solely from Bach, and this
explains the pains he took in turning to account the productions of others and remodelling them for Bach's purposes; and of this procedure his treatment of Franck's
hymns is not the only example. Bach also took an interest
in the writing of Johann Jakob Rambach, several of whose
devotional works he had in his library. He never used one
of Rambach's cantata texts, however, although they are as
good as anything of their kind. But he seems to have
drawn Picander's notice to a pretty madrigal by Rambach
("Erwünschter Tag") :—

> O wished-for day,
> To be engraved on marble,
> Or metal that will ne'er decay—

for the same idea occurs in the text of one of Picander's
Christmas cantatas (" Christen ätzet diesen Tag") :

> Christians, grave ye this great day
> In brass and stone that will not perish.

In a cantata by Rambach, for the Feast of the Purification,
one of the arias begins thus (" Brechet, ihr verfallnen
Augen") :—

> Rest, O eyes so dim and weary,
> Close in slumber's sweet repose.

---

[314] *E.g.*, the poem written by J. D. Schieferdecker and E. G. Brehme for
music, in the castle churches at Weissenfels and Sangerhausen, in the years
1731-1735. Bach was Capellmeister at Weissenfels, and in that capacity had
to perform certain duties at Court.

And in one of Bach's cantatas on the same feast there are
these lines (" Schlummert ein, ihr matten Augen ") :—

> Slumber now, O eyes so weary,
> Close in soft and sweet repose.[315]

Bach had composed music to an ode by Gottsched for the
obsequies of Queen Christiana Eberhardine, and afterwards
wished to put the music to some other purpose ; Picander
gave his assistance and wrote a new poem, so that the
funeral ode became a Passion according to St. Mark.[316]
He was just as willing and ready to put new words to compositions on his own texts, if the music could thereby be made
available for other purposes.

It is worth while to draw attention to the difference which
existed between the sister arts of music and poetry as
regards their art-ideals. Music as applied to religion had
attained a height which must be allowed to be unapproached
before or since, in respect both to depth and richness of
substance, and to variety and breadth of form. The art of
sacred poetry, however, so far from rising to a similar level,
had sunk, under the successors of Neumeister, to be a false
and hollow mockery. It would not be too much to say that
the influence of the cantata-poem upon the development
of poetry at that time was really ruinous. For these
collections of texts, although made for the special purpose
of musical treatment, ere long asserted their claim to be
regarded as independent creations. Originally printed
separately, in order to enable the congregation to follow
the words during the music, they soon came to be considered as devotional works on their own account, and
were, in fact, sold as such in large numbers. Very many

---

[315] " *M* Joh. Jacob Rambachs, | *HALLENSIS*, | Geistliche | Poesien, |
Davon | Der erste Theil | Zwey und siebenzig *CANTATEN* über | alle Sonn-
und Fest-Tags-Evangelia ; | Der andre Theil | Einige erbauliche Madrigale, |
Sonnette und Geistliche | Lieder | in sich fasset." (Magister J. Jacob Rambach
of Halle's Spiritual Poems, of which the first part consists of seventy-two
cantatas on all the Gospels, for Sundays and Festivals ; the other part contains
several madrigals, sonnets, and sacred hymns.) Halle, 1720, pp. 218 and 257.
B.-G., XX.,[1] p. 37.

[316] This matter has been cleared up in a conclusive manner by W. Rust, in the
preface to B.-G., XX.,[2] p. VIII. f.

of these texts were never set to music; for Picander wrote cantata-poems even for the Sundays on which, as he knew very well, there was no music in church—viz., for the Sundays in Lent and the three last in Advent. Those who chiefly threw themselves into this branch of poetry were persons who either had no poetic faculty at all, or in whom whatever talent there might be inclined to another kind of work; to the last class belonged Picander, as well as another writer well known at that time, Daniel Stoppe, of Silesia. The gigantic advance made by Brocke in his "Irdisches Vergnügen in Gott," and by Gellert in his odes and songs—not to mention Klopstock, who came somewhat later—can only be perfectly estimated by a comparison of their works with the great mass of the cantata-poems in vogue in Bach's time. Still, it must be admitted that the new spirit which appeared in the works of these men was unsuited and opposed to musical setting; their poems were to attain their end by their own poetical inspiration, independent of other aids. During Bach's period, artistic feeling and emotions in the domain of religion found vent almost exclusively in music, and from the moment when sacred poetry made itself felt as a prominent influence religious music began to decline. The overpowering predominance of the musical factor in this kind of work is very clearly seen in Bach's relations with his Leipzig poet. It might have been fatal to him, for it is not possible that church music can be genuine and good which utterly disregards the particular religious sentiment or emotion called up by the poetry; indeed, Keiser, Telemann, and Stölzel, although their gifts were by no means small, had succumbed to this very danger. Bach triumphed over it, because, however fully and comprehensively he represented all the musical inspirations of his time, he yet remained faithful to the foundation of all Protestant church music, namely, the chorale.

Bach composed in all five complete "year books" of church cantatas for all the Sundays and holy days.[317] Now, by

---

[317] Necrology, p. 168.

deducting the six Sundays in Lent and the last three in Advent, and adding in the three feasts of the Virgin, and also the festivals of the New Year, Epiphany, Ascension, St. John, St. Michael, and the Reformation festival, we get a total of fifty-nine cantatas to the ecclesiastical year at Leipzig. It follows, then, that Bach must have written on the whole 295 church cantatas. Of these at least twenty-nine belong to the period before his coming to Leipzig ; then the maximum of those written at Leipzig must be put at 266. As Bach was twenty-seven years working at Leipzig, he would have written on an average ten cantatas in a year. Telemann, who was four years older than Bach, wrote nearly seven "year-books" of cantatas in 1718 alone;[318] and in 1722-23 Johann Friedrich Fasch wrote a double set of church compositions, for the morning and afternoon, and when Saints' days occurred, often four cantatas in one week.[319] This comparison of mere numbers is only given to confute the opinion of Bach having been a voluminous and rapid writer. The number of his works is indeed very large, but it is spread over a long life. The talents of Telemann, Fasch, and other of his contemporaries who were prolific in production, were of a shallower kind, and their work is therefore no proper standard of measurement for that of Bach. But even when compared to geniuses of nearer equality with himself, such as Handel and Mozart, Bach appears as a more deliberate worker, though at the same time a more clear and certain one. His scores do not give the impression that he made many preparatory sketches or experiments with the chief subjects, as Beethoven did, for example. They seem to have been written down when the work had been completed in its outline and general features in the composer's mind, but yet not so far that nothing could be added to it during the actual process of writing it down. The cases in which he discarded and altered the entire original design of any piece are comparatively rare,[320]

---

[318] Mattheson, Grosse General-Bass-Schule, p. 176.

[319] Gerber, N. L. II., col. 92.

[320] The first sketches of the cantatas " Die Himmel erzählen die Ehre Gottes " and " Man singet mit Freuden vom Sieg " met with this fate.

but alterations of detail are of frequent occurrence. When, after a lapse of some time, he took up one of his works, he never omitted to try it afresh, and, when occasion required, to improve it; compositions on which he laid great importance he used to rewrite again and again, refining and adorning them into perfection. This careful forethought is illustrated also by the fact that he very frequently took a share in the work of transcribing the parts. The Cantors always had among their scholars one or more musical copyists, and Bach did not omit to keep his pupils very hard at work at this employment on occasion; and even in the year 1778 Doles recalls to mind the quantity of notes that Bach made the Thomasschule boys transcribe.[321] His sons, too, had to give their assistance, but his best copyist was his wife; her handwriting, which helped in the production of the parts of all the first Leipzig cantatas, meets us even in the church compositions of Bach's later years, larger and stiffer, but as firm and accurate as ever. Where so many hands were helping, many musicians would have spared themselves the mechanical labour of writing out the parts, which must have taken much of his time from composition. Those 266 Leipzig cantatas are the work of the truest artistic industry devoting itself solely to the subject in hand; a mighty monument built up stone by stone. It has not remained until our day in an unimpaired condition, for all that are at present known of Bach's cantatas, even including the six cantatas of the Christmas Oratorio and the more important fragments, only reach the number of 210.

Bach's trial piece was performed on the Sunday next before Lent (February 7), 1723; it was the cantata "Jesus nahm zu sich die Zwölfe."[322] The cantata "Du wahrer Gott und David's Sohn"[323] seems to have been at first intended for this occasion; it is recognisable as having been written at this period, and while he was yet at Cöthen.

---

[321] In a written apology addressed to the Council on July 15th, 1778. See Council deeds " Die Schule zu *St. Thomae* betr. *Fasc.* II."

[322] B.-G., V.,[1] No. 22. P. No. 1290.

[323] B.-G., V.,[1] No. 23. P. No. 1551.

It consists of a duet for soprano and alto, a recitative for tenor, and two choruses, one free and one on a chorale; it shows the master at a height that none of his former works had approached. The text is not particularly adapted for musical setting—Scriptural words are wanting altogether, and the rhymed verses are in "madrigal" form, occasionally changing into Alexandrines. Here, more than in most cases, Bach had to give form to the whole, and it is quite peculiar. The Sunday (Estomihi, as it is called) is the one next before Lent, when the minds of the people are to be prepared for contemplating the sufferings of Christ. In the gospel for the day it is related how Jesus, with His disciples, is drawing nigh to Jerusalem, there to await His Passion. A blind man sits by the wayside, and appealing to Christ, as He is passing by, to have mercy upon him, receives his sight. These ideas form the germ of the religious feeling of the work: the fervent cry for help, and the presentiment of the tragedy that is approaching. The duet (in C minor *Adagio molto*) is accompanied by two oboes, which with the bass have an independent and more animated movement, surrounding the broad phrases of the melody and the sustained tones of woe in the vocal parts, which are in imitation. There is less emotion in the recitative, except at the end where it rises to passionate intensity. The prominent feeling of this piece is not however given out by the voice, but by the first violin and the oboe, which play the melody of the chorale " Christe du Lamm Gottes " very softly above the vocal recitative. This bold combination of chorale and recitative is a new effect, even in Bach, but it followed almost naturally from his melodic manner of treating recitative, and after he had ventured upon a recitative-duet.[324] Its effect is very powerful; the whole feeling of the Passion, so tragical and yet so full of comfort, comes over the hearer like a flood. The chorus (in E flat major) now rises in a perfect cycle, its chief section being repeated in a solid homophonic style, while the central portion consists of imitative two-part

----

[324] See Vol. I., p. 557.

interludes between the tenor and bass. Yet this chorus, with its mighty pathos, is not the climax of the emotional progress of the work. The expectation of Christ's passion and death is brought out as the strongest element; the E flat chorus is immediately followed by the chorale chorus in G minor on " Christe du Lamm Gottes." On account of the shortness of the melody, all three verses are gone through, which is rare with Bach. The first verse, sung more or less in homophony by the chorus, has an independent instrumental accompaniment of a mournful, wailing character; in the second verse the course of the lower parts is more animated, the upper part (with the melody) being imitated in canon both by the oboe and the first violin ; by the former, at the third note of the melody in the fourth below, and by the latter, at the sixth note in the third above; in the third verse, which closes in an Amen, the lower parts have a different, but quite as vigorous a counterpoint, while above the *Cantus firmus* the oboes give out a new melody of the highest intensity of expression, and sharply contrasted in its rhythm. The feeling rises throughout from sadness to intense grief, and at last is changed into a pious prayer, pleading for reconciliation with God. A new treatment of the chorale form is shown in the first verse, and one subsequently much used and largely developed by Bach ; here, however, it is only used in very modest proportions. In the second verse enormous skill is shown in polyphonic combination; it is evident that this form comes directly from organ-music, and Bach treated this very chorale, together with many others, in his " Orgelbüchlein."[325] The last verse, on the other hand, is in the manner of the older composers, and is only superior to their works in the constantly melodious character of its instrumentation. Moreover, it must not be overlooked that between the second and fourth numbers of the cantata deep poetic connection subsists which has been already noticed in different cantatas of the Weimar period;[326] the chorale melody, which in an earlier movement was given to the instruments alone,

---

[325] See Vol. I., p. 600.   [326] See Vol. I., p. 544.

is sung at the close, being used at the beginning to give a tone to the emotional aspect of the work, and at the end to bring out clearly the devotional feeling. In every respect this cantata is a trial piece well worthy of Bach; compared with the one which he actually employed for that purpose, it is easy to see why he judged it necessary to keep this cantata in reserve for a time. It was too grave, deep, and elaborate. Bach knew the taste of the Leipzig public, accustomed as they were to varied styles of operatic music and to Kuhnau's soft and tender tunes.

In the cantata "Jesus nahm zu sich die Zwölfe," he adapted himself more to this taste. The fugal chorus in the first number shows a simplicity of counterpoint which is of very ordinary occurrence in the works of Telemann, but which surprises us in Bach. An agreeable tenor aria is followed by an easily intelligible chorale number, in which the chorus in four simple parts is accompanied by the uppermost instrumental parts in counterpoint of semiquavers, which is continued in short interludes. This was a form much in vogue at the time; Bach himself had formerly made use of it,[327] and in this instance it is only enriched so far that passages, mostly of an independent though not very characteristic order, are allotted to the second violin and the viola. The other numbers are deeper, especially the opening of the first, an unison chorus for tenor and bass; the most important part of this is in the instrumental portion, which is very delicately interwoven and is much less like an accompaniment than an independent piece. From this number alone we can see in truth that the composer understood his business. The work as a whole is well suited to its purpose, but it can in no respect be considered of equal merit with the first one, which seems to have been first performed on the Sunday before Lent, 1724.[328]

We cannot now be sure what was the music for Whitsuntide with which Bach began his labours in the University church.[329] The only cantata which is likely to have been

---

[327] See Vol. I., p. 491. [328] See App. A., No. 19.
[329] See ante, p. 214.

used is " Erschallet ihr Lieder, erklinget ihr Saiten," but there are convincing reasons for placing the date of composition two or three years later. He began his church work as Cantor of the Thomaskirche on the first Sunday after Trinity. It has not, it is true, been expressly recorded that the first church music conducted by him and favourably received by the congregation was of his own composition ; but this may be taken for granted according to the customs of the time.[330]   There exist two cantatas for the first and second Sundays after Trinity, the last of which is dated by Bach himself 1723. The first is so exactly similar to it as regards the text and the musical form, both in outline and in detail, as well as in feeling, that no doubt can be entertained that they both belong to the same period, especially when we remember Bach's characteristic way, before alluded to, of producing several examples at once of any new form previously unused by him.[331]   The chief novelty of form in this case is that we here meet, for the first time in Bach's work, with the church cantata in two divisions. We know already that on the high festivals part-music was sung before as well as after the sermon, and that it was allowed in this latter place even on ordinary Sundays and holy days. But to cast one single work in so large a mould, as that it could be divided into two independent parts, was at variance with previous customs, in Leipzig, at least. It seems to me that Bach, in this innovation, followed the method of the oratorio composers whose works, destined for the Catholic form of worship, were so arranged that the sermon came between the two parts.[332]

---

[330] *ACTA LIPSIENSIVM ACADEMICA.* 1723., p. 514.—" On the 30th of the said month (namely May), as on the first Sunday after Trinity, the new *Cantor* and *Collegii Musici Direct.,* Hr. Joh. Sebastian Bach, who came from the Ducal Court at Cöthen, performed his first *Music* here with great applause." (See *Ante,* p. 215, Note 64.)—In Sicul, *ANNALIVM LIPSIENSIVM MAXIME ACADEMICORVM SECTIO* XX.   Leipzig, 1726, p. 479, it is stated that this performance took place in the Nikolaikirche.

[331] See App. A., No. 20.

[332] The division which was usual, even in the 17th century, of oratorios into two parts, in contradistinction to the triple division of operas, is explained by this custom, which obtained, in Italy, at least, throughout the whole of the 18th century.   See Burney, Present State of Music in France and Italy, p. 365.

The Gospels for the first two Sundays after Trinity are more than usually rich in deep and beautiful thoughts and in striking contrasts. The librettist unfortunately did not understand how to take advantage of this in the interests of music. In both he devotes his energies to didactic trivialities, which have but a loose connection with the Scriptural narratives, and might just as fitly have been written for many other Sundays. In the first cantata, " Die Elenden sollen essen, dass sie satt werden "[333]—" The poor shall eat and be satisfied "—(in E minor), reflections of a common-place kind are made, with reference to the story of the rich man and Lazarus, upon the worthless and transient character of earthly riches, upon Jesus as the essence of all good, upon a good conscience and contentment. Bach triumphs over this heterogeneous medley in four well contrasted arias, the first of which is ingeniously and fancifully built on the following motive :—

and in six recitatives. The chorale " Was Gott thut, das ist wohlgethan "—" That which God doth, is still well done "— plays an important part in the work. It appears first at the close of the first part, and in a new combination of Pachelbel's style, with that especially peculiar to Georg Böhm.[334] This movement is repeated again at the close of the second part, and a chorale fantasia[335] on the same melody serves as an introduction to the same part, not set for the organ, but for the string quartet with the trumpet—the quartet taking the independent and polyphonic accompaniment and the trumpet the chorale melody. The thread of the cantata, broken off by the sermon, could not be re-united in a more skilful or artistic manner. The introductory chorus, however, arouses the liveliest interest of all, speaking as it does in affecting tones of consolation in sorrow. The emotion of sorrow, as might have been

---

[333] B.-G., XVIII., No. 75.   P. No. 1670.
[334] See Vol. I., p. 206.   [335] See Vol. I., p. 610.

expected in Bach, is more or less prominent both in the
orchestra—which in the first movement of the chorus
progresses independently in faltering pulsations—and in
the agonised and sustained melodies in the voice parts.
But a promise of joy gleams brightly through the sorrowful sounds (compare especially bar 53 ff.) and in the
broad theme of the fugal movement which follows :—

Eu - er Herz soll e - - wig-lich le - - - - - - -(ben)

the sick and the weary soul inhales full draughts of the air
which is to bring new life and health.   But yet a certain
veiled character predominates, and in the interrupted cadence
(in bar 13 of the fugue) it has even a tone of piercing grief.
From this point, however, all the forces of the music
combine, and finally pass by a lovely modulation into
D major ; the major sixth which occurs in the soprano
part, an interval strictly forbidden by the old rules for the
formation of melodies, but used moderately often by Bach,
has here a powerful effect of light and liberty.

Not only in the division into two parts and the insertion
of an instrumental movement, but also in the number of its
choruses and chorales, its recitatives and arias, and the
order in which these forms are arranged, the cantata (in
C major) for the second Sunday after Trinity, "Die Himmel
erzählen die Ehre Gottes"[336]—"The heavens declare the
glory of God"—agrees with the one just spoken of.   Nay,
the arias, whether intentionally or not, are in the same keys
as those of the other work, their order alone being different.
Here, again, the most important part of the whole is the first
chorus, although scarcely any connection subsists between
its words and the Gospel for the day.   As before, the chorus
consists of an opening section with free imitations and an
independent instrumental accompaniment, agreeing with the
other even in the time—and of a fugue; there, however, the
entry of the full choir is preceded by a movement for soprano

and alto, while here some of the basses begin alone.[337] The resemblance is seen even in similar phrases (compare bars 24 ff of the C major, with bars 26 ff of the E minor cantatas). The whole piece is very full and brilliant, and the fugue theme is strong and vigorous. An effect noticed in the cantata "Ich hatte viel Bekümmerniss"[338] is repeated here, and once again in a new work that we shall consider next in order to the present ("Ein ungefärbt Gemüthe"); the fugue is begun by solo voices, the tutti parts coming in gradually at the recurring entrances of the theme, giving the effect of a slow *crescendo* such as that produced on the organ by the gradual drawing out of more and more stops. This fugue also bears a resemblance to some of the earlier fugues, in that the trumpet is used as a fifth part in the working out. The chorale sung at the close of each part is set in a simple and familiar form. The instrumental movement at the beginning of the second part is a trio for oboe d'amore, viola da gamba, and double-bass, one of the forms of chamber music transferred to the church, of which we have already met with several examples in Bach. Bach, not long after, used this piece in one of his organ sonatas,[339] not, however, without considerable alterations. Many of these alterations are absolute improvements, in various ways, upon the older work; the calmer basses and the generally lower position of the upper part reveal its devotional purpose, for the second part of the cantata was performed during the Communion.[340]

---

[337] Bach had at first intended to begin the chorus immediately with a fugue with an independent accompaniment on the instruments. This was to have been the theme:—

Die Himmel er - zäh - - - - - - - len die Eh-re Got- tes.

[338] Compare vol. I., p. 534.

[339] B.-G., XV., p. 40 ff.

[340] Both cantatas were well known in an altered and abridged form, the first beginning with the first recitative, under the title "Was hilft des Purpurs Majestät," and the second, as "Gott segne noch die treue Schaar," beginning with the opening of the second part. The latter was also used as a Reformation cantata. See Breitkopf's catalogue. Leipzig, Michaelmas, 1761, p. 20.

It appears that Bach came again before the public with a
new work fourteen days after this, on the fourth Sunday after
Trinity (June 20).[341]   The librettist of the two former cantatas could no longer satisfy him, so he turned back to
Neumeister's poems, which he had tried and found successful.   The text " Ein ungefärbt Gemüthe "—" A pure and
guileless spirit "—taken from the fourth of the five year books
of church cantatas, is elegant in versification but is anything
but a model of poetic feeling.   Bach viewed this didactic,
prosaic dissertation in the light of his own musical imagination.   To the two arias which the cantata contains he set
fine and affecting music; the first of these (F major), with
which the work opens, delights the hearer with its pleasant
and contented expression.   This may be called a trio for
violin, viola, and bass, and the second a quartet for two
Oboi d'amore, viola, and bass, so little prominence is given
to the voice part.   This method was here necessary from
the inferior quality of the text; and from the relationship
between the chief subject of the first aria and that of the last
movement of the B minor sonata for violin and clavier,[342] it
may be concluded that Bach was devoting himself now more
especially to instrumental writing.   The third number, a
chorus on the text in Matt. vii., 12, " Alles nun, das ihr
wollet "—" Therefore all things whatsoever ye would that
men should do to you, do ye even so to them "—is very
animated, energetic, and striking, especially in the double
fugue, which forms its second part ; on the other hand, the
short phrases in which the chorus and the orchestra answer
one another at the beginning, remind us of the style of the
older church cantatas, while bars 11—18 have a resemblance
to bars 11—25 of the second chorus in Bach's earlier cantata
" Ich hatte viel Bekümmerniss."   The closing chorale is
simple in form, like that in the cantata " Jesus nahm zu sich
die Zwölfe."[343]

For the seventh Sunday after Trinity (July 11) in this year,

---

[341] B.-G., Vol. I., No. 24.   [342] B.-G., IX., p. 80 ff.
[343] See App. A., No. 21.

Bach chose a text from Franck's "Evangelische Sonn- und Festtags-Andachten," which had provided him with the groundwork of two compositions in Weimar.[344] Franck had intended it for the third Sunday in Advent, so that its adoption for another occasion involved the alteration of the first two arias. Recitatives, which do not usually occur in Franck's texts, were inserted, and in them we seem to discern the hand of the prolix compiler of the cantatas for the first and second Sundays after Trinity; their insertion renders the text sufficiently long to serve for a cantata in two parts. The first chorus "Aergre dich o Seele nicht" (G minor)—"Fret thyself no more, my soul"—is remarkably short, dispensing with any full working out, such as we are accustomed to in Bach. After a prelude the chorus starts with a phrase of three bars, which by means of striking suspensions is intended to produce the impression of vexation and anger. In Bach's vocal pieces it may often be noticed that on the one hand their character is derived not so much directly from the text as from the church teaching for the Sunday, or some other more general poetic idea, often merely from the necessity of musical contrast; while, on the other hand, certain special ideas provide the basis for characteristic musical subjects which direct and pervade the working out, giving outward colour rather than intrinsic purpose to the sentiment—an intimate union of the general and the particular. This is the case here; for as the idea of vexation is only viewed negatively, it could give no character to the whole, but it did give occasion for an opening of great musical interest. In contrast to this, there now comes in a declaimed fugato on the same words, full of Bach's emphatic intensity; the instruments are given an elaborate fugal movement on another theme in contrast to the air; the double-bass alone going on in its own course. After one working out, the close follows in D minor, and in a short homophonic phrase, the words which give the reason for those that have gone before are given out; then the whole process is repeated in C minor, leading back to the original

---

[344] See Vol. I., pp. 570 and 642.

key ; six bars more by way of epilogue, and the piece is at
an end. In spite of the unusual and concise form, the
emotional picture is complete ; we are sensible of the sure
hand of a master not only in the elaborate detail, but in the
whole structure. Altogether, the cantata, generally, stands
above most of those that preceded it, and is worthy to
rank with the cantata, "Du wahrer Gott." The recitatives
are throughout very expressive, and at times deeply touching,
especially the *arioso* endings ; particularly that of the second
recitative with the anticipations of the harmony in the bass, so
ingeniously contrived to impart colour to the accompaniment.
The three arias vie with one another in depth and intensity
of expression, but the gem of the solo numbers is a duet (in
C minor) for soprano and alto, " Lass Seele kein Leiden von
Jesu dich scheiden"—" My soul, let no sorrow e'er part thee
from Jesus." It is in the rhythm of a gigue, and has that
melancholy grace which is peculiar to so many of Bach's
pieces in dance-form. Lastly, the chorale with which the
first part of the cantata closes is of great interest. Here,
for the first time, we meet with the chorale fantasia since
it was transferred to vocal music. In the cantata " Du
wahrer Gott," Bach had indeed shown a predilection for
this new production, but in the works which followed had
gone back to the simpler forms. An instrumental piece, of
a pious and innocent character, is played by the violins
and flutes, with bass, answering each other; and the melody
of " Es ist das Heil uns kommen her," steals in with the
verse :—

> Ob sichs anliess, als wollt er nicht,
> Lass dich es nicht erschrecken.
>
> Although He seems to will it not,
> Yet let not this affright thee.

The *cantus firmus* is in the soprano, and the other voices have
counterpoint, mostly imitation ; the melody in diminution.
In the score there is no chorale at the close of the whole
work, but, by analogy with the cantatas for the first and
second Sundays after Trinity, it may be assumed with
certainty that the chorale of the first part was to be repeated.
    Another of Franck's texts was set for the thirteenth Sun-

day after Trinity (Aug. 22). It is, however, not quite certain whether this work was written before the following year, when it was performed first on the 3rd of September. But I consider the first to be the more probable date.[345] For this work Bach returned to the "Evangelische Andachts-Opfer,"[346] the poetry of which was more suitable for music. The work is altogether without chorus, except at the very end, where a simple chorale is sung to the fifth verse of the hymn, " Herr Christ der einig Gott's Sohn "—"Lord Christ, the only Son of God." The Gospel narrates the parable of the Good Samaritan, and the whole musical work is full of Christian tenderness and compassion. In the first aria in G minor, "Ihr, die ihr euch von Christo nennet, wo bleibet die Barmherzigkeit "—" Ye upon whom Christ's name is called, where is your love and charity "—we seem to hear the Saviour Himself speaking, with divine tenderness and true human warmth of love and sympathy, yet not without a touch of sadness :—

Ihr, die ihr euch . . . von . . Chri - sto nen - net,

In the second aria (in D minor), " Nur durch Lieb und durch Erbarmen werden wir Gott selber gleich "—" Only by our love and pity are we made like God Himself "—the Redeemer's teaching is applied by man to himself; and in the third it is delivered with joyous conviction as a duet, and in a strain that seems to have originated from the melody of the first movement :—

"Hands not grudging, ever ready." These two themes are worked out with a persistency unusual even in Bach, for the most part in canon on the unison or the octave, and in the duet also in contrary motion; they are heard unceasingly, now in the voices, now in the instruments, like those words of St John, "Little children, love one another."

---

[345] See App. A., No. 22.
[346] See Vol. I., p. 540.

The re-modelling of the beautiful Weimar cantata, " Wachet, betet,"[347] can with moderate certainty be assigned to this year. Since no church music was performed in Leipzig on the last three Sundays in Advent, Bach employed it for the twenty-sixth Sunday after Trinity, as it fits the Gospel for that day very well. The alteration consists essentially in this, that by the insertion of recitatives and the chorale "Freu dich sehr, O meine Seele"—"Now rejoice, O soul and Spirit"—the work is enlarged into a two-part cantata. To one recitative, one of the finest ever written by Bach, a chorale is added on the instruments, which raises the passionate personal emotion into the province of religious worship, while, on the other hand, it is enriched and individualised by it. Bach himself thought very highly of this cantata, and in later years performed it again and again.[348]

In addition to these eight cantatas there are yet two works, dating from the first year in Leipzig, which owe their existence to church ceremonies of an exceptional character. On the 24th of August in each year—St. Bartholomew's Day—the election of the new Town Council used to take place, and, on the Monday or Friday next following, a festival service was held before the members of the new Council took their seats. In the year 1723 this Monday fell on August 30,[349] and for this occasion Bach wrote the festival cantata " Preise, Jerusalem, den Herrn "[350]—"Now praise the Lord, Jerusalem "—a work equally remarkable for its vigorous and brilliant choruses and for its fervent and melodious solos. That the form of the work was intended for a festal occasion is shown very plainly by the character of the separate numbers. It opens with an overture in the French style, for the performance of which an orchestra

---

[347] See Vol. I., pp. 571 and 643.

[348] See Appendix A., No. 23.

[349] It was held on the Monday after St. Bartholomew's Day in the years 1724, 1725, 1726, 1727, 1731, and 1739; and on the Friday in the years 1728, 1729, and 1730. See the deeds of the Council " Rathswahl betr. 1701, Vol. II.," and Nützliche Nachrichten von Denen Bemühungen derer Gelehrten und andern Begebenheiten in Leipzig. In the year 1739." P. 78.

[350] B. G., XXIV., No. 119. P. 1684.

consisting of four trumpets, drums, two flutes, three oboes, string quartet, and organ is requisite. The splendidly pompous *Grave* movement is played by the instruments, till at the *allegro* (12-8) the chorus enters with the words of Psalm cxlvii. (12—14), worked out not so much in fugal style, as with free imitation and episodical use of the chief subject which was first given out by the bass; this goes on until the recurrence of the *Grave* movement, played as before on the instruments alone, and filling the part of a postlude. It is not the first time that we meet with this bold transference of a thoroughly secular instrumental form into church music by Bach; for the same thing is done in the cantata "Nun komm der Heiden," written for Leipzig in 1714.[351] An essential difference is observable, however, in that the overture form in the earlier work is united with a chorale, and also that the voices take part in the *Grave* movement. The number of which we are speaking in this "Rathswahl" cantata inclines more strongly towards the secular side, because it comprises a chorus in free style, and more distinctly towards the instrumental side, in that the chorus does not take part in two of the chief sections into which the work is divided. This was allowable, since its purpose was not in the strictest sense devotional; besides, a fundamental religious sentiment, if nothing more, is preserved throughout the *allegro* by the polyphonic style displayed in it, which is all Bach's own. No more sacred character than this would befit the recitatives and arias which follow, of which the words set forth the happy circumstances of the town of Leipzig. But for his amazing gift of pure musical invention, Bach would have found it almost impossible to produce such a charming piece as the second aria "Die Obrigkeit ist Gottes Gabe, ja selber Gottes Ebenbild"— "Authority is God's ordaining, yea, and His image here on earth"—for he could hardly have got his inspiration from the words. But whenever it was possible to get any poetic impulse from the text, he availed himself of it, as is shown by the first aria "Wohl dir, der Volk der Linden, wohl dir,

---

[351] See Vol. I., p. 507.

der hast es gut "—" O dwellers by the lime trees, O blest, O favoured race." There are few pieces of so agreeable and sunny a character as this; the low oboes (*Oboi da caccia*) here employed by Bach lend it an idyllic character, yet a grave one as befitted the circumstances, so that it differs perceptibly from the aria of *Pales* in B flat from the cantata "Was mir behagt,"[352] which in other respects it closely resembles in feeling. This aria (in G major) is joined to the second (in G minor), which we have already mentioned, by an entirely separate movement; a piercing trumpet call introduces a bass recitative "So herrlich stehst du, liebe Stadt"—"So fair thou art, beloved town"—which is then accompanied by sustained harmonies on the two flutes and two English horns, in addition to the figured bass, the jubilant trumpet call recurring at the close; the strings are silent during this movement. After the G minor aria the whole body of instruments and voices reunite immediately in a splendid movement cast in the form of the *da capo* aria. The first section consists of a fugue, whose theme :—

The Lord hath done great things   for   us

is apparently found from the first line of the chorale "Nun danket alle Gott." Such an independent use as this of parts of a chorale melody is extremely rare in Bach (in the motett "Nun danket alle Gott" he once did something similar to this); the chorale was to him consecrated, as it were, to the church, and where he introduces it he is wont to set it unaltered as the central point of his own composition. In departing from his usual method in this case, he doubtless felt impelled by the mingled sacred and secular character of the whole work. The second section of the cantata forms, in its homophony, a contrast to the first; a motive of vocal character given out by the trumpets in the instrumental ritornels :—

---

352 See Vol. I., p. 566.

is worked out in this section with great skill. The strictly
devotional feeling finds its first expression at the close of the
cantata in a few lines from "Herr Gott dich loben wir."

During the years 1722-3, the Church of Störmthal near
Leipzig had been restored, and at the same time a new
organ had been erected, the building of which had been
undertaken by Zacharias Hildebrand, a pupil of Gottfried
Silbermann, for 400 thalers. A certain Kammerherr von
Fullen, who was resident at Störmthal, had provided the
requisite sum of money, and after the completion of the
work requested Bach to try the instrument. On November 2, the Tuesday after the twenty-third Sunday after
Trinity, a public service took place for the dedication of the
organ, and Bach wrote a cantata for the occasion : " Höchst
erwünschtes Freudenfest "—" Hail, thou longed-for feast of
joy"—and conducted the performance himself. The organ,
" certified " by him " as an excellent and durable instrument
and highly commended," is in existence in all its essential
parts to this day ; it underwent thorough repair in 1840
at the hands of the organ builder, Kreuzbach, who at the
same time expressed himself favourably with regard to the
organ. It says a great deal for the respect in which
Bach's person and name were and are still held in
Saxony, that the tradition of his having been at Störmthal
has remained there through more than a century and a
half.[353] The cantata, which Bach must have taken his
forces from Leipzig to perform, is written with especial care,
owing, perhaps, to the high position of the personage who
had given him the order.[354] It is, moreover, of intrinsic
importance, and Bach, who always liked to turn the compositions written for special occasions to account for his
regular duties, subsequently arranged it for Trinity Sunday,
and often performed it in its altered shape on that day.
We may learn much from comparing this work with the

---

[353] This was told me by Pastor Ficken, of Störmthal, to whose kindness I also
owe the extract given above from the accounts of the church there.

[354] Both the autograph score and the original parts are in the Royal Library in
Berlin. To the parts are appended the text printed on a folio sheet.

"Rathswahl" Cantata. Here, again, there is no strictly
devotional purpose, and the fundamental forms are even
more thoroughly secular, although purified and adapted to
church use. The opening again consists of an overture in
the French style, and the way in which the voices take
part is similar, excepting that when the *grave* recurs at the
close, they are introduced in the last bar, to heighten the
whole effect. Besides this the *allegro* is here a true *fugato*,
and the interrupting trio-passages are not omitted, so that
the overture style is more strictly adhered to, even in detail.
By the continual recurrence of the chief subject :—

the first aria has in some degree the character of a rondo,
though the aria-form is retained. The second aria is entirely
in the rhythm of a gavotte :—

The third keeps up the character of a gigue against the
following theme used as a bass ritornel :—

Finally, the fourth has the movement of a minuet :—

Thus we have here the remarkable phenomenon of a cantata in the form of an orchestral suite, except that recitatives are introduced and that each of the two sections closes with a chorale. Bach probably intended in this way to suit the taste of the noble patron of the church at Störmthal, just as he had suited that of the Leipzig people with his trial cantata; for, under Augustus the Strong, French music was in great favour at the Court of Dresden. In so doing Bach did nothing whatever against his natural instinct, which was to weld together in his own style all the musical forms of the time. It was, therefore, in no way unsuitable when he subsequently performed this " organ dedication " cantata on Trinity Sunday. It is not undevotional, and yet it lacks that highest degree of sacredness which can only be given when the composer's imagination is set in motion by an event of universal importance to the Christian church.

Bach had entered on his post in the ferial portion of the ecclesiastical year. Remarkable as was the activity displayed by him as a church composer during this period, yet he had no opportunity of showing himself in his full greatness until the beginning of the ecclesiastical year 1723-1724. It is self-evident that he would celebrate the first occurrence of the festal days as far as possible with music of his own. On this assumption we can, with moderate certainty, assign most of the festal cantatas to this year. On his first Christmas Day in Leipzig, the chief music was his cantata " Christen ätzet diesen Tag in Metall und Marmorsteine "—" Christians, grave ye this great day In brass and stone that will not perish."[355] The particular emotion of the composition is revealed in a

---

[355] B.-G., XVI., No. 63.

duet occurring in it for alto and tenor. The words are as
follows :—

> Ruft und fleht den Himmel an,
> Kommt ihr Christen, kommt zum Reihen,
> Ihr sollt euch an dem erfreuen,
> Was Gott hat anheut gethan.

> Come, ye Christians, praise and pray,
> Come with singing, come with dancing,
> With your joy and praise enhancing
> That which God hath done to-day.

The universal feeling of Christmas joy seems thus dramatised by the image of a festal procession mingling in
sacred dances, and, as it were, obeying the commands of
the Psalmist : " Praise Him in the cymbals and dances ;
praise Him upon the strings and pipe." The festal dance,
represented by a graceful waving figure in the duet, comes
out powerfully and splendidly in the ritornels of the first
chorus. Without deviating from this character the chorus
itself is formed from quite different melodies which are
worked out very effectively in canon; it contains exhortations
to Christmas rejoicing, and as each section is concluded the
jubilant dance again breaks forth immediately. The last
chorus, too, is influenced by the same idea, which, however,
is soon changed ; for the festal procession crowding together
seems bowed in devout adoration before God; this is represented by a very characteristic double fugue full of fervent and
intense expression. In the second part of the chorus another
double fugue corresponds to this on the words " Lass es
niemals nicht geschehn," &c.—" Let it never come to pass
that Satan shall torment us "—which is coloured by the
dramatic expression suggested by the word " torment." The
other numbers of the cantata, two recitatives and a skilfully
worked duet for soprano and bass, are of a more general
religious character ; their subjects, which are peculiar to
themselves, being prolonged and developed in the oboe and
instrumental bass parts. For the rest, the style of the
work unmistakably approaches that of oratorio, and this it
is which makes it especially remarkable among Bach's
cantatas, although it has a very considerable amount of

intrinsic musical value. It is noticeable that there is no chorale throughout.[356]

On high festivals, after the sermon, the *Sanctus* was sung in a florid style as an introduction to the Communion (ante, p. 270). There are a number of such Sanctuses composed by Bach, one of which I believe may be identified as that composed for Christmas Day, 1723. Like the cantata, it is in C major, and the instrumentation is almost the same; it is remarkable for its bright festal character, which culminates in the *Pleni sunt coeli et terra.*[357]

The performance of the cantata "Christen ätzet diesen Tag," with its attendant *Sanctus*, took place during the morning service, and was sung by the first choir in the Nikolaikirche. In the evening the cantata was repeated by the same choir in the Thomaskirche; and after the sermon the hymn of the Virgin was sung, set in its Latin form and in an elaborate style. For this purpose Bach wrote his great *Magnificat*, which, since it has become generally known, has rightly been reckoned one of the highest inspirations of his genius.[358] For the occasion of the festival of Christmas, for which it was intended, Bach expanded the Bible text by inserting four vocal numbers in suitable places, the words of which bore especial reference to the Leipzig form of service. These are (1) The opening verse of the hymn "Vom Himmel hoch"; (2) the verse " Freut euch und jubilirt, Zu Bethlehem gefunden wird Das herzeliebe Jesulein, Das soll euer Freud und Wonne sein"— " Rejoice with pious mind, To Bethlehem go now and find The fair and holy new-born Boy, Who is your comfort, peace, and joy "; (3) the *Gloria in excelsis Deo*; (4) the lines *Virga Jesse floruit, Emanuel noster apparuit, Induit carnem hominis, Fit puer delectabilis. Alleluja.* Although these words are some German, some Latin, and have no outward connection of form, yet Kuhnau had built upon them a

---

[356] See App. A., No. 24.

[357] B.-G., XI.,[1] p. 69 ff.   See App. A., No. 19.

[358] B.-G., XI.,[1] p. 3 ff, is the form in which it was afterwards cast by Bach. It was published in its original form by N. Simrock, at Bonn, in the year 1811. P. 40.

Christmas cantata, retaining the exact order given above.[859] They are very suitable in feeling, for they give a kind of dramatic character to the events of the Christmas night. Several points of detail go to prove that Bach took the words directly from Kuhnau's cantata. One of these is in the form of the angel's song *Gloria in excelsis*. The Greek words καὶ ἐπὶ γῆς εἰρήνη, ἐν ἀνθρώποις εὐδοκία are wrongly rendered in the Vulgate by the words *et in terra pax hominibus bonæ voluntatis*. The meaning of this will be either "Peace on earth to men of good-will," or "Peace on earth to the men with whom God is well pleased," while the true meaning is (as in our English version) "Peace on earth, and good will towards men," as Luther rightly translated it (Friede auf Erden und den Menschen ein Wohlgefallen). The Vulgate version, however, is nearly always retained, even in Protestant churches, when the words are set to music. The cantors, who for the most part built their texts on the model of the Romish composers, were severely blamed by the theologians for thus introducing errors or stamping them with their approval, whether from ignorance or negligence; but it was justly answered that from the musician's standpoint the Vulgate version had a more melodious rhythm.[860] Kuhnau, however, had amended the reading of the Vulgate in the cantata referred to, replacing it by the words *bonæ voluntes* in accordance with the Greek; and Bach, who in all his other *Glorias* retained the words *bonæ voluntatis*, here follows the correct reading. So far, however, as we may gather from the musical phrasing, either the sense was not quite clear to him or he felt himself raised above and beyond it by the greatness of his musical ideas; for he phrases the words thus: *et in terra pax hominibus, bona voluntas*, approaching near to the original sense, but not quite reaching it; so that we may perceive that the Vulgate version was running in his head, and that he set the texts given to him as a whole, without paying any especial heed to the theological

---

[859] The cantata exists in the separate parts in the Town Library at Leipzig.
[860] S. Rango, Von der *Musica*, alten und neuen Liedern, &c. Greiffswald, 1694, p. 22 ff.

battles which raged round him. A second piece of evidence is found in the lines *Virga Jesse*, &c. This is a fragment of a longer Christmas hymn, given by Vopelius in its entirety.[361] It runs thus :—

Virga Jesse floruit,	The stem of Jesse hath flourished,
Emanuel noster apparuit,	Our Emanuel hath appeared,
Induit carnem hominis,	And hath put on human flesh,
Fit puer delectabilis.	And become a lovely child.
Domum pudici pectoris	The home of the Virgin chaste
Ingreditur Salvator et	Receives the Saviour and
Autor humani generis.	Creator of the human race.
Ubi natus est Rex gloriæ ?	Where is the King of glory born ?
Pastores, dicite !	Ye shepherds, say ?
In Bethlehem Juda.	In Bethlehem Juda.
Sause,[362] liebes Kindelein,	Slumber, little baby dear,
Eya, Eya,	Eya, Eya,
Zu Bethlehem Juda.	In Bethlehem Juda.
Virga Jesse floruit,	The stem of Jesse hath flourished,
Emanuel noster apparuit,	Our Emanuel hath appeared,
Induit carnem hominis,	And hath put on human flesh,
Fit puer delectabilis,	And become a lovely child,
Alleluja!	Alleluja!

Kuhnau only used the last four lines, and it would have been more than strange if Bach had hit upon the same fragment quite independently. But the order in which Bach inserted the four passages into the *Magnificat* is precisely that adopted by Kuhnau. This is not the last time that we shall see Bach treading in Kuhnau's foot-prints, as in this instance. Just as he cherished and revered the traditions of his family, and was always ready to learn whatever he could from the works of older and contemporary masters, so now, when a great master had preceded him, it was foreign to his nature to study to appear as an innovator, or, trusting in his own power, to leave the work of his predecessor disregarded. It is true that his inmost nature was different from Kuhnau's, and his adherence to his method of working could only be superficial ; it is, however, none the less

---

[361] Neu Leipziger Gesangbuch, 1682, p. 77 ff.

[362] Meaning to " sing in sleep," or "sing one's self asleep," still remaining in ordinary use in the low-German " susen."

important for the understanding of Bach's character. In this instance Kuhnau's Christmas music was connected with certain Leipzig church customs which must have been interesting to Bach, for their own sake. The Latin-German Christmas hymn above quoted is, in part at least, a lullaby sung at the cradle of Christ, and, since it was included by the Leipzig Cantor, Vopelius, in his Leipzig hymn book, it must have been in ordinary use there. It was an old Christian custom to place a manger in the church, and to perform the events of Christmas night as a drama or mystery. Boys represented the angels and proclaimed the birth of the Saviour, and then priests entered as the shepherds and drew near to the manger; others asked what they had seen there (*Pastores, dicite*); they gave answer and sung a lullaby at the manger. Mary and Joseph were also represented: Mary asks Joseph to help her to rock the Child; he declares himself ready, and the shepherds sing a song.[363] This custom of "Kindleinwiegen," as it was called, traces of which have remained into the present century, was in full force in the beginning of the previous century in Leipzig. It was one of the customs which the Council wished to abolish in the year 1702.[364] That their proposal met with but little favour has already been told. This particular custom of "Kindleinwiegen" actually survived to Bach's day, for we find a *lullaby* in his Christmas Oratorio. As it is spoken of in connection with *Laudes*, it can only have taken place at the close of the service in the Nikolaikirche. The cradle hymn which used to be used on this occasion is the old and favourite one, "Joseph, lieber Joseph mein, hilf mir wiegen mein Kindelein."[365] It is evident that the hymn *Virga Jesse floruit* must have been intended for the same purpose. That it was actually so

---

[363] Compare Weinhold, Weihnacht-Spiele und Lieder. Graz., 1870, p. 47 ff.

[364] "That sundry fanciful Latin *Responsoria, Antiphonæ*, Psalms, *hymni* and *Collects*, as also the generally so-called *Laudes* at Christmas time with the 'Joseph lieber Joseph mein,' and 'Kindlein wiegen,' be henceforth discontinued in public service." See ante, p. 264.

[365] It is reprinted in Schöberlein, Schatz des liturgischen Chor-und Gemeindegesanges. Part II., p. 164 ff.

used in the Leipzig Christmas service is not, indeed, expressly stated; but we may assume it with certainty. So much at any rate is clear; the words put together by Kuhnau for a Christmas cantata and adopted by Bach reflect the simple old custom, still popular at that time in Leipzig, of representing dramatically in church the angelic message and the adoration of the shepherds; but in a more ideal way, being, as it were, its poetic and musical counterpart. Viewed in this light, Bach's *Magnificat* gains a special meaning, which lends a greater depth to the feeling of this mighty composition. If we compare the four pieces he inserted—which form a contrast to it both by their partly German text and by their substance—with the materials and forms used in the principal body of the work itself, we shall perceive a striking difference. With the exception of the *Gloria*, which to a certain degree requires the assistance of the instruments, all these pieces are accompanied only by a figured bass.[366] It had long been a favourite custom in the Lutheran church to sing the music on Christmas night with antiphonal changes, whether between the choir and the people or between a large and a small choir, these being usually placed at a distance from each other.[367] This custom, originally followed with only short sections of hymns, gradually grew as time went on, until longer pieces were performed in this way. In Leipzig itself performances with responsive choirs were of no unusual occurrence (comp. ante, p. 284). Now the Thomaskirche, where the *Magnificat* was first performed, contained a smaller organ built above the "high choir," so that it was opposite to the great organ. We know that this was only used on high festivals. It evidently then was used for no other purpose than for these alternating antiphonal performances of vocal music. From this I gather that Bach, when he brought his *Magnificat* to a hearing, made these four Christmas hymns sound down from the smaller organ loft, the contracted dimensions of

---

[366] In "Vom Himmel hoch" the bass is not once figured, showing that the organ took no share in the accompaniment.

[367] Examples are given in Schöberlein, loc. cit., p. 52 f. and 96 f.

which admitted only a small band of singers and few
instrumentalists. This is the easiest way of explaining the
arrangement of the score and his subsequent treatment
of these numbers. They certainly seem to have been
composed at the same time as the *Magnificat*, and intended
to form one with it, but Bach did not write them in
the score in the places they were intended to occupy.
In the autograph score they run consecutively, from the
twelfth page, along the bottom stave, below the *Magnificat*,
and are marked with references to the points at which they
are to be inserted. If they were to be sung from the smaller
organ-loft they could only be performed in the Thomaskirche; in the Nikolaikirche, where the great musical performance took place in the afternoon of the second day of
Christmas, they had to be omitted altogether, since there
was no similar situation in the church from which to sing
them. And further: since an elaborate *Magnificat* was sung
both at Easter and Whitsuntide, and Bach intended his
work to be available for these feasts also (besides this, so
far as we know, he only wrote a small *Magnificat* for soprano
solo, which is not known to exist), and since these interlude
numbers were only suitable for Christmas time, it is conceivable that in a later recension of the work he should
leave them out altogether.[368]

The *Magnificat* is written for five-part chorus with accompaniment of organ, strings, two oboes, three trumpets, and
drums, to which two flutes are added in the later recension.
The opening chorus is set only to the words *Magnificat anima
mea Dominum*. Its external form is that of the Italian aria,
but is only thoroughly intelligible when reference is made
to the concerto form. The instrumental introduction has
less the character of a ritornel than that of a concerto tutti.

---

[368] The autograph scores of the work, both in its first conception and in its
altered form, are in the Royal Library at Berlin. In the latter the work is
transposed from E flat to D, besides which it is enriched in respect of
orchestration; the part-writing is elaborated here and there, and in several
places it is made more complete in other respects, or else altered. This
alteration took place about 1730. On the lost smaller *Magnificat*, see Rust in
the Preface to B.-G., XI.,[1] p. xviii.—And Appendix A., No. 24.

We have already seen how Bach developed and re-modelled
the concerto form,[369] and how it was one of his chief objects
of study in Cöthen, and from this circumstance it is very
natural that having just come from thence he should use
the form which had become so familiar to him there.   There
are not two contrasting subjects, but the whole material is
exhibited in the tutti, the jubilant character of which is
indicated by this motive :—[370]

But in the treatment of the chorus with regard to the
orchestra, the concerto idea is shown in the plainest way
possible. The first entry of the chorus follows this like
that of a solo, accompanied only by a figured bass, and its
melodic form accords with the opening of the tutti just as is
the case in the real concerto. Two bars later the instrumental tutti comes in anew, but breaks off after two bars to
allow the choir to be heard alone in another subject taken
likewise from the tutti.[371] It then continues its course
until the sixteenth bar of its united progress with the
chorus, but so that the latter is the subordinate element
as regards musical importance. It follows the course of the
instrumental parts, now in unison and now in octaves ; not
indeed renouncing its independence altogether, but freeing
itself and then becoming re-united to the instrumental parts
in passages of the most wonderful lightness ; but the chorus
is here by no means a musical factor of equal importance
with the orchestra, as it is, for example, in the opening
chorus of the cantata " Ärgre dich o Seele nicht "; it only
gives definiteness to the poetic emotion—though it indeed
does this in the most decisive way possible.   In the second
section the conditions are changed.   Here the chorus
predominates even in respect of the music, the subject

---

[369] See ante, p. 125.

[370] I quote in the key of the later recension.

[371] Compare with this the first movement of the violin concerto in E, B.-G
XXI.,[1] p. 21 ff.

of its second entry being diligently worked out, while the orchestra comes in again in concerto style in little snatches taken from the great tutti. The third section is like the first, excepting that the working out leads from the subdominant into the original key; the last fifteen bars of the instrumental tutti form a postlude.

To appreciate Bach's power of building new forms, we must compare with this the chorus in the cantata "Wer sich selbst erhöhet" in which concerto-like elements are worked in, as they are here.[372] The aria for second soprano which now follows—*Et exultavit spiritus meus in Deo salutari meo*— is in the same key—a rare thing with Bach. It carries out the feeling expressed in the opening, but transfers it from the region of general joy and exultation to that of the quieter and more childlike joy of Christmas. We know the way in which this feeling is expressed by Bach too well not to recognise it here.[373] In order to leave no doubt of the composer's intention, this aria is immediately followed by the chorale " Vom Himmel hoch da komm ich her," the first of the inserted numbers. The *Cantus firmus* lies in the soprano; it is in four parts, in Pachelbel's form, and treated with evident love and delight; the counterpoint is throughout formed from the lines of the melody in diminution, and treated imitatively with great art, except that in a few cases the harmonies are somewhat daring. This number is also in the principal key, forming one group with the two that preceded it. We must bear in mind, too, that the chorale " Von Himmel hoch" was one of the hymns usually sung before the sermon, on Christmas Eve, by the congregation, if we are to appreciate the effect it must have produced when it came in, sounding down from the top of the church in the midst of the Latin songs, which were inaccessible to the direct sympathies of the congregation.

Now another style begins. An aria for the first soprano

---

[372] See ante, p. 13.

[373] See Vol. I., pp. 510 and 561, and in the Christmas oratorio (B.-G., V.⁹) especially the chorale, p. 37 ff. In the Simrock edition of the score of the *Magnificat*, the last four bars of the opening ritornel are omitted, it would seem by oversight.

gives out the words *Quia respexit humilitatem ancillae suae. Ecce enim ex hoc beatam me dicent (omnes generationes).* The fact that the church, from the earliest times, included the Song of the Virgin in the liturgy, divested it of its personal character, and Bach, as his work shows, viewed it in its broadest signification. On the other hand, he was tempted by the operatic forms of church music to give it individuality. Whenever this occurs—and we shall often have occasion to notice it—the treatment is never dramatic throughout, but is confined to a single number of the work. This subjective tendency was one of his chief motives in musical composition. Bach always pierced deep into all the Biblical and ecclesiastical relations of his texts, in order to gain suggestions for new forms in art; but it was his sense of musical connection or contrast which ultimately ruled his choice. In Bach's compositions, even though we may not perceive the inmost motives of each separate part, we always receive the impression of a 'musical organism rounded, complete, and intelligible in itself; interpolations, which are otherwise than obvious and easily understood, are never so important as to disturb the harmony of the whole, like an unsolved enigma. We saw in Bach's solos that an outward smoothness of form, moulded by a master's hand, conceals a passionate and ever-varying emotion; and here again, in the midst of a work made up of many parts, and whose aim appears to be simple and clear, we discover a store of varied powers; it is only by the discovery of these powers that we can thoroughly appreciate Bach's spirit, with its own individual impulse and activity. The feeling of the first aria was innocent Christmas rejoicing; in the second the composer is inspired by the idea of the Mother of God. Scarcely ever has the idea of virgin purity, simplicity, and humble happiness found more perfect expression than in this German picture of the Madonna, translated, as it were, into musical language. Somewhat allied to this in fundamental feeling is the aria in B minor from the cantata "Alles was von Gott geboren,"[874] but

---

[874] See Vol. I., p. 563.

the direct reference to a particular individual and the effect óf the *oboe d'amore* in the accompaniment give this aria of the *Magnificat* a greater intensity of feeling and a quite different character. The words *omnes generationes* are not sung by the soprano, but are taken up by the whole choir; thus the dramatic fiction, which gave the aria its peculiar character, is here again discarded. The choral movement composed on these two words alone is not less deeply felt, though it is conceived in another way, as representing the entrance of an innumerable company of people moved by one and the same idea. It is very characteristic of Bach that this idea is not cast in the form of a hymn of praise, as the preceding words might have suggested. This perhaps might have been Handel's method; but Bach, with his less subjective nature, represents only the idea of a great and universal movement. By the theme not entering alone, but being always surrounded by three moving parts, we are flung, as it were, into the midst of the throng. The working out is not fugal: at first the different parts seize upon the chief subject as it comes within their range; they overtop one another in gradually ascending entries; and at last they build themselves up in canon on a dominant pedal. A gifted editor of the *Magnificat* has expressed his opinion that Bach meant here to represent the all-conquering power of Christianity driving the nations against one another in deadly battle.[375] I cannot go so far as this, chiefly because a movement with this character does not seem to me to suit the object of the whole work, which is to represent the joy of the Christmas festival. And I have found that the character of this chorus in performance, although grave and mighty in its rush and flow, is yet not properly speaking wild or vehement. Bach, following his musical nature, gives to movements of this kind a more excited character than others—as, for instance, Handel— would have done. Certain alterations made in this particular movement, in the later recension, seem to me to be especially

---

[375] Robert Franz in his thoughtful little pamphlet: Mittheilungen über Johann Sebastian Bach's "Magnificat." Halle, Karmrodt. 1863.

instructive. In bars 6 and following from the end, the bass was originally this :—

om - - - - - - nes, om - nes, om - nes, ge - ne - ra - ti - o - nes :

on the pause the second soprano remained on d″, the instruments keeping silence until the entry of the last bar but one. And in bar 3 from the beginning the expression was harsher, this being the original passage in the bass part :—

(generatio) - - - *nes.*

We cannot suppose that Bach meant to express any different feeling by the two versions. Nor can technical reasons account for the alterations. He must rather have found that the expression had, here and there, exceeded its limits and required moderating.[376]

The bass aria, constructed on a *basso quasi ostinato*, that reminds us of Böhm—*Quia fecit mihi magna qui potens est et sanctum nomen ejus:* "He that is mighty hath magnified me and holy is His name"—breathes a fresh joyfulness into the feeling of the music, which in the last movement had become graver, and leads up to the Angels' song "Freut euch und jubilirt"—"Rejoice and be ye glad"—which ends a second group. This hymn, for only two soprani, alto, and tenor, is full of imagery; it seems to

---

[376] I take this opportunity of drawing attention to a clerical error in this chorus, on Bach's own part in the writing out of the later recension, which error has been transferred to the edition of the Bach Gesellschaft. In bar 6, the second half of the alto part runs as follows:—

But as is shown both by the accompanying first flute and by the older score in the alto part, it should be:—

float in a realm of light above the dimmer earth; a fifth part is given to the *continuo*. Bach may perhaps have had in his mind the old custom when boys, dressed as angels, sang Christmas hymns in the festival service. This beautiful piece bears a remarkable resemblance to Kuhnau's work; in Bach the theme of the first section is as follows :—

Freut euch und ju - bi - lirt, freut euch und   ju - bi - lirt,

in Kuhnau :—

Freut euch und ju - bi - lirt, ...

The intermediate subject in both is full of deep feeling—Kuhnau indicates it as *affettuoso*—and the finale in both is a regular fugato, though Bach has carried it out the more thoroughly. The mercifulness of God is praised in a very melodious duet for the alto and tenor in E minor, almost homophonous throughout, with an accompaniment of violins *con sordini*, and flutes; the words *timentibus eum*—" On them that fear Him"—offer an opportunity for closing with an elaborate and picturesque treatment of a very interesting character. As a contrast to this, the chorus *Fecit potentiam* represents the power of the Almighty bringing the pride of man to nothingness; and then, for the third time, the treatment leads up to a hymn sung by celestial beings, in the Latin *Gloria in excelsis Deo*. The chorus *Fecit potentiam*—" The Lord hath shewed strength "—displays in its principal theme a sort of sweeping and irresistible energy, with a peculiar crushing force in the accompanying chords and the rhythm of the instrumental bass. There is a poetical detail worthy of note in the way in which the instruments, divided into two portions, imitate the contrapuntal melody of the upper part :—

Fe - cit po - ten - ti - am

at the third note in contrary motion, as if to represent

the idea that there is no escape from the hand of the Lord. Among other striking details, the attention is especially rivetted by the closing *Adagio,* where the idea of arrogance is expressed with forcible verisimilitude by the pompous, widely spread notes of the dispersed chord. Here again we have an instance where the separate words of the text are taken advantage of to serve as the motive for a peculiarly effective musical close. In after years Bach composed a *Magnificat* in German [377] (in part paraphrased) for the Festival of the Visitation, in which the same portion of the text gave him the opportunity for an equally picturesque setting. It is in recitative and contains a very elaborate Melisma, which was a favourite way of concluding recitatives.[378]

A fourth group is composed of two arias and the verse "*Virga Jesse*" set as a duet. The first aria has a very vigorous, nay resolute, character; it has undergone many alterations in the process of re-arrangement, resting partly on practical grounds only, and by no means invariably striking as improvements. In the second aria, which was conceived in a softer vein of feeling, flutes were introduced by Bach, even in its first state. An expression of longing is stamped very beautifully on the principal idea by a striking turn of the rhythm :—

E - su - ri - en - tes

The abrupt close—an illustration of the words *dimisit inanes* —"sent empty away"—is an innovation in the second treatment; originally the flutes were carried on to the last note. The final bars of the duet are lost; the voices rise and fall

---

[377] B.-G. I., No. 10.

[378] Franz suggests (op. cit. p. 19) that Bach had by mistake attributed the words of the Vulgate *mente cordis sui* to God, for it would have been a great fault in taste to emphasise the idea of arrogance by the display of the sublimest means of expression at his command. Such a mistake is, however, hardly conceivable in a man so versed in his Bible as Bach, and even in classical Latin *sui* would be right. To me the feeling of the extended chord is quite clear; the impulse which led Bach up to this Adagio close was not derived from the individual passage, which only serves to colour its expression, but from the fundamental idea of the whole.

above a slow and lulling *continuo* which, as in the aria
Quia fecit, is *quasi ostinato.*

Up to this point a simple Christmas joy has been the
ruling idea through all the various movements, but when
the last Christmas hymn, properly speaking, has died away
a new element of feeling comes into play. At Vespers a
sermon was to be preached on the Epistle, which enlarges
on the work of Redemption as being the final aim of Christ's
incarnation. The only words which distinctly refer to
this in the *Magnificat* are in the verse *Suscepit Israel
puerum suum recordatus misericordiae suae.* Their suggestiveness did not escape Bach's notice. He takes them for
a chorale arrangement, in which two soprani and an alto
voice have the counterpoint, while a trumpet (or in the
second arrangement two oboes) softly plays the old church
melody to the *Magnificat.* Much has been said as to the
idea conveyed by this particular form.[379] Bach employs it
when he desires to give utterance to a mystical and abstract
emotion. In his German *Magnificat* he has treated the
same passage in the same way, with evident reference to
this previous composition. But the effect produced is not
precisely similar, because the chorale has already been
introduced and re-appears again at the close. In the Latin
Magnificat the chorale does not occur anywhere but in this
place; the unexpected melody, therefore, sounds doubly
suggestive, pathetic, and melancholy; though the whole
number, from its high position, is singularly translucent
and visionary. It steals into the midst of the happy
triumph which has hitherto possessed our feelings, as a
shadow glides across a sunlit meadow, but the original
sentiment is immediately restored by a powerful five-part
fugue without concertante instruments. The *Magnificat*
is closed, according to the custom of the church, with
the usual Doxology, *Gloria Patri et Filio,* &c. Bach has
set the threefold *Gloria* to grand rolling passages in triplets,
towering up in repeated imitations, and sinking to rest in
broad harmonies—a composition of exceptional grandeur

---

[379] See Vol. I., pp. 459 and 544.

and power. In *Sicut erat* he returns to the opening chorus, reconstructing its principal motives into a gorgeous and glowing whole.

The part played by the *Magnificat* in the evening service determined the form of this composition. A cantata was performed before the sermon, and, if the service was not to be made too long for custom and convenience, Bach could not allow himself to expatiate too largely on his musical ideas; all the more so because he proposed to extend the text by introducing four Christmas hymns. The *Magnificat* is consequently emphatically distinct from the rest of Bach's grand church compositions by the compactness and concentrated power of the separate numbers—particularly of the choruses—by the lavish use of the means at command, and by its vividly emotional and yet not too agitating variety. It stands at the entrance of a new path and a fresh period of his productivity, at once full of significance in itself and of promise for the future development of the perennial genius which could always re-create itself from its own elements.

If the cantata for the first day of Christmas had seemed to resuscitate that side of Christianity which rejoices with mirth and dancing before the altars of the healing Godhead, and if in the *Magnificat* the popular feeling of Christmas festivity had found its expression against a background, as it were, of simple festal usages, in the cantata "Dazu ist erschienen," which was probably composed for the second day of Christmas, 1723, we see Christ represented as the radiant hero sent into the world to conquer the powers of darkness.[380] "That was the true light which lighteth every man that cometh into the world. . . . And the Word was made flesh and dwelt among us, and we behold His glory, the glory as of the only begotten Son of the Father, full of grace and truth." The cantata is made to illustrate these fundamental ideas of the Gospel, and some of these words serve as the text of the first recitative; the grand chorus which follows is on the words of I. John iii., 8:

---

[380] B.-G., VII., No. 40.

"The Son of God was manifested that He might destroy the works of the devil." Bach has concentrated the feeling of the work in this one chorus, more than he has done in the case of any of his other cantatas, for chorales are used much more freely than usual, no less than three, each in four parts, being introduced in it; but, with one exception, they are new melodies not in general congregational use.[381] For novelty, boldness, and breadth of structure this is far superior to all the choruses of the *Magnificat* or of the first Christmas cantata. The instrumental introduction is not a proper ritornel, but has something of a concerto character, like the first chorus in the *Magnificat*, in which Bach seems to have tried his wings before a wider flight. Then the chorus works out the motive which the instruments have given in a compressed form. At a first glance it appears as though the instrumental prelude were wrought out of independent materials, but on closer examination we may convince ourselves that the subject of the chorus is in fact contained in it, as a kernel in its shell. The first phrase of the chorus is almost exclusively homophonous in character, then it occurs alternately with the orchestra in an interchange of the very shortest phrases; but on the words "destroy the works of the devil," uttered in defiant declamation, the answering bodies unite and combine in unison—which in Bach is a very rarely used device— radiating from thence like a sheaf of rays from the focus of a lens, chasing the shades of night and pouring a flood of brightness on all around. From this latter portion a double fugue is worked out, as the first portion of the chorus is from the Prelude. The first theme is constructed by augmentation, while the second preserves the original time. It sets out with wonderful boldness on the unprepared

---

[381] Erk has proved that the melody "Schwing dich auf zu deinem Gott "— "Lift thy spirit up to God "—was not, as Winterfeld says, composed by Bach ; see his admirable essay on Bach's Chorales, Part I., p. 121, under No. 114. The final hymn, the fourth verse of "Freuet euch ihr Christen alle," by Keimann and Hammerschmidt, had become popular less as a congregational hymn than as a sacred chorus tune. The first chorale is the third verse of the sixteenth century Christmas hymn "Wir Christenleut."

seventh, and, as if this were not enough, the first horn follows it in sixths, and a wild triumphant battle turmoil is worked out. Then, exactly as in the *Magnificat*, it passes from the subdominant back to the first part. When it is said that this chorus gives us the true heart and root of the whole composition, this is so far true that its musical elements continue to leaven the cantata throughout. After a haughty and scornful air for the bass " Höllische Schlange wird dir nicht bange "—" Serpents of hell will not affright thee "—we have a recitative with an accompaniment, of which the rhythm is derived from some of the instrumental figures in the chorus, and the motive of the last aria is also traceable to certain elements of that grand composition.[382]

For the third day of Christmas we have another cantata, which was probably composed in this year, or, at any rate, during the earlier part of Bach's residence in Leipzig, and performed there and then.[383] This again offers a strong contrast to the Christmas music previously described. It has little to do with the incidents of the festival itself; the previous compositions had sufficed in this particular. It alludes in an encouraging manner to the love of God, who is fain to be the Father of His human creatures, and the imperishable grace which Jesus wrought for them by His incarnation. This gives rise to a tone of grave collectedness and devoted faith which prevades the whole work. As in the cantata "Dazu ist erschienen," a more extensive use of the simple church hymn is made here than in Bach's other works, and this, in itself, points to its having been composed at the same time and to words by the same author. Three different chorales are introduced in the course of the work: the first, which is the last verse of " Gelobet seist du Jesu Christ," immediately follows the introductory chorus, a fine and solemn fugue on the words " Sehet, welch eine Liebe hat uns der Vater erzeiget, dass wir seine Kinder heissen "—" Behold what manner of love

---

[382] See Appendix A., No. 25.
[383] B.-G., XVI., No. 64.

the Father hath bestowed upon us, that we should be called the sons of God"—in which the voices are reinforced by the strings and the trumpets with the cornet. The effect of this chorale depended in great measure on the circumstance that it was sung by the congregation before the intoning of the Gospel, and consequently the sentiment of the Gospel was brought vividly before them in a glorified foreshadowing. The second chorale consists of the first verse of the hymn " Was frag ich nach der Welt "—" What care I for the world "; it follows closely on an alto-recitative, in which rapid rising and falling passages in the bass figure forth the transitoriness of all earthly things that pass away " like smoke." It was in the same spirit as that in which Bach had on a former occasion given a contrapuntal setting to the organ chorale " Ach wie flüchtig, ach wie nichtig," [884] and subsequently composed the introductory chorus to a cantata on this same chorale,[885] that he now worked out the soprano aria which here follows. The last chorale, which forms the last number, is the fifth verse of " Jesu meine Freude," a favourite chorale with the master.[886]

As in this year Christmas Day fell on Saturday, there was only one Sunday after Christmas; the next music had to be composed for the New Year's festival of 1724. Among Bach's New Year's cantatas there is but one of which we can assert with any certainty that it must have been written between 1724 and 1727, this is " Singet dem Herrn ein neues Lied "—" Sing to the Lord a new song."[887] It may, therefore, be mentioned in this place. The first chorus—in D major 3-4 time—is founded on words taken from Psalms cxlix. and cl. At first the voices are used in a rather homophonous and massive way, but on the words " Alles was Odem hat lobe den Herrn "—" All that have voice and breath, praise ye the Lord "—a fugue begins. In two places the grand composition is interrupted by all the voices de-

---

[884] See Vol. I., p. 602.

[885] B.-G., V.,[1] No. 26.

[886] See App. A., No. 26.

[887] A fragment of the original score and some of the original parts exist in the Royal Library at Berlin.

claiming in mighty unison the first two lines of the chorale
" Herr Gott, dich loben wir "—" Lord God, we sing Thy
praise." In the second number these lines are used for
a four-part chorus interwoven with recitatives. The third
movement is an alto aria, of a gay and almost dance-like
character, and compact in form (A major, 3-4); it is accompanied only by a quartet of strings. A bass recitative then
leads into a duet of a deeply emotional character (D major,
6-8) for the tenor and bass, with violin *concertante*, " Jesus
soll mir alles sein "; and after another recitative for the
tenor the piece concludes with a second verse of the New
Year's hymn " Jesu nun sei gepreiset." This work is in no
respect inferior in importance to the Christmas compositions
just discussed, and Bach himself thought it worthy to serve,
after some revision, for the first day of the Jubilee in memory of
the Augsburg confession, on June 25, 1730. Picander undertook the necessary alterations in the text. It is not improbable,
indeed, that he had also written the text for the New Year's
cantata, for it is included in his works ;[388] indeed, the last
recitative of the older form of it follows out much the same
train of thought as we find at the end of a piece in
Picander's "Erbaulichen Gedanken,"[389] written for the New
Year of 1725. This last recitative also forcibly reminds
us of the first recitative in the *Rathswahl* cantata " Preise
Jerusalem den Herrn," and it would seem from this that
the same poet wrote this also.[390]

Bach came forward with another grand new composition
for the Feast of Epiphany, on January 6. It refers to the
Epistle for the day, and not to the interesting Gospel
narrative, and so is better adapted for Vespers than for
the first service. The eye of the Prophet sees the crowd
of nations over whom the light of the new doctrines dawns
and spreads, the thousands across the seas that are converted
to Christ, and the might of the heathen that are gathered
in to Him ; unfortunately the poet has not sufficiently

[388] Vol. I., p. 207, of the collected edition of his poems.
[389] Leipzig, 1725, p. 78.
[390] See p. 173 of this Vol., and Appendix A., No. 27.

concentrated these grandiose images, and has availed himself of the greater portion of the space afforded to him for a moralising homily, to the great detriment of the work as a whole, though it was perhaps suggested by the doctrinal purpose of the Epistle in the service. From the very first recitative this cantata " Sie werden aus Saba alle kommen" —" They shall all come from Sheba "[391]—has a grave and deliberate character, but no remarkable originality; and even the closing chorale does not lead us up to a coherent and definite festal feeling, but carries on the general sentiment which is suggested by the last aria. It is difficult to understand why, in this place, Bach did not introduce some change. It would almost seem as though he on his part had wished to insist on the feeling of the Epistle in the cantata, though it had to be performed at morning service. But the beginning—a chorus on the last verse of the Epistle with a chorale immediately following—is of lofty and peculiar beauty. Dense masses seem to come crowding on to do homage to the Saviour, " Bringing gold and frankincense, and to declare the praise of God." First on the key note and then on the dominant, with close imitations in canon, the pilgrims seem to come pouring in, almost treading on each other's heels; a few small gaps occur in the tumult of the fugue which follows, and then in the last bars they sing, as with one voice, the Glory of the Lord. A solemn and mystical brilliancy is given to the whole picture by the use of the horns, flutes, and *Oboe da caccia*. The introduction, immediately after, of the short chorale " Die Könige aus Saba kamen dar"—" Kings from afar have come to Thee "—sounds strange. Though in poetic purpose it follows what has gone before as the fulfilment of a prophecy, in musical effect the small and simple form is swamped by the broader and richer one. Here, again, it is the connection it bears to the service which explains and justifies it. The hymn appointed for use at the Epiphany was *Puer natus in Bethlehem*, and this chorale is the fourth verse of that hymn (*Reges de Saba veniunt*). The hymn

---

[391] B.-G., XVI., No. 65. P. 1280.

was sung at the beginning of the service by a chorus
a cappella, and the return to it here has a symbolical significance which would suffice to counterbalance the great
chorus; but it is indeed more than justifiable, it is indispensable in this place to give the work a thoroughly sacred and
festal character. The recitatives and aria bear, it is true,
the stamp of church use, but they are but slightly connected
with this particular festival. The first chorus gives a
wonderfully artistic form to the leading idea of the Epiphany;
but the mode in which an incident has been musically
embodied in it approaches very remarkably the oratorio
style, of which the distinguishing mark is the way in which
it directly depicts the emotion an event gives rise to, without the modifying stamp of church use. This chorale is
treated on a method which, lying between the two, defines
them both; it strictly confines the human emotion within
the limits of church use, while it concentrates the devotional
feeling on the festival of the day. Its oratorio style gives
this first chorus an affinity with the Christmas cantata
"Christen ätzet diesen Tag"—"Christians, mark this happy
day." They have other resemblances in detail. When the
first chorus in the Christmas cantata runs thus:—

and the theme of the fugue in the Epiphany cantata thus:—

the same principal idea can be traced in both, though
dressed in a different garb; indeed, here the same idea
is used again, treated in canon (from bar 27).[392]

The next festival of the church year was the Purification
of the Virgin. This was held on February 2, which, in
1724, fell upon the Tuesday after the fourth Sunday after

---

[392] See Appendix A., No. 28.

the Epiphany. The music which Bach seems to have composed for this day, "Erfreute Zeit im neuen Bunde,"[898] is an off-shoot from the first chorus of the *Magnificat* and the cantata for the second day of Christmas, and a pendant to the cantata for dedicating the organ, of November 2 of the previous year. There we had a cantata in the form of an orchestral suite; in the first chorus of the *Magnificat* and in the Christmas cantata we had an imitation of the first movement of a concerto. The music for the festival of the Purification has assumed the form of a complete Italian concerto; and, as if Bach was resolved to force this on the hearer's consciousness, he adds a violin part *concertante* to both the first and third movements, one being an aria for the alto and the other for the tenor. The resemblance to an instrumental concerto is indeed so conspicuous that we might almost be tempted to think it had been founded on one, and remodelled from its first form for church purposes. This, however, is not the case. The use of the aria form, it is true, would not suffice to disprove it, since it occurs in real concertos by Bach, as, for instance, the violin concerto in E major. But the regular and normal ritornels, though worked out on the same method as those in the *Magnificat* and Christmas cantata, prove that it is an original composition.

The modification and application of the form must be regarded as most masterly, and admirably suited to the text. The words of the venerable Simeon are a suggestive theme for verses intended to express the belief in a blessed death as secured to us by Christ; and both poet and composer have treated the motive grandly and broadly. It is conspicuous in the text, but is not the predominant idea ; at least, as much importance is given to the feeling that faith is effectual in bestowing strength and happiness in this life ; but Bach has worked exclusively on the former ground, and to embody it musically the powerful and, at the same time, plastic style of an opening concerto movement offered a form as admirable as it was novel. This was not quite the case

with the third or *giga* movement, here represented by the
tenor aria " Eile Herz voll Freudigkeit "—" Haste my heart
with eager joy "—for in the first place the common factor
in the conception of the text and of the music is, in this
case, the rather superficial one representing the idea of
" haste"; however, even in this, an irrepressible and elastic
nature asserts its power. The piece which divides the two
arias, in the same way takes the place of the concerto *adagio;*
more, however, by the contrast it offers to its surroundings
than by its inherent nature. The song of Simeon was sung in
the Leipzig liturgy as preliminary to the Collect.[394] In the
second section of the cantata Bach takes up the first three
verses of it, gives them to the bass, and has them accompanied by an independent instrumental subject in two parts,
worked out now in strict canon and now in free imitation.
This is interrupted by recitatives. The severely sacred character of the elaborate counterpoint to the old melody puts
the listener into the fitting vein of feeling for the first and
third movements. A fine effect is produced by the melody
of the three verses being repeated, not in the same position,
but each time in a lower one, each time more calmly and
dimly, as it were, like the dying thoughts of one who
" departs in peace."

Another short recitative follows the tenor aria, and then
comes the fourth verse, in four parts, of the chorale " Mit
Fried und Freud ich fahr dahin," which was the appointed
congregational hymn for this festival, for Vespers only. It
is not without interest to note the arrangement of the keys
in the different movements of this cantata. The first movement, the alto aria, is in F major; the second, the chorale
arrangement, in B flat major; the third, the tenor aria, is
in F major again, and the final four-part chorale is in D
in the Doric mode. When a cantata included only two
arias, and the second was not the final movement of the
whole composition, Bach usually avoided composing them
both in the same key, and its occurrence here is farther proof
that the type of the Italian concerto was floating in his

---

[394] According to Vopelius, p. 112.

mind. The first three numbers form of themselves a musical entity, and what follows is an external addition.[395]

It is not known what Bach composed this year for the festival of the Annunciation; for the present we will pass over the Passion music which he had performed on Good Friday and go on to the first day of Easter. Here a truly grandiose work meets our view, the cantata " Christ lag in Todesbanden "—[396] " Christ lay in bonds of darkness." It is certain that Bach composed this in the early years of his life in Leipzig, and we discern, moreover, that his ideas reverted to Kuhnau in this work in the same way as in the *Magnificat* at Christmas. It is, therefore, highly probable that it was composed for April 9, 1724.[397] A MS. of the year 1693 has been preserved containing a sacred composition by Bach's predecessor, in which the same chorale constitutes the central idea.[398] The first and last stanzas of the hymn form the beginning and the close, and between them there are independent lines in verse-form, themselves a paraphrase of the ideas of the older hymn. It begins with an instrumental sonata in the old form; the first verse is sung by the soprano alone with an accompaniment of two cornets and continuo in this rhythm—

and this is immediately followed by a *vivace* Allelujah in four parts. In comparing this first section of Bach's cantata—the short introductory symphony, the composition of the second verse, and the Allelujah at the close of the first— we at once detect that he has allowed himself to be inspired by Kuhnau's work, which he must have found among the music in the St. Thomas' Library. However, this special musical impulse has not carried him beyond the first movement, though the whole cantata betrays a constant endeavour to recover the earlier forms of expression which

[395] See App. A., No. 29.

[396] B.-G., I., No. 4.   P. 1196.

[397] See Appendix A., No. 30.

[398] In the Royal Library at Berlin.

he had in fact long since left behind him; and in this respect it evades comparison with any other of his works. We may be very sure, from the profound nature of the artist, that in doing this, what he aimed at was something more than a mere rivalry with his esteemed predecessor. The melody of the chorale is one of the most ancient in existence; it is easy to recognise it as a modification of a hymn already well known in the twelfth century, "Christ ist erstanden"— "Christ is risen." If the high antiquity of this tune was known to the composer—as is certainly very probable—he would no doubt feel the fitness of stamping on the whole composition he developed from it a correspondingly antique character, and this he thought could best be done by the adaptation and revival of forms which were not yet wholly cast off by the modern time, but which yet had some flavour of antiquity. Since, too, in the morning service, both these old hymns were sung, and at Vespers "Christ lag in Todes-banden" was again used by the congregation in the churches both of St. Nicholas and St. Thomas, the melody gave utterance to the festal feeling of this special day above all other festivals, and guided the emotional side of the whole service into the right path.

An antique character is impressed on it merely by the constitution of the orchestra. It is well known that in the seventeenth century harmony in five parts was almost invariably preferred to four, and for this reason two violas were frequently added to the two violins. Bach himself had followed this custom in some of his earlier cantatas, as in the Advent music " Nun Komm der Heiden Heiland "— " Come, O Saviour of the nations "—written in 1714, and the Easter cantata " Der Himmel lacht "—" The Heavens laugh "—in 1715. The cantata for Sexagesima, which was written still earlier, " Gleichwie der Regen und Schnee vom Himmel fällt "—" Like as the rain watereth "—has four violas, the violins being altogether absent. In the Leipzig cantatas it is an exception when the two violas are em-ployed, and this is one of the exceptions. None but stringed instruments are introduced; the trumpets and cornet belonging to them are only used in a few passages

to support the voices. The composer has carefully avoided all
the "madrigal" types of music, as likewise the arioso and all
solo singing strictly speaking. The seven verses of Luther's
hymn serve exclusively for the text, and he works out the
melody in seven numbers, each different from the other, so
that this is the only work by Bach which is literally and
thoroughly a church cantata in the sense in which Buxtehude, Pachelbel, and Kuhnau used the word.[899]

The introductory *Sinfonia* is quite in the style of Buxtehude's sacred music, and it must remain doubtful whether
Bach purposely returned to the forms of expression of an
earlier period, or used a work of his youth as the foundation
of it. This melody, played by the first violin :—

—the feeling of the first two bars; the repetition of the same
phrase; the interrupted progressions; the episodical dis-
memberment of the first line of the chorale, which is, as it
were, only caught in passing; and, finally, the brevity of the
piece, which altogether contains but fourteen bars—all this
is so foreign to Bach's later style of writing, that the second
hypothesis seems the more probable of the two.

Each of the seven verses undergoes a special treatment.
The first and fourth are in the style of Pachelbel; the full
choir is employed in them, and in both without any independent instrumental accompaniment. In the first the *cantus
firmus* is given to the soprano; in the fourth to the alto. In
the second verse, for the soprano, alto, and *continuo*, the lines
are dissected and worked out in Böhm's manner. The third
is constructed on the principles of an organ trio, and the
only voice employed is a tenor, which has the *cantus firmus*;
the fifth verse, on the contrary, is sung by the bass alone,
the melody lying in the first violin of the accompanying
strings; but the lines of the air do not follow each other

---

[899] See Vol. I., p. 305.

immediately, but are separated by interludes, in which the
first violin has an independent part. These interludes, as
well as the opportunity afforded by the prelude, are taken
advantage of by the bass voice, which sings each line in
anticipation, whereas in the passages where the melody is
given to the instruments, a counterpoint is allotted to it ;
thus each line is repeated twice, and both times on notes of
the same value, and the fact that the instruments are the
true exponents of the chorale, and not the voice, is only
recognisable from the place in the scale in which it appears
on the instruments. In this number also we find in certain
pregnant passages an extension of the melody in Böhm's
manner. The sixth strophe is given to the soprano and
tenor ; the delivery of the chorale is distributed between
them, the tenor taking the first two lines and the soprano
the third and fourth ; the fifth again is for the soprano, the
sixth for the tenor, and they both sing the last two. This
alternation, however, only applies to the lines of the chorale
itself; the two voices are for the most part employed together
throughout ; the voice which is not singing the melody sings
in counterpoint, and also leads the two first couplets with
the melody sung in the manner of a prelude, but on the
fourth above or the fifth below the chief part. In the seventh
verse, the whole chorus sing the simple finale.

These treatments of the chorale bear abundant traces of
the earlier style. They lie partly in the numerous imitations
of Böhm's effects and partly in certain combinations of the
instruments in the first chorus. While the second violin and
the viola for the most part support the voices, the first violin
goes on its own way high above the general body of sound; at
the same time it drags the second violin into its own rhythm,
and so develops a movement such as we have often met with
in Bach's earliest cantatas.[400] The entrance of the strings,
too, in the second bar, reminds us of Buxtehude's tendencies
towards mere fulness of tone, irrespective of the thematic
value of melodic phrases. On the other hand, again, the
cantata displays a wealth of chorale forms which the old

---

[400] See Vol. I., pp. 444 and 453.   B.-G., XXIII., p. 169.

masters were far from having at their command ; nor had
they any intuition of the dramatically sacred sentiment
which we here meet with at every line. The type of the
first chorus is, it is true, that of Pachelbel ; still, this is not
perceptible in the first two lines, since the *cantus firmus*
starts on the very first note, and scarcely any dependence on
the theme is perceptible in the parts which have the
counterpoint. But when, as an introduction to the following
lines ("der ist wieder erstanden und hat uns bracht das
Leben"—"Who hath risen again and brought us life"—) they
strike in with a broad fugal subject which is at last crowned
by the soprano with the expected melody—when all the
parts begin to extend, and spread, and overflow with
independent vitality—then we discover what a deep poetical
intelligence has here pervaded and animated the whole. The
extension of the lines in the second stanza is, in the first
instance, a recurrence to the standard of the old type of
chorale, but it is also subservient to the poetical idea. On
examination of the separate phrases, it is easy to perceive
that they consist for the most part of five bars or of five
half-bars. The text speaks of the impotency of men against
spiritual death, which has overcome them and holds them
captive ; hence this broken and abrupt rhythm, which
seems to hold the music spellbound. In the sixth verse we
find the same artifice, but with what a different aim !

So feiern wir das hohe Fest	Come let us keep the holy feast
Mit Herzensfreud und Wonne,	With joy and exultation,
Das uns der Herre scheinen lässt,	Our Sun is risen in the east,
Er ist selber die Sonne,	He is our soul's salvation,

says the poet, and after each section of the melody a long
train of light seems to fall across the path. I have spoken
of the treatment of the fifth strophe as the expression of
a mystical emotion. It is so here ; a mysterious parallel
is drawn between the Paschal Lamb of the Passion and
its saving power, and the sacrificial death of Christ. The
instruments, like an invisible choir, glorify the mystery
which is proclaimed by the bass ; but he does not speak
of it as a Catholic priest would, but with a personal
and Protestant participation in it ; this arises from the

fervency with which Bach throws himself at once into the purport of the text. The image of the Cross is vividly given by a dislocated *melisma*, full of anguish ; that of Death by a leap of a diminished twelfth down to the darkest depth ; that of Death overcome, by a d¹, held through several bars, and almost boastful in its effect. In bars 43 and 52, the voice imitates, as it were, the movement of the mystic type.

Indeed, the cantata is full of picturesque details throughout. In the third verse, the " Form of Death," which alone remains when all living powers have been overcome by death, is represented by a peculiar counterpoint, which seems to shrink away humbled and confounded. " Die Schrift hat verkündigt das Wie ein Tod den andern frass, Ein Spott aus dem Tod ist worden "—"The Scripture hath declared to us that as One Death hath swallowed all, death is now mocked at." Thus begins the fourth verse ; the parts enter in counterpoint on the first line, impressively and powerfully, like the shout of a herald ; on the second they entwine in a close maze in canon, in which the parts seem to swallow each other in turn ; in the third they dance gaily and victoriously, disdaining the *cantus firmus* ; in the fourth stanza, the *cantus firmus* derives a peculiar effect from the circumstance that it is carried on, not in the fundamental key, but in that of the fifth above. This bold and striking combination obviously serves a poetic purpose, for " it was a great and fearful fight that death and life were waging." If we listen to the cantata all through, as a whole, the effect is at first somewhat monotonous, in consequence of the persistency of the chorale melody and of the key of E minor, and from the uniformly low and gloomy pitch of feeling throughout. A dim and mournful light, as of the regions of the north, seems to shine upon it ; it is gnarled and yet majestic, like the primeval oak of the forest. From the total absence of all Italian forms, it bears a German and exclusively national stamp. Such a product of art could never have matured under a southern sun—a work in which the Spring festival of the church, the joyful and hopeful Easter-tide, is celebrated in tones at once so grandiose and so gloomy.

The cantatas written by Bach for the second and third

days of Easter, 1724, are lost, as well as that composed for Ascension Day; those for the first and third days of Whitsuntide we have, on the contrary, and also one for Trinity Sunday, all of which seem to have been written in this year, or, at any rate, early during his residence in Leipzig.

The composition for "Erschallet ihr Lieder, erklinget ihr Saiten "—" Sing out, all ye minstrels, your lutes now be sounding "—belongs to the first day of Whitsuntide.[401]   The verses are probably by Franck; they are not, to be sure, included in any of the printed collections of his poems, still, we are not forced to conclude that Franck published all his cantata texts.   A glance at the "Geist- und weltlichen Poesien" shows us that he was fond of setting Bible verses, not merely at the beginning and end of a text, but of introducing them here and there, and enlarging upon them in words of his own.   An uniform musical composition was hardly to be expected from this process, but Franck never very well understood how to work hand in hand with the musician.   In the cantata, "Erschallet ihr Lieder," the Bible text, "He that loveth Me, keepeth My word," which ought properly to have crowned the whole, takes quite a subordinate place.   As is very frequent with Franck, the words for the arias are not in the *da capo* form, but like the verses of a hymn; there are no recitative passages at all. Franck's peculiar manner is most conspicuous in the duet, and if we compare the dialogue it contains with some of the verses of a Whitsuntide cantata in his "Geist- und weltlichen Poesien" we cannot but recognise the same hand in both. As we shall presently see, again, this is not the only unpublished text by Franck which Bach made use of in Leipzig.

The duet, which reminds us of the music of the chorus, "Himmelskönig," is the most important movement of the cantata.   The soprano and alto sing together above a *basso quasi ostinato*, while an independent instrumental part works out the Whitsuntide chorale "Komm heiliger Geist, Herre Gott"; in a subsequent rearrangement, he gave the bass

---

[401] The original parts are in the Royal Library at Berlin.

and chorale to an *obbligato* organ. The artistic elaboration of this complicated movement is enhanced by Bach having introduced a variety of highly-coloured detail into the chorale in Buxtehude's manner; at the same time, he has not used the whole long tune, but only the first three lines and the last two, treating the repeated "Hallelujah" at the end as a single line. It is worthy of remark that he used the same abridged form in the original arrangement of his chorale fantasia for the organ on the same melody, but there the "Hallelujah" also is omitted.[402] The whole movement is instinct with a fervency and ecstasy which astonish us even in Bach. Buxtehude's mode of treatment was peculiarly suited to express such emotions; the liberty it gave the imagination facilitated the carrying out of such intricate combinations, by allowing small deviations from the strict order of the time, as in the "Hallelujah," or even a break in the melody, as in bar 9. The solo songs are equally full of characteristic beauty, as the tenor aria, where the passages for the united violins float by like airs of spring, and the magnificent bass aria, accompanied only by trumpets, drums, and bassoons. The chorus, which is repeated at the close, recalls that in the Christmas cantata "Christians, mark this happy day"; it is, however, less important in character. It must be observed, as reminding us of the Easter-day music—"Christ lay in bonds of darkness"—that we here again have two viola parts.[403]

The music for the second day of Whitsuntide, 1724, again is wanting, while that for the third may have been preserved in the cantata "Erwünschtes Freudenlicht,"[404] which at any rate was written at about this period. At the same time there can be no doubt of the fact that it is a remodelling of a secular cantata. For what occasion the original was composed is not known; not a trace of it survives. But

---

[402] The omission of the "hallelujah" justifies us in assuming that Bach had arranged the first four lines, and wished to give the last of them a closing tune which should lead back into the original key, for the fourth line is almost exactly the same as the one before it.

[403] See App. A., No. 31.

[404] The original score and parts are in the Royal Library at Berlin.

that it was actually founded on a secular cantata is evident
from the popular dance-like character of the duet, and still
more from the gavotte measure of the final chorus. Another
particularly strong evidence is that it recurs with a different
text as the closing chorus of a secular composition written
in 1733—that is to say, the first twenty-four bars of it do.[405]

This proves that it was originally written for a secular
purpose. Bach himself must have had a particular liking
for the subject, for often as it occurs with him to transform
a secular into a sacred piece, it is equally rarely that he
transfers a number from one secular cantata to another.
The chorale which precedes the gavotte was not inserted
till later, when the work was adapted to church purposes,
but it was insufficient to alter essentially the tone of perfectly
worldly cheerfulness of the whole piece.

To the same period, and probably the same year, belongs
the Trinity cantata " O heilges Geist- und Wasserbad "—
" O fountain of the Spirit's grace "—of which the text
is again taken from Franck's " Evangelische Andachts-
Opfer "[406]—a flat and empty poem to which Bach has written
a pleasing and graceful though not very important composition. The opening subject, an aria for the soprano, is
a remarkable piece, an extremely artistically wrought fugue
with strettos, inversions, and countersubjects. The two
other airs proceed more simply, but exhibit throughout the
same finish of detail. The chorus only comes in in the
simple final chorale, and the feeling of the whole is mild
and temperate.

This closes the series of the festival cantatas which can
be assigned with more or less certainty to the first complete
ecclesiastical year in Leipzig. We may now consider the
works composed for ordinary Sunday use, belonging—or
appearing to belong—to this year.

---

[405] Lasst uns sorgen, lasst uns wachen," written for the birthday of the Elector
of Saxony, September 5, 1733. The text is in Picander, Part 4, 1737; the
autograph score and parts are in the Royal Library at Berlin. The circumstance that the beginning of the final chorus is a clean copy, proves that it
was not first written for this cantata.

[406] See App. A., No. 32.

I.—The Sunday after New Year's Day, January 2, 1724, I should place here the cantata "Schau lieber Gott, wie meine Feind"; a grand and boldly planned tenor aria, "Stürmt nur, stürmt ihr Trübsals-Wetter," and an alto air of wonderful melodious charm, are associated with three simply set chorales, one of which is placed at the beginning, the second after a bass arioso included in a recitative, and the third at the end. There is no chorus on the chorale nor on any independent subject, and the arrangement of the movement is different from what is usual with Bach.[407]

II.—First Sunday after Epiphany, January 9, 1724, "Mein liebster Jesus ist verloren." As in the former cantata, the chorus has only two simple chorales, one of which forms the close and the other is the third number. The arias are of great beauty; the tenor begins in a mournful and genuinely Bach-like longing strain:—

Mein lieb-ster Je - sus ist ver - lo - ren, o Wort, das

mir . . Ver-zwei-flung bringt.

The following lines : "O Schwert, das durch die Seele dringt "—" O sword, that piercest through the soul," &c.— are evidently suggested by Joh. Rist's hymn, "O Ewigkeit, du Donnerwort, O Schwert, das durch die Seele bohrt." Bach composed two cantatas beginning with this chorale. In one of these, that for the twenty-fourth Sunday after Trinity,[408] the anxious expectancy with which man watches for the coming of the Judge is expressed by a light quivering motion of semiquavers on the strings. Bach here employs precisely the same image to the analogous words, and in composing the cantata for Trinity Sunday, 1732, this earlier work may have recurred to his mind. Another

---

[407] The original parts are in the Royal Library at Berlin. See App. A., No. 33.

[408] B.-G., XII.,[2] p. 171.

striking resemblance occurs in the tenor aria which precedes
the last chorale with this passage :—

In a duet in the cantata "Liebster Jesu, mein Verlangen,"
which also belongs to the first Sunday after Epiphany,[409]
the same passage occurs elaborately worked out, and we
cannot doubt that the repetition was intentional. It may
also probably be recognised in the fugue in F sharp major
of the second part of the Wohltemperirte Clavier, where
the polyphonic progression is interrupted twice by a long
homophonic section worked out almost without any thematic
connection with the subject quoted above; and again this
cantata reminds us of a third composition: compare the
following passage :—

with the first subject of the Violin Sonata in A major, particularly bar 8.[410] The passage occurs in the alto aria:
"Jesu, lass dich finden"—"Jesu, let me find Thee." A
tender and feminine grace breathes through this composition.
It is felt from the first in the principal subject :—

and the piece acquires throughout a soft ethereal brilliancy
from the accompaniment, consisting only of violins and
violas with two *oboi d'amore*, and the rocking movement of
the principal parts :—

which is carried on by the violas, gives it a peculiar
character.

The parents of Christ, so runs the Gospel narrative,
went up with Him to the Passover at Jerusalem. There

---

[409] B.-G., VII., No. 32, p. 55, P. 1663.
[410] B.-G., IX., p. 84. See ante, p. 113.

they lost their Son, and after long seeking "found Him at last in the temple sitting in the midst of the doctors both hearing them and asking them questions." With gentle reproach, Mary says to Him "Son, why hast Thou dealt thus with us? Behold Thy father and I have sought Thee sorrowing." And the Child justifies Himself in words almost of reproof. "And His mother," we are told, "pondered these words in her heart." The writer of the text has treated the incident symbolically as representing the longing of the soul for Christ, and Bach has adopted this as the fundamental feeling of his composition. Indeed, we know how ready he always was to find some special purport in the Bible text itself, or in the ecclesiastical significance of the Sunday, and here, when we see moreover that the above quoted aria is immediately followed by the words from the Bible in which Jesus reproaches His mother, "Wist ye not that I must be about My Father's business," we cannot for a moment doubt that it was the image of the blessed Mother—so vividly set before us in the Gospel narrative—which floated before the fancy of the deep-souled composer. It is an instance similar to that of the B minor aria in the *Magnificat* (see ante, p. 377).[411]

III.—Fourth Sunday after Epiphany, January 30, 1724, "Jesus schläft, was soll ich hoffen"—"Jesus sleeps, what can I hope for?"—Jesus is sailing across the sea with His disciples—a storm rises, but He is asleep. They wake Him in their terror, He reproves them for their little faith, speaks to the sea and it is still. The hearer, whose mind is full of this picture, when he listens to this cantata will be startled by the first aria, for it is quite beside the situation as thus depicted. It is a dusky night piece, the Saviour sleeps and some weird apparition wrings cries of terror from the lonely watchers. It is not till the second aria that the musical work corresponds somewhat more closely to the Gospel narrative, and here all the means at command, even the voice part, are engaged in representing the sea surging in a storm. In the following movement the connection

---

[411] See App. A., No. 34.

is even closer; we hear Christ speak, "O ye of little faith wherefore are ye so fearful?" and in the magnificent E minor aria we see Him rise majestically to rule the winds and waves with words of might. It is vain to seek here any thread of dramatic purpose which might give unity to the whole. It is indeed the very privilege of the composer that he may treat the Gospel narrative itself, in its simple or its symbolical meaning, as the amalgamating factor; he may view his subject from different sides, and need regard none but musical requirements in arraying and ordering the pictures he sets before the hearer. In this cantata Bach has shown how with the smallest means he could produce the grandest results. It is beyond question one of the most stupendous productions, not only of his art but of German music at any time. In every bar it may be said that his genius reveals its full power. No one can listen without deep emotion to the chorale "Jesu meine Freude" which comes in with consolatory effect.

IV.—Quinquagesima Sunday, February 20, 1724, "Du wahrer Gott und Davids Sohn." This cantata, composed a year before, has already been discussed (see p. 350).

V.—Jubilate Sunday (third after Easter), April 30, 1724, "Weinen, Klagen, Sorgen, Zagen"—"Sorrow, weeping, anguish, terror."[412] There are clear proofs indicating that this cantata was composed at the same time as that for Whitsunday, "Erschallet ihr Lieder"—"Sing out, all ye minstrels"—though at the same time we are tempted to trace in it, as in "Christ lag in Todesbanden," a remodelling of an earlier work. The autograph score, which is preserved, is a beautifully executed, fair copy. If it is founded on an older composition, this must have been written during the Weimar period, perhaps about 1714; the spirit and style of the words betray the hand of Salomo Franck. The symphony is one of those broad and richly harmonised *adagios* in which Bach rose superior to Gabrieli's church

---

[412] B.-G., II., No. 12. The statement in the preface that in the autograph score only the symphony has a figured bass is not wholly correct. The figuring, though it is imperfect, extends throughout the first recitative and first aria. As to the chronology, see App. A., No. 31.

sonatas in one movement, not without assimilating in some degree the purport and feeling of the introductory *adagio* of the Italian chamber sonatas. Now this form occurs most frequently in his earlier sacred works.[413] The first chorus is in three divisions in aria-form, and the first and third sections are a *passacaglio* adapted to the chorus and orchestra. A parallel to this also exists among Bach's earlier works: the *chaconne* at the end of the cantata "Nach dir Herr verlanget mich."[414] In both, difficulties of form are got over in a masterly manner; still this *passacaglio* is the more interesting from a musical point of view, and more thoughtfully harmonised. Its pathetic and tearful feeling, revelling in melancholy, is also characteristic of that period of Bach's life when he was still engaged on church music of the older type, and was developing his own line of feeling in the forms it offered. I have spoken in another place of the internal connection of this *passacaglio* with a chorus in the Mühlhausen Raths-wechsel cantata, and with an air by Erlebach (Vol. I, p. 351). Its bass part is one of Bach's favourite motives; it occurs also in the cantata "Nach der Herr verlanget mich"; there, however, it is the theme of a fugue for the first chorus; again we find it in the cantata "Jesu, der du meine Seele," where other details also remind us of the chorus "Weinen, Klagen."[415] The arias follow each other, as was Franck's wont, without any recitatives inserted between. The alto aria is remarkable because the instrumental ritornel has a different idea in it to the voice part, and the same is the case in the Weimar Easter cantata "Der Himmel lacht, die Erde jubiliret." Finally, this work resembles the cantata "Nun komm der Heiden Heiland" in the circumstance that it closes in a different key from that it begins in, and falls naturally into two divisions of the first four and the last

---

[413] For instance, in "Ich hatte viel Bekümmerniss" (see Vol. I., p. 531), "Himmelskönig sei willkommen" (Vol. I., p. 539), and in "Der Herr denket an uns" (Vol. I., p. 371). Compare also Vol. I., p. 124.

[414] See Vol. I., p. 443.

[415] Compare bar 83 of "Weinen, Klagen" with bar 25, &c., and bar 57, &c., of "Jesu, der du meine Seele."

three movements (see Vol. I., p. 507). Thus we find
throughout traces which connect it with an earlier period
of Bach's writing.   It is further noteworthy that in bar 17
of the alto aria an imitation in canon of the voice part,
beginning on the fourth quaver, implies the use of an organ
accompaniment; this proceeding frequently occurs, not only
in Bach, but in other music of the time, in closing cadences
and particularly in recitatives.   In evidence we may quote
the end of the recitative in the cantata "Gott der Hoffnung
erfülle euch":—[416]

VI.—Second Sunday after Trinity, June 18, 1724, "Siehe
zu, dass deine Gottesfurcht nicht Heuchelei sei"—"Take
thou heed, that thy fear of God be not hypocrisy."   This
cantata is evidently a companion piece to that for Trinity
Sunday, "O heilges Geist- und Wasserbad," but it is
worked out in grander forms, and is more important and
full of meaning.   Still, an extraordinary resemblance is
perceptible in the structure of the first movements, which
are quite exceptional and highly complicated.   What in the
Festival cantata is a soprano aria, in this is a four-part
chorus, with an independent bass in some passages.   The
theme of the fugue is worked out in both pieces *in motu recto
et contrario,* and in each a second theme is introduced,
which afterwards combines with the first to form a double
fugue.   A certain relationship is also traceable in the themes,

---

[416] See App. A., No, 21.

at any rate, in the principal themes. In the Festival cantata the theme is as follows :—

in the other :—

But the progression of the parts is in the former more intricate and close, almost overwrought indeed ; the fugal aria might almost be called a study for the choral fugue which is so broad, free, and imposing. But it is not in this only, but in the two arias and the closing chorale that Bach has fully displayed his unsurpassed powers of combination ; particularly in the second aria, in which the soprano and bass have a real quartet with two *oboi da caccia*, which is quite admirable in its lavish use of harmonies and modulations. The cantata resembles the former one in ending in a different key from that in which it begins.[417]

VII.—Twelfth Sunday after Trinity, August 27, 1724, " Lobe den Herrn, meine Seele "—" Praise thou the Lord, O my soul." This cantata owes its sumptuous and festal character less to its appropriateness to this particular Sunday than to the circumstance that it is evidently intended also for a Rathswahl cantata. The service usual on this occasion took place, in 1724, on the 28th of August, and the cantata was then performed a second time. A third performance took place about 1735 ; it no doubt did not serve for Sunday use, but only for the Rathswahl service. For in the re-arrangement which it underwent for this occasion the reference to the city government was brought out more distinctly in the text, so that its application to the twelfth Sunday after Trinity is altogether lost. The solo movements of this cantata are of no conspicuous importance. But in the first chorus Bach has put forth all his powers: it is a double fugue worked out

---

[417] The autograph score and some of the original parts are in the Royal Library at Berlin.

on broad proportions with an aria-like opening, and it is one
of the most brilliant and powerful pieces of the kind that
remain of his writing.[418]

Having followed Bach through the first complete church-
year of his residence in Leipzig, we may henceforth study
all that he wrote in the way of cantatas in larger groups,
according to periods. Such a group may be very properly
limited by the date of the death of the Queen Christiana
Eberhardine, September 7, 1727, when a public mourning
of four months began, during which all church and organ
music was silenced.[419] Of four of the cantatas composed
until this time, the year and day of their performance can
be exactly determined, and it can be approximately ascertained as regards several. As has been said, Picander
published for the years 1724—1725 a "collection of edifying
thoughts," which appeared in weekly parts. If we may
hazard a guess that he had written for Bach so early as for
the Rathswahl of 1723, and New Year's day, 1724, we can
point out in this collection the first texts which Picander
can be proved to have written for Bach at all. The
"Erbaulichen Gedanken" had no pretensions to be fitted
for music, excepting in so far as they included hymns in
stanzas, and the introduction of a hymn in verses into the
musical setting of a sacred "Madrigal" involved many
anomalies. For this reason Picander found himself obliged
to give a "Madrigal" form to the poems in stanzas contained in the "edifying thoughts" for St. Michael's day,
by shortening, compressing, and transposing them with
certain additions to some of the lines.

On comparing, as I have been able to do, the text of the
cantata as it stands with that in Picander's collection, we
find that the first two verses have been re-written to suit
the ideas suggested by the Epistle appointed for the Festival.
But the words of the soprano aria correspond exactly with
the third verse in the "Erbaulichen Gedanken," while the
tenor recitative is the first verse transformed by a facile

---

[418] B.-G., XVI., No. 69, P. 1667. See Appendix A., No. 37.
[419] See Appendix A., No. 33.

hand into the "Madrigal" form; this is the case, too, with the last two strophes, which have been adapted to the soprano recitative, while the tenor air is a new and independent verse. The closing chorale consists of the eighth verse of the hymn "Freu dich sehr, O meine Seele." There is not the smallest doubt in my mind that the cantata text and the verses in the collection were alike written for the Feast of St. Michael of 1725, and that while the former was intended only for Bach to compose to, the latter was intended for publication as a separate work. Picander wrote too quickly and readily in the Madrigal form for it to be possible that he should in later years have worked again on a poem which, even in its original form, was, on the whole, but meagrely adapted to the requirements of a cantata.

I have already taken occasion to point out that Bach derived the impetus to this composition from a work by his uncle, Joh. Christoph Bach.[420] We know that he had that composition performed in Leipzig, and that it produced a great effect. Its influence, in his mind, betrayed itself in the first place in the construction of the text, in which Picander certainly followed the prompting of Bach; and which, contrary to custom, refers more to the epistle than to the Gospel for the day, so far as it was possible to reconcile this with the use of the verses he had at hand. Besides this, the effort to produce dramatic and oratorio-like tone-pictures is conspicuous throughout the composition. Even in the first chorus, where the text offers an idea which suggests a figurative movement in the music, it is eagerly seized upon. And yet the result is not properly an oratorio chorus. It is not the objective—or, may we say, epic—concentration on the matter in hand which is so effective, but a torrent of feeling, roused by some stupendous event, which roars and rushes by, reflecting the quavering picture in vague and broken outlines. On comparison with Joh. Christoph's composition the chorus plainly reveals the characteristics and limitations of Sebastian's

---

[420] See Vol. I., p. 51.

genius. A composer of oratorio, like Handel, would have
made nothing of it, even if the external conditions had
offered themselves ; but Bach's style was precisely what
was required in church music. In the soprano air, to the
quaint words :—

Gott schickt uns Mahanaim zu,	God shields us with the Mahanaim,
Wir stehen oder gehen	Whether we stay or go
So können wir in sichrer Ruh	We walk in safety all the same,
Für unsern Feinden stehen.	Nor fear our ghostly foe.—
	(Gen. xxxii., 2.)

the image of " Mahanaim "—the angelic hosts which guard
humanity at every step—is beautifully set before us by a
close tissue of music woven out of the principal melody.
The tenor air is even more profoundly significant in its
combinations. The orchestra accompanies the voice with a
Siciliano, which is almost independent of it, while the
trumpet rings out the melody of the chorale " Herzlich lieb
hab ich dich o Herr"—" Thee, Lord, I love with all my
heart." This calls our thoughts, not to the first verse, but
to the last :—

Ach Herr, lass dein lieb Engelein	Thy ministering angels send
Am letzten End die Seele mein	O Lord ! my parting soul to tend ;
In Abrahams Schooss tragen,	To Abraham's bosom take me.
Den Leib in sein'm Schlafkäm-merlein	My body in the grave shall spend
Gar sanft ohn einge Qual und Pein	The days in quiet, till the end
Ruhn bis am jüngsten Tage !	When the last trump shall wake me.
Alsdann vom Tod erwecke mich,	And grant me then with gladden'd eyes
Dass meine Augen sehen dich	To see Thy glory in the skies
In aller Freud, o Gottessohn,	O Lord ! in perfect joy and peace ;
Mein Heiland und Genaden — Thron !	My Saviour, fount, and throne of grace !
Herr Jesu Christ !	Lord Jesu Christ !
Erhöre mich, erhöre mich !	O hear Thou me ! O hear Thou me !
Ich will dich preisen ewiglich !	Thee will I praise eternally.

The length of the stanza resulted in an unusual expansion
of the aria. It is requisite to conceive of the chorale melody
as forming the nucleus of it in order not to feel the movement
altogether too long. However, we can perceive how this
combination serves as a preparation for the closing chorale,

which leads our thoughts away from the warlike images of the commencement to the peace of the blessed dead.[421]

The second cantata text which Picander arranged in part from the collection of his poems belongs to the seventeenth Sunday after Trinity, 1725, and begins with the Bible text " Bringet her dem Herrn Ehre seines Namens " (Psalm xxix., 2). In 1725 the seventeenth Sunday after Trinity fell on September 23, so this cantata must have been performed six days before that for Michaelmas. Thus, if we had closely followed the chronological order we ought to have studied it first. Since, however, the text is a less evident instance of the method on which Picander worked, and the composition generally would give rise to few observations of any interest, it is more fitly placed after the St. Michael's cantata. The subject of it is the feeling of rejoicing in the Lord in His Sanctuary, and though it is far from being so grand a work as the St. Michael's cantata, it is nevertheless of such high merit as to hold its place well by the side of it. The first chorus has a particular soaring swing, with a stamp of vigorous nationality; it is an effective union of homophonic sections and fugal subjects on very productive themes. The alto aria, accompanied by three oboes and figured bass, breathes of the solemn and joyful Sabbath feeling of the worshipping Christian.[422]

The third of the four cantatas written between 1724 and 1728, of which we can exactly fix the date, belongs to the beginning of February, 1727, and the text is by Picander. This, like the cantata "Lobe den Herrn, meine Seele," of 1724, has a two-fold purpose; it was intended both for a church cantata and for occasional music. In its first application it belonged to the feast of the Purification, February 2; and in the second it was adapted to a mourning ceremonial held only four days later. Johann Christoph von Ponickau, the elder, Lord of Pomssen, Naunhoff, Grosszschocher and Winddorff, Chamberlain, *Hof- und Appellationsrath*, had

---

[421] B.-G., II., No. 19. The autograph score and original parts, which are in the Royal Library at Berlin, offer no special evidence as to the date of the work.

[422] See Appendix A., No. 38.

died in October, 1726, in the 75th year of his age, and was
buried October 31, in the family tomb at Pomssen.   He
had acquired many honours in Saxony, and had become a
highly respected and important personage.   Picander himself had good reason to be grateful to him, and gave
expression to this feeling in his mourning ode.   On February
6, 1727, a solemn mourning service was performed in
memory of the deceased, in the church at Pomssen;
Picander wrote for the occasion the text beginning " Ich
lasse dich nicht "—" I will not leave Thee except Thou
bless me "—and Bach composed the music.[423]   It would
seem as though he had done so less from an impulse of his
own than to oblige the poet who was his friend, and for
his part was more engaged in considering how the music
could be made at the same time to serve the purposes of
the church service.   The text avoids all personal allusions—
probably by Bach's desire—and without the alteration of a
single word could be used for the Purification a few days
previously.   The composition throughout has no specially
solemn character ; it is a grave and meditative composition
in the strain of feeling of the words of the aged Simeon—
" Lord, now lettest Thou Thy servant depart in peace." There
is no chorus whatever but the last chorale.

Fourthly, we must mention the cantata " Herz und Mund
und That und Leben," which was probably written for the
Fourth Sunday in Advent, 1716, in Weimar; but it had
undergone a very comprehensive revision in Leipzig, and,
as music was not used in the Advent season, it was now
adapted to the Visitation of the Virgin Mary.   Though it is
not absolutely certain, it is extremely probable that this was
not done before 1727.[424]

There now follows a series of church cantatas, of which
all that can be said with any certainty is that they were
written between 1723 and 1727.

---

[423] S. Schwartz, Historische Nachlese Zu denen Geschichten der Stadt
Leipzig; Leipzig, 1744, 4, p. 33.   The autograph of Bach's cantata is not
known to exist.   I only have seen it in a copy preserved in the Royal Library
at Berlin.

[424] See Vol. I., pp. 574 and 643.—Appendix A., No. 31.

I. For the New Year, " Herr Gott dich loben wir." In speaking of the cantata " Jesus nahm zu sich die Zwölfe "— " Jesus called to Him the twelve "—it has already been pointed out that Bach by no means disdained to accommodate himself on occasion to the taste of the Leipzig public, and of all his church compositions that are known to us, this, for the New Year, is the one in which an intentional return to Telemann's mode of writing is most manifest. Not, to be sure, in the first movement, which is a splendid chorale for the chorus on the first four lines of the *Te Deum* ; in this form Bach could borrow nothing from Telemann, nor, indeed, could Telemann have followed in his steps, even at a remote distance. But a quite different spirit seems to speak to us in the second chorus, " Lasst uns jauchzen, lasst uns freuen "—" Come rejoicing, come with gladness." The alternation of the bass and the full choir, the pleasing style of the melody, the incisive style of expression, the handling of the chorus—all this is deceptively like Telemann's choral subjects,[425] though on a closer inspection we at once find traces of Bach's more powerful mind. Bach's connection with Telemann did not rest merely on personal friendship ; he by no means undervalued him as a composer, and transcribed with his own hand one of Telemann's cantatas for use in his Leipzig performances.[426] Again, in the very tuneful and fervent tenor air "Geliebter Jesu, du allein," we cannot fail to detect a reflection from the solo airs by Keiser and Telemann. Comparing this with the tenor aria of the cantata discussed, No. IV. (pp. 404 and 350), we at once perceive a certain affinity in their vein of feeling.[427]

II. Third Sunday after Epiphany, " Herr wie du willt, so schicks mit mir "—" Lord, as Thou wilt so let it be."[428]

---

[425] Only to give one example, I would refer the reader to Telemann's Whitsuntide cantata "Ich bin der erste und der letzte"—"I am the first and the last "—and particularly the chorus " Auf, lasst uns jauchzen."

[426] " Machet die Thore weit "—" Open wide the gates"—which exists in Bach's autograph in the Róyal Library at Berlin.

[427] B.-G., II., No. 16. P. 1286. See Appendix A., No. 40.

[428] B.-G., XVIII., No. 73. P. 1676. See Appendix A., No. 19.

The chorale chorus at the beginning, which refers, though
only incidentally, to a passage in the Gospel, displays a form
which in many respects is new. It is intersected throughout
by recitative portions which carry out the ideas suggested
by Melissander's hymn. We often meet with such a scheme
in Picander's sacred texts; the last aria of "Ich lasse dich
nicht" is on a similar plan, and so is the beginning of a
text written for the third Sunday after Epiphany, 1729;
we may, therefore, conclude that the words of this cantata
are by him. The chorale is in four parts, and so far
homophonic as that the voices are never interfered with
by imitative elaborations. The instruments are perfectly
independent. Before and between the lines a ritornel comes
again and again, always the same, but differing in key after
each line, and it does duty as an accompaniment to the
recitatives. A singular use is also made of one of the subjects
of the chorale. A horn, which supports the *Cantus firmus*,[429]
and at first plays a little prelude, asserts itself now and
then as a subsidiary supported by the strings, giving out
the first lines of the melody in a dismembered form and
in diminution. This is particularly the case with the notes
that fall on the words "Herr wie du willt":—

which are brought in in diminution over and over again.

At last, long after the chorus has done its part, it seems
suddenly to understand the idea that the composer has been
incessantly suggesting to it by the instruments; three
times again, at long intervals, we hear it briefly ejacu-
lating "Lord, as Thou wilt," breaking off at last on
the dominant seventh, when the instruments come in with
a rapid closing cadence. But the whole purport of this
singular tone-picture is not disclosed till we come to the
bass aria, which precedes the final chorale. The text
consists of three verses of four lines each, all beginning

---

[429] Bach afterwards allotted the horn part to the Rückpositiv of the organ
of St. Thomas'.

with the words "Lord, as Thou wilt." Bach designates
this movement as an *Aria*, though it is in fact a form of
his own invention. He works out in it the idea of the first
chorus in such a way as plainly shows that this hymn was
in his mind when he wrote the chorus. The theme is given
out by the voice without any preliminary notes in the
instruments:—

Herr, so   du willt,

they immediately take it up and repeat it in diminution, but
the rhythm only:—

and they work it out with pertinacity. The accompaniment
in semiquavers is also borrowed from the first chorus. The
feeling of a man who bows in humble submission before the
incomprehensible counsels of the Almighty is here expressed
with the deepest fervour. From the passage where the
strings *pizzicato* imitate the tolling of a knell, a sort of
vision of peace seems to be revealed through the dismal gate
of death.[430]

III. Third Sunday after Epiphany, "Alles nur nach
Gottes Willen "[431]—" Lord, Thy will alone obeying." This
text is from Franck's "Evangelisches Andachtsopfer," and
certainly one of the most suggestive. It follows out the
same line of thought as the former cantata, and it would
almost seem as though one had influenced the other; at the
same time, the feeling in the former is emphasised rather in
the sense of a pious resignation to the sufferings of life, while
in this work that blissful contentment is praised which has
its root in the assurance that the hand of a loving father
is to be traced in everything. The imaginative features
and gloomy colouring of the former cantata do not exist
here, but a trustful and childlike devotion of most touching

---

430 Compare Vol. I., p. 553.
431 B.-G., XVIII., No. 72, P. 1299. See App. A., No. 41.

power. This feeling finds its strongest expression in the soprano aria " Mein Jesus will es thun "—" This will my Saviour do, my sorrows He will sweeten "—one of the most lovely vocal pieces Bach ever wrote ; but the remainder is no less delightful in its way : the less tranquil alto aria " Mit Allem was ich hab und bin "—" With all I have, and as I am "—the arioso which precedes it, in which rhythms of two and three time respectively are intermingled with such wonderful effect, and the preliminary chorus which marches on in such magnificent breadth, and overflows with fervent feeling.

IV. Septuagesima Sunday, " Nimm was dein ist und gehe hin "—" Take that thine is, and go thy way."[432] The cantata begins with a fugue, in which the resolute, nay stern, repudiation of the fancied claims of the workmen for fairer payment is treated with almost dramatic force. It is a pity that the writer of the text should have so inadequately grasped the deeper meaning of the Gospel parable of the householder who hires labourers for his vineyard, that he could find nothing better to say about it than the praises of contentment ; this must necessarily impair the interest of the music. What Bach did with the trivial couplets is of course full of ingenuity and purpose, but it does not stir us deeply ; still, this cantata seems to have become very popular, and the text was used by several composers.[433]

V. Sexagesima Sunday. " Leichtgesinnte Flattergeister " —" Empty thoughts of worldly folly." The bass aria at the beginning, figuring the empty and foolish thoughts that scatter the blessings of the Divine word to the winds, is a characteristic composition, full of individuality. The finale is an independent chorus in the Italian aria form ; it is a

---

[432] The autograph score in the Royal Library at Berlin. Published in " Kirchengesänge für Solo- und Chor- Stimmen mit Instrumentalbegleitung von Joh. Seb. Bach." Berlin, Trautwein, No. 1. See App. A., No. 19.

[433] The first chorus of this work of Bach is quoted as a model by Marburg, for its admirable declamation, " Kritische Tonkunst," Vol. I., p. 381. He speaks of a public performance of it. The beginning of the alto aria " Murre nicht, lieber Christ," is quoted by Sulzer, " Allgemeine Theorie der schönen Künste," Part IV., p. 267, Leipzig, 1779, but to another setting. I have not been able to make any farther inquiries in this direction.

fugue, but simple and popular in subject, and must originally have belonged to a secular work.

VI. First Sunday after Easter, " Halt im Gedächtniss Jesum Christ "—" Keep in remembrance Jesus Christ." Here again we have a work which must satisfy every requirement, even as regards the text. The beautiful Gospel narrative of how, after His resurrection, Jesus appeared among His disciples, bidding them " Peace be with you," and strengthening their faith, is clearly reflected in the text, which is made up of well-chosen passages from the Bible, suitable chorales, and melodious verse. It reminds us of Franck's manner, and if Picander wrote it he surpassed himself. There is but one solo in this cantata—irrespective of a few short recitatives—a beautiful tenor aria. In the first chorus—a splendid fugal movement freely worked out on two principal themes—Scheibe would have found a perfect example of that " poetic embellishment and graceful expression " which he demanded as the conditions of adequate and expressive church music. About half-way through the work, the Easter chorale " Erschienen ist der herrlich Tag "—" The glorious day has now arrived "—is brought in with great effect. From the words of the recitative which leads up to it we see that the same chorale must have been previously sung by the congregation. This was not prescribed by rule, so Bach must have expressly determined that this hymn should be used on this occasion.[434] The next chorus is extremely peculiar; it is designated as an *Aria*, from the verse form of the text. The bass sings the words of Christ, " Peace be on you all," to a tender and deeply felt melody below a soft floating accompaniment on the flute and oboes. Against this, the three upper voice-parts express by word and note their faith and confidence in Christ's protection and aid; the whole dies away in the lingering benediction of the bass, and then the chorale " Du Friedefürst Herr Jesu Christ "—" Thou Prince of Peace, Lord Jesu Christ "—once more briefly concentrates the leading idea of the cantata.[435]

---

[434] See ante, p. 231.
[435] B.-G., XVI., No. 67, P. 1293. See App. A., No. 19.

VII. Second Sunday after Easter, "Du Hirte Israel"—
"Shepherd of Israel." A sacred pastoral, which exhibits
a beautiful combination of tenderness and gravity, grace and
depth. The rhythm of the first chorus is, properly speaking,
not to be regarded as in 3-4 time, but as 9-8, since the
beat throughout is chiefly in triplets, and the rhythmical
figure ♩♪ according to the custom of that time should be
read ♩, ♪ (see Vol. I., p. 563). By this means, and by the
heavy droning bass like a bagpipe, the stamp of pastoral
music is delicately impressed on the composition. Besides
its wonderful melodic charm, this chorus is at the same
time a masterpiece of artistic structure. In the vocal parts,
homophonic sections alternate with fugal workings out; three
schalmei (oboes) are added to the three upper parts to
give them support and colour. The stringed instruments
meanwhile involve them in a glittering network of rising
and falling figures, always however perfectly independent.
Bach had never before composed such a work ; it is a fresh
evidence of his inexhaustible imagination. We may compare
the pastoral symphony of the Christmas oratorio as the only
worthy pendant to this movement in feeling and in the
delightful magic of its harmonious development, as well as in
the combination of different qualities of tone. The bass air
has in many respects a similar character, while, on the other
hand, the tenor aria which comes between it and the chorus
expresses that dejected sentiment which is naturally aroused
by such passages in the Psalms as "Though I walk through
the valley of the shadow of death, I fear no ill," and "As the
hart panteth for the waterbrooks, so longeth my soul for
Thee, O God"; and it is certain that Bach had these passages
in his thoughts, since the text is to much the same effect,
and a stanza of Psalm xxiii. versified forms the close of the
cantata.[436]

VIII. Second Sunday after Easter, "Wo gehst du hin?"—
"Where goest thou?" The text, like those of many of Bach's
cantatas, reveals a lamentable incapacity on the part of the
writer for grasping the idea of the Gospel and giving it a

---

[436] B.-G., XXIII., No. 104, P. 1680. See App. A., No. 19.

poetic form. After a slight reference to it we find ourselves
once more in the beaten track of exhortation to think of
heaven, and reflections on the transitoriness of all earthly
things. It is a source of constant astonishment how Bach
was always equal to the occasion, and could always produce
new and still new forms and styles to give life to this
poetical monotony. The work is a solo cantata, for,
excepting the closing chorale, no chorus—in many parts, at
any rate—is employed. The first and third sections claim
our particular attention; in the former Bach has found it
possible to compose an aria on a text of four words, which,
moreover, merely put a question, " Wo gehst du hin ? "
It has a singular effect from the phrases, in three bars
each, of which it is constructed. In the third number the
soprano sings the third verse of Ringwald's hymn " Herr
Jesu Christ ich weiss gar wohl," while the instruments
carry on a two-part counterpoint. In this piece we meet
for the first time with a complete and deliberate transfer of
the organ trio to vocal music ; in the cantata " Erfreute
Zeit im neuen Bunde " we found scarcely more than an
attempt at it. It was during the early period of his residence
in Leipzig that he composed his six great organ sonata
trios; hence we here see the outcome of his labours in
this direction.[487]

IX. Rogation Sunday, " Wahrlich, wahrlich, ich sage
euch, so ihr den Vater bitten werdet "—" Verily, verily, I
say unto you, that ye shall pray to the Father." This is a
work which bears the most obvious and close relationship
with the next preceding one, both in purport and date. The
arrangement of the text is precisely the same ; first a text
taken from the Bible, then an aria, chorale, recitative, aria,
and final chorale. The means of which Bach has availed
himself are also identical, even the arias are for the same
voices, but in reversed order ; each, however, begins with a
solo in the bass and ends with a simple four-part chorale.
The chorale subject in the middle, on the last verse of

---

[487] The original parts of the Cantata are in the Royal Library at Berlin.
See App. A., No. 19.

" Kommt her zu mir, spricht Gottes Sohn," reveals in both
cases a form borrowed from the organ ; in this cantata
three parts are employed in the counterpart, but the melodic
character of the parts is nearly related in the two.   In the
cantata " Wo gehst du hin ? " it begins thus :—

In " Wahrlich, wahrlich," it is thus :—

Bach was wont to give Bible words in the arioso form to
one single voice, because any adaptation of the opera forms
might so easily seem profane ; and when, for once, he
deviated from this rule in the cantata " Wo gehst du hin ? "
it certainly arose from the peculiarities of the text.   It is
true that the movement which stands at the beginning of
" Wahrlich, wahrlich," is not an arioso ; but the dignified
attitude which befits the composition of a Bible text is
attained in another way—a way, it is true, in which none
but such a master as Bach could venture to walk ; he has
entangled the song in a regular four-part instrumental
fugue, and so worked it out that for the most part it
constitutes an independent fifth part ; it is only now and then
that it flows in unison with the instrumental bass, and thus
distinctly recalls the usual type of the old-fashioned sacred
arioso.   A companion piece to this original composition is
not wanting ; we find it in the first movement of the cantata
" O heilges Geist- und Wasserbad"; it therefore seems
probable that the two works were written within a short
time of each other.[438]

X. Sixth Sunday after Easter, " Sie werden euch in
den Bann Thun"—"They shall cast out your name as evil "
(G minor).   This text again is precisely similar in its construction to those of the last two cantatas, and the
composition also displays a general resemblance to them,

---

[438] B.-G., XX.,[1] No. 86.   See App. A., No. 19.

particularly in the two arias. The opening piece is a duet
for the tenor and bass, afterwards taken up by the chorus.
The greatest polyphonic skill prevails throughout the duet,
which may be compared with that in the duet in the
cantata "Du wahrer Gott und Davidssohn" (see p. 350).
The chorus, on the other hand, with its popular style of
arrangement and easily understood polyphony, reminds us of
the choruses in "Jesus nahm zu sich die Zwölfe" (see
p. 353) and "Ein ungefärbt Gemüthe" (see p. 358). Something perfectly new is revealed to us again in the middle
chorale movement "Ach Gott, wie manches Herzelied."
It is a free imitation, not of any organ trio or quatuor but
of Böhm's type of chorale treatment.[439] The simple chorale
itself is sung by the tenor, accompanied only by a figured
bass, and that in phrases developed by diminution from the
first line of the chorale, which by their chromatic dis-
locations are intended to convey the idea of "heart-
sickness." As the verse consists of only four lines the
subject is soon over, almost too soon for its whole
significance to be grasped and understood. In a cantata
written much later, Bach worked out this melody in the
same way,[440] only, instead of one voice, he employs a four-
part chorus. But in the later composition the effect produced is greater, because recitatives are inserted between
the lines of the chorale, and the hearer consequently has
time afforded him to take in the original structure of the
form. The closing chorale of the present cantata is the last
verse of Flemming's hymn, "In allen meinen Thaten."[441]

XI. First Sunday after Trinity, "O Ewigkeit, du
Donnerwort"—"Eternity! that awful word." Rist's hymn
is the basis for the text, the first, second, and sixteenth
verses being transcribed bodily; the remainder, excepting
verses seven and eight which are omitted, is cast in the
madrigal form. We must recognise Picander's hand in
this work, for it is worked out in precisely the same

---

[439] Compare Vol. I., p. 206.
[440] "Ach Gott wie manches Herzeleid," A major; B.-G., I., p. 84.
[441] B.-G., X., No. 44, P. 1659. See App. A., No. 19.

way as the Michaelmas cantata "·Es erhub sich ein Streit." The work is in two portions, each concluding with a verse of a chorale set to the same harmonies; thus quite in the manner frequently found in Bach's earlier Leipzig cantatas. It is evident that in this one he worked *con amore;* in it a passionate agitation is combined with a mighty and imposing solemnity. Through four arias and a duet the image of the awfulness of the Divine Judge and of eternal torment is brought home to the personality of the hearer, and displayed with all the dramatic vividness the limitations of church music admit. The separate numbers are in strong contrast to each other, so that although it is the same idea which is varied in them, our keenest interest is kept up to the end; and it adds to the vigour of the expression that, as a whole, it is brief and abrupt. Even in the opening chorus we are already made to feel that personal and passionate conception of the subject which, to a certain extent, we always meet with in Bach, but which is the especial stamp of this work. We need only study the phrases given in the counterpoint on the first and third lines of the chorale to the three deepest parts; the tremor which takes possession of the instruments in bars 13, 17, 23, and 27, and the terrified flight, as it were, of the combined rhythm in bar 90. Besides, this chorus affords the third instance in the course of Bach's early years at Leipzig of the adaptation of the French *ouverture* to church music. In the cantatas " Preise Jerusalem den Herrn " and " Höchst erwünschtes Freudenfest " it is not, however, founded on a chorale; here, as a chorale is amalgamated with the overture form, the cantata affords a striking pendant to the Advent cantata " Nun komm der Heiden Heiland," written in 1714.[442]

XII. Feast of St. John the Baptist, " Ihr Menschen rühmet Gottes Liebe "—" O men, declare God's loving-kindness "—a cantata of less importance, and which offers hardly any opportunity for special observation. Its character is cheerful and pleasing, the forms simple and easy to under-

---

[442] See Vol. I., p. 507.

stand. It is only in the middle duet with *oboe da caccia*
that the master has displayed his higher art; and this even
is marred by a certain dryness, which we cannot wonder at
when we consider the vapid emptiness of the words. A
graceful feature may be mentioned in the way in which the
bass recitative which precedes the final chorale appears as
a sort of prelude to the first line. The form of the chorale
itself is that already known from the cantata " Jesus nahm
zu sich die Zwölfe."[443]

XIII. Eighth Sunday after Trinity, "Erforsche mich Gott
und erfahre mein Herz"—"Search me, O God, and know my
heart." It would be possible to select from among Bach's
cantatas a group which might be designated "orthodox
compositions," and this one would be included in it. It
is full of a stern zeal verging on severity, which is peculiar
to Bach among the sacred composers of the time, and
which, in this cantata, is most conspicuous in the important
opening chorus. The conception of the Bible words,
Psalm cxxxix., 23, to which it is composed, was suggested
by the Gospel for the day, which is directed against false
prophets—one of the most fertile themes for an orthodox
preacher.[444]

XIV. Ninth Sunday after Trinity, "Thue Rechnung!
Donnerwort"—"Day of reckoning! awful word." The
text is from Franck's "Evangelischem Andachtsopfer,"
hence, we must suppose that the work is an early Leipzig
composition. Apparently Bach wrote it in the same year
as the cantata "Ihr, die ihr euch von Christo nennet"
(see p. 361).[445] It has no chorus but the final chorale. Of
the solo pieces, the tenor aria is unsatisfactory by reason of
its truly amazing text, "Capital und Interessen"—"Capital
and interest of my sins, both great and small; I must soon
account for all!" The bass aria, on the contrary, and
the duet for soprano and alto are splendid examples of
force and of characteristic treatment.

---

[443] The original parts are in the Royal Library at Berlin. See Appendix
A., No. 19.

[444] The original parts in the Royal Library at Berlin. See Appendix A., No. 19.

[445] See Vol. I., Appendix A., No. 26, p. 640.

XV. Ninth Sunday after Trinity, "Herr, gehe nicht ins Gericht"—"Lord, enter not into judgment." This has the character of a fervent and supplicatory penitential prayer, and the orchestra begins in G minor with the two upper parts worked out in canon; in the closing cadenza the four-part chorus comes in with "Enter not into judgment with Thy servant, O Lord," Psalm cxliii., 2. It derives nothing from the instrumental subject but the motive of the canon treatment, the other parts are constructed out of freshly introduced ideas over a ground bass. At the end of six bars the voices are silent again, while the instruments repeat their inarticulate penitential hymn on the fifth above. It then is worked out in double counterpoint, and the same is done in the chorus which comes in again eight bars later, the soprano answering the tenor, the alto the soprano, and the tenor the alto. The instruments then borrow a rhythmical motive from the chorus, and work it out into an independent picture which is welded with the chorus into a masterly whole. Once more there is a brief pause in the chorus, while the instruments carry on their motive, at the same time referring distinctly to a certain passage of the opening subject—bar 5. Now, for the third time, the chorus comes in, emphasising and freely working out the principal subject; at last it gives out its own penitential cry, going through it completely in the middle range of compass, as if it flowed straight from the hearts of the singing host. The chorus ended, the feeling is allowed to die softly away on a long organ point on the dominant. An admirably constructed *adagio* subject is immediately followed by an animated fugue "For in Thy sight shall no man living be justified." We might place at the head of this movement, as an appropriate motto, the words "I, the Lord thy God, am a jealous God"; the treatment of the resolute theme leads in many places to passages which rage and roll like angry billows. Once we suddenly come to a long *piano* passage—an extremely rare device with Bach—and this presently sinks even to *pianissimo*, as though man were cowering to hide from the dreadful eye of God. The remainder of the cantata is in no way inferior to the impressive effect of this opening chorus.

Wie zittern und wanken,	The sinful must languish,
Der Sünder Gedanken,	In torment and anguish;
Indem sie sich unter einander verklagen,	They turn on each other with impotent railing,
Und wiederum sich zu entschuldigen wagen.	Or plead their temptations with bitter bewailing.
So wird ein geängstigt Gewissen Durch eigene Folter zerrissen.	Thus racked by its self-accusation Their guilt works its own condemnation.

So runs the text of the first aria, to which Bach has set a composition of the greatest originality. A tremulous semiquaver figure on the violins goes on throughout, while the soprano, with an oboe concertante, sings a boldly constructed and impressive melody. No figured bass is added, the lowest part is given to the viola in a steady slow *tremolo* of quavers. A secret terror, and at the same time a profound grief pervades the whole air. A change comes over it with the accompanied recitative for the bass which follows : " In Jesus ist Trost, er öffnet uns einst die ewigen Hütten." None but Bach could have found tones of such deep pathos to express these words ; they introduce an artistically constructed aria for the tenor, overflowing with the sentiment of restored calm. Its rhythm is particularly noteworthy. The words it begins with : " Kann ich nur Jesum mir zum Freunde machen "—" If only Jesus be my Friend and Saviour " —Bach has adapted to a phrase of which the periods fall into a half and a whole bar in common time :—

Kann ich nur Je - sum mir zum Freun-de ma- chen,

and the three notes of the first half-bar are subsequently used very ingeniously for episodic phrases. The closing chorale combines the two main ideas of the cantata—dread and reassurance are both expressed in it. The vocal part speaks of reassurance, and the violins which re-echo the soprano air in trembling semiquavers keep up the feeling of fear. But by degrees the beating heart becomes calmer

and more peaceful; the semiquavers sink to triplets of
quavers, then simple quavers, then to tied (♩ ₃ ♪) triplets,
and finally in the last bar to crotchets. It is clear that
Bach intended to keep the memory of the soprano air alive
to the very last, because at the end the chorale is played on
the instruments without any figured bass, but with the viola
for the deepest part.

It is impossible sufficiently to admire the successful combination of antagonistic feeling in this composition; it
opens before us a realm of music utterly unknown to any
of Bach's forerunners and contemporaries. The song of
Orestes in "Iphigenia in Tauris," "Le calme rentre dans
mon cœur," is justly praised as Gluck's *chef d'œuvre* in
dramatic music, but he was not the first to disclose under
a musical aspect the inmost depths of the inarticulate
complication of human feeling; half a century before him
Bach had solved the problem with no less mastery.

I must not here omit to notice a singular reminiscence of
Handel's Passion music to Brocke's text, part of which Bach
had copied with his own hand, probably in the later Cöthen
period. The progress of the melody of the soprano air is
free and animated, but one passage startles us by its studied
and almost forced style, which does not duly harmonise with
the rest. It is in bar 28, &c., which is as follows:—

so wird ein ge-äng-stet Ge-wis-sen

In Handel's Passion this passage occurs:—[446]

den-ket, dass die Straf schon kei-met

I feel convinced that Bach in this place was carried away
by his remembrance of this very beautiful and impressive
passage; that Handel's work was exerting an influence on
him throughout this composition it is fair to conclude from
the use of the oboe in imitation, and the feeling all through
is very similar. This bears important testimony to the

---

[446] German Händel Society's edition, part XV., p. 80, bar 3.

interest which Bach took in the works of his great contemporary, and the reader will remember that it is not the
only instance.[447]

XVI. Tenth Sunday after Trinity, "Schauet doch und
sehet, ob irgend ein Schmerz sei, wie mein Schmerz"—
"Behold and see, if there be any sorrow like unto my
sorrow." This cantata is a companion piece to the previous
one, and they were undoubtedly composed at the same time;
they are alike in structure and in feeling too, so far as the
different characteristics of the subjects admit. In the
Gospel for the day, Jesus prophesies with weeping the
coming destruction of Jerusalem; the text, as adapted to
this conception, is very unskilfully managed. It alludes
first to the former destruction by Nebuchadnezzar, and then
makes an awkward transition to the coming fall under Titus,
drawing from it an application to the judgment impending
over all mankind, of whom Jesus will nevertheless tenderly
shield the pious. As the musical treatment gives the
greatest weight to the beginning, the work as a whole lacks
directness and clearness of dramatic purpose. This is much
to be regretted, for in the conception and working-out of
individual parts the cantata is one of the most striking and
thrilling works that Bach ever created. The whole essence
of the lamentation of Jeremiah is compressed into the first
chorus (in D minor) with quite incomparable force; every
note is tearful, and every interval a sigh. As in the cantata
"Herr gehe nicht ins Gericht," the chorus consists of a
slow subject developed in canonic imitations by the voice
parts, and of a lively fugue. The first has sixty-six bars, the
second seventy-six, in 3-4 time—thus it is of some considerable length; and yet it is not more than enough to
convey the sentiment which it has to express. In certain
carefully chosen passages the chorus is supported by a
trumpet and two *oboi da caccia*, while the stringed quartet
and two flutes play round and about the *adagio* subject in
graceful and appropriate arabesque. Certain sobbing
passages on the flute remind us distinctly of the chorale

---

[447] See ante, p. 175. B.-G., XXIII., No. 105. See App. A., No. 19.

for chorus in the Passion according to St. Matthew, "O
Mensch, bewein dein Sünde gross";[448] but in the Passion the
sentiment is qualified by thankfulness for the Redeemer's
death, while in the cantata there is no comfort for the
burning anguish that torments the soul; these two wonderful
compositions stand in contrast like the Old and New Covenant.
Next to the chorus our attention is most rivetted by the grand
bass aria "Dein Wetter zog sich auf von weitem." The
main idea, rising in thirds from the B of the instrumental
bass:—

Dein Wet- ter   zog   sich   auf . .   von   wei - tem

has in it something mysteriously terrible which scarcely any
other composer could have found means of expressing; this
feeling is enhanced by the long-drawn f'' high above all in
the trumpets,[449] like a shaft of light piercing the dark storm-
clouds and giving, as has been aptly observed, "a red hue
as of blood."[450] The chromatic rise and fall in the middle,
bar for bar (45 to 54 and 67 to 76), of the instrumental bass
is highly effective. The alto air, G minor, which is accompanied only by the flutes and oboes without any figured bass,
paraphrases the words of Christ, "How often would I have
gathered thy children," &c., Matt. xxiii., 37, and has a
soothing though solemn character, as befits the context. In
the closing chorale—the ninth verse of Meyfart's hymn,
"O grosser Gott von Macht"—we again hear the flute
passages of the opening chorus in brief interludes; this is a
reference to the beginning, similar to that in the final chorale
of "Herr, gehe nicht ins Gericht."

---

[448] This chorus was originally written for the Passion according to St John,
and was already in existence when Bach composed the cantata in question.
More will be said on the subject when we deal with the Passion music.

[449] Bach here indicates, as in the opening chorus and final chorale, *Tromba
o Corno da tirarsi*. The *Corno da tirarsi*, which is frequently put in by him—
for instance, again, in the cantata "Halt im Gedächtniss Jesum Christ"—was
the same instrument, or a similar one, as the *Tromba da tirarsi*, in which a
combination was attempted of the trumpet with the trombone. Kuhnau speaks
of it in the "Musikalischer Quacksalber," p. 82.

[450] Lindner, *Zur Tonkunst*, p. 124. Berlin, Guttentag, 1864.

It has already been explained (ante p. 322) that even in a composition for choral singing, all use of ornament need not be excluded ; two passages of the first chorus here are examples of this. In bar 37 in the tenor, and bar 51 in the alto, the falling intervals of thirds are filled up by the addition of "accents"; in the voice parts these are not indicated, though they are in the accompanying oboes.[451] Of course they must be used in every part, or no intelligible harmony could result, though it is true they thus cease to be embellishment and become part of the tune ; but the limit line was often overlooked by Bach (see ante p. 316).[452]

XVII. Thirteenth Sunday after Trinity, "Du sollst Gott deinen Herren lieben"—"Thou shalt love the Lord thy God." The style of this cantata is conspicuously different from all we have hitherto discussed. The arias are considerably simpler than we are accustomed to find them in Bach. In one of them two instruments are introduced *concertante* (probably two oboes) with the soprano: this they carry on almost uniformly in parallel thirds or sixths, and we nowhere find that they work out any polyphony worth mentioning. The sentiment verges on that quiet ecstacy which is peculiar to Bach's earliest church compositions, when he was still lingering on the borders of the old cantata. The soprano aria even reminds us very plainly of "Jesu dir sei Dank gesungen," from the cantata "Uns ist ein Kind geboren."[453] The condition of the autograph offers no evidence in support of the idea that Bach has here remodelled an older composition, unless we detect it in the haste with which it has been written, and which seems to indicate lack of leisure. As regards the first chorus, however, the difference of style consists in its presenting itself in a perfectly new form, ingeniously

---

[451] In the second passage the oboe part is as follows—

which seems to imply that the shake should begin on the passing note above.

[452] B.-G., X., No. 46, P. 1660, App. A., No. 19.

[453] See Vol. I., p. 491.

conceived, and worked out in a masterly manner. The text is taken from the Gospel, "Du sollst Gott deinen Herrn lieben"—"Thou shalt love the Lord thy God with all thy heart, and all thy soul, and with all thy strength, and with all thy mind, and thy neighbour as thyself" (Luke x., 27). Now it was not unknown to the composer, who was well versed in his Bible, that the incident which called forth this injunction is reported in a more extended form by the Evangelists Matthew (xxii., 35—40) and Mark (xii., 28—34); and the precept which follows, "On these two commandments hang all the laws and the prophets," was full of significance to him. He brought in the melody of Luther's hymn, "Dies sind die heilgen zehn Gebot," in the bass in minims, as a *Cantus firmus*, working out the chorus in quavers from the first line of the chorale, and finally gave out the chorale in crotchets on the *Tromba da tirarsi*. Thus its very essence pervades every portion of the composition, and closes it in on every side; and the thought that all God's laws are embodied in these two precepts acquires the most figurative musical presentment which is in any way possible.[454] It is clear that the form, regarded from the purely musical stand-point, is that of the organ chorale; we have, indeed, two real organ chorales by Bach on this same melody. One is in the third part of the "Clavierü-bung,"[455] and belongs consequently to the latest period of Bach's work. The other is in the "Orgelbüchlein,"[456] and so must have been written at Weimar. The later one treats the melody in strict canon on the octave in the inner parts. In the earlier organ chorale the melody lies in the upper part, and the counterpart is worked out from the first line. This chorus, therefore, as regards its musical treatment, holds a middle place between the two organ chorales. A working out in strict canon form between the instrumental bass and trumpet was inadmissible, since, in the first place, neither the value of the notes nor the

---

[454] W. Rust has given a sympathetic interpretation of the deep meaning of this chorus. B.-G., XVIII., p. xv.

[455] B.-G., III., p. 206.

[456] P. S. V., Vol. V. (No. 244). See Vol. I., p. 600.

intervals are the same; and, in the second place, the trumpet repeats the first line after each of the others in order to emphasise very expressly the words "These ten are God's most holy laws"; finally, the whole melody is repeated once more straight through, above an organ point on G. This playing with fragments of the melody, so to speak, rather points to the influence of the Northern school. So, indeed, does another circumstance. Bach divides the fourth line—

hoch auf dem Berg Si - na - i

in a singular manner into two sections, treating the first four notes separately, and connecting the last three with the *Kyrie*. No reason for this, either poetical or musical, is discernible; it is simply a whim of that capricious art which the Northern composers were so ready to yield to; and, in fact, something similar occurs in a chorale arrangement by Buxtehude.[457] Bach has followed the same course again in the organ chorale in the "Clavierübung," whence we may conclude that he had the cantata chorus in his mind when he wrote it.[458]

XVIII. Sixteenth Sunday after Trinity, "Liebster Gott, wann werd ich sterben?"—"Ah, Lord God, when shall I see Thee?" This cantata seems to have been composed very nearly at the same time as that for the Thirteenth Sunday after Trinity, "Ihr, die ihr euch von Christo nennet."[459] Its subject consists in meditations on Death, only very remotely suggested by the narrative of the widow's son, of Nain. A verse of Neumann's hymn "Liebster Gott, wann werd ich sterben," is used both at the beginning and end in the original form; verses two, three, and four, on the contrary, are so paraphrased on the "madrigal form" that verse two serves as the text for a tenor air, verse three

---

[457] *Te Deum laudamus.* See Spitta's edition of Buxtehude's Organ Compositions. Vol. II., p. 53, bar 5.

[458] B.-G., XVIII., No. 77, P. 1675. See App. A., No. 19.

[459] See ante, p. 361.

for an alto recitative, the first half of verse four for a bass air, and the second half for a soprano recitative.

The aria-like form of the hymn was due to Daniel Vetter, who has been frequently mentioned in this work (and who died in 1721) as organist to the church of St. Nicholas, in Leipzig. Vetter had been a pupil of Werner Fabricius, and at his death, January 9, 1679, he had succeeded him as organist (on August 11 of the same year).[460]   He was a native of Breslau and composed this hymn at the request of his friend Wilisius, the cantor of St. Bernhardin at Breslau, for his funeral, 1695. It had become widely known and suffered much defacement, for which reason he republished it in 1713, in the second part of his Musicalischen Kirch- und Haus-Ergötzlichkeit[461] set for four parts. Bach must have known this four-part aria, for it is the same which appears at the end of his cantata, in a somewhat altered form, but easily recognisable. Here again we perceive that Bach held his Leipzig predecessors in due honour. In the first chorus the melody is treated in the form of a chorale fantasia (compare p. 361). This is a very remark-able composition—the sound of tolling bells, the fragrance of blossoms pervade it—the sentiment of a churchyard in spring time. The character of the piece may no doubt have been largely determined by the fact that it is not strictly a chorale but a sacred *aria* which is under treat-ment, but this does not sufficiently account for it. Rather might we suppose that the tender encouraging tone of the Gospel story had suggested the feeling, particularly when we regard the whole cantata; for its gentle grace, not unfrequently passing into a blissful childlike playfulness, contrasts strangely enough with the stern gravity of Bach's other funeral cantatas. A knell is imitated in exactly the same way as in the Weimar cantata "Komm du süsse Todesstunde" by *pizzicatos* on the strings, and rapidly reitera-ted high notes on the flute. Two *oboi d'amore* float along above the strings, now crossing each other in flowing melody,

---

[460] Archives of the University and of the Town Council of Leipzig.

[461] Winterfeld, Ev. Kir. III., p. 487, and Musical Supplement, p. 140.

and now united in soft passages of thirds and sixths; the
piece of music thus evolved almost suffices of itself to fill
our souls with peacefulness. Indeed, the musical impression
of the whole rests upon it; it consists of sixty-eight bars,
while the homophonic chorus, which comes in interruptedly
and gives us the original melody with no embellishments
but a few delicate *Melismata*, includes altogether no more
than twenty bars. Nevertheless its words of death attune
our feelings to that peculiar vein of melancholy which we
experience beside the bier of a child or a youth. The tolling
of the bell goes on in the basses all through the highly strung
aria given to the tenor, and sometimes even appears in the
voice part, bars 29-31. The melodious and elaborate bass
air and the two recitatives fully correspond in beauty to the
other pieces.[462]

XIX.—Sunday after Christmas, "Gottlob, nun geht das
Jahr zu Ende"—"All praise to God, the year has gone."
This is the last we have to mention of Bach's cantatas
that are composed to texts by Neumeister,[463] and as regards
the use of the chorus it is the finest. The principal chorus
is the second number, but such is its weight, that the finished
beauty of the preceding soprano air hardly asserts itself,
and all that comes after sinks into nothingness. Bach
had taken the composition of the chorus in hand earlier
than the rest of the work, and had sketched it first
separately, for in the complete score it shows hardly any
corrections and has all the appearance of a fair copy. At
the conclusion of this gigantic work the master himself
looked back on it with proud satisfaction—he has done what
he scarcely ever did—counted up its 174 bars, and noted
them at the end. It is a chorale for chorus on "Nun lob
mein Seel den Herren"—"My soul now praise the Lord"—
and resembles a motett in so far as that the instruments—
strings, three oboes, cornet, and three trombones—work with
the voices, and it is only the figured bass which is here and
there allowed a way of its own. The type is that of the

---

[462] B.-G., I., No. 8. P. 1199. See App. A., No. 43.
[463] See Vol. I., p. 487.

Pachelbel organ chorale, elaborated to the highest degree of which it was capable within the limits of the motett form. Particularly we may note, as belonging to this form, the picturesque musical rendering of the separate lines of the verses by the use of contrapuntal parts, which interpret the forgiveness of "us miserable sinners" by acute chromatic passages, or pour out the consolations of God as it were in a stream over wretched humanity, and then soar up "like to the eagle." Bach subsequently wrote several pieces of this kind,[464] and they are worthy of the first-born, but not one surpasses it.[465]

On September 7, 1727, a general mourning of four months began for the Queen Christiana Eberhardine. The interruption this occasioned of course made a break in the long series of Bach's Leipzig compositions; this is, therefore, a suitable place to pause for a retrospect. Our final judgment as to the Weimar cantatas was much to the effect that in them the ideal of church music in Bach's hands had already been found, excepting in the one particular of the treatment of the chorus.[466] In spite of the occurrence in them of many important choral numbers, these are on the whole outweighed by the solo pieces, in which the form gives us an impression of perfect maturity; and the student who has thoroughly examined them will find very little that is new as regards form in Bach's later compositions for solo voices. Then it became evident from the Cöthen cantata, "Wer sich selbst erhöhet,"[467] that Bach, from his having long occupied himself in composing for the organ and other instruments, had acquired a complete mastery of the art of working out independent choral compositions in the most grand and elaborate forms. In the cantatas written during the first four years of his life at Leipzig, we again find that unlimited wealth of invention which the artist derived from his power of applying the

---

[464] "Ach Gott vom Himmel sieh darein," B.-G., I., No. 2. P. 1194, "Aus tiefer Noth schrei ich zu dir," B.-G., VII., No. 38. P. 1694.

[465] B.-G., V.,¹ No. 28. See App. A., No. 41.

[466] Vol. I., p. 565.

[467] See ante, p. 12.

forms of instrumental music to his sacred compositions in a
way previously undreamt of; we find him unhesitatingly
adapting parts of the chamber sonata, and utilising it as an
instrumental opening to the second part of the cantata, "Die
Himmel erzählen die Ehre Gottes." He blends the elements
of the first movement of the Italian concerto with true
choral forms, as in the Magnificat and the Christmas piece,
"Dazu ist erschienen der Sohn Gottes"; he casts whole
cantatas in the concerto form, as "Erfreute Zeit im neuen
Bunde," or in that of the orchestral suite, as "Höchster-
wünschtes Freudenfest." He combines the French *ouverture*
with an independently conceived chorus or even with a
chorale, as "Preise Jerusalem, den Herrn," "O Ewigkeit,
du Donnerwort"; he makes the *giga* serve its turn as a
sacred duet, "Aergre dich, o Seele, nicht," and the *passecaille*
as the basis of a chorus of lamentation, "Weinen, Klagen."
In the cantata "Die Elenden sollen essen" he uses the
instruments of secular music for a chorale *fantasia*, and in
the Michaelmas music, "Es erhub sich ein Streit," he takes
a *Siciliano* for counterpoint to a chorale melody; he avails
himself of everything that he or his predecessors had ever
invented in the whole realm of the organ chorale for his
sacred vocal music. We meet once more with the type
created by Pachelbel and with those of Buxtehude and
Böhm in new and figurative modifications, sometimes pure,
as in "Erschallet ihr Lieder"; sometimes mixed, as in
"Die Elenden sollen essen," "Christ lag in Todesbanden,"
"Du sollst Gott deinen Herrn lieben." The chorale, trio,
and quartet which Bach constructed in so masterly a way
for the organ we find again in the cantatas, "Wo gehst du
hin?" and "Wahrlich, wahrlich, ich sage euch," but now
in a vocal form. He welds the orchestra and chorus together
with a mighty hand to unite in the chorale fantasia; he calls
upon the instrumental chorale to accompany the irregular
figures of the recitative ("Du wahrer Gott und Davidssohn");
he inserts the appealing phrase of the recitative, which has
a personality of its own, between the sections of the chorale
chorus ("Herr, wie du willst, so schicks mit mir"), and
he impresses on the solo voice the polyphonic form of the

instrumental fugue ("O heilges Geist- und Wasserbad,"
"Wahrlich, wahrlich, ich sage euch"); and among them all
we find the old well-known forms of the aria, the arioso, the
recitative, and the simple chorale, but always filled with new
meaning from a perennial fount of inexhaustible inventiveness, made deeper, broader, and grander, and either linked
together by a deep and inherent poetical purpose, or
connected with one of his newly invented forms. All this
may be detected on a narrower and less ambitious scale
in his Weimar cantatas, but what distinguishes the Leipzig
compositions from these in a very conspicuous manner is the
lavish introduction of powerfully and boldly outlined choruses.
Only a small proportion of the cantatas hitherto discussed
are devoid of such numbers. It need hardly be said—for it
is evident from the descriptions given above—that a variety
worthy of Bach is to be found in them; at the same time—
and this is characteristic of this group of cantatas—the
freely invented choruses are decidedly the more numerous
class. The chorales for chorus which occur in the cantatas,
"Du wahrer Gott und Davidssohn," "Christ lag in Todesbanden," "O Ewigkeit, du Donnerwort," "Du sollst Gott
deinen Herrn lieben," "Liebster Gott, wann werd ich
sterben," "Gottlob, nun geht das Jahr zu ende," and in a
few other places, are beyond a doubt thoroughly thought-out
subjects, some of them very grand, and each and all such
as Bach alone could compose; nor must it be forgotten that
the final chorus of the first portion of the Passion according
to St. Matthew is also to be attributed to this period. But
when we set them all in the scale against the mass of
independent choruses written at the same time, we see at
once that Bach's inclinations tended towards the latter.
Their form varies, but on the whole the fugue is evidently
preferred to any other, and is often prefaced by an *adagio*.
It is highly significant as indicating Bach's attitude of mind
towards the chorale that there are among these cantatas,
some—and these by no means unimportant ones—in which
a chorale is altogether wanting ("Christen ätzen diesen
Tag"), and not a few in which it plays quite a secondary
part. Bach found in Leipzig a public which next to Kuhnau,

preferred Telemann's music above all other. Telemann's
strength lay in a certain style of brilliant chorus, superficially
graphic and highly effective to the general public from its
obvious and picturesque imagery. Now, though Bach may
never have thought of taking him for a model in this, still,
the tendency of popular taste, which he had already taken
into account in his examination cantata, may have been an
incentive to him to occupy himself chiefly with the composition of independent choruses, while he did not disdain
to copy with his own hand a piece written for Advent by
Telemann. There are indeed features in his choruses and
solo pieces which have a certain air of Telemann about
them; this is most conspicuous in the cantata, " Herr Gott
dich loben wir." But we have also seen that he derived
something from Kuhnau, and once made use of a composition
by Vetter that had become popular. This open mind as
regarded the works of his contemporaries and his anxiety to
learn from them as much as possible, or at least to show his
respect for them, and through them for the public, is a trait in
his character which has not till now met with due recognition,
though it is as characteristic of his art as of his nature.

VI.

BACH'S CANTATAS—(CONTINUED).

WE are now entering on the year 1728, and approaching the
period when the work was written which to all appearance
Bach himself valued most highly among his sacred compositions. We must however defer (as he did) giving our
attention to the Passion according to St. Matthew, and must
first occupy ourselves with the church cantatas composed
between this and 1734. It may here be pointed out, however,
that this great work must have prevented the composition of
any other church music, at any rate after the last months of
1728; all the more so since for the new year of 1729 he had
to compose the music for the great mourning ceremonial at
the obsequies of Prince Leopold von Anhalt-Cöthen, and to
conduct it at Cöthen in person. It is therefore no wonder

that we can only indicate one single cantata which may be attributed with tolerable certainty to 1728 : " Wer nur den lieben Gott lässt walten," for the fifth Sunday after Trinity. In this again we find clear tokens that Picander must have written the text, though it is true that it is not to be found in the cycle of cantata texts which Picander began on the Feast of St. John the Baptist, which fell immediately before the fifth Sunday after Trinity in 1728. Still, such poems were not invariably written solely with a view to composition, and still less with the idea that they would one and all be set to music and performed within that same year.[468] Besides this, Bach exercised considerable influence over the poet who for a long time lived in his immediate neighbourhood ;[469] it never occurred to him to set everything Picander put into rhyme as soon as it was written, and he expected something more than the details to be adapted to his wishes; no doubt he generally sketched the foundation lines of the purport and feeling of the whole. The cantata " Wer nur den lieben Gott " affords an instance in support of this. It is not wholly devoid of reference to the Gospel for the day, but its general tendency leads us tolerably far from it. Bach, in the first place, desired to make Neumark's consolatory hymn the central point of a composition, and Picander has used all the seven verses for the text; the first, fourth, and last, in their original form. He also preserved the words of the fifth, and almost all those of the second, only he has woven in with them recitatives in madrigal form, and he has dealt freely with the meaning of the third and sixth, though he has preserved some of the original phrases. The attitude taken up by Bach with regard to the separate verses of the melody is precisely analogous. In the sixth, a few fragments of the tune are incidentally introduced into a soprano air (bars 23-25, 28-30, 35-37, and again 31-32 in diminution) ; the tenor aria, for which the third verse is used, reminds us generally of the chorale by the retention of the verse form, and besides this, at the beginning of each section of the

---

[468] See on this point Appendix A., No. 45.

[469] In the Burgstrasse; see Das jetzt lebende und florirende Leipzig, 1736, p. 14; 1746-47, p. 11.

verse, reminiscences of the corresponding parts of the melody are brought in transposed, the first time into the major key. Verses three and six are given to a solo voice which alternates between the long-drawn phrases of the chorale tunes and the more animated lines of the recitative. The rest of the stanzas give us the chorale form complete; the last verse being a simple four-part subject; the fourth is on the model of the Pachelbel organ chorale—the soprano and alto singing counterpoint motives to the lines of the melody, which is at the same time played by all the instruments, and the first is set to a modified form of chorale fantasia.

Such an undeviating reference to the same chorale melody throughout a whole work has only once before come under our notice, in "Christ lag in Todesbanden." But the difference is evident at a glance. We there meet only with regular church chorale forms; however great their freedom and variety of treatment, a strict *Cantus firmus* is present throughout. Here, on the contrary, the chorale appears as the general starting point of personal devotion. This is not the case however in all the numbers, for the fourth and seventh verses are within the strict limits of congregational feeling; but the rest express a frame of mind which strives to give to religious consolation a form that may answer to subjective needs. In each the chorale serves only as the nucleus—the motive and incentive to the aria, but in such a way as that this motive is not concealed, but must be felt and understood by the hearer, or the piece will fail of its due effect. In the recitatives to each line of the melody appropriate reflections are added, by which means the chorale as a whole is dissevered and lost; for in the bass recitative all its parts are not even brought in, and in the tenor recitative each line appears in a different key. Even in the opening chorus this character is plainly discernible. If the form of the chorale fantasia was to be successfully transferred to the chorus and orchestra, their relations had in the nature of things to be so adjusted that the delivery of the independent tone picture which expounds the fundamental feeling of the chorale should be given to the instruments, while the chorus filled the rôle of *Cantus firmus*. This could

be effected in various ways, for instance, by a simple four-part
treatment, but contrived in such a manner as that some of
the parts give out the calm flow of the melody, while others
surround it with more rapid figures, in the course of which
they may, of course, sometimes approach or coincide with
the parts given to the instruments; it is only necessary to
maintain the general principle of contrast. In the present
instance we see that, irrespective of the independent instrumental accompaniment, the voices prelude each line with an
introductory subject in which they have a fugal arrangement
of the line that follows. The impression produced is that
the subjective sentiment, after having first dwelt upon the
meaning of each separate line, rises to the level of the lofty
general feeling of a congregation of worshippers. I confess
frankly that I find it difficult to comprehend and enter into
this chorale chorus, as a whole, but the composer's purpose
does not seem to me to admit of a doubt. It need scarcely
be pointed out that the musical character of the cantata is
thus throughout contemplative. The fervency which pervades each separate portion of it acquires from this a
peculiar colouring which is most easily and plainly discernible in the beautiful and touching aria in E flat major. In
Bach's time musicians had already begun to write compositions in the grand style for household worship.[470] Although
the cantata "Wer nur den lieben Gott lässt walten" was
used as church music, in feeling it borders on the domain of
private devotion. As his letter to Erdmann tells us, and as
is proved by the large number of various kinds of instruments which he possessed, Bach had musical performances
in his own house. It is very possible that he conceived and
composed this cantata more with a reference to this than for
its church purposes.

So far as we can judge from our present knowledge of
Bach's church music, he composed music to nine of the
cantata texts by Picander which first appeared in 1728-29.
Four of these he probably wrote in 1731, the other five I
assign to 1729 and 1730, of which years no cantatas can

---

[470] For instance, Telemann in his Harmonisches Gottes-Dienst, Hamburg, 1725.

be proved to exist excepting a few pieces for festivals, while a considerable number remain of the following years. A Christmas Cantata, " Ehre sei Gott in der Höhe," survives only in a fragment,[471] but the chief part of it was transferred to a later piece composed for a wedding ceremonial.[472] The alto air " O du angenehmer Schatz " is one of those lovely cradle songs, one of which we have already met with in the cantata " Tritt auf die Glaubensbahn."[473]

We have a cantata for the New Year which is remarkable for a dignified and powerful fugue at the beginning with this theme :—

Gott, wie dein Name, so ist auch dein Ruhm bis an der Welt En - de.

However, Bach seems to have set aside this cantata in an unfinished state, and not to have worked it up till a later period when he added a soprano air from the cantata " Der zufriedengestellte Aeolus " and the final chorale from the New Year's piece " Jesu nun sei gepreiset."

A cantata for the third Sunday after Ephipany, " Ich steh mit einem Fuss im Grabe "—" With one foot in the grave I stand "—is full of the solemnity of death, and at the same time of believing expectation. It opens with a symphony which proceeds in the style of the first adagio of a chamber sonata. This is immediately followed by an aria in the form of a chorale quartet, in which the soprano delivers the chorale " Machs mit mir Gott nach deiner Güt "—" Do with me, Lord, just as Thou wilt "—other words in " madrigal " form being added by the tenor—a highly poetic composition from the sinking motion and halting rhythm of the contrapuntal parts.[474]

---

[471] In the possession of Herr Professor Epstein. See App. A., 46.

[472] B.-G., XIII.,[1] No. 3.

[473] See Vol. I., p. 560.

[474] I only know this cantata through a score by Franz Hauser, who found the parts in the Thomasschule in 1833; they are no longer there. It was probably composed in 173?, and, if so, was first performed on January 22, 1730. In 1729 Bach would have been too busy with the mourning music; and in 1731 there was no third Sunday after Epiphany.

The cantata for Quinquagesima Sunday, "Sehet, wir gehen hinauf nach Jerusalem"—"Behold, we go up to Jerusalem"—is no less meritorious. In every portion of it the affinity to the Passion music (St. Matthew) is conspicuous, it is full of the same sentiment that pervades that work. The cantata begins with the same words as that for Quinquagesima of 1723: "Jesus nahm zu sich die Zwölfe"—"Jesus called unto Him the twelve"—and the words in which Christ declared to His disciples His approaching passion. Here too they are set to an expressive arioso which derives its peculiar character from a wandering motive in the bass; recitatives for the alto carry on the feelings called up by the Bible words. A very beautiful and softly flowing chorale trio on the sixth verse of Gerhardt's Passion hymn "O Haupt voll Blut und Wunden"—"O Thou whose head was wounded"—an indescribably pious and deeply felt Bass aria "Es ist vollbracht das Leid ist alle"—"It is finished, Thy pain is over"—and the simply set chorale "Jesu deine Passion"—"Jesus, Lord, Thy Passion"—with a short recitative for tenor, constitute the remainder of this cantata, which though of no great extent is very beautiful, and exhibits to the full the genius of Bach.[475]

The music for the third day of Easter, "Ich lebe, mein Herze, zu deinem Ergötzen"—"I live, O my heart, for thy joy and thy gladness"—is one of the freshest and brightest of the master's works; the bass aria "Merke, mein Herze, beständig nur dies" is full of swing, and even has something dance-like about it; we almost fancy we can see sturdy and happy figures dancing in the spring. Like the two preceding cantatas, this one also is written for solo voices only, not counting the usual final closing chorale in four parts.[476]

---

[475] The autograph is wanting. A MS. copy by Christian Friedrich Penzel, Cantor of Merseburg, who was foundation boy at St. Thomas' from 1751 to 1756, is in the possession of Herr Joseph Hauser, of Carlsruhe.

[476] This work is known to me only from a recent MS. in Zelter's collection. In this the chorale "Auf, mein Herz, des Herren Tag" and a chorus "So du mit deinem Munde bekennest Jesum" are introduced before the opening duet.

We now may go on to the cantatas of the years 1731 to 1734, and will first consider those compositions which again are based on Picander's series of texts. The cantata for Septuagesima " Ich bin vergnügt "—" I am content "—(for Jan. 21, 1731, or Feb. 10, 1732), occurs in Bach's composition in an altered form, which Picander himself arranged however. In this delicately treated composition we find, what rarely happens with Bach, that it is set throughout exclusively for a soprano voice. We shall learn when speaking of another cantata " Ich habe genug "—" I have enough "— which belongs to this period, that this was done with special reference to Anna Magdalena Bach, and that the piece was actually written for her ; for it was at this time that Bach's household band and singers, of which his wife and children were the mainstay, were in the prime of their powers. Anna Magdalena had kept up her practice as singer in the Church services, and she had never appeared in public in any other way since, from being a court singer at Cöthen,[477] she had become Sebastian's wife.[478] Still, she exercised her talents in private music, and her husband took care in his compositions to give her the opportunity. The cantata " Ich bin vergnügt " has more distinctly the stamp of music for domestic performance than the former one. It is only by supposing that Bach had this purpose immediately in view that we can explain the modification made in the text, in which the original arrangement is exactly preserved, and almost the same ideas are worked out ; and it is of the same length. But, excepting the final chorale—which is the last verse of the hymn " Wer weiss, wie nahe mir mein Ende "—all the phrases in which God is directly addressed are altered or omitted. The whole, as

There can be no doubt as to the genuineness of the chorale, but I have serious hesitation in accepting the chorus : the mode of working out the melody and the fugue is not Bach's, but more like Telemann. From these two pieces at the beginning, the cantata is sometimes designated by the first lines of them ; see Mosewius, J. S. Bach in seinen Kirchen-Cantaten und Choralgesängen, p. 21, where they are assigned to the first Easter day, or to Easter generally.

[477] That this had been the case is proved by a notice found in the Baptismal register of the Cathedral Church of Cöthen, of Sept. 25, 1721.

[478] See Gerber, Lex., I., cap. 76.

it stands, is a devout meditation culminating in the chorale as a prayer.[479]

The cantata for the second day of Whitsuntide, "Ich liebe den Höchsten von ganzem Gemüthe"—"I love Thee, my Saviour, with all my affection"—(May 14, 1731, or June 2, 1732), begins with a symphony borrowed from the first subject of the third Brandenburg concerto,[480] which Bach has enriched with much art by the addition of two horns and three oboes. Such an application of secular music to church purposes was not new to him; we have already seen an attempt made in this direction in the Weimar cantata "Der Himmel lacht" and "Gleichwie der Regen."[481] At this time, when he was acting as director of the Telemann Musical Union, it must have seemed to him a very obvious course, and we shall soon meet with several instances of it. In this cantata we have no complete chorus, but in the aria for bass "Greifet zu! Fasst das Heil, ihr Glaubenshände"—"Grasp and hold. Hold it fast, it is salvation"—we have a composition of the highest class. The accompaniment is given to violins and violas in unison with a figured bass. The ritornelle is in two sections: a broad melody of four bars—

and a more animated and vigorously marked subject of eight bars; from these materials—figuring on the one hand the blessings of divine grace, and on the other the eager reception of it through faith—the whole air is developed. The four-bar melody is taken up by the voice part, but occasionally the instruments are employed, and a splendid effect is produced where here and there they come in unexpectedly with the air in a rich body of sound; or again, as in bar 94, follow the voice in canon. In the recitative which precedes it we observe that Bach has left three lines without music; the first of the omitted lines is exactly like

[479] B.-G., XX.,¹ No. 84. App. A., No 46.

[480] See ante, p. 133.

[481] See Vol. I., pp. 541 and 492.

the first of those that follow, so that here we probably have merely an oversight due to haste. Bach often went hurriedly to work on recitatives and arioso passages; of this we find an interesting example in the arioso of the cantata "Gottlob, nun geht das Jahr zu Ende."[482] He here wrote the words under an empty stave and without any repetitions; when he did this he was not yet quite clear as to the music he should set it to, for when he set to work to compose it he scratched through, shifted the words, and added repeat-marks until the text fitted the music.[483] In the Michaelmas cantata, "Man singet mit Freuden vom Sieg," Sept. 29, 1731, the Saturday before the Nineteenth Sunday after Trinity, we have again a complete chorus; this is not a new composition but taken from the Wiemar cantata "Was mir behagt ist nur die muntre Jagd," the secular cantata which he had composed for such a very different purpose, and which he had also utilised for the church cantata "Also hat Gott die Welt geliebt."[484] Here it forms the finale, set in F major, and it must be admitted that the music is admirably suited to the fifteenth and sixteenth verses of Psalm cxviii.

A comparison of the revised form with the original is highly instructive and interesting, as it always is in such cases with Bach, although we cannot say that the remodelling has been very thorough. It is transposed into D major, the horns are exchanged for trumpets, a third trumpet and a drum are added, some sections are enlarged, the parts are worked out rather more briskly, and certain alterations have resulted from the new text and the new key; finally, towards the close we have a very effective *unisono* in the chorus, and this is about all. The stroke of genius lies in the keen perception which discerned in the old piece its fitness for the new purpose. Bach, however, had at first intended to compose an altogether new chorus to the verses of the Psalm. The beginning of this exists on a sheet of paper which he afterwards made use of for a secular cantata. This cantata, called "Der

---

[482] B.-G.,[1] p. 266.

[483] The original score and parts of the cantata "Ich liebe den Höchsten" are in the Royal Library at Berlin. See App. A, No. 46.

[484] Vol. I., p. 568.

Streit zwischen (the contest between) Phöbus und Pan," was composed in 1731, and it is from it that we know the date when this Michaelmas cantata was written. It is clear that other occupations caused Bach to leave this sketch for the chorus incomplete, and that then, when pressed by time, he fell back on an earlier work.[485] Among the solo subjects the soprano aria in A major, "Gottes Engel weichen nie," is remarkable for its sweetly melodious and gently floating character. The last number but one, too, a duet between alto and tenor with bassoon obbligato, is as artistic as it is expressive, with its penetrating but simple treatment of the melody; it is in G major, and the final chorale is in C major. As this cantata, like the former Michaelmas cantata "Es erhub sich ein Streit," turns entirely on the desire that the angels may bear the souls of the departed to the abode of the blessed, the persistent descent towards the subdominant has undoubtedly been meant by Bach to have a mystical and poetical significance, and it does in fact produce that effect. The last chorale consists of the third verse of Schalling's hymn "Herzlich lieb ich, o Herr" ("Ach Herr, lass dein' lieb' Engelein")[486]

The fourth cantata on the remaining text by Picander: "Ich habe meine Zuversicht"—"I have a perfect confidence"—is for the twenty-first Sunday after Trinity, Oct. 14, 1731, or perhaps Oct. 29, 1730. The composition is interesting because it is the first among those composed in Leipzig in which an organ obbligato is introduced; this, indeed, could not be done before 1730, since it was not till that year that the *Rückpositiv* of the organ of St. Thomas' was fitted with a manual of its own, and so could be used independently of the great organ. The cantata "Ich habe

---

[485] This sketch is also in D major; the trumpet begins:—

Of the voice parts only the first note of the bars is written with the word " Man " under it. The score of " Phöbus und Pan " exists in the Royal Library at Berlin.

[486] The autograph of this cantata is not known to exist. A copy by Penzel is in the possession of Herr Joseph Hauser, of Carlsruhe.

meine *Zuversicht*" was intended to be introduced by the clavier (or violin) concerto in D minor,[487] which underwent a special re-arrangement for this purpose. A similar use made of chamber music has already been mentioned in "Ich liebe den Höchsten." The fact that the whole concerto is placed at the beginning, and not merely a movement from it, reveals an intention of letting the congregation hear to full advantage the improvement in the organ; and we may infer from this that the cantata must have been performed in 1730, immediately after the alterations in the *Rückpositiv*, but we do not know exactly when they were finished. The obbligato organ is silent during the first air, but in the second it combines with the alto voice in a trio of conspicuous beauty.[488]

As soon as Bach found himself enabled to introduce the organ obbligato in church music we find him using it tolerably often. He arranged older cantatas for it, as " Erschallet ihr Lieder"; but he also composed several new ones with an organ part *concertante*. In a few of these—as in the one just discussed—he adapted chamber compositions for instrumental symphonies. This is evidently the case in the cantata for the twelfth Sunday after Trinity, " Geist und Seele wird verwirret "—probably August 12, 1731.[489] Though the instrumental symphonies of the first and second sections are neither of them extant in their original form, we can detect that they have been transferred to the cantata from the fact that here they are written in fair copy.[490] In form they constitute the first and third movements of a concerto, and the middle movement Adagio may have been the A minor aria, a Siciliano such as Bach has used for the middle of a concerto in other cases besides this. A clavier concerto in E major has, between two allegro subjects, a Siciliano in C sharp minor.[491]

[487] B.-G., XVII., No. 1.

[488] See App. A., No. 47.

[489] B.-G., VII., No. 35. See App. A., No. 46.

[490] Only a fragment of the first movement is preserved in the original form. It is B.-G., XVII., p. xx.

[491] B.-G., XVII., p. 45.

This concerto too has been utilised for church music, and in all its movements. The two first are included in the cantata for the eighteenth Sunday after Trinity, " Gott soll allein mein Herze haben," Sept. 23, 1731, or Oct. 12, 1732; the first, transposed into D major, and enriched by the addition of three oboes, being the introductory symphony. The vocal piece that follows is Arioso in 3-8 time, interspersed with recitative in common time. In the following aria, D major common time, the obbligato organ comes in again; this, however, is a perfectly new composition. On the other hand, in the second aria, in B minor, 12-8, the Siciliano of the concerto undergoes a remodelling and extension (from thirty-seven to forty-six bars) which is stamped with genius. The voice part, which begins as follows :—

Stirb . .   in   mir, . .   stirb . .   in   mir, Welt   . .

is newly inserted.[492]   A recitative and the chorale " Du süsse Lieb schenk uns deine Gunst " (the third verse of Luther's hymn, " Nun bitten wir den heiligen Geist ")

---

[492] The editor of the concerto in the B.-G. edition has failed to detect the relationship between this air and the Siciliano of the concerto. After pointing it out it is hardly possible to regard his assertion as accurate, that the cantata is the earlier and the concerto the later work, B.-G., XVII., p. xv. So much as this is, at any rate, self-evident, that the E major concerto could not well have preceded the cantata as it now stands, even allowing for such simplifications as the different nature of the organ would demand. The melody of the B minor air, in spite of all the mastery displayed in it, gives us too closely the impression of a supplementary composition for us to think it possible that the whole number, as we find it in the cantata, is in its original form, and that it was subsequently simplified for the concerto. A middle course, which relieves us from this dilemma, is afforded by the supposition that the clavier concerto in E major now exists complete only in a later re-arrangement, as can be proved to have been the case with the D minor concerto, and that, in adapting it for the cantata, Bach followed the original casting of it. Such an earlier form of the Siciliano exists, and is to be found B.-G., XVII., p. 314. There can be no reason for doubting that the first six bars of the clavier part of the older form were filled up by pauses, since here the clavier has only the accompaniment in figures, which would sound badly on the organ. In later years Bach collected his clavier concertos in a volume, and may probably have remodelled this one at that time. See App. A., No. 48.

conclude the work. It may be assumed that in the A minor air of the cantata "Geist und Seele" we have a similar case of adaptation, with all the more reason because the resemblance in structure of the two cantatas is obvious at a glance; it extends even to the vocal melodies made use of, since both are for an alto voice, only the final chorale is wanting. We meet with the last subject of the E major concerto in the cantata for the twentieth Sunday after Trinity, "Ich geh und suche mit Verlangen,"[493] which must, therefore, have been written in the same year as the former one, and have been performed for the first time only a fortnight later. It here forms the introductory symphony, and is filled out by the addition of an *oboe d'amore;* but with respect to the solo part it is treated more simply, which must be partly ascribed to the different conditions of the organ. In the course of the work the obbligato organ plays its part in newly composed and engrafted pieces, some of these being solos for the soprano or bass voices, some dialogues for the two, as representing the Soul and Jesus. The cantata includes no chorus. However, in the last piece for the soprano we hear the final verse of the chorale "Wie schön leucht't uns der Morgenstern," while the bass sings, in a vein which may almost be called fervid, this paraphrase of Bible words :—

Dich hab ich je und je geliebet,	From all eternity beloved
Und darum zieh ich dich zu mir.	I, loving thee, have longed for thee.
Ich komme bald	Now, lo! I come
Ich stehe vor der Thür,	And say " prepare for me,
Mach auf, mach auf, mein Aufenthalt!	Open thy heart to be my home."

A stringed quartet with *oboe d'amore* and organ concertante complete this highly significant picture.

I have already mentioned, in another place, that Bach, who when he conceived his three violin sonatas was quite as much possessed by the feeling of the clavier or the organ as by that of the violin, subsequently re-arranged them in fact as clavier and organ pieces.[494] He adopted

---

[493] B.-G., X., No. 49.
[494] See ante, p. 80.

the same course with the prelude to the suite for violin
alone, in E major; he has transposed it for the organ to
D major, and furnished it with an orchestral accompaniment
of strings, two oboes, three trumpets, and drums; and in
this state it forms the instrumental symphony to the Rathswahl cantata performed on Monday, Aug. 27, 1731, "Wir
danken dir Gott, wir danken. dir "—" We thank Thee, Lord
God, we thank Thee, Lord."[495] Though this is a less remarkable work than the transformation of a clavier solo into a
clavier concerto for the clavier, violin, and flute, with a
stringed orchestra (see Vol. I., 420), this symphony nevertheless sets Bach's powers of combination in a very clear
light.   As in a clavier concerto with orchestra there must
be a special instrument for the figured bass to be played
upon, so, usually, when Bach uses an organ obbligato in
church music, the great organ is also introduced to support
and connect the whole.   In the cantata " Wir danken dir
Gott" this certainly cannot invariably have been the case,
for it was performed twice again (Aug. 31, 1739, and in
1749) in the church of St. Nicholas; during the performance
of Divine service on the occasion of a change of council,
and the organ there had no independent *Rück-positiv*.[496]
The symphony has a festal and lively character, and
leads up very fitly to the cantata, which gives expression to
gratitude towards God in gushing songs of triumph, and
solemn, majestic choruses, emphasizing this feeling rather
than the occasional purpose of the composition. The
principal chorus is on the words from Psalm lxxv., and
we must take this verse—" But I will declare for ever; I
will sing praises to the God of Jacob "—as the starting
point of the sentiment of the whole great work.   Bach

---

[495] B.-G., V.,[1] No. 29. W. Rust, in B.-G., V.,[1] p. xxxii., and B.-G., VII.,
p. xxvii., expresses an opinion that the violin prelude was arranged from the
symphony.   But this is contradicted plainly by the circumstance that the violin
suites were completed long before 1731 (See App. A., No. 4).   The date of the
performance is given from the documents of the Leipzig Rath "concerning
the Rathswahl (election of councillors) 1701."

[496] A. Dörffel has noted the first repetition, Musikalisches Wochenblatt.
Leipzig, 1870, p. 559.   The second we know of from a text-book of 1749
accompanying the autograph score.

works out two themes in fugue, one after the other, without their ever coalescing to form a double fugue. On the contrary, the response always follows in artistic stretto movement, which beyond a doubt—as in the cantata " Sie werden aus Saba alle kommen" (see ante p. 217)—was founded on a dramatic feeling.[497] The first of the two themes is formed on an ancient type of the old church chorale, of which Handel also made extensive use.[498]

Hardly two weeks later, September 9, 1731, Bach must have conducted a cantata for the sixteenth Sunday after Trinity, in which again an organ obbligato is introduced: " Wer weiss, wie nahe mir mein Ende"—" Who knows how near my end is?"[499] In this we find no revised chamber composition; the alto aria accompanied by organ obbligato and *oboe da caccia* is a perfectly fresh invention.[500] If we are not altogether deceived, Bach's hand is also to be traced in the text, which is recognisable as a modified version of a poem by Neumeister. The words set by Bach are as follows:—

Willkommen! will ich sagen,	When Death shall come to call me
Wenn der Tod ans Bette tritt.	I will hail him as a friend,
Fröhlich { folg ich / will ich folgen } in die Gruft,	When he leads me to the tomb
Wenn er ruft.	I will come.
Alle meine Plagen	Still shall pain and grieving
Nehm ich mit.	Go with me ;
Willkommen! will ich sagen,	When Death shall come to call me
Wenn der Tod ans Bette tritt.	I will hail him as a friend.

[497] The indication of the time suggests a somewhat quick *tempo*. Bach says in his Generalbasslehre ch. iv., that the way of indicating a (rapid) tempo in common time by a 2, was used by the French in pieces which are to go quickly and gaily, and the Teutons have imitated it from the French. So that he himself felt that he had but imitated the French in this matter. See App. B., XII., Cap. 4.

[498] See Chrysander, Handel I., p. 393.

[499] B.-G., V.,1 No. 27. See App. A., No. 48.

[500] In the B.-G. edition it has escaped notice that in the score the aria has the title *Aria à Hautb. da Caccia e Cembalo obligato*. On the other hand, on the autograph organ part we find *Organo obligato*, and on the cover for the parts, likewise in Bach's hand, *Organo oblig*. It is certainly surprising that the organ part is not transposed, but in E flat major. This was probably done to please any player who might perform the concertante part on the Cembalo, while Bach himself played at the performance in the church and transposed it at the time.

The metrical construction of the text is unskilful, and the expressions are awkward, since, if the tomb is to be considered as the longed-for goal of rest, the pains of the deceased cannot follow him thither; it is clear that the poet, in altering the verses, has only written what occurred to him as fitting the rhyme to "tritt"; Picander with his knowledge of form would scarcely have done this. But we find in the composition that expression, peculiar to Bach, of a fervent longing for death, reaching a pitch which, so far as my knowledge goes, is not to be discerned in any other work by Bach, whether earlier or later. The Gospel for the day refers to the youth of Nain, and it may be remembered that we spoke before of another cantata on the subject, for the same Sunday, "Liebster Gott, wann werd ich sterben." A more striking contrast than that between the two is scarcely conceivable. The older cantata is pervaded by a youthful sentiment, painful though sweet, while in the later composition we have the feeling of one who, having bid the "false world farewell," longs to depart. There can be no doubt that Bach made this strong contrast intentionally, for the finales of the two cantatas plainly show that when he wrote the later one he had the older one in his mind. The close of the first consisted of an air by Daniel Vetter; here we have a five-part composition by Johann Rosenmüller "Welt ade! ich bin dein müde." They were Leipzig musicians to whom Bach in this way paid a kind of homage.[501] The whole work is composed with the same devotion as the aria. In this frame of mind Bach was more at home than in any other. If we try to picture to ourselves what the most concentrated form might be of the feeling which lies at the base of the two Passion-musics, and of the funeral ode, we shall find that it is incorporated in this cantata. A token that Bach actually *lived in* the sentiment he embodied in this composition is to be found in certain points of resemblance to those greater works. Only one or

---

[501] Rosenmüller's composition is to be found in Vopelius, p. 947. Bach has reproduced it unaltered; a small difference in the sixth bar arose beyond a doubt from a slip of the pen. See Rust, B.-G., V.,[1] p. xxvii.

two need be here pointed out. 1st. The beginning of the
final chorus of the Passion according to St. Matthew on
the one hand, and on the other the beginning of the first
movement of the cantata, and again bar 66 of the bass
aria. 2nd. The motive for the two flutes in the first chorus

of the mourning ode and that for the

oboes in the first chorus of the cantata (from bar 13),

and the way in which it is worked

out.[502]   3rd. The first bar of the aria " Es ist vollbracht "—
" It is finished "—in the Passion according to St. John, and
bars 35 and 78 of the bass aria in the cantata.   Still, the
whole speaks even more clearly than the details.

Bach must have been so greatly pleased with the effects
of the organ concertante that his inventive genius found more
and more ways of turning it to account.   For the sixth
Sunday after Trinity, probably of 1732 (July 20), he wrote a
solo cantata for an alto voice, " Vergnügte Ruh, beliebte
Seelenlust "—" Contented rest, with sweet and heart-felt
joy "—in which he introduced an obbligato organ subject for
two manuals, as an accompaniment to the second aria.   This
however has to be performed on the great organ : all is subsidiary to the figured bass, and violins and violas in unison
have the lowest part.   This most original combination led
to the production of a composition which is not only remarkably artistic, but also deeply emotional ; and it stands
among worthy surroundings, for the whole cantata is one of
the most beautiful of its kind.[503]

---

[502] The mourning ode was worked up again for the Passion according to St.
Mark, and was then first performed in 1731.

[503] See App. A., No. 48.—The autograph score is in the Royal Library at
Berlin.   There also is a later recension of the work (from Fischhoff's bequest)
in which the cantata is transposed from D major to C major.   Besides this
the first movement alone remained intact : it is followed by a new recitative,
and then by a great final chorus, which is none other than the opening chorus
of " Herz und Mund und That und Leben " in ¾ time, and with slightly altered
text.   I know not for what occasion this recension was made, nor, consequently,

It happened at this time that Bach had become sickened with the trivial rhyming of the "madrigal" cantatas, on which for nearly ten years he had been almost incessantly engaged, and begun to yearn for stronger poetic diet. The old Protestant church hymns supplied him with what he required. Consequently, he occupied himself in the musical treatment of a number of the best sacred verses of the sixteenth and seventeenth centuries. He had already made use of the whole of the words of the hymn in the Easter cantata " Christ lag in Todesbanden"; and in " O Ewigkeit, du Donnerwort," and " Wer nur den lieben Gott," he had used a part of a hymn. But in these cases he had always worked up the melody side by side with the words, by which those works were rendered quite distinct from the group of cantatas now to be characterised. In these Bach adopts the text of the hymn rather as a mere poem on a sacred subject, to serve him as the germ from which he may develop an independent composition. He does not wholly ignore the melody proper to the hymn; on the contrary, these cantatas always include at least one movement in which it appears in its fullest form, but they also contain others in which it is almost or altogether set aside. Johann Adam Hiller, one of Bach's successors in office in Leipzig, says: " Old and new spiritual songs have also been treated as cantatas by certain composers; I confess that this kind of composition seems to me one of the fittest for church use, only the composer should refrain entirely from the use of recitative. Recitative has none of the characteristics that are proper to this kind of song, no symmetrical periods, no lines of perfectly equal length, no jingle of rhymes, and it is therefore extremely displeasing when we hear four-lined verses, for instance, which rhyme line for line, delivered in recitative."[504] Since the works of the great cantor were at

---

whether Bach was the originator of this transformation. It is quite possible that he was, for, since the cantata " Herz und Mund " was used in Leipzig for the feast of the Visitation, the amalgamated work may have been performed in 1742, when the Visitation (July 2) followed immediately upon the 6th Sunday after Trinity (July 1).

[504] Hiller, Beyträge zu wahrer Kirchenmusik. Zweyte vermehrte Auflage. Leipzig, 1791, p. 7.

hand, we cannot doubt that these words were aimed at him. But what he blames—namely, the treatment in recitative of verses of hymns—Bach has certainly not avoided, any more than he thought proper to adhere to the rules laid down in 1754 by the Musical Society of Leipzig as to the construction of cantata texts, although he was a member of the society. Hiller's reflections were justified, however; the madrigal form in sacred texts had been retained principally for the sake of the recitative. It is clear that Bach's chief object was to have texts of fuller meaning to work upon, but it never occurred to him to give up any part of the musical form. As his style of recitative differed essentially from that in common use, he had no need to consider that the poetical and musical forms were in perceptible contradiction to each other.

He composed two hymns of the sixteenth century in the cantata form of his time. The paraphrase of Psalm xxiii. written by Wolfgang Musculus, " Der Herr ist mein getreuer Hirt "—" The Lord my faithful shepherd is "—was adopted for the second Sunday after Easter, and was first performed on April 8, 1731, or April 27, 1732.[505] The hymn " Ich ruf zu dir, Herr Jesu Christ "—" On Thee I call, Lord Jesu Christ "—was arranged for the fourth Sunday after Trinity, July 6, 1732.[506] The setting of the fine hymn by Johann Olearius, " Gelobet sei der Herr, mein Gott, mein Licht, mein Leben "—" All praise to Thee, O Lord, my God, my life, my glory "[507]—for Trinity Sunday, 1732. Joachim Neander's hymn, written in 1679, " Lobe den Herren, den mächtigen König der Ehren "—" Praise ye the Lord, the Almighty King of glory "—was composed for the twelfth Sunday after Trinity; it may have been performed for the first time in 1732, on August 31.[508] Paul Flemming's hymn, on the

---

[505] B.-G., XXIV., No. 112. P. 1682. See App. A., No. 46.

[506] The autograph score in the Royal Library at Berlin has these words written at the end, " Il fine SDGl. ao 1732." The original parts are in the Library of the Thomasschule at Leipzig. See App. A., No. 44.

[507] The original parts are in the Library of the Thomasschule, and a copy by Penzel, dated 1757, is in the Royal Library at Berlin. See App. B., No. 48.

[508] The original parts are in the Library of the Thomasschule. See App. A., No. 46. This cantata, and " Lobe den Herren meine Seele " (see ante, p. 407),

occasion of starting on a journey, "In allen meinen Thaten,"
written in 1633, was set by Bach in 1734, but for what
particular event is not known.[509]   Martin Rinckart's hymn
"Nun danket alle Gott" (1644)—"Now thank we all our
God"—and one by Jacob Schützen, "Sei Lob und Ehr dem
höchsten Gut" (1673)—"All praise and glory be to Thee"—
have also no trace of any special occasion or purpose.   It
can only be said, as regards the date of their composition,
that this must have taken place at about the time we are
now considering, while Johann Heermann's "Was willst du
dich betrüben" (about 1630)—"Why art thou so dejected?"
—and Rodigast's "Was Gott thut, das ist wohlgethan"
(1675)—"That which God doth is still well done"—appear
to be of later date.[510]   It is common to all these cantatas
to begin a grand chorale in chorus treated in the form of a
chorale fantasia.   In "Nun danket alle Gott" only, this
form has been so far altered that freely invented subjects
for the chorus introduce and interrupt the treatment of the
chorale and come in again as a finale.   In the cantata
"In allen meinen Thaten" the chorale fantasia assumes
the aspect of a French *ouverture,* and the chorus is built
into its fugal allegro with admirable art.   This piece
reminds us perceptibly of the opening chorus of "O Ewigkeit, du Donnerwort," which, however, we concluded we
must assign to an earlier period.

The finale chorales display a greater variety—they sometimes appear as simple four-part compositions; in "Lobe
den Herren," and in "In allen meinen Thaten" they are
expanded and made splendid by the addition of three
independent instrumental upper parts; again, we have them

---

were evidently connected with the change of Council.   The twelfth Sunday
after Trinity in 1732 was the first after St. Bartholomew's day, when the
change by rotation commonly took place, so the service for the occasion was
performed on the 25th.

[509] B.-G., XXII., No. 97.   P. 1674.   See App. A., No. 49.

[510] "Sei Lob und Ehr," B.-G. XXIV., No. 117.   P. 1690.   "Was willst du
dich betrüben," B.-G., XXIII., No. 107.   P. 1685.   "Was Gott thut, das ist
wohlgethan," B.-G., XXII., No. 100.   P. 1669.   "Nun danket alle Gott," is in
the original parts, in the Royal Library at Berlin, unfortunately not complete.
See App. A., No. 44.

in the chorale fantasia form; or, as in "Gelobet sei der Herr" and "Was Gott thut," they are treated in a manner which reminds us of Böhm, a certain phrase being given to the orchestra and repeated after each line, besides being played with the lines when possible. But, excepting in the opening and final movements, the melody of the hymn recurs only twice in its complete form—namely, in the second and fourth verses of "Lobe den Herren"; in the latter instance it is given to a trumpet concertante. In most other cases no heed is given to it at all; this is the case throughout the cantatas "Der Herr ist mein getreuer Hirt," "Ich ruf zu dir," "In allen meinen Thaten," the rest of the verses serving simply as a text for independently invented arias, duets, and recitatives; often, too, the composer has indulged in a whimsical sporting with the melody, allowing it to come out now more strongly and then more softly. In this way Bach developed a new phase of church music. Up to this time we have not met with anything like it, excepting a slight example in the cantata "Wer nur den lieben Gott," and I there pointed out its æsthetic importance.[511] From the musical point of view, the Suites offer us something analogous, where the beginning of each dance of the series has a certain connection with that of the Allemande. The florid opening phrases commonly have reference to the first line or the first two lines of the chorale. For example:—

Chorale Melody.

Ge - lo - bet sei der Herr, mein Gott, mein Licht, mein Le - ben.

Third aria of the Cantata.

Ge - lo - bet sei der Herr, mein Gott, der e - wig le - bet.

---

[511] The resemblance to the chorale "Nun danket alle Gott" in the Rathswahl cantata "Preise Jerusalem" (see ante, p. 364), need not be dwelt upon, as this chorale occurs nowhere else in the cantata. Its only meaning is a symbolic or poetical one.

Chorale Melody.

Was Gott thut, das ist wohl - ge - than.

Fourth verse of the Cantata.

Was Gott thut, das ist . . wohl-ge - than.

In the cantata " Lobe den Herren " the melody—

Lo - be den Her - ren, den mäch - ti - gen Kö - nig der Eh - ren

is once transposed into the minor, and worked out as a duet, thus :—

Lo - be den Her - ren, der künst - lich und fein dich be - rei - tet.

In the fifth verse of " Sei Lob und Ehr," which begins with a recitative, we come suddenly on a phrase which is directly connected with the first four notes of the melody :—

Sei Lob und Ehr dem höch-sten Gut

the bass imitates it, and an arrangement grows out of it which reminds us vividly of the chorale treatment of Bach's early time.[512] But other lines besides the first are sometimes touched on lightly, and, as it were, in passing by; in this respect the fourth verse of " Was Gott thut " is worthy of attention. In verse five of " Was willst du dich betrüben," which begins with a very ingenious fantasia on the first lines, and then develops it freely as an aria, it occurs that at the close the last line of the chorale comes in quite unadorned and simple, as though the fancy of the composer had sunk back to its source. Again, the second verse of " Nun danket alle Gott " is formed on a free

---

[512] See Vol. I., p. 214.

utilisation of the chorale melody in such a way as that it is heard throughout this grand and wonderfully brilliant work, sometimes full and clear, and sometimes veiled in sound.

Meanwhile the master must have been fully aware that this method of dealing with the hymn and chorale had its objectionable side. Though he continued during several years to return to it from time to time, still a glance at his later works as a writer of cantatas reveals that we must regard those that have now been described as the creations of a period of transition or digression, outside and beyond which lay a still more perfect type. Even during the first Leipzig period we come upon a few works in which the form is already plainly discernible, which became to Bach in his latter years the very ideal and type of the church cantata. In these, too, a hymn with its appropriate tune forms the nucleus, but the hymn text is not made use of for airs or recitatives, nor, on the other hand, is the hymn tune sacrificed to fanciful embellishments. On the contrary, words and compositions which, though independent, are developed out of the church hymn, are used to serve the more personal emotion which is aroused by the congregational feeling; the chorale preserves its unapproachable and unalterable nature, though it still pervades the whole as a unifying power, even where neither the original words nor the original music are to be heard.

Very closely approaching to this ideal form is the magnificent composition which Bach prepared for the twenty-seventh Sunday after Trinity of 1731, November 25. This Sunday, as is well known, but rarely occurs in the ecclesiastical year; and for this reason, and because of its poetically and mysteriously solemn Gospel, Bach felt himself prompted to compose for it a creation of the very highest order. Nicolai's three-verse hymn "Wachet auf, ruft uns die Stimme"—"Wake, arise, a voice is calling"—has, with just feeling, been selected as the basis of the work; this has an obvious connection with the Gospel story of the ten virgins (Matthew xxv., 1—13), and it leads on and up to the beatific contemplation of the Song of

Solomon and of the Revelation of St. John, chap. xxi.[513]
Between the stanzas are inserted recitatives and dialogues
between Christ and the Bride, duets of the highest art,
which breathe of chaste fervency without ever trenching
on the domain of personal passion.   The three verses of
the chorale are precisely at the beginning, middle, and end,
and figure the mystical tone that pervades the whole work,
and which is required by the ideas of the solemn silence of
the night when the Heavenly Bridegroom is looked for, and
the unspeakable joys of the glory of the New Jerusalem.
The first verse is a chorale fantasia : this motive—

which comes in on the fifth bar, infuses a feeling of mysterious
bliss into the majestic rhythm of the orchestra, and this
feeling overflows again and again in happy and expressive
passages.   The soprano has the melody, while its dramatic
purport is indicated by the other voices in figures of wonderful significance.   In the second verse, which is a trio for
tenor voice, violins, and bass, the mystical sentiment is most
fully brought out.   It is like the dance of souls in bliss,
swaying to and fro with a strange and mysterious expression
on the low notes of all the violins— all Zion and the faithful
have passed with Christ into the joys of the heavenly
banquet.   The last verse, in which " Gloria, mit Menschen
und Engel-Zungen "—" Glory, with tongues of Men and
Angels "—is sung, appears in unadorned simplicity.   The
splendid melody has here once more an opportunity of
producing its effect by its own beauty.

The cantata " Was Gott thut, das ist wohlgethan," of
which I spoke above, is, so far as its opening and final
subjects are concerned, only an extended and embellished
remodelling of earlier pieces.   The closing movement occurs
in, the cantata " Die Elenden sollen essen "—" The poor

---

[513] The cantata, the original parts of which are preserved in the Thomasschule
Library, is as yet published only in Winterfeld, Evang. Kirchenges., III ,
Appendix, p. 172 ff, and in P. 1691.   On the date of composition, see Appendix
A., No. 44.

shall eat and be satisfied"[514](1723). The first movement—but in a simpler form—also introduces a work which may have been written two or three years earlier, about 1733. (?) It repeats the type of the cantata "Wachet auf" in a somewhat simpler development, making use of only two verses of the chorale. We find them at the beginning and at the end in the same form as in that cantata, and between them come a number of vocal movements in "madrigal" form.[515] A third composition beginning with the same chorale must have served for the twenty-first Sunday after Trinity, and have been performed for the first time October 21, 1731, or November 2, 1732.[516] It contains only one verse of the chorale, which is at the beginning and set in the form of a chorale fantasia; still the instrumental tone-picture is not in the first instance strictly homogeneous, and during the first section of the tune it has more of the character of a ritornel. In the remainder of the work the chorale melody is nowhere used again, not even at the close, for the cantata ends in a bass aria. Hence it is imperfect as to form, a mere sketch which has never received the final touches; even the separate movements are inferior to the other two cantatas in musical value. A cantata for the sixth Sunday after Trinity, on the other hand, "Es ist das Heil uns kommen her"—"Now is salvation come to us"—gives us perfect satisfaction by its masterly completeness and fulness of form. If similarity in the aspect of details is any evidence of a similar period of composition—and with Bach this is certainly the case—this cantata must have been written in the same year as "Wachet auf"—viz., 1731. Only the first and twelfth verses of Paul Speratus' hymn are used and placed at the beginning and end of the work, while between them, among other pieces in madrigal form, an admirable duet in canon finds a place; but the treatment of the first verse resembles that of the first verse of "Wachet auf" in a surprising degree; particularly in the two-part imitations,

---

[514] Composed in 1723. See ante, p. 355.

[515] B.-G., XXII., No. 99.   P. 1670.

[516] B.-G., XXII., No. 98.   See Appendix A., No. 48.

and partly in the accompanying rhythm of the instrumental subject.[517]

A new and deeply thoughtful composition for the sixteenth Sunday after Trinity (probably September 28, 1732) "Christus der ist mein Leben"—"Christ, who is my life"—must be mentioned in this place, although as to form it hardly belongs here. It begins with a chorale chorus on that hymn, but besides this three chorales are used in it, all among the most beautiful and best known funeral hymns of the Protestant church. By this means the sentiment of the cantata, poetical and musical alike, is enhanced to powerful intensity; still, we cannot fail to observe an absence of unity. The importance of the chorale in Bach's cantatas is different and greater than what could arise merely from the combination of a well thought-out poem with a fine melody; it has to serve as the common centre for the more subjective arias and recitative. It is even justifiable to introduce a different chorale at the end from that with which the cantata opens; in such cases the feeling is developed from the starting point of the strictly church sentiment in such a way as that it returns again to that narrow and confined province of religious art. It can only prove a disturbing element when, instead of this one starting point, two or three are taken. We know how Bach could revel in images of mortality and death; he has here again given the reins to this sombre mood, and has gone so far in the first chorale chorus as entirely to destroy the proportions of the four lines of the chorale by a long extension for the sake of the word "Sterben"—"Dying." The way in which this chorus passes into the solo without any musical break is very delicate and imaginative; first into an arioso, then a recitative, which is immediately followed by a fresh chorus in the simple style of Pachelbel, on the words "Mit Fried und Freud ich fahr dahin"— "With joy and peace I pass away." The third chorale "Valet will ich dir geben"—"Farewell to thee addressing" —is treated as a trio, and it is impossible to overlook its

---

[517] B. G., I., No. 9. P. 1281. See Appendix A., No. 44.

affinity with the chorale trio in "Wachet auf." At the close comes the fourth verse of the hymn " Wenn mein Stündlein vorhanden ist "—" When my last hour is close at hand." [518]

Though from this time forth it became more and more firmly established that the first movement should assume the form of the chorale fantasia, still the craving for variety in Bach was sometimes so strong that he assigned the first place to other forms; this is the case with a piece written for the first Sunday in the year, January 4, 1733. In this the vocal portion associated with the instrumental work is in two parts only, the soprano singing the first verse of the chorale, "Ach Gott, wie manches Herzeleid "—" Ah ! Lord, how many a pang of heart "—while the bass sings against it in a fashion of its own, admonishing us to patience and endurance. The same kind of contrast is once more brought out musically in the final movement, which again is not a chorale fantasia, but a bass air, and the chorale is worked into it by the soprano voice. The text of this chorale consists of the second verse of Martin Böhm's hymn, " O Jesu Christ, meins Lebens Licht "—" O light of life, my Saviour dear "—while the melody is the same as at the beginning. From the character of alternate complaint and consolation which are worked into this cantata—though only in the principal movements—this work has been styled the *Dialogus*.[519] It did not remain alone of its kind ; Bach wrote another *dialogus* for the twenty-fourth Sunday after Trinity (probably November 23, 1732), in which the characters are " Hope" and "Fear." The bass alone appears as opposed to them, and we may suppose it to represent that " Voice from Heaven " which, in Rev. xiv., 13, utters the words here given to the bass to sing. The first movement is constructed in a way exactly analogous to that of the former cantata. The alto sings the melody " O Ewigkeit, du Donnerwort "; this, however, is not repeated at the close, where we have Joh. Rudolph Ahle's expressive aria " Es ist genug" in a four-part setting.[520]

---

[518] B.-G., XXII., No. 95. P. 1673. See Appendix A., No. 50.

[519] B.-G., XII.,² No. 58. P. 1195. See App. A., No. 48.

[520] B.-G., XII.,² No. 60. P. 1285. See App. A., No. 51.

We have now done with the chorale cantatas, and, before
concluding, must glance briefly at a group of church pieces
which are based entirely, or chiefly, on free invention.   In
most of these a text from the Bible has supplied the poetical
motive, and in accordance with the custom which was
general, and which Bach himself by his practice acknowledged as well-founded, the idea is usually embodied in the
chorus form.   Among these, two works stand pre-eminent.
First, a cantata for the tenth Sunday after Trinity (probably
July 29, 1731), " Herr deine Augen sehen nach "—" O Lord,
are not Thine eyes upon the truth ? " (Jer. v., 3)—belongs to
that class of works which I have ventured to designate as
orthodox compositions (see ante, p. 423).[521]   If Picander
compiled the text he must have surpassed himself; in the
recitative, it is true, the commonplace method prevails,
but the airs have a strict metrical structure and vigorous
phraseology.   Besides the text for the principal chorus,
another passage is quoted from Rom. ii., 4-5, while Picander
usually contented himself with one Bible text.   Since Bach
was planning an exceptional work of art he may, perhaps,
for once have stirred up his colleague to unwonted vigour,
while in the cantata " Schauet doch und sehet "—" Behold,
now, and see "—he revels in insatiable lamentation as if he
desired to do full justice to the words of the prophet, " Mine
eye runneth down with rivers of water for the destruction
of the daughter of my people " (Lam. iii., 48-49).   He here
appears as the ardent, almost fanatical, preacher of repentance.
As usual, the first chorus gives the key to the prevailing
sentiment; it is arranged in a masterly and quite new way.
A prelude expresses in a connected whole the principal ideas
which afterwards and separately form the basis of the chorus,
transposed in various ways.   We often meet with this
method of procedure in Bach, but it is astonishing to find
two elaborate fugue subjects interwoven in the working out.

---

[521] It is one of the many services rendered by Rust to have restored this
cantata to its original form; previously it was only known to the general public
through the edition of A. B. Marx, Kirchenmusik von J. S. Bach, No. 2, Bonn,
Simrock.   It is now published B.-G., XXIII., No. 102,   P. 1679.   See App. A.,
No. 48.

Their themes—

and

are of extraordinary boldness and overwhelming energy, and it is impossible to overlook the oratorio-like stamp of this stupendous chorus. It is conspicuous in the aria and in the bass arioso, often rising almost to dramatic energy. The tenor aria is characterised by certain peculiarities of form. The text is as follows:—

Du allzu sichre Seele	Thou all too boastful spirit
Erschrecke doch!	Be dumb with fears,
Denk, was dich würdig zähle	Remember the due merit
Der Sünden Joch!	Of sinful years!
Die Gottes-Langmuth geht auf einem Fuss von Blei,	Though God's long-suffering may linger with foot like lead,
Damit ihr Zorn hernach dir desto schwerer sei.	'Tis only that His wrath may crush thy guilty head.

The first of these lines was not graphic enough for the vein of agitation which Bach desired should predominate throughout this cantata; he therefore began on the second, and with a musical phrase which paints terror with emphatic significance. The aria offers us one of those cases—rare in Bach—where the principal musical thought, which is introduced as a prelude in the ritornelle, remains throughout conspicuous in the instrumental part, and hardly appears at all in the voice part. The chief melodic phrase

---

522 The objections raised by Hauptmann to the passage in bars 37—44 have been removed by Rust, who refers it to the general plan of the whole; still, it cannot be denied that there is something strange in the anticipation of the words "Du schlägest sie," &c.—" Thou hast stricken them but they felt it not; Thou hast plagued them but they amended them not"—which, besides, are not once treated separately with the expression which they suggest.

here seems to have been devised to give us the words in
their right order—

(Du allzu   sichre   See- le,   er - schrecke   doch!)

and if this suggestion is the right one, this aria is an
instructive example of the way in which, to Bach's mind,
the vocal and instrumental aspects of a work presented
themselves as an inseparable unity.

The other cantata, which I rank as equal to this one, is
based on the words of Psalm xxxviii., 3. Its purport is
much the same as that of the former cantata, and we now
must imagine that the repentance, preached with such
fervency in that, has penetrated and filled the soul of the
sinner. "Es ist nichts gesundes an meinem Leibe," &c.—
"There is no soundness in my flesh because of Thine anger;
neither is there any rest in my bones because of my sin"—
is his cry.[523] The chorus is a double fugue, complete in
itself, and full of contrite expression. From bar 15
onwards, the four-part chorale "Ach Herr mich armen
Sünder"[524] is given out at regular intervals by the flutes,
cornet, and three trombones, and is heard through the
fugue, which in parts is accompanied by particular phrases
on the strings. The four-part subject is equally complete in
itself, and, like the fugue, might be performed independently
with a satisfactory effect; nevertheless, the two bodies of
sound amalgamate as if they had grown from one and the
same root. The depth of the effect produced when the sacred
penitential hymn comes in, sung, as it were, by invisible
voices above and beyond the abased multitude entreating
from the dust, is indescribable and unfathomable. It appears
in augmentation in the instrumental bass before each
couplet of the first section of the tune.

---

[523] B.-G., V.,[1] No. 25. P. 1650. See App. A., No. 44. The water-mark is
distinguishable only on the wrapper of the original parts.

[524] No other hymn can possibly be intended. The melody also belongs, as
is well known, to the words "O Haupt voll Blut und Wunden"—"O Thou
whose head was wounded."

Even now all is not told. The two themes of the fugue are derived from two lines of the chorale—the former from the second and the latter from the first. The way in which this is done serves to remind us of the construction of the melody of the cantata, which is founded on the entire text of a church hymn; for this reason it appears to me probable that the cantata " Es ist nichts gesundes" belongs to the same period—and that a limited one—as this. The composition evolved out of all these musical and poetical motives is extremely remarkable and unique in its way. The movement "Es ist der alte Bund," out of the cantata "Gottes Zeit" (see Vol. I., p. 457), cannot be compared with it, because in that the chorus subjects appear rather as mere interludes in the chorale; but here we see the forms borrowed from the chorale fantasia and transferred to the chorus and orchestra in an inverted position: the chorus fulfils the duty of the instruments, and a body of instruments takes that of the chorus. It is neither a freely worked-out chorus on a Bible text, nor is it a chorale chorus; it is something compounded of the two and superior to each, which we vainly strive to comprehend. A beautiful bass aria with an instrumental bass independently worked out, full of character, brings the overwhelming conception of the first movement home to the personality of the hearer; this air still lingers in the same domain of feeling, but it passes gradually into a consolatory vein, in which the work is brought to an end.

A brighter picture is put before us in the cantata for Ascension Day, " Wer da glaubet und getauft wird "[525]— "He that believeth and is baptised." In the principal chorus two melodies are worked out in contrast—one broad and calm, and the other animated and eager; they are treated throughout under the same conditions as are displayed in the beautiful bass air of the Whitsuntide cantata " Ich liebe den Höchsten " (see ante, p. 444). Even the poetic sentiment is the same, and the two cantatas must belong to about the same period. The particularly *singable* chorus

---

[525] B.-G., VII., No. 37. P. 1693.

is associated with a rich six-part accompaniment, and the whole body of sound has a very splendid and ample effect, while the words of the Gospel, " Go forth into all lands, and preach the Gospel to every creature," are delivered in an animated rhythm that flows fully and freely onwards. In the middle we have a two-part chorale—the fifth verse of " Wie schön leuchtet der Morgenstern " ; the lines extended by *melismata* are given out now by the soprano and now by the alto, with imitations in the other parts, while in the bass a characteristic episode is wrought out of the first line of the chorale.

A very remarkable chorus opens a cantata for the twenty-first Sunday after Trinity, " Ich glaube, lieber Herr "— "Lord, I believe; help Thou mine unbelief " (Mark ix., 24).[526] It expresses the sentiment of doubt and wavering in a way which is as unmistakable as it is masterly, for the parts wander about separately and, as it were, aimlessly, and only combine into compact figures now and then, and for a short while. The same idea is given by other means in the tenor air, of which the text serves to give us the key to the meaning of the chorus. Here we have a chorale fantasia at the close, on the seventh verse of " Durch Adams Fall ist ganz verderbt."

The cantata on the words from Psalm xcvii., 11-12, " Dem Gerechten muss das Licht "—" Light is sown for the righteous, and gladness for the upright in heart "—was written neither for a Sunday nor a festival, but for a betrothal. It has a superlatively festal and brilliant stamp, and reminds us of the style of the cantata " Lobe den Herrn meine Seele," of the year 1724. It opens with a couple of splendid fugues (in common time and 6-8), in which, as in some few cantatas of the early Leipzig period, the fugal treatment is begun in a small chorus and is gradually transferred to the great chorus.[527] The closing chorus, which is homophonic, is broad and powerful, and between them

---

[526] B.-G., XXIII., No. 109. P. 1686. See App. A., No. 44. The water-marks do not occur in the autograph score, but are very plainly in the original parts.

[527] See ante, p. 187.

stands a bass aria in the Lombardic style,[528] so-called, combining a flow of melody which reminds us of Italian grace with a conspicuously festive character. A wealth of warmth hangs over the whole work, which, however, in its present form can hardly be regarded as in its original state, since it must have resulted from a revision of a composition which belongs indeed to the very earliest Leipzig period.[529] The history of its origin seems to have been the same as that of the funeral cantata " Herr Gott, Beherrscher aller Dinge," which, in part at least, is founded on an older Rathswahl cantata, " Gott, man lobet dich in der Stille," and, in part, on an adagio from the violin sonata in G major.[530] The alliances which have arisen between different works of Bach, through remodelling and transferring, are often extremely intricate. The Rathswahl cantata just mentioned must, to all appearance, have also served as the second Jubilee cantata for the centenary anniversary of the Augsburg Confession, June 26, 1730, and may finally have been once more worked up into the form in which we now have it for its original purpose. The Bible text, Psalm lxv., 1, is not here set for a chorus—this seems to have been prohibited by the purport of the words—but as an alto solo, of which the florid character most expressively conveys the feeling of festivity. The principal chorus follows, on words in madrigal form.

It may here be observed that the triad of Jubilee cantatas of which Bach conducted the performance on three successive days in 1730[531] are to be traced to earlier works from which they have been remodelled. The first, " Singet dem Herrn ein neues Lied "—" Sing to the Lord a new song "—is the New Year's cantata for 1724,[532] and the third " Wünschet Jerusalem Glück "—" Wish thou joy to Jerusalem "—is a Rathswahl cantata for August 25, 1727, which was

---

[528] See Vol. I., p. 419.

[529] B.-G., XIII.,[1] p. 3. P. 1662.

[530] B.-G., XXIV., No. 120. Compare B.-G., IX., p. 252 ; also ante, p. 117 ; and see App. A., No. 52.

[531] See ante, p. 243.

[532] See ante, p. 386.

repeated on a similar occasion, August 18, 1741 ;[533] this, and the piece in the original state, have both been lost. There is yet a fourth re-arrangement which we may assign to 1730. The assertion is no doubt well founded that in this year the celebration of the Reformation festival was considered of special importance and kept accordingly ; and it is evident that the cantata " Ein feste Burg ist unser Gott "—" A stronghold sure is our God "—must have been intended for some such extraordinary solemnity.[534] Bach took the music he had composed at Weimar to " Alles was von Gott geboren "—which, as it was intended for the third Sunday in Lent, he had not yet been able to use in Leipzig—and he added new movements to the first and fifth numbers. These are chorale choruses on the first and third verses of Luther's hymn. The bold spirit of native vigour which called the German Reformation into being, and which still stirred and moved in Bach's art, has never found any artistic expression which could even remotely compare with this stupendous creation. The first number, including 228 bars, is in the Pachelbel form, excepting that the *Cantus firmus* is carried on in canon by the trumpet and the instrumental basses; it stands up like some impregnable giant fortress. The second chorus, No. 5, is a chorale fantasia with episodical treatment of the first line of the tune ; the whole chorus sings the *Cantus firmus* in unison, while the orchestra plays a whirl of grotesque and wildly leaping figures, through which the chorus makes its way undistracted and never misled—an illustration of the third verse (" Und wenn die

---

[533] With a few omissions and additions, see Nützliche Nachrichten von Denen Bemühungen derer Gelehrten, &c., p. 82, Leipzig, 1741.

[534] B.-G., XVIII., No. 80. P. 1012, and in English translation published by Novello. See Vol. I., p. 641. It is certainly possible that this cantata may have been written for the year 1739, with reference to the Jubilee of the two-hundredth anniversary of the adoption of the Evangelical doctrines in Saxony. The service took place in the principal churches on Whitsunday, May 17, but by express order without any special ceremonial. The University commemorated this event on August 25 ; Görner had composed a Latin ode for the purpose ; see Gretschel, Kirchliche Zustände Leipzigs vor und während der Reformation im Jahre, 1539, p. 292. Leipzig, 1839.—It will be presently shown that the Reformation cantata " Gott der Herr ist Sonn und Schild " was composed neither in 1730 nor 1739.

Welt "—" If all the world with friends were filled ")—as grandiose and characteristic as it is possible to conceive.[535]

Before quitting the subject, there are two other revised arrangements of chorales, of which we can only say that they seem to have been brought out about this time—that is to say, about 1730. Bach made use of his beautiful serenata written at Cöthen, " Durchläuchtger Leopold," for a cantata for the second day of Whitsuntide ("Erhöhtes Fleisch und Blut"), and for the same purpose turned the final duet into a chorus.[536] The birthday cantata for the Princess of Anhalt Cöthen he adapted for the first Sunday in Advent, enriching it with two admirable arrangements of the chorale " Nun komm der Heiden Heiland " and two simpler chorales. One of these arrangements is a chorale fantasia with a *Cantus firmus* given to the tenor. In the other, on the contrary—a rare occurrence with Bach—the chorale tune is treated in the manner of a motett, line for line, for a soprano and an alto. We are here reminded of the beautiful two-part chorale subject in the cantata " Wer da glaubet und getauft wird "—" He that believeth and is baptised "—but the development is more completely worked out in the Advent cantata.[537]

When words from the Bible were used for solo songs, the established form was the bass arioso, and, in general, Bach did not deviate from this practice. Still, his observance of it was often merely superficial—that is to say, he avoided the designation *aria*, but actually wrote pieces of music which must be regarded as independent arias. This is the case with the solo of the cantata " Herr, deine Augen sehen nach dem Glauben," which bears the title *Arioso ;* with the solo in the Rathswahl cantata "Gott man lobet dich in der Stille," which has no designation at all, and which is exceptionally given to an alto voice, and again with the song which opens a cantata for the twenty-second Sunday after

---

[535] The cantata was published about 1822 by Breitkopf and Härtel, of Leipzig, and was the first engraved and published after Bach's death. Rochlitz gives a section to the subject (Für Freunde der Tonkunst, Vol. III., p. 229).

[536] See ante, p. 7, and App. A., No. 44.

[537] B.-G., VII., No. 36. P. 1292. See ante, p. 158.—See App. A., No. 44.

Trinity "Was soll ich aus dir machen, Ephraim "—" How shall I give thee up, Ephraim?" (Hosea xi., 8). On the other hand, the introductory solo of a cantata for the fifth Sunday after Trinity, "Siehe, ich will viel Fischer aussenden"— "Behold, I will send forth many fishers" (Jerem. xvi., 16)— is simply entitled an aria. Both these works belong to this period, still the exact date of composition can only be given with any approach to certainty in the case of the second (July 13, 1732).[538] From the fact that the solo arias are among the most beautiful that Bach ever wrote, we can see that he must have worked at them with the devotion due to the sacred text on which they are founded. They have certain peculiarities of form which are not always accounted for by the structure of the text. The cantata " Siehe, ich will viel Fischer aussenden," which is altogether a very remarkable work, contains two such solo pieces on Bible words. The second begins with two bars, common time, in G major, as introductory, while the remainder is in D major. The first consists of two grand pieces in D major and G major, but the whole cantata is very remarkable as regards the arrangement of the keys and the distribution of the orchestral accompaniments. But in this instance there is no covert meaning to be found in the singularity. The peculiar feeling which finds expression in the first movement will have due justice done to it, in connection with a similar phase of sentiment, when we have occasion to discuss a portion of the Passion according to St. Matthew.

These two last cantatas are, with the exception of the closing chorales, mere solo cantatas. We still have to add to them a few of the same kind, which are however composed to madrigal poems : "Ich armer Mensch, ich Sünden- knecht "—" I, wretched man, the child of sin ! "—for the twenty-second Sunday after Trinity (October 21, 1731, or November 9, 1732), "Ich will den Kreuzstab gerne tragen "— " How gladly will I bear the cross ! "—for the nineteenth

---

[538] B.-G., XX.,¹ Nos. 88 and 89. As to the former, see App. A., No. 48; to the latter, No. 44. The watermark is only distinguishable in the horn part. This cantata cannot have been composed in 1733, because in that year the Reformation festival fell on the twenty-second Sunday after Trinity.

Sunday after Trinity (October 7, 1731, or October 26, 1732),[539] "Jauchzet Gott in allen Landen"—"Sing to the Lord in every land"—for the fifteenth Sunday after Trinity,[540] and, finally, "Ich habe genug"—"I now have enough"—for the Purification (1731 or 1732).[541] The cantata "Jauchzet Gott," a fiery solo cantata for a soprano voice, has no connection with the Epistle or Gospel for the day, it passes into a chorale fantasia on "Nun lob, mein Seel, den Herren," and closes it with a Hallelujah subject fugally treated. It must have been intended properly for some other occasion which we can no longer even guess.[542] A somewhat sombre feeling is common to the other three cantatas, and all three bear the stamp of having been composed by Bach at the happiest period of his mature powers and fullest contentment. If one of them is inferior to the others it is "Ich armer Mensch," in which the succeeding movements are not quite worthy of the first aria with its fervent and contrite emotion. In the other two the glowing and thoroughly dignified character of the texts particularly deserves to be pointed out. The expressive passage, at the close of the first aria in "Ich will den Kreuzstab," stands out in beauty, both of rhythm and melody, like a sigh of deep happiness after final relief, and it returns with wonderful effect at end of the last recitative. This evidently was never intended by the author: it is Bach who here has once more outdone the poet. We also trace an unmistakable poetical purpose in the scheme by which the work is made to die away with the sixth verse of the chorale "Du O schönes Weltgebäude" on the subdominant of the principal key.

The music for the Purification is based on the prevailing sentiment of the hymn of Simeon. It is interesting to

---

[539] B.-G., XII.,[2] Nos. 55 and 56. The second is P. 1664, see App. A., No. 44.

[540] B.-G., XII.,[2] No. 51. P. 1655. See App. A., No. 44.

[541] B.-G., XX.,[1] No. 82, P. 2149. See App. A., No. 46.

[542] The indication *et in ogni tempo* shows this. The text was altered at a later date, see B.-G., XII.,[2] p. 9. From the alterations in the first aria we might conclude it was intended for the festival of Michaelmas, according to this it may have been repeated in 1737, when St. Michael's Day and the fifteenth Sunday after Trinity fell on the same day.

compare it with the earlier cantata "Erfreute Zeit im neuen Bunde" (see ante, p. 390), as showing us how Bach could conceive of the same sacred occasion from two such different points of view. In the former the flow of feeling is cheerful and hopeful of life ; in this it is weary, and happy only in the contemplation of approaching death. The aria "Schlummert ein, ihr matten Augen "—"Close in rest, ye weary eyelids"—expresses this sentiment with indescribable beauty. This cantata was originally composed for Anna Magdalena Bach ; then the master arranged it for a mezzo-soprano or alto voice, and finally for a bass. With reference to its use in church, the last must be considered the most proper, since the text is a paraphrase of Simeon's words, and the connection with the Gospel for the day is thus made most obvious from the musical point of view ;[548] but it was no doubt really intended for sacred chamber or domestic music. It is very significant that Bach has expressly designated this a *cantata*, which he never did with his church music, properly so-called.

This brings me back to a circumstance already touched upon. A vein of feeling which points rather to family than to congregational worship is conspicuous in certain works of the middle Leipzig period. It is evident in the cantata " Wer nur den lieben Gott lässt walten," and it could only be this which prompted the master—quite contrary to the practice of both his earlier and his later years—to introduce into some of his cantatas the whole of certain church hymns, but with the different portions of the chorale tune modified with the utmost ingenuity, while giving them an entirely new musical connection. Formerly, he had dealt with the chorale as with a dogma from whose impeccable unity it was permissible to borrow portions—that was strictly orthodox ; now he merged it in subjective emotion—this was proper to the spirit of private worship. Naturally, this would find expression principally in the form of solo song. Bach had already written many solo cantatas at an earlier time ; but, with the single exception of the Weimar cantata, " Ich weiss, dass mein Erlöser lebt," in not one of them

---

[548] See App. A., No. 53.

could it be pointed out that one and the same voice was to perform the whole piece. This constitutes an essential difference, for by the mere fact of several voices taking part in the same subject—even though it be only one after the other—the subjective feeling is abstracted from the expression of the sentiment. In the cantatas of the middle period it was to a certain extent different.

The first which can be called a solo cantata in the strictest sense of the word, since only one voice is employed in it, was the Septuagesima cantata "Ich bin vergnügt" —" I am content "; and that this was in the first instance intended for private use seems very clear from the alterations made in the text. By degrees, seven others were added to it, among which the composition " Ich will den Kreuzstab" was actually marked by Bach himself as *Cantata à Voce sola è stromenti* ; it is striking, too, that a considerable number of them (" Geist und Seele," " Gott soll allein mein Herze haben," and " Vergnügte Ruh ") are written for an alto or mezzo-soprano voice. We also find three for a soprano (" Ich bin vergnügt," " Jauchzet Gott," and " Ich habe genug "), the last being also arranged for alto and for bass. If we may suppose that the soprano cantatas were composed in the first instance for Bach's wife, the alto cantatas were perhaps intended for his daughter Katharina, of whose proficiency as a singer her father himself bears favourable testimony. Besides the arrangement of " Ich habe genug," we meet with only one cantata for the bass and one for the tenor—" Ich will den Kreuzstab " and " Ich armer Mensch." But I do not believe that these can have been all the compositions written at this period. Three pieces certainly come into the same category : one a composition for a soprano voice for the twenty-third Sunday after Trinity, " Falsche Welt, dir trau ich nicht "— " World so false, I trust thee not "—which has, as an introduction, the first movement of the first Brandenburg concerto, just as the cantata " Ich liebe den Höchsten " has the first movement of the third Brandenburg concerto;[544] an

---

[544] B.-G., XII.,[2] No. 52.

alto cantata for no special occasion, " Widerstehe doch der
Sünde "—" Stand and fight against temptation "[545]—as well
as the well-known beautiful aria for an alto voice, " Schlage
doch, gewünschte Stunde "—" Haste to strike, oh, longed-
for hour "—in which I believe the style of Franck is to
be detected in the text.[546] It is self-evident that this
aria cannot have been intended for church use, for there
is no part of the service where it could have been introduced; it is too short for the regular church music, which
had to last from twenty-five to thirty minutes, and the text
is not suited for any extraordinary occasion of mourning.
It may be regarded as certain that Bach, though as
much inclined as ever to introduce a musical imitation
of the sound of bells, would never have brought a real
bell into the church to produce the effect, while in the
family circle no one would have objected.[547] All the
other cantatas for solo voices may have been used in
divine service; this would no more have been a breach
of good taste than the adaptation of secular cantatas to
church purposes. It has already been said that Bach's
style was penetrated throughout by a spirit of sacred
feeling and that it remained sacred, in a certain sense, even
when he meant to be secular; but within these broad limits
we can detect many subtle differences by which Bach
certainly distinguishes his secular music from what he wrote
originally for church use, and such distinctions also exist
between that and those compositions which give rise to the
comparisons here drawn.

[545] B.-G., XII.,[2] No. 54. This work is inserted in Breitkopf's list for Michaelmas, 1761, not under the heading of Church music, but at p. 10, under the
heading of " Smaller sacred cantatas and arias."

[546] B.-G., XII.,[2] No. 53. Also in Peter's " Alt-Album."

[547] In Breitkopf's list previously quoted, we find on p. 23, " Trauer-Arie:
Schlage doch gewünschte Stunde, à *Campanella*, 2 *Violini*, *Viola*, *Alto solo*,
Basso," and not "*Organo*." It is singular that this composition, which is so
undoubtedly Bach's, has no original warranty for his name; in Breitkopf's list
even there is no author's name. Forkel's opinion that the mention of the
Campanella of itself proves it to belong to a period when Bach's taste was
still imperfect is thus justified. Forkel, Uber Joh. S. Bach's Leben und
Kunstwerke, p. 61. Still, it is very certain that in its full and mature state it
is not a youthful work.

Moreover, the period, which in point of time fell about half-way in Bach's labours as a writer of cantatas, is also a middle stage in the character of his work; since here the different tendencies meet which, before and afterwards, we see the master following with remarkable distinctness and singleness of aim. Still, all such limitations have, of course, only a relative value, and require that we should allow them a certain elasticity and mutability. Even in this middle period we find cantatas with freely invented choruses on both Bible and verse text in considerable numbers, and in examples which for grandeur and profundity are inferior to no earlier works of the same character. But, by the side of these, the chorale cantata, properly so-called, is already conspicuous, and it was to this that in his later years Bach gave more and more preponderance. The years between 1727 and 1734 are the richest and most fruitful of Bach's life; this is amply proved by a consideration of the church cantatas only, and it will be fully confirmed as we study other domains, in which his inexhaustible genius laboured during the same period.

VII.

PASSION MUSIC BEFORE BACH.—THE ST. JOHN PASSION—THE ST. MATTHEW PASSION.

It has been customary, in investigating the history of Bach's Passion Music, to rest satisfied with referring its origin to a dramatic interpretation of the Gospels with a side glance at the oratorio and at the opera. But the matter is not so simple; many and diverse elements must have co-operated for the evolution of such creations as these, which we must admire as the culminating efforts of Protestant Church music.

The custom of singing the history of the Passion according to each of the four Evangelists on the four days of Holy week, seems to have been established in the church tolerably early in the middle ages. The object was to set the story as clearly as possible before the intelligence of the people, since the Latin words were understood by very few. One priest sang the narrative portion, a second the words of Christ, a third those of other individuals; while the utterances of the populace—the crowd or *turba*—were repeated by the choir. The Protestant church kept up this peculiar form of Passion service. Luther, it is true, considered it unnecessary that all four Gospel narratives should be sung, and attributed no particular importance to the performance.[548] Nevertheless Johann Walther, as early as in 1530, had composed the Passion according to St. Matthew and that according to St. John, with a German text for church use; the first being intended for Palm Sunday and the second for Good Friday.[549] The same composer, in 1552, arranged a Passion music in four parts to a German text compiled from the four Gospels.[550] In the course of the sixteenth century the German text of the Passion came into universal use by the Protestants. So early as 1559 we again meet with a St. Matthew Passion at Meissen;[551] in the year 1570 we find the first printed edition so far as is known;[552] others followed in 1573 and 1587.[553] From this the Passion performances must have continued in vogue in the Protestant churches throughout the seventeenth century. In 1613 Melchior Vulpius brought out a St. Matthew Passion; two Passions by Thomas Mancinus— St. Matthew and St. John—were published in 1620; in 1653 Christoph Schultz, cantor at Delitzsch, had a St. Luke Passion printed at Leipzig; and in Vopelius, Neuem Leipziger Gesangbuch, of 1682, we find Passions after St. Matthew

---

[548] Deutsche Messe und Ordnung des Gottesdienstes 1526. Vol. XXII., of Luther's collected works, p. 243, Erlangen Edition, by Heyder, 1833.

[549] O. Kade, Der neuaufgefundene Luther-Codex, p. 126. Dresden 1871.

[550] S. R. Eitner in den Monatsheften für Musikgeschichte, 1872. P. 59 of the Supplement.

[551] In a MS. in the Court Library at Vienna and which came thither from Meissen. Ambros, Geschichte der Musik, Vol. III., p. 416.

[552] Also according to St. Matthew, composed by Clemens Stephani, printed at Nüremburg. Chrysander, Händel, Vol. I., p. 427.

[553] In the hymn books of Keuchenthal und Selneccer: Winterfeld, Ev. Kir., Vol. I., p. 311.

and St. John.[554] And no less a musician than Heinrich Schütz treated the history of the Redeemer's sufferings in four compositions, after the four Evangelists, which still exist, though it is true only in MS.[555]

This custom continued in practice until late in the eighteenth century. In Leipzig, as has been already said (p. 273), the singing of the Passion music was first discontinued in 1766; but at Dosdorf, near Arnstadt, the cantor, Kramer, composed a work of this kind so late as 1735, and this exactly corresponds with the Passion text printed in the Arnstadt Hymn-book of 1745, above which it is stated that "in most of the districts and villages belonging here (*i.e.*, to Arnstadt) every year on Good Friday, it is customarily chanted *in stylo recitativo*."[556]

As to musical, form these Passions are so absolutely stereotyped that it would be difficult to imagine why they were printed so often and so often newly composed—if we may so call it—if it were not that the custom had struck such deep root into the life of the church. Almost all of them are in the transposed Ionic mode—F major. The separate voices recite the plain-song, and the phrases, which have very little melodic movement, resemble each other with scarcely any variation. The narrator — the Evangelist—has the tenor part, Christ sings in the bass; the remaining personages are represented by an alto voice, even Pilate's wife and the two maid servants; although as a rule, in the sixteenth and seventeenth centuries, the alto parts were sung by men. As an exception,

---

[554] I myself possess original impressions of the Passions by Vulpius and Schultz. Those of Mancinus appeared in the *Musica Divina* (Wolffenbüttel, 1620) and are reprinted in Schöberlein's Schatz des liturgischen Chor-und Gemeindegesangs. Pt. II., p. 362.

[555] They are to be found in a MS. copy in the Library at Leipzig, written probably about the end of the seventeenth century by Zacharias Grundig, the date 1666 on the title page of the St. Matthew Passion can at any rate refer only to this; for the St. John Passion, which is still extant in autograph, is dated April 10, 1665. See Chrysander, Jahrbücher für musikalische Wissenschaft, Vol. I., p. 172.

[556] Herr Stade, town cantor of Arnstadt, possesses the autograph of Kramer's Passion. The words of the Passion according to St. Matthew, here spoken of, are in the Arnstadt Gesang-Buch of 1745, p. 679.

we occasionally find these persons represented by a treble
solo, for instance, in the Passions by Walther, 1552, Schultz,
and Kramer.[557]   In the part writing rather more development and variety are to be found.   In some, even the *turbae*
are treated in such a simple style of pure recitation that
they could hardly claim to be called part music if some
more definite melodic phrase or characteristic series of
harmonies were not here and there observable.   Melchior
Vulpius makes the two false witnesses—whose words were
usually sung by the chorus in four parts—sing together in
two part imitation.   In very critical situations he repeats
the words several times.   When the people call for Barabbas,
the chorus repeats his name six times in a passionate
syncopated rhythm, and when they cry for the last time
" Crucify him," the choir divides into two parts, the lower
voices calling after the higher ones ; then they re-unite and,
whereas throughout the rest of the work a four part treatment prevails, we here have a setting in six parts.   The
same occurs in the corresponding passage in Schultz.   The
close commonly consisted of a short act of thanksgiving,
called *Gratiarum actio* ; and throughout these Passion compositions the Latin names of the persons were preserved
—a token of their early church origin—*ancilla, servus, Pilati
uxor, latro, centurio* or *miles.*

The words of the thanksgiving were " Thanks be to our
Lord Jesus Christ, who hath redeemed us from the torments
of Hell."   Even when the music was of corresponding
brevity this offered an opportunity for expressing a purely
lyric sentiment, which gave rise to the development of more
lavish musical resources.   In the seventeenth century, indeed,
these meagre words often proved inadequate for the utterance of fervid and eager emotion, and we find in their place
verses from hymns with a kind of motett setting, as in
Schütz ; or even an original verse in hymn form, as in a very
remarkable manner in Schultz.   The opening consisted, in

---

[557] I have not myself seen Walther's Passion ; in that the treble is said also
to sing the High Priest's part (see Eitner, Op. cit. p, 61), but I think there must
be some error here.

the same way, of a devotional chorus to correspond to the finale. For this the text would consist merely of the announcement "The sufferings of our Lord Jesus Christ, as they are declared to us by the holy Evangelist," or "The sufferings—sometimes the bitter sufferings—and death of our Lord Jesus Christ, according to the holy Evangelist," or to that effect. The importance of the announcement was intended to be emphasised by the choral singing. However, the introduction of the choir was not immutable either at the beginning or the end; it even occurred—as in the Leipzig St. Matthew Passion by Vopelius—that the beginning and end were in unison plain-song.

Music being generally introduced to grace the services of Passion week and to represent those events of the life of Christ from which they took their rise, this form could no longer be considered adequate so soon as music had reached a higher development. Consequently, at the earliest period of composition for several voices, side by side with the old plain-song Passion, there arose settings of the Latin texts which were treated throughout in the motett style, and in part writing. This style was also adopted by the Protestant composers with the words of the German Bible. The oldest German Passion music of this kind known to me is by Johann Machold, published at Erfurt in 1593.[558] In his preface the composer refers to a Passion by Joachim von Burck "which had been written a few years previously," and had served him as a model; that, therefore, must also have been in the motett style.[559] Machold composed the Passion according to St. Matthew, which Burck had not done, and lived in the hope that it might sometimes be performed alternately with Burck's, so as "not always to fiddle on one string." From this it may be inferred that

---

[558] In the Royal University Library at Königsberg. It is in five parts; the alto part is wanting to this copy.

[559] Walther, Lexicon, p. 119, mentions a German Passion by Burck, printed at Erfurt in 1550. As Burck was born in 1540 or 1541 this cannot be accurate. If for 1550 we read 1590 this would agree with the music alluded to by Machold. A Passion by Burck is said to exist in the Rathsbibliothek at Löbau.

such settings of the Passion had an established place in the
service as well as the plain-song Passion. The beginning
consists, as in these, of the chorus announcing the subject,
and at the end there is a hymn-subject on the words—

> O Jesus Christ, God's only Son,
> We humbly sue before Thy throne,
> That through Thy bitter cross and pain,
> Our souls may life and comfort gain.

No very high degree of artistic merit can be attributed to
Machold's unpretending work; but more can be said
for a St. John Passion in the same style, written in six
parts by Christoph Demantius, and brought out at Freiberg
in Saxony in 1631.[560] This also begins with the announcement "Hear the sufferings of our Lord Jesus Christ from
the Gospel of John the Evangelist," which plainly indicates
that Demantius contemplated not merely a setting of the
Gospel narrative, but actually a musical remodelling of the
old chanted Passion; the words "newly composed for six
voices" inform us of this.   The detailed character of the text
naturally precluded the broad motett treatment; the narrative portions are rapidly got over, the speeches of the
persons stand out in dramatic and animated phrases, in
which we find repetitions both of the text and of musical
subjects; still, solo singing is wholly excluded, and the
introduction of persons is indicated by smaller groups of
voices, the body of the chorus being divided.   The end,
here again, is a general reflection referring to the words in
John xix., 35, "We believe, Lord; do Thou give increase of
faith. Amen."

A Latin St. John Passion exists by Gallus, of 1587;[561] it
is composed in the same manner, and the consideration of
the works by Machold and Demantius naturally leads us
back to it. The subject matter is divided into three sections,
and the case is the same in the Passion by Demantius,

---

[560] A copy in the Church Library at Pirna; the bass part is unfortunately
wanting.

[561] *Secundus tomus Musici operis Authore Jacobo Händl. Pragae, Anno*
MDLXXXVII.   There is a copy in the University Library at Königsberg.
Compare Winterfeld, Joh. Gabrieli, Part II., p. 204.

indeed, the divisions occur at nearly the same passages; the first ends with the words of Christ "Why smitest Thou me?"; the second begins with the leading of Christ before Caiaphas and ends with the high priests' words "We have no king but Cæsar"; the third includes the crucifixion and death of Christ. It is to be observed that Machold's Passion is also in three sections, and, so far as the difference in the text allows, is divided at about the same places, so the assumption seems well founded that this was a form that had become established by custom; and though the number of German Passions in the motett form at present known to us is but small, we may, nevertheless, suppose that at one time they were in very general use, and the Passion by Demantius shows that this was not alone in the sixteenth century. It was the first method adopted for dealing musically with the history of the Passion, with all the means available at the period. As such it has an important historical interest, both as regards later church music and the oratorio.

As a middle stage between the chanted and motett forms of Passion music, we may mention those compositions in which the Evangelist's narrative and the speeches of Christ were alike recited in plain song, while all the rest were in parts. This form too—which was employed, among other Catholic composers, by Orlando Lasso and Jakob Reiner— found imitations among the Protestant musicians. To this class belong the well-known Passion by Bartholomäus Gese, written in the year 1588.[562]

Thus, we find three forms existing at the time when concerted church music found its way into Germany from Italy, and their elements are easily recognisable in the works of Heinrich Schütz, the greatest German Protestant composer of the seventeenth century. His "Seven words of Christ on the Cross" treats, it is true, only a section of the history of the Passion, still the work must be considered as belonging to that category.[563] Of the plain-chant Passion,

---

[562] Published by F. Commer. *Musica sacra*, Berlin. Vol. VI., p. 88.
[563] In parts in the Library at Cassel.

it retains the one-part recitation for the Evangelist and for the speeches of the persons; while of the motett type it preserves the use of the repetition of the four-part setting in the narrative portion; and like the Passions of the older type, has the devotional choruses at the beginning and end. A verse of the Protestant hymn "Da Jesus an dem Kreuze stund"—"When Jesus stood before the cross"—is used for the opening chorus, and another verse for the close, but only as having appropriate words, and without any reference to the tune. But what is new, and a result indeed of the concerted style, is the instrumental accompaniment, and the symphonies so full of meaning which occur after the first and before the last chorus; new too, and an outcome of the dramatic style, is the abandonment of the plain-song, which has given way to the recitative invented in about 1600.

But this work, which, as we see, combined such very different elements in a new form, had already had a predecessor, resembling it in artistic treatment though not in its materials. In the "Historie der fröhlichen und siegreichen Auferstehung unsers einigen Erlösers und Seligmachers Jesu Christi" (1623)—"History of the joyful and triumphant resurrection of our only Saviour and Benefactor, Jesus Christ"—the plain-song is still preserved, although it shows a marked disposition to pass over into the mode of the newly devised monologue. The first and last chorus are in the old manner, as are also a dramatic chorus of youths; the speeches of persons are some of them in several parts without any dramatic emotion, as in the Passions in motett form; while the figured bass accompaniment has sprung from the soil of the new style of music.

It is only at the first glance that the four Passions by Schütz seem to keep wholly within the limits of the old liturgical form. The Evangelist recites, while in the speeches of individuals or groups of persons single singers come in; there is the devotional chorus at the beginning and end, and no instrumental accompaniment. But on closer examination we perceive that, at any rate in the St. Matthew Passion, the separate singers no longer use the old plain-song, but actually sing the more modern recitative, and that

the old style of writing is only apparently adhered to. A
very limited amount of melodic movement is proper to the
plain-song; it is only at the beginning and end of a phrase
that melodic intervals are introduced, and these consist
of a few frequently-recurring formulas, while the end of the
phrase falls almost without exception on the key-note or the
fifth. In those portions of Schütz's St. Matthew Passion
which are intended to be recited, we detect an unexpected and
varied melodic movement, which almost seems to demand a
figured bass accompaniment, and in which, indeed, only a
few turns remain to remind us of the plain-chant. It
is no longer an equable sacred calm, but an eager personal
emotion that pervades it. This is perceptible in the repetition
of words and phrases, which is wholly incompatible with
chanting. For instance, Judas sings—

or—

In the St. Luke and St. John Passions we likewise find
the modern recitative concealed under the mask of the
plain-chant; still, it is more old-fashioned in character, and
in the St. Mark Passion the old style of chanting is preserved in all its simplicity. The St. Matthew and St. John
Passions again are not in the usual mode; the first is in a
transposed Doric, the latter in the Phrygian. If we turn
from the solo songs to the dramatic choruses, here again
a vivacity and keenness of expression are to be remarked
such as could only have become possible under the development of concerted music. In the St. Mark Passion, which
is richest in passionate choruses, these are singularly contrasted with the unisonous monotone of the solo portions;
while in the other works—and most completely in the
St. Matthew Passion—the contrast is softened down by the

old form of plain-chant being enlivened to the more modern
monologue; even the choruses at the beginning display that
free and bolder style of part progression which was introduced by the concerted style. At the opening of all four
of these Passions the announcement is set to music, but the
customary thanksgiving occurs only at the close of the
St. Mark Passion, which thus adheres more closely to the
older type; for the others Schütz has chosen verses of
church hymns: for the St. Matthew Passion the last verse
of "Ach wir armen Sünder"; for that according to St. Luke
the ninth verse of " Da Jesus an dem Kreuze stund," with a
slight variation in the text; and for that according to St. John
the last verse of "Christus der uns Selig macht." But his aim
in so doing was not—or was in a very small degree—to effect
a closer alliance with congregational singing; it was in the
last of these three instances only that he made use of the
chorale melody, working it out as a motett. He set the
other verses to original music, and we find the same in the
Seven Words and in his other works. Church hymns at that
time always afforded, next to Bible words, the most available
text for German church music; but Schütz's efforts were
already tending towards the introduction of the Italian
madrigal style into Germany, and he hailed with delight
Caspar Ziegler's first attempts of the kind.[564] In these
Passions there is a peculiar mixture of old and new, but the
new predominates, and this, as Schütz understood it, was
not church music nor the church sentiment; it was partly
sacred, but partly secular—the Oratorio.

In the farther course of the seventeenth century, the
musical transformation of the German Passion music, and
the gradual advance through its various phases of Protestant
church music in general, continued to progress side by side
at an equal pace. The vocal recitative preserved in all
essentials the *arioso* character it had acquired in Schütz's
hands; even in church cantatas down to 1700, recitative,
properly speaking, does not occur. The instrumental accompaniment became universal; some modest attempts at

---

[564] See Vol. I., p. 469.

making it more independent are perceptible, and in suitable places short symphonies appear. In the choruses, which were by preference in five parts, the same feeble and etiolated character is perceptible, as we have seen in the cantatas—homophony preponderates; here and there we have short imitations, insignificant sub-divisions, and frequent ritornelles.

The characteristic form of this period is the sacred aria; it is now introduced into the Passion; I first find it used under its own name in a St. Luke Passion of 1683 by Funcke, Cantor of Lüneburg.[565] A Passion setting from Rudolstadt, of 1688, is already abundantly supplied with arias in several verses.[566] The simultaneous appearance of the same form of development at two places, tolerably far apart, allows us to conclude that the custom of inserting sacred songs into the Passion music had already been for some time widely spread. Among the arias we may include the "little hymn of thanksgiving for the bitter sufferings of Jesus Christ," which forms the close of the St. Matthew Passion, by Giovanni Sebastiani, written in 1672.[567] For although the *gratiarum actio* in a song form had long since ceased to be new, up to this time it had lacked the instrumental accompaniment peculiar to the aria. Besides this, in Sebastiani's work, a number of chorales are inserted "for the arousing of greater devoutness"; these, like the thanksgiving—all but its last verse—were to be performed by the treble only, with an accompaniment of four "deep viols" and figured bass; thus they were to be sung as arias. This is a new phase in the development of the German Passion music. Writers have hitherto been content to establish the fact without explaining it, for which reason we must dwell on it for a moment. The mode in which Sebastiani adopted the chorale into his Passion cannot of course have been original; it presupposes a stage of development in which the

---

[565] A copy of the text is in the Library of the Johanneum (school) at Lüneburg.

[566] A copy of the text is in the Royal Library at Sondershausen. On the title page is added "as in use for musical performance from day to day in Holy week," thus indicating a custom already some time established.

[567] A copy of this work, which, since Winterfeld's investigations, has been frequently mentioned, exists in the Royal Library at Königsberg.

chorales, here treated as arias, were sung by the whole
congregation, as their very nature required that they
should be. And the congregation did in fact participate in
this way in the old chanted Passion. The regular order of
the divine service provided, indeed, that the congregation
should sing, both before and after the Passion, a hymn
having reference to it; for the chanting of the Passion in
Holy week took the place of the lessons from the Gospels
read on Sundays. But this was not thought enough.
Since the chanting was a long affair, in order to keep the
interest of the congregation alive and to enhance the
edifying effect, pauses were made at certain places where
the assembled Christians struck in with a suitable hymn.
Of this fact we have evidence, of which the value is rather
increased than diminished by its dating from a period later
than Sebastiani's Passion. For all that could avail to
uphold true church music under the revolutionary movement which, in the beginning of the eighteenth century,
threatened to annihilate it, undoubtedly rested on old and
tried foundations. A little volume of Passions brought out
in 1709, at Merseburg,[568] contains narratives of the Passion
abridged from the four Gospels as they were at that time
in use at Merseburg. It is immediately clear that these
were sung in the old plain-song form, I might say in the
oldest; for the thanksgiving is lacking from the end, and
the introit, which is introduced into the St. Matthew
Passion only, " Höret das Leiden "—" Hear ye the sufferings "—is not sung by the choir, but intoned by the
Evangelist *choraliter*.[569]   Arias are wholly excluded, but
not chorales; these, however, are not printed in their place,
but the first lines of the verses are given in brackets and
usually there is an indication in the margin with the words
" Here shall be sung verse * * of hymn * * "   They
mostly consist of one or more verses of Stockmann's hymn

---

[568] Auserlesene | Passions- | Gesänge, | wie auch | Die Historie vom blu- |
tigen Leiden und Sterben | unsers Heylandes Christi | JEsu, | und wie solche
von dem Chor, | nach dem *MATTHÆO, MARCO, LUCA* und *JOHANNE*, |
abgesungen wird, Merseburg, 1709. In the Count's Library at Wernigerode.

[569] As it is in the St. Matthew Passion by Vopelius.

"Jesu Leiden, Pein und Tod "—" Jesu! Suffering, pain and death "—in which the whole history of the Passion is told in verse ; in this way the congregation is enabled to follow the course of the events. But other hymns of five, six, seven, and even ten verses are indicated, which were to be sung at full length, and towards the end of the St. John Passion a hymn containing twenty-one verses " Nun giebt mein Jesus gute Nacht "—" And now the Saviour bids good night "—is ordered to be sung. Besides these chorales we also find in certain places one or two verses of hymns printed complete ; possibly the chorus alone were to sing these for the sake of variety.

The same kind of interest was sometimes shown by the congregation in other ways. At the first performance of a Passion music, to words in madrigal form, in a town of Saxony, part of the people present sang quite calmly and devoutly in the first chorale, but presently expressed their displeased surprise at the rest being so different from what they were accustomed to.[570] Sebastiani himself published a small book in 1686, " Kurze Nachricht, wie die Passion . . . in einer recitirenden Harmonie abgehandelt und nebst den darin befindlichen Liedern gesungen wird " (A short account of how the Passion is to be treated in harmonised recitative and sung, together with the hymns to be found herein), from which we may conclude that the congregation were at liberty to join in the hymns.[571] And even as the Passion acquired an increasingly rich musical treatment the custom was here and there adhered to, and the congregation sang in the chorales.[572] But the more the sacred aria gained ground the less this practice could be kept up ; Sebastiani's music is quite on the border line. His chorales no doubt are all of early origin, but the mode of their performance

---

[570] Gerber, Historie du Kirchen-Ceremonien in Sachsen, p. 284.

[571] To be seen in the Royal Library at Königsberg.

[572] Gerber, op. cit., p. 283. " As at this time folks have begun to perform even the Passion story—which was formerly so fine *de simplici et plano* and chanted simply and devoutly—with all sorts of instruments in the artistic manner, and sometimes to mix in a Passion hymn, so that the whole congregation sings with the instruments."

is no longer that of the ancient chorale. The whole
character of chorale singing had assumed the aria type ;
all the new tunes, which were composed at this time in
considerable numbers and of great beauty, were, in fact,
arias, and no objection was made even to calling them so ;
as, for instance, Paul Gerhardt's chorale " Ein Lämmlein
geht und trägt die Schuld "—" A white Lamb comes to
bear our guilt "—to the old melody of " An Wasserflüssen
Babylon."[573] Chorales for a soprano solo with an instrumental accompaniment occur not only in Sebastiani's
Passion, but in the church cantatas of the period, as in
those of Buxtehude ; but here they appear in such a connection as entirely to exclude the idea of any co-operation on
the part of the congregation. That this should be the case
was but natural, since the aria is the expression of individual
feeling, and thus, at last, in Seebach's Passion (to be fully
described presently) even the separate *dramatis personæ*,
" Jesus, John, the Virgin Mary, and the Bride of Christ,"
sing now in recitative, now arias, and now chorales.

It is undeniable that, in the last quarter of the seventeenth
century, chorales play a considerable part in the Passion
music. This, however, may not prove that the congregation
had any more intimate share in it, nor that it had become
more closely amalgamated with the service. On the contrary,
like the introduction of the aria, it seems to prove a gradual
evanescence of the animating spirit of church community,
and it was the aria which helped the chorale to assert and
hold its place in church music. Certain forms of music, in
which formerly the congregation had taken enthusiastic part,
they now were satisfied to hear sung, and could listen to
them with calm sympathy. The Protestant chorale began
at the same time to find in the organ the importance it was
losing in vocal music.

Wherever the chorale is set in several parts in these
Passion works, it is always in the simplest possible form.
Though Eccard and Hassler set chorales in *contrapunctum*

---

[573] In the Rudolstädt Passion of 1688, at the beginning of *Actus* III., the
indication stands " to begin with Paul Gerhard's *Aria*."

simplicem and gave the melody to the upper part, still the others had always some intelligent and tuneful progression, and there was an abundance of strong and original harmony. Now the most meagre progression was deemed sufficient, and the most commonplace harmonies. In the first instance this may have arisen from a desire to make it convenient to the congregation to join in. But that this was very soon lost sight of is proved by the parts as well as the printed texts; for the chorales—like the portions ascribed to the Jewish populace, the youths, and the high priest— have the simple indication *Chorus;* and soon the case was the same with the Passion music as with the church cantatas; for no composer ever took the co-operation of the congregation into consideration in writing a chorale, but, on the contrary, conceived of it in a spirit absolutely opposed to congregational singing.[574] The chorale now appeared in the place of the old announcement and thanksgiving, or if these were piously retained, there was at least one chorale into the bargain. As a thanksgiving " Nun wir danken dir von Herzen "—" From our hearts we thank the Saviour "—(the last verse from the hymn " Jesu meines Lebens Leben ") was in almost universal use; as an introduction any appropriate hymn might be selected. The voices were supported by the instruments, which at most had some brief and insignificant solo interludes. Rarely we find a paraphrase of a hymn with an original setting, as at the close of a St. Matthew Passion, by J. C. Rothe, of 1697.[575]

The most perfect Passion music that remains to us in the style of the older church cantatas is no doubt that by Kuhnau, according to St. Mark. It was written for Good

---

[574] In the preface to a series of cantata texts which were printed in 1696 for the Hofcapelle at Gotha under the title: " Erbauliche Uebereinstimmung der Sonn- und Fest-Tags-Evangelien," and compiled by Witt (in the Library at Wernigerode), which consist chiefly of chorales and Bible texts, it is written " it is necessary too that those who sing should themselves devoutly ponder on what they sing, and that the hearers should not give heed to the sweet music only, but still more to the noble matter of the song."

[575] The autograph is in the Library of the Castle Capelle at Sondershausen. This paraphrase is founded on the usual verse " Nun ich danke dir."

Friday, 1721, and so about twenty years too late, but nevertheless it won the approbation of connoisseurs (see p. 336).
The eighteen arias it includes are for one, two, three, and
four voices. They all have the character of hymns in verse
and, with one exception, have ritornels. This single exception is the four-part aria "O theures Blut, du dienst zum
Leben "—" O precious Blood, of life the fountain "—in
which the close affinity of the sacred aria to the true chorale,
as it was at that time sung, is very conspicuous; there is
nothing in it to make it less proper for congregational use
than, for example, the hymn "O Traurigkeit, o Herzeleid"
—" O bitter ruth and grief of heart." Besides these
eighteen arias we find twenty chorales, the last of which
is that just named, "O Traurigkeit"; however, it does not
strictly speaking belong to the work, which ends with "Nun
ich danke dir von Herzen." Kuhnau, who opened the performances of Passion music in part writing in Leipzig with
his St. Mark Passions, evidently intended to bring them
into closer connection with the customary services there, and
this hymn had, as has been said (p. 274), its fixed place
in the Good Friday service. For the same reason he
inserted, after the alto aria which follows the words "And
Jesus cried out and gave up the Ghost," the hymn "*Ecce
quomodo*" of Gallus—a highly suggestive idea which no
one seems to have had before him, at least I have not met
with this motett in any other Passion music.

With the year 1700 began a period during which the
theatrical music of the Italians became infused into church
music in an ever spreading flow. Under the name "theatrical music" I include the Italian oratorio, which, however,
was widely distinct from the opera, not only by the subject
matter and a few broadly developed choruses, but by its
presentment on a stage never having become an established
custom. It was of course self-evident that the narrative
of the Passion offered admirable material for a German
oratorio on the Italian pattern, and Ch. F. Hunold at once
set to work and wrote the words of the "Bleeding and dying
Jesus" ("blutigen und sterbenden Jesus"), in which not the
recital of the Evangelist alone, but the Bible words and

even the chorale were dispensed with, and the whole material cast in one mould like an Italian oratorio. Keiser set this poem to music, and it was performed at Hamburg in Holy week, 1704. But it is an injustice to regard Hunold as the pioneer in this new line of work; he simply transferred to the Passion a process which had previously been tried with success in the church cantata. The gifted originator, therefore, of this new form was not Hunold but Neumeister, who had published his first cycle of "madrigal" cantata texts in 1700. As Hunold was his great admirer, and in 1707 published, without his leave, Neumeister's work "Die allerneueste Art zur reinen und galanten Poesie zu gelangen," there can be no doubt that he simply imitated him. Neumeister's first annual series—and indeed his second also, published in 1708—are quite independent alike of Bible texts and chorales, and are wholly original verse. We have seen what angry reprobation this practice incurred from various sides as a profanation of the church; and the same vehement antagonism arose against the new form of Passion writing, but without any result worth mentioning. It is indeed very true that, besides those in the Italian oratorio form, many Passion texts continued to be compiled, in which the recital of the Evangelist and the Bible words were retained as well as the chorales. But this could hardly be regarded as a general concession to the opponents of the new form. Still, among the poets of the time there were certainly not too many who could go even half way towards the satisfactory accomplishment of such a task. The impulse towards new texts of compositions of the narrative of the Passion proved a strong one, and it was partly for convenience sake only that music was set to the older form. It certainly was not respect for the words of the Bible, as something reverend and sacred, which prevented its utter deposition, or else the traditional arioso in solo singing might have been retained for Bible words, as was done in the church cantatas. No one will assert that the perfectly secular—not to say flippant— way in which most of the composers after this date set the deeply pathetic history of the Passion to a sort of recitative betrays any feeling for the sublimity of the language of the Bible.

On the other hand, both the Bible words and the chorale offered undoubted advantages to the musician; a regard for these induced Neumeister to make use of them again in the third and fourth series of his cantatas. Still, this combination of Bible words, chorales, and original verse could not henceforth have become the normal and immutable form if musicians had not recognised in it the ideal form of that period. For the time, however, the Italian oratorio remained the fundamental prototype of all who wrote and arranged Passion-texts, and who had any pretensions to be considered poets. Postel's Passion according to St. John, which Handel composed, still stood on the debatable ground, though it was written certainly not later than Hunold's work, and probably one or two years earlier; and a few years later Benjamin Neukirch and Johann Ulrich König still sailed in the wake of the Italians. Neukirch in his " Weinende Petrus "—"Weeping Peter"—treated, not the Passion properly speaking, but, as it were, a reflection of it. Peter and Judas Iscariot have both sinned against Christ : they are tortured by conscience, and Judas is driven by it to kill himself. Belial and spirits of hell would fain ensnare Peter too into despair, but the comforting words of John and of Mary Magdalene, as they remind him of the infinite love of God, give him fresh courage to suffer, to endure, and to conquer. This work is in fact nothing else than a sacred opera; it even falls into three acts, or incidents, like an opera; while the oratorio usually has but two sections, and each act has a different scene. Scenic effects are throughout taken into account; thus at the beginning we are told : " Peter goes, in melancholy thought, to a desert place, and presently begins—" and at the end of the first act, " Peter goes off sadly on one side, and Judas, full of despair, on the other." Besides these two, the following persons appear : Philip the younger, Zion, Belial, and the allegorical figures of Despair and Faith. The first act ends with a chorus of youths, the second with a chorus of the demons of hell, and the third with a chorus of angels and the righteous; the

work consists of recitatives, arias, and one duet. There are
no chorales; all the verse is original. When and by whom
the text was composed I know not; on the title page it is
said to be "for devotion on the Passion."[576] König called his
poem honestly an oratorio, and farther bestowed on it the
designation of "Tears under the cross of Jesus." We are
told that these words were set by Keiser and performed in
1711, "on Monday, Tuesday, and Wednesday in Holy week,
at vespers." The contents actually consist of the history
of the Passion; chorales are introduced, and in part the
words of the Bible narrative are retained, though certainly
in a very singular manner, for they are used as stage
directions between the songs. For instance, after an aria
sung by Mary the mother of Cleophas, it is added in
brackets, "They that passed by blasphemed Him," where-
upon, Mary goes on in recitative till soon after the words
given to her are again interrupted in a similar manner :—

> Great Heaven! and can this really be,
> Can Christ while hanging on the tree
> Be mocked by all the scum of earth?
> (And one of the malefactors blasphemed him.)
> The malefactors now begin
> To blaspheme Him who knew no sin.
> (Then answered him the other.) &c.

These notes were intended for those who were following the
performance in the book of words, supplying the place of
dramatic action, and König considered this subordinate
service quite good enough for the Bible words.[577]

---

[576] The "Weinende Petrus" must have been written in 1711 or 1712 at
latest, for the third act alludes to the Emperor Joseph I. in such a way as to
show that he must have lately died; Joseph I. died in the spring of 1711. The
text was first printed as an appendix to the "Adachts Ubung | Zur Kirchen
Music. | In Cantaten, Oden und | Arien. Franckfurt und Leipzig, 1721." It is
to be found in the Count's Library at Wernigerode.

[577] "Theatralische, geistliche, vermischte und galante Gedichte von König."
Hamburg and Leipzig, 1713, p. 307. "Thränen Unter dem Creutze JESU, In
einem *ORATORIO* Montags, Dienstags und Mittwochs zur Vesper-Zeit In
der stillen Woche Musicalisch aufgeführt. M.DCC.XI." In the Town Library
of Leipzig. Winterfeld mentions a "verurtheilten und gekreuzigtens Jesu "—
"Judgment and crucifixion of Jesus "—by Johann Ulrich König, as performed
in Hamburg with Keiser's music in 1714. I have not seen this poem.

He found imitators; in 1719 Joachim Beccau brought out a poem of the Passion after the four Evangelists, in which all the events are inserted in this way; for instance :—

> *Jesus.* Whom seek ye ?
> *The Host.* Him that is called Jesus.
> *Jesus.* I am He. (And they fell to the ground.)

In Beccau, indeed, as may be seen by this quotation, the whole is dramatised. Peter, Jesus, Mary, and Judas sing arias ; there is an animated dialogue between them, with choruses of various kinds. Besides this, there is a lyrical devotional song for Sulamith, who often takes an eager part in the proceedings and speaks between the speeches of the others. The piece begins with a *canzonetta* of the disciples at the last supper, and closes with a chorale of believers, " O hilf Christe, Gottes Sohn "—" Help, O Christ! thou Son of God." [578]

The Passion oratorio of Johann Georg Seebach, Erlebach's son-in-law, is on the whole constructed on the same lines ; it was brought out in 1714.[579] The speeches of the actors are a paraphrase of the Gospel text ; the narrative is partly given, as in König and Beccau, as a kind of stage direction, but in part is supposed to be known to the hearer. Besides this, the personages sing independent arias, as well as chorales—as if it mattered not which—and there are several scattered throughout the work. The action begins with the institution of the Lord's Supper, and the oratorio opens with a hymn of praise by the disciples, in the aria form, as in Beccau.

It is impossible not to see that Beccau and Seebach wrote under the influence of an older work, of which I have intentionally reserved all mention till this place. In 1712, Barthold Heinrich Brockes, a member of the Town Council

---

[578] *Beccau*, Zulässige Verkürtzung müssiger Stunden | Hamburg, 1719, p. 83. " Heilige Fastenlust | oder: das Leyden und Sterben unsers Herrn JEsu Christi | nach der Historie der Vier Evangelisten." Royal Public Library at Dresden. (Sacred Lenten Diversion on the sufferings and death of our Lord Jesus Christ.)

[579] Johann Georg Seebach, Der leidende und sterbende JESVS. . . . In einem *ORATORIO* und in geistlichen Liedern zur Erweckung heiliger Andacht ans Licht gestellet. Gotha, 1714. In the Library at Wernigerode.

of Hamburg, compiled what was, according to the views of that time, a model text: "Jesus tortured and dying for the sins of the world."[580] Keiser was the first to set it to music, and it was performed in Holy week both in 1712 and 1713. He was followed by Telemann and Handel in 1716, and Mattheson in 1718; a remarkable setting of this much admired work also exists by Stölzel,[581] and finally, as we shall presently see, Sebastian Bach was not unacquainted with it. What Brockes' capabilities were as a poet, he subsequently showed in his "Irdisches Vergnügen in Gott" ("Earthly joys in God"). The Passion text, it cannot be denied, is skilfully arranged and well fitted for music; but the turgid language, overloaded with glaring imagery, by which the sublimity of the subject is sensibly depreciated, makes the poem distasteful to us, though it was precisely this which delighted his contemporaries. It has long since been estimated at its true value,[582] and I may, therefore, restrict my observations to these few words. Brockes adopted the independent oratorio form which had now for some years been popular, but, intimidated perhaps by his opponents, he did not want to abandon entirely the older customs. He, therefore, retained the recital of the Evangelist, but gave him a paraphrase of the Bible words—a kind of compromise which could not satisfy either party, and in which, so far as I know, he found but one single imitator. The admiration excited by this poem was founded on other characteristics. It frequently occurred that a selection of aria texts from this work was introduced into Biblical Passions; a St. Mark Passion by Telemann, composed before 1729, contains—besides the Gospel words, a number of chorales, and a few arias by an unknown author—seven passages derived from Brockes.[583]

Thus the German Passion had developed through the

---

[580] "Den für die Sünden der Welt gemarterten und sterbenden Jesus, aus den vier Evangelisten in gebundener Rede vorgestellt."

[581] The autograph is in the Royal Library at Königsberg. Stölzel divided his work into four parts, and the second and fourth are unfortunately wanting.

[582] By Winterfeld, Ev. Kir. III., p. 128; and Chrysander Händel, I., p. 429.

[583] This Passion is in my possession in a copy made in 1729 by J. P. Hasse.

influence of the Italian oratorio into a very singular com-
pound. The most ancient and modern forms stood side
by side; the simple and the ornate, the sacred and the secular
were worked out in juxtaposition. It had become possible
by these enhanced means of art to appeal to the emotions
from the most opposite sides. But it had not yet been
given to any man to co-ordinate and amalgamate this mass
of elements from a high stand-point, not even to Handel; and
by subsequently making use of all that was best in his
Passion music for other works he showed that he was
conscious of this. The chorale here plays the most per-
plexing part; its uses from the musical and poetical side
alike were not to be undervalued. Seebach says very
astutely in the preface to his Passion oratorio "a well-
known and well-designed poem has in truth no small effect;
it has a very lively one, and quickens the hidden heart of
man like a refreshing balm. It is as though our faith took
breath once more, our love grows fervent and our hope
blossoms out in sacred admiration of God's glory, grace,
mercy, long-suffering, and kindness. Yea, in so far as the
poet is able to connect the chorale with his own thoughts,
a well-composed oratorio or cantata will often wring tears
and sighs from the heart of a child of God, particularly
when the music is of equal weight with the words of the
poetry." But it was just this—the musical treatment—
which the composers could not succeed in. They had
borrowed the chorale from the Passion form which had
existed before 1700; and the simple guise in which they
had found it there was suitable to the music among which
it stood; but it no longer matched with the varied and
passionate character of the new type of Passion. However,
as the composers could make nothing else out of it they
had to leave it as they found it. To stand still is to go
back, and we are positively startled at the more and more
wretched garb in which the noble figure of the chorale
was condemned to appear in their works. Thus the
original church element, which had existed in the
modern Passion form, dwindled away; and the elements of
oratorio it contained did not fare much better. When

Scheibe gives the name of *Oratorio* to Kuhnau's St. Mark Passion, which had its root in an older and very different period, this shows that he had hardly a shadow of an idea of what is indispensable to the oratorio, and yet he was one of the most keen and intelligent men of his time. The conception of the oratorio was so completely lost to the multitude that most people ceased even to understand the meaning of the name. Count Heinrich XII. of Reuss established at Schleitz a scheme of church music by which, on Sundays, first a chorale was sung, then the Gospel was read (or more probably intoned), then an aria was performed, and the whole concluded with a chorale; and the text compiled and printed for this purpose he called an *oratorio*.[584] Gottfried Behrndt published in 1731 a collection of sacred poems, some of which had, however, been written much earlier, and these were called on the title page "*Oratorien* so-called." These "so-called oratorios" are very simple church cantatas in Neumeister's style. But it is to be noted that Behrndt does not use the Latin word *Oratorium* or the Italian *Oratorio*; he connects its etymology with the Orator—*i.e.*, the speaker or preacher.[585] Accordingly, the Passion necessarily degenerated into a religious cantata, although it long retained, superficially, much in common with the older and purer form. "The death of Jesus" ("Der Tod Jesu") by Ramler and Graun is such a cantata; this was written in 1756, and must be regarded as affording

---

[584] *ORATORIUM* | Welches, | nach Anleitung | derer Sonn- und Fest- | tägigen | Evangelien, | zu Erweckung | einer Christlichen Andacht, | aufgeführt wird | In der Schloss-Capelle | zu Schleitz. | Schleitz, *s. a.* Auf der gräflichen Bibliothek zu Wernigerode.

[585] Gottfried Behrndt, *Zitt. Lusat.*, Poetische Sonn- und Fest-Tags- | Betrachtungen | über die verordneten Evangelien | durch das gantze Jahr, | In so genandten Oratorien | bestehend. Magdeburg, 1731. In the Library at Wernigerode. In explanation of his misuse of the term, one more circumstance may be mentioned, namely, that works of the oratorio class were at that time not unfrequently performed on the regular school speech-days by the choirs of pupils. This was the case, for instance, with a poem and music by Constantin Bellermann, "Die himmlischen Heerschaaren," performed in 1726 at the Gymnasium at Göttingen (see Marpurg, Kritische Briefe, Vol. III., p. 13). Heiland speaks of similar performances in the programme of the Wiemar college, 1858. P. 16.

a fair standard of the Holy week music of the second half
of the eighteenth century. The chorales it contains, the mis-
applied survivals of an earlier period, might still have some
edifying effect, but their importance as church music is
wholly lost. In 1759 Doles conducted a performance of
an original Passion on Ramler's text in St. Thomas' church
at Leipzig; I even fancy that a few portions of Graun's
music were transcribed bodily into it.[586] In 1766 the primitive chorale Passions were abolished once for all, and with
reason. When Graun's style of art began to be pre-eminent
all true intelligence must have vanished to the last trace.

From the very first the old church form of the Passion
had contained a dramatic germ capable of development.
In the middle ages the Passion miracle play had grown out
of it, without its ceasing to exist in its simple identity. The
reading of the Gospel with distributed parts—and not of the
history of the Passion only—survived the ruin which over-
took the so-called " mysteries " of the sixteenth century, and
had preserved enough of their characteristics to bring them
to a second bloom, so far as was possible under totally
altered circumstances. It is evident, from the Latin text of
Carissimi's oratorios, and still more from the *Historicus*
(the Historian or Evangelist) who appears in them, that the
semi-dramatic musical style of the Italians in the seventeenth century did not remain outside all connection with it.
But the attempts of a similar character made in Germany
in the seventeenth century must not be regarded in this
connection as an imitation of the Italians. It is quite
certain that the Italian oratorio was not unfrequently performed with scenery and action; but long before any
Italian oratorio existed at all, performances of the Passion
with action had been customary in the churches of Germany.
I do not of course refer to the medieval Passion plays—
though they too originally had a liturgical purpose, and
were performed in the churches until they freed themselves from ecclesiastical control, and then rapidly became
secularised and degenerate—but to the simple Gospel

---

[586] The text of this performance is preserved in the Library at Wernigerode.

readings with distributed parts. It is a fact that has only recently become known, that dramatic representations of the Passion took place in Protestant neighbourhoods after the Reformation. Such a performance took place on the fifth Sunday in Lent, 1571, at Zittau. The composition was by a certain Paurbach, and had long been in existence. Ten years previously, Christoph Bornmann, tavern-keeper of the "Freiberg cellar" at Dresden, had made it a present to the Church of St. John at Zittau. The stage was erected near the altar, and the actors were the three lowest masters of the school and two treble choristers.[587] It is not stated whether the performance took place before or after divine service; but this is of no importance. The real interest of the matter lies in this, that evidently the feeling still survived of the connection between the old dramatised Gospel readings and the Passion play, for it is only under this supposition that such an attempt is explicable.

Because the sacred plays of the people during the sixteenth and seventeenth centuries were of but small importance in the development of dramatic art in Germany, but little attention has been paid to them, with the single exception of the Oberammergau play. And yet a due regard to them is indispensable to a complete comprehension of the German Passion music and its allied forms; and even the first beginnings of the German opera must undoubtedly be referred to it.[588] In Thuringia, Upper Saxony, and Silesia the popular sacred drama throughout the seventeenth century was universally delighted in, even when its progress was checked by the scholastic drama. It was not merely venerated as a piece of respectable antiquity, and allowed as such to subsist, but it grew and lent itself to the needs of the time. A Christmas drama from Arnstadt in Thuringia, of which I possess a copy, made in 1700, reproduces the general outlines common to most of the popular Christmas

---

[587] Reinhold Zöllner, Das deutsche Kirchenlied in der Oberlausitz, Dresden, 1871, p. 31.

[588] See Chrysander, Händel, I., p. 78, and Weinhold, Weihnacht-Spiele und Lieder, p. 290.

dramas, but betrays itself in language, versification, and
music as a new arrangement of well-known motives which
cannot have originated long before 1700; and yet its
essentially popular character is plainly to be seen from
the fact that two peasants and two shepherds who figure
in it speak the Thuringian dialect.[589]   In the same way,
in the Zuckmantler Passion play, we have one of the
re-arrangements of an older work which were made in the
seventeenth century; this is even more clear from the
music than from the language.   There are seven arias altogether bearing the stamp and feeling common in the
middle of that century.[590]   No doubt, however, it was not
so much the specially dramatic element, as a general
popular tone and treatment, that the Passion music and its
allied forms at their most flourishing period had borrowed
from the contemporary sacred drama.   A time when the
creative instinct, which flooded and obliterated every other
artistic tendency, was so purely musical was especially
unfit for the development of a new type of dramatic poetry;
such germs of it as could assert their existence could, for a
time, only expand in Handel's oratorios and Bach's church
music—to forms indeed of transcendent beauty, but to the
total exclusion of scenic representation and with a general
tendency to resolve everything into lyric forms.

In short, the position held by the medieval " Mystery "
in the life of the people was not very different from that
of the Passion music of the seventeenth and eighteenth
centuries—making due allowance for the progress and
changes that had meanwhile taken place in art.   In both
we see an obvious dependence on the Church; each had
for its principal subject the Life of Christ, and was performed at fixed church festivals.   In both, the liturgical and
sternly ecclesiastical element acquired by degrees a greater
admixture of the secular.   Just as in the " Mysteries " we
trace, first the explanation of the Latin Bible and sacred

---

[589] In a volume of collected pieces in the Ministerial Library at Sondershausen.

[590] Zuckmantler Passionsspiel, edited and elucidated by Anton Peter.
Troppau, 1868-9.

words by a context in German, then the interpolation of independent verses, and, finally, an entire suppression of the church element and complete secularisation ; so in the Passion music we first find the interpreting congregational hymn side by side with the Gospel narrative, then the introduction of the independent sacred aria, and by degrees of the various richer forms of modern music ; till at last the church element is felt as a disturbing one, and is as far as possible set aside. But the latter process of development is distinct from the former; for a man had now appeared on the scene, capable at the right moment of giving worthy utterance at once to the sacred and the secular feeling, and of restoring the church element to all its dignity, without in any way detracting from the fulness, splendour, and richness of the secular adjuncts.

It has been said above that from the seventeenth century onwards, the development of the German Passion performances ran parallel with that of Protestant church music, and this is equally true as applied to Bach : for the musical style of his Passion music is identical with that of his church cantatas. But this was new altogether, evolved from organ music and the chorale, and hence truly churchlike; while in it, at the same time, all the musical forms of the period were purified and re-invigorated. By transferring them to the Passion, he achieved the amalgamation and natural coalescence of all the heterogeneous elements which in the lapse of time had become agglomerated under that name. At the same time, the style was eminently German; for if ever anything was a national product, the organ music of the seventeenth and eighteenth centuries and the popular hymns of the reformed faith were essentially German. Thus, when we find that the influence excited by the German sacred plays on the Passion performances and other allied forms was, properly speaking, only fully revealed in Bach, the internal process and connection are very intelligible. The more his contemporaries ran after the Italian opera and Italian oratorio, the farther they found themselves from the national spirit ; Bach would not yield to the momentum given by foreign art, though he did not ignore it ; but the point from which he started and the work he produced were invariably conceived from the essentially German views of art. The ineradicable hold these had on his mind is the evident result of his inheritance from a long race of artists, and here again we see how important to a thorough comprehension of Bach's individuality is a just estimate of his ancestry. None but a man who could take his stand on a tradition founded in an unbroken intimacy with the life of the people, and in whom their feelings, deeds, and thoughts had become an innate and inseparable part of his being, could, at such a period of general ferment as the beginning of the eighteenth century, have restored to a form of art so vacuous as the Passion had become all the dignity and mastery of the German genius. Bach's Passions and kindred works are indeed a revival of the medieval sacred drama of the best period, but on an immeasurably higher level—nay, it may be said they are the very culmination and crown of their kind. Bach was careful not to attribute the title of oratorio, at any rate, to his Passion music. His compositions for Christmas, Easter, and Ascension-tides have, it is true, kept that name—in fact, at that time there was no other or more suitable term in use; I shall venture in the following pages to revert to the more comprehensive designation of "mysteries," alike for the Passions and for these three oratorios.

According to the Necrology in Mizler (p. 168), Bach left five compositions of the Passion, and we cannot doubt the statement of this, our best authority, because the number corresponds with that of the annual series of cantatas (see ante p. 348). After his death, his sons, Friedemann and Emanuel, divided these cantatas between them, and the Passions were no doubt included. Emanuel had the original scores of the St. John and the St. Matthew Passions. He treasured them faithfully and they still exist. The original manuscript of the other three fell into the hands of the dissipated Friedemann, who now grew wilder than ever; they were sold for a trifle, and two have entirely disappeared. A St. Luke Passion in Bach's handwriting may be the third;

but whether this is a genuine work by him is a question still unsolved. I hope to bring it a little nearer to a solution, but first I have a few words to offer as to the lost settings of the Passion.

On Good Friday, 1731, a Passion music was performed in St. Thomas' Church on the text of the Gospel of St. Mark; Picander, who in 1729 had compiled the St. Matthew Passion text for Bach, had also written this one.[591] It is in two parts, the first being sung before the sermon and the second after. Besides the narrative from chapters xiv. and xv. of the Gospel, which was sung in recitative and which includes twelve dramatic choruses, this text contains a lyric chorus at the beginning and end, six arias, and sixteen chorales. Now it is almost inevitable that, if Picander wrote this text for St. Thomas', and if it were really printed and set to music, Bach must have written the music; this is nearly certain when we consider Bach's official position and his relations with Picander. And the hypothesis is raised to a certainty by the identity we can trace between the text of the opening and closing choruses, and of the second, third, and fourth arias, with the corresponding choruses, and the three arias in the funeral ode for Queen Christiana Eberhardine (1727). Although the feeling and purport of those is different, there is a similarity in the metrical structure which leaves no room for doubt that Picander adapted his text to the music already composed by Bach; and this is particularly conspicuous in the last line of the final chorus.[592] Picander has here exercised his skill, which was often turned to similar account, in the most commendable way. Hence we may regard the musical portion of the St. Mark Passion as not wholly lost, since five lyrical pieces of it are preserved in the funeral ode,

---

[591] It is to be found in the third part of his poems, p. 49, with the title: "*TEXTE* Zur Passions-*Music* nach dem Evangelisten Marco am Char-Freytage, 1731."

[592] Rust deserves the credit of first detecting this resemblance (see B.-G., XX.,[2] p. 8). In Breitkopf's list for the New Year, 1764, p. 18, we find "*Anonymo*, Passions-Cantate, *secundum Marcum*. Geh. Jesu, geh zu deiner Pein." The beginning of the text is the same as in the mourning ode, and so is the music down to the employment of two viol-di-gamba and a lute.

though this is indeed but a meagre substitute for a complete work rich in recitatives, dramatic choruses, and chorales.

Besides this there exists a third Passion text by Picander, hitherto unknown : the first in point of order, since it was written for Good Friday, 1725.[593] A remark made some pages back applies to this work ; it is constructed entirely on Brockes' model, and, so far as I know, Picander in this stands alone.   The Bible narrative is brought into the madrigal form, and is to be recited by the Evangelist.   The *dramatis personæ* are John, Peter, Jesus, and Mary.   Still, Peter has rather the more important part ; that of Jesus is, by comparison, meagrely worked out, and of all the important and pathetic situations in which the Gospel story represents Him, hardly one is done justice to—indeed, the rhymed narrative of the Evangelist touches on the most important events with a superficiality that is hardly credible.   For instance, all the incidents between the seizure of Peter on the Mount of Olives and his denial of Christ are summed up in the feeble line, " And Jesus went out calmly, and came to the high priest, Caiaphas."   There are no dramatic choruses whatever, while, on the other hand, the lyrical reflections given to the allegorical figures of Zion and the Soul occupy a wide space.   There are only two chorales introduced, fewer therefore than in Brockes' text ; the second is Picander's original composition, and vapid enough. Neither of them are skilfully brought in ; he calls the whole thing an *oratorium*.   A comparison with the prototype is very unfavourable to Picander.   In that of Brockes we cannot but recognise that all the musical factors are skilfully brought out, and the separate incidents depicted with vivid, though too often painfully glaring, colours ; the flat lyrical monotony of Picander's poem closely borders on the religious Passion cantata of a later date.   It is noteworthy, though from a quite different point of view, how many resemblances it bears to the text of the St. Matthew Passion ; the words of the closing chorus are almost identical in both.

---

[593] Sammlung Erbaulicher Gedancken über und auf die gewöhnlichen Sonn- und Fest-Tage.   Leipzig, 1725.   For the complete text in German the reader is referred to the original German of the present work, Vol. II., App. B., x. 1.

Now, did Bach compose the music for this text? It is not possible to give any certain answer, but it is not improbable, if we suppose that it was intended to be set to music. The composers in Leipzig at the time who might have done it were Görner, Schott, and Bach. Görner, at any rate, is out of the question, since he did not institute Good Friday performances till 1728, and as regards Schott, so far as is known, Picander had never any connection with him; but it can be proved that he had written other texts for Bach in the same year as this very Passion. We must also pay due regard to the following remarkable circumstance: Bach's St. John Passion was probably projected during the last months of his residence at Cöthen, and was certainly first performed on Good Friday, 1724, as will presently be amply proved. It began originally with that grandiose chorus "O Mensch, bewein dein Sünde gross"—"O man, thy heavy sin lament"—which Bach subsequently placed at the end of the first part of the St. Matthew Passion when he passed it under revision in 1740. It has hitherto been supposed by those who have paid any attention to the manifold uses made of that chorus that it was transferred direct from the St. John to the St. Matthew Passion, but a closer examination of the MS. materials show that this is not the case; on the contrary, Bach had already had the St. John Passion performed in 1727, with the introductory chorus as it now exists, and the chorus "O man, thy heavy sin," had therefore been removed at a time when the St. Matthew Passion (written in 1729) had not yet been thought of. It is certain that when he changed the chorus, which remains one of the grandest of his compositions, it was not because it appeared to him unsuitable, but because it asserted its claim to some other use. The chorale "O man, thy heavy sin," is a Passion hymn, and can have found its use in the church only in the Holy week. Now the only concerted church music performed at that season was the Passion, at vespers on Good Friday; hence this chorale chorus must necessarily have found its place here, and consequently Bach must have written another Passion between the years 1724 and 1727, in which it could be introduced. This hypothesis coincides

very well with the date of Picander's first poem, written in
1725. It is quite conceivable that Bach, dissatisfied with the
meagre amount of sacred purpose in the poem, wished to
give it a more characteristic style by opening it with this
masterpiece of chorale writing. In this case he may simply
have set aside Picander's text for the chorus, "Sammelt
euch, getreue Seelen"—"Gather together, true believers"—
still, it was not unusual in the Passions to allow a composition on a madrigal text to follow immediately after the
chorale at the beginning, and in the same way a funeral
hymn, set as a choral aria, not unfrequently preceded the
closing chorale at the end. The fact that the poetical form
of this Passion is unlike that of Bach's other Passions need
not rouse our suspicions. Certainly, Brockes' type of
Passion, with its paraphrases and modernising of the Bible
words, was not Bach's ideal; but that he could nevertheless
condescend to it, is proved by his Christmas oratorio. If we
remember, moreover, that it was precisely in his first year
at Leipzig that, to please his public, he now and then lent
himself to the Hamburg vein of writing, many things
combine to render it probable that Bach supplied the music
to Picander's text of 1725, and that we may consider this to
have been one of the lost settings of the Passion.

If I here venture to interrupt the course of my narrative
with some critical observations, I only do so on the assumption that the question as to the number of Bach's settings of
the Passion, their date and fate, is one of very general interest.
Four can be proved with more or less certainty, and the fifth
may be the St. Luke Passion above mentioned, of which,
however, the genuineness has hitherto been doubted. I shall
here take occasion to discuss this more fully. I have already
said that a MS. of this music exists in Bach's writing.[594] It
bears no express notice that it is his own composition, but on
the other hand we find on the title the letters J. J. (*Jesu Juva*),
which Bach was accustomed to add only to his own works,
and not to copies from those of other composers. Besides

---

[594] In the possession of Herr Joseph Hauser, private singer to the Grand
Duke at Carlsruhe. See App. A., No. 54.

this, in a list of MS. musical works which was printed by Immanuel Breitkopf at Michaelmas, 1761, on page 25 we find " Bach, J. S. Capellmeisters und Musicdirectors in Leipzig, Passion unsers Herrn Jesu Christi, nach dem Evangelisten Lucas, *à* 2 *Traversi*, 2 *Oboi*, *Taille*, *Bassono*, 2 *Violini*, *Viola*, 5 *Voci ed Organo*." The list of instruments corresponds exactly with those in the Passion under discussion, but not the vocal parts, as there are nowhere more than four; but any one who had occasion to note the numerous errors in Breitkopf's list[595] will find no difficulty in thinking that 5 may be a misprint for 4. A doubt as to the authenticity of the work can hardly be founded on these details; but the music itself is strange and puzzling : its very simple forms reveal a tender and soft expressiveness, but it is far away from the power, fervency, and solemn grandeur of the St. John and St. Matthew Passions. Judging from this alone we should be disinclined to regard the St. Luke Passion as genuine. But we have become familiar with a mass of works of Bach's youth, and if we compare the St. Luke Passion with them it appears in quite another light. Although the score which exists was undoubtedly written at Leipzig, nothing compels us to assume that it was composed there. In Weimar, where he displayed no small industry as a composer of cantatas, he also occupied himself greatly with the whole class of Passion Music. He wrote out at Weimar, with his own hand, the parts of a St. Mark Passion by Keiser " Jesus Christus ist um unsrer Missethat willen verwundet "—" He was wounded for our transgressions "—and must therefore have had it performed there.[596] We must unquestionably assign the St. Luke Passion to the first half of the Weimar period. Though in many respects it is evidently inferior to the cantatas " Nach dir, Herr," "Aus der Tiefe rufe ich," and " Gottes Zeit," we must consider that in this, his earliest work of the kind, Bach would naturally cling closely to the type of Passion

---

[595] Thus, for instance, on p. 20 in the cantata " O Wunderkraft der Liebe " (" Herr Christ der einge Gottessohn," B.-G., XXII., No. 96, P. 2142), we find "*à* 3 *Voci*" instead of " *à* 4 *Voci*."

[596] See App. A., No. 55.

music prevalent at the time, while in the province of the
cantata he could already move with freedom. We cannot
justly estimate the St. Luke Passion unless we assign it a
place about half-way between these and his earlier Weimar
cantatas. Then its weak points will seem explicable, and
our comprehension will be opened to its more important
features.

As regards the text, the early date of its composition is
stamped on the face of it. The independent lyric pieces
in it are but eight; two arias for the soprano, one for the
alto, three for the tenor, an important opening chorus, and
a chorus for the women who followed Christ to His Crucifixion. The Gospel narrative, Luke xxii. and xxiii. to v. 53,
is all brought in, and no less than thirty-one chorales are
introduced. Such a lavish use of chorales almost always
occurs in the older Passions of central Germany which
had not yet come within the influence of the Italian
oratorio, and it was subsequently adhered to in many places
where the new style found no favour. In the Rudolstadt
Passion of 1729 there are twenty-eight chorales; in the
Gera setting twenty-five; in the Gotha Passion of 1707
nineteen; in the Schleiz Passion of 1729 twenty-seven; in
the Weissenfels Passion of 1733 thirty; Seebach, in 1714
—who was strongly influenced by Brockes—inserted no less
than forty-nine in his setting. Original verses stand
in inverse proportion: sometimes they are altogether wanting, but as time went on they increased in numbers, and
finally supplanted the chorale altogether. Bach's St. Luke
Passion, which is but slenderly provided with lyric verse,
still shows in places clear traces of Italian influence; as
when, after the words "And there followed Him a great
company of people and of women," a chorus of soprani
and alti sing :—

Weh und Schmerz in dem Gebären	Our pangs and woe in travail
Ist nichts gegen deine Noth.	Are as nought beside Thy pain.

Here the women who are brought in as the speakers have
original words to sing, while all the rest of the dramatic
music is set to Bible words alone. From these tokens we

may assign the text to about the year 1710. Certain
important Passion hymns recur naturally with more or
less regularity in every setting; and besides this, in certain
neighbourhoods some chorales seem to have been particular favourites, with passages from the Litany and the
Te Deum. In the Rudolstadt Passion, after the narrative of Judas hanging himself, come the lines from the
Litany "From the crafts and assaults of the devil, from
murder and sudden death, and from everlasting damnation,
good Lord deliver us." Farther on, after the passage
telling how John took home with him the Mother of Jesus,
come the lines "To defend and provide for the fatherless
children and widows, We beseech Thee to hear us, good
Lord! To have mercy upon all men, We beseech Thee to
hear us, good Lord!" Again, after Pilate's question "What
is truth?" the words "Thou art the King of glory, O Christ!"
and two other suitable verses are quoted from the *Te Deum.*
In the Gotha Passion according to St. Matthew, of 1707,
after the history of the crucifixion, ch. xxvii., v. 38, the
chorus comes in with "By Thy cross and passion, in our
utmost need, help us, O Lord God!" In the same way in
this St. Luke Passion, in two places we find lines from the
Litany, and three times words from the *Te Deum*—the last,
it may be observed in passing, exactly to the same melodic
setting as exists in the organ arrangement of that hymn by
Bach, which is still extant.

I have not succeeded in discovering who can have been
the writer of the lyrical portions of this work; it was not
Franck, in spite of some resemblance to the poems in his
sacred and secular verse. Texts of such uniform metre and
shallow purpose were not in his line. Still, there is a
recognisable resemblance between these and the aria texts
of the cantata "Nach dir, Herr, verlanget mich," which also
belongs to Bach's early Weimar period.

Any one who is familiar with the glowing style of
melody which characterises Bach's recitatives will at once
recognise it in those of the St. Luke Passion. It cannot
be denied that the harmonic sequences, above which the
recitative is carried on, are sometimes rather loose and

halting, and instead of the usual final cadence proper to the recitative, an arioso close occurs more often than usual, without the melody having assumed the arioso form early enough to confirm it. We get an impression that it is the work of a composer who has had but little practice in writing recitatives; and this agrees with the facts of the case, for in the earlier church cantatas to which Bach had hitherto devoted himself there is, as we know, no recitative. The style of the Biblical dramatic choruses is equally unskilful. In a few we still recognise that more general church-feeling which prevails in the Passions of the seventeenth century; others—indeed the greater number—are marked by a dramatic vividness which, it is true, does not rise to the mark of the choruses in the St. John and St. Matthew Passions, but still is conspicuously higher than that of contemporary composers. The chorus of lamenting women set to the poem above quoted is not very important, but it is well thought out, and its peculiar instrumentation—two flutes, violins, violas, and no bass—gives promise of later master-pieces, such as the soprano arias in the Ascension Oratorio, and the cantata "Herr, gehe nicht ins Gericht"—"Enter not into judgment, O Lord." The opening chorus, too, reminds us of this cantata; of course no one will expect to find in it anything like the stupendous chorale figures of the later Passions, but those who find much to admire in the four-part aria of the cantata "Denn du wirst meine Seele"—"Thou shalt not leave my soul in hell"—and the C major chorus of "Uns ist ein Kind geboren"—"Unto us a child is born"—cannot hesitate to accept this also.

The *Da capo* form predominates both in the two choruses and in the arias; the length of the pieces is small, but not smaller than in the cantatas "Nach dir, Herr, verlanget mich," or "Uns ist ein Kind geboren." The first two, it is true, show small trace of Bach's essential characteristics, they rather remind us of Handel's earliest work; and the soprano aria "Selbst der Bau der Welt erschüttert"—"Nay, the earth itself is quaking"—must be called meagre and insignificant. The rest of the arias, on the other hand, are so full of power and individuality that no one but Bach

can be named who could have written them. Particularly
noteworthy is the use here made of the bassoon. In his
Weimar period Bach showed a special predilection for this
instrument; it is possible that he had at the time a
remarkably good player at his command. In the cantata
"Nach dir, Herr," it is introduced obbligato, and again
later, more artistically, in "Mein Gott wie lang, ach
lange." The chorales throughout are more simply harmonised than we are accustomed to find them in Bach. But,
do we not find the utmost harmonic simplicity in the closing
chorale of "Denn du wirst meine Seele"? and it cannot
be denied that the treatment is careful. Moreover, Bach's
deep sense of fitness is so unmistakably revealed in the
way in which they are introduced that in view of this
alone all remaining doubts as to the authenticity of the
work must surely vanish.

In the St. Luke Passion Johann Flittner's hymn "Jesu
meines Herzens Freud"—"Jesus, Thou my heart's delight"
—constitutes, as it were, the focus of the church sentiment,
recurring in the most important situations in fresh developments, as the melody "O Haupt voll Blut"—"O Thou whose
head was wounded"—does in the St. Matthew Passion; and
Stockmann's hymn "Jesu Leiden, Pein und Tod"—"Jesus,
suffering pain and death"—in the St. John Passion. It
recurs no less than four times—first, after Christ's words,
"Where is the guest-chamber where I may eat the
Passover with my disciples?" xxii., 11 (with the third
verse "Weide mir"—"Pasture me"); then after the words
"With desire I have desired to eat this Passover with you
before I suffer" (with the fourth verse "Nichts ist lieb-
licher"—"Nothing fairer is than thine"); again, after the
scornful address of the soldier, "If Thou be the King of the
Jews, save Thyself!" (with the fifth verse "Ich bin krank"—
"I am sick, O heal thou me"); and lastly, after the prayer
of the repentant thief, "Lord, remember me when Thou
comest into Thy kingdom" (with the second verse "Tausend-
mal gedenk ich dein"—"Often have I cared for thee"). The
tender grace of this hymn, which can hardly be termed a
chorale, is characteristic of the spirit of the Passion music

of the time,[597] and particularly of this St. Luke Passion. It
was known and loved in many places, but it can never have
been a church hymn, properly speaking, and in general
use, for the reason that hardly any tune underwent so much
variation as did this one. It was originally written in the
minor, but was soon transposed into the major key. Each
of these forms, which held their place side by side in many
parts of Germany, shows many variations in the details
both of rhythm and melody.[598]   In the St. Luke Passion
Bach used only the major tune, and, as we might expect,
has given it a different form each of the four times he has
introduced it. But, whereas in his later works he was wont
to alter the harmony only, here the changes are chiefly in
the melody and rhythm. This is simply explained by the
early date of the work; when he composed the St. Luke
Passion, Bach was not yet wholly free from the influence of
those organ composers—principally the North Germans—
who, with their taste for arbitrary ornamentations, obeyed
their own immediate musical promptings rather than the
permanent needs of the congregation.[599]   It is not merely in
the tune of this hymn of Flittner that melodic and rhythmic
alterations of the chorale are to be found. The Passion hymn
" Herzliebster Jesu "—" Jesus, beloved "—occurs in the
second part of the St. Luke Passion in common time and its
usual melodic form, while, in the first part, it is in 3-4 time
and has two alterations in the tune. Arbitrary deviations from
the normal tunes occur in other chorales in the same work.
The deeper Bach penetrated into the church feeling and

---

[597] Two verses of it are also used in the Rudolstädt Passion of 1688.

[598] Dretzel, Des Evangelischen Zions Musicalische Harmonie, p. 316;
Nürnberg, 1731; gives three forms of the major and two of the minor. In
Mühlhausen the minor form was in use in Joh. Rudolf Ahle's time, Winterfeld,
Ev. Kir. II., p. 467, and at Gotha, as in Witt's Cantional, 1715, p. 203, at
Sondershausen, as we see from Gerber's Chorale book, which was never printed,
but exists in my possession in a MS. of 1745. Freylinghausen's hymn book,
on the other hand, in the Halle edition of 1741 has the major tune ; but it is not
to be found in the earlier edition of 1710. Bach himself has the minor melody
under No. 696 of the Naumburg-Zeitzer hymn book (known as Schemel's) of
1736, and in his Choralgesängen, Vol. III., 264, of 1786, the major tune. In no
two of these editions do the tunes exactly agree.

[599] See Vol. I., pp. 312 and 592.

value of the chorale, the more strictly he adhered to that form of the melody which he had once adopted; and then it was only in exceptional cases that he allowed himself to alter a single note of the *Cantus firmus*. Such an exception occurs in the seventh line of the seventh stanza of his chorale cantata " Christ lag in Todesbanden."[600]

In reviewing the instances in which Bach has introduced chorales into the St. Luke Passion, we are first struck by the close of the first part: Peter has denied his Lord, he goes out and weeps bitterly; an important tenor aria prolongs the emotion, and then, as a closing chorale, comes the sixth verse of Schwämmlein's hymn " Aus der Tiefe rufe ich "—" From the depths I cry, O Lord ! " But it is not in four parts; it is for one voice only and is sung by Peter. This is evidently a deeply considered feature and full of sentiment. But here again we recognise the connection between Bach's work and the Passions composed on the pattern of the early church cantatas; it reminds us of a similar passage in the Passion composed by Sebastiani of Weimar. The subjective character is rendered prominent by the free transformation of the two last lines of the text. Here we see the hand of the poet who compiled the text for Bach, and to him we must also refer a few other chorale texts which belong to no well-known hymns. Bach had a farther opportunity of revealing his deep religious feeling in a still more striking manner, in the course of the story of Peter's denial—in the passage where we are told how that Peter, who had previously avowed himself ready to follow his Lord to prison and to death, followed Jesus into the High Priest's palace; here we are to discover whether he is strong enough to keep his pledge. At this point the chorus sings in unison, and in the " Collect " tone, the words of the Lord's prayer "And lead us not into temptatoin, but deliver us from evil." The solemn and impressive effect of this short movement is intensified when we turn to the place in the Gospel of St. Mark xiv., 38, which Bach must

---

[600] B.-G., I., p. 124., P. 1196. The expressive Melismata with which Bach loved to ornament his chorales of course do not here come into the question, since they neither change nor conceal the fundamental form of the melody.

certainly have had in his mind : Christ, praying in the
garden of Gethsemane, finds His disciples asleep; He turns
first to Peter—" Watch and pray," He says, " lest ye enter
into temptation.   The spirit is willing, but the flesh is
weak."   But the most deeply felt adaptation of the chorale
Bach has reserved till near the end of the work.   The
Evangelist sings " And having said thus, He gave up the
ghost."   Here we have, in four parts, the chorale " Ich hab
mein Sach Gott heimgestellt "—" All care for me I leave
to God "—performed only by wind instruments, oboes and
bassoons.   After this symphony is ended the chorus sings,
still in four parts, the twelfth verse of the same chorale :—

> Derselbe mein Herr Jesu Christ
> Für all mein Sünd gestorben ist,
> Und auferstanden mir zu gut,
> Der Höllen Gluth
> Gelöscht mit seinem theuren Blut.

> My Saviour, Christ the crucified,
> To purge my sin has bled and died;
> And He is risen for my good.
> Hell's fiery flood
> Is slaked by His most precious blood.

It is this which first suggests the real meaning of the
instrumental subject which is repeated after the singing.
Then the narrative goes on as far as the descent from the
cross, interrupted once more by a chorale.   A tenor aria,
full of the stricken fervent feeling which is so essentially
Bach's, goes on :—

> Lasst mich ihn nur noch einmal küssen,
> Und legt dann meine Freud ins Grab.

> Ah, grant me but once more to kiss Him,
> And then the grave must hold my Joy.

Nine bars after, the oboes and bassoons begin once more
the same chorale, and carry it on with a few breaks till the
end.   This combination of independent verse sung by voices,
and a chorale for instruments only—the chorale having
already acquired a peculiar dramatic chiaroscuro from its connection with what has gone before—could have been conceived
and worked out by no composer of the eighteenth century

excepting Bach himself. A farther and strong evidence of his authorship is to be found in the fact that a very similar combination occurs in the cantata " Gottes Zeit "— " God's time is the best "—and that in both cases it is the same chorale that is so treated, and the reader will recollect that this cantata was also written in the early Weimar period.[601] As it is altogether more mature in style we may conclude that the St. Luke Passion was written earliest. It cannot fail to strike any one who compares them that the form of the chorale is different in the two. In both it varies from the original melody ; but both the forms were in use together with the original tune in that neighbourhood. The melody in the cantata at first is identical with that of " Warum betrübst du dich, mein Herz," and I presume that Bach selected it on that account.[602] This is not the only indication of an internal connection between the St. Luke Passion and the *Actus tragicus*. The celebrated treatment of the closing words " Ja komm, Herr Jesu "—" Yea come, Lord Jesus "—has its counterpart at the close of the chorale " Stille, stille ! ist die Losung "—" Silence, silence ! is our watchword." Here all the voices are silent excepting the soprano, which has the words " Silence ! Silence ! " alone, above the bass, having previously begun the chorale in the same manner and with the same words.

If we acknowledge the St. Luke Passion as a genuine composition by Bach, the number attributed to him by the Necrology is complete. For, though in a list of the compositions by Seb. Bach, published in 1790 by his son, Philipp Emanuel, we read, on p. 81, " A Passion according to St. Matthew, *incomplete*," we may consider this to mean merely the first sketch of the great St. Matthew Passion to

---

[601] See Vol. I., p. 456.

[602] The use of this tune in Thuringia is not only established by Witt's Cantional, but also by Michael Bach's motett " Unser Leben ist ein Schatten." Rust very justly regards Bach's use of it as a fresh proof that the cantata " Gottes Zeit " was written in Weimar, B.-G., XXIII., p. xl. The form adopted in the St. Luke Passion is to be found in Freylinghausen Gesangbuch, 1741; but in the tenor aria Bach deviates from this in one passage.

Picander's words.   Otherwise Emanuel Bach must have possessed three Passions and Friedemann only two, which is contradicted by the perfectly trustworthy account of the way in which the property left by their father was divided. At the same time it must remain uncertain whether the MS. spoken of was actually incomplete, or whether, as the grand closing chorus of the first part was not yet inserted, it may not have misled the writer of the catalogue into thinking so.   We must pay due honour to the St. Luke Passion as the first attempt in this direction of a great genius.   Bach himself thought it worthy of revision even after he had written his greatest work of the kind.   In the course of that revision, which was probably carried out during the years 1732-1734, he may have improved it in some details, but the whole aspect of the work tells us that it can have undergone no radical change ; it is true, however, that it would hardly lead us to anticipate the height to which Bach was able to rise as a composer of the Passion subsequently, at Leipzig.   This is revealed in the St. John and St. Matthew Passions, to which we will now turn our attention.   It is by a singular and happy chance that these three Passions have been preserved to us, for the process of Bach's development is broadly stamped upon them.   As has been already said, the narratives of St. Mark and St. Luke had no place in the liturgy used at Leipzig.   Bach, who loved to establish the most intimate alliance between his own music and the services of the church, of course did not overlook this circumstance.   It is therefore highly probable that he himself attributed the highest importance to the two later works, and we may indulge in the belief that in them is preserved to us the very best that he thought himself capable of in this branch of his art.   The other two Passions seem not long to have survived their author, even in the scene of his labours.   In the year 1780, Doles, the Cantor, had only three performed ; the St. Matthew, St. John, and possibly the St. Luke Passions.[603]

---

[603] Rochlitz, Für Freunde der Tonkunst, Vol. IV., p. 282.   "As a boy, under Doles, I only made acquaintance with three Passions."   This he says when

If the hypothesis is a correct one that Bach did really compose the music to Picander's Passion text of 1725, the Passion music which he conducted on Good Friday, April 7, 1724, can only have been that according to St. John; and this assumption is so far confirmed by the state of the MS. that it acquires the certainty of an established fact. This was the fourth year in which concerted Passion music had been performed in one or another of the Leipzig churches. When Kuhnau first introduced it, in St. Thomas', in 1721, the Council agreed that these Passion performances should take place every year in the two chief churches alternately, so in 1724 it must have come to the turn of St. Nicholas'. Since, however, the organ there was of very limited compass, Bach preferred to remain at St. Thomas', and had made all his arrangements, and had sent out notices by issuing the printed books of words. The superintendent of St. Nicholas, however, would not forego the honour; he laid his protest before the Council, and within four days of the performance Bach had to submit to remove to the church of St. Nicholas, to carry out as quickly as possible the necessary preparations, and to print new programmes.

The form in which the St. John Passion was performed for the first time was not that in which we now know it. Before it finally crystallised it had undergone various vicissitudes. We have every reason to suppose that Bach had already written it in Cöthen, in fact at the time when he decided on applying for the post of cantor to St. Thomas' and expected to receive the appointment. His application was made at the end of the year 1722, and he no doubt reckoned that he should be in office in Leipzig by Good Friday, 1723, and must be prepared for that event. Hence, the work would have been composed in the early months of 1723. As we know, however, Bach's call was delayed till May, so he could not make use of his work till Good Friday, 1724. This history of its origin accounts for a

---

speaking of the St. John Passion, which must therefore have been one of the three, and of course the St. Matthew, his greatest and most famous work, was another. The St. Luke Passion was still procurable in the Leipzig music shops. at any rate, as late as 1760, as is shown by Breitkopf's list mentioned above.

number of peculiarities in the work. In the first instance, the composer had to hurry it on if he wished to have it ready in time, and, since there was no poet equal to the task in Cöthen, he had to do the best he could himself with the text. The Bible narrative was before him, and he was more competent than any one else could be to select the appropriate chorale verses; the original verses presented the only difficulty. To find these he naturally turned to the favourite Passion poem by Brockes. This supplied him with the texts for the arias "From the bondage of transgression," "Haste, ye deeply wounded spirits," "Beloved Saviour," "My heart, behold how all the world," *Arioso*, and the next song "Dissolve, O my heart," with the words of the last chorus "Rest here in peace."[604] Bach did not borrow any of these verbatim from Brockes; the last three are very independently dealt with, and the first two altered in details. The changes do not always seem to be for the better; though in some instances he has mitigated a few harsh expressions in the original. Still, they are not on the whole unworthy of the praises lavished on them at a later period by Birnbaum;[605] it is true they do not satisfy our highest requirements as to the co-ordination of idea and suggestiveness of expression, but they show a delicate taste for musical verse. A few comparisons of the two works will show this more plainly. After the death of Christ is accomplished, in Brockes' text the believer is made to ask in an indirect way whether the work of redemption is indeed finished. "Thus," as he puts it, "asks the daughter of Zion, and the Saviour bows His head in sign of assent." As Bach has it, the question is directly addressed to the Redeemer: "Beloved Saviour, wilt Thou answer, as Thou hast now the cross endured . . . Shall all the world redemption see? Thou canst for anguish now say nothing, yet dost Thou bow Thy head and say in silence, Yea."

---

[604] "Von den Stricken meiner Sünden," "Eilt, ihr angefochtnen Seelen," "Mein theurer Heiland," "Mein Herz, indem die ganze Welt," "Zerfliesse, mein Herz," "Ruht wohl, ihr heiligen Gebeine." The English text is quoted throughout from Novello's edition.

[605] See ante, p. 238.

The final chorus is founded on Brockes' model, only so far as the second half is concerned; the first portion is on the usual pattern of those closing verses which Bach no doubt had in his memory; and the five remaining aria texts cannot be referred with certainty to any earlier poems, though the aria "Zerschmettert mich" may have been suggested by a verse of Franck. Bach may have relied for the most part on his own inventive powers. This, however, cannot be actually proved, nor is it indeed certain that it was he who wrote the text modified from Brockes. But we here meet with the same want of skill in the use of words as has been already alluded to, and the construction is that of a man whose head was well furnished with Bible texts and hymns, but who was not apt at combining them into a whole. But a man who was only slightly experienced in putting verses together could not have compiled this text; and as I shall presently bring forward evidence based on a MS. by Bach himself, that on another occasion he certainly made an attempt at poetry,[606] of quite the same stamp as that which we are now discussing, we have every reason to suspect this to be his handiwork.

In the setting of the Bible words, and even of the chorales, Bach subsequently found but little to alter essentially. But this was not the case with the pieces in madrigal form, in which the words of the text, hastily thrown together, had as it were run away with him. Three of these he dispensed with entirely, and not, certainly, because they were of inferior musical merit; their character must have seemed to him unsuited to their place. In lieu of two of them he inserted new solos of a different stamp, one of which—"Consider, O my soul," with the aria that follows it—is, again, a paraphrase from Brockes. This he seems certainly to have written himself, and it cannot be said that the attempt is any more successful than the former ones. Brockes' words are in the very worst taste, but Bach's verge on utter nonsense.[607] Another portion

---

[606] *A propos* of the cantata "Vergnügte Pleissenstadt."

[607] The text of the arioso, for bass, is moreover wrongly given in the edition of the B.-G., XII.,[1] p. 55. The original parts and score both give the words

of the madrigal verses were subsequently cut out by Bach
and replaced by an instrumental symphony ("Mein Herz
indem "—" My heart, behold"—with the preceding recitative and the soprano air following it), but he afterwards
restored them on the original plan.   He must also certainly
have laid a revising hand on the opening and closing
choruses.   Both these were grand chorale choruses.   The
last "Christe, du Lamm Gottes," now forms the last
number of the cantata for the Sunday before Lent "Du
wahrer Gott" (see ante p. 351); indeed, it must surely have
belonged there from the first and have been transferred
from thence to the Passion, merely because the composer
laid that cantata aside for the time as beside his immediate
purpose; but after failing to bring out the Passion in 1723
the chorus was restored to its original position, and probably
was never once performed as a portion of the Passion.
The opening chorus, "O Mensch, bewein dein Sünde gross,"
was, we may imagine, made use of by Bach for his third
Passion, written in 1725, and finally incorporated in the
revised form of the St. Matthew Passion, as the closing
chorus of the first section, transposed from E flat major to
E major.   Its place in the St. John Passion was taken
by a new chorus, "Herr unser Herrscher"—"Lord, our
Redeemer"—with a simple chorale to close the whole work,
"Ach Herr, lass dein lieb Engelein"—"Lord Jesus, Thy
dear Angel send."   Most of the alterations here enumerated
were made for a second performance of this Passion, which
seems to have taken place on Good Friday, 1727.   Bach
afterwards conducted it at least twice again, and each time
made some few farther alterations; the dates of these
performances cannot be exactly ascertained, at least one,
however, must have taken place in 1730.[608]

The old custom of giving the narrative of the Evangelist
and the speeches of individuals in recitative, while those
of a number of persons were sung by a choir in parts, put

" mit bittrer Lust und halb beklemmtem Herzen" and afterwards "wie dir aus
Dornen, so ihn stechen, die Himmelsschlüsselblumen blühn."   It is equally
incorrect in Winterfeld, Ev. Kir. III., p. 368.

[608] See App. A., No. 56.

many and great difficulties in the way of any attempt to
create a well proportioned and homogeneous work of art.
The composer was absolutely dependent on a text which
was not written for musical treatment, and in which he
could not venture to alter any essential features.   Many
portions of it compelled him to employ all the wealth
of musical means, while in others, of which the purport
was no less weighty, he had to confine himself to simple
recitative.   Short, and even subsidiary passages, were dis-
proportionately prominent from having to be treated in
chorus, while some deep and vital utterance ran a risk of
passing disregarded in the modest delivery of a solo voice.
Thus it became a leading function in the inserted chorales
and madrigal pieces to restore the balance; they had to
rivet the attention of the hearer to the important points,
to define and concentrate the separate incidents of the
drama, and to distribute light and shade alike on the whole
and on the details.   It cannot be concealed that in this
respect the St. John Passion leaves much to be desired.
In more than one passage the images mingle in confusion—
as Christ's examination before Annas, with Peter's denial;
Christ's appearance at the Judgment seat, with His crucifixion; and, again, the episode where Christ from the cross
commends His mother to the care of John, does not stand
out distinctly.[609]   We cannot always consider the places
where the madrigal verses are brought in as well chosen.
The recitative "Simon Peter also followed Jesus" introduces
the description of Peter's denial, and when we find inserted
here a song of hopeful faith :—

> I follow Thee also, my Saviour, with gladness,
> And will not forsake Thee my Life and my Light—

while the incident it leads to is one of contemptible weakness and cowardly retractation, it needs no very subtle sense
of fitness to perceive that a transient feeling is made
prominent at the cost of the whole effect, and all the more
so since two arias are thus made to follow each other almost

---

[609] B.-G., XII.,[1] pp. 29, 31, 83, 102, and 104. Novello's edition, 29-32,
85, 98, 111.

without interruption. Even where the place seems appropriate for the insertion of a lyric piece the verses themselves are not satisfactory. After Jesus has been smitten by one of the High Priest's servants, the feeling of the situation is very finely concentrated in the chorale "O Lord, who dares to smite Thee." But this was immediately followed by a second portion of a chorale, on the seventeenth verse of "Jesu Leiden, Pein und Tod," in which the bass sang below the *Cantus firmus* of the soprano an independent text, which, though it referred to the Saviour scourged and crowned with thorns, was by no means suited to this place. The words "went out and wept bitterly" were originally followed by a passionate aria "Zerschmettert mich"—"Fall on me, O ye hills"—which gave the sentiment a turn quite different from that which was led up to by the setting of the foregoing words from the Bible. All these things point to the perplexity in which Bach found himself as to the necessary poetical additions, when he undertook the composition of the St. John Passion. He had actually no text for the more important places, and for the others he had none that were appropriate. The numerous alterations which the work constantly underwent prove that it did not satisfy him. Much he certainly improved in time: the first aria here named he eliminated, in spite of its great musical merit, and the second he replaced, with much taste, by a song of lamentation. Still many imperfections remain.

It is very evident that it was this difficulty as to the lyrical antithesis which led Bach to a quite peculiar treatment of the dramatic choruses. Of these, the St. John Passion includes a considerable number, highly artistic, vigorous, and characteristic compositions. The breadth and solidity with which most of them are worked out are very striking—almost as if they were oratorio choruses; and it need hardly be said that the words themselves, so far as any connection with the narrative is concerned, do not involve any such treatment, since they suggest movement rather than passive strength; indeed, a glance at the St. Matthew Passion shows that Bach was quite clear on the subject. But the need for some broad lyric forms was imperative and had to be satisfied, as well as might be, with the means at hand. From this point of view it becomes intelligible how such comparatively tame and unemotional words as " Let us not divide it, but cast lots for it who shall have it," or "It is not lawful for us to put a man to death," can have been set to choruses so full of musical purpose. There is still another proof that Bach, when he wrote the choruses of Jews, ranked as first in importance the musical form he required to give, rather than any striking dramatic rendering of a mass of people. It is that he has reset almost every one of these compositions once or oftener to other words, with small alterations and such amplification or abridgement as the text may have required; thus, the chorus " If this man were not an evil doer " to the words " It is not lawful "; the chorus " We salute Thee, King of the Jews " to " Write not the King of the Jews "; the chorus " We have a law" to the words " If thou let this man go." Besides this, Bach has constructed a short subject of four bars which he introduces in no less than four choral passages, which are sung respectively by the soldiers who take Jesus prisoner, by the populace outside the palace of Pilate, and finally by the high priests, under the most diverse conditions; and the accompaniment given to these in semiquavers on the upper instruments is also used with episodical extensions for the grander chorus " It is not lawful for us to put any man to death." It cannot be asserted that the music is equally well suited to all the different texts. The repetition of the phrase to which the reiterated cry of "Crucify Him" is set is founded on internal fitness, and it is not positively repugnant to the poetic sense, even in other instances; but we feel it quite unsuitable when we find the music to the words " We salute Thee, King of the Jews," afterwards adapted to the text " Write not," &c. For in this instance the fundamental feeling is entirely different; in the first instance it is malicious scorn—which, indeed, the music admirably depicts so far as its means allow; in the second it is remonstrance or a secret anxiety; Bach has here sacrificed suitability of character to musical solidity and unity.

Of the four Gospel narratives of the sufferings and death of Christ, that of St. John is the least detailed and animated. A mass of significant circumstances, well suited for musical treatment, is passed over in silence; as, for instance, the institution of the Lord's supper, the agony in the garden of Gethsemane, and the convulsions of nature at the moment of Christ's death. Bach felt this as a serious deficiency, and to compensate for it in some degree he transferred, at the right place, the description of the earthquake from St. Matthew, and set the words which close the episode of Peter's denial with true musical feeling: "Then Peter thought upon the word of Jesus, and he went forth and wept bitterly."[610] On the whole, he could not of course remedy the meagreness of the narrative; but this circumstance must be taken into consideration to explain the fact that the St. John Passion is far inferior to the St. Matthew, or even to the St. Luke. Its highest permanent value does not lie in the general construction; as a whole, it displays a certain murky monotony and vague mistiness. This must be confessed even though we are fully conscious that such a work must be viewed from quite a different standpoint to an oratorio or a musical drama. It is true in considering a Passion setting we must never forget that it is church music, which does not admit of any radical differences in the treatment of the epic, lyric, and dramatic elements; but, on the contrary, must express everything, even the most opposite ideas, within the spell-bound circle of impersonal generalities. Hence it ought not to be regarded as want of style when the recitative of the speaking persons is not sharply distinguished from that given to the Evangelist by its greater animation, if the Evangelist himself seems impressed by them; the words of the Bible have the same importance, no matter who it is that speaks them. The composer must remain at full liberty to render the expressions of the soldiers or high priests by a full chorus as well as

---

[610] The words of Jesus were "In this night before the cock crow thou shalt deny me thrice." They are wanting in St. John's Gospel, and as Bach has omitted to borrow them from St. Matthew the passage he has inserted has no connection or sense.

those of the populace; it is sufficient that the contrast between individuals and numbers should be generally indicated. Nor can any objection be made where a grand chorus is constructed on a short sentence, such as "Crucify Him," since, even from the church point of view, it can be full of high symbolical significance. All the dramatic elements which underlie the text of the Passion music can only approximate a true dramatic utterance, but cannot assume its most vivid and natural expression. Meanwhile, though granting all this, we find, remaining within the limits thus imposed, ample opportunity for subtle distinctions and gradations; this has been incontrovertibly proved by Bach himself in the St. Matthew Passion; but the St. John Passion cannot be admitted to be of the highest perfection in this respect.

The adaptation of Brockes' poetry in the St. John Passion has given it a certain resemblance to the Italian oratorio, inasmuch as the aria "Haste, ye deeply wounded spirits," represents a dialogue between the Daughter of Sion and the souls of the believers. The division into two portions which, in the same way, we find in the St. Luke Passion, must also be referred to the Italian oratorio, in that the first portion was intended to be performed before the sermon and the second after it. The custom of the Protestant church did not correspond to this; hence, when the narrative of the Passion was divided, it was into six sections, one for each day of Passion week; or sometimes even more, some being performed on the previous Sundays in Lent.[611] Of course, when we consider the actual process by which the text of the St. John Passion was evolved, any considerable influence from the Italian oratorio is out of the question; it is far more conspicuous in the St. Matthew Passion. I mention this merely as characterising the difference between the earlier and the later works, and not as a merit or a demerit

---

[611] The Rudolstadt Passion of 1688 is divided into six parts (Actus). Count Heinrich XII. introduced at Schleiz a Passion in twelve sections, the first to be sung on the first Sunday in Lent and the last on Good Friday. The text exists in the Count's Library at Wernigerode. Both these are composed to "harmonies of the Gospel"—*i.e.*, texts compiled from all the four Gospels.

in either.   But as a result the St. John Passion has a less modern air according to the standard of the time.

This becomes more than negatively evident in the chorales which are used to introduce and close each part, and which (excepting the first, "O Mensch, bewein dein Sünde," which was afterwards cut out) are set simply in four parts.   If Bach had been minded to follow out the old custom in every particular, he would, at the end of the whole work, have introduced either the usual thanksgiving, or with a nearer allusion to the burial of Christ, Rist's chorale "O Traurigkeit, o Herzeleid!"—"O anguish sore, O grief of heart."   The choral aria over the sepulchre, which precedes the final chorale—and which occurs very similar in form in many of the Passion settings of Central Germany at the end of the seventeenth and beginning of the eighteenth centuries—owes its existence to an ancient ceremonial—*i.e.*, the performance of the interment in front of the altar (auf dem Chor), at which stage of the proceedings a motett was sung on the chorale "O Traurigkeit."   I have not discovered that this was still customary at Leipzig in Bach's time, but that the ceremony had left its record in the close which continued in use in the Passion music is very certain. The remembrance of it must, therefore, have survived in Leipzig, since it was an established thing that after the Passion music was ended the congregation sang the hymn "O Traurigkeit," and this was obviously the reason why Bach would not introduce it again at the end of the St. John Passion.   Much later, at a time when Passion settings were already performed in concert halls, it became common to designate the finale by the name "By the sepulchre."[612] Nowadays, if this dirge is not omitted and, at the same time, the closing chorale is retained, two choral pieces must be sung in succession, as Bach has planned in the St. John Passion; and the same thing is observable in many other Passions of the time of the old church cantatas. The close relationship which the St. John Passion bears

---

[612] Israel, Frankfurter Concert-Chronik of 1713 to 1780.   Frankfurt a. M 1876, p. 33 (a concert programme of March 26, 1743).

to these is also discernible in the recitation of the Bible
text, which renounces all attempt to give prominence to
the speeches of individuals—Christ, for instance—by the
use of additional effects, and is throughout content with
a simple fundamental bass.

But it is only by this reticence that Bach adheres to
the early practice, and not in the form of the recitatives
themselves. After pointing out those peculiarities of the
St. John Passion which cannot entirely satisfy our highest
demands, we must all the more emphatically insist that
in everything which relates to musical style, in invention,
and in the elaboration of the separate compositions, Bach
proves himself to have reached the heights of ripe and
perfect mastery. The treatment of the recitatives, as
in the cantatas, is of Bach's best period; but any one who
should look for a difference in manner corresponding to
that between a contemplative passage, a narrative, or a
dramatic speech will be disappointed. The composer has
not neglected such opportunities as the Gospel text affords
for more impressive phrases or more incisive accentuation;
and, besides frequently giving strong relief to important
passages by special melodic or harmonic combinations, he
often depicts the idea of movement—such as going back-
ward, falling to the earth, the drawing or sheathing of
swords, interment, smiting, scourging, or fighting—by
graphic musical phrases, usually in the voice, but occasionally in the accompanying bass. Emotions also, which
are only indirectly connected with an image or a statement,
are expressed as opportunity offers; thus, the word "dying"
is illustrated by a lingering, longing *melisma*, "Crucifixion"
and "Golgotha" by a painful and dislocated turn. When
the servants warm themselves by the fire Bach sets the
words to a figure which is obviously intended to convey the
sentiment of comfort, though we might not perhaps suspect
the intention if the same phrase did not recur when
Peter warms himself (pp. 30 and 34 of Novello's English
edition). Much more, resembling this, is left to be divined.
When on the words "Every one that is of the truth heareth
my voice," spoken by Jesus, a wailing *melisma* is brought

II.

out,[613] there is certainly no direct instigation in the text itself. Possibly the composer had in his mind the passage in the Gospel of St. Luke, where Christ weeps over Jerusalem saying, "If thou hadst known the things that belong unto thy peace," xix., 42. Now and then Bach even diverges into the theatrically dramatic, and introduces declamatory figures which seem to require the addition of gesture for their full effect; thus, in Peter's reiterated cry "I am not"; the phrase "Now Barabbas was a robber," and the *a-parte* passages which are carefully indicated by the directions *piano* and *forte*.[614] Still, from all these examples it is not possible to deduct any fixed principle of treatment, for Bach quite as often leaves words and sentences, which would well bear some characteristic accent or melisma, to be chanted in commonplace recitative. The supreme and sole principle of form that governs throughout is the result of his own innate tendency towards vigorous melodic movement. Everything else is merely a means to this end; if it were not so it would be inconceivable why Bach should sometimes introduce picturesque details which have no dramatic musical purpose, and which, in themselves, are mere sports of the composer—*e.g.*, when the word "the Pavement" (in German the word "Hochpflaster") is declaimed in such a way as that the first syllable is sung on G sharp, reached by a leap of a sixth, and the other two on C sharp.[615] A stronger development of the melodic element suited the style of the church recitative, and it was a favourite method to let the closing fall die away into an *arioso* passage, in which it is impossible not to recognise an affinity to the character of the cadence in the Gregorian church mode. It was from such cadences that the elaborate —nay, too elaborate—*melismata* had been derived, and Bach employed them in setting the phrases "and wept bitterly" (p. 37), and "Pilate took Jesus and scourged Him" (p. 57). But even a reference to the style of the church recitative

---

[613] B.-G., XII.,[1] p. 53, bar 9.   Nov. ed., p. 56, bar 3.

[614] B.-G., XII.,[1] p. 33, 54, 119, 122.   Nov. ed., pp. 36, 57, 121, 123, &c.

[615] See B.-G., XII.,[1] p. 78, bars 4-5.   The word "Hoch" is thus strongly emphasised in the German.

is insufficient to explain the matter as it lies before us. Bach's recitative—I can only repeat my former expressions,[616] for I find none more apt—has in it something of the character of a prelude or an independent fantasia. The composer wanders through the realm of musical imagery and gives himself up to realising it, now in one way and now in another—prompted to do so now by some important factor, and now by something wholly unimportant, and without ever renouncing his right to absolute free-will. We can find no reason in the nature of things why in one place he should devote all the means at his command to an exhaustive illustration of some emphatic word, while in another he passes it over with complete indifference: it was his good pleasure, so he did it.

I have already alluded to the oratorio character of the dramatic choruses in the St. John Passion; still there is something in them which does not bear the true stamp of the oratorio. They are all characterised by a polyphony of exceptional complexity and a certain compactness of structure, so far as is compatible with broad working out. It may be admitted that by this means the fanatical Jews, in their craving for a victim, their wild accusations and threats, are graphically depicted. But this is not the real reason which made Bach write in this particular manner, for the chorus of the soldiers who cast lots for Christ's coat is constructed in the same way. Though Bach had been forced, from the lack of lyric text, to find a substitute for it in the deeper musical treatment of the dramatic chorus, he must, on the other hand, have seen very clearly that he could not deviate very widely from the narrow dimensions of the forms properly associated with the poetic essence of these choruses without detriment to the whole. It is the mixture of breadth and concentration, arising from a compromise between the oratorio and the dramatic styles, which gives the Biblical choruses of the St. John Passion so peculiar an aspect. These grandiose forms, which are full to overflowing of musical sense and

---

significance, testify to a stupendous creative power, but at the same time have something oppressive and sultry about them. The large space they fill in the whole work stamps the greater part of it with their peculiar character.

The chorales are almost all set simply in four parts, and are such as Bach could write at the height of his powers. By a marvellous pliancy in the treatment of the parts, and an inexhaustible wealth of harmonic resource, he was able to distribute over the whole a fresh and varied vitality with a subtle and significant illustration of details; and at the same time to work out the chorales, each as a whole, in most effective contrast to the rest. The best example of this is offered by the chorale "Ach grosser König"—"Thy bonds, O Son of God"—which is permeated by a vein of ecstatic love; and that wonderful hymn, touching in its extreme simplicity, "In meines Herzens Grunde"—"Within our inmost being." Indeed, the choice of the chorale is worthy of the great master, both as regards the text and the melody. Stockmann's hymn on the· Passion "Jesu Leiden, Pein und Tod" forms, as it were, the pivot of the church feeling of the work; originally it recurred four times with four different verses. One verse Bach subsequently took out, as well as the aria "Himmel reisse"—"Rend, ye heavens." It is ·now twice repeated in a simple form, and finally, after the words "And He bowed His head and departed," as a chorale fantasia; for the bass sings an aria to the organ, while the soft and meditative chorale in four parts is woven in with it.

As regards the solo songs, they probably all (with the exception of the aria "Ach windet euch nicht so" and that which subsequently took its place "Consider, O my soul") are among the best that Bach ever wrote. How they can ever have been supposed to betray the manner of an earlier period[617] it is hard to discover, for they almost all depart, more or less, by their grand, free, and novel form, from the traditional type of aria. The very first "From the bondage of transgression" is interesting as to its form, and

---

[617] Winterfeld, Ev. Kir., III., p. 364.

important from the episodical transition from the second to the third part. The aria "Zerschmettert mich" derives, from the frequent changes of time and the bold close of the voice part on the dominant, a character of personal passion devoid of all conventionality; in novelty and captivating ingenuity it is superior to that which subsequently took its place "Ah, my soul!" though this too, its other merits apart, is distinguished by its ingenious construction. We are insensibly led on from the second part into the third, which here consists only of the opening ritornel, while the song continues its course independently. The construction of the aria "It is finished" is again quite peculiar, with its *adagio* subject, accompanied only by the organ and viola di gamba, contrasted with an *allegro* to the whole orchestra of strings, returning at the close with startling effect to the *adagio*. The bass aria "Haste ye deeply wounded spirits," with its stressful rhythm and the impressive questioning of the chorus, is so full of dramatic force that scarcely any other solo piece out of Bach's Mysteries will bear comparison with it. The two *arioso* numbers also: "Consider, O my soul" and "My heart behold," are compositions of the most striking character and deep musical feeling.[618] The highly artistic, and, indeed, over-refined, setting which characterises most of these pieces no doubt prevents their having that simple charm and popular effect which is the specialty of almost all the solos in the St. Matthew Passion. The impression they leave is profound and grave, and their prevalent feeling is gloomy; they reveal a near affinity to the duet in the cantata "Du wahrer Gott und Davidssohn," which was, indeed, composed at the same period. There is hardly any interest to be found in comparing Bach's settings of Brockes' text with those of other composers. Not only do they surpass them immeasurably in richness and

---

[618] The former is to be accompanied by two *Viole d'amore*, lute, and bass. In the absence of the lute Bach has given the part to a cembalo, and an autograph part for that instrument is in existence. Later, after 1730, he transferred it to an organ obbligato; the autograph part exists—it is in D flat major and has the indication in Bach's handwriting "To be played on the organ with the eight and four foot Gedackt." The harpsichord part is in E flat major.

depth, but, in consequence of the profound church feeling that prevades his style, they stand forth as something totally distinct when compared with the operatic religionism of the other German masters. The solitary grandeur in which Bach dwells as a composer of church music is only rendered more clear by a comparison with similar works by Keiser, Telemann, Mattheson, Stölzel, or even by Handel.

The St. John Passion includes only two madrigal choruses. The dirge, "Rest here in peace," which immediately precedes the finale chorale, is an aria for chorus which, however, is not in the stanza form, but in that of the Italian *da capo* air. A very simple form of structure was here an accepted law of style ; the upper part has the melody accompanied by the lower voices in free and graceful movement ; the ritornel comes in at the usual places. The length of this number is all the more surprising. It is in five instead of three sections, for the second is repeated as a fourth in a different key ; the whole thus attains the enormous length of 172 bars. It is an inexhaustible lament and leavetaking over the grave ; flowing passages in quavers on the strings sink softly down to the lowest depths, mingling with the tearful tenderness of the vocal parts like the dull, slow fall of clods on the coffin. Bach evidently did not trouble himself with the fact that the burial of Christ was effected in a manner different from ours, for there can be no doubt that he intended to represent a descent into the grave. A very remarkable composition lies before us in the opening chorus, which Bach wrote for the second performance of the St. John Passion. The text is as follows :—

> Lord our Redeemer, Thou whose name
> In all the world is glorious,
> Show us in this Thy Passion
> That Thou, the true and only Son.
> For evermore.
> E'en from humiliation sore,
> Dost rise victorious.

The first lines resemble the eighth Psalm, and were, no doubt, borrowed from it; the key is G minor. The voices roll onward above long-held pedal points—now in impressive

outcry and massive homophonic subjects, piled up in figures
of semiquavers; now in proudly-mounting themes or broadly
flowing passages, worked out in canon, in fugue, or in free
imitation: a mighty picture of divine power and glory. The
orchestra is quite differently treated; a vague and incessant
rushing movement is heard throughout the work, generally
in three parts on the violins and violas, and always in the
medium or lower notes, with brief excursions into the basses
and rapid passages in the lower flutes and oboes, while
above this the wind instruments hold long-drawn notes of
lamentation almost uninterruptedly. What Bach's general
intention was is obvious at first sight; he proposed to depict
at once the· majesty and might of the Son of God, and His
utter humiliation under the bitterest sufferings of which
humanity is capable.

Nay, we can hardly err even in our interpretation of the
semiquaver movement in the instruments. It was a favourite
trope with the sacred poets of the time to figure the miseries
of human life as the waves of the sea which threaten to
surge up and overwhelm man; the narrative of Christ
crossing the sea was what proximately suggested this. A
great part of the cantata previously discussed, "Jesu schläft"
—"Jesus sleeps"—is founded on this conception, and in
the cantata, "My spirit was in heaviness,"[619] we find an
aria with the same purport. It was, of course, an easy and
pleasing task to represent the motion of the waves by
musical means; in the last-named aria this is done by a
figure on the violins, which bears considerable resemblance
to that which predominates in the first chorus of the
St. John Passion. We therefore can have no doubt as to
the meaning which was conveyed in this heavily-rolling
instrumental figure. Bach has given the antagonistic images
and sentiments which he desired to render to antithetical
bodies of sound; the element of divine supremacy was to be
expressed by the voices; the instruments were to lend the
expression of human suffering. Nor is it contradictory to
this interpretation when we find that in some passages the

---

[619] See Vol. I., p. 532. English edition by Novello.

voices unite with the stringed instruments; for, when sung, the semiquaver figures acquire a different character, and all the more so when, as here, they occur only in a transient form and in alternation with a rich variety of other figures. This is not, indeed, the first time that we have met with such a combination in Bach; in the final chorale of the cantata "Enter not into judgment," the same idea prevails. Of course, we have not here two different conceptions merely superficially connected; both have arisen from one common idea, and are only contrasted for the sake of greater effect. The power of imagination which could enable Bach to amalgamate two such opposite images into one is truly marvellous; but there is yet another thing which excites our astonishment in no less degree. I have already pointed out again and again how Bach loved, in his cantatas, to epitomise and concentrate the whole domain of feeling in the opening chorus, and so to define the limits to which the development of the work in hand might extend. The introductory chorus of the St. John Passion serves the same end; it is, as it were, the prologue to the drama. Beyond a doubt, it was only after deep consideration that Bach decided on selecting this text, which bears neither on the sentiment of lamentation, on a feeling for the sufferings of Christ, nor on our blessedness as won by this sacrifice of Himself, but merely on the contrast between the eternal omnipotence of the Son of God and His temporary humiliation. In point of fact, even in the setting of this chorus we nowhere find any expression of warm sympathetic emotion; it is full of a dark unapproachable grandeur, and remains, in that respect, unique among Bach's works.[620] But it rehearses with impressive distinctness the sentiment of the whole work—a work which is not always synthetically constructed nor elaborated with all the charm of variety, but which stands out in a grandiose outline, though in a dim and lurid chiaroscuro which contrasts strangely enough with the

---

[620] Even Winterfeld (Ev. Kir., III., p. 366) has pointed out this feature in the introductory chorus to the St. John Passion, and has subjected it throughout to a very sympathetic analysis. His objections to the views of Rochlitz seem to me ill-founded; however, their differences might well be reconciled.

ideas of tenderness and love that we are accustomed to associate with the character of the writer of this Gospel.

At the time when Bach decided on composing a Passion according to St. Matthew, he had at his disposal what he had conspicuously lacked in the case of the St. John Passion; the assistance, namely, of a skilled and sympathetic poet, with whom he had already co-operated for some years. Picander's talent was less than mediocre, but Bach asked for nothing more than facility of outward poetic form, and this he could command. The main outlines of the scheme of the Passion were long since established by tradition, and, in spite of the tendencies of his time, Bach was fully convinced that the Biblical core of the work could not be tampered with if the church feeling of the significance of the sufferings and death of Christ was to be fully brought out in the highest and most comprehensive form. He himself possessed, in the highest degree, that knowledge and sentiment which were needed to give the utmost intensity to the fundamental Protestant tone of the work by the interpolation of appropriate chorales at suitable places. Besides this, he was sufficiently imbued with the spirit of the popular sacred drama to require of his poet all possible regard for it. How much of the construction of the text is due to Bach and how much to Picander is hardly capable of demonstration in detail, but we may regard it as certain that Bach had a very considerable share in it. The mere fact that Picander's text was printed again and again, not only without the Bible text, but without the chorales, proves that he felt no particular interest in the form it had assumed by the addition of the chorales.[621] But Bach in some degree influenced the independent poetry; it must have been he who insisted on the adaptation of Franck's hymn " Auf Christi Begräbniss gegen Abend "—" Towards evening at

---

[621] He had the St. Mark Passion printed with the Bible words and chorales, although it is to be presumed that Bach himself also selected these. But in this Picander's poetical contribution was so small that it would not have been worth printing by itself. The St. Mark Passion is not included in the collected edition of Picander's poems.

Christ's burial"—and it seems as though he had not been content to make use of Franck's text only once in the Passion; for the recitative "Thou blessed Saviour, Thou," agrees in feeling, and even in certain turns of thought, with one of Franck's madrigals, in the same way as the recitative "It was in the cool of eventide" corresponds to the above-named dirge. It is incontestable that their co-operation resulted in a text which satisfied Bach's requirements in every particular, and which we must recognise as being in every way suited to its purpose, whatever our opinion may be of Picander's trivial rhymes.

The story of the Passion according to St. Matthew was sung in Leipzig every year on Palm Sunday, treated chorally. The close connection with divine service which it thus acquired must have been a special incitement to Bach to bestow on it a consistent and thorough artistic treatment; though, indeed, a sufficient inducement lay, no doubt, in the subject itself, for the narrative of St. Matthew far exceeds those of St. Mark or St. Luke in fulness and vividness. Bach divided the story into two parts, but not according to the break in the chapters xxvi. and xxvii.; he ends the first section with the taking of Jesus and the flight of the disciples (xxvi., 56). The hearing before Caiaphas, Peter's denial, the judgment of Pontius Pilate, with the episode of the death of Judas, the progress to Golgotha, Crucifixion, Death, and Burial of Christ, are all included in the second part, while the first comprises only the conspiracy of the High Priests and Scribes, the anointing of Christ, the institution of the Lord's Supper, the prayer on the Mount of Olives, and the betrayal by Judas. This division alone proves the judgment exercised in the treatment. In a work planned to represent the most stupendous events, and engaged throughout with none but the saddest emotions, every possible contrast had to be made the utmost use of. The first section is contrasted with the second as a prologue with the crisis; in one a solemn stillness reigns, in the other a passionate stir; in the former the lyric, in the latter the dramatic element. The number of independent poems is considerable, no less than twenty-eight if we consider

the recitatives in verse as separate pieces. Besides this we
have fifteen chorales. With so abundant a supply of lyric
compositions, Bach found himself in a position to treat all
the separate events in a quite different way from that he
had used in the St. John Passion, defining them clearly
and dividing them with a satisfactory close. Only in
two places do we find an incident without a concluding
lyric. The narrative of the death of Judas is followed by
the aria " Give, O give me back my Lord," in connection
with the restoration of the " price of blood," since the Bible
words which follow, no doubt, seemed less proper as an
introduction to a suitable meditation. Bach follows up the
description of Christ's death very appropriately with the confession of the heathen set to guard Him: " Truly this was
the Son of God," and he connects the proceedings of the
women who had been present at the Crucifixion with the scene
of the Burial, which is quite fitting, because the two
Marys have a further part to play in the narrative of the
Resurrection.

The grandeur and breadth of the poetical matter are
adequately met by the musical means made use of.[622] Bach
has arranged it for double chorus, and given to each chorus
its own orchestra and its own organ accompaniment. He
has made a truly astounding use of these two main masses
of sound, both to emphasise all that has poetic value, alike
from the lyric and dramatic point of view, and to express in
music the many elements which compose the mighty picture.
In the unanimous utterances meant to characterise the
vehemence of the fanatical persecutors of Christ, the
choruses commonly sing together in polyphony, only coalescing in a compact four-part structure at the culminating
points of their passion. In less emotional portions, Bach
was satisfied to employ only one choir, as when the
servants of Caiaphas address Peter " Surely thou also
art one of them, for thy speech bewrayeth thee." The
scornful words at the foot of the Cross: " He calleth for

---

[622] The St. Matthew Passion is contained in Vol. IV. of the B.-G. edition;
and it has been published with English words by Messrs. Novello & Co. This
edition is quoted throughout.

Elias," are given to the first choir, and those which immediately follow: "Wait, let us see if Elias will come to save Him," are sung by the second. The disciples are represented only by the first choir; but in all the chorales, except where supplementary lyrics are interwoven, and except in the deeply significant dramatic chorus "Truly this was the Son of God," the choirs combine in one mass of sound. In the grand "madrigal" tone-pictures at the beginning and end, and towards the close of the first part, they work together as a double chorus with a grandiose progression of parts, and in the opening number a third chorus of one part only—*soprano ripieno*[623]—is associated with them. Turning to the solo songs we find all the Biblical personages, with the exception of the false witnesses, supported by the first choir. The "madrigal" recitatives and arias are pretty equally divided between the two choirs, with a trifling preponderance in favour of the first. This detail, which is commonly neglected in performances of the work at the present time, is, nevertheless, not unimportant, since the choirs, of course divided into two bodies, were placed on the right and left sides of the organ choir.

Bach did not write for solo singers, who should stand out in contrast to the chorus. His *concertists* sang with the chorus, and only came forward for the moment when it was their turn to sing; it must, therefore, have had a characteristic effect when the solo voices rang out in the spacious church from one side and then from the other, and this would be all the more striking when a single voice was heard above its own proper accompaniment from one side, while on the other the whole chorus joined in with its full orchestra. For instance, when in the scene on the Mount of Olives one voice in the first choir sings "O grief! Now pants His agonising heart," and from the other side the chorale rises up, like the penitential prayer of a kneeling congregation, "O Saviour, why must all this ill befall Thee?" the effect must have bordered very closely on the dramatic.

---

[623] P. 4 of Novello's edition.

Bach has succeeded in subtly characterising the various poetical elements which, in the course of time, had become infused into the form of the Passion music, without injuring the fundamental unity of the style. He did not hesitate to introduce a certain number of madrigal recitatives side by side with those from the Bible. He has even added to their colour by the addition of instrumental effects, and yet left it possible that each class shall be immediately recognisable. The Evangelist and the other persons who are introduced as speakers sing in *recitativo secco;* when Jesus speaks, to distinguish Him from the others, a stringed quartet is brought in, but the accompaniment is mostly restricted to held chords, though in certain passages it adds a graphic illustration of the words, and in the institution of the Lord's supper it works round the voice part, which gradually develops into a long arioso in a highly artistic four-part subject. The accompaniments to the words of Christ are chiefly used to give colour; the "madrigal" recitatives, on the other hand, have an obbligato accompaniment in which a motive is usually worked out, which bears a figurative reference to some important image in the words. These recitatives are thus a degree nearer to an organic composition and constitute a very natural transition to the form, complete in itself, of the arias which they lead up to. The accompaniments are frequently given to wind instruments, so as to produce a distinct contrast to the words of Christ; a sufficient variety is thus produced, and a musical antithesis corresponding to the different importance of the recitatives. And this applies to the chorale portions as well as to the solo parts. Bach, who had at his command an incomparable wealth of forms of chorale treatment, has, nevertheless, in the St. Matthew Passion refrained from using any other than a simple choral setting. By far the greater number of chorales are set in a severe style, and accentuate the congregational feeling in all its modesty and force. Twice, however, in the chorales at the opening and close of the first part, he has extended this simple form to a chorale fantasia, thus giving free expression to personal sentiment. Even these two numbers again are

quite dissimilar; since in the final chorus of the first
part the subjective element finds its chief expression in the
instrumental picture, while in the introductory number it
lies with the two principal masses of the chorus, each having
its own text.   While Bach thus bridged over the gap between
the strictly sacred and the independent chorus, he succeeded,
by combining the lyric solo and the simple chorale for chorus
("O grief now pants"), in effecting a union between these
two antagonistic elements; and in the opening chorus of
part II. ("Alas! now is my Saviour gone!") between the
aria and the chorale treatment of Bible words in general,
without effacing the peculiar essence of each.   The choruses
in madrigal form roll by in the broadest waves of sound,
but in the simplest possible treatment; in the dramatic
chorus he indulges in the contrapuntal profundity which
beseems the Bible words, and yet he resolutely confines
himself to the concisest expression possible.   Apart from
a few certainly quite new and peculiar developments the
musical forms in the St. Matthew Passion differ in no
respect from those in the cantatas.   But what is amazing
is the evident economy of artistic means in their application.
A distinct organisation prevails throughout, and at the
same time a delicate treatment of the outlines and a tender
toning down of contrast which are far above anything that
can be mentioned in the St. John Passion.   This circumstance is in the highest degree characteristic of the whole
impression produced.

There is scarcely anything left to be added with regard to
the Bible recitatives in the St. Matthew Passion to what
has been said in discussing the St. John Passion.   But as
one critic has tried to detect in them a clear and definite
characterisation of the various Biblical personages,[624] it may
here be expressly insisted that nothing of the kind was done
by Bach, or even intended by him.   The Passion has,
it is true, borrowed certain features from the drama, but
it is not really a drama for all that.   All that he proposed
to do by way of distinguishing the actors is effected by the

---

[624] Mosewius, Johann Sebastian Bachs Matthäus-Passion, musikalisch-
ästhetiscn dargestellt. Berlin, 1852, p. 70.

distribution of the speeches to different voices, and by the addition, when Christ speaks, of a more highly coloured and sometimes even quite independent accompaniment; but from this to dramatic individualisation is a long step. This can only consist in the development of a special basis of feeling for each of the different *dramatis personæ*, on which the mode of expression for each shall be modelled in every particular. If this cannot be proved to exist, all the supposed characterisation dwindles down to a suitable accentuation of the words and phrases of the actors. And this, even, is by no means so constant as to justify us in regarding it as a ruling principle, always before his mind. The essential character of his recitative can only be perfectly understood by considering it as a musical improvisation under dramatic conditions, and, even then, as an improvisation within the pale of strict church forms and style; for it is only by considering its church use that we can account for the fact that the narrative of the Evangelist is given with the same fervent utterance as the speeches of individuals, a fact which is sufficient by itself to contravene all notions of dramatic treatment. Throughout the Evangelist's narrative we may note an emotional unction which often is nothing more than this, but often, on the contrary, is concentrated in a special sentiment. The agony and terrors of Christ in Gethsemane, Peter's bitter tears of repentance, and Christ's Crucifixion are not so much related by the Evangelist as experienced by him, with all the devout fervour of the sympathising Christians. He has not translated the cry " Eli, Eli, Lama sabachthani," as Handel has done in setting the Passion[625] compiled by Brockes; but he lets the feeling of the appeal find an echo, as it were, in his own breast ; and we see too that the melody was invented for the German rather than the Hebrew words, for it does not perfectly agree with these in accent. When Peter denies the Lord for the third time, the Evangelist reiterates the phrase of recitative a fifth higher, on the words "And

---

[625] Handel-Gesellschaft, XV., p. 134.

immediately the cock crew," thus reminding him of Christ's prediction by a mocking echo of his own pitiable weakness. Now such a treatment was only possible to Bach because he regarded the words of the Evangelist and those of the actors from the point of view of the Protestant believer, and not from that of the dramatist.

Even the stringed quartet accompaniment which, as a critic has elegantly said, floats round the utterances of Christ like a glory,[626] does not proceed from a dramatising tendency. The notion of *characterising* the omnipotent God by mere human means would certainly have seemed to Bach a blasphemy in itself; besides, the style of music given to Christ is precisely the same as that of the other persons. But, just as in earlier times Christ's words had been delivered in several parts with the idea that the use of this fuller effect gave them, musically speaking, a higher value; reverence for the person of the Redeemer has here prompted the composer to attune the minds of the hearers to special devotion when He speaks. This, however, was not in itself a novel mode of proceeding. It is not necessary to go back to the "Seven Words" by Schütz for an example, and it is hardly likely that Bach can have known the work; if Bach had a model in his mind he is more likely to have found it in Telemann's St. Mark Passion (in B flat major). Still, Telemann frequently set the words of Jesus to an arioso, a means which Bach has only used to give greater prominence to the words spoken at the institution of the Lord's supper. Both composers have dispensed with the string quartet in one place, different, however, in each; Telemann at the brief reply made by the suffering Saviour to Pilate: "Thou hast said." In this place Bach, it is true, ceases the continuous accompaniment, but throws in short chords before and after it; on the other hand, Bach stops the accompaniment on words uttered in the depth of crushed humiliation, "Eli, Eli, Lama sabachthani." Both are highly graphic, but Bach's feeling, which makes him

---

[626] Winterfeld, Ev. Kir., III., p. 372.

extinguish, as it were, the glory round the Redeemer's head, at this instant is by far the most figurative.[627] As far as regards the general management of the accompaniment, Telemann, of course, cannot measure his strength against Bach by a long way; with him it is no more than a superficial means of emphasis, while in Bach it really rouses a feeling of higher devotion;[628] and if Bach was not altogether original in his idea, he certainly was in his method of dealing with it.

Though the treatment of the Biblical recitative in the two Passions according to St. John and St. Matthew is essentially the same, in the choral numbers on Bible texts we see a conspicuous dissimilarity. No form of composition used in them shows more convincingly that Bach's Mysteries form a class of art apart from the dramatic choruses—so called for brevity—in the St. Matthew Passion. Consider the passage where the Jewish people, prompted by the high priests and elders, demand the release of Barabbas. The Evangelist makes them reply to Pilate's question with the single word "Barabbas"; the situation is no doubt full of emotion, and an oratorio writer might have been prompted to let the electric tension of the moment discharge itself in a chorus. But it must necessarily be embodied in a form in which the chorus could have its full value as a musical factor, in a broadly worked out composition and on a text of somewhat greater extent. The dramatic, or operatic, composer would have given it the utmost brevity, since it stands midway in the critical development of an event; he would have to con-

---

[627] Bach has, at this passage, given held chords to the organ which has a particularly solemn effect, as it elsewhere has only short chords. That the unsupported recitative of the St. Matthew Passion was intended to be accompanied on the cembalo and not on the organ, is an unfounded hypothesis of Julius Rietz, B.-G., IV., p. xxii; for the organ part which still exists contains the recitative accompaniments complete. I need only refer the reader to p. 299 of this volume to prove that the idea rests on an altogether false assumption.

[628] The principles which guided Telemann are rendered more obvious by his St. Mark Passion of 1759 (in G major), in which he gives a stringed quartet accompaniment not merely to all the words of Christ, but to other important and significant passages.

sider the progress of the action as well as the expression
of feeling: an excited populace thronging wildly and
tumultuously round the governor. A sudden roar and brief
turmoil of voices would be the kind of movement best suited
to his purpose. Bach, composing a devotional Passion,
makes the whole chorus groan out the name of Barabbas
once only, on the chord of the minor seventh, led up to by
a false close. This of course is not oratorio style, but
even in a dramatic work such brevity would be inadmissible at such a crisis. Bach commonly pays no regard to
the scenic situation, a freedom of which, in this case,
he availed himself to concentrate the utterance even beyond
the limits of dramatic usage. He depicts in the strongest
manner the savage feeling of the populace by giving
them a dramatic identity, and at the same time suggests
the sudden horror which seizes the believing Christians
at their answer. It is a master-stroke, equally admirable
for the decisive rightness of the feeling for form which
it reveals and the overwhelming force of its utterance.
Although it is directly suggested by the text itself, it never
occurred to any composer of eminence before Bach; all
have composed a longer choral movement by repeating the
word "Barabbas" several times.

The chorus "Let Him be crucified" which, after a few
bars of recitative, follows this soul-shaking cry, and its
repetition later on, is a fresh example of the style peculiar to
the Passion music. It is a fugue subject of eight bars, in
which the parts, from the bass upwards, come in with strict
regularity on the closing note of the subject in the previous
part, thus giving us the impression of a coherent musical
whole artistically worked out.[629] The shortness of the
movement is sufficient to prevent our feelings lapsing into
calm, and this is enhanced by the fact that the response
to the theme is not constructed by strict rule, for the subject
starts in A minor and we are ultimately flung aground,
as it were, on the dominant of E minor. This of itself

[629] Marx (Kompositionslehre II., p. 276) finds expressed in this the solemnity
of popular justice. Solemnity indeed there is, but it is that of Protestant
church music.

accentuates a dramatic element, which is brought out in full force when the chorus is repeated; the words of the Evangelist, "But they cried out all the more and said," require an increased emphasis. In the oratorio style, where musical principles are paramount, this would have had to be brought out by a more complicated and intensified effect in the music itself. Bach simply repeats the chorus, but a tone higher. He actually depicts the populace in its natural excitation. The sense of their utterance remains the same—they only shout in shriller pitch, starting on B, with which he ended the first time; he now closes the chorus on C sharp (in the bass), the dominant of F sharp minor. In this passage a comparison with the St. John Passion is particularly instructive. In that also the chorus "Crucify Him" occurs twice. The composition is very similar on both occasions, but the first time it is in G minor and the second, half a tone lower, in F sharp minor. Here no enhanced effect has been attempted. The secret of this strange proceeding lies in the order of the modulations of the whole of the second part of St. John. For the sake of the general principle of musical construction Bach has not only sacrificed all dramatic emphasis, but even counteracted it, in the same way as a short time previously he has repeated the chorus "We have a law" to other words, but a semitone lower.

The influence of the dramatic aspect is shown in a peculiar way of closing the choruses in other passages of the St. Matthew Passion, besides those at the Crucifixion. Not unfrequently they end on the dominant of the key, even when the text does not contain a question, and thus produce an impression of something unfinished and leading on to a sequel. Bach has also used this effect almost throughout the St. John Passion.

But besides this, again, in the St. Matthew Passion, choruses occur where the progression of the modulation does not return on itself, but leads to some new end—where, consequently, a psychological progression is depicted and not a single feeling. The chorus "His blood be upon us and upon our children" carries us on, from the gloomy surging of hatred and blind impulse to murder, to an insolent defiance of the law of divine retribution. In the choral number " Sir, we remember," the picture of the chief priests and Pharisees talking themselves into vehement zeal has led Bach to modulate at last quite out of the key of E flat major, which is undoubtedly the original. The mixture of breadth and conciseness, which is characteristic of the choruses of the St. John Passion, we must regard as a not perfectly successful amalgamation of the oratorio and dramatic styles. In the St. Matthew, the problem is throughout triumphantly solved ; an elaborate musical scheme for a long chorus is nowhere to be traced in the dramatic portions, and where the choruses are of any length it is the result of the length of the words to be sung. They are marked throughout by the utmost concentration, but combined with a severity and artistic treatment of the musical texture which always bears a direct proportion to the importance of the poetic sense to be interpreted, while both are in keeping with the purest church feeling.

As regards the different expressions of emotion which depend on individuals or situations, to do them full justice we must study them through the double medium of church feeling on one hand, and a conception midway between the drama and the oratorio on the other. Even then they exhibit a very sufficient differentiation. The choruses of disciples are often distinguished by a feeling of humble devotedness which, in the passage where they desire to prepare the Paschal Lamb for their Lord, has a vein of solemnity, and which, when they hear that there is a traitor among them, is tinged with anxious sadness. In the choruses of the persecutors, fanatical hatred is revealed in all its varying shades ; it rises to terrific rage when they demand that Christ shall be crucified—none but a transcendent genius could come so near to naturalistic expression without overstepping the limits imposed by the style of the whole work.[630] As soon as the Jews are certain of their victim

---

[630] It has long been supposed that the dislocated form of the theme and the crossing of the parts in their progression might be intended to have a graphic effect. The similarity of the theme with that of the Crucifixion chorus in the

their fury turns to fiendish triumph; and a solemn conviction
is stamped on the short chorus of the heathen: " Truly this
was the Son of God."

As in the Passions according to St. Luke and St. John,
so in that according to St. Matthew, Bach has distinguished
one of the chorales introduced from the rest by frequent
repetition, thus making it the centre of the church sentiment
of the whole work. Among the fourteen simply set chorales
included in the work in its original form, the melody " O
Thou whose Head was wounded " occurs five times; it was
a favourite melody with Bach, and there is no other that,
throughout his long life, he used so frequently or more
thoroughly exhausted as to its harmonic possibilities for
every variety of purpose. It comes in three times in the
second part: first when Jesus silently bows to His fate
at Pilate's decision. Here it is used with the words of
the first verse of Gerhardt's hymn " Commit thy ways to
Jesus," one of the few passages in this incomparable work
to which perhaps exception might be taken. It was a
beautiful idea to associate the pious submissiveness of Jesus
with a congregational meditation on it; but the soft and
heartfelt tone of Gerhardt's hymn, with its admonitions to
patience under human affliction, is not commensurate nor
appropriate to the solemn pathos of the situation and the
awfulness of the sufferings of the Son of God. Apparently
Bach felt chiefly the need for bringing in the melody; in
the hymn " O Haupt voll Blut und Wunden" there was
no suitable verse, and he seized, not very happily, on another
well-known hymn by the same writer. The second time the

St. John Passion is striking. The disposition to a picturesque treatment at
that time sometimes found expression in a kind of writing for the eye; thus
Mattheson once figured the " rainbow," marked by the scourging on the
Redeemer's back, by a series of notes, which, as written, showed the form of an
arch (see Winterfeld, Ev. Kir. III., p. 179). The leading idea of Bach's
Crucifixion theme—

make the sign of the cross when the first and last notes are joined by a line and
the two middle ones by another; nor is there anything displeasing in the
conceit, since the musical idea is a sound one.

chorale is sung is in the second section, immediately before the progress to the Cross, when the soldiers have crowned the Saviour with thorns and mocked Him and smitten Him; and we here have the first two verses of the hymn addressed to the Head of Christ.[631]

Nothing more suitable could be found for this place, and the effect is consequently deeply touching. The third time it is the last chorale in the work, and it comes in after the words "But Jesus cried with a loud voice and departed," with the ninth verse of the hymn "If I should e'er forsake Thee, Forsake me not, O Lord." This climax has always been justly regarded as one of the most thrilling of the whole work. The infinite significance of the sacrifice could not possibly be more simply, comprehensively, and convincingly expressed than in this marvellous prayer. Bach has chosen for it a particularly low pitch, and while he has in other places treated the mode as Ionic, as it was originally, he has here, certainly after full consideration, worked out the solemn and twilight effects of the Phrygian.[632] The three moments marked by the entrance and recurrence of this melody, are the three decisive crises in the treatment of the second part.

---

[631] The English version slightly alters the sense. The following is rather more literal:—

  " O wounded Head, and bleeding,
   Weighed down with pain and scorn,
  Thou'rt crowned by cruel mockers
   With piercing boughs of thorn !
  O Head ! thy radiant glory,
   With honour crowned of yore,
  Is now sweat-stained and gory—
   I hail Thee and adore ! "—*Translators.*

[632] It is an error which has grown to an almost universal custom to have this chorale movement sung *a cappella*. Setting aside that it is unfaithful to the original, as it certainly is, it decks out the passage by the use of an effect quite unlike Bach, and gives it a touch of sentimentality which could nowhere be in worse taste than here. Bach's chorale settings can produce their special effects only by that peculiar colouring which results from the mixture of human voices with the organ and the tones of instruments, and which cannot find a substitute in anything else. The instruments have besides, in Bach's hands, so much to say of their own individuality that they constitute an intelligible symbolism when they come in unanimously with the four voice parts.

The passages in the first part where it is introduced are in the scene on the Mount of Olives. Jesus says " Ye shall all be offended because of Me this night : for it is written, I will smite the shepherd, and the sheep of the flock shall be scattered abroad." The figure of the shepherd leads to the introduction of the fifth verse :—

> O Lord, Thy love's unbounded,
> So full, so sweet, so free.[633]

Then follows the prediction of Peter's denial, and Peter and the other disciples pledge themselves to be faithful; this is followed by the sixth verse—

> Though all men should forsake Thee,
> Yet will not I, O Lord.

In the St. John Passion—after the narrative of Peter following Jesus when He is led captive to the palace of the High Priest, where he subsequently denies Him, we have the aria " I follow Thee also, my Saviour, with gladness," and it has been already pointed out that this sequel can hardly be thought satisfactory. On a comparison with the corresponding passage in the St. Matthew Passion, it seems quite clear that Bach could not carry out the idea he had in his mind for lack of adequate verse. It was not the reflections arising out of this particular incident, but those suggested by the course of events generally that he desired to express. This is made quite clear by the original closing chorale of the first part, which, after the statement " Then all the disciples forsook Him and fled," begins " Jesum lass ich nicht von mir " :—

> Never will I quit Thee, Lord,
> Walking ever at Thy side.[634]

The Christian congregation stands in conscious contrast to the disciples : they fled while it remains unalienated from Jesus. Thus, through the whole of the events on the Mount of Olives, the atoning sentiment prevails that the

---

[633] " Erkenne mich, mein Hüter, Mein Hirte nimm mich an "—" Know me for Thine, O Saviour, My Shepherd keep me safe."

[634] This composition, never hitherto published, is given as a Musical Supplement, No. 3, to this work.

very sufferings endured by Jesus at the hands of those who had once loved and honoured Him are what bind Him the more closely to His people. Now we begin to understand what is signified when the chorale is introduced for the second time with precisely the same setting as at first, and only a semitone lower (E flat major instead of E major). The contemplation of human weakness revealed in the disciples fills the people with humility; but even in humiliation they remain firm.

Next to this chorale, the one which fills the most important part is Johann Heermann's hymn, "Herzliebster Jesu, was hast du verbrochen?"—"O blessed Jesus, what is Thy transgression?"—with the first, third, and fourth verses,[635] and we have also Gerhardt's hymn, "O Welt, sieh hier dein Leben," twice, with the fifth and third verses. The other three chorales, like the original closing chorale of the first part, are not strictly Passion hymns, but of more general import, and all chosen with a fine sense of fitness.[636] At the end of the first part Bach subsequently put what had been originally the opening chorus of the St. John Passion. The intention of the two verses of the chorale "O Haupt," which are introduced into the first part, is certainly thus rendered rather less evident. However, the grand proportions of the whole work acquire a more impressive culmination, and Bach must certainly have desired not to omit from a work of so exhaustive a character the best known and most venerable of the hymns on the Passion; such a hymn is Sebaldus Heyden's "O Mensch bewein dein Sünde gross," which was frequently sung even in the old chanted Passions, though in Bach's time it was no longer used on Good Friday in the chief churches of Leipzig. The composition which Bach has set to the first verse of this hymn is not a simple four-part chorale, but a chorale fantasia on the grandest

---

[635] "Mysterious act of God's Almighty mercy," and "O Saviour, why must all this ill befall Thee?"

[636] "O Father, let Thy will be done," verse 1 ("Was mein Gott will, das g'scheh allzeit"); "The world accuses falsely, Lord," verse 5 of the hymn "In dich hab ich gehoffet, Herr"; and "If I should e'er forsake Thee," verse 6 of "Werde munter, mein Gemüthe."

scale and of the richest style. The tone-picture given to the instruments is woven out of a motive which seems to owe its origin to an illustration of " weeping "; and while this represents the general feeling, the alto, tenor, and bass voices of the combined chorus are busied with working out the individual shades of sentiment, the *Cantus firmus* being given to the soprano. This mighty movement, saturated with the most intensified feeling of the divine Passion, has so long been universally regarded as an integral portion of the St. Matthew Passion, and it so admirably fits its place, musically speaking— particularly as it is a splendid finish to the first part—that we are scarcely conscious of the fact that, in one respect, it cannot conceal its original purpose; the poetical purport of the words refers almost exclusively to things which are antecedent to the Passion properly speaking. The verses ought to form an introduction to a rhymed narrative of it, and are therefore out of place here, where the history has already begun; and the contrast must have been still more perceptible at a time when the purport and feeling of Heyden's hymn were more familiar to every one than they are now. Bach did not transfer the chorus directly from the St. John Passion; he seems to have used it first for a fifth Passion setting, now lost. It was not till near the end of his career that he added another embellishment to his greatest Protestant church work, by adding this; thus framing the first part between two chorale choruses of the very grandest type; for the opening chorus also is nothing more, as to musical structure, than a treatment of the chorale " O Lamm Gottes unschuldig," though it is, to be sure, a treatment in which the counterpoint is carried on by two choirs with their own texts, and two orchestras, while a third choir in a single part sings the *Cantus firmus*. When we compare it with the chorale in the Little Organ Book, constructed on the same melody (twenty-seven bars long), no words are too strong for admiration of the colossal power which was equal to such an elaboration of form, and which, within the development of one man's mind, was able to produce what in other cases required the evolution of generations—for instance, consider the history of the symphony. We shall return to a closer analysis of this chorus; but, for the present, it may lead us from the study of the chorale numbers to that of the numbers in madrigal form, since it combines both of these in itself.

The madrigal words have been given by Picander to the Daughter of Sion and to the believers; in this we may perhaps trace his dependence on Brockes. At the same time the idea is not systematically carried out as it is in Brockes and, indeed, in Picander's own Passion text of 1725. It remains conspicuous only in six numbers— important ones it is true — and it would here have resulted in a distinctly oratorio-like effect if Bach had consistently throughout given the words of the Daughter of Sion—a strictly allegorical personage—to a solo voice, as Handel did in his setting of Brockes' Passion. But he has not composed them all as songs for a single voice, but also in the choral and duet forms; and in the solo songs he varies the voice, thus generalising the personal feeling. From a few trifling changes made also in the text it is made additionally clear that he was throughout inclined to express the feelings of the congregation.[637]

From a poetic point of view no separation can subsist between the individual believers and the body of the Christian church,[638] for the believers have church hymns to sing as well as independent verses ("Lamb of God" and "Mysterious act"); it is only in a musical sense that the distinction is marked. A general observation has already been made as to the style of the madrigal choruses; while conciseness and an intricate treatment are combined in the dramatic choruses, in these breadth and simplicity have joined hands; they are intended for sacred arias and are so entitled in the text. It was, of course, impossible to give

---

[637] At the beginning of the second recitative "Although mine eyes with tears o'erflow" Bach changed "mine" into "ours." In Novello's edition the singular is restored in the English. In the second recitative of Part II. (p. 98) Bach substituted the words "to show *us*" for Picander's text which simply said "t show" ("Um uns damit zu zeigen," for "Um damit anzuzeigen").

[638] Winterfeld, Ev. Kir., III., p. 372, assumes this to be the case.

them the verse form in such a work, and the poet has therefore disregarded this consideration : they are in the Italian aria form. Bach has, however, succeeded in keeping up a connection with the older form by adhering to the homophonic method of setting and the simplest possible phrasing. In this way a new style has been originated in this department, bearing fresh witness to Bach's inexhaustible genius. In the whole realm of church music there is nothing that can be compared with these choruses; they have the broad dimensions of Bach's cantata choruses, and at the same time are as simple and as intelligible as a ballad.

The first time such a chorus comes in is when Jesus is praying in the garden of Gethsemane. It is introduced by a recitative for a tenor of the first choir, full of sympathy for the Agony of Jesus, and which is interrupted by chorale lines sung by the second choir, "O Saviour! why must all this ill befall Thee?" (p. 43) and then the anguish is merged in the resolution to cling to Jesus alone and find rest in Him from the torments of the consciousness of sin. Here again a tenor comes in with the soothing, lulling passages, from the second chorus, which represent the "falling asleep of sin." We listen with rapture to the flowing *sostenuto* melody of the upper parts, and scarcely perceive that the same melodic charm is equally present in all the others. They might equally well fill the place of upper parts and, in fact, become so by various changes of position in the course of the double counterpoint.

When Jesus has been taken another grand madrigal choral piece comes in. Two voices in the first choir begin their lament "My Saviour Jesus now is taken." It is supported by a lower part on the violins and violas which certify their connection with the notion of "being led away captive" by syncopations, and then by slowly progressing quaver passages—one of the many examples of Bach's manner of extracting a musical idea from the external factor in an event contemplated from within, and of then freeing himself from its influence and working out only its lyrical features. The deep melancholy of the two solo voices is broken by short and vehement cries from the second choir, "Leave Him!

leave Him, bind Him not." Then both choirs burst out in a *vivace*, and with righteous indignation call upon Heaven to hurl down thunder and lightning on the traitor and his accomplices. The music wars and raves like the wind and storm ; nevertheless the form is very simple : an aria of which the second and third divisions are compressed into one—the choral treatment is perfectly homophonic apart from the fugal beginning ; the two choirs sing in parts, each by itself, in a compact body, and only unite at the close. Any one knowing Bach only from his cantatas would hardly trust in his capacity for producing from such simple combinations an effect which is one of the most thrilling in the whole realm of music. And how miserably do the undignified execrations, which in other Passion settings have to be sung by a solo voice in this place, compare with this picture, traced as it were in flames of fire ! [639]

The third madrigal-choral number of the St. Matthew Passion is the final song by the tomb of Christ. This also has an introduction, a brief recitative for different voices in turn, with short choral subjects full of yearning, and of that deep feeling which checks all but subdued utterance as we stand by the grave. The intimate connection of the final chorus with that of the St. John Passion is self-evident. The character has, however, become far calmer and simpler, the contrast in style with the dramatic choruses more decided, the sense of woe more pious, and more confident in the work of redemption wrought by Christ—a combination of beatitude and sorrow which none but Bach could ever achieve and which is most conspicuous in the words " Hope returned, Here the weary close their eyes." And although we gain from this chorus an impression of breadth which is precisely suited to the rest of the work, it is considerably shorter than the corresponding one in the St. John Passion. The inexhaustible flow of lamentation there leaves a remnant of unsatisfied feeling which is only relieved by the chorale which succeeds it. In the St. Matthew Passion this is not

---

[639] Picander evidently took as his model the text of Peter's aria in the Passion by Brockes.

needed; the sentiment soars slowly upwards, and is amply
worked out within the established limits of the aria form.
To close a Passion-setting with an aria instead of a chorale
was quite opposed to all tradition, and we must not under-
estimate this fact. It contributes in an important degree
to give to the St. Matthew Passion that tenderly human
stamp which distinguishes it from the St. John Passion.
It seems to me that the simplicity of form of all these
madrigal choruses does not arise merely from a general
necessity for musical contrast—I see in it also a sign
that Bach desired to have them recognised as an extended
form of sacred aria; and there is fresh and striking evidence
in favour of this in the introduction to Part II. of the
St. Matthew Passion. The alto solo of the first choir
sings with the whole of the second choir, but the solo sings
a lyric text and the choir sings Bible words.[640] Another style
of choral writing is here at once perceptible; subjects of a
motett character, beautifully complete, come in with a consolatory effect, answering the Daughter of Sion, while her
strains drop one by one, like hot tears, with an expression
quite different from that deep and tearless grief with which,
in the first part, she gazed after Jesus as they bound Him
and led Him away.

One more of the solo arias included in the St. Matthew
Passion claims the co-operation of the chorus. In the
figure of Jesus, hanging with out-stretched arms upon the
Cross, the Daughter of Sion beholds the image of Love
ready to embrace in His mercy those who crave redemption. She calls on the " forsaken broods "[641] to shelter
themselves in Him, and the believers interrupt her with
ejaculated questions. The musical idea is of the same
character as " Haste, ye deeply wounded spirits," in the
St. John Passion. It was Brockes who introduced this
style, and he found many followers, among them Rambach,
and Picander also, in many parts of the St. Matthew text.
However, in the opening chorus, and again after Christ is

---

[640] Song of Solomon, VI., I.
[641] Compare Matthew xxiii., 37, " As a hen gathereth her chickens."

apprehended, the short choral ejaculations participate in a
connected manner with the regular chorus, and have a
definite place in the development and completing of the
composition. The impression given when the number is
considered solely as a musical work—which is an indispensable condition with a form of art which is to produce
its effect apart from action—is one of urgent longing, exactly
like that of the bass aria in the St. John Passion.

The grades of feeling traversed by Bach in the solo songs
of the St. Matthew Passion are all the more impressive,
because every sentiment of joy in its various shades is
wholly excluded; they are all based on the emotions of
sorrow. The most fervent sympathy with the sufferings
of the Son of Man, rising to the utmost anguish, childlike
trustfulness, manly earnestness, and tenderly longing devotion to the Redeemer: repentance for the personal sins that
His sufferings must atone for, and passionate entreaties for
mercy; an absorbed contemplation of the example offered
by the sufferings of Jesus, and solemn vows pronounced
over His dead Body never to forsake or forget Him—these
are the themes Bach had to treat. And he has solved the
difficult problem as if it were child's play, with that inexhaustible wealth of resource which was most at his command
precisely when he had to depict the sadder emotions. In
no other of his works (unless it be in the Christmas
oratorio) do we find such a store of lovely and various
solo airs, nor did Bach even ever write melodies more
expressive and persuasive than those of the arias in the St.
Matthew Passion. If here and there the stream of tune-
fulness flows somewhat less richly, as in the tenor aria
" Rejoice, rejoice," it is because the contemplative character
of the text has led to it. A critical note is, however,
demanded by the bass aria "Give, O give me back my Lord."
It comes in after Judas has restored the " price of blood "
to the Chief Priests and testified that Jesus was innocent,
and the words express the desire that Jesus should be set
free, since even a Judas must acknowledge His innocence.
Now, all the other madrigal texts express sentiments and
reflections which, it is true, are connected with certain crises

of the history of the Passion, but still contain permanent truths of Christianity. This one alone is not the utterance of a member of the Christian communion—who has not lost Christ through His captivity and death but who, on the contrary, has not till now truly found Him—it is that of a person who has stood by during the events recorded; a disciple perhaps or some other follower of Jesus. The influence of the dramatised oratorio is here perceptible, and not quite satisfactory. The hearer is obliged to change his point of view; in the other arias it is based on the general facts and bearing of the work of redemption; here, on the contrary, it is limited to the feeling aroused by the immediate incident.

All the madrigal recitatives have obbligato accompaniments in which, as has been said, wind instruments are employed in preference to the strings, in order to distinguish them as vividly as possible from the Biblical recitatives of Christ. Space will not admit of an analysis here of all the picturesque features and ingenious phrases in which they are so rich; where he thought the work would gain by it Bach did not shrink from the boldest strokes, such as the startling enharmonic modulation at the end of the recitative "All gracious God!"

The recitative "'Twas in the cool of Eventide" (p. 167) requires, however, some more detailed explanation; the text is on the model of Franck's. It is a well-known trait in the Teutonic mind that it loves to regard nature, external to man, as sympathising in the joys and sufferings of humanity, and to think of its phenomena as animated by a spirit akin to the human soul. The nations of antiquity and the Romans, who in their metaphysical conceptions had borrowed from them largely, were strangers to this characteristic; their attitude towards nature was determined solely by the pleasures she offered, or the burdens she imposed. This vein in German poetry is prominent or subordinate in proportion as the poem moves chiefly on national or on foreign ground. While the medieval poems, particularly those of the Minnesänger, are full of this sentiment of natural symbolism, and while in popular songs it was still preserved, in the artificial poetry of the seventeenth

century it disappeared more and more, not to revive till
the second half of the eighteenth century, and then to
shoot forth once more in full vigour from the same soil—
the national ballad. A parallel process is observable in
music. So long as Italian ideas were paramount in the music
of Europe we find hardly a single attempt at expressing the
romantic moods and aspects of nature. Suggestions of this
kind occur in Gluck—in the "Orfeo" and in "Armida"—
and again in Cherubini, who had certain German proclivities
—in "Elisa"—but it is not till we come to the accompanied
vocal music of Weber and Schubert that this feature is
fully revealed, while in Haydn's Oratorios the antique
view of Nature is still sensibly felt. It is, therefore,
especially noteworthy that here and there in Bach's music
the romantic feeling for nature is already unmistakably
perceptible ; nay, this may even be said of some of his
ancestors.[642] An instance of such imagery—revealing the
core of Bach's thoroughly German spirit—is offered in this
very recitative. The softened violins float and linger like
the tender mists of twilight; there are no figured bass
chords to overweigh the dreamy web of sound, only the
long drawn tones of the organ and stringed bass lend it
support. The feeling that is breathed out from this composition is not, in the first instance, the religious sentiment
of peace and redemption spoken of in the text. It is the
sense of evening; the deeper sentiment is only brought out
musically through this medium, and the emotions that stir
the heart of the Christian are infused into the picture of
nature. An instance, in many respects similar, is offered by
the opening chorus of the cantata "Bleib bei uns"—"Bide
with us "[643]—in which the sombre tones of the united violins
and violas alternating with three oboes, which at first move
very softly through several bars and then are long held,
give us a feeling as of falling shadows. But here it is less
the peaceful sense of evening calm than the unearthly tremor
which accompanies the gradual fading of daylight.

----

[642] See Vol. I., p. 71.

[643] B.-G., I., No. 6. Also as " Bide with us," with English words by Rev. John
Troutbeck, D.D.   (Novello & Co.)

I have already taken occasion to point out another instance of the same kind; a cantata for the fifth Sunday after Trinity begins with the verse from the Bible "Behold I will send for many fishers, saith the Lord," &c. (Jer. xvi., 16). Bach has not used these words, according to his usual custom, for a simple dignified arioso; he has worked them up into a grand tone-picture in two divisions, in which we are first led to see the tossing surface of the sea, and then to listen to the horns echoing through the wood. These nature-pictures do not merely supply him with a definite musical motive; they constitute the romantic aspect of the feeling he desires to depict.[644] In the tenor aria of the Whitsuntide cantata "Erschallet ihr Lieder,"[645] and the soprano aria of another Whitsuntide cantata "Also hat Gott die Welt geliebt" (transferred from the secular cantata "Was mir behagt"[646]) we feel, as it were, the breath of May. And the Easter cantata "Der Himmel lacht" contains passages in which we almost seem to feel the airs of Spring.[647] A threatening and stormy mood breathes through the cantata "Schauet doch und sehet," and in the bass aria "Dein Wetter zog sich auf von weitem."[648] Even in several instrumental pieces this romantic vein is very perceptible; conspicuously, for instance, in the Pastoral Symphony of the Christmas Oratorio. As this spirit has something pantheistic in it, it is quite intelligible why in such works as these—which stand on the foundation of the old Lutheran doctrine — a very small space can be allotted to it. Still, the occasions are numerous when it is impossible to ignore its presence. They suffice to show us the contrast between Bach and Handel as to their views of art, both sacred and secular. A poem like "Allegro e Pensieroso," which in its most beautiful passages takes for its subject the harmonious sympathy of nature with humanity, could not have failed to call forth a romantic response in the region of music, if any such conception had ever existed in the sphere

---

[644] See ante, p. 472.   [645] See ante, p. 398.   [646] See Vol. I., p. 568.
[647] See Vol. I., p. 541.   [648] See ante, p. 428.

of Handel's ideas; but Handel stood too firmly on an Italian basis for this to be possible. He has derived a multitude of musical motives from the realm of nature, but he is far from knowing how to vivify them with any mysterious reflex action of the human soul. His music is worked out in clear and classical lines; the composer stands face to face with nature, gazing at creation with a steady eye, as its master and not as an integral portion of it; the mystic absorption into the great universal mind which is essential to the romance of nature has left not a trace. To interpret its moods in musical forms demands more complicated lines than Handel loved to work in, and above all a greater wealth of colour. Everywhere in Handel we find a blooming and abundant sweetness of melody, but no very great variety of handling; Bach is the greater colourist, and the effect of his works results in a high degree from the richer effects he has lavished on them.

These reflections lead us back to that great tone-picture in madrigal form in Part I., which follows closely on the capture of Jesus :—

> My Saviour Jesus now is taken.
> Moon and stars
> Now refuse to yield their brightness.

Since the events narrated occurred on the day of the Passover, the full moon must have shone down on Christ when he prayed by night on the Mount of Olives. We must suppose Him to have been taken towards the end of the night, since the moon had already set. By taking this into consideration Picander has introduced a popular trait into his poem; the Teutonic mind would recognise a deep symbolism in the coincidence of a natural pheno-menon with the transcendently important occurrences in Gethsemane—nature mourning over the sufferings of Jesus.[649]

---

[649] This or similar ideas were frequently worked out by the German poets. The pretty popular song is well-known :—

> " Our Saviour Christ went forth to pray,
> And soon began His agony,
> The greenwood mourned and grassy sward,
> That Judas could betray his Lord."

That the desolate feeling that pervades Bach's composition was determined by this idea in the poem, I cannot venture to assert. We may rather suppose that it was Bach's influence which led to this application of the popular *motif*. It is impossible not to see that the opening chorus also reflects some popular usage. The text, which treats of the progress to the Crucifixion, where Jesus bears His own Cross, amid the lamentations and tears of the Daughters of Jerusalem, Luke xxiii., 27, does not seem particularly suitable as an introduction to the whole history of the Passion. It gives prominence to a single incident, and that not the most important, in a drama full of movement; and we are led on through Part I. and half of Part II. before we arrive at the progress to the Cross. Usually the Passions were introduced by a chorale, or else with an exhortation in verse to contemplate the sufferings of Christ; and a text like the present must have seemed altogether strange if it had not borne a reference to the ancient custom of the Good Friday processions. The Passion plays were so conducted, in many parts of Germany, that only a preliminary portion was performed in the church, while the principal action was played in a procession, arranged to go to a raised spot outside the church, called the Calvary or Hill of the Cross. This procession was planned on the Biblical narrative of the progress to the Cross; the different personages, distinguished by their clothes or by emblems—among them a representative of Christ with the Cross—marched in tra-

---

"Christus, der Herr im Garten ging." Des Knaben Wunderhorn. Part I., Ed. II., Heidelberg, 1819.

Friedrich Spee (1592—1635) in a "Lamentation for Christ's agony in the garden," makes the Saviour Himself say:—

> The lovely moon will soon be gone,
>   And rise no more for sorrow;
> The stars this night have hid their light,
>   In grief for Me to-morrow.
>
> No song is heard, no piping bird,
>   The woods in silence languish;
> The wild beasts grieve in hole and cave,
>   And share in all My anguish.

"Der schöne Mon, wil vndergohn," in Trutz Nachtigal. Cöllen, 1649, p. 227.

ditional order, chanting hymns of lamentation. At certain
spots the procession halted and performed the more dramatic
scenes. These, however, always included those incidents
which had occurred before the progress to the Cross,
so that the whole thing might suffice as a concentrated
representation of the history of the Passion, ending with
the Crucifixion on Calvary and the Burial. Remains
of these processions continued to be kept up in Schleswig
as late as the beginning of this century, and in the lower
Rhine provinces till the end of the seventeenth.[650] We have
no present means of knowing how far any traces of the
Good Friday processions had survived in Thuringia and
Saxony. But it is quite clear that the text of the introductory chorus of the St. Matthew Passion could only have
been based on a view which attributed to the procession of
the Cross, and its sequel, everything that was essential in
the history of the Passion. What Bach constructed musically is a stupendous picture of a surging crowd moving
onwards with hymns of lamentation. But, at the same
time, he has clung to the custom of opening the Passion
with a chorale. A third chorus in unison joins in with
the intricate maze of the other two choirs and the double
orchestra, with the chorale "O Thou, begotten Son of God."
As it was a favourite method in Leipzig to place separate
choirs in different parts of the church to sing together, it is
extremely probable that the chorale was sung by the small
choir, which was placed opposite the grand organ. It must
also be said, to Picander's credit, that he has shown great
skill in adapting the different portions of the madrigal text
to the lines of the chorale. The chorale is made to stand
out both outwardly and logically as the power which
governs the whole, and in this way this grand composition
was most intelligibly brought within the limits of Protestant
church music.

It is not improbable that Picander, who in other portions
of the poem took Franck and Brockes for his models, here

---

[650] Peter, Zuckmantler Passionsspiel. Troppau 1868, p. 10. Also Rein, Vier
geistliche Spiele des 17, Jahrhunderts. Crefeld, 1853, p. 9.

actually imitated certain popular hymns. Setting aside the form of question and answer, the text of the opening chorus has quite the stamp of the hymns sung in the Good Friday processions.[651] It also contains one expression which clearly betrays its primitive and popular origin. According to old German custom, it was the part of the relatives of a deceased person to "help" in the wailing over the corpse ; and the expression is frequently used in the composition of Passion texts, particularly in the Marien Klage, "Mary s Lament."[652] Picander makes the Daughter of Sion sing " Come, ye daughters, help me to lament." That he had in his mind some poem of the kind I have no doubt, and all the less because a similar poem certainly—though probably unconsciously—influenced his mind when writing the words for the aria " Blute nur, du liebes Herz "—" Break and die, thou dearest heart." Picander is always clear and lucid in his own verse, but where he imitates or paraphrases he is apt to lose himself. In the words :—

> Break and die, thou dearest heart !
> Ah ! a child which thou hast trained,
> Which upon thy breast remained,
> Now a serpent has become,
> Murder is the parent's doom—

the wildest confusion certainly prevails. We do not immediately see whether it is the heart of the believer, or of the Daughter of Sion, or of Jesus Himself that is spoken of; judging from the last two lines, Picander can only have meant the heart of Jesus, though the expressions in the second and third do not correspond to this idea. The phraseology is in fact in great measure that of a " Mary's Lament," and made use of in this very sense by Picander himself in the soliloquy he puts into the mouth of the

---

[651] Compare in Rein, the hymn on p. 20. "Schaue Sion deinen König."

[652] " *Maria cantat :* Johann's beloved cousin mine, Help me bewail my grief and thine," from a MS. of St. Gall of the fifteenth century printed in Mone, Schauspiele des Mittelalters, Vol. I., p. 200. " Weep, ye faithful sisters, and help me, a poor troubled soul; help me to bewail my grief, my loss which is grown great, and my heart's pain." In a Low German Marienklage in a MS. from Wolfenbüttel published by Schönemann, Hanover, 1855.

Virgin Mary, in the Passion of 1725. It is difficult to answer the question as to what Bach with his keen intelligence can have understood by these meaningless words, for which he, nevertheless, evolved one of his finest arias.

There is still another passage full of naïve simplicity in the St. Matthew Passion, which, however, is attributable solely to the composer. After Peter has denied the Lord, the Evangelist tells us "And Peter remembered the words of Jesus, which said unto him 'Before the cock crow thou shalt deny me thrice,'" and he has set the words to a musical figure which mimics the crowing of a cock. In the scene on the Mount of Olives, too, to which these words refer, there is the same graphic figure, and in the corresponding passage in the St. John Passion there is a bass figure in semiquavers which is inexplicable but on the supposition that it represents the crowing of a cock; the intention is, therefore, unmistakable. Those who regard such an interpretation, as beneath the dignity of Bach's genius,[653] may be asked to remember that Schütz, in his three Passions, and Sebastiani also have made use of a similar though less assertive kind of imagery. We may also ask whether it is less extravagant when Bach represents the idea of a "high" pavement, and even of a "high" priest by the use of high notes, and finally point to the character of Bach's recitative in general, such as I have attempted to show it. In spite of all this, however, we must admit that there is something rather startling in the mimicry of an animal's cry, and that the contrast it offers to the solemn gravity of the whole work threatens to fall into absurdity. But the direct connection with popular traditions of art gives the proceeding a deeper meaning, and even a certain justification, if we rightly comprehend the principles on which Bach bases his work. The crowing of the cock in the sacred plays formed a favourite crisis, with the populace at any rate, by reason of its simple naturalism,[654] and it is no wonder that they objected to its

---

[653] As Mosewius, Johann Sebastian Bach's Matthäus Passion, p. 6.
[654] Mone, Schauspiele des Mittelalters. Vol. I., p. 108.

omission even in the Passion music. Scheibe, to give an instance of certain ancient Franconian modes of expression, gives us the narrative of a musician from Schleswig: "He once conducted the performance of a Passion music, and in order to render the crowing of the cock very plainly and naturally he hid one of his musicians behind the organ, who at the proper time imitated on nothing but the pipe of the hautboy the crowing of the cock with such naturalness that all the hearers were put into the utmost astonishment, and gave due praise to his happy idea." [655] Certain performances of the sufferings of our Lord existed in Saxony down to the twentieth year of the present century, the remains of the Passion plays. They were given by perambulating choirs of singers, and in these the three crowings of the cock, mimicked on a pipe by one of the singers, was always looked for with excitement, and received with great delight and applause. [656]

Bach's St. Matthew Passion as a whole is, therefore, in a remarkable degree a popular work; and this character does not rest solely on its connection with certain national aspects of thought, or in the faithful preservation of church traditions that had grown dear, but on the whole character of the music. With all its profundity, breadth, and wealth, and in spite of all the art lavished upon it, it never belies the lucidity and simplicity which are its mainstay, and at the same time seizes and grasps with amazing certainty that leading sentiment which pervades the whole history of Christ's sufferings and death—namely, atoning love. Though violent and thrilling emotions are not absent, they only serve to make the tender fundamental feeling stand out as all the more perfect and impressive. The contrast it thus presents to the gloomy St. John Passion is a marked one. It is needless to repeat once more how it surpasses that in many other respects, and how in it all the demands of the most complicated form of art that is conceivable are amply satisfied, and in the most masterly

---

[655] Scheibe, Critischer Musikus, p. 58.
[656] See a paper in the Musikalisches Wochenblatt, 1870, p. 337, by Kriebitzsch, who remembered having witnessed it himself.

manner. Favoured by a happy concurrence of circumstances, Bach has created, in the St. Matthew Passion, a
masterpiece such as it is granted to the human race to
have bestowed on them but rarely as the centuries grow
and wane; and a monument at the same time of the
German national character which will perish only with
the spirit that gave it life.

The first performance of the St. Matthew Passion took
place on Good Friday, April 15, 1729, at afternoon service.
It would be rash to suppose that the hearers could at once
appreciate it in all its significance. At the same time
its reception seems to have been even less favourable
than Bach was justified in expecting, since the Town
Council did not feel moved to grant certain modest requests
of the composer with regard to matters musical (see p.
241). Time alone brought due recognition of the St.
Matthew Passion, and though it may have never become
very widely known—the difficulty of performing it, and
the insufficient means of most of the church choirs at
the time, must have hindered that—it took a firm root
in the soil of Leipzig and was performed by the Cantors
of St Thomas' till the end of the seventeenth century.[657]
Vesper service began at a quarter-past one, and under
ordinary circumstances lasted till about three; since at
a quarter-past three the University Church service began.
But with the St. Matthew Passion the Good Friday
vespers must have lasted more than four hours, since
the music alone demands about two hours and a half
for its performance. Its abnormal length would therefore
reverse the usual and due proportions of the Passion music
to the service; while the original idea—founded, indeed,
in the nature of things—pointed to the embellishment
of the service by the introduction of music, here we have
a sacred concert to be performed with the addition

---

[657] See note, p. 518. In Mizler, Mus. Bib., Vol. IV., p. 109, an incomparable
Passion music is mentioned, which, by reason of the vehemence of the
emotions it expressed, had a good effect as chamber music, but a bad effect in
a church. It is possible that this may have been the St. Matthew Passion.

of the church service. Actually, indeed, the St. Matthew Passion trenches closely on the limit line where church music ceases and concert music begins ; nor is this by reason of its musical style, which is still throughout church-like, but from the self-sufficing sense of art, for art's sake, which is revealed in it. As far as possible it exhausts and completes its subject by its own methods, and, in attaining the effect it aims at, it hardly retains the church element, excepting as a background determining the feeling. It hovers so near the borderland of secular music that the attempt must certainly have been made occasionally to produce it in the hall or room used by the Musical Union, or even in Bach's spacious dwelling. This characteristic affords fresh support for the opinion, derived from experience, that a work of art, in which the ideal type of its special form is brought to absolute perfection, bears in it the germ, which, in growing, entails its destruction.

The reader may here remember that, irrespective of the Passion performances which had long existed in the New Church since 1728, Görner had instituted Good Friday music at Vespers in the University Church. It follows that the latter service would have clashed with the performance of the St. Matthew Passion on account of the great length of Bach's work, so that after 1730, when Görner became organist at St. Thomas', he could not be available for the organ accompaniment of all the great Passion performances. But Bach conducted the performances of his own great works in St Thomas', preferring it for the sake of the greater space. Thus in 1731 he produced the St. Mark Passion ; then, probably in 1734, the revised St. Mark Passion ; and, possibly in 1736, a third performance of the St. John.[658] The St. Matthew Passion, in the altered and extended form in which we now possess it, could only have been brought out at the earliest in 1740.[659]

---

[658] See Appendix A., No. 54 and No. 56, towards the end.
[659] See Appendix A., No. 57.

VIII.

BACH'S COMPOSITIONS FOR CHRISTMAS, EASTER, AND ASCENSION.

THE deep congregational feeling which lies at the root of Bach's Passions underlies also his grand compositions for Christmas, Easter, and Ascension; at the same time the conditions of its manifestation are somewhat dissimilar. There is certain evidence that, in the medieval church, Gospel recitations were performed, with a distribution of parts, at Christmas, Easter, and Ascension, as well as during Passion week; but the Protestant church did not avail herself of them in the same way. At least, I have found no instance of their use at Christmas or Ascension during the first century and a half after the introduction of the reformed faith. It is not till the end of the seventeenth century that they occur in Thuringia,[660] and we can hardly suppose them to have had then any recognised connection with the customs of the older church; they must rather be regarded as merely suggested by the ancient and favourite Passion form. This explains why Bach should have given the works in question the title, then so foreign, of Oratorio. There was no designation at his service derived from church tradition and custom, so he borrowed the name of the form which seemed to have a comparatively close affinity to that which he had evolved. In this one respect the connection of the oratorios with the liturgy for the three festivals is far less deeply rooted than is that of the Passion music with its corresponding liturgy; on the other hand, the affinity to certain other national

---

[660] Rudolphstädtischer | Christ Abend, &c. (the Rudolphstadt Christmas, that is to say, the joyful narrative of the incarnation and birth of our Lord and Saviour Jesus Christ, brought together out of the Evangelists Matthew and Luke, and mingled with suitable hymns. As it is performed [musicirt] at the meeting of the preparation or eve of the Christmas festival in the Hof Kappelle of the Counts of the Schwartzburg, at Rudolphstadt; printed at Rudolphstadt) Heinrich Urban. Im Jahr, 1698. In the Ministerial Library at Sondershäusen. From this title we gather that it was not a solitary, but a customary performance.

church usages is all the more conspicuous in parts. The sacred dramas, in so far as they comprehended the whole work of Redemption, went back beyond the Incarnation, to the Old Testament types and preparatory events ; but as they did not extend beyond the Ascension of Christ, the occurrences of Pentecost were not included. Bach, again, has left no Whitsuntide "oratorio," and from that we might infer that he had followed the popular tradition ; but we must guard against too confidently assuming this to have been his intention, since at the end of the seventeenth century even Whitsuntide music on the pattern of the Passion was not unknown.[661]

I have already observed (p. 499) that the part-reading of the Passion gradually developed into the Passion plays of which the church was originally the theatre. The Christmas, Easter, and Ascension dramas had the same origin; but as the requirements were far simpler for the ceremonies and processions needed in their dramatic presentment, it is easy to understand that they could be included, entire, within the limits of the liturgy ; while the Passion liturgy, to counteract the degeneracy of the drama as performed outside the church, was restricted again to the merest indications of dramatic purpose. The Christmas story offers only four incidents : the Birth of Christ ; the announcement of the angels to the shepherds ; the visit of the shepherds to Bethlehem ; and the adoration of the three wise Kings. The symbolical dramatisation of these events had for a long time wholly or partly fallen into disuse in the Protestant service. What survived at Leipzig in Bach's day I have already spoken of when discussing the *Magnificat* (p. 372). Besides the custom of lulling the holy child, a symbolic ceremony representing the angels' message must also have been known there. It consisted in placing boys, dressed as angels, and divided into four choirs, in four parts of the church—for instance, in front of the altar, in the

[661] In the Ministerial Library at Sondershäusen a printed text exists (Rudolphstadt, 1690, printed by Johann Rudolph Löwe) of the same character as the Christmas music mentioned in the preceding note.

pulpit, in the officials' seats, and in the organ-loft—when
they sang the Christmas hymn, *Quem pastores laudavere*, line
for line alternately.[662] That this was done in Leipzig we
know from Vopelius,[663] but this does not prove that it was
customary in Bach's time. But, besides these liturgical
ceremonies, there were the Christmas plays outside the
church, which also represented these four principal events
in a popular style, and with the utmost simplicity and
freedom. Since, too, the festival of Christmas had absorbed
into itself many primeval German heathen customs and
ideas, it was rooted more deeply and firmly in the national
life than the Passion plays; it consequently flourished more
vigorously, and had been familiar to the children of the
Thuringian race from the earliest times. Circumstances
were, therefore, particularly favourable there for the institution of a Christmas mystery as part of the church service,
which should prove an exhaustive means of expressing the
ideas and sentiments of the people with the highest artistic
perfection.

The Christmas Oratorio was written in 1734.[664] The
Biblical text is from Luke ii., 1 and 3—21; Matthew ii., 1—12.
This text is not divided into two sections on the plan of the
Italian Oratorio as the Passions are, but falls into six
sections for the three days of Christmas, New Year's day,
New Year's Sunday, and the festival of the Epiphany; each
division thus constitutes a complete composition for one of
six days, and this is how it was usually performed. It has
indeed been asserted that the Christmas Oratorio is merely
a series of superficially connected, but really independent,
cantatas. In our day, when church usages are neglected or
forgotten, such an opinion cannot seem surprising, and
the title of " Oratorium," though given by Bach himself, is
misleading. But the church regarded the whole period till

---

[662] 1589, in Brandenburg, as we learn from Schöberlein, II., p. 52,
corresponding to the German version of the hymn *Nunc angelorum gloria*, in
the Arnstadt hymn-book of 1745, p. 22 f.

[663] Neu Leipziger Gesang-Buch. 1681, p. 44.

[664] B.-G., V.[2] Novello's octavo edition is here quoted for the English text.

Twelfth night—from Christmas Day, that is, till the Epiphany —which had been held as a feast even in heathen Germany —as one festival season of which the Birth of Christ was the central idea. Though the Catholic church had given certain Saints' days a place within these twelve, the Protestants endeavoured to remove them so as to devote them solely to the person of Jesus. Thus it was now in Leipzig. On the three days of Christmas the Birth of Christ was illustrated: on New Year's day, the Circumcision; on the first Sunday in the year and the feast of the Epiphany, the persecution by Herod and the adoration of the Kings; and on all these days the Christmas hymns were sung.[665] Thus, irrespective of the fact that the six portions of the Christmas Oratorio deal with a progressive series of events, they must be held, according to church views, to constitute a whole, as being intended for the six consecutive days. This church idea is indeed indispensable to the proper comprehension of the work; we must not approach it, any more than the Passions, with the expectation of finding a concert-room oratorio. What Bach did here for Christmas he had already done for the usages of Holy week, as I have already observed (p. 527).[666]

The madrigal pieces are for the most part transferred from secular occasional music. The opening chorus of the third part and two arias are derived from a *Drama per Musica* written by Bach, and performed by the Musical Union for the Queen's birthday, on December 8, 1733; four arias, a duet and a chorus are transferred from a work of a similar character composed for the birthday of the heir-apparent, September 5, of the same year, and one aria from a complimentary cantata to King Friederich August III., on his visit to Leipzig, October 5, 1734. Of the remaining six pieces it is probable that four were transferred from other

---

[665] See ante, p. 277. The fact that the Christmas hymns were again sung on the feast of the Purification (Feb. 2) must be regarded as a last echo of Christmas.

[666] As the Christmas Oratorio was composed for a year when there was no Sunday after Christmas till after New Year's day, in after times so long as Bach lived, it could only be completely given in years when this occurred again—three times, namely, 1739—40, 1744—45, 1745—46.

compositions which no longer exist in their original form.[667] The text for the cantata on the Queen's birthday was evidently written by Bach himself,[668] while Picander wrote the text of that for the Electoral Prince, and probably that of the complimentary ode.[669] Hence it follows, almost of course, that Picander and Bach must each be responsible for the alterations in his own portion of the text of the Christmas Oratorio; this view is confirmed by the text of the first chorus which is partly founded on Ps. c., 2, and partly bears an evident resemblance to two arias by Georg Ahle, which can hardly have been known to Picander, though they would be to Bach, Ahle's immediate successor at Mühlhausen.[670] Whether the secular compositions which have found their way into the Christmas Oratorio may not already have been altered from still earlier works, at any rate in part, is a question that cannot be decidedly answered in the negative. At any rate the final chorus of the *Drama* for the young prince—which to be sure is not adopted into the Christmas Oratorio—had already been used in the Cantata "Erwünschtes Freudenlicht," of course with other words, and even this was not its original place and use.[671]

It might seem as though, under these circumstances, the Christmas Oratorio must fail in unity of treatment; and it must be granted that many details in the madrigal portions betray the fact of their having been originally set to other texts. The words of the first chorus were at first " Tönet ihr Pauken, erschallet Trompeten !"—" Sound all ye drums,

---

[667] No such transfer is probable in the case of the alto aria of the third part, "Keep, O my spirit." In the autograph it is conspicuous for the multitude of corrections of the original conception; and that it was Bach's intention to introduce something entirely new in this place is evident from a previous sketch of another aria in B minor, 3-8, which, however, remains a fragment and was subsequently struck through by Bach. The opening chorus of the fifth part also, "Glory be to God Almighty," has, in the autograph, no appearance of being taken from a former work. Compare Rust's Preface to B.-G., V.[2]

[668] As will be shown presently when the occasional cantatas come under discussion.

[669] Although this text is not included with the other in Picander's poems, the style prohibits our attributing it to Bach.

[670] See Winterfeld, Ev. Kir., III., p. 344.

[671] See ante, p. 399.

and shout out ye trumpets"—and the music suits these words, beginning with kettledrums, immediately followed by the fanfare of trumpets — while it scarcely suits those now substituted " Jauchzet, frohlocket, auf !"—" Christians, be joyful." The opening chorus of Part IV. had for its text " Lasst uns sorgen, lasst uns wachen"—" Let us be wary, let us be watchful"—and the idea of watchfulness is figured by two staccato quavers, but the word " loben "—" praise Him"—in the altered text, does not seem to require this mode of utterance. In the cantata for the Crown Prince we find the words " Auf meinen Flügeln sollst du schweben"— " Thou on my pinions shalt be carried"—and the music which represents a floating and soaring motion with graphic dignity is set in Part IV. of the Christmas Oratorio to the text " Ich will nur dir zu Ehren leben," &c.—" 'Tis Thee I would be praising ever, My Saviour give me power and skill, and all my heart with ardour fill." In the same cantata Hercules sings " Ich will dich nicht hören, ich will dich nicht wissen " :—

> Mine ears may not hear ye,
> My heart shall not know ye,
> Prohibited joys ye shall never be mine ;
> Wreathing serpents, long since crushed and sore defeated,
> Seek not my spirit to lull and entwine.

The accompaniment (p. 103) at suitable places depicts the twining of the snakes, and to the altered words, " Strengthen me, that Thy mercy worthily to praise I may endeavour," the significance of the phrases is lost.

Still, the mere fact that Bach himself never hesitated before such trifling incongruities is extremely instructive for the true comprehension of his music. Ready as he was to sprinkle his works with picturesque figures, he did not do so as a result of fundamental principles based on a sense of the graphic power of music. Those figures are transient flashes, and their presence or absence cannot alter the value or intelligibility of the composition in its integrity. In studying Bach, when we meet with some conspicuously melodious line or some strikingly harmonious tune, that happens to coincide with an emphatic or emotional word, we are too ready to attribute to them a much closer and deeper connection than can ever have dwelt in the purpose of the composer ; if in Bach's recitatives we often find that the relation of the music to the words is quite secondary— almost accidental—how much more is this the case in the consecutive pieces ! Any one who has listened to the first alto aria of the Christmas Oratorio must have been delighted with the tender expression given to the isolated cry, " The fairest, the purest." (p. 15, l. 4.) The music and text, as they stand, seem inseparable ; and yet in the original form these notes belong to the words " I will not, I may not," and suit them, too, extremely well. Often enough the rendering of these subtle associations is left to the inter- pretation of the singer—Bach's music neither forbidding nor requiring it. Nay, the dramatic feeling suggested by the text is allowed to influence the construction of the musical composition as a whole less by Bach, on the average, than by other masters of his own or of a later time. The aria here quoted seems in the secular cantata to express, in the words of Hercules, his contempt for the delights of pleasure, and in the Christmas cantata the desire of the Daughter of Sion to receive her longed-for Bridegroom with due honour ; and yet all will agree in feeling that there can hardly be a more characteristic piece of music than this, only the character lies in the music itself.

Now, when Bach transferred a piece complete and bodily from one work to the other, the question, with him, was chiefly whether it fitted the musical context and—since its original purpose was secular—whether its style was not antagonistic to a sacred work. As to this I must refer the reader to what has already been said in Vol. I. (p. 569). Bach's whole mode of expression was built on true church feeling ; whether he wrote sacred or secular music, whether he composed organ fugues or chamber sonatas, the funda- mental church sentiment developed directly from the nature of the organ pervades all his works, and he consequently could write nothing that jarred with it. On the other hand, his secular occasional pieces were not genuinely secular ; as such they scarcely fulfilled their aim, and the composer only restored them to their native home when he applied them to church uses. In the face of the inexhaustible inventive wealth, and the profound sense of artistic responsibility, testified in Bach's works, no one would dare to assert that such transfers were made for mere convenience sake, or for lack of time. They were made with a perfect feeling that the compositions in question would not be seen in their right place till they were set for church use. At the same time we cannot deny to Bach a certain distinction between his sacred and his secular styles. Irrespective of the general vein of feeling which would govern him in the act of composition, Bach must naturally have felt moved in a very different way when he was writing for the delectation of a musical union, or for the edification of a band of Christian worshippers, when singing in honour of the Electress of Saxony, or celebrating the glory of the Infant Christ. The character of the secular cantata is lighter and more sportive; but even within the cycle of church life there were suitable opportunities for striking this key of feeling, and Christmas afforded one above all others. The festal cheerfulness and innocent sweetness which are the principal features of the Christmas oratorio, and exhaustively express the very essence of the Christmas festival, are most happily attained by this very transfer of secular compositions. It is true that pieces by Bach are not wanting in which the style seems more decisively determined by the words ; still, in changing the use of these due caution has been exercised, and the altered words have been skilfully adapted to characteristic pieces. The cradle song of Part II. was indeed, as originally composed for the birthday cantata, a lullaby to the Crown Prince.

No other work by Bach contains a richer collection of charming and easily comprehended melodies than the Christmas oratorio. Still, it is not alone in its musical aspect that its popular character lies; wherever it was possible, reference has been had in the words as well as in the music to the traditional ceremonies connected with the Christmas plays and hymns. The custom of cradling the Child was reflected in the cradle song of Part II., "Slumber, beloved," a composition of enchanting grace and the sweetest melody.[672]   It does not certainly fill its proper place, which is in Part III.; but musical considerations must have prevented Bach's inserting it there.   In Part II. its introduction is led up to by a bass voice, which delivers the call to the shepherds, and charges them when they are come to Bethlehem to sing "in sweet harmonious tone, and all with one accord;"[673] the following song, however, is certainly not appropriate in any way for choral singing. The only thing here needed was to supply a reason for its introduction; Bach has by preference given the song itself to the Virgin Mary, since it is written for an alto voice, while in the Birthday Cantata it was written for a soprano, a minor third higher.   In the Christmas dramas and pastorals it was a stereotyped detail that after the appearance of the angels the shepherds should be encouraged to go to Bethlehem.   Thus, in a play used in Schleswig we find:—

> Laufet ihr Hirten, lauft alle zugleich,
> Nehmet Schalmeien und Pfeifen mit euch, &c.

> Hasten, ye shepherds, rise, hasten away,
> Take with you reed-pipe and tabor to play,
> With joyful accord
> At Bethlehèm.
> And there, in the stable, worship the Lord.

And in a pastoral :—

> Up, O shepherds, rise and hasten,
> Jesus newly born to greet;
> He in yonder stall is lying,
> Fall in worship at His feet. [674]

If we compare these with the text of the tenor aria in Part II. of the Christmas oratorio we cannot doubt their association :—

> Haste, ye shepherds, haste to meet Him,
> Why should you delay to greet Him ?
> Haste the gracious Child to see.

---

[672] The precursor of this lovely composition is to be found in the Weimar Cantata, "Tritt auf die Glaubensbahn." See Vol. I., p. 560.

[673] Reminding us of Luther's "Righteous Susanna," who sang "her heart's delight in sweetest tones."

[674] Weinhold, Weihnacht-Spiele und Lieder, pp. 119 and 434.

The matter is of some importance, because Bach himself wrote the words for the aria taken from the cantata for the Queen's birthday, and consequently it is probable that he undertook the other paraphrases ; we must therefore ascribe the introduction of this suggestive reminiscence to him.

The bass aria of Part I. belonged to the same cantata ; in this Jesus is praised as "Mighty Lord and King, all glorious ": here, too, the words must be the composer's. The lowliness in which Jesus came into the world must always have offered a significant and obvious contrast to the idea of His divine omnipotence; it seems, however, as if Bach had had an ulterior view. The three wise kings—whose coming had been dramatically treated in the primeval church liturgy, and who had subsequently become very popular personages even in the processions outside the church walls —bring, as we know, three gifts to the Infant Christ : gold, frankincense, and myrrh ; gold symbolising His sovereignty, incense His divinity, and myrrh His redeeming sufferings and death on the Cross.[675] In Part I. of the Christmas oratorio we hear nothing, it is true, of the three kings ; but we have already seen that Bach seems to have cared more for giving general expression to certain popular and church aspects of the subject than for assigning to them any particular position. The premonition of Christ's death, immediately after His birth, has assumed a very striking form in Part I. by the adaptation of the melody of " O Haupt voll Blut und Wunden,"[676] to the words of greeting, " How shall I fitly meet thee ?" which falls across the bright festal tone like a dim shadow. It must have seemed unnecessary to bring out

---

[675] Thus rendered from the Latin Christmas hymn in an old German version, reprinted (from the Andernacher Gesangbuch of 1608) by F. Böhme Altdeutsches Liederbuch, Leipzig, Breitkopft and Härtel, 1877, p. 640.

" Als ein könig brachten Gold,
weihrauch dass er opfern solt
myrrhen dass er sterben wolt."

" Gold they brought for Royalty,
Incense for Divinity,
Myrrh to show that He should die."

[676] That of the chorale, " O Lord ! Thy love unbounded," in the St. Matthew Passion (p. 18 of Novello's Edition).

the idea of Christ's divinity by any specially suggestive
subject, but it was all the more obvious to emphasise His
royalty, and there was surely room enough for this in the
whole work.   And yet the feeling of Part I. may not unfitly
be expressed in the saying of the Apostle, " He made Himself
of no reputation and took upon Him the form of a servant."
Framed, as it were, in festal joy, it is a picture of humility
and self-abasement that meets our gaze ; but the objection
taken to the bass aria as not corresponding to this is surely
much diminished when we point out the affinity which
subsists between it and the first chorale, on the ground of
popular feeling.[677]

In Part II., when the angels have proclaimed the birth of
Christ, the aria just mentioned, "Haste, ye shepherds, haste
to meet Him," is introduced by the following bass
recitative :—

> What God to Abraham revealed,
> He to the shepherds doth accord
> To see fulfilled.
> To shepherds, lo ! our gracious Lord
>   His purposes unfoldeth ;
> That blessing which, in days of old,
> He to a shepherd first foretold,
>   A shepherd first beholdeth.

This text also seems to contain an obscure reference. The
insipid antithesis of Abraham as a shepherd, and the
shepherds of Bethlehem, can hardly have been the whole
motive of the poem ; the author must rather have had in
his mind an idea of praising the shepherd's calling
generally.   In the Christmas plays it was the custom for
the shepherds watching by night to sing a *Cantilena de laude
pastorum*, to while away the time.[678]   Thus, to be perfectly

---

[677] Winterfield, Ev. Kir., Vol. III., p. 347, raises this objection, and thinks
the fact of the aria being taken from another work lies at the root of its
inappropriateness; but his hypothesis as to how Bach could have allowed
himself such an error of taste is answered if what is said above be correct.

[678] Such a piece exists in a Bavarian Christmas drama, beginning " Lasst
uns singen von den Hirten " :—

Weinhold, op. cit., p. 176.

> " Let us sing the shepherds' glory,
> Who have been renowned in story."

in sympathy with the instrumental symphony which opens the second part, we shall do well to imbue our minds with the sentiment on which the scene of the shepherds by night was based in the Christmas plays. A combination of opposite factors—which presented no difficulties to the naïve minds of the people—of the grace of the Eastern idyl with the severity of the starlit boreal winter's night, gave the fundamental feeling of this symphony. This wonderful composition, woven as it were of silver rays, and enchanting us by harmony of hues, is full of calm rejoicing, and yet unutterably solemn, child-like, and overflowing with yearning. The romantic feeling for nature, which so unmistakably breathes from it, also prevades the magnificent chorus of angels, " Glory to God in the highest ! " where the sparkling accompaniment makes us feel as if we are gazing into the vault of stars.

The ground covered by the Gospel narrative of Christmas events is much narrower, and the incidents themselves are less tragical and vivid than those of the Passion ; hence the lyric element becomes more important, and, as a whole, it decidedly tends to the style of the church cantata. Bach was well aware of this ; indeed, he has brought this element into greater prominence than the circumstances required. Even connected portions of the Gospel, treated as such by Bach himself, are not unfrequently interrupted by reflections in verse, which never occur in the Passions. Bach has not by any means invariably availed himself of the opportunities offered for varying the sung recital by the introduction of a chorus. In Part II. he even lets the Angel's speech, begun in the soprano, be continued by the Evangelist, the tenor ; certainly this takes place after the announcement made by

---

And then it enumerates all the shepherds named in the Old Testament. And that this was a popular theme in more recent times is proved by the well-known shepherds' dance by Johannes Falk :—

> What can be of fairer fame,
> What can give a nobler name
> Than to come of shepherd lineage ?

the Angel has been interrupted by a recitative and an aria.[679]
After this Bach may have thought it unsuitable to bring in
the Angel again without the intervention of the Evangelist.
But if it had been incumbent on him to carry out a dramatic
fiction, he would undoubtedly have arranged the separate
numbers differently throughout. In Part V. Herod calls
together the chief priests and scribes, and enquires of them
as to the birthplace of the Messiah. They answer, " In
Bethlehem of Judæa : for thus it is written by the prophet,
'And thou Bethlehem, in the land of Juda, art not the
least.'" St. Matthew ii., 6. According to rule these words
ought to have been sung by a chorus, but they are given to
the Evangelist. The reason is not, as it seems to me, that
Bach undervalued the dramatic element. In the Christmas
story the most popular personages, next to Mary, Joseph, and
the Child, were the herald angels, the heavenly host praising
God, the shepherds, the three kings, and Herod ; and, so far
as the Gospel text allowed, Bach has introduced them all.
But he must have seen reason to fear that a chorus of chief
priests and scribes would produce a puzzling and bewildering
effect, since these persons were of no importance in the
incidents directly concerning the birth of Christ, and his
object was to remain strictly within the cycle of popular
feeling. In this way, no doubt, he left a powerful vein of
dramatic animation untouched ; but it is the predominant
lyrical character of the work which enables us to comprehend
the easy freedom with which Bach inserts pieces, such as
the cradle song, or the praises of Christ as King, in places
where, in the due course of events, they do not belong. He
took his stand on the ground of the church cantata, in
which all the incidents of the Gospel are accepted as known,
and the emotions raised by them are made use of from a
purely musical point of view.

The Christmas Oratorio falls naturally into three divisions
of the subject ; the narrative of the birth of Christ and its
announcement, which compose the story of Christmas Day
strictly speaking, are treated in the first three parts. The fourth

---

[679] B.-G., V.,² p. 66.   Novello's Edition, p. 34.

relates the naming of Jesus, and the fifth and sixth the visit
of the three kings. Bach has rounded off the whole work
into unity in a very unmistakable manner, by making the
first chorale of Part I. recur at the close of Part VI. in the
form of a brilliant and festal chorale fantasia. Otherwise
each section has its own particular character. In the first
three the Christmas feeling prevails most vividly; this is
effected in great measure by the chorales, which are interspersed in far greater numbers than in the last three,
and which are almost all familiar Christmas hymns.[680]
Most of them are simply set in four parts with highly
ingenious applications of the church modes. The melody of
" O Haupt voll Blut und Wunden" is harmonised by Bach
in the Phrygian mode, thus excluding all doubt as to his
purpose in introducing it. Where the same tune occurs in
Part II., with the words of a verse from Gerhardt's hymn,
" Schaut, schaut, was ist für Wunder das?" the harmonies
have Mixolydian chords, and the same mode is strongly
stamped on the last chorale but one of Part III. (p. 78),
where the last verse of the hymn " Fröhlich soll mein Herze
springen" is sung to the melody—somewhat modified by
Bach—of " Warum sollt ich mich denn grämen"; and in
both these cases we feel that the character of fervent
humility, which the chorales derive from this mode of
treatment, is rendered especially beautiful and impressive
from the places they fill.[681] Unlike the St. Matthew
Passion the Christmas Oratorio contains one single-part
chorale. When the Evangelist has recited " And she
brought forth her first-born Son . . . and laid Him in the

---

[680] Luther's melody of " Gelobet seist du " comes in twice (Nos. 7 and 28),
" Vom Himmel hoch " three times (Nos. 9, 17, and 23), " Fröhlich soll mein
Herze springen " (No. 33, with another tune) and " Wir Christenleut " (No. 59)
each once. Besides these the words of the Advent hymn are very poetically
set to the tune of " O Haupt voll Blut und Wunden "; and the tune of Rist's
hymn, " Ermuntre dich, mein schwacher Geist," has been adapted to " Break
forth, O beauteous morning light " (No. 12), as has been observed by L. Erk.
Bach's mehrstimmige Choralgesänge. Part I., p. 115, No. 27.

[681] See Winterfeld's well-considered comparison, Ev. Kir., V. III., p. 348,
350, and 302. It makes no difference that he has given a wrong text for the
first of these two hymns.

manger because there was no room for them in the inn,"
two oboes with the basses and organs come in with an
exquisite composition of the most tender and modest fervency, to which the soprano calmly sings the sixth verse of
"Gelobet seist du"—"For us, to earth He cometh poor"
(p. 19)—and between the lines the bass sings a devotional
recitative. Chorale subjects, such as we usually find in Bach,
close Parts I. and II. Here, again, the chorale appears
in simple four-part treatment, but with interludes and
a coda on instruments founded on motives or echoes of the
first number of the respective sections. In the first instance
we have verse xiii. of the hymn "Vom Himmel hoch"; in
the second, verse ii. of Gerhardt's hymn, "Wir singen dir,
Immanuel," but the tune is again that of "Vom Himmel
hoch," and not that originally written to it;[682] to make it
fit the text Bach has omitted the final "Hallelujah."

In Part III. we again detect the purpose of connecting
the musical feeling of the end with the beginning; for it
does not conclude with a chorale; it is the opening chorus
that is repeated—a rare thing with Bach. Parts V. and VI.,
devoted to the history of the three kings, are in no respect
inferior to the first three. The lyrical choruses are full
of artistic beauty and swing. Among the solo pieces
a terzet in dramatic style (p. 130); "Ah, when shall we
see salvation," and a four-part fugal recitative are of
conspicuous importance. On the other hand, Bach has
neglected to avail himself of the events on which the
work is based as completely as in his Passion music. The
cantata character is more conspicuous here than in the first
three sections, and the specially Christmas feeling resides
more in the general tone of the music than in the chorales.
The two Christmas hymns principally used in the Leipzig
churches, "Vom Himmel hoch," and "Gelobet seist du," do
not occur at all. Of the four that are introduced, indeed,
only one is really a Christmas hymn (Gerhardt's "Ich steh
an deiner Krippen hier"—"Beside Thy cradle"), one is an
Epiphany hymn, the other two have no distinctively festal

---

[682] "Erschienen ist der herrlich Tag."

text; and even the tunes ("Gott des Himmels" and "O Haupt voll Blut") are not Christmas tunes. In the Epiphany hymn Bach has chosen to alter the words of the chorale (p. 122, "All darkness flies"), and in "This proud heart" he has had to repeat the last note of each of the last two lines in order to make the words and the tune fit each other.

Part IV. has least of the character of church festival music. The Biblical matter consists of a single verse from the Gospel of St. Luke, ii., 21, which relates the circumcision and naming of Jesus. Not much material could be worked out of this, and Bach has almost entirely set aside all adjuncts from the liturgy. No Christmas hymn, indeed no true chorale, is introduced in it. We find, it is true, two verses of hymns by Rist; the fifteenth verse of "Hilf, Herr Jesu," is used for the finale (p. 105) in a similar form to those of Parts I. and II., and the first verse of "Jesu du mein liebstes Leben" is divided into independent subjects for a soprano arioso, with a bass recitative in counterpoint, "Immanuel, beloved name" (p. 91). But in both these cases Bach has not used the regular church tune, but others of an aria stamp, which, as they are to be found nowhere else, have long been regarded with justice as of Bach's own invention.[688] This section, therefore, bears more strongly the stamp merely of a religious composition; it is full of grace and sweetness, and can only have derived its full significance for congregational use from its position in context with the rest of the work.

I have already taken occasion, more than once, to point out that towards the middle of his Leipzig period Bach showed a disposition to divert church music into the channel of sacred domestic music, or—as we may say on the other hand—to raise the home music he performed and loved to the dignity of the church style. Part IV. of the Christmas oratorio is fresh evidence of this tendency. One feature by which it is manifested in the details deserves notice, in spite of its inconspicuous nature. In the verse of

---

[688] Since Winterfeld; see Ev. Kir., Vol. III., p. 354.

the final chorale Rist begins every line with the name in whose honour the day is held sacred, "Jesu, guide my every action; Jesu, still abide with me," &c.   Bach alters "Jesu" (the vocative) to "Jesus" (the nominative).   Thus Rist addresses a supplication to the Redeemer, Bach merely utters a pious wish, and it is not till the last line that he uses the form of prayer.   This, as we have seen, is the same frame of mind as that which guided the paraphrase in the cantata "Ich bin vergnügt."[684]   Traces also occur elsewhere in the Christmas oratorio of a free mode of dealing with sacred property, which plainly betrays Bach's tendency towards a sentiment of family edification; it is for this reason that I have intentionally noticed the liberties, greater or smaller, which he has taken with the chorales: "Thee with tender care," p. 78; "With all Thy Hosts," p. 55; "All darkness flies," p. 122; and "This proud heart," p. 139.   Whether Bach could have introduced such a composition as the soprano aria "Ah, my Saviour," with a double echo of a second soprano voice and an oboe, into any work other than this very peculiar Part IV. may well be doubted.   Of course, childlike naïveté is in its place in the Christmas festival if anywhere, and it is touching to note how the grave and thoughtful master has allowed himself to yield so completely to this festal feeling as to admit such sportive movements into the work.   Indeed, he has not simply copied the echo in its natural form, but has conceived of it in an independent manner as a subject motive.   In the first instance the aria had its place in the occasional cantata for the birth of the Crown Prince.   This *Drama per musica* deals with the narrative of Hercules choosing between Vice and Virtue.   After Pleasure and Virtue have exercised their persuasive powers, Hercules, who has not yet decided what he shall do, says :—

> Faithful Echo of this glade,
> If I should be soon betrayed
> An I were content to go
> Where this sweet voice bids, say No.
> *Echo*—No.

---

[684] See ante, p. 443.

> But if then the warning voice,
> On through toil and weariness,
> Guides me to a better choice,
> Then, I bid thee, answer Yes.
> *Echo*—Yes.

Here the situation fairly allows the presence of the Echo; if Bach had transferred the aria into the Christmas oratorio merely for the sake of its pleasing music, and so disjoined it from the scenery that befits it, it would have been an obvious breach of good taste. But he did not do this. The person who sings the hymn tune in the oratorio is the Bride, who goes forth to meet her Beloved. To verify the correctness of this interpretation we must go back to the origin of such Echo songs. It is to be found in the Trutz Nachtigall of Friedrich Spee. In one of the sweetest poems contained in this collection, " the spouse of Jesus talks in the forest with an echo or reverberation."[885]

Der schöne Frühling schon begunnt,	The bonny spring had well begun,
Es war im halben Märzen,	And March was half way thorough,
Da seufzet ich von Seelengrund,	And from my deepest soul I longed
Der Brand mir schlug vom Herzen.	To cast away my sorrow.
Ich Jesum rief	Jesus! I cried,
Aus Herzen tief,	And deeply sighed,
Ach Jesu! thät ich klagen:	" *Ah, Jesu*," humbly praying;
Da hört ich bald	And lo! I heard
Auch aus dem Wald	An answering word,
Ach Jesu! deutlich sagen.	" *Ah, Jesu!*" plainly saying.

This play of words is carried on in a very pleasing way through a multitude of appeals and answers till the last verse :—

> 'Tis well, sweet echo, to my call
> That answerest from thy bower,
> With thee I oft will play at ball,
> For many a happy hour.

---

[885] Trutz Nachtigall, 1649, p. 10. This is the second verse; there are twenty in all.

> And this the ball
> That ne'er shall fall
>   Between us, Jesus' name
> From me to thee,
> From thee to me,
>   'Tis ever Jesus' name.[686]

Echo songs soon became a favourite conceit with poets; Franck has several times availed himself of this *motif;* in a "Sacred echo to the cooing turtle dove"[687] the plagiarism from Spee is self-evident.

What has been said above as to the elements of Bach's secular cantatas, namely, that by transferring them to sacred ones he actually restored them to their natural sphere, is equally true of the echo song, but in a quite different manner: the source of these poems lay in the domain of sacred poetry. That Bach, and the poet who turned the words of the aria into their sacred form, must both have known Spee's poem I consider as probable, if only because it involves the glorification of the name of Jesus, and so gives the leading idea of Part IV. of the oratorio. Certainly Bach's composition is its worthy counterpart.

Dramatised Gospel recitations had from the earliest times held an important place in the Easter solemnities of the Protestant Church, though they were less general than in those of Holy week. This is to be accounted for by the fact that the Easter Gospels are the direct sequel of the narratives of the Passion. We have Easter compositions in the style of the older Passions by Scandelli and by Schütz, both Capellmeisters at Dresden; and in Vopelius' Leipziger Gesangbuch, of 1681, there is one which must still have been sung at Leipzig at that time, but which must have been written considerably earlier. The text is harmonious and the musical treatment remarkable, because the Evangelist is represented by a baritone and not by a tenor, while the

---

[686] The English reader will be reminded of George Herbert's *Heaven*, the last poem but one in " The Temple."

[687] Geist-und weltliche Poesien. Part I., p. 80. Compare the Song of Solomon II., 14.

speeches of the individuals are in several parts. Christ's
words are given in four parts and the rest in two.[688] But these
Easter readings had already fallen into disuse in Kuhnau's
time, and it is impossible to say at what stage of divine
service they may have been introduced. On the other hand,
in the so-called sacred concerto of the seventeenth century
a form was developed which, by the omission of all purely
narrative portions, approached very nearly to the dramatic
musical *scena*. Schütz and Hammerschmidt worked in this
form with great success.

We have, by Hammerschmidt, a small Easter drama
called a *Dialogus*, which is put together from the words of
the Evangelists, and deals with the great event of the
Resurrection.[689] Mary Magdalene, Mary the mother of James,
and Salome (Mark xvi., 1) have come to the sepulchre to
anoint the body of Christ. After an introductory symphony
begins a three-part song, " Who shall roll us away the stone
from the door of the sepulchre ?" To which two men in
shining garments answer, " Why seek ye the living among
the dead ? He is risen, He is not here." The women
lament, " They have taken away the Lord and we know not
where they have laid Him." The answer to this is a chorus
on the Easter hymn, " *Surrexit Christus hodie Humano pro
solamine. Alleluja.*" This constitutes, as it were, the first
scene ; the next is between Mary Magdalene and Christ
(John xx., 13 and 15—17). She now laments and entreats
alone, " They have taken away my Lord and I know not
where they have laid Him. Sir, if thou hast borne Him
hence, tell me where thou hast laid Him, and I will take Him
away." The risen Saviour replies to her with the questions,
" Woman, why weepest thou ? Whom seekest thou ?" And
then sings slowly and significantly " Maria." She recognises
Him and cries out " Rabboni !" several times repeated, while
He charges her to announce His resurrection and approaching ascension to the disciples. The little work ends with

---

[688] Vopelius, pp. 311—365. As to the probable date of this "Auferstehung"—
Resurrection—Winterfeld gives some information in Ev. Kir., Vol. II., p. 556.
[689] Hammerschmidt, Musikalische Andachten. Freiberg, 1646. No. 7.

a repetition of the chorus " *Surrexit Christus.*" It is one of those which led and prepared the way for the oratorio in Germany. Although it was undoubtedly written for church use it has nothing that bears any special indication of it ; the " *Surrexit* " is not introduced in the usual manner, but in a newly devised way, and rather as being merely a suitable text, as is frequently done by Hammerschmidt and Schütz ; it nowhere exhibits any striking polyphonic treatment, nor any well-composed melody, but a good deal of clear dramatic emphasis. This work is in many respects closely allied to Bach's Easter oratorio. In this, also, the narrative portions are wanting, only the two Marys, Peter, and John, appear in person ; there are no chorales, and the portions given to the chorus are, when measured by Bach's standard, of remarkable simplicity. The text consists, not of Biblical quotations, but solely of poems in madrigal form, and the resemblance of the whole work to the Italian model is immediately perceptible. Of all Bach's compositions this has the fairest right to the name of " Oratorio," though not, to be sure, in Handel's sense of the word.

The text, of which the author is unknown, is meagre enough. All that is most beautiful and significant in the history of the Resurrection, and that has been given above in the outline of the *Dialogus*, has not been made any use of. It begins with a duet between John and Peter, who are informed of Christ's resurrection by the women, and who run joyfully to the sepulchre to convince themselves (John xx., 3 and 4). There Mary the mother of James, and Salome, reproach them with not having also purposed to anoint the body of the Lord and thus testifying their love for Him. The men excuse themselves, saying that their anointing has been "with briny tears, and deep despair and longing." Then the women explain that these, happily, are no longer needed, since the Lord is risen. They gaze into the empty tomb ; John asks where the Saviour can be, to which Mary Magdalene replies—what the men have long known :—

> " He now has risen from the dead.
> To us an angel did appear
> Who told us, lo ! He is not here."

Peter directs his attention to the "linen cloth," and this leads him to recall the tears he had shed over his denial of Jesus—a very tasteless episode. The women next express their longing to see Jesus once more; John rejoices that the Lord lives again, and the end is a chorus :—

> Thanks and praise
> Be to Thee for ever, Lord!
> Satan's legions now are bound,
>   His dominion now hath ceased,
> Let the highest heaven resound
>   With your songs, ye souls released.
> Fly open, ye gates! Open radiant and glorious!
> The Lion of Judah comes riding victorious.

It cannot but surprise us to find that Bach could have been satisfied with such a text. He has embodied the history of the Passion in a stupendous work, and he knew that the Resurrection had been sung at an earlier period, for he knew and made use of Vopelius' hymn book. It might be supposed that this would have been reason enough for his treating the history of the Resurrection in a worthier and more dignified way. Nor is this a work of his youth ; the forms show the handling of a mature master, and from the MS. we may see that the work must have been written about 1736.[690] I can only find an explanation in the regulations for divine service at Leipzig ; there was, in fact, no opening for a comprehensive work in the style of the St. John or the St. Matthew Passions. The *Magnificat* was performed at Vespers, and in the morning there was only time for a piece of about the length of a cantata, which could not even be in two sections, since after the sermon the *Sanctus* had to be sung. It is clear that Bach, having written " Mysteries " for Christmas, Holy week, and Whitsuntide, simply wished not to omit Easter ; and as he could not deal with the Gospel narrative in so extensive a form as he thought desirable—and as he found adopted by Vopelius—he preferred giving the form of an Italian oratorio, of which less was expected and demanded, to selecting a portion of it.

In the Easter plays the race between Peter and John to the sepulchre was a favourite event for representation ; on this

---

[690] See App. A., No. 58.

occasion Peter appears as the weaker and less important personage. I do not think it merely accidental that Bach's work should begin with a lengthy duet between the disciples as they run to the sepulchre ; nor, again, that Peter's part is given to the tenor and John's to the bass, while in the St. Matthew Passion the reverse plan is adopted. Bach subsequently obscured the popular sentiment which lay at the root of this, the principal event treated in the work ; for he re-arranged the duet as a four-part chorus, though the circumstances, of course, allow us to suppose that, besides the two disciples and the two Marys, other of Christ's followers would have hastened to the sepulchre.[691] As regards the church feeling in a text which avoids both Biblical words and chorales, it certainly can only arise from the circumstance that it treats of an event of supreme importance in the church. Bach's music had to do its utmost and best to support it. Of course we cannot expect grandeur and depth, as in the cantata "Christ lag in Todesbanden," or even the triumphant spring-like joy of the Weimar cantata "Der Himmel lacht," since the words are absolutely devoid of any incitement to either. Bach has given to the whole a fresh and innocent character, suggested, perhaps, by the words :—

Lachen und Scherzen	Laughter and gladness
Begleitet die Herzen	Now drive away sadness
Denn unser Heil ist auferweckt.	For lo ! the Lord hath waked from sleep.

A symphony in the two movements, together with the first vocal number, constitute a complete instrumental concerto. Among the arias, that given to Peter is distinguished by being a soft lulling cradle song, such as Bach was fond of writing. Singularly enough the principal motive is the same as that at the beginning of the Coffee Cantata which Bach composed about 1732 ; this of itself is definitive as to the

---

[691] In the parts, as last written out for this alteration, Bach did not note the names of the four *dramatis personæ*, nor in the score, but only in the earlier parts ; but we need not conclude from this that he had altogether given up the dramatic scheme of the work. This would render the first and second recitation perfectly unintelligible.

cheerfulness of the feelings with which he composed the Easter Oratorio. The final chorus, freely worked out in the form of the French *ouverture*, is attractive from the breadth and splendour of the first subject ; compared with this, the Fugato is surprisingly brief, and produces no profound effect.[692]

In the Ascension Oratorio Bach, on the contrary, has adhered to the old liturgical forms. The historical matter was, in this case, of such limited extent that it could easily be worked out within the narrow bounds allowed by the regular service for Ascension Day. The Biblical narrative is compiled and harmonised from St. Luke xxiv., 50—52 ; Acts i., 9—12, and Mark xvi., 19. Bach has made no use of the customary hymns "Nun freut euch " and "Christ fuhr gen Himmel "; after Christ's ascension has been related we have the fourth verse of Rist's hymn, " Du Lebensfürst, Herr Jesu Christ ! " and at the end the last verse of Sacer s " Gott fahret auf gen Himmel." It is not known who wrote the texts in madrigal form, consisting of one chorus, two recitatives and two arias, nor can anything exact be stated with regard to the date of the composition. The style displays the fullest maturity in the master, hence we may assume that the Ascension Oratorio, like those for Christmas and Easter, was written in 1729.[693] Like the Christmas Oratorio, it has at the beginning a madrigal chorus in the Italian aria-form, and at the end a choral-fantasia. The opening chorus, which may have been transferred to this place from some occasional music, is a masterpiece in its way, a combination of tuneful simplicity with polyphonic elaboration ; in the upper parts the jubilant melodies flow on without interruption with the most artless phrasing, and yet the lower parts evolve a rich and independent vitality.

It is remarkable that the solo pieces are not devotional, but dramatic in conception. In the alto aria, and the bass

---

[692] B.-G., XXI.[3]

[693] The autograph has the characteristics of Bach's later writing, but beyond this gives no data as to its chronology. The work is B.-G., II., No. 11. I may here observe that there is in the Royal Library, at Berlin, a figured organ part in autograph, which has not been made use of in editing the work.

recitative which precedes it, Jesus is implored not yet to depart from among those who believe in Him; in the soprano air consolation is derived from the reflection that Jesus, though He has ascended into heaven, is still present in spirit to the faithful. In the St. Matthew Passion, in one passage only ("Give, O give me back my Lord"), the same view is taken, and there seems hardly justified. The arias in the Christmas Oratorio, "Haste, ye shepherds" and "Slumber beloved," had their origin in popular tradition, and in the solos of the Ascension Oratorio we must recognise a dramatic expansion of the simple narrative in the same spirit of the sacred plays. In fact, we actually meet with such an expansion in a medieval Ascension-play, where first Peter (compare the bass recitative in Bach) and then the Virgin Mary (compare the alto aria) bewail the departure of the Redeemer.[694] Both the arias are full of splendid harmonies; the first breathes an overpowering fervency, the second a magical radiance of glory, and the contrast between the two shows Bach's power and poetical feeling for colour. The chorale, "Nun lieget alles unter dir"—"Now art Thou Sovereign over all"—is set in as low a range as possible; the aria, which is accompanied only by the flutes, violins and violas—dispensing with the basses—soars up to the realms of light. In one we have the image of the disciples left below, in the other that of the transfigured Saviour floating upwards.

IX.

BACH'S MOTETTS.

IN order to fill up the whole cycle of all Bach's labours as a church composer during the years 1723—1734, it is necessary, after having considered his "mysteries," to pass in review his motetts. A critical examination of these is rendered difficult by many external circumstances. Some of the motetts have been lost or have at any rate disappeared;

---

[694] Mone, Schauspiele des Mittelalters. Vol. I., p. 261.

many pass for Bach's which would seem to be spurious; of those which are undoubtedly genuine only the smallest portion are yet existing in Bach's writing, and the greater part of them have been handed down in a very incomplete and unsatisfactory condition; while of one alone do we know the date of composition.[695] This one belongs however to the section of his life between the years 1723—1734, and since most of the others bear the stamp of his full maturity of style they cannot be placed far from this one in regard to date.

At all events Bach did not begin to turn his attention to the composition of motetts for the first time in Leipzig. It was impossible that one who employed his energies in vocal church music so early in life, and so thoroughly as he had done both at Mühlhausen and at Weimar, could leave unnoticed the Motett—a form of composition which, in spite of transformation and disfigurement, remained so full of vitality, and which was an indispensable part of the church services at that time. It is also not improbable that an early composition of this kind by Bach is contained in a motett, " Unser Wandel ist im Himmel "—" Our conversation is in heaven." The text is taken from the Epistle for the 23rd Sunday after Trinity (Philippians iii., 20 and 21); the work is divided naturally into two fugues, the first of which is preceded by a short homophonic movement, while between the two is inserted the second verse of the chorale " Herr Gott, nun schleuss den Himmel auf," simply set in four parts. In the " Orgelbüchlein " Bach treated the same melody, though in a somewhat altered form; this is no sort of evidence against its Weimar origin, for Bach, even in his Leipzig time, employed varying forms of one and the same melody (e.g., " Warum sollt ich mich denn grämen," " Helft mir Gotts Güte preisen "). The four-part writing of the chorale somewhat resembles that of the Passion according to St. Luke. In the fugues the parts are now and then treated with too little care, and their working out is not always quite successful, but on the whole they are

---

[695] See Appendix A., No. 59.

flowing and animated musical pieces, not unworthy of
Bach. This is especially true of the second fugue; it shows,
too, an intimate connection with the fugal movement " Herr,
höre meine Stimme," from the Weimar cantata "Aus der
Tiefe rufe ich Herr zu dir."[696]   Not only are the key and the
indication of time identical, but the character of the theme
and the movement which prevails throughout present a
striking similarity, and in the motett the idea of agitation is
represented in a realistic manner, like that of Telemann,
as that of entreaty is in the cantata. Again, the close of
the preceding number in the cantata agrees to some extent
with the end of the first fugue in the motett. Several
passages, too, where the vocal bass part lies above the
tenor, and is yet to be considered as the root of the harmony,
make it probable that it was intended to be accompanied
by a 16-foot *Basso continuo*.[697]

In the services of the churches of St. Thomas and St.
Nicholas the motett had its regularly appointed place at
the beginning of the early service and of vespers, after the
organ prelude. Besides this a motett was occasionally sung
on the high festivals during the communion; this was always
the case on Palm Sunday and Holy Thursday. The motett
was only omitted altogether when the organ was not played.
There were also occasions for the composition of motetts
outside the circle of church ordinances, and especially in
the case of funeral ceremonies; and one of Bach's motetts
really owes its existence to the burial of the rector, Johann
Heinrich Ernesti (d. Oct. 16, 1729). Bach however turned
it to an ecclesiastical purpose, as was his wont with other
" occasional " compositions. The position in the service
occupied by the motett, limited it as regards length; nor
could the motett be of great musical importance, since it

---

[696] See Vol. I., p. 450.

[697] In parts, which may have been written about 1800, in the Library of
the Singakademie in Leipzig. Inscription: " *Motetto di Bach.*"   On the same
sheet are also written, " *Ecce quomodo moritur* " by Gallus, and " *Tristis est
anima mea*," by Kuhnau. Although no Christian name is added, it cannot be
doubted that the copyist of the parts, the exemplar of which must have
been preserved among the archives of the Thomasschule, referred it to
Sebastian Bach.

only served the purpose of an introduction. Many of Bach's motetts are, however, of such grand proportions and are worked out with such an exhaustive treatment of the special feeling suggested by the Church ordinances that they cannot possibly have served merely as an introduction to the service. They must be regarded rather as pieces to be performed before the sermon in place of the cantata, and we know from Bach's own words that he occasionally substituted the one for the other.[698]

The motett of Bach takes its rise from his cantatas, and, like them, primarily from his organ music. This explains the relation it bears to the motett form as that is generally understood. It is only indirectly connected with the motett of the seventeenth century. That was influenced by the concerted vocal music of the time, and reflects its half-developed forms with moderate completeness both of outline and detail.[699] In so far indeed as Bach's cantatas owe their origin to these, they have something in common ; but Bach's motetts, like his cantatas, are absolutely free from the dramatic elements which appear in Schütz's and Hammerschmidt's sacred concertos and madrigals, and which also found their way into the motetts of the time. Whereas in the cantatas the forms of organ music have scarcely more than a subsidiary influence, they here make themselves felt in their full power. The organ-style governs the whole ; it determines the characteristic formation of the melodies and the polyphony, always founded upon the laws of harmonic progression ; and, above all, it has re-established the chorale in its full significance. Bach's cantatas were a central form of art, which included and made use of every musical element of a living and progressive character which existed at the time. Even the motett had been absorbed into the Bach cantata, and it was afterwards not so much born fresh from it as set free once more from its trammels. It re-appeared, not as an independent form of art, but as an offshoot of the Bach cantata.

---

[698] See ante, p. 247.
[699] See Vol. I., p. 55.

So far as it is possible to venture on an assertion, owing to the incompleteness of the materials, the history of the motett bears out this view. The name motett first occurs in Bach as applied to a piece of really concerted church music, namely, to the Rathswechsel cantata of 1708 ; the title is also borne, in the autograph by the cantata "Aus der Tiefe rufe ich Herr zu dir," the very work of which we are so strongly reminded in the motett "Unser Wandel ist im Himmel." The chief reason of this is to be found in the text of this work, but yet the changed application of the title would be inexplicable had not Bach been actuated by the idea of uniting the form of the motett with that of concerted music.[700] We first meet with a choral movement in genuine motett style in the Weimar cantatas "Ich hatte viel Bekümmerniss" and "Himmelskönig, sei willkommen,"[701] then in the first inserted piece in the great *Magnificat* "Vom Himmel hoch," then in the treatment of the fourth verse of the Easter cantata "Christ lag in Todesbanden," and again in the second movement of the cantata "Gottlob nun geht das Jahr zu Ende."[702] This last number was afterwards turned into an independent work, after having been re-modelled in such a manner that the *Basso continuo* could be entirely left out.[703] Bach subsequently prefixed to the cantatas "Aus tiefer Noth schrei ich zu dir" and "Ach Gott vom Himmel sieh darein"[704] chorale choruses in motett style, which afterwards obtained celebrity as inde-

---

[700] See Vol. I., p. 345 and 449. The title "motett" for the Cantata "Aus der Tiefe" is given in Aloys Fuchs' catalogue of autographs, which is found in MS. in the Stadtbibliothek in Leipzig.

[701] See Vol. I., p. 531 f. and 539.

[702] See ante, pp. 376, 394, and 433.

[703] In MS. in the Amalienbibliothek in the Joachimsthal Gymnasium in Berlin, Nos. 24 and 31. Title : "*Choral.* | Sey Lob und Preiss mit Ehren. | vom Herrn | Bach." For the first verse of "Nun lob, mein Seel, den Herren," the fifth verse is substituted. Important changes have been made in several places ; in particular, the closing symphony is entirely different. For this reason we might suspect Bach to be the remodeller, if some other features of the work did not make it improbable.

[704] B.-G., VII., No. 38, and I., No. 2. P. 1694 and 1194.

pendent works.[705]   But texts of Scripture set in motett form occur also in the cantatas.   The Christmas cantata " Sehet, welch eine Liebe,"[706] opens with a number of this kind, and another number in motett form, " Wenn aber jener der Geist der Wahrheit kommen wird," stands in the middle of a work for the fourth Sunday after Easter (" Es ist euch gut, dass ich hingehe").   All that Bach has left us in the motett form is throughout written in the same style.   The texts consist either of Bible words only or of Bible words combined with a chorale, or else of a sacred aria-text joined to these two, or lastly of the aria-text alone.   All the texts are in German.   As the motetts sung at the beginning of divine service, even in Bach's time in Leipzig, were for the most part in Latin, he may very likely have been prompted to write some also in that language.   In the year 1767 a certain one heard, at the early Christmas service, a Latin motett for two choruses by Bach, and " was thrilled to his inmost soul," and considered that nothing could compare with the lofty devotion and the beauty which pervaded it.[707] They are, however, all lost.

Of four-part motetts only one remains: the 117th Psalm, " Lobet den Herrn, alle Heiden "[708]—" Praise ye the Lord, all ye heathen "—a grand work, which flows onward uninterruptedly in one movement in the old style, except that the Hallelujah movement at the close is disjoined from the rest.

There are two motetts in five parts ; both have a chorale for their groundwork, but are in all other respects very dissimilar.   In one the words chosen are taken from Ecclesiasticus l., 24—26, " Now therefore bless ye the God of all, which only doeth wondrous things everywhere,

---

[705] In a MS. of Agricola's in the Amalienbibliothek, Nos. 37 and 38.   The chorale movement " Aus tiefer Noth " is still followed by the terzet, which occurs in the same cantata.

[706] See ante, p. 385.

[707] Gerber, N. L. I., col. 222 f.

[708] Published in 1821, in score and parts, by Breitkopf and Härtel, in Leipzig. It must have been done from Bach's autograph, which however has not hitherto come to light again.

which exalteth our days from the womb, and dealeth
with us according to His mercy. He grant us joyfulness of
heart, and that peace may be in our days in Israel for ever :
That He would confirm His mercy with us, and deliver us at
His time !" Martin Rinckart, as is well known, paraphrased
this passage in the two first verses of his hymn " Nun
danket alle Gott "—" Now thank we all our God "—and
this hymn forms the groundwork of the motett. It not
only concludes with the third verse of the hymn set in
simple harmony, but its first section is pervaded with
reminiscences of the first line of the chorale melody. This
mode of treatment may justify the supposition that the
motett dates from about the year 1730, since in the cantatas
also Bach liked to employ fragments of chorale tunes as
free motives.[709] To what extent his thoughts, in the composition of the motett, ran on the words of the hymn is
shown by the fact that in one passage, obviously unintentionally, he substitutes the words of the hymn for those of
the Bible ; he wrote, namely, thus : " Who wondrous things
hath done, wherein His world rejoices," which occur indeed
in the hymn, but not in Ecclesiasticus.[710]

In the other five-part motett Johannes Franck's devotional
hymn " Jesu meine Freude"—" Jesus, my joy"—is set in all
six verses. Its musical treatment displays of course great
variety. The first and last verses are set in four-part harmony,
" simplici stilo," as Bach himself used to designate pieces of
this kind,[711] the harmony being the same for both verses,
although the lower parts display rich animation and transcendental fervour. The same may be said of the second verse
in five parts, and the fourth in four, although the lower
parts, especially in the fourth verse, exhibit a still
greater individuality and many graphic and characteristic
touches. In the fifth verse the principal key of E minor
changes to that of A minor, for the purpose of giving
the Cantus firmus to the alto part ; the two soprano parts
and the tenor have counterpoint consisting for the most

---

[709] See ante, p. 457 f.
[710] The motett has hitherto remained unpublished. See Appendix A., No. 60.
[711] See Vol. I., p. 557, Note 271.

part of freely invented phrases, which however vary with each line of the tune, so that the whole form is different from that which we have termed the chorale fantasia, and which we found employed so frequently in the cantatas. The third verse is treated quite freely, taking the lines of the chorale in only the most general way as its motives, without strict regard to the exact intervals or length of these lines. The imitative and homophonic styles are used alternately, and unison even is employed to complete a picture which for power, variety, and individuality has not its match among Bach's motetts. In this work that resemblance which we noticed before to Buxtehude's chorale cantata "Jesu meine Freude" is more prominent than ever,[712] but the soft and tame emotion of the older master does not show to advantage beside this warlike strength and eager desire of conflict. Between the six verses of the chorale Bach introduces freely invented passages in five and three parts, on words from Rom. viii., 1, 2, 9, 10, and 11, the first of which agrees as regards musical material with the last.[713] In these he discourses with the fervency of faith on the importance of Christ's atoning work. The congregational feeling infused into these subjects, as being appropriate to their general dogmatic purport, is pointedly applied to the practical Christian life by the intervening verse; and thus the germ of Protestant Christianity is embodied in this great work. Bach uses all the power of his inmost convictions to give expression to the teaching of Luther in its utmost rigour and purity. But with this keen dogmatic certainty he combines the deepest personal devotion to Christ. In no other of his works do we so plainly see how completely the two parties into which the church of his time was divided—namely, orthodoxy and pietism—had ceased to exist for him. Even if we knew nothing more with regard to the position taken by Bach in church disputes, an attentive

---

[712] See Vol. I., p. 307 ff.

[713] It has been already mentioned (Vol. I., p. 67) that Michael Bach also used the chorale "Jesu meine Freude" as the nucleus of a motett. It is a simple work for double chorus in one movement, which Sebastian may indeed have had in his head when composing this work in this too the key is E minor.

consideration of this motett would suffice to guide us to the right opinion.[714] It is indeed a work "for all time," allotted to no particular day in the ecclesiastical year, though occasion for it may have been given by the eighth Sunday after Trinity, the Epistle for that day being taken from the eighth chapter of the Epistle to the Romans. Of course it was not intended as an introduction to the service, but as a substitute for the concerted music between the reading of the Gospel and the sermon.[715]

The four remaining motetts are set for double chorus. Among them is found the one mentioned above, which Bach wrote for the funeral of the Rector Ernesti. It consists of two sections, the words being taken from Rom. viii., 26 and 27 ; the first only is set for double chorus, the second being a four-part fugue. Bach afterwards added the third verse of the chorale " Komm heiliger Geist, Herre Gott"; judging from the words of the latter the motett was probably used for Whitsuntide, but it may also have served for the fourth Sunday after Trinity, the text being taken from the Epistle for that day. Another of these motetts begins with a number on Ps. cxlix., 1—3 (" Sing to the Lord a new song "), consisting of no less than one hundred and fifty-one bars. This is followed by the third verse of the chorale " Nun lob nein Seel," interrupted by fragments of the first chorus introduced as interludes, yet held together by a connected text, which is written according to the metric scheme of Rist's hymn " O Ewigkeit, du Donner-wort," although the melody which belongs to these words is not employed in the music. Next comes another double

---

[714] See Vol. I., p. 365, ff.

[715] This Motett is notified as Sebastian Bach's work in Breitkopf's Catalogue for the New Year 1764, p. 5. The MS. is in the Amalienbibliothek, Nos. 10, 12, and 30. There are three copies, which have, notwithstanding their many clerical errors, a great importance as regards authenticity. Published in score by Breitkopf and Härtel (" Motetten von Johann Sebastian Bach," No. 5). The text has here undergone much modernising ; Bach set it correctly in its original form. Also the titles of the separate numbers, and the indications of time, with the exception of the word " chorale " over verses 1, 2, 4, and 6, and an " Andante " over the three-part number, " So aber Christus in euch ist," are modern additions.

chorus on Ps. cl., 2, and finally a closing fugue in four
parts on v. 6 of the same Psalm. The work is apparently
a composition for the New Year.[716]   A third motett " Fürchte
dich nicht, ich bin bei dir "—" Fear not, for I am with
thee "—is set to Is. xli., 10, and xliii., 1 ; in the last verse
the treatment is again in four parts, but in such a manner
that the three lower parts work out the subject as a *Fugato*,
while the soprano sings the last two verses of Gerhardt's
hymn " Warum sollt ich mich denn grämen." The chief
subject of the *Fugato*, on the words " For I have redeemed
thee," referring to the crucifixion of Christ, is free and
chromatic. From the third verse before the end onwards,
Bach makes an arbitrary alteration in the expressive melody
of the chorale ; its key now appears as E major, while it
begins in A major. By this means it gains the mixolydian
character much more distinctly than in the Christmas
Oratorio.[717]   Grief for Christ's sorrow and lowly devotion
to His person are thus united into one emotional picture,
which gives a deep and genuinely Protestant foundation to
the trust in God which was before expressed. As regards
the form, we again have a chorale fantasia in the style
developed by Bach in his organ music. At the same time
it must be understood that the soprano and the three other
parts are not contrasted together as two dramatic factors,
but that their poetic and musical import is merged in a
more universal religious feeling. That Sebastian Bach, by
this method of viewing and treating subjects of this kind,
drew a sharp line of demarcation between himself .and his

---

[716] The autographs of both motetts are in the Royal Library at Berlin. They
are published by Breitkopf and Härtel as Nos. 1 and 6 of the collection before
mentioned, but with spurious time-indications and many alterations of the
text, which are probably due to J. G. Schicht, Cantor of the Thomasschule,
1810—1823. Below the second section of the last motett, in the autograph
score, stand the words " The second verse is like the first, except that the
choirs change about, the first choir singing the Chorale, and the second the
Aria." The second verse must probably have been the fourth verse of
the Chorale, but Bach must have found that in this way the work would be
too long, for in the original parts the interchange between the choirs is not
found. The connection of the Psalm-verse which follows is, in fact, not very
obvious.

[717] Compare ante, p. 583.

uncle, Johann Christoph, who set part of the same text,
and also interwove a chorale melody to form a motett, has
been explained before.[718] For the last of the motetts for
double chorus Bach used an aria text, and in this case dispensed with a chorale altogether. The text consists of two
stanzas beginning "Komm Jesu, komm, mein Leib ist
müde"—"Come Jesu, come, for I am weary." The poet,
who is unknown, may have written these words with a special
view to their being set to music. They cannot have been
intended for congregational use, for their metre suits none
of the Protestant chorale tunes that existed in 1750. The
music to the second stanza in aria form is evidently Bach's
original composition. The first stanza is fully developed
for double chorus, and the picture which it presents of
fervent longing for death is as majestic as it is deeply
moving.[719]

In the treatment of an ordinary motett one fundamental
principle held good : the separate sections or lines of the
text were to be worked out fugally, not, however, to the
exclusion of shorter homophonous passages. In motetts
for double chorus, on the other hand, the working out was
done by means of alternating the two bodies of the chorus,
which were opposed to one another, as self-contained and
complete entities, the two being usually only united at the
chief cadences. By this means there was very little scope for
thematic development ; there exist, indeed, excellent motetts
of the seventeenth century which exhibit nothing of that
kind at all. Sebastian Bach followed out this principle.
With that keen penetration which went to the very heart

---

[718] See Vol. I., p. 93.   This motett is notified as Seb. Bach's work in
Breitkopf's Catalogue of 1764, p. 5, and was published in Breitkopf and Härtel's
collection as No. 2.   The MS. is in the Amalienbibliothek, No. 15—17, to which
is added a note in Kirnberger's writing with regard to the origin of the chorale
employed.

[719] Designated as Seb. Bach's work in Breitkopf's Catalogue of 1764, p. 5,
and published by Breitkopf and Härtel as No. 4, but with altered words.   The
MS. score in the Amalienbibliothek, No. 18—21, must have been put together
from the separate parts, for above the beginning stand the words *Soprano
Chorimi*, which the careless copyist apparently read for *Soprano Chori I mi*,
and transferred to the score.

of all new forms and followed them out to their ultimate consequences, he never once divided his body of voices into a higher and a lower chorus, as was frequently done by the older masters ; and it was but seldom, and in a way of his own, that he introduced a fugue in more than four parts. In this method there was, indeed, a danger of the choruses becoming united into one mass; but a fugue in which all the parts took an equally active and independent share would be a conscious transgression of the ruling principle of the form, being not so much a union of all the parts to one whole, as the resolution of two factors into eight. Wherever Bach employs a fugal movement in which all eight parts have a share, as for instance in " Komm Jesu, komm," bars 44—57, and in " Der Geist hilft," bars 76—84 and 124 ff., it always happens that the separate parts of the choruses are treated antiphonally. The individuality of Bach's style is most prominent in the motetts for double chorus, because here he was impelled most strongly towards the use of homophony. I use this word only to denote the absence of imitative writing. It is not intended to convey the impression that there is any lack of melodic movement in the separate parts. It is just this movement which is no less conspicuous in the homophonous than in the fugal portions, and which testifies with the greatest certainty to the origin of Bach's motett style. These passages did not originate in the nature of the human voice, which excels most in the simplest movements, and particularly in gradations of strength reached by imperceptible degrees in colouring and *nuance*—they took their rise in the conception of a musical instrument which has no means of embodying the whole force of emotion but by varying degrees of mere external movement within the limits imposed by unalterable strength of tone. The church organ is the parent of these passages that flow up and down and across each other ; and its influence may be traced even in the minutest details of their form. In the organ the lack of power to give proper expression to melody and rhythm leads naturally to a greater prominence of purely harmonic effects. Though Johann Christoph Bach, and others of his

time, strove to gain their effects by homophonous movements, a clearly recognisable melody, of however simple a
form, is always heard persistently in the upper part. In
Sebastian Bach there occur passages—as at the beginning
of " Singet dem Herrn "—which can only be regarded
as waves of harmony twisted into melody. The astounding boldness of the part-writing finds in this view its
explanation and only justification. The grand harmonic
portions, developed with the surest and truest instinct,
afford firm points of support, or rather of suspension, at the
beginning and the end, between which the separate parts
can disport themselves at will. Contact and collisions between the parts, nay, even transgressions of the elementary
rules of part-writing—notice the octaves between the
extreme parts in bars 26—27 of the motett " Singet dem
Herrn "—are not avoided, provided only that the harmonic
progression is clearly intelligible as a whole. We cannot
but notice that the whole is full of life and movement, but
in many passages the effect of Bach's motetts in no way
depends upon the exact perception of how that movement is
obtained. Combinations of parts such as these :—

720

or :—

721

are not written by Bach in other places. In the same way
he gets his effects of increased power in a manner similar to
that employed on the organ. The four-part fugues, chorales,

---

720 Motett " Singet dem Herrn," bar 72.
721 Motett " Komm Jesu, komm," bar 150 ff.

or arias, at the close of the motetts for double chorus, represent, as it were, the full organ. When in the elaborate fugue "Die Kinder Zion sein fröhlich," from the first chorus of "Singet dem Herrn," more and more parts from the second choir are brought in to strengthen the entrances of the theme, the method may be compared to that of increasing the force in the course of an organ piece by drawing out one powerful stop after another.

It has been stated in another place[722] that at that time in Leipzig, as everywhere else, it was the custom to accompany the motett on the organ or some other supporting instrument. Bach's position relatively to this custom has been a matter of doubt. When he set free the motett from the church cantata, forming it, as is most evident, upon the style of the organ, never scrupling to let the bass part rise above the tenor, though it is always to be regarded as the continuous root of the harmony; when choral numbers, from cantatas like "Aus tiefer Noth" and "Ach Gott vom Himmel," could become widely known by the name "motett," even with a figured bass, which was partially, at least, independent of the vocal parts; and when his pupil Kirnberger expressly testifies to the co-operation of the organ, the doubt seems superfluous. Indeed, an organ accompaniment exists for the Psalm "Lobet den Herrn alle Heiden," and there is a figured organ part written by Bach himself for the motett "Der Geist hilft unsrer Schwachheit auf." Of course this can only have been intended for use in church. The performance at funeral ceremonies took place at the house of mourning; for this the instrumental parts which also remain to us—two violins, viola, violoncello, for the first choir, and two oboes, tenor, and bassoon—may have been employed, in which case it remains uncertain whether or no they, as well as the organ, took part in the church performances. The organ part is very interesting. On the one hand it offers an example rarely given by the composer of how agreeably a figured bass may be added to his motetts for double chorus without being independent in any way,

---

[722] See ante, p. 279.

since the organ part contains only one semiquaver which is not also in the vocal bass. On the other hand, the figuring, which in the passages where it is used follows the fundamental harmony, regardless of some rather serious false relations, shows clearly by what considerations Bach was led in writing his parts. If we consider the relation between the two vocal bass parts, it appears very similar to that which exists in Bach's cantata choruses between the vocal and instrumental bass parts. To write the two bass parts so that they frequently came together either in unison or in octaves was indeed usual before his time. But the way in which Bach often makes one of the bass parts separate from the other for a short time, in order to execute some rather important phrase or other, and then flow on again, united to the other (see "Singet dem Herrn," bar 122 ff.); the way in which one joins in with the other on the figured notes, thus simplifying the phrase (see the first of the examples given above, and also "Fürchte dich nicht," bar 34 and "Komm, Jesu, komm," bar 60); the way the bass of one of the choirs is brought in alone to complete the harmony of the other (see "Fürchte dich nicht," bar 57)—all this can be called neither unity nor duality of parts; it is a free method of treating the parts under his control according to the necessity of the moment, such as we also notice in the treatment of the figured bass, with regard to the vocal bass in the cantata choruses. Here, indeed, the figured bass is the dominant part, whereas in the motetts for double chorus this part is taken now by one of the basses, now by the other, sometimes even by both together. But Bach could only fall into this style of writing while the idea of his accompanied cantata choruses was in his head.

If we consider the fugal movements that occur in the motetts, not a few of them are so arranged that the one part which has the theme does not lead off quite alone, but supporting harmonies are supplied by the other parts. Thus it is in the second section of the motett "Jesu meine Freude" ("die nicht nach dem Fleische wandeln"), vocal harmonies surround the opening of the fugue from which real parts are gradually evolved. In the fugue "sondern der

Geist," &c., from the Funeral Motett, the theme given out by
the soprano of the first choir is accompanied by all the other
parts of the same choir. In the fugue " die Kinder Zion
sein fröhlich " (in " Singet dem Herrn"), the whole second
choir at first only accompanies the first in harmonic masses,
until the separate parts are gradually drawn in by the
irresistible flood of sound, and made to take part in the fugal
development. But Bach usually constructs the fugal movements of his cantatas above or among the accompanying
harmonies of the figured bass or of the instruments. If we
compare the opening chorus of the cantata " Wer sich selbst
erhöhet "[723] we shall have an almost exact counterpart to
the motett fugue last alluded to. We see in this how the
individual characteristics of Bach's concerted music are
repeated again, even in detail, in his motetts.

In spite of this, the question as to the accompaniment of
Bach's motetts is not yet dismissed. Though in Breitkopf's
printed catalogue of 1764 some of these works are entered
under the name " Motetts without instruments," this proves
very little. For, as may be seen on the next page of the
catalogue, compositions with organ accompaniment are also
comprised under this name, so that the plural " Instruments "
is to be taken in its strictest meaning. Nor is the fact of the
organ not being expressly mentioned in Bach's pieces any
reason for denying that it was used, for, as has been shown,
it was very often taken for granted. The fact of its
having to provide the necessary completion of the harmony
has nothing to do with the point. The question is simply
whether the quality of the vocal writing is not such as to be
only fully explained and justified by the addition of the organ
effect. A strong piece of evidence on the other side is, however, that among the original parts of the motett, " Singet dem
Herrn," which are preserved in their entirety, no organ part
is found. And more important still is the testimony of Ernst
Ludwig Gerber, who in 1767 heard a motett for double
chorus in Leipzig, and remarked that the Thomasschule
boys " were wont to sing " these compositions by Bach

---

[723] B.-G., X., No. 47. P. 1698.

without any accompaniment. This expression cannot be misunderstood, and at the same time it points to a custom which had prevailed for a long time. Thus there exist contradictory testimonies with regard to this question.

The whole of Bach's creative work is pervaded by a tendency to cast off all that is unnecessary and redundant attaching to the forms, to limit the means of expression to what was indispensably necessary, and in the highest possible degree to spiritualise what was material. It was this tendency which prompted him to cast off the figured bass harmonies with the clavier obbligato in the sonatas for violin and viol da gamba, and to write sonatas and suites for violin and violoncello without any accompaniment whatever. His predecessors preferred to write motetts with rather than without an independent figured bass part. Only a single work of his is known in which the figured bass is necessary to its completeness, at any rate in a portion of it—this is the Psalm " Lobet den Herrn alle Heiden"; the motett movements, which were originally parts of cantatas, are not referred to here. For the rest, all that is requisite to the tone-picture was to be done by the voices alone. It is perfectly conceivable that Bach should have allowed himself to be led by that spiritualising tendency so far as to eliminate from his motetts even the admixture of that quality of tone, and of that colouring, which first gave them their individual style. This would have been no more than what he had previously done in the case of his solo sonatas for violin and violoncello, the style of which in the same way was derived less from the nature of those instruments than from that of the clavier and organ. We must constantly bear in mind that Bach's fancy lived and had its being in the tone of the organ, and that as he listened to the unaccompanied motetts—or to the sonatas—his mental ear would vividly supply, in addition to their audible effect, that quality which had originally given them life and which, though separated from them, yet hovered around them like a delicate perfume. It is certain that the motetts could only produce their full effect when accompanied on the organ. Without this their right appreciation would depend chiefly upon the ease with which their technical difficulties could be overcome, and upon the extent to which the voices could assimilate themselves in quality to the restful flow of the organ; also, upon the degree in which the hearer can succeed in saturating his imagination with the feeling of organ music, and so supplying what is unattainable by the instruments used.

For the rest Bach's motetts are the only compositions of his that have at no time vanished completely from the world of music. The cantors of St. Thomas' after him always held them in honour, and had them sung, though certainly not always *con amore*. Rochlitz, calling to mind his practice in the Thomasschule, remembered particularly the motetts "Singet dem Herrn," "Der Geist hilft unsrer Schwachheit auf," and "Sei Lob und Preis mit Ehren," with a certain mixture of feeling, however, for the difficulty of these works caused the boys much trouble.[724] When Mozart went to Leipzig in 1789, the Cantor Doles had the motett "Singet dem Herrn" sung for him, and he was so charmed with it that he studied all the motetts by Bach that the Thomasschule possessed. Then came a time when it seemed as though Bach would again meet with more general appreciation. This was the period when a transient admiration for Bach was created by Forkel's work; it passed, however, very quickly. But that the motetts were not forgotten, even later than this, is shown by their first appearance in print, in an edition prepared by Schicht in 1802 and 1803. Outside Leipzig, too, they seem to have been moderately well known; in Saxony, at least, as was natural from the fact that a great number of Saxon cantorates were held by men who had formerly been scholars in the Thomasschule. Marschner, when a boy at Zittau, sang Bach's motetts, under the direction of Friedrich Schneider, the choir prefect; and in a MS. choral-book preserved at Nieder-Wiesa, in Saxony, dating from the end of the last

---

[724] Rochlitz, Für Freunde der Tonkunst, II. (Edit. 3.), p. 134 f.—The Motett "Wie sich ein Vater erbarmet," mentioned by him, in addition to the above, is only the second part of "Singet dem Herrn." It seems that this comprehensive work was at that time only performed piecemeal.

century, is found the text of the motett " Komm Jesu, komm," adapted to a newly invented melody, and turned into a chorale.[725]

X.

" OCCASIONAL " COMPOSITIONS.

DURING the years 1723—34 an abundant wealth of compositions in the domain of church music was brought to perfection by Bach's genius. These works bear most certain and eloquent witness to the fact that Bach was here in his element. His obtaining the post of Cantor at St. Thomas's just in the ripest years of manhood must be regarded as no less happy a contingency than his having been summoned to Weimar and Cöthen, which served the purpose of giving to his nature its first free development and its contemplative depth. As compared with the result of this eleven years' work in Leipzig, the disappointments and unpleasantnesses which the office necessarily involved are seen to be of very small actual importance. Bach really valued his post and considered it a favourable one, and, as we shall soon see, felt himself bound to sing the praises of Leipzig. The plunge into the unknown which he had ventured upon "in the name of the Most High "[726] was really a fortunate one, although at times it seemed to him to be otherwise. In order to get a clear idea of his life and work, it is necessary that his productiveness in the way of church music should be dwelt on at full length, and shown to be the power which drove all other kinds of work into the background ; by this means alone can light and shade be rightly thrown upon the path of his development. For this reason detailed reference will not be made here to the numerous instrumental compositions which date from about this time. It will be more suitable to leave the consideration of these to the end, and the more so because Bach never, even at the end of his life, ceased to

---

[725] See Jakob and Richter, Reformatorisches Choralbuch. Berlin, Stubenrauch. Part II., No. 918.

[726] See ante, p. 254.

produce works of high importance in this branch of art. The case is different with regard to the " occasional" compositions for voices and instruments. The greater number of these date also from the Leipzig period; besides which, they are in part, at least, so closely connected with the church compositions, that even on this account they would claim examination in this place.

The " occasional" compositions, which were intended to celebrate some specially important event in the life of an individual, or of some public institution, are both sacred and secular. To the first class accordingly belong the funeral compositions: " Dem Gerechten muss das Licht " and " Herr Gott, Beherrscher alle Dinge "; the funeral cantata for Herr von Ponickau, " Ich lasse dich nicht" (1727); the burial motett for the Rector Ernesti, " Der Geist hilft unsrer Schwachheit auf" (1729); and the cantata for the dedication of the organ at Störmthal (1723): while the compositions for the annually recurring election of the Councillors (Rathswahl-cantaten), and those written for special ecclesiastical festivals, cannot be included in this category, although in a certain sense they too may be called " occasional " cantatas. Mention has before been made of the works just alluded to, for some of them were employed afterwards as " Rathswahl " cantatas, while some were used in their entirety for church purposes.[727]

We know that a portion of the Passion according to St. Mark is nothing more than an adaptation of an " occasional" composition.[728] This Passion music no longer exists, but the composition which was thus adapted is completely preserved as the music for the death of Queen Christiana Eberhardine. It would be valuable from this cause alone; but it deserves recognition also from the fact that it has an ecclesiastical and political *raison d'être*. Queen Christiana Eberhardine, of the family of the Margraves of Brandenburg-Bayreuth, had been married to Frederick Augustus since 1693. When her husband had, in 1697,

---

[727] See ante, pp. 468—9, 411—12, 602, 365—67.
[728] See ante, p. 505 f.

ascended the throne of Poland and embraced the Catholic religion she had remained true to the Evangelical church. She had no desire for honours that were to be purchased at the price of her religion ; and, although she could not persist in her refusal to bear the title of Queen, she never set foot in the kingdom of Poland. Even before her husband had cut himself off from her by his connection with the Countess Königsmark she had completely separated herself from him, and lived quietly at Pretzsch near Wittenberg. It was not long before her son, the successor to the throne, whose earliest education she had undertaken, abjured the religion of his father, which he did in 1717. A living religion of the heart, and firmly rooted convictions, were her Protestant doctrine, as she showed on the occasion referred to, in a letter in which, being well versed in Scripture, she sought to point out the errors of the Catholic Church, and adjures her son, "for his own poor soul's sake, and for his poor mother's sake, whom else he would bring down with sorrow to the grave, to return again to Evangelical truth."[729] By their perversion to Catholicism the Electors of Saxony lost the leading position which they had held in Protestant Germany since the Reformation, and which now passed into the hands of Prussia. Though the prince gave many pacifying assurances that his change of religion was a purely personal circumstance, and that everything would remain as it had been of old in the country, the people of Saxony were so zealously Protestant that they could not but regard with suspicion a movement which seemed to favour or at least to allow the introduction of Catholicism. At the Saxon diet of the year 1718, very violent accusations and petitions were brought on this question.[730] Protestant preachers, zealous for the faith, did their best to stir up excitement and hatred. The doubts raised by the Leipzig Council in 1702 with regard to the propriety of the services there being conducted in Latin, which made them resemble

---

[729] The letter is quoted entire by Förster, Frederick August II., Potsdam, Reigel, 1839, p. 245—249.

[730] Gretschel, Geschichte Sachsens, II., p. 589, ff.

the Catholic services too closely[731] appear in a new light
under these conditions.   A year before the queen's death
religious fanacticism had even led to murder and insurrec-
tion.   The archdeacon of the Kreuzkirche in Dresden,
Magister Joachim Hahn, was stabbed on May 21, 1726, by
a Catholic whom he had converted to Lutheranism, and who
had afterwards been in doubt as to his spiritual condition.
This deed created a fearful tumult, which had to be quelled
by   military   power.[732]   In   these   circumstances   it   was
natural that the Saxon populace should regard the steadfast
queen with special respect and love, and should be deeply
moved by her sudden decease. The general mourning which
was commanded lasted from September 7 to January 6.[733]
On October 17 the town of Leipzig showed its respect for
the departed princess by a grand public funeral ceremony ;
compared with this the indifference shown on the occasion
of the king's death, six years later, is sufficiently significant.
In the year 1697 when, after the election of the King of
Poland, a *Te Deum* was appointed to be sung in the Saxon
churches, the congregations, with unequivocal demonstra-
tions, sang Lutheran and other Protestant hymns after it.[734]
But the funeral ceremonies for the queen, who had remained
true to her faith, were performed in a devotional Protestant
spirit.   The poem set by Bach avoids, and that designedly,
all that might give offence to the king, but does not omit to
celebrate the queen, " the pattern of a great woman," as the
" defender of the faith."

The ceremony did not bear a strictly devotional stamp ;
it was arranged in the same way as the academic "speeches,"
and took place in the University church, the University
having taken the principal part in its arrangement.[735]   On

---

[731] See ante, p. 264.

[732] Gretschel, loc. cit., p. 592 f.—Picander celebrated the event in a dull and
bombastic poem (Part I., p. 212—231).

[733] See Appendix A., No. 33.

[734] Gretschel, loc. cit., p. 475.

[735] The printed matter relating to this ceremony—viz., (1) the Latin introductory speech by the Rector of the University ; (2) the text of Gottsched's
Ode, as it was distributed among those present in the church ; (3) the eulogy

occasions such as this it was usual to set to music, not
cantata texts in the modern madrigal form, but Latin odes.
Bach had previously set a Latin ode for the birthday
festivities of Duke Friedrich of Saxe Gotha.[736]   The general
interest taken in the funeral ceremony must have been the
reason why the German language was considered more suitable on this occasion.   Gottsched, who had been for several
years lecturer in the University, and was Senior of the
Deutsche Gesellschaft, wrote the ode ; it cannot be praised
for any great flow or wealth of ideas, but its general
character is worthy of its subject, and its diction is correct.[737]
The composition is divided into two parts, of which the
first was sung before and the second after the funeral
oration.   This was delivered by Hans Carl von Kirchbach,
" Assessor of the Royal and Electoral Upper Court of Mines
(Oberberggerichts) at Freyberg."

Bach finished the composition on the 15th of October,
only two days before the funeral.   As the parts had then to
be written out we may see in this case with how few preparations this kind of musical performance was usually
given.[738]   He gave the work the cantata form by ingeniously
dividing the strophes of the ode into choruses, recitatives,
and arias.   This seems to have been an innovation as
applied to poems of this kind, for a reporter mentions
expressly that the ode was composed " in the Italian style."

---

and lament delivered by Hanns Carl von Kirchbach ; (4) a funeral ode by *M.*
Samuel Seidel—is all found together in one volume in the Royal Public Library
in Dresden (*Hist. Saxon.* c. 232).   The order of the ceremony is described by
Sicul, Das thränende Leipzig, 1727.

[736] See ante, p. 215.

[737] It was reprinted in an elaborated form in "Oden der Deutschen Gesellschaft in Leipzig."   Leipzig, 1728, p. 79 ff.

[738] At the close of the autograph score stand the words, "*Fine SDG. aõ*
1727. *d. Oct.* 15. *J S Bach.*"   On the title-page Bach gave the date of performance as October 18.   That he was mistaken in the date is indubitable since
the recovery of the original printed form of the ode, which gives the date as
October 17 (see above, note 735).   If the ceremony had been obliged for any
reason to be put off for a day, Sicul would surely have mentioned it in his
elaborate description.   This rectifies and completes the statement made in
the Preface to B.-G., XIII., 3.

The Italian style is also prominent in the use of the clavicembalo, which Bach himself played, and on which he must have accompanied the recitatives and arias, as was done in the Italian opera : the organ, probably, was only introduced in the choruses. The place which the work holds, half-way between secular and sacred music, by comprising continual references to God, and by the employment of chorales, while it is only a mortal person who is celebrated, but who is brought, as it were, into the region of the church, is explained by the circumstance that[739] the deceased queen had been very fond of music. Bümler, the Capellmeister at Anspach, was in her service from 1723—25, and in the summer she used frequently to invite members of the Dresden orchestra for her own pleasure.[740] This may have given a special incitement to the composer. The music to the Trauerode (funeral ode) is one of Bach's finest works. In the broad phrases of the first chorus, to which a full and florid colouring is given by the employment of gambas and lutes, a feeling is breathed forth which is closely related to that of the final chorus in the Matthew Passion. But in the chorus in the Trauerode, even though it is an introductory movement, there is a more vehement and passionate sorrow. This also comes out in the second recitative, which the instruments accompany with passages resembling the sound of bells ; the high flute begins, and is followed by a gradually increasing number of instruments going from the highest to the lowest, in figures of different kinds; last of all comes in the bass in long pulsations, and this sea of sounds flows on further in peculiarly sorrowful modulations, until it gradually ceases. The undeveloped sketch for this is found in the Weimar Cantata " Komm, du süsse Todesstunde," in describing which we spoke of the æsthetic justification of this graphic realism.[741] As the funeral ode goes on the feeling becomes calmer, particularly in the choruses, which are now smoother and more quiet,

---

[739] Sicul, loc. cit., p. 22 f. See Appendix A., No. 6.
[740] Hiller, Lebensbeschreibungen. Leipzig, 1784, p. 56 and 197.
[741] See Vol. I., p. 549 ff.

the last being quite in the simplest style. The prophecy
here uttered by the poet :—

> Doch Königin du stirbest nicht,
> Man weiss, was man an dir besessen,
> Die Nachwelt wird dich nicht vergessen.

> But, noble Queen, thou diest not ;
> We know what we possessed in thee,
> Posterity shall not forget thee.

has been fulfilled, although in a manner somewhat different
from that which he intended. It is the art of Bach which has
given immortality to the figure of the good queen, and I
believe that the privilege of being so gloriously remembered
will not be lost to her by the fact that the Trauerode,
since it has become known again, is sung to a modern
text of quite general religious import. No æsthetic reason,
it is true, can be brought against this practice, and Bach
himself employed the work for church purposes set to
another text. The bitter reproaches which have been justly
poured on a later and less intelligent period for a similar
procedure with Handel's funeral hymn for Queen Caroline
are not applicable here.[742]   Handel's music can only be
properly appreciated in its full depth and beauty by him
who remains conscious throughout that it was dedicated to
the pious memory of a noble personage. Instead of this
free and broad human feeling, in Bach we find a strictly
devotional sentiment; his music always speaks the same
language.   But the Protestant queen who remained true to
her faith, and inspired Bach to such a masterpiece, might
surely appear to subsequent generations worthy of an hour's
remembrance.

A second funeral composition of yet greater length was
written by Bach a year later, in honour of Prince Leopold,
Anhalt-Cöthen.   A lasting intercourse had been kept up
between Bach and his cultured patron, even after he had

---

[742] Chrysander, Handel II., p. 445.—Among the German capellmeisters and
cantors of that time it was the general custom to employ funeral compositions
written for distinguished personages, with altered texts, for church cantatas.
Johann Ernst Bach's funeral music on the death of Duke Ernst August
Constantin, of Weimar (1758), also met with this fate.

left his court. The title of "Royal Capellmeister of Cöthen," which he continued to bear, bound him to perform certain honorary duties. Thus he composed a cantata for November 30, 1726, the birthday of the princess; and in the cradle of her first-born, the hereditary Prince Emanuel Ludwig (b. September 12, 1726), he laid an autograph copy of the first Partita in the "Clavierübung," which had just then appeared in print, together with a dedicatory poem written by himself, from which his relations with the princely house appear to have been of a most friendly kind. In May, 1727, at the time of the "Jubilee" fair, Prince Leopold was in Leipzig, where he heard the festival music which Bach had performed on May 12, in honour of the king, who was also present.[743] This seems to have been their last meeting. The death of the Prince took place unexpectedly soon after this, on November, 19, 1728. The funeral ceremonies at Cöthen, at which Bach conducted his compositions himself, did not take place till the following year; the exact date is not known. It has of late been made extremely probable that this work, which has for some time been lost, was for the most part made up of portions of the then newly composed St. Matthew Passion. Here, accordingly, the same relations subsist between the two works as between the Trauerode of 1727 and the St. Mark Passion; only in this case the church composition was certainly the older of the two.[744]

Turning now to the considerably larger number of secular "occasional" cantatas, I must first mention, by way of supplement to a former chapter, a work which belongs

---

[743] Sicul, *ANNALIVM LIPSIENSIVM SECTIO* XXIX., Leipzig, 1728.

[744] For the discovery of this adaptation we are indebted to W. Rust; see B.-G. XX.,[2] p. X. f. The only circumstance which can be adduced against the result of Rust's research is that Forkel, who possessed the funeral music in autograph, and also knew the St. Matthew Passion, did not remark on their identity. Certainly Forkel's knowledge of the St. Matthew Passion may have been only very superficial, see his work on Bach, p. 62. Rust mentions (loc. cit. p. XIV.), among the lost "occasional" compositions of Bach, a third funeral cantata ("Mein Gott, nimm die gerechte Seele") adducing Breitkopf's Catalogue of Michaelmas, 1761. The cantata is indeed mentioned there (p. 23), but without the name of the composer.

indeed to the Cöthen period, but which has only lately come to light.[745] Since both the title and the opening are lost, the occasion and purpose of its composition can only be guessed. Thus much, however, is clear, that it tends to the glorification of the whole princely house of Anhalt-Cöthen. It is possible that Bach dedicated the cantata, a work of considerable extent, which, to all appearance, was written before the end of the year 1721, to the honoured family at the close of the year, and that he himself wrote the words, which leave much to be desired in both substance and form. The words of the last recitative (" Ja sei durch mich dem theursten Leopold ") show in the clearest way the purpose of the cantata. This delicate composition, which is full of lovely ideas, and in which a duet between alto and tenor (E flat major, common time) is remarkable for its especial beauty, is set throughout for solo singers, even the four-part number, at the close, being intended for single voices. In this the cantata agrees with the birthday cantata " Durch-lauchtger Leopold,"[746] and shows, moreover, that Bach when in Cöthen had no available chorus at his service. As that had been used for a Whitsuntide Cantata, so this was afterwards turned into a work for the third day of Easter (" Ein Herz, das seinen Jesum lebend weiss ") in Leipzig, without all its numbers being used however.[747] Here I must once more point out that the cantata mentioned earlier (" Steigt freudig in die Luft "), which Bach wrote for the first birthday which the second wife of Prince Leopold celebrated in Cöthen, was afterwards re-arranged several times.[748] The first of these re-arrangements was made for the birthday of a master,

---

[745] I discovered it in 1876 in the collection of autographs belonging to Herr W. Kraukling, of Dresden, who was kind enough to entrust it to me for a considerable time. See App. A., 61.

[746] See ante, p. 6.

[747] The autograph score of this Easter Cantata is in the Royal Library at Berlin.

[748] In Picander I., p. 14, it is expressly stated: " For the first birthday festival of the Serene Princess, at Anhalt-Cöthen, 1726." Now since her birth-day was on Nov. 30, and her marriage took place on June 2, 1725, it follows that on Nov. 30, 1725, the Princess cannot have been at Cöthen. Compare ante, p. 158.

perhaps of Gesner ;[749] the second transformed the work into a church cantata for the first Sunday in Advent.[750] There lived in Leipzig a lawyer, Johann Florens Rivinus (b. July 28, 1681), who was appointed *Professor ordinarius* to the University on June 9, 1723. He must at that time have been exceedingly popular, for on the evening of that day the students performed a serenade in his honour.[751] At least ten years after this the students again waited upon him with music on his birthday; for this the Cöthen Cantata underwent its third re-arrangement, and hereby regained its original secular character.[752] Bach seems to have had a special liking for this work, which, although pleasing, is not of great importance, possibly because such agreeable remembrances were connected with it.

Bach's secular "occasional" cantatas belong almost exclusively to the class of dramatic chamber-music. They are founded either upon some action, represented by means of a number of personages who come on and speak in character, or else upon a situation which is explained by the speeches of various persons. While, in general, vocal chamber-music stood half-way between sacred and dramatic music, this kind of composition leans more strongly towards the side of the opera. Of course such pieces were of much shorter extent, and rather resembled the last act of an opera. The plot and the characters were by preference taken from ancient mythology, although they were treated for the most part allegorically. Dramatic situations and style were demanded in as great a measure as for a work for the

---

[749] See ante, p. 262. Noticed in Breitkopf's Catalogue of Michaelmas, 1761, p. 33, among "Cantatas for promotions and days of honour " ("Promotions-und Ehrentags-Cantaten ").   [750] See ante, p. 471.

[751] Vogel, *Continuation* Derer Leipzigischen Jahrbücher von *Anno* 1714 bis 1728. MS. in the Leipzig Town Library. Fol. 32[b]. The text of the cantata written on this occasion is there given, without mention of the composer. Winterfeld, Ev. Kirchenger III., 262, suspects Bach to be the composer, but hitherto the suspicion has received no kind of confirmation.

[752] The words begin "Die Freude reget sich, erhebt die muntern Töne." The text of the cantata are in the Royal Library at Berlin. The parts are no longer complete, but, under existing circumstances, the loss is not very great. B.-G., XII.,[2] p. V., Note, is to be corrected accordingly. Bach was also a personal friend of Rivinus, and in 1735 asked him to be godfather to his son, Johann Christian.

stage; only costume, action, and scenery were wanting; and the last not entirely. It does not follow, from these compositions being reckoned as chamber-music, that they were always performed in the music-room. There is one essential difference between the musical performance of our time and of the past, in that a much greater freedom and variety prevailed then with regard to the place of the performance. At that time the ties connecting music with social life were much more numerous than they are now. Whereas now almost all the music which is performed outside the domestic circle—except it be either ecclesiastical or theatrical—is confined to the concert-room, where the public assembles for the special purpose of hearing it; at that time people chose the street, the garden, the wood, or even the lake or river, according to whether the music to be performed referred to a public ceremony, a wedding, a birthday, a hunting expedition, or any other festivity. If the work were of a dramatic kind the place of the performance was regarded as the scene, and the incidents of the piece had to be such as were suitable, though it was only in exceptional cases that such performances took place in costume. For a just appreciation of the character and effect of Bach's dramatic cantatas it is necessary to keep this mode of performing such works constantly in mind. It involved the procedure—so strange to us—of bringing in, not only the full chorus, but also solos in recitative and aria style, accompanied with instruments and the chorus in the open air. The usual weak and often simple treatment of the voices and instruments could not, of course, produce that far-reaching fulness of tone which is needed in an unlimited space under the open sky. Yet the skilled composer had to take care to suit his effects to the place of performance, and certain strange details in the Bach cantatas with which we are now concerned become intelligible in connection with this necessity.[753]

---

[753] Scheibe (Critischer Musikus, p. 450 ff.) goes so far as to give exact rules as to the different treatment of works of this kind, according to whether they were to be performed on the water or on land, in a room or in the wood, in a garden or in an open space surrounded with trees.

Apart from these peculiarities, the employment of certain rules of style underlies the dramatic cantatas, since they belong to the class of chamber-music. They had to unite the solidity of the sacred style with the ease and elegance of that of the theatre. In them we see the musical root and foundation from and on which the Handelian oratorio arose ; its connection with the dramatic chamber cantatas is revealed even in external style by the circumstance that Handel had his "Acis and Galatea" performed in a suitably decorated scene, although in this case it was an artificial one.[754]   But Handel, it must be owned, embodied the full import of the ancient myths in works which were intended for the whole cultured world, while in Bach an allegory supplies the dramatic motive, and the purpose of the work is to do homage to some particular person and to delight a small and select circle.   While Handel is in his element here, Bach can hardly appear in any other capacity than that of a musician whose services are given to order.   He would not have been the grand musician that he was if he could have contented himself with the composition of dramatic cantatas. For the public concert, which in England enabled Handel to elevate these and similar kinds of musical work to a branch of art of the first rank, was wholly wanting in Germany.   The only place from which a man with Bach's comprehensive musical gifts could exercise an influence on the German people was the church choir.   The influence of this, his own special province, pervaded all he undertook, consciously or unconsciously to himself.   Accordingly he made use of the greater part of the secular cantatas for church music, without radical alteration, and they are seen to be in their right place.   It follows from this that in their original form they cannot have been very suitable to the purpose for which they were written.   Indeed, Bach's chamber cantatas, so far from keeping their proper central position, lean strongly towards the church style. The characteristic treatment of the persons and situations which is required in the more dramatic of them shows indeed in its great sharpness and contrast that the artist

---

[754] Chrysander, Handel, II., p. 266.

has worked with mature deliberation; still it exhibits nothing more than the versatility of his inventive faculty in his own province. It fulfils but one requirement of the dramatic style; it is very much too heavy for the circumstances; the light play of the emotions is turned into serious pathos, and the comic into the grotesque. Although many of the figures appear full of character when compared with one another, yet they in no way show that Bach's talent would have been suitable to opera; on the contrary, it cannot be doubted that he was wanting in the class of sentiment which is an indispensable condition of that sphere of art. It is consequently impossible to hold up Bach's chamber cantatas as models of their kind. They are works full of value and charm, but only for him who brings himself into sympathy with Bach's individuality. This by way of introduction to the examination which we are about to make of the separate works.

We have seen already how Bach always took trouble to assure to himself the goodwill of the student-world of Leipzig.[755] It evidently has to do with this when we find him, even in the first years of his residence there, before he had undertaken the conducting of Telemann's Musical Society, occupied frequently in helping the students' enterprises by means of his art. Among the popular teachers at the University was the Doctor of Philosophy, August Friedrich Müller, whose nameday fell on the 3rd of August.[756] In the year 1725 his pupils wished to honour him with a musical work on this occasion, for which the ever-ready Picander made the text, which was set by Bach.[757] It was a dramatic cantata, evidently intended to be performed in the open air, and this is confirmed by the strong treatment of the accompaniment. The characters in the piece are

---

[755] See ante, p. 214.

[756] Müller was born in 1684 and died in 1761. On October 19, 1731, he became Professor extraordinary. His scientific works are noticed in the " Leipziger Neue Zeitung von gelehrten Sachen," III. 224, 519. VI. 654, 672. XVII. 760. XX. 103. In Ch. E. Hoffmann's " Geographischer Schau-Platz Aller vier Theile der Welt," Andere Theil., an engraving of him is given.

[757] Picander's Gedichte, I., p. 146 ff. B. G., XI.,² 139 ff.

drawn from ancient mythology. Pallas wishes to celebrate
a festival on Helicon with the Muses in honour of the
learned man. It is feared that it will be interrupted by a
violent autumn tempest (a fear, by the way, that appears
somewhat premature at the beginning of August); the
fierce winds are heard murmuring in their prison, and
Æolus, their ruler, promises that they shall soon be set free;
however, after Zephyrus, the god of the warm summer
breezes, and Pomona, the protectress of the fruits of the
earth, have both entreated in vain, he consents, on the
representations of Pallas, to leave the pleasant repose
of the season for a time undisturbed. The chorus of winds
and the recitative of Æolus, with which the cantata opens,
are taken by Picander from a well-known image in Virgil
(Æn. I., 56 ff.). The winds are in a mountain dungeon,
where they wrestle with one another, and vent their un-
tamable fury upon the locks and bolts of their prison.[758]
Æolus is rejoicing in the expectation that they soon will be
set free:—

> When through the world they rush and roar
> The rocks and hills are firm no more,
> But all things fly before them.

By these figures and ideas Bach was moved to create
tone-pictures of strange grandeur. In what follows, too,
Picander prepared the composer's way very efficiently
to some beautiful musical contrasts, even introducing some
striking features into the more detailed character-drawing.
The aria of Zephyrus, with its softly breathing figures and
tender, charming colouring, is one of Bach's loveliest
pictures of nature; and Æolus becomes in his hands a
wild unmannerly churl. His demeanour, it is true, is more
suitable for a tragedy than for a cheerful garden festival,
and when he is induced, by the single name " Müller," to

---

[758]   *Hic vasto rex Æolus antro*
Luctantes ventos, tempestatesque senoras
Imperio premit, ac vinclis et carcere frenat.
Illi indignantes magno cum murmure montis
Circum claustra fremunt.

hush the uproarious winds in their cavern,[759] the effect becomes irresistibly comic.[760]

Nine years later Bach brought his work again to a hearing on a much more important occasion. On January 17, 1734, Friedrich August II. was crowned King of Poland, as August III., in Cracow. For the festivities of the Leipzig University, which began on February 19, Görner had to provide a Latin ode.[761] Already in January, when the approaching coronation became known, Bach had prepared the Musical Society for a festival performance which was to take place so soon as news should arrive that the coronation was over. The necessary alterations in the text were undertaken by himself. Æolus was transformed into Valour, who, in the first recitative, instead of the raging of the winds, described the deeds done by her in the war with Stanislaus, the opposing king, and his party. Zephyrus had to take the *rôle* of Justice, and Pomona that of Mercy, Pallas alone remaining in person to beg the king's protection on behalf of the Muses. The name " August" now referred no longer to Professor Müller, but to the king of Poland. By this means the music, of course, lost all its dramatic character, but it is also evident that Bach did not consider the chief importance of the work to lie in this quality ; if he had, the alteration of the text would have been a barbarism which could the less be justified because he was not obliged by any kind of command to celebrate this festal occasion.[762]

---

[759]   *Celsa sedet Æolus arce,*
          Sceptra tenens : mollitque animos, et temperat iras.

[760] E. O. Lindner (Zur Tonkunst, p. 129), gives it as his opinion that the aria, " Wie will ich lustig lachen," has a wild humour, compared with which Handel's lauded Polyphemus sinks almost to the level of the ordinary Italian *buffo* air. But I do not understand how the whole can so be lost sight of compared with the details. The greatness, never to be surpassed, of Handel's Pastoral arises from the perfect harmony existing between the subject and its musical treatment. Bach used stronger materials in his treatment, but it is not usual to adorn a summer house with church steeples.

[761] Mittag, Leben und Thaten Friedrich Augusti III. Leipzig, 1737, p. 333 f. Note.

[762] The original printed form of the text is in the Royal Public Library at Dresden, *Hist. Polon.*, 672, 17. That Bach is the poet is clear from the form

On another occasion, in the year 1726, Bach made himself serviceable to the students. Gottlieb Kortte, a scholar, born in the year 1698, at Beeskow, in Lusatia, who had studied first theology and philology in Leipzig, and afterwards jurisprudence at Frankfort on the Oder, was promoted on December 11, 1726, to be professor extraordinary of law at Leipzig. From the comprehensive knowledge he had acquired, and his personal merit, he was already considered an ornament to the University. During his few remaining years this opinion was confirmed, and his early death, which took place on April 7, 1731, " was greatly bewailed by the young students, with whom he was very popular, and by all who knew the thoroughness of his erudition."[763] The performance in honour of the ceremony of his promotion took place, of course, in the Great Hall of the University, and, as was suitable to the scene, the personages of the dramatic cantata performed on the occasion are only allegorical: Diligence, Honour, Happiness, and Gratitude. Though Bach gave a pompous character to this work he did not write it all afresh, but employed[764] the third movement of the first Brandenburg Concerto, which he adapted to the opening chorus with great skill, although with a certain license of genius. The second trio of the dance-numbers appended to the Concerto was introduced as the ritornel of the duet. The alto aria, which is independent, so far as can now be determined, of any other work, has the rhythm of a minuet, and, with its softly sounding phrases in the form of fanfares, reminds us of the united violins and violas in the second gavotte in the

---

of the title. The poet's name was never omitted on occasions of this kind, and it was much more likely for the composer not to be mentioned. From the fact that a blank space is left for the date, we see that the text was printed before the day of the coronation was known.

[763] Leipziger Neue Zeitung von gelehrten Sachen XVII., p. 264. The November number of the *Acta Eruditorum* of 1731 contains, in an *Elogium* G. *Cortii*, his biography, which has served as the source of later notices. See Sicul, Leipziger Jahr-Geschichte, 1720, pp. 92, 127, 212. Kortte's writings were mostly of a philological kind (Ausgaben von Ciceros Episteln, Sallust, Lucan, &c.).

[764] See ante, p. 130.

orchestral suite in C major.[765] The whole work opens with
a march such as usually accompanied festival entrances and
exits, that is to say, rather a fanfare prolonged into a march-
form of two sections than a composition of purposeful
and compactly articulated melody : the march in Erlebach's
great Homage-music (Huldigungsmusik) of 1705 is cast in
a similar form.[766] The cantata was afterwards performed
again under Bach's direction, with an altered text, for the
name-day festival of King August III. (August 3).[767]

The Cantata " Siehe der Hüter Israel " seems to have
been written for a similar occasion as the music for Kortte.
It was for four voices, string orchestra, and harpsichord, but
has been lost.[768]

Five months after Kortte's promotion there took place a
new student festivity with music by Bach. On May 3, 1727,
King August II. arrived in Leipzig, meaning to stay a few
days for the Jubilee fair. On May 12 was his birthday.
As he had had a severe illness in the beginning of the year
at Bialystok, in Poland, the patriotic Leipzigers purposed
to make unusual efforts to celebrate this birthday with due
solemnity. In the morning there was a festal ceremony
in the University church, with a Latin ode of Görner's
composition, and a Te Deum with firing of cannon and
pealing of bells. In the evening, at eight o'clock, the
students belonging to the academical common table performed a dramatic cantata outside the king's lodgings, which
were then, as usual, in Apel's house in the Market (No. 17) ;
for this Bach composed the music and conducted it in
person. The music is lost : the poem was written by a

---

[765] See ante, p. 141.

[766] See Vol. I., p. 351.

[767] That it was really August III. and not August II. is shown by the tenor
recitative, " Ihr Fröhlichen, herbei." The military events here alluded to only
fit August III., and are evidently the tumults which prevailed during the first
year of his reign. Besides, in the year 1733, the king's birthday was celebrated
by a performance of Picander's Cantata " Frohes Volk, vergnügte Sachsen "
(Picanders Gedichte, IV., p. 14 ff.), so that Bach's altered composition was not
apparently used till later.—B.-G., XX.,[2] p. 73 ff.

[768] In Breitkopf's Catalogue of Michaelmas, 1761, p. 33, it is entered under
" Promotions- und Ehrentags-Cantaten."

certain Christian Friedrich Haupt. Picander's indefatigable
pen was not idle; he prepared a festival poem in
Alexandrines. The town was illuminated. It has been
already mentioned that Prince Leopold was present in
Leipzig on the day.[769]

With a single exception, no "occasional" compositions
written by Bach for the students especially can be pointed out
during the following years. From the year 1729 he had, in
the old Musical Society of Telemann, the solid assistance
which he needed for his work, and at the same time suitable
material for cases when he considered it advisable to come to
the front with musical "attendances" (i.e., occasional performances). In the first and second years of August III.'s
reign this happened at least five times with reference to the
royal family. It is evident that this assiduity was connected
with Bach's personal position. On July 27, 1733, he had
presented the first two movements of the B minor mass
to the king in Dresden, with the petition that he would grant
him a Court-title, which might ensure him against being
further troubled by the Leipzig Council; and he no doubt
thought to add to the urgency of his request by the festival
performance got up by him in Leipzig. We have already
spoken of the Coronation Cantata performed in January,
1734. But before this, on September 5, 1733, he had brought
to a hearing a dramatic cantata "Hercules in indecision,"
set to words by Picander, for the Electoral Prince's
birthday (b. September 5, 1722).[770] The convention of the
Collegium musicum took place in the course of the summer
out of doors, in Zimmermann's garden, and the Cantata,
also, is evidently intended for an open-air performance.
The characters in the drama—Hercules, Pleasure, and Virtue
—are excellently drawn, and the contrasts are more vivid
than in Handel's "Choice of Hercules";[771] the whole work
glows with freshness and wealth of idea. But, as a whole, it
again betrays a transcendental feeling which suits neither

---

[769] Sicul (Das frohlockende Leipzig, 1728) describes the festivities.

[770] Picanders Gedichte, IV., p. 22 ff. The autograph score of the music is in
the Royal Library at Berlin.

[771] Händel Gesel schaft, XVIII.

the subject nor the purpose of the work. We may, there-fore, congratulate ourselves that, with the exception of the final chorus and the recitative, it was all transferred into the Christmas Oratorio composed a year later.[772]

Three months later, December 8, 1733, the *Collegium musicum* again kept the birthday of the queen with a dramatic cantata, " Tönet ihr Pauken, erschallet Trompeten." On this occasion, too, Bach was the librettist, and he only finished the work the day before the performance.[773] Irene, Bellona, Pallas, and Fama are in-troduced. The lovely music, with the exception of Bellona's aria " Blast die wohlgegriffnen Flöten," and the recitatives, was made use of for the Christmas Oratorio.[774]

During the visit of the royal pair to Leipzig, which lasted from the 17th to the 26th of May, the musicians of that place seem to have been as inactive as they were on the occasion of the allegiance ceremony, held in Leipzig on April 21, 1733. But when the king and queen again visited the town, on October 2, 1734, the queen wishing to celebrate the anniversary of August III's election to the Polish throne, on the 5th of October, Bach had an opportunity of supplying the students with a serenade, to be performed to their Majesties. It was got up in haste. The unknown manu-facturer of the text wrote it quite at random, his only object being to get in the necessary amount of words; in one place, in the last recitative, he wrote such nonsense that the composer was obliged to make some alterations in them. The production was a cantata, half lyrical, half dramatic; what personage may be intended at the beginning of the last number but one the poet has not revealed. It was impossible even for Bach to write entirely

---

[772] Comp. ante, p. 573 and 586.

[773] The autograph score, in the Royal Library at Berlin, bears at its close the note " *Fine DSGl.* 1733 d. 7. *Dec.*" The authorship is betrayed, as in the case of the altered Æolus-Cantata, even in the title of the original printed copy, which is in the Royal Public Library at Dresden, as well as in the awkward putting together of the text, and more especially in some Thuringian Provin-cialisms, such as " zum Axen " for " zu den Axen," " zum Sternen " for " zu den Sternen," " seyn " for " sind."

[774] Comp. ante, p. 575

new music in the given space of time—three days. He, therefore, made use in part, at least, of older works, of whose original purpose we cannot however speak with certainty. The original aria " Durch die von Eifer entflammten Waffen " was soon to find a place in the Christmas Oratorio. The opening chorus " Preise dein Glücke, gesegnetes Sachsen " was subsequently, and, as it seems, in its original shorter form, introduced into the B minor mass.[775]

Only two days after this, on October 7, was the birthday of the king, who was still staying in Leipzig. For this occasion Bach had, apparently some time before, prepared a dramatic cantata, and performed it with his Society on that day. In beauty and importance the music may rank with the " Hercules in indecision," and the cantata for the birthday of the queen. The rivers Vistula, Elbe, and Danube sing the praises of Augustus in turn, in whom they profess to have each an equal share ; the Vistula and the Elbe, as being the chief rivers of Poland and Saxony, and the Danube, because the queen, Maria Josepha, was an Austrian princess. Their pretensions are very properly rejected by the Pleisse, the river of Leipzig, and the work, having opened with a four-part song, calling upon their fountains and streams to join in the king's praise, closes with their good wishes for the king's happiness, also sung in four parts ; so they are permitted to return to their banks and cliffs, although it beseems them to flow with a gentle murmur " for wonder and fear." This first piece is a charming and romantic picture of nature ; now it moves with a gentle swing, and now with rushing violence, with the loveliest play of colour. Bach repeated the work for the name-day of the king (August 3) in the year 1736 or 1737; as far as we know he never made it serve for church music.[776]

---

[775] The autograph score, with the title " *Drama per Muscia overo Cantata gratulatoria*," is in the Royal Library at Berlin ; a copy of the text, written by Bach himself, is bound up with it. As to the ceremony itself, see Mittag, op. cit., p. 485 f., a passage which Bitter (II., 40 f.) was the first to point out. Compare also ante, p. 573.

[776] B.-G., XX.,[2] p. 3 ff. See App. A., No. 62.

When the king and queen came to Leipzig, in 1738, for the Easter fair, Bach waited upon them with a Serenade, which even gave rise to a printed criticism. A year afterwards Magister Birnbaum, in a work devoted to Bach's art, expressed his opinion of this composition in these terms: "That the Court Composer (der Herr Hofcompositeur) composes in a moving, expressive, natural, and orderly style, and not in debased, but in the best taste, is shown particularly and undeniably in the Serenade publicly performed by him at the Easter fair, before our most Serene and Royal Rulers, on the occasion of their gracious visit to Leipzig, which composition met with thorough success."[777] The music has, however, been lost.

Lastly, Bach turned his attention to the old Weimar cantata "Was mir behagt ist nur die muntre Jagd," with the view of performing it with the Musical Society for the king's nameday. Whether the king was August II. or III. we cannot, however, be sure, but probably the latter, because Bach, as we have noticed, took all possible trouble to please this monarch.[778]

In the way of occasional cantatas written between the years 1723 and 1734, which became publicly known, as having been suggested by public personages or events, the dedicatory music for the rebuilt Thomasschule (July 5, 1732) only remains to be mentioned.[779] The private occasional compositions of Bach consist of some secular wedding cantatas; according to old custom they were intended to be sung during the wedding feast. They comprise only

---

[777] Scheibe, Critischer Musikus, p. 997.

[778] See Vol. I., p. 567. There were other festival performances of music after this: on April 30, 1741, when the students performed a serenade for the Electoral Prince and Prince Xaverius, on the occasion of their being in Leipzig for the first time (the text is in the Royal Public Library in Dresden), and in 1747, when, on the first coming to Leipzig of the Electoral Prince and his wife, an academic ceremony was held in the Paulinerkirche (the text, as before, in Dresden). But whether Bach composed the music for these cannot even be surmised. Since the publication of Vol. I. of this translation, the cantata "Was mir behagt" has been published in B.-G., XXIX. p. 1.

[779] See ante, p. 262.

solos. The oldest of them is certainly the cantata "Weichet nur betrübte Schatten,"[780] belonging possibly to the Cöthen period. Johannes Ringk has preserved it to posterity in a MS. dating from the year 1730. Ringk, born at Frankenhayn, in Thuringia, was formerly a pupil of Peter Kellner, of Gräfenrode, a gifted admirer of Sebastian Bach, who himself wrote out many of the master's works. It was apparently through Kellner that Ringk became acquainted with the cantata. If Kellner was cantor at Gräfenrode when he first knew the cantata, it must have been between 1727 and 1730, for he entered on his post, at the earliest, in 1727.[781] He had formerly, however, worked at Frankenhayn, Ringk's home, where in 1726 he wrote out Bach's sonatas and suites for violin solo ; and there exists a copy of one of Bach's organ-fugues made by Kellner in the year 1725.[782] And as he had in 1719 been a pupil of the organist, Schmidt of Zella, in the Thuringerwald, who seems to have been for a long time intimate with Bach,[783] the materials of the evidence lead us rather far back.[784] The text is a pleasing poem about spring, which subject naturally leads to the spring of love in two hearts ; it is also remarkable for a refinement of expression not very frequent in poems of the kind. The work, set only for a solo soprano voice, is pervaded even in the first number by a gentle breath of romance. Evidence of its early origin is found not only in the concise forms of the arias, but also in another circumstance. The sixth of the violin sonatas with clavier obbligato[785] is known to have been twice remodelled by Bach, and at last furnished with an Allegro, the first subject of which is taken from the C major aria of this cantata. I have previously mentioned the bridal feeling which pervades this sonata,

[780] B.-G., XI.,[2] p. 75 ff.

[781] Gerber, N.L., col. 715.

[782] See Appendix A., No. 4.

[783] Probably the same Schmidt who, on November 9, 1713, wrote out a Præludium of Bach's. See Vol. I., p. 434 ; note 135.

[784] In the collection of Grasnick (now in the Royal Library at Berlin) there is a clavier fugue by Bach in B flat major, in Ringk's writing, which is evidently a work of his earlier period.

[85] See note, p. 116.

especially in the middle movement, *Cantabile, ma un poco Adagio*. It would seem that Bach, in remodelling the sonata for the last time, experienced this feeling, and was thereby prompted to use for the last Allegro a subject taken from an actual wedding composition which was written about the same time. A second agreement is also re-markable; the chief subject of the D major aria, given in the prelude to the oboe, is found again as the chief subject of the bass aria in the cantata " Liebster Gott, wann werd ich sterben." [786]

Although the musical portion of a secular [787] wedding cantata for February 5, 1728, has disappeared, an interesting circumstance attaches to Picander's poetry for it. The newly-wedded pair referred to were the Herr Johann Heinrich Wolff, of Leipzig, and the daughter of Hempel, the Royal and Electoral Commissioner of Excise, at Zittau. [788] The marriage took place at noon, being performed by Archdeacon Carpzov in Schellhafer's house, " by royal command." [789] This was situated in the Klostergasse, and was a favourite place for convivial gatherings; Görner used to hold the meetings of his *Collegium musicum* there, and the wedding banquet, at which Bach's cantata was performed, must have been given at the same place. The personages introduced in the cantata are the rivers Pleisse and Neisse, according to which it would appear that the bride did not live in Zittau before her marriage. What is of greater importance, however, is that Bach himself afterwards remodelled the text to do honour to the Town Council of Leipzig. The Pleisse became Apollo (tenor) and the Neisse Mercury (alto), representing respectively Learn-ing and Commerce, the two pillars of the town's fame. The text, preserved in Bach's own writing, gives an

---

[786] See ante, p. 431 ff.

[787] It was formerly in the possession of Aloys Fuchs, in Vienna.

[788] Picander II., p. 379 ff. The printed text contains only the initials of the names; in order to complete the verses and the rhyme it is necessary to insert the words " Hempelin " and " Wolff." This is followed by a second poem on the same occasion: " Der Liebes-Congress zwischen dem Cupido, Wolff und Hampelmann."

[789] Marriage Register, St. Thomas' Church, 1728, p. 172.

interesting opportunity of seeing the musician engaged in the troublesome work of hammering out verses and rhymes. It is sufficiently remarkable that he could permit himself to sing the praises of Leipzig, and that of the Council which had caused him so much annoyance in his own person, with such hyperbole of expression as to write these words as the text of an aria :—

> Mit Lachen und Scherzen
> Mit freudigem Herzen
> Verleib ich mein Leipzig der Ewigkeit ein,
> Ich habe hier meine Behausung erkoren
> Und selber den Göttern geschworen,
> Hier gerne zu sein.

> With glad jubilation,
> And true gratulation,
> I wish thee, dear Leipzig, perpetual youth.
> Here have I been content to fix my household fane,
> And sworn to the gods in all truth,
> Content to remain.

Even when he put the words into the mouth of Mercury, no one would ever conceive the idea of their referring to a place which he himself found unbearable. This parody is a complete and reliable testimony to the fact that Bach was very well pleased with Leipzig at this time.[790]

I would draw attention in this place, to a third secular wedding cantata, " O holder Tag, erwünschte Zeit," for soprano, although it was written much later, probably not before 1749. The young bridegroom to whom reference is made must have been a patron of music, for these words occur in the work :—

> Man, loved and honoured, prosper in thy way,
> Ever remaining true to noble harmony, &c.

Express allusion is made to the despisers and disparagers of music, which seems very appropriate to the particular year 1749, since, in the spring of this year, Biedermann the Rector, at Freiberg, had heaped gross insults upon musicians in his pamphlet, " *De vita musica.*" If we may venture to

---

[790] The autograph, a folio sheet written on three sides, was in the possession of Herr Grasnick, of Berlin. It is now in the Royal Library there.

draw a conclusion from the careful and even elegant style in which the manuscript was prepared by Bach, he seems to have attached a special value to this composition, which in truth is of great beauty.[791]   With another text treating only of the praise of music (beginning " O angenehme Melodei "—" O melody, delightful power"), Bach brought this cantata to a hearing on three different occasions.   Once it was done for a scion of the family of the Counts Flemming, in which music was loved and cultivated.[792]   One aria is borrowed, and that is from a composition for the ceremony of allegiance of the year 1737.   A protegé of Count Brühl, Johann Christian Hennicke, who had gradually risen from the position of a lackey to that of a Count of the Empire, received homage on September 28 of this year, on the occasion of his coming into possession of Wiederau, which had been granted to him as an hereditary feoff.   For this ceremony Picander and Bach made a cantata, in which were introduced Destiny, Happiness, Time, and the river Elster; and in which the composer was extraordinarily successful, especially in the choruses at the beginning and the end, which are full of swing and freshness, and in the alto aria, which is remarkable for originality, elegance, and beauty of tone.   We shall come across it again in the guise of a church cantata.[793]   There is another

---

[791] The autograph is in the Royal Library at Berlin ; the paper on which it is written is of the same kind as that of a harpsichord part to Bach's " Musikalisches Opfer," which is in the same place.   That work was composed in 1747.

[792] For example, by General Field-Marshal Jakob Heinrich von Flemming (died 1728), and by the Governor of the town of Leipzig, Joachim Freidrich von Flemming (died 1740).   Only the soprano part (some of which is in this autograph) of the altered form is preserved in the Royal Library, in Berlin.   The writing and the paper alike are those of Bach's latest period, the cover alone, with the watermark, M A, being a remnant of earlier days.   Since the music remains the same under all the alterations, with the exception of the last recitative, no loss has taken place, as is erroneously asserted in B.-G. XX.,² p. XIV.   Since the publication of the original of this work, the Wedding Cantata has been published in B.-G., XXIX., p. 69.   See also App. II. to the same volume.

[793] B.-G., V., No. 30 and Preface.—On Hennicke see Gretschel, III., p. 17. There is another poem on him in Picander, V., p. 350 f.

composition for a ceremony of allegiance, the so-called
Peasant's Cantata (Bauerncantate) of the year 1742, which
we cannot even touch upon in this place, for its style is so
widely different from the other occasional cantatas as to
demand an extended description in another place.

Besides these secular occasional compositions, Bach wrote
some chamber cantatas, both in German and in Italian,
of which, as they were not suggested by outward circumstances, the chief intention and purpose is to be found
in the works themselves.   Their number is not large.
Impelled by other ideals, Bach could but rarely feel prompted
to write independent music of this kind.   When he
did so, it is not surprising, considering his keen interest
in the productions of other persons and nations, and the
zeal with which he had formerly studied the instrumental
chamber-music of the Italians, that he should also turn
his attention to Italian chamber-music of a vocal kind.
This tendency shows itself in the fact of his setting music
to Italian texts.   That Italian poetry, as such, was a
thing he did not care for is proved by the fact that
at least one of the texts is apparently from the pen
of a German, who was by no means a perfect master
of Italian.   One of these cantatas, "*Andro dall colle al
prato*," set for soprano with accompaniment of two flutes,
string quartet, and bass, is lost.[794]   In another, "*Amore
traditore*," a bass voice is accompanied by the harpsichord,
which is treated in parts as an obbligato instrument.
This is not, we believe, an innovation of Bach's, but
it is found moderately often, both in the Italian composers
of that time and in the Germans who formed themselves
on the Italian style; thus it occurs in Porpora, Conti,
Heinichen, and others.[795]   The fact is rather that even

---

[794] It was mentioned in Breitkopf's Catalogue for Michaelmas, 1770, p. 17.

[795] A cantata, "*La dove in grembo*," for a solo voice with a very brilliant
harpsichord accompaniment, by Heinichen, is preserved in the king of Saxony's
collection of music at Dresden.   The first of the twelve cantatas by Porpora,
which appeared in London in 1735, contains recitatives with an equally rich
and elaborate harpsichord accompaniment.

Bach appears to form himself on the pattern of the Italians in the harpsichord acccompaniment which he appends to the second aria in his cantata. In other circumstances it was not his manner to write an obbligato part chiefly in broken harmonies, nor was he especially fond of using the obbligato treatment, except now and then. The breadth of form exhibited in the work points to the time of his fullest maturity; he first came to a thorough knowledge of Italian vocal music through the intercourse which was kept up between Dresden and Leipzig.[796] Traces of this familiarity with Italian forms, and especially resemblances to Lotti, are found here and there, even in his church cantatas. An aria for Marziano from Lotti's *Alessandro Severo* :—

agrees, as far as this opening is concerned, in all essential points with the opening of the bass aria in Bach's church cantata " Liebster Gott, wann werd ich sterben," and with the D major aria in the chamber cantata " Weichet nur, betrübte Schatten." In the opera of *L'Ascanio*, composed by Lotti, for Dresden, in 1718, the first aria begins thus :—

thus resembling the opening of the D minor aria in the fourth part of Bach's Christmas Oratorio. In the *Sicut erat in principio*, in the *Magnificat*, Bach, in repeating the subject of the first movement in a compressed form, was imitating

---

[796] " *Amore traditore* " is published in B.-G., XI.,² p. 93 ff. The autograph does not exist. It is noted as Bach's in Breitkopf's Catalogue for the New Year, 1764, p. 32.

the Italian church composers. The same thing is done in Leonardo Leo's *Dixit Dominus* for double choir and instruments (in C major), and in a five-part *Dixit*, by Lotti (in A major).[797] The latter work exercised an influence on Bach in other respects when writing his *Magnificat*. The grand close of a chorus, on the words *Dispersit superbos mente cordis sui*, has its model in Lotti's five-part chorus *Conquassabit in terra capita multorum ;* the aria *Quia fecit mihi magna* is built on a bass theme which is similar to an alto aria in Lotti's work :—

798

It may here be noticed that a mass in G minor, by Lotti, was written out by Bach's own hand, in the middle of his Leipzig period, a circumstance which affords tangible evidence to confirm the fact of his having been much occupied with the music of the Italian master.[799]

A third Italian chamber cantata by Bach treats of an actual occurrence. This can, however, only be made out dimly from the text, which is evidently put together by a German, and consists of awkward and sometimes incorrect and meaningless Italian, with the admixture of scraps extracted from original Italian poems. A friend wishes to return to his native country, that is, from Germany into Italy. He is supposed to have been resident for some time in Anspach, and to congratulate himself on being once more able to be of service to his country, the more so that his work in foreign lands has not met with due recognition and support. But the poet tells us that the favourable opinion of some illustrious personage which he has gained while in Anspach will assist him in achieving great things in his

---

[797] Both works, in old handwriting, are in the king of Saxony's collection at Dresden. The autograph score of Leo's *Dixit* is in the Fitzwilliam Museum, at Cambridge, and the work, edited by Mr. C. V. Stanford, has been published by Messrs. Novello.

[798] See ante, pp. 379—81. Handel also seems to have known this *Dixit*. The theme of the " Amen " fugue in " The Messiah " is nearly related to the closing fugue in Lotti's work.

[799] The transcript is in the Royal Library in Berlin.

own country. Personal circumstances in connection with
Bach seem to play some part in this. The Italian taste
was in the ascendant in the band of the Margrave of
Anspach, under Pistocchi and Bümler (1696—1745), and
Torelli worked there also at the beginning of the century;
but the words "*Tuo saver al tempo e l'età contrasta*" forbid
us to apply the words to any Italian musician whom Bach
may have befriended, if, that is to say, we may take the
words of this bungling poet literally. The composition, set
for soprano solo, flute and quartet of strings, betrays a
thorough study of Italian chamber music. The fusion of
Bach's original style with the Italian in this work makes it
incomparably more interesting than the Cantata "*Amore
traditore*." The melodies have the breath of Italy about
them ; this is especially felt in the second part of the first
aria and throughout the second, while the introductory
symphony (in B minor), a piece in the style of the first
movement of a concerto, and bearing a remarkable resemblance to the first movement of the violin concerto in
D minor,[800] is in Bach's own style.[801]

Bach was probably incited to the composition of German
chamber cantatas by the musical portion of his family circle.
The very elaborate cantata for soprano about contentment
("Ich bin in mir vergnügt, ein andrer mache Grillen"—
"Let others have their whims, I still will be contented"),
which may have been written for Anna Magdalena Bach,
claims attention less on account of any particular musical
charm than from the fact of its being still in existence.[802] The
music is pleasing and suitable to the words, and that is all.
But the fact that he felt moved to set this text with
its commonplace garrulity is characteristic of Bach, whose
domestic nature knew how to prize most highly the tranquil
repose of family life, notwithstanding the place in art which
he had achieved, and all the honours showered upon him by
princes and great people.

---

[800] See ante, p. 128.

[801] The work is in a MS. in Forkel's collection, in the Royal Library at
Berlin.

[802] B.-G., XI.,[2] p. 105 ff.

Besides these pleasures, all the luxuries produced in various parts of the world occasionally introduced temptation into the contented family circle. The small differences which might arise between a father and children afforded Bach the material for a comic cantata. In the seventeenth century a new luxury was introduced into European society in the shape of coffee. As wine and tobacco[803] had already been extolled in song, the musician conceived the idea of doing the same with coffee. It would seem that the French had preceded him in this respect. In a collection of *Cantates françoises* (*Troisième livre*, No. 4) which appeared in Paris about 1703, the praises of coffee were sung in a very elegant style. The Germans were not long in following the example; in 1716 Johann Gottfried Krause wrote a text for a Coffee cantata.[804] But among all the German towns Leipzig was most remarkable for a particularly strong fancy for foreign productions. Although the luxury of coffee was limited, until the seven years' war, to the well-to-do classes, yet as early as 1697 the Leipzig Council sought to derive profit by taxing the "undue number of coffee houses"; and in 1725 Leipzig contained no fewer than eight licensed coffee houses.[805] In this Picander found material for satire. He published in the first volume of his poems (1727), under the title of "Von allerhand *Nouvellen*," a kind of journal in villanous rhyme, in which, under the form of correspondence from people of all countries, he satirised the existing state of things in this respect. Thus the news came from Paris: "A few days ago a royal mandate came to the parliament, which ran thus—'We have long noticed, and with sorrow, that many an one has been ruined simply by coffee. In order to stop this evil in time, we command that no one shall dare to drink coffee, the king and his court alone excepted. But permission may be obtained,' &c., &c. Then there arose a

[803] On Bach's Tobacco song; see ante, p. 151. A cantata by Stölzel, for a bass voice beginning " Toback du edle Panacee " is in the Royal Court Church Library at Sondershäusen.

[804] " Poetische Blumen von Joh. Gottfried Krausen, Erstes *Bouquet*. Langen-Saltza 1716," p. 129.

[805] Gretschel, loc. cit. II., p. 524.

long wail; 'Ah! cried the womenfolk, take our bread from us, for without coffee our life is dead.' . . But all this broke not the king's determination, but the people died like flies. As in time of pestilence they were thrown in heaps into the grave, and the womenfolk took on dreadfully until the mandate was torn down and destroyed, when the deaths ceased in France." Several years later he turned it into the subject of a comic cantata, and Bach set it to music in 1732. There was nothing new in treating circumstances and events of low life in this kind of comic vein. The "Jenaische Wein- und Bierrufer" by Nikolaus Bach was of the same class.[806] Other cantatas treated of the tooth-drawer, of the watchman in love, of the "female Magister," even of the "woman who makes cakes to cure the worms in Leipzig"; and the fun was not always of the most refined description.[807] In Picander's Coffee Cantata, one Father Schlendrian wants to cure his daughter Lieschen of the passion for coffee, which she shares with all the ladies of Leipzig. All his threats are in vain except the last, that she shall never have a husband; this seems at last to have an effect upon her; but she has laid a trap for her father, and while he goes to look after an eligible son-in-law she puts it about that "no lover need come to the house unless he will promise to me in person, and insert it in the marriage settlements, that I am to be allowed to make coffee as I like it." The last phrase is not by Picander, who concludes his poem with Lieschen's promise to give up coffee-drinking for a husband. Bach, probably, had something to do with the end, preventing the joke from becoming vulgar by the addition of the waggish ending; at all events it does credit to his taste that he set this, rather than the original form of the poem, to music. The two characters, besides which there is another, a narrating tenor, are kept clear and distinct, and drawn with great power. The old fellow grumbles and blusters about, Lieschen indulges in anticipations of enjoyment; Schlendrian takes council with himself, and seems of great importance in his own eyes, while the daughter rejoices over

---

[806] See Vol. I., p. 135.
[807] Breitkopf's Catalogue for Michaelmas, 1761, p. 34 f.

the bridegroom she is to expect; she has the liveliness and innocence of youth, he the heaviness and acerbity of age. This original couple seem to have delighted the world. In the *Frankfort News* of 1739, may be read the notice: "On Tuesday, April 7, a foreign musician will give a concert in the Kauffhauss under the N. Krämen, at which, among other things, will be performed a drama, Schlendrian and his daughter Lissgen; tickets 30 Kreuzer, the words 12."[808] It is not, indeed, expressly stated that the work to be performed by the "foreign musician" was Bach's composition; but who else would ever have put music to a poem treating of the state of things in Leipzig, and written by a Leipzig poet especially for Bach?[809]

A dramatic chamber cantata of larger calibre entitled "The strife between Phœbus and Pan"—("Der Streit zwischen Phöbus und Pan")—has a cheerful and partly satirical character. Picander wrote the words in 1731, and it was first performed at the summer meeting of the Musical Society in that year.[810] The old Greek myth, of course, is that Phœbus Apollo, as the god of the lyre, and Marsyas, the inventor of flute-playing, entered into competition; Apollo having gained the victory, by the terms of which he could do what he liked with his conquered rival, flayed Marsyas alive. The later myth changes Marsyas for the rural god Pan, who is subdued in the same way by Apollo; but the penalty is not inflicted on him, but on the Phrygian king Midas, on whom asses' ears are bestowed, because he thought Pan's playing the more beautiful. In this form Picander treated the myth, using as his classical authority Ovid's Metamorphoses, XI., 146—179. Besides the characters already mentioned, he

---

[808] Israël, Frankfurter Concert-Chronik von 1713—1780. Frankfurt am Main, 1876, p. 28.

[809] The Coffee cantata appeared. edited by S. W. Dehn, published by Gustav Crantz in Berlin, and in a second edition, thoroughly revised and corrected, published. by C. A. Klemm, in Leipzig. See App. A., No. 63. It has been published in B.-G., XXIX., p. 141; and in an English form, edited by Mr. Samuel Reay, Mus. Bac., and published, together with the "Bauern Cantate," by Weekes & Co.

[810] See Appendix A., No. 46. Published B.-G., XI.,[2] p 3. ff.

introduces the Lydian mountain-god Tmolus, as the ar-
bitrator of the dispute, and—for which no authority is
given by Ovid—Momus, the god of mirth, and Mercury to
preside over the contest. The cantata opens with a fresh and
graphic chorus of winds, which are very soon driven back
into their confinement, in order to leave the music of the
rivals free to echo and re-echo in nature's perfect stillness.
Then the two competitors enter. Pan boasts of the mighty
power and effect of his pipe, and charms Momus by singing
a merry song. Mercury commands the contest, which is,
however, carried out not with instrumental but with vocal
music. Phœbus begins by singing an aria to his beloved and
beautiful Hyacinthus; Pan thereupon sings a merry dance
aria, in the middle of which he derides his opponent's
grave and solemn tunes. This is followed by the verdict.
Tmolus, in a congratulatory aria, declares Phœbus the
conqueror, Midas, on the contrary, votes for Pan, on which
he receives his punishment. Mercury and Momus point the
moral, and a finale on Apollo's art closes the work, which
is a masterpiece of characteristic variety, only granting
that Bach's style is suitable for such things. As far as its
poetic character goes, we might include it in the same
category with Handel's "Acis" and "The Choice of
Hercules," were it not for the fact of its being an allegory.

   This time the purpose of the work is not to sing the
praises of an exalted personage, but to do honour to
a much maligned branch of musical art. Pan's flute
delights the forest and the nymphs; he represents music
of an agreeable kind, and easy to be understood by
everybody; his light and untutored song pleased Midas
so much that "he perceived it at once." The art of
Phœbus unites beauty of melody with noble grandeur and
depth; it is fit "to satisfy the gods." Both kinds of art
are justified, but must always be opposed to one another;
still, where the art is duly cherished, the last will be
recognised as more important than the first. This would
be the one pervading idea of the drama were it not that an
intentional purpose is visible of mocking at Pan's music,
and representing it as worthless, while extolling that of

Apollo in the hearing of his ignorant censurer. The introduction of Mercury also probably contains some reference to particular circumstances. The myth says nothing of his having taken any part in the transaction. He is indeed the father of Pan, but he could not, as such, take the opposite side, as he exclusively does. But as the god of commerce he personifies the Leipzig world of business, as Apollo does that of learning; in his remodelled version of the cantata "Vergnügte Pleissenstadt," Bach introduces them both in this signification. If the only object of the work was to exhibit Phœbus and Pan as contrasting elements in music, this might have been done in strict accordance with the myth, by performances on the lyre (or lute) and on the flute; or, if the parts were to be sung, it might have been expected that the instruments of the rivals would have played an important part in their songs. The fact that Bach did not do this, although he was generally so easily induced to take his musical motives from external circumstances, shows that his intention was not so much to depict the character of Apollo and Pan as to enforce the contrast between the grave, serious, and elaborate style on the one hand, and the light and merely pleasing on the other. He himself represented the former, as he could not be unaware, while the latter was represented by the opera composers and nearly all the rest of the musical world of the period. Pan is the patron of this class, while Apollo is Bach, who portrays himself in the beautiful aria in B minor which is written with evident purpose, and in the same way he laughs at himself with quaint irony in the middle section of Pan's song ("When the notes too doleful sound, And their mouths seem tightly bound, Strains of joy do not resound").

Who is Midas? Of course it must be some Leipziger, for Midas's aversion can only refer to Bach's vocal music, and this was not yet known outside Leipzig, although his instrumental music had already met with universal admiration. We only know one inhabitant of Leipzig who lifted up a voice of censure against Bach's vocal compositions, and that is Johann Adolph Scheibe. He was the son of

Johann Scheibe, the organ builder, whom we have so often mentioned, and was born in 1708; since the autumn of 1725 he had studied in the University, and at the same studied with a view to becoming a musician. On the death of Christian Gräbner, the organist of the Thomaskirche, in 1729, Scheibe, among others, applied for the situation. Bach was among the judges. Scheibe's trial playing seems not to have made a favourable impression; at all events, the post was given, not to him, but to Görner.[811] He remained, however, in Leipzig until 1735, giving lessons on the clavier, and having compositions of his own performed.[812] In 1737 he began to publish the "Critischer Musikus" in Hamburg, and in the sixth part of it he attacked both Bach and Görner, accusing the latter of being a conceited ignoramus,[813] and the former for his intricate and pompous style of writing, which was, according to him, both vain and tedious, as it was against reason. This opinion, which made a great commotion in certain circles, and caused a paper war, to which we must return later on, must be considered in connection with Scheibe's personal experience in Leipzig, although it is not unintelligible from a musical point of view alone. We must weigh it after knowing what he himself says, with commendable candour, of his earlier opinions. "Several years ago," he writes on July 28, 1739, "there lived in a certain famous town a certain man, whom I can the better describe from having been associated with him from youth, and have known him even as myself. I will call him Alfonso for the nonce. From certain circumstances he was obliged to devote himself to music . . . . . When he himself began to remark his own daily improvement, a secret jealousy of the excellencies of others appeared at the same time in him . . . . When he heard praise bestowed on the merits of skilful men, he immediately became envious, for the simple reason that he did not possess such capabilities." Further on: "At last the jealousy that held him captive was changed into a

---

[811] See Critischer Musikus, p. 410.

[812] Gerber, Lex. II., col. 413.

[813] See ante, p. 211.

passionate desire of emulation, which impelled him to imitate
the excellencies of great men. And gradually he so overcame his envy that he was able to hear the praise of able
men without becoming red in the face, and at last he could
even praise them himself with an honest heart, and give
them the admiration they deserved." Scheibe expressly
admits that this feeling had prompted him to action:
" Perhaps my readers recognise me in Alfonso. And very
likely my actions at that time bore a great likeness to
those of Alfonso."[814] According to this, he must at that time
have done all he could against Bach, and been sorry for it
later; and those views of art which he still defended, even
at Hamburg, when he had become more enlightened, he
may have upheld and asserted with increased vehemence,
especially as he may have been irritated at coming
off so badly in the trial of organists. It is quite conceivable
that Bach and his Musical Society were annoyed by these
views, although they were only enunciated by a youth
of three-and-twenty. Scheibe was an able fellow, and as
such had influence with the students, and might have got up
a party against Bach.[815] Now without the students Bach's
Collegium musicum could not exist. Indeed, these motions
of opposition made themselves felt in wide circles. Ludwig
Friedrich Hudemann, Doctor of Laws in Hamburg, a
capable musical amateur, and an old friend of Bach, as
is shown by a canon dedicated to him in the year 1727,
published "Proben einiger Gedichte," in 1732, at Hamburg,
in which are included lines "To Herr Capellmeister J. S.
Bach." From references in this poem it is probable that
he .knew all about Picander's poem on the goat-footed
Pan, and Midas with the asses' ears.

The allegorical and polemic point spoils the harmonious
impression of the cantata, in spite of its freshness,
wealth of beauty, and drastic comedy (the pointed asses

---

[814] Critischer Musikus, p. 445 and 446.

[815] I notice that even George Friedrich Einicke, for instance, who did not
go to the Leipzig University until 1732, went both to Bach and Scheibe in
order to complete his musical education. See Marpurg, Kritische Briefe über
die Tonkunst, II., p. 461.

ears on p. 52, bars 19 ff. and afterwards, are exceedingly funny), and causes it to rank on this account below Handel's work of similar kind. But on this very account it is of peculiar biographical interest. The differences which Bach had in 1714 with the church Elders at Halle and in 1725 with the University of Leipzig, and the lengthy dispute with the Rector Ernesti, soon to be related, betoken a certain combative nature, as well as a touch of the pettifogging orthodoxy of his time. We have here a case in which he believed himself capable of defending his artistic procedures and methods against his antagonist. He did not fly to his pen, like Mattheson; he was too genuine an artist for that. But he did not, like Handel, leave his compositions to speak for him entirely alone. He carried on his defence by means of a work of art, with a special tendency.[816] To this work threads attach themselves which connect it with a later time, and we shall see the feeling it betrays appearing again and again. The next period, the last of his life, has, however, an essentially different aspect from this, the richest and happiest of his creative life, which we conclude with the characteristic work " Phöbus und Pan."

---

[816] S. W. Dehn pointed out this explanation of the cantata, " Phöbus und Pan," in the October number of Westermann's Magazine for 1856. He went on partially wrong premises, and for this he incurred E. O. Lindner's censure (Zur Tonkunst. Berlin. Guttentag. 1864. p. 87 ff.). But yet in the main Dehn took the right view. Dr. E. Baumgart attempted to put him on the right track again, in a delightful little treatise, which also contains an elaborate and delicate musical analysis ("Uber den Streit zwischen Phöbus und Pan," Verhandlungen der schlesische Gesellschaft für vaterländische Cultur. Philosophisch-historische Abtheilung. Breslau, 1873).

APPENDIX (A, TO VOL. II.)

1 (p. 13). "**Wer sich selbst erhöhet.**" The preface to Helbig's series is dated March 22, 1720. Thus the cantatas must have been intended for the church year 1719 to 1720; they were at first printed separately, and then collected into a little volume with a preface, as was then usual. Bach, therefore, cannot have composed this cantata before 1720, and hardly later than 1722, since he was already living in Leipzig by the seventeenth Sunday after Trinity of 1723, and there had other texts at his command; besides, the character of the autograph is opposed to this assumption. There are no circumstances, it is true, to prohibit the idea of its having been written during the two intermediate years, still we do not know of his having undertaken any journey which might have prompted him to compose it. Moreover, it is to be observed that such series of cantata-texts, which at that time sprang up like mushrooms, were rarely remembered beyond the year for which they were written, unless they were the work of some distinguished poet, more particularly when, as in this case, they were not used in the place where they were written. The autograph, which is in the Royal Library at Berlin, is of such a character that we almost involuntarily associate it with the Carlsbad journey. Besides the difference in the writing and whole appearance from those of the Weimar and Leipzig periods, we are struck by the peculiarity of the paper, of which the last sheet and a half are quite unlike the others as to appearance and watermark, while the writing is the same; so it is evident the composer's paper came to an end while he was writing it, and he was forced to get more of a different kind. The watermarks of the first portion do not ascribe it undoubtedly to Cöthen (a kind of paper which he certainly used there is recognisable by the "Harzmann," as it is called—a figure of a savage clothed in a skin, and holding a fir tree in his hand; Bach used this for the birthday serenata for Prince Leopold). They are, on one sheet the eagle, and on the other all sorts of outlines, among which a D is plainly traceable; quite unusual marks. The last sheet and a half bear a shield with the crossed swords on one half of the field, thus betraying its manufacture in Saxony. Whatever view we take of these details, it is clear that the autograph was written under exceptional conditions.

I must add a further observation on the Bach-Gesellschaft edition of this cantata. The first aria is, in the score, accompanied only by an organ obbligato; but the part belonging to it is not for the organ but quite certainly set for the violin; indeed, the word "*organo*" has been written over it by a more recent hand. It would be inexplicable why the bass should be wanting, as it is, and why the right should play alone; why, again, the many ties and staccato marks, which have no sense as applied to the organ, should be marked in the part, though wanting in the score, why in the second portion of the aria so many double notes should have been altered, if it were not to render it feasible for the violin; for instance, in bars 128-129 instead of—

and, finally, why the parts should be written in D minor, and the part written out for the organ bass in C minor. If any performance ever took place with an obbligato organ accompaniment, Bach himself must have played it and transposed the part at sight. I, however, think it was a mistake to deviate from the score in favour of the part copy. The considerations adduced in the preface to the cantata (p. XXIV.) show it to have been quite unnecessary.

2 (p. 32). **The F minor toccata.** A MS. authority is Andreas Bach's book. An autograph which has now disappeared (see Grie-penkerl's Preface) contains, besides the toccata in F sharp minor, another organ chorale on "Valet will ich dir geben" in B flat major, which certainly was written in Weimar; and Bach would naturally have written out together two pieces composed at the same time. It is against all probability and analogy that two toccatas con-structed alike should not have originated at the same period; and, if for this reason alone, the assumption is obvious that it should have been at Weimar, even though the direct evidence of Andreas Bach's book is lacking. There is indeed a third toccata in F minor, and of similar structure so far as that it begins with an ornate subject, which however soon gives way to severer imitative passages, followed by a slow movement in 3-2 time with full broad chords and throughout sustained in character, while the finale is an animated fugue. This toccata is preserved in two old MSS., neither of which, however, names Bach as the author. One, in the possession of Dr. Rust, he inherited from his grandfather, F. W. Rust, erewhile Kapellmeister at Dessau; it is inscribed "*Toccata con Fuga in F moll*"; nothing more. The other is in the Royal Library of the Institute for Church Music at Berlin; it is only called a "toccata," and bears on it the name of "Dobenecker." But there was a third MS. in the possession also of F. W. Rust, of which now only a copy of the fugue remains; this Herr Schubring of Dessau had from him in his life-time, and he expressly said that the composer was Sebastian Bach. The question now is whether the internal evidence of the work itself is such that it can be unhesitatingly attributed to Bach, in spite of various doubts. I consider it to be so; and I see no particu-

lar difficulty in the name "Dobenecker" in the Berlin MS.[1] It may very well be the name of its owner at one time or another, who may have been all the more tempted to name himself on the title-page, because—as we see from Rust's MS.—the toccata was anonymous. Christian Friedrich Dobenecker may have been this owner, but nothing is known of any composer of that name. If the work is by Bach we must refer it back to the first Arnstadt period, and any resemblance of form we may find in it to the toccatas in F sharp minor and C minor can only be accidental and superficial. The polyphony of the first movement is, to be sure, skilfully managed, though it is not free from awkward and halting passages, easily detected by an ear familiar with Bach's masterpieces; it has besides a considerable resemblance in texture to that C minor prelude (P. S. V., C. 4, 243, No. 5) which, with its fugue, appears to me to belong to the earlier Arnstadt time. The middle movement, which, with its obscure imitations and heavy harmonic masses, reminds us in parts of certain toccatas by the southern masters—for instance, Georg Muffat—has various harsh phrases, and the fugue betrays so clearly, to any one who is accustomed to Bach's various manners, the traces of his beginner's hand that it is unnecessary to go into details. Still, it is Bach's genius that shines through it all; and we can but suppose that Kittel was mistaken in his statement as to the D minor toccata, which is a far riper work. As the matter at present stands, I could not venture to give the F minor toccata a place among Bach's authentic works; we must wait, and some new material may perhaps come to light to support the view. The MSS. themselves do not agree, and indicate certain changes by the composer. Rust's copy is the original form; in the Berlin copy the first bar of the fugue theme (of three bars long) is repeated, and a better phrase is thus constructed, not to speak of other small improvements; and the missing MS. agreed with this. In the Berlin copy it is obviously wrong that the movement in 3-2 should be placed at the end, and there are many other errors. It contains besides a fugue in G minor which must also be attributed to Bach, and it has in fact a conspicuous resemblance to the closing fugue of the E minor toccata, excepting that it is stiffer and less mature. Both the toccata and fugue were edited from the Berlin MS. by Fr. Commer (*Musica Sacra*, I., No. 9), and Dobenecker named as the composer; but they are not correct.

3 (p. 36). **Bach's fingering and execution.** What Quantz says in the passage alluded to is as follows :—" In performing running

---

[1] A merchant named Dobenecker lived in Leipzig in Bach's time. A son of his, named Christian Friedrich, went to the University there in 1728, and in 1735 was still living in the place. Compare also what Huttman says in the Musicalischer Quacksalber, p. 163 : " He did just as much in the matter as certain village schoolmasters who sign their names to all their copies of music simply because they have written them out."

notes it is not right to lift the finger off at once; rather should the player place the tips of them on the farthest part of the keys, and withdraw them towards him till they glide from the keys. I refer this method to the example of one of the greatest of clavier-players, who used and taught it." That this meant Bach is proved by the index to the book, where, under Bach (Johann Sebastian), this passage is referred to. The description by Forkel of the action of his fingers corresponds with this, but Quantz restricts it to the execution of runs, while Forkel very rightly regards it as a general characteristic of Bach's *technique*. It is only in this sense that we can understand the application to the clavichord of this particular drawing inwards of the finger—it would be useless on the quilled harpsichord or organ, were it not that perfect equality of touch could only be acquired by this means. The real value of the method lay in its wide applicability. Its merit is most conspicuous in passage-work on the clavichord, and the most obvious to a superficial judge, because in the unavoidable jangling made by the tangents in striking the strings, the longest possible pressure of the keys is absolutely indispensable for the distinctness of the sequence of notes. It is therefore intelligible why Quantz, a flute-player, should speak of it in that sense only. But when Ph. Em. Bach confines this withdrawing action of the fingers to certain occasions—he calls it "the rapid touch, by means of which the fingers glide off the keys as quickly as possible, and which always must be used with a certain degree of strength" (II. 1, § 36)—when he directs it to be employed only in rapid changes of the fingers on one key (I. 1, § 90), at the last time of striking the upper note of a shake (II. 3, § 8), in the ornament of the "Schneller," or trill (II. 8, § 1), and in giving out quick subjects (III., § 1), not regarding it as a general rule of playing, we see that his style of fingering must have differed from his father's. This, already explained, will shortly be made clearer from other considerations. Forkel's surprise is therefore ungrounded. Much that Philipp Emanuel wrote has been taken for Sebastian's teaching, and thereby erroneous opinions have become widely spread.

4 (pp. 69, 72, and 81). **The dates of the sonatas for strings.** After what has been said about the thoroughness of Bach's nature, which never allowed him to relinquish a form of art when once he had taken it up till he had worked it out in every direction, it cannot be doubted that two works so similar in character as the six violin soli, and six for violoncello, must have been written in succession. But the second series was not, in fact, written for the violoncello, but for the *viola pomposa*, invented by Bach himself. What has been said above concerning this is taken from Gerber. He had heard from his father, who was Bach's pupil at Leipzig from 1724 to 1727, and who was still living, that his master had at times given the place of the violoncello to the *viola pomposa*, to facilitate the clearer per-

formance of the difficult and rapid bass figures, more particularly those that lie high, in his church compositions (see Gerber, Lexicon I., cols. 491 and 90). If we suppose the *viola pomposa* to have been invented in about 1724, as the younger Gerber does (Lexicon II., App., p. 85), the composition of these two works must have fallen within a period of Bach's life when his whole mind was taken up with the transition to a new and busy sphere of life, and with the effort to accommodate himself to it. That this is improbable is evident at a glance. Besides this, we may certainly assume that the first five violoncello soli, which Bach himself could not play, were written with reference to some skilled master of that instrument—such as Abel, of the Cöthen band—since many other of his most important pieces of chamber music can be proved to have been composed in Cöthen; and, on the whole, nothing can be more natural than that the composition of a musical specialty should have taken place in a town where the motive for writing them was stronger than in any other. The contrary and very remote possibility that the two works should have been composed at the later Leipzig period is disproved by the fact that the violin soli occur, copied out, in the often-mentioned collection made by Joh. Peter Kellner, now in the possession of Herr Roitzsch, with this note, "Franckenhayn den 3 Juli, 1736" (with the exception of the B minor suite, and in this order: G minor, A minor, C major, E major, D minor); nay, that even so early as 1725 this same Kellner had copied for himself an organ fugue arranged from the G minor sonata (see B.-G., XV., p. 25). Finally, further proof is found in the state of an autograph of the violin soli. Any one who has studied the master's autographs can scarcely be mistaken in his handwriting, as it is known to us from the vast mass of his compositions at Leipzig; and the small variety in the sorts of paper he used, with their different watermarks, are another and tolerably certain standard. The Royal Library at Berlin possesses an autograph of the violin pieces in which the writing is altogether different from that of the Leipzig period, while it displays a decided affinity in its sharp and pointed character to the second copy of the "Inventionen und Sinfonien," mentioned in note 102 to p. 60. The watermark too, a double eagle, is different in Leipzig autographs: I have only met with the single eagle, and that but rarely. This may be the first fair copy which Bach made. Georg Pölchau, the professor of music at Hamburg, acquired this manuscript in 1814, from among the papers left by Palschau, the clavier-player of Petersburg, which were being disposed of to the butterman. It consists of twenty-three leaves, not all written over, for regard is always had to the necessity for turning over; hence it happens, too, that each piece, when the end of a page is reached without its being finished, is continued on another page in such a way that by placing them side by side it can be read straight on without turning over. The title is wanting in the superscription of each piece; Bach only names, with much precision, the pieces in

G minor, A minor, and C major, as *sonatas;* for in each of these two slow movements alternate with a quick one; while the others, which are made up of dances, he calls *partien.* The autograph of the last of these, in E major, is wanting; and the last twelve bars of the D minor chaconne are written in an unpractised, childish hand, perhaps Friedemann Bach's. A second and complete original MS., likewise in the Royal Library at Berlin, comprises a title-page and twenty-two other leaves, and the writing, watermarks, and title-page all refer it to Leipzig. The title, written by another hand, runs thus: " *Pars* 1. | *Violino Solo|* *Senza Basso | composée | par | Sr. Jean Seb: Bach. | Pars* 2. | *Violoncello Solo. | Senza Basso. | composée | par | Sr. J. S. Bach.|Maitre de la Chapelle|* *et | Directeur de la Musique | a | Leipsic."|;* and below, to the right hand: " *écrite par Madame | Bachen. Son Epouse."* The MS. is in the hand of Anna Magdalena Bach. Here, again, there are three sonatas and three partien. The title indicates that the violin and violoncello soli are united in one work in two parts; but the latter do, in fact, constitute a separate part, written out likewise by Anna Magdalena, with the title: " 6 | *Suites a | Violoncello Solo | senza | Basso | composées | par | Sr. J. S. Bach. | Maitre de Chapelle."* | There are nineteen leaves not written all over; the word "Suite" is added by Bach himself to each separate piece. The second *"autograph"* of the solo violin, sonatas and partien is therefore not so at all; it was written by Bach's wife, all but the title and a few directions, which have been added in a strange hand. So far as I can see, Sebastian has only added a few details to the sonata in C major.

5 (p. 103). **Bach's treatment of figured bass.** There are still extant the complete autograph scores of three chamber-trios with clavier obbligato. A sonata in G minor for viol-da-gamba and clavier has a figured bass (B.-G., IX., p. 203) where one of the above-described passages is to be found, but there alone. A sonata in G major, for the same instruments, shows no trace of figuring (B.-G., IX., p. 175), because no such passages occur in it. The six sonatas for violin and clavier exist in a MS. of which the last movement of the last sonata only was written by Bach, though he revised the whole; the figured bass is only indicated here and there, and he may have thought it unnecessary to complete it; the little there is, however, suffices to show that the same principle prevails. There is yet another very valuable ancient MS., the bass of which is more completely figured, and in it, too, the figures are only added to the bass at the first entrance of the theme in each part (*vide* B.-G.). It is certainly only an accident that the figuring is lacking in the E major sonata; and here the chords must be filled up in bars 1—4 and 35—49 (with the exception of the single bar in which the right hand is alone) and 120—123, of course in as decisive and simple a way as possible. But this cannot be required in places where the accompaniment makes a complete harmony of itself, like the beginning of the third movement of the A major sonata,

the beginning of the second section of the last movement in the C minor sonata (at least not for the first two bars), at the beginning of the first movement in the viol-da-gamba sonata in D major (B.-G., IX., p. 189); or where both parts are separated from one another by about an octave, and that their relative and interdependence must be plainly brought out, as at the beginning of the finale of the G major violin sonata, or the corresponding place in the B minor flute sonata (B.-G., IX., p. 15); which last, since it exists in autograph, confirms in the strongest possible way the justice of our remark, by the omission of figuring in the bass part at this point. A nearly complete autograph also exists of a trio for flute and clavier in A major (B.-G., IX., pp. 32 ff. and 245 ff.), the first movement of which has a figured bass in some passages. These passages are when the flute enters with one of the two contrasting themes (for the movement is written in concerto form) namely, at the beginning and for the introduction of the middle section; and here moreover the character of the form gives an accompaniment by itself. On this model the first movement of the flute sonata in E flat major (B.-G., IX., p. 22 ff.) should be played, where all passages are to be accompanied, even when the clavier part ceases in the right hand. Separate cases in which a single full chord should be struck find confirmation in the *largo* in four parts (and in that movement alone) of the violin sonata in F minor, by the direction at bar 8 " *accomp*.," and the natural indicated in bar 58, from which it is clear that in this and all ambiguous passages the violin is to be united with the bass by a few simple harmonies. The viol-da-gamba sonata in D major, which exists in a carefully written MS. of the Thomasschule pupil, Christian Friedrich Penzel, dating from the year 1753, is figured in bar 22 of its third movement, which may be a genuine indication, although the two parts harmonising is perfectly sufficient. Lastly, in the third movement of the G major violin sonata (according to the first arrangement in B.-G., IX., 252 ff.) we find, and in very unusual places, a figured bass, which is justified here by the unique plan of the piece. And this is the whole list of passages of this kind; its scantiness is clear evidence of how diligently and constantly Bach strove after pure and uninterrupted three-part writing. I repeat once more that all the instances consist only of passages where the obbligato part for the right hand is silent. To add parts and fill up the harmony in the case of these characteristic passages is quite inadmissible, in my opinion, and contrary to the intentions of Bach in outline and in detail alike. I cannot agree with the opinions put forth by Herr W. Rust on this subject (B.-G., IX., pp. 16 and 17).

6 (p. 110). **Bach's use of the organ and harpsichord.** Within the last few years an opinion has prevailed that in his compositions Bach used both the harpsichord and the organ; the harpsichord always for arias and recitatives; and the most wonderfully fanciful notions on the subject were given to the world with more assurance than truth by a writer in the "Allgemeine Musikalische Zeitung," Nos. 31

and 33, for 1872. It would seem that an essay by Franz Chrysander gave rise to them, in which he sets forth the manner in which Handel desired to have the organ used in "Saul" (Jahrbücher für Musikalische Wissenschaft, I., p. 408). The total outcome of these very interesting communications, based as they were on Handel's own private copy, is just what has already been said in the text of this work—that Handel did not regard the organ as a central feature of his orchestra in oratorio, but merely used it as he might any other instrument, where he thought it would produce its due effect—hence only to any great extent in the choruses and instrumental movements; and in these cases very frequently it is only for strengthening the bass. This is the sole object with which he introduces it in the few solo pieces in which it is brought in; while the proper instrument for such accompaniments is the harpsichord. The variety of ways in which Handel sometimes uses the organ, sometimes discards it—sometimes in one part only, sometimes in full chords—shows the sovereign master who knows the exact place for everything. But he had derived the principle of his treatment from the Italians, who transferred both their chamber music and their theatrical traditions to their church music. In Hamburg, the most important home of the opera in Germany, all that Handel justly claimed for his new ideal form of art had been simply copied from the Italians in the strictest limits of church music; and the harpsichord had soon so completely displaced the organ that in 1739 Mattheson thought he ought to put in a good word for it, and in the Vollkommene Capellmeister (p. 484, § 29) wrote that: "for various reasons it would not be bad if in churches small and neat organs, answering readily to the touch, and without harsh stops, could be combined with the clavicembalo." Bach, on the other hand, always adhered to the pure German principle, and would have nothing to say to a permanent harpsichord for church music, any more than he would have anything to do with theatrical music. I do not know that Chrysander has anywhere drawn any inference as to Bach's method from Handel. That any one else should have done so is the more incomprehensible because more than a hundred cantatas by Bach are now published in the Bach-Gesellschaft edition, and afford an ample mass of evidence from which any one can derive information on the subject. Since, happily, a great number of cantatas exist in autograph, or in copies revised by the composer, the organ parts—transposed a tone higher and figured from the first bar to the last—are beyond dispute so far as Bach is concerned. For why the busy composer should have given himself the trouble of transposing and figuring-in pieces which were not suited at all to playing on the organ it would indeed be difficult to say. When we find both a figured organ-part and another figured part in "chamber" pitch, this of course does not mean that both were played when the piece was performed, but that the harpsichord part was used for the rehearsals which did not take place in the church. And this regular co-operation of the organ was insisted on by Bach throughout his life, not merely at Leipzig, whence most of the examples are derived, but at Weimar also. The Advent cantata for 1714, in which a list of all the instruments to be employed is to be found on the outside page, specifies the organ and no other instrument; and the shifts that Bach was put to in writing out his scores, in consequence of the " cornet " pitch of the castle organ, have been described in Vol. I., App. A., No. 17. Now, in the cantatas which belong to the earlier phase of his work, there ought never to be any question of the harpsichord, even if the autograph score and printed parts of the Mühlhausen Rathswechsel cantata did not afford the fullest evidence as to the unrelaxed use of the organ. Nothing could have given rise to the introduction of the harpsichord into the church but the adoption of the Italian aria and recitative—forms that had grown up in opera music and were wanting to the older church cantata. Nor can even the semblance of a precedent be discovered for performing the cantata—for instance, "Gottes Zeit ist die allerbeste Zeit "—without an organ. If farther evidence were needed it might be derived from Bach's own words in the Mühlhausen specification (see Vol. I., p. 355 f.); he says of the 8-feet " Stillgedackt," introduced into the new Brustpositiv, that it " sounds well in combination "—meaning, with the church music as performed by singers and instrumentalists. The character of the stops introduced proves that solo movements were intended. It has been shown, in the proper place, that in Mühlhausen Bach started on the path from which all his life he never deviated. Very rarely does it occur that the figured organ-bass is absent from any single number in the cantata; among the published cantatas one such instance occurs (B.-G., V., I., p. 200). But neither in the score nor in the parts do we find a trace of the introduction here of a harpsichord; even if this had been the case, a few unimportant exceptions could not avail against the rule; apparently, however, Bach himself undertook to accompany on the *positiv* organ, which was generally the task of the organist. Only in one single instance do we know of the introduction of the harpsichord, and this only serves to prove that Bach did not usually employ it. It is in the mourning ode on Queen Christiana Eberhardine, of which it is said in Sicul's Thränende Leipzig (1727, p. 22): " Soon after was performed the mourning music, which this time was composed by the Herr Capellmeister, Johann Sebastian Bach, after the Italian manner, with *clave di cembalo*, which Herr Bach himself played, organ, *violes-di-gamba*, lutes, violins, *fleutes douces*, and *fleutes traverses*." He had set the ode " after the Italian manner "—as is particularly stated on account of the exceptional circumstance—because, without having in itself any sacred element, it was to be performed in a church, and for these hybrid circumstances the hybrid style of the Italians seemed the fittest.

How far the unsuitable use of clavier music in churches had extended in Germany I am unable to ascertain with accuracy. As Bach was the only composer who wrote in the true church style, it ought not to surprise us if he alone had given the organ its due and proper share in it. But it must be said, to the honour of his Thuringian countrymen, that they at any rate have always duly valued the only really church instrument as such. Perhaps the harpsichord may never have found its way into their churches; at any rate, I have before me cantatas of the years 1768 and 1769, which have no accompaniment whatever but the organ. It may at any rate be considered certain for the first half of the last century; for the author of the " Gespräch von der Musik zwischen einem Organisten und Adjuvanten " (Erfurt, 1742), who was perfectly familiar with Thuringian life, takes an organ accompaniment for granted—as at p. 29, where he warns the player not to hold the chords in accompanying recitative, so that the hearers may understand the words. Even G. H. Stölzel, who had travelled through Italy, does not seem to have been unfaithful to the traditions of his native land ; the word *cembalo* was, however, very loosely used. Thus Altnikol, in his copy of his father-in-law's cantata, " Ein feste Burg ist unser Gott " (B.-G., XVIII., No. 80), could write for the upper of the two bass parts in the first chorus, *Violoncello e cembalo;* for the lower, *Violone ed organo.* In the rehearsals the cembalo must have set off at once, strengthening the violoncello bass, and not have waited until the entry of the *canto fermo* in a lower register; in the church, the organ would fill the place of the harpsichord. On the other hand, we can now understand what Kittel means when, in the passage quoted in the text out of the " Angehende Praktische Organist," he says that a pupil always had to accompany on the harpsichord when Bach was conducting a cantata. It means of course, though inaccurately put, nothing more than a rehearsal; Bach's interruption as there described, and the feeling of the pupil, could only refer to a rehearsal.

But it would be quite unwarrantable to call in the evidence of Philipp Emanuel Bach in matters concerning his father. In studying the methods of fingering of the two men we saw clearly that their views were not identical. Nor could they be, for the son diverged into new paths different from his father's. He gave himself little more trouble with the organ ; his whole endeavour was directed to the clavier, now becoming more and more independent; he had no more intimate connection with church music than his father's and his own contemporaries had; besides all this, it is a significant fact that he lived more than twenty years in Hamburg. He nevertheless made the most various demands on the harpsichord as an accompanying instrument. He says: " The organ, the harpsichord, the fortepiano, and the clavichord are the instruments most in use for accompaniments. The organ is indispensable in church use for fugues, strong choruses, and particularly in combinations; it gives grandeur and maintains steadiness. But whenever recitatives and arias are used in churches, and particularly when the middle parts form a simple accompaniment, and give the voice part perfect liberty for variations, there must also be a harpsichord. We hear only too often how bad the effect is in such a case without the harpsichord accompaniment" (Versuch über die wahre Art, &c., II., p. 1). The last sentence puts his meaning beyond a doubt. The harpsichord was not to be used instead of the organ in arias and recitatives to accompany from a figured bass; it was only to come in where an organ accompaniment was, in the nature of things, out of the question, and it was given to other instruments—no doubt the stringed quartet. Here, particularly in very simple accompaniments, a reinforcement by the harpsichord was needed, or the effect of sound was too meagre. It is quite in accordance with this—indeed, only intelligible on these grounds—that, at p. 259, he should give rules for accompanying a recitative on the organ in connection with other *tenuto* instruments. For the usual style of the church composers of the eighteenth century—if indeed we may speak of their style—the use of the organ in solo movements was highly inconvenient; it kept all expression and execution within the strict bounds of sacred feeling and of those forms and limitations which are the very essence of church music; all frivolity and sentimentality must vanish before its grave and dignified tones. But these writers had no suspicion even of this high ideal significance of the organ in the construction of a sacred cantata; and Kirnberger—who for two years had, as Bach's pupil, assisted in his church services every Sunday and had derived all his musical views from him—exclaims indignantly: " Hitherto always has church music been accompanied by the organ as its foundation and support. In these days of modern enlightenment, when a piece of sacred music must be just like a comic opera, the organ is considered quite unfit for the accompaniment, whereby a band is degraded from its dignity and the musical abortions go at once to the beerhouses."

7 (pp. 57 and 125). A three-part sonata for violins and bass, in A minor, exists in the Royal Library at Berlin, in Seb. Bach's own MS. It is written on the same particularly stout yellow paper as the autograph also preserved there of the six-part *ricercar* from the " Musikalisches Opfer " (press-mark, P. 226), consequently it dates from the last years of Bach's life, about 1747. That the piece was composed by him is certified by the title-page, written in another hand. But this certainly is an error; not a breath of Sebastian's genius animates any portion of it. Probably one of his sons may have been the author—it would not be the only instance of the father having copied one of their works in affectionate sympathy. The themes are given in A. Dörffel's thematic catalogue (App. I., p. 3, No. 5). The same library possesses a small brochure in oblong quarto, with " Inventionen " for violin and figured bàss, without naming the composer. This too is written out by Bach himself. The character and shape are the same as in the second autograph of the " Clavier Inventionen und Sinfonien " (see note 102 to p. 60). It is, to say the least, very doubtful whether they can be

his original compositions, from the manner in which the pieces are named. The volume begins with "*Inventio seconda*"; it is in B minor, and consists of—*Largo, Balletto; Allegro, Scherzo; Andante, Capriccio; Allegro.* Then follow two blank pages, but for the most part ruled; and immediately after "*Inventio quinta*," in B flat major: the first movement has no designation; *Aria, Giga; Presto, Fantasia; Amabile.* Then comes "*Inventio sexta*," in C minor: a first movement; then *Lamentevole, Balletto; Allegro, Aria; Comodo assai, Fantasia.* This invention is on four leaves, the last page however is blank. Finally "*Inventio settima*," in D major: the first movement has no designation ; *Presto ; Bifaria,*[2] *Largo ; Andamento, Presto ;* on four leaves, the last only partly written on. This ends the volume; the beginnings of the themes are given in the thematic catalogue (App. I., p. 3, Nos. 8 to 11). It is easy to see that here we have only a copy which was not even taken from an original collection; it is impossible, to be sure, to assert that the compositions absolutely cannot be Bach's; he may possibly have proposed to make a selection from an older MS. for some particular purpose, and the musical style is at any rate of his time. But it is highly improbable, if only from the elaborate designation of the movements, which was quite foreign to Bach's habit, and still more from the insignificance and meagreness of the pieces as to motive and form, and the character of the phrasing, which is quite unlike Bach's scheme of expression. The general form is that of the violin sonata in restricted proportions. The most interesting detail for us is the name "*Invention*." It proves to a certainty so much at any rate as this, that Förkel's definition of the terms is radically inaccurate when he says (p. 54): " The name *invention* was given to a musical subject which was so constructed that out of it, by imitations and transposition of the parts, the course of a whole piece might be developed. The remainder was all working-out, and needed no new inventiveness when the composer knew the proper method of development." This definition is evidently founded on Bach's clavier *inventions.*

8 (p. 125). **Authorship of the C major Trio.** I can here supplement the MS. material on which the Bach-Gesellschaft have based their edition of the C major trio. In the Gotthold Library at Königsberg, in Prussia, there is a collection of preambles or preludes to chorales written out by Gotthold himself—No. 498 in J. Müller's catalogue. Among these, on folio 11, we find the C major trio, entitled " Trio von Gollberg " ; the name being evidently a slip of the pen for Goldberg. He was the well-known pupil of Sebastian, for whom were written the thirty variations of the fourth part of the Clavierübung; he was a native of Königsberg. Since the authorship of this trio by Bach has long since been fully established, it is evident

---

[2] *Sic* (meant probably for Bizzarria, whimsicality). The term was sometimes applied to pieces of music, as we learn from Walther in his Musiklehre, 1708.

that we have here a fresh instance of a confusion which we so often meet with in studying MSS. ; Gotthold must have copied from a MS. by Goldberg, and in the course of time the name of the copyist has slipped into the place of the composer. Goldberg, as a pupil of Bach's, would carefully have made his transcript from a very good copy, and therefore it is not without its value in the reproduction of the text, the autograph being lost. It is not figured. A few of the variants from the established text have some internal justification ; but none of them bear on any essential point. As the MS. is accessible for comparison, I need say no more about it here.

9 (p. 143). **Writing and watermark of the " Partien."** The unpublished orchestral Partie, in D major, I only know from the copy which came into the Berlin Library from the papers left by Fischhoff. Its genuineness is, however, amply proved, irrespective of the character of the subjects, by the circumstance that Bach has worked up the overture in his most admirable manner in the cantata " Unser Mund sei voll Lachens." This fine work must, therefore, be promoted from its place among the doubtful works in the appendix to the thematic catalogue (Ser. VI., No. 3). As regards the time when the Partien were written, the autograph parts of the other D major Partie point, by their watermark, M A, to Leipzig. In those of the B minor Partie, on the other hand, the writing displays the Cöthen style of hand-writing; it is preserved with the former in the Royal Library at Berlin ; the character is sharp and pointed, and stiffer than that of the later Leipzig period. The naturals, which Bach subsequently wrote by the method of first making the connected strokes ⌐ and adding the other

angle thus ⌐ often occur here in their old form, thus ♭ . The later

and peculiar form of sharp, which results from the vertical strokes not being drawn long enough, and so often failing to touch the lower horizontal strokes, does not yet prevail. Still, both these later methods of writing occur here and there among the other, so that a transition stage is plainly revealed. The watermark, too, is quite peculiar, and I have found no other like it in the Leipzig autographs. If we now duly consider the probability that Bach, as chief of the Prince's orchestra in Cöthen, may have written such a work, it seems very likely that the B minor partie should have been transcribed there. The autograph of the C major partie is wanting, but a certain simplicity of treatment would seem to indicate an earlier, rather than a later, origin. The two in D major, which are characterised by a richer instrumenta-tion, may both have been composed in Leipzig.

10 (p. 152). **Authorship of " Willst du dein Herz," Giovannini.** In the larger of Anna Magdalena's music-books, on the inner pages of the two leaves which now immediately follow p. 111, we find the well-known song, " Willst du dein Herz mir schenken." On

the middle of the outer page of the first leaf are the words: "*Aria di G(i)ovannini.*" The leaves are now loose, but they have belonged to the book, for on the last page we find begun for the second time the aria "Schlummert ein, ihr matten Augen," which is continued on the following page. A few pages must originally have been left blank on which the song was afterwards written, and these with a few other leaves torn or cut out. The music and words are neither in Bach's writing nor his wife's, the words being in Roman hand; and the lines for the music are more closely ruled than those commonly used. The book passed from the Bach archives of Ph. Em. Bach into the hands of KarlFriedrich Zelter, the director of the Berlin Academy of Singing; these leaves were then already loose, as he himself states. The idea that the music and poetry both were Bach's also is Zelter's, who, in a note which is still with the copy, hazards the following conjecture: "Giovannini may have been Joh. S. Bach's pet name turned into Italian; and the poem as well as the composition may have been written by him at the time when he was betrothed to Anna Magdalena, who is said to have sung very well. The copy, which is in a girlish hand, may be by the hand of his beloved. If this hypothesis is well-founded, such a memorial of the happiest period of the great man's life is not to be rejected, though Dr. Forkel will have it that Seb. Bach never wrote such a song." What Zelter only put forward. as a possibility was considered proved when A. E. Brachvogel had adopted it as the theme of a romance in his novel, "Friedemann Bach"; and Ernst Leistner made this song—as a composition and poem by Joh. Seb. Bach—the turning point of a play in two parts (Leipzig, O. Leiner, 1870). It is also sold in the house at Eisenach, supposed to have belonged to the Bachs, as a "Memorial of Johann Sebastian Bach's birthplace"; it is sung in private circles and even in concert rooms and applauded for its touching antiquity; but, in spite of all this, unprejudiced hearers have always shaken their heads, for this music cannot be by Bach. That it is not his, any one may see who will study the MS. with an unprejudiced eye, and besides, the name of the composer is clear and plain on the title-page. Giovannini was an Italian gentleman of the middle of the eighteenth century, who resided for a long time in Germany, and who is mentioned with respect as a violinist and composer (Gerber, L. I., col. 510; N. L., II., col. 332). He was a master of the German language, and made many experiments in composing songs. In the third and fourth parts of the Odensamm-lung, edited by Johann Friedrich Graefe, 1741 and 1743, we find seven odes with music by him, and in the preface to the fourth part the editor gives us some personal details concerning him. Ernst Otto Lindner has included two of these compositions in his Geschichte des deutschen Liedes im XVIII. Jahrh (Leipzig, 1871—Musical Supp., p. 103, compare also p. 31 and 33 of the text); and we at once recognise in them the style of the composer of "Willst du dein Herz." How and when the song found its way into Anna Magdalena's book cannot, of course, be determined; probably not until after her death, when the book had passed into other hands, for the rest of the contents are of an earlier date, as has been said. From the circumstance that the four verses of the song are written in a Roman hand it may perhaps be inferred that the copyist, who certainly was not very expert, transcribed it from Giovannini's original, since he, no doubt, would have used this character for German as well as for his mother tongue. The poem, of which the playful grace ranks it above the music, I consider to be a translation from the Italian. The character of it, in my opinion, is not reconcilable with the state of German literature between 1750 and 1780. And it is quite incomprehensible to me how any one can seriously imagine that Bach could have written such a song,—Bach, whose poetical tastes had been formed on hymns and cantata-texts, by Neumeister, Franck, and Picander, and whose mode of expression, not to speak of the matter expressed, is known to us from his letters and official documents. I much regret that Dr. W. Rust (in the preface to the B.-G., Vol. XX., 1, p. xv) should have declared in favour of the genuineness of this song; all the more so because I had previously indicated to him Giovannini as its real composer, and because there was no particular reason for mentioning it there at all. He opines that in certain places the notes reveal Seb. Bach's handwriting; I, as I have said, am of the opposite opinion. I flatter myself I am sure of general agreement when I say that I have here settled once for all the question as to the writer of "Willst du dein Herz." In November, 1873, the Deutsche Zeitung of February 12, 1873, was sent me from Vienna, in which Herr Franz Gehring had already pointed out the similarity of style in "Willst du dein Herz," and in the songs by Giovannini, published by Ernst Otto Lindner.

11 (p. 159). **Autograph of the French Suites.** This is the most important autograph copy now extant of the whole work. A MS. containing only four of these suites is now in the possession of Professor Wagener, of Marburg. Whether this is written throughout by Bach himself, as used to be supposed, I must frankly doubt. It certainly only seems to me that it is older than the copy in Anna Magdalena's Clavierbüchlein. From this in the course of time a few sheets, being loose, have been lost; hence the copy is imperfect The sixth suite, in E major, is altogether wanting, and several others are incomplete. But the usual order of the six suites is here already retained. The D minor suite has evidently been at the beginning, but the *allemande* is wanting and the first portion of *courante*, and from the second part of it we also miss 1 and 2-3 of a bar, the remainder is paged by Bach 4, 5, 6, 7, 8, 9. Since, however, the same suite recurs in Anna Magdalena's larger book, the gap can be filled up. The C minor suite must have come next, and here the *allemande* and the first part of the *courante* are again wanting, and only twelve bars and the preliminary

portion of a bar of the *gigue* are to be found; the remainder must have
been on a lost leaf. Before the gigue Bach has noted: " N.B. Hierher
gehöret die fast zu ende stehende *Men. ex. c. b* " (" N.B. Here belongs the
minuet in C minor which is almost at the end "). The minuet is in fact in
quite a different place in the book; from this notice I infer that the rest
of the suite had to come after this beginning. Here again the larger book
is of use to supplement the smaller one; only partially, it is true, since
it contains only so far as the sarabande of the C minor suite, pp. 96 to 100.
The B minor suite must have followed with this superscription :—

" Suite pour le Clavessin par J. S. Bach."

The *Courante, Sarabande,* and *Anglaise* are wanting, excepting the
last twenty-two bars of the second part of the Anglaise; the two
minuets, on the other hand, are in the book, but farther on among
other pieces, and were probably composed later. The Gigue, again,
is perfect, after bars 10 and 28 of the first part of it, and bars 12 and
28 of the second, the next two bars are in each instance inserted in
German "Tabulatur" on the upper or lower margin. Then follows
"Suite ex Dis (D minor) pour le Clavessin," and then "Suite pour
le Clavessin ex G♮." Both these are perfect.

12 (p. 166). " **The Wohltemperirte Clavier and Friedemann's Büchlein.**" In the edition of the Wohltemperirte Clavier,
published by Hoffmeister and Kühnel, of Leipzig, 1801, Forkel, who
edited it, has given the preludes in C major, C minor, C sharp major,
C sharp minor, D major, D minor, E flat minor, E minor, F minor, and
G major in a shorter form. He supposed them to be the final form in
which they were projected by the composer (see his work on J. S. Bach,
p. 63). But this is in direct contradiction not only to musical feeling,
but to all the autographs of the Well-tempered Clavier. Nor has he
based his views on a due study of the documents. A MS. which passed
from his hands into the Royal Library at Berlin is, in the first place,
somewhat incorrect, and, in the second place, contains only the
Preludes in C sharp major and E flat minor of all those in question.
At the same time it is difficult ever to imagine that such serious
alterations, and in so many pieces, could have been made without any
reference whatever to the composer. The Little Clavier Book of
Friedemann Bach, which has not hitherto been utilised, gives us the
wished-for solution. It shows that, in fact, a shorter form of several of
the preludes was left by Bach. The question now arises whether this
shorter form represents the original sketch or merely a re-arrangement
intended not to overtask the powers of the younger pupils. But
here again the little book helps us out to comparative, if not absolute,
certainty. For, on the one hand, all the preludes which exist in an
abridged form are not to be found in Friedemann Bach's book—that
in G major is altogether wanting—and, on the other hand, several
are here in the more extended form, thus C sharp major is

complete in one hundred and four bars (the beginning is thus in the

right hand:—) and C sharp minor in thirty-nine

bars. E flat minor breaks off at the thirty-fifth bar, with the passage in semiquavers, on the chord of the diminished seventh; enough, however, is given to show that it is not in the form given by Forkel, and the same is the case with the F minor Prelude, which breaks off on the pedal C in bar 18. The C major Prelude also shows a considerable deviation from Forkel's version, with additions which are at once seen to be improvements; for instance —not to speak of minor changes—after each of the bars 4, 6, and 8, a bar is inserted by which the effect of the veiled melody is essentially enhanced. We thus see that in modifying the preludes none but purely musical motives have been acted on; and, as it is proved that in a few of the preludes the Forkel form, as we may call it, proceeded directly from the composer, from the character of the alterations it is not too bold to infer that this is the case in all. The Prelude in D major, which occurs in both the longer and shorter form, is, unfortunately, so fragmentary in Friedemann's book—ending at bar 19—that it is impossible to determine which form was intended. In the C major prelude, again, we have three forms to discriminate, that of Forkel, that of Friedemann Bach, and that finally arranged for the Well-tempered Clavier. Thus the case is precisely the reverse of what Forkel supposed; the shorter preludes were the earlier, and the longer were the later. Some MSS. of the preludes, in their first state, must have come into his hands, perhaps directly from Friedemann Bach, and he took them for later and revised arrangements, misled by having seen similar instances in other of Bach's works.

13 (p. 166). **The hitherto unknown autograph of the Well-tempered Clavier**, of which I am here enabled to give information, was formerly in the possession of Hans Georg Nägeli, of Zürich. So far as I can gain any information as to his acquisition of the Bach autograph, he seems to have procured it in 1802, through a friend, Professor J. K. Horner, of Hamburg, from the only daughter of Ph. Em. Bach, who was then still living there. This lady, Anna Karoline Philippine Bach, after her father's death, in concert with her mother, carried on a sale of the musical papers of Ph. Em. and of Sebastian Bach, and continued to do so alone after her mother's death in 1795. This I gather from a notice in No. 122 of the *Hamburger Correspondent* for 1795 (given by Bitter in Emanuel und Friedemann Bach, II., p. 127); and it is very probable that the two Eisenach autographs of Joh. Christoph Bach now in my possession, were first derived from this source (see Vol. I., p. 130, note 159).

This autograph of the Wohltemperirte Clavier was purchased of Nägeli's son in 1854, by Herr Ott-Usteri, of Zürich, and, thanks to the kind intervention of Herr Hofrath Sauppe, of Göttingen, he was persuaded to entrust it to me for a short time in the autumn of 1869. Since then Herr Ott-Usteri has died, in the summer of 1872, and, as I learn, bequeathed all his collection of autographs to the Town Library of Zürich.

This MS. has a wrapper, cover, and title-page also in autograph, which must originally have served for the two portions of the well-tempered clavier, for it runs as follows: "Zweymal XXIV | *Praeludia* $\frac{1^r \text{ Theil } 24}{2^r \text{ Theil } 24}$ (then, in another hand, below the word *Praeludia*) und *Fugen* | aus | allen 12. *Dur* und *moll* Tönen. | vors *Clavier* | von | *Joh. Seb. Bach* | *Dir. Mus.* in Leipzig | ." The addition of "und *Fugen*" is in another hand, while in the work itself the fugues are written together with the preludes in such a way that at the end of the prelude "*Fuga seq.*" is frequently written. Both prelude and fugue are often written on the same sheet, so it is clear that this cover did not originally belong to this MS. but to another which contained the preludes only. This proves that Bach did not regard the preludes as inseparable from the fugues, but even at some period had collected them into an independent work. The same hand that added these words has written on the inside of the cover a paged table of contents, thus :—

> "*Praelud.* 1. 2 Seiten *Fuga* 1. — 2 Seiten
>   2. 2   •   • 2. — 2 • "

and so forth; and stated the total of the pages in sheets. It has also added, over the D minor Fugue, which is written by Bach, the words "bleibt weg." All the contents of the wrapper are not, however, in autograph; the first six preludes and fugues are written in another and much younger hand, probably that of a copyist; the writing is very round, the paper crisper, the staves ruled to a different scale and far more carefully. Bach's writing begins with the D minor Fugue, which thus occurs twice—a word as to this presently. The index of pages is not fitted to Bach's MS., with which it does not agree, but to that of the copyist. The number of pages is generally greater than in Bach's MS., since Bach's writing is proportionately smaller and closer than that of the copyist. Consequently we must suppose the owner originally to have possessed the whole first part of the Wohltemperirte Clavier, only in the copyist's writing, and to have added "und Fugen" on the title-page and the table of contents in accordance with this. Subsequently he inserted what had been written by Bach himself. As regards this I firmly believe that Bach, for some unknown reason, did not write any more than we here find, but intended to add what was wanting. For instance, while the autograph everywhere shows a very economical use of space, the first leaf, before the D minor Fugue, is ruled but not written on. Here the Prelude belonging to it was intended to come; since, however, this is too long for a single page we may conclude that he intended to write in the whole of the remainder, and had calculated that this was space enough.

Like all Bach's fair copies this is clearly, and in some parts beautifully, written. Over each prelude the name is written in a large bold Roman hand with its number, and in the fugues the number of parts is added, excepting in the case of the twelfth and twentieth: thus "*Praeludium* 7." "*Fuga* 7, *à* 3." After the 10th, 20th, 21st, 23rd, and 24th preludes is written "*Fuga seq.*" once, after the E flat major Fugue the number of bars is marked, 37. It is evident from its whole aspect that the MS. was written during the Leipzig period; quite clear from the character of the writing, less so from the watermark—a shield with crossed swords on the sinister field—(the cover is of different paper and has the double eagle on one side). But if we compare the contents with those of the other autographs, which are so carefully described in the introduction by Fr. Kroll to the edition of the Bach-Gesellschaft, the different readings afford conclusive evidence that this Zürich autograph (Nägeli's) is the latest and best of all. It may possibly have been Ph. Em. Bach's private copy which he took with him when, in 1735, he quitted his father's house; granting the correctness of this hypothesis, we may assert with the more confidence that this copy had been made by Seb. Bach not long before. The most important of the variorum readings are not to be found in any of the other MSS., nor in any printed edition so far as Kroll's admirable edition enables us to judge, although they are conspicuous improvements, as I shall proceed to show. This can only be accounted for by supposing that this autograph was removed from the reach of Bach's pupils—who were chiefly instrumental in multiplying and copying his works—soon after it was written. It is, besides, reasonable to imagine that Bach should have given to his two elder and most distinguished sons, between whom his musical papers were subsequently divided, a copy of the Clavier work to which he attached so much importance. That belonging to Friedemann Bach passed first into the hands of Müller, organist to the Cathedral at Brunswick, who died there in 1835, and by him was bequeathed to Prof. Griepenkerl, after whose death it was acquired by the Royal Berlin Library.

A Second Autograph now in the possession of Prof. Wagener, of Marburg, was probably the composer's private copy. This was written in 1732. The Zürich autograph must, at any rate, have been written later than this. According to Griepenkerl, Forkel had seen a MS. bearing at the end the note "Scripsit 1734." This cannot have been Friedemann's autograph, since it has no such note; nor can it be objected that it is imperfect towards the end, for it is quite clear that nothing has been lost and afterwards supplied by a strange hand; on the contrary, Bach himself, with visibly increasing impatience, has written as far as bar 68, inclusive of the A minor Fugue, and the rest has at once been added by another hand, no doubt Friedemann's.

Then the volume, or rather Cahier, has lain by for some time and afterwards been completed by the same hand. This is plainly discernible by the arrangement of the MS. and the various kinds of paper used in it; nor does the Zürich autograph contain this note, nor, again, that of Fischhoff, of which the genuineness is accepted. Hence, unless an autograph written in 1734 is lost, that which Forkel saw either was not genuine or it was Wagener's, and he mistook 1734 for 1732; this seems to me the most probable idea.

However, the Zürich autograph had not been without influence on the present text of the Well-tempered Clavier though to be sure it is infinitesimal. I am much deceived if the two earliest German editors had not seen it—used it I really cannot say—namely, Ch. F. G. Schwenke, the musical director and successor to Ph. Em. Bach at Hamburg, who in 1800 supervised Simrock's edition, and Nägeli, who soon after brought out an edition of his own. That Nägeli should not have done so till the autograph was in his possession is extremely probable, its influence betrays itself in both, in a number of small alterations, common, and at the same time peculiar, to them both; I shall here indicate a few of these. We are forced to reflect that diplomatistic accuracy was at that time a thing unknown in the province of music, and that mere guess-work was the only guide to comprehend how these editors could have taken up such trifles and passed over the more important alterations.

Since in this place my first object is to prove that the Zürich autograph is preferable to all the others, I have not attempted to give a complete list of all the variorum readings. I shall not reproduce the places where the embellishments differ or are lacking; such minutiæ and the omission here and there of tie-marks, are evident oversights, and are besides comparatively rare. Another opportunity will doubtless offer for mentioning these. Everything else I have set down in its order, the readings from the Zürich autograph being quoted first which occur only in the Zürich autograph (and here and there in the editions by Schwenke and Nägeli) and then a number of those whose genuineness, though authenticated by several authorities, still admits of a doubt which may now be diminished or dispelled. I have used as a basis Kroll's edition for the B.-G.

D minor Fugue, bar 31, second crotchet, in the right hand

(N.B.—The notes of the upper part are always supposed to be in the treble clef.) This reading, which contradicts the sequence of the episodical treatment, is perhaps only an oversight.

E flat major Prelude, bar 9, third crotchet, right hand,

Nägeli's reading no doubt was derived from this (see the variants given by Kroll). Bar 56, tenor last crotchet, G is a whole crotchet, matching bar 65 where the E flat is always given as a whole crotchet.

E flat major Fugue, bar 21, right hand, bars 6

and 29 show why this is an improvement.

E flat minor Prelude, bar 37, left hand, there is no seventh in the three chords, which seems to me grander and better considered;

Nägeli has adopted this, bar 38, right hand,

a closing chord without a fermata; so in Nägeli.

E major Prelude, bar 3, left hand, E major Fugue,

bar 6, left hand, twelve semiquavers on d'; bar 13, left hand, the seventh quaver f sharp, both perhaps mere slips of the pen.

E minor Prelude, bar 16, right hand,

This is an evident improvement, as corresponding with the earlier bars:

bar 37, left hand, a closing chord with a minor third; thus

in Nägeli and others.

F major Prelude, bar 13, left hand, bar 17, left hand,

in the tenth quaver F as analogous to bar 7; it is probably on this ground that Czerny has already altered it.

F major Fugue, bar 45, right hand,

F minor Prelude, bar 5, left hand, first half-bar, Bar 14,

right hand, first beat The closing bars of this piece have

been hastily written and many notes are missing; the D flat in the eighth semiquaver in the bass is an error likewise.

F minor Fugue, bar 13, in the third beat of the tenor, a flat is a full crotchet. Bar 36, the two lower parts are as follows:—

so that the *a* flat in the tenor goes to *b* flat, a progression which might have been carried out by an *e* flat in the bass instead of *e*. In bar 44, the uppermost part in the second crotchet has *d″* written as a minim, which is certainly only a slip of the pen, and the same in bar 46, where the first note in the bass *c* is written as a crotchet.

F sharp major Prelude, the time is marked 12-8, in contradiction to the real time of the piece, an oversight which may perhaps have arisen from the recollection of the measure originally intended; and it may be in connection with this that the last bass note is here, as in the other autographs, written . Bar 28, left hand, the second note *c* sharp to avoid the octave with the upper part. Bar 29, right hand, the second semiquaver *e″* sharp seems to be an error.

F sharp minor Fugue, bar 29, second half right hand,

is at any rate finer and more logical. Compare bars 32 and 33, the last note in the alto *a′*.

G major Prelude, bar 7, left hand, the last six semiquavers are only the repetition of the previous six to avoid the two octaves; one instead is introduced, but only one.

G major Fugue, bar 8. There is B in the bass in all the other autographs, but here there is *b″* in the treble, which truly suits the whole feeling better.

G minor Prelude, bar 5, in the right hand:—

is a charming effect of rhythm. And similarly in bar 6, right hand, in the last beat, and in bar 8, left hand, last beat, which deviations are both given by Nägeli (see Kroll, p. 230). Bar 15, right hand, last beat:

G minor Fugue, bar 21, the first note in the alto is *a″* flat, instead of the universally accepted A flat.

A flat major Prelude, bar 36, in the alto, has no *f′*, apparently an oversight when compared with bar 38.

A flat major Fugue, bar 6, the last note of the tenor is *a* flat, crotchet; this is better, for the theme is more prominent. The slur also over the *a″* in the upper part is found here, as in some MSS. and editions, and serves the same end. Bar 13, right hand, last beat:

 bar 35, in the alto, second beat: in imitation of

the bass figures in the last beat of the previous bar.

G sharp minor Prelude, bar 2, right hand, the first note in the alto is only a quaver to avoid hidden octaves with the bass.

G sharp minor Fugue, bar 7, second half in the tenor, is better as being a more melodious progression. Bar 15, the first two quavers in the tenor are *c* sharp, possibly, however, by a mistake, although it sounds well. Bar 32, left hand, ![notation] is by far the least harsh of all the versions of this remarkable passage.

A major Prelude, bar 9, left hand, the *e'* is sounded on the fourth quaver after the previous semiquaver in the middle part. See also Nägeli and Simrock. The effect in performance is exactly the same as that of the more correct version given by Kroll after the other autographs. Bach often allowed himself such liberties, in order to exhibit his musical intentions to the eye of the player. So in this Zürich autograph he writes the 29th bar of the F minor Fugue, right hand :—

![notation]

A major Fugue, bar 50, right hand, the sixth quaver is *c''* sharp to make it correspond to the progression of the middle part in bar 53. On the other hand, in bar 43, fifth quaver, *g'* sharp, is certainly an error.

A minor Prelude. The nine quavers from the seventh of bar 22 to the seventh of bar 23 are struck out, which indeed hinder the course of the final development, and besides that sound very harshly, for the seventh on F is either not at all or only partially resolved. For this reason the F is changed into A in Fr. Chrysander's edition (Wolfenbüttel, L. Holle), but I know not on what authority. There is a fermata on the last chord, as in Nägeli and Schwenke's MS.

A minor Fugue, bar 41, in the third beat, the *c* in the bass is a quaver.

Bar 59, in the tenor, ![notation] is harsh, but not impossible. Bar 63, in the alto, the eight semiquavers in *e''*; the seventh, as it seems, has to be prepared. Bar 64 in the third beat of the tenor part *d'*, a crotchet; the skip to *a* is, as a matter of fact, superfluous. Bar 69 is the tenor, ![notation] Bar 81 in the upper part, ![notation] the strict stretto is discarded, perhaps because we have heard enough strettos before.

B flat minor Prelude, bar 1, left hand, second quaver, no d' flat; in the following bar the progression of parts is somewhat differently managed. Bar 24, the ties to the notes $\genfrac{}{}{0pt}{}{g'\ \text{flat}}{e'\ \text{flat}}$ are wanting, and there is a fermata over the last chord.

B flat minor Fugue, bar 20, left hand, is to be pre-

ferred, because it carries on the crotchet movement in thirds longer. Bar 36, right hand, the last quaver but two, f'', not f'' flat, is better as preparing for A flat major. In bar 74—75 there is no tie between f and f.

B major Fugue, bar 4, in the tenor, is better,

since the chord of the six-four is avoided.

B minor Prelude. The direction *Andante* is lacking. B minor Fugue, bar 63, second half in the upper part, a'' alone as a crotchet, coming in anew in the next bar to keep the imitation more strictly.

D minor Fugue, bar 35, the reading of the Zürich and the Fischhoff autograph agree and confirm each other; a little harshness more or less is not of great account in this fugue.

E flat major Prelude, bar 34. The reading agrees with that of the Wagener and the Fischhoff autograph. Kroll pronounces it (p. xxiv) quite correct, and has put it into his text as the chief reading.

E flat minor Prelude, bar 10, right hand, the last chord is a complete E flat minor chord with b' flat as the lowest note, but of not much weight because it has been written in later with different ink. These traces of a foreign hand occur also in the F sharp major Prelude and in the Fugue, and are evidently corrections of Bach's errors from too quick writing, but of course I attach no further value to them.

E flat minor Fugue, bars 20 and 21, 41 and 48, all the autographs agree against the reading adopted by Kroll.

E major Fugue, bars 16, 26, and 27, are alike except that in the last of these the fifth quaver in the bass is dotted, to correspond with the foregoing bass. E minor Prelude, bar 5, right hand :—

and with a little variation in the autographs, bars 7, 9, and 11 agree with all the the autographs, except in bar 9, before the opening B in the right hand there is an accent marked. Forkel says (p. 63) that the E minor Prelude was at first overloaded with running passages, and afterwards simplified by Bach. In this there is, as we see, a grain of truth, but Forkel took the first sketch in Friedemann's book for the simplified form, and we do not know whether the ornamentation in the extended form really proceeded from Bach himself. Forkel must have heard something of the story from Bach's sons, but either understood or applied it wrongly, as was frequently the case with him.

E minor Fugue, bar 21, right hand, g' sharp as the eighth semi-quaver, which is adopted by Kroll as his chief reading. The same with bar 40, right hand, g' the third crotchet.

F major Fugue, bar 42, agrees with all the autographs against Kroll's reading.

F minor Prelude, bar 22, the final chord is minor against the majority of the MSS.

F minor Fugue, bar 32, the bass has g flat in the second beat. Bar 41, alto, has c' in the third beat.

F sharp major Prelude, in bars 5, 17, and 29, there are no slurs between the ninth and tenth semiquavers.

G major Fugue, bar 82, agrees with all the autographs against Kroll's reading.

G minor Prelude, bars 13 and 14, the c in the bass remains; this is also in Simrock's edition. Bar 19, a fermata on the last b, agreeing with the Fischhoff autograph.

G sharp minor Fugue. The last bar is major, so is the Fischhoff's autograph, and a few MSS. of Nägeli and Simrock.

A major Fugue, bar 53, the fourth crotchet in the middle part is g sharp ; so that the erasure in Friedemann Bach's autograph can hardly be the work of the composer.

A minor Fugue, bar 69, in the last beat to the upper part as is in Kroll's chief reading.

B flat major Fugue. The final chord has no fermata. B flat minor Fugue, bars 50 and 51, without a stretto are thus:—

In bar 59 the second crotchet of the alto is d'', agreeing with all the autographs, as in Wagener's, which Kroll follows. A sharp can be clearly seen. I believe that this most diligent editor has been misled into an erroneous judgment in respect to the corrections inserted by a second hand in the Wagener autograph. As the reader will have remarked, the Zürich autograph always confirms the first reading. If the corrections are later improvements by the composer, it is inconceivable why none of those in the Zürich autograph should be indentical.

14 (p. 225). **Leipzig Musical Unions.** In the Leipzig Directory (Das jetzt lebende und florirende Leipzig) for 1723 we find p. 59 "The ordinary Collegia Musica in Leipzig are two: I. Under the direction of Herr George Balthasar Schott, organist of the New Church ; in the summer on Wednesdays, from four to six, in the garden of Herr Gottfried Zimmermann, in the *Wind-Mühl-Gasse*, and in the winter on

Fridays, from eight to ten, in the Coffee house in the Cather Strasse. II. Under the direction of Herr Joh. Gottl. Görner, organist of the Church of St. Niclas; on Wednesdays, from eight to ten, in Herr Schellhafer's house in the Closter Gasse." The notice is almost identical in the edition of 1732, excepting that under No. I. Bach and not Schott is named as the director; and again in that of 1736, only that under No. II. it is added "also during the winter months on Mondays, from eight to ten, at Herr Enoch Richter's Coffee house, in Herr D. Altner's house in the Market Place."

The first part of Mizler's Musikalishe Bibliothek contains on p. 63 the following: "Report of the Musical Unions of Leipzig. The two Musical Unions or Meetings, as here held every week, continue to flourish. One is directed by Herr Johann Sebastian Bach, Capell-meister to the principality of Weissenfels and musical director in the churches of St. Thomas and St. Nicholas; and it is held, out of fair-time, once every week at Zimmermann's coffee house in the Cather Strasse on Friday evenings from eight to ten, and in fair-time twice a week, on Tuesdays and Fridays, at the same hour. The other is directed by Herr Johann Gottlieb Görner, director of music in St. Paul's church and organist of St. Thomas'. This is also held once a week at Schell-hafer's hall in the Closter Gasse, on Thursday evenings, from eight to ten, and in fair-time twice a week, namely, Mondays and Thursdays, at the same hour. The members who constitute these unions are for the most part students of the place, and there are always good musicians among them; so that often, as is well known, skilled per-formers appear from among them, and every musician is permitted to perform in public in these meetings, and for the most part there are hearers present who can judge of the merits of a skilled musician." In 1746 this register tells us (p. 69): "The ordinary *Collegia Musica* are three: I. Will for the future meet under the direction of Herr Gerlach, organist to the New Church, at Herr Enoch Richter's in the Catharinen Strasse, in the summer-time on Wednesdays, in his garden in the back Street, from four to six, and in winter, on Fridays, in the Coffee house, from eight to ten. II. Is held on Thursdays, from eight to ten, under the direction of Herr J. G. Görner, organist of St. Thomas', at Schell-hafer's house in the Closter Gasse. III. On Thursday also a meeting will be held from five to eight, under the direction of the Merchants' Guild and others, at the Three Swans in the Brühl, where the greatest masters when they come here may be heard, and where the attendance is considerable and they are listened to with great attention." The directory for 1747 mentions the same three *Collegia Musica*, but instead of Gerlach "Herr Trier" is named as the director of the first union. This was Thomas Trier, of Themar, who, after Bach's death, came forward as candidate for the post of Cantor to St. Thomas', and afterwards was organist at Zittau. For several years the Leipzig Directory fails us. But from the notices here collected it is clear that it was Telemann's union which passed out of Schott's hands into those of Bach, from Bach to Gerlach, and finally to Trier. These two young musicians were pupils of Bach, and this seems to prove that Bach maintained a certain influence over the society, and had only withdrawn from the personal management because he must have observed that it could no longer hold its own against the new ones which were then becoming effective.

In the performances at the New Church after Schott's time, five instrumentalists were employed, appointed by the Council. In 1736 a sixth was engaged in consequence of Gerlach's representations. After 1738, four students, who composed the choir, received a honorarium of twelve thlrs.; in 1741, two more violins were appointed, with four thlrs. a year, but they were required occasionaliy to perform as singers, and in 1744 eight thlrs. a year were granted to two musicians who were to play the stringed bass and the organ. Thus the musicians in the New Church, appointed by the Council, now consisted of fourteen persons, four singers and ten players. These facts are extracted from the accounts of the New Church.

15 (p. 282). **The Leipzig Organs.** Rust has very acutely inferred that some alterations of the same kind must have been made about this time in the organ of St. Thomas' (see his Preface to B.-G. XXII., p. xiv). In the oldest score of the St. Matthew Passion, which exists in Kirnberger's MS., we find as yet no double organ part, while in the Rathswahl-Cantata, on the contrary, "Wir danken dir Gott," two organs, one *obbligato*, the other for accompaniment, are employed. The former work was first performed in 1729, the latter in 1731. And in the accounts of St. Thomas' for Candlemas, 1730 and 1731, we find the following item: "50 thlrs. to the organ builder, Johann Scheibe, for repairs, according to the vouchers of Zettel and Görner, the organists." Thus the *Rückpositiv* is not named here, and what was done to it was not in fact repairs. However, we must not take the accountant's style so literally. He writes concerning the great restoration of the St. Thomas' organ finished in 1721: "217 fl. 3 ggr. or 190 thlrs., were furthermore paid to Joh. Scheibe—in agreement with the new contract made with him, altogether 390 thlrs—for the entire and complete repairing of the great organ, with four new bellows, and 400 new pipes for the mixture." These "400 new pipes for the mixture" include, however, an independent Sesquialtera for the *Rückpositiv*, which—as Rust was the first to remark—had no Sesquialtera in the year 1670, while Bach ordered this stop to be used on the *Rückpositiv* in the Matthew Passion. An experienced organ builder, whom I consulted, told me that, at that time, the alterations here spoken of could quite easily have been made for the sum of 50 thlrs. Only, indeed, with one keyboard, and that for the manual: for, if a separate pedal-stop had been put into the *Rückpositiv*, such as Scheibe put into the organ of the Neuekirche, which had, however, an independent *Rückpositiv*, the

thing would have cost more. This agrees entirely with the use which Bach subsequently made of the *Rückpositiv*. But this must refer to the Thomaskirche organ, for the organ in the Nicolaikirche had no *Rückpositiv* which could be played alone, and in the accounts no trace can be found of its *Rückpositiv* having been made fit for such a treatment in Bach's time.

16 (p. 286). **Organ-pitch in Leipzig.** In the Preface to B.-G., I., p. xiv., Moritz Hauptmann goes upon the assumption that the Nicolaikirche organ stood in chamber pitch, and concludes from this that of the double parts for the figured bass, which are frequently found in Bach's cantatas, the transposed part was used in the Nicolaikirche, and the other in the Thomaskirche. He may have founded his opinion upon the fact that the organ in the Nicolaikirche, which was replaced in 1862 by a new one, stood in chamber pitch. But this organ was not the same one that stood in the Nicolaikirche in Bach's time. On the contrary, the old organ, the specification of which is given in the text, was replaced in the year 1793 by a new one, built by the brothers Trampeli, of Adorf, for 7,000 thlrs. It must have been badly built to require renewing in less than seventy years. But there is nothing to show that the old organ stood in chamber pitch. In the seventeenth century the "chorus pitch" was still in ordinary use, so that the organ must have been altered to chamber pitch during the repairs of 1725. But at that time this pitch was still very little used, and we may be sure that if it had been introduced here in 1725, the fact would have been mentioned somewhere or other. Probably the first organ in chamber pitch in Saxony was one built by Silbermann, at Zittau, 1741, and its pitch was considered a curiosity. (See Sammlung-einiger Nachrichten von berühmten Orgel-Wercken in Teutschland. Breslau, 1757, p. 103.) There was also no reason whatever for changing the pitch of the organ in the Nicolaikirche, and thus making it different from the Thomaskirche organ, for at times the same church music had to be accompanied on each organ by turns; and considering the difficulty, especially in old organs, of lowering the pitch, which involved lengthening the pipes, it could only have been called a foolish waste of money and trouble. If in any way the chorus pitch were found to be a difficulty in the case of concerted church music, we may be sure that it would not have been allowed to remain in the Neuekirche. But the organ there, which was built in 1704, had this pitch, and kept it even after the thorough repair which Scheibe undertook for the sum of 500 thlrs. in 1722 (see acounts of the Neuekirche from Candlemas, 1721 to 1722, and the inserted documents that contain the contracts and advices). The specification of this organ is given in Niedt, Musikalische Handleitung Andere Theil. 2nd edition. Hamburg, 1721, p. 189.

17 (p. 325). **Clef and Pitch of Instrumental Parts.** Kuhnau's Christmas Cantata "Nicht nur allein am frohen Morgen," for chorus, two violins, viola, bass, two oboes, two horns, drums, and

continuo, is in A major; the score and parts are in the Town Library of Leipzig. All the stringed instruments as well as the figured continuo are set in this key. The violins and oboes are to play from the same

parts, as is indicated by the signature;   That is to say,

the oboes play in the key of G without any signature—*i.e.*, in C major, which in the low chamber pitch sounded like B major; the strings, on the contrary, and the organ, in A major at chorus pitch, which in the same way sounded B major. In the cantatas "Erschrick mein Herz vor dir," "Ich hebe meine Augen auf," "Und ob die Feinde Tag und Nacht," which also exist in the Town Library at Leipzig, the organ parts are likewise in the original key, so that the violins had to be tuned to chorus pitch. This is not the case in the cantata "Welt ade, ich bin dein müde"; here the continuo is in G, the strings in A, the flutes and oboes in B flat, but from this disposition we perceive that the wood wind instruments were in the low chamber pitch. Bach's cantata "Höchst erwünschtes Freudenfest," which was originally written for the dedication of an organ at Störmthal, is in B flat major. When Bach conducted it on the feast of Trinity at Leipzig, he had only oboes at chamber pitch at his disposal, as is proved by the notes "*tief Cammerthon*" added in his own hand. Thus the B flat sounded as A, and the part for the organ which was at chorus pitch had to be written in G major, as is in fact the case. That this G major copy was prepared for a Leipzig performance is shown by this note inserted above the second portion, "*Parte 2da sub Communione.*" Hence all the stringed instruments, in order to be able to play from the copies which already existed in B flat major, had to be tuned a semitone lower, a process which Bach in fact prescribes by the words "*tief Cammerthon.*" When, on a subsequent occasion, he once more conducted this cantata, he had oboes at his command in high chamber pitch, and so wrote out very carefully a new figured bass part in A flat major, while the strings could remain at their normal pitch. This fresh part is remarkable, moreover, for having a bass figure only in the recitatives, the figures being generally replaced by a voice or instrumental part above the bass, and two portions have neither. It may also have served as the conductor's copy, particularly as the cantata is abridged, and the different sections have been displaced. Finally, as regards the pitch of the trumpets (compare Vol. I., p. 343, note) a MS. note may here be quoted as supporting what is said in the text. It is on a Whit Sunday cantata by Kuhnau, now in the Berlin Library ("Daran erkennen wir"), and runs as follows: "1. N.B. This piece is set for the violins (and all the strings) at chorus pitch, and for the voices and bass, in the key of B flat. 2. The trumpets are written in C natural. Thus a particular mouthpiece must be added to the trumpets so that they may sound a tone lower in the chamber pitch, and the drums must be tuned a tone lower, down to chamber pitch.

3. The *hautbois* and *bassons* must tune to chamber pitch, and in writing out the parts the music must be transposed a tone higher, so in this way all may agree."

18 (p. 331). **Accompaniment on the Harpsichord.** Gesner says that while he conducted Bach played either the organ or the clavier, which agrees very well with the circumstances, if by the *clavier* we understand the keyboard of the separate *Rückpositiv*. But the mention of a pedal does not agree with this, as the *Rückpositiv* had no pedal. Still the picture of Bach sitting at the great organ and thus playing the figured bass part cannot be reconciled with the rest of Gesner's description, and is hardly conceivable in itself; for, if he was to conduct thirty or forty performers, and keep them in order by movements of his hands and head, beating time and indicating emphasis, he cannot have kept his back turned upon them. Gesner's account is more compatible with solo organ-playing; it is quite possible that he should think of Bach's grand performances on the organ when wanting to give an instance of how various functions might be fulfilled at once, and that he overlooked the importance of accuracy in the picture as a whole.

In this place I must refer the reader to a statement already quoted from Kittel (ante p. 104, and note 6 of this Appendix) that when Seb. Bach conducted church music he always had an accompaniment played by one of his best pupils. For the purpose mentioned in the text this statement is useless, since, as I have already said, Kittel's remark can only refer to rehearsals, for this reason—irrespective of any others—that when Kittel was studying under Bach the harpsichord had been removed from St. Thomas. He wrote the above more than fifty years afterwards, so it is not surprising that his memory should have failed him. Still the notice is interesting within its limits, as proving that Bach stood to beat time at the rehearsals and entrusted the figured bass playing to a pupil. The scene of these rehearsals must have been the school hall; and yet there was no harpsichord there in Bach's time. An inventory of the instruments in the Thomasschule was added to the accounts of the school every year, and from 1723 till 1750 it is always as follows:—

Musical Instruments.

1 *Regal*, old and quite done for.

1 *dito*, bought *āō*. 1696.

1 *Violon āō*. 1711.

1 *Violon āō*. 1735, bought at the auction (not included in previous years, of course).

2 *Violons de Braz* (? iron fiddles).

2 *Violins*, repaired *āō* 1706.

1 *Positiv*, upright, with 4 stops and tremulant, yellow striped with gold, bought *āō* 1685.

1 *Positiv*, in the form of a *Thresores* (? in trapeze form), with four handles, which gives a stopped 8 ft. tone.

1 Another with a 4 ft. tone.

1 *Principal*, 2 ft. tone, bought *āō* 1720, to be used at family weddings.

Now since, irrespective of Kittel's evidence, the rehearsals—excepting the chief rehearsal on Saturdays in the church—would hardly have been carried on with only the accompaniment of a *Positiv*, particularly when Bach's intricate compositions were being practised, it follows that the scene of them must have been Bach's own residence, in which several harpsichords were at command for all the purposes of practice.

19 (p. 353). **Bach's Probationary Cantata, and Cantatas written between 1723 and 1727.** The autograph score of the cantata " Du wahrer Gott und Davidssohn," is written on paper with the watermark of the wild man with the fir tree. This mark occurs in no paper used by Bach at Weimar or at Leipzig. On the other hand, we find it in the autograph of the Cantata " Durchlauchtger Leopold " (see note 1 of this Appendix), and in that of another piece of occasional music written at Cöthen, and not long since come to light again, " Mit Gnaden bekröñe der Himmel die Zeiten "; thus it is a token of the Cöthen period. Now the following observations may also be made note of: 1. In Cöthen itself Bach had no opening for the performance of church cantatas; what he wrote there were composed for other places. 2. Bach must have passed his tests at Leipzig on Estomihi (or Quinquagesima) Sunday, 1723. 3. He wrote the score of " Du wahrer Gott " with unusual care, with a view to some special occasion, but he did not quite complete it; the final chorus is wanting. It is clear that it was not Bach's original intention to close with the chorus in E flat major, and that the final chorus owes it existence to a later idea, from the fact that the closing initials, *S. D. G.*, were not put at the end of the chorus in E flat major. Besides, the chorale brought into the recitative by the instruments would be quite vague in intention if the introduction of this chorale in the final chorus had not been planned from the beginning; indeed, the cycle of keys presented by the different subjects of the cantata is only completed by the chorale in chorus closing in C. 4. From the character of the original parts we see that some of them only were written at Cöthen, while the rest were finished during his early years at Leipzig. 5. The texts of the cantata under discussion, and of that finally used as his test of proficiency, " Jesus nahm zu sich die Zwölfe," are evidently by the same poet, and we know the date of this latter cantata on the best authority.

The conclusion is obvious. When Bach had made the clean copy of " Du wahrer Gott," as far as the closing chorus, he changed his mind, wrote another piece, and put the first aside for a more fitting opportunity; when this offered, in Leipzig, he completed the parts and performed it no doubt on Estomihi Sunday, 1724. I observe that W. Rust has already come to the same conclusion (see preface to B.-G., V.,[1] p. xxi).

Two original scores exist of the cantata " Jesus nahm zu sich die Zwölfe," both in the Berlin Library. One is autograph throughout, and the almost total absence of corrections, as well as the ruling of the bars in the first chorus, show that it is a fair copy. It is not possible to determine exactly when it was made; we can hardly base a definite opinion on the watermark—a shield with crossed swords—though it is not improbable that it indicated the Cöthen period (compare notes 9, 41, and 57 of this Appendix). The second copy is written by Anna Magdalena Bach, and Sebastian has only written in one or two passages—*e.g.*, a line of the text on p. 7, and the careful figuring of the bass which extends as far as bar 42 of the first aria. From the watermark this score was written at an early period in Leipzig; and, at the beginning, in Anna Magdalena's writing, are the words: "N.B. This is the probationary work for Leipzig."

The watermarks in the paper of the original MSS. afford, perhaps, the most valuable data for the chronology of Bach's cantatas; a thorough investigation and comparison of the MSS. reveal the fact that a few marks, very distinct in character, constantly recur. From this we may infer that at different periods Bach used quantities of certain sorts of paper, and consequently that those MSS. which are written on paper with the same watermark belong to the same period. This sign of course is not absolutely infallible in every case, but, in the state in which the chronology of Bach's works is at present, much is gained even when we have succeeded in grouping them within different periods. When once this is done other means may be more successfully adopted for the more exact determination of the date of composition, when any such exist. I hope that I have succeeded in thus dividing and grouping them, and I will now deal more fully with the first section of the Leipzig period. I must begin by saying that to identify these marks I have had to look hundreds of MSS. several times over, because many which at first seemed undecipherable or worthless after fresh observations became clear and important.

The first period extends from 1723 till October, 1727, and the latest example is the score, written in this month, of the mourning ode for Queen Christiana Eberhardine. The watermarks of the MSS. within these limits are, on one half of the sheet, this sign :—

and on the other a half moon. These marks occur in the original MSS. of the following :—

1. Aergre dich, o Seele, nicht
2. Christen ätzet diesen Tag
3. Christ lag in Todesbanden
4. Dazu ist erschienen der Sohn Gottes
5. Die Himmel erzählen die Ehre Gottes
6. Du Hirte Israels
7. Du sollst Gott deinen Herren Lieben

8. Du wahrer Gott und Davidssohn
9. Ein ungefärbt Gemüthe
10. Erforsche mich Gott
11. Erfreute Zeit im neuen Bunde
12. Erwünschtes Freudenlicht
13. Halt im Gedächtniss Jesum Christ
14. Herr gehe nicht ins Gericht
15. Herr wie du willt
16. Herz und Mund und That und Leben (Remodelled for Leipzig)
17. Himmelskönig sei willkommen (Remodelled for Leipzig)
18. Höchst erwünschtes Freudenfest
19. Jesus nahm zu sich die Zwölfe
20. Jesus schläft, was darf ich hoffen?
21. Ihr Menschen rühmet
22. Leichtgesinnte Flattergeister
23. Lobe den Herrn, meine Seele (XII. Sunday after Trinity)
24. *Magnificat* in E flat major (D major)
25. Mein liebster Jesus ist verloren
26. Nimm was dein ist und gehe hin
27. O Ewigkeit, o Donnerwort (F major)
28. O heilges Geist- und Wasserbad
29. und 30. *Sanctus* in C major and D major
31. Schauet doch und sehet
32. Schau lieber Gott, wie meine Feind
33. Sehet, welch eine Liebe
34. Siehe zu, dass deine Gottesfurcht nicht Heuchelei ist
35. Sie werden aus Saba alle kommen
36. Sie werden euch in den Bann thun (G minor)
37. Singet dem Herrn ein neues Lied
38. Wachet, betet (Remodelled for Leipzig)
39. Weinen, Klagen
40. Wahrlich, wahrlich, ich sage euch
41. Wo gehst du hin?

To prove the practical use of this critical text it can be shown that other marks exist on these compositions which assign them to the period between 1723—1727. Of five of the number we know the date precisely. The original score of "Aergre dich, o Seele, nicht," and "Die Himmel erzählen die Ehre Gottes," bear the date 1723, that of "Mein liebster Jesus" 1724. "Höchst erwünschtes Freudenfest" was composed for the dedication of the organ at Strömthal, near Leipzig, as we learn from a note in the composer's hand in the score, and copy of the words for the voices ; and the church accounts of that place inform us that this took place November 2, 1723. The cantata "Jesus nahm zu sich die Zwölfe" was performed at Leipzig on Estomihi Sunday, 1723, as is noted by Anna Magdalena Bach. It has been shown that it is probable that some of the original parts of "Du wahrer Gott" date from 1724. The words of "Ein ungefärbt Gemüthe" were by Neumeister, written in 1714, and are to be found in the Fünffachen Kirchenandachten (p. 334). The text of "O heilges Geist- und Wasserbad" is by Franck, and was written in 1715; it exists in his "Evangelischem Andachts-Opffers." It is natural that in the early Leipzig period, when Bach was not yet in intimate relations with Picander, and could not at once find in the place a writer whose texts might suit his needs, he should return to poems already known to him. This can be proved to have happened in two other cases. The words of "Aergre dich, o Seele, nicht," which bear the date 1723, are also by Franck, as also those of "Ihr die ihr euch nach Christo nennet," and I shall presently show that this last must have been composed in 1723 or 1724 at the latest. Consequently it seems probable that the cantatas "Ein ungefärbt Gemüthe" and "O heilges Geist" must belong to the early Leipzig period. Thus, of the forty-one compositions in the list, eight may, from other marks, be assigned to a time before 1727, and the same can be proved with a number of others. The marks are of an external character; but internal evidence also exists to a considerable extent. As this, however, is derived from the characteristics of the separate works, I will discuss them in the body of the work. What has been said will suffice to show that we are justified in assigning MSS. which are on paper with the same marks to approximately the same period.

20 (p. 354). **Oboe d'Amore in two Cantatas.** W. Rust has pointed out, and with justice, the resemblance in the complicated notation for the oboe d'amore as indicating the connection of these two cantatas (B.-G., XVIII., Preface, p. xiii). For this instrument both the G clef on the second line and the C clef on the first line were used.

The oboe d'amore was pitched a minor third lower than the ordinary oboe, thus C minor sounded as A minor, G minor as E minor. Bach here uses this instrument for the first time, and, to make it easier to read the part, he added the C clef as well, a plan he afterwards discarded. The intention is perfectly evident from the middle portion of the Cantata "Die Himmel erzählen," where, if the oboe parts had been correctly assigned to the C clef, a sharp would have to be added. This has not been done; Bach was satisfied with a reminder merely of the unusual pitch. However, such double notation was not unusual, particularly for the oboes (see No. 17 of this App., and Vol. I, p. 628), and, as in the present instance, could only be intended to facilitate the performance of the part on an ordinary oboe or violin when no oboe d'amore was at hand. Whether this was Bach's purpose cannot be decided, for the orchestral parts are wanting. If the different parts of the Cantata "Die Elenden sollen essen" had not been lost, we could perhaps determine what is meant by the words "*col accomp.*," which occur at the beginning of this score, under the first line of the instrumental bass. Was this a hint to the copyist of the bass part, as the score has no figures—that he should add the figures corresponding to the instrumental harmony ; or does it rather indicate something like *colla parte*, and did Bach thereby intend a freer performance of the Ritornel, as is quite conceivable from the passages given to the first oboe ? The watermarks on the autograph MS. are on one page a W, on the other a horse.

21 (p. 358). **The Cantata " Ein Ungefärbt Gemüthe,"** if it was not composed in 1723, must have been written in 1726 or 1727—since we are here dealing only with the period between 1723—1727 (see No. 19 of this Appendix). For, in 1724 the fourth Sunday after Trinity fell on the Feast of the Visitation, and in 1725, on St. John Baptist's Day, so that no ordinary church music would be performed. Still, it is improbable that Bach, who was by this time acquainted with Picander, should have selected this insignificant text by Neumeister. In Neumeister's "Neue Geistliche Gedichte " (V. I.), we find on p. 105 a text for Whitsunday, "Gott der Hoffnung erfülle euch," and a setting of this, bearing Bach's name, exists in the Amalien Library at Berlin (oblong folio volume, 43). This composition is not at all like Bach, and certainly not his ; in style it greatly resembles a cantata in the same volume, " Herr Christ der einge Gottssohn," which was discussed in Vol. I., p. 633. It would seem that out of the Fünffache Kirchenandachte, Bach also composed that for the seventh Sunday after Trinity ; but at present we only know of the existence of the music from its being mentioned in Breitkopf's list for Michaelmas, 1770, according to which it was set for four voices, two flutes, two violins, viola, and bass.

22 (p. 361). **" Ihr, die ihr euch von Christo nennet."** The date of this cantata is derived from a particular mark in the part for the second oboe ; this part being extant in the Berlin Library among the autograph score and original parts. At the end of this part

we find : *Il Fine*, and this monogram which supplies the

initials W. F. B., and is a boyish triviality on the part of the copyist, William Friedemann Bach. The title and the words " *Aria tacet*," " *Recit aria tac :*" " *Recit tacet*," with the violin or G clef, what is now the first section ; the two flats, the common time mark ¢, the indication "*Aria all unis :*" and, below, the *volti* and the larger *Fine* under the monogram, are all in the writing of Anna Magdalena Bach ; the rest is by Friedemann, and in a very stiff and childish hand. In the summer of 1723, Friedemann was in his thirteenth year ; we may therefore infer that his mother, who was a good musician, set him the part as he was to write it. With regard to the watermark, see No. 43 of this Appendix.

23 (p. 362). **Wachet, betet.** The first performance of this remodelled piece must have taken place either in 1723 or 1725, since the

twenty-sixth Sunday after Trinity did not again come into the Church year till 1728. I incline to the year 1723, because I believe that Bach, during the early years at Leipzig, never let this Sunday, which occurs comparatively seldom, pass without performing some composition of his own, and all the less because the character of the services of the day must have strongly affected his imagination. The evidence of a second performance of the remodelled work lies in the early obbligato violoncello part, and one of the figured organ bass parts in B flat. These parts are on paper with the watermark M A which is the distinguishing sign of a group of cantatas about 1730 (see No. 44 of this Appendix). Between 1725 and 1736, the only years in which there were twenty-six Sundays after Trinity were 1728 and 1731, so the second performance must have been on one of these days.

24 (p. 369). **Christmas Day Cantatas.** It may be assumed as certain that during the early years of his official residence at Leipzig, Bach composed the cantatas and other part music at any rate, for all the more important festivals, since it was universally the custom for the Cantor or Capellmeister himself to supply the greater part of the music needed for the church year. And when a man like Fasch could compose during the first year of office a double series of cantatas, that is to say, above 100 (see Gerber, N. L. II., col. 92), Bach was certainly not the man to be behindhand in the matter. Besides, he himself says in a *Promemoria* dated August 15, 1736, and to which his squabble with Ernesti gave rise, that the cantatas which he performed with the first choir were mostly of his own composition. All then that is required is to select the right ones from among the festival cantatas. Bach wrote five annual series, at least five therefore for each festival. There are indeed six extant for Christmas Day, as follows :—

1. Christen ätzet diesen Tag.
2. Ehre sei Gott in der Höhe.
3. Gelobet seist du, Jesu Christ.
4. Jauchzet, frohlocket, auf preiset die Tage.
5. Unser Mund sei voll Lachens.
6. Uns ist ein Kind geboren.

No. 6 is an early work written at Weimar (see Vol. I., p. 487), and cannot come under consideration here, unless we assume, what is most improbable, that Bach, in his new office, could find nothing better for the first celebration of one of the greatest Church festivals than a *rechauffé* of a not very important early work. No. 2 is the setting of a text written by Picander for Christmas Day, 1728. No. 3 bears the marks of having been composed between 1735 and 1750 (see note 4 of Appendix A to Vol. III.). No. 4, which belongs to the Christmas oratorio, was composed in 1734, according to Ph. Em. Bach. No. 5 contains, as the fifth movement, a duet, "Ehre sei Gott in der Höhe," which is an extended re-arrangement of the setting of *Virga Jesse floruit* belonging to Bach's great Latin *Magnificat*. This was written for vespers at Christmas, at Leipzig; hence the Cantate No. 5 cannot have been written for Christmas, 1723, as this would make the remodelled work older than the original.

Only No. 1, therefore, can possibly have been written for this first Christmas in Leipzig, and this inference is borne out by the watermark of the original parts (see No. 19 of this Appendix), and by the circumstance that the part of the oboe in the A minor duet was subsequently given by Bach to an organ *obbligato*, and this would not have been possible before 1730, when the *Rückpositiv* in St. Thomas' was altered ; so the cantata must have been written before that year.

We only have one other setting of the *Magnificat* by Bach, and it is doubtful whether there ever were more than these two. The marks on the score assign it to a period between 1723 and 1727 (see No. 19 of this Appendix), and the probability that it must have been written for Christmas, 1723, is increased by its being connected with a cantata by Kuhnau.

25 (p. 385). **St. Stephen's Day Cantatas.** There are but four cantatas for the second day of Christmas, St. Stephen's Day :—

1. Christum wir sollen loben schon.
2. Dazu ist erschienen der Sohn Gottes.
3. Selig ist der Mann, der die Anfechtung erduldet.
4. Und es waren Hirten in derselbigen Gegend.

Of these No. 1 has the watermark of a half moon without the corresponding mark on the other half sheet, which refers it to 1735—1750 (see note 3 of Appendix A to Vol. III.). No. 4 belongs to the Christmas oratorio,[3] and so to 1734. In No. 3 the watermark is the shield with crossed swords, and if any date may be founded on this it would at any rate not be the first half-year in Leipzig, as will be shown in No. 41 of this Appendix. No. 2, therefore, remains, and the watermark confirms this.

26 (p. 386). **St, John's Day Cantatas.** There are four Cantatas for St. John's Day :—

1. Herrscher des Himmels erhöre das Lallen.
2. Ich freue mich in dir.
3. Sehet, welch eine Liebe.
4. Süsser Trost, mein Jesu kommt.

No. 1 belongs to the Christmas oratorio. (No. 24. Hear, King of Angels. (Ed. Novello.) No. 2 was composed at the same time as the *Sanctus* in six parts, which Bach afterwards used in the B minor Mass; this *Sanctus* was written between 1735—1737. No. 4 is set aside by the watermark—the shield with crossed swords. No. 3 has been included in the list in note 9, Picander probably wrote the text, which displays a certain resemblance with one known to be by him for 1729.

---

[3] No. 11. " And there were shepherds." (Ed. Novello.)

27 (p. 387). **New Year's Day Cantatas.** There are five complete New Year's Cantatas :—

    1. Gott, wie dein Name so ist auch dein Ruhm.
    2. Herr Gott, dich loben wir.
    3. Jesu, nun sei gepreiset.
    4. Lobe den Herrn, meine Seele.
    5. Singet dem Herrn ein neues Lied.

And besides these the chorus " Fallt mit Danken," out of the Christmas oratorio (No. 36, "Come and thank Him." Ed. Novello.) Of No. 5 Rust thinks that only the four voice parts and two violins ever existed (see Preface to B.-G. XII.,[2] p. v.). However a considerable portion of the autograph score remains in the form of a separate cantata "Lobe Zion deinen Gott," in the Berlin Library. But the absence of any title, and also of the initials *J. J.* at the beginning, shows that this is not perfect, as well as the fact that the cantata begins with an aria in A major and ends with a chorale in D major, while three oboes, three trumpets, and a drum are introduced into this chorus, the remainder being accompanied only by the strings. The connection of this score with the imperfect parts of " Singet dem Herrn " seems to have been recognised by L. Erk (Joh. Seb. Bach's " Mehrstimmige Choralgesänge und geistlichen Arien," Th. II., p. 124). It is very evident, if only from the identity of keys, and of the watermark which are alike; and again from a comparison with the text of the cantata written by Picander for the first day of the Jubilee of the Augsburg Confession, 1730, which is throughout merely a recasting of the verses in this New Year's Cantata. It is clear not merely that the two sets of MS. belong to the same composition, but also that the cantata " Singet dem Herrn " is not lost, as has hitherto been supposed. Even the closing chorale has been preserved in the Trinity cantata "Lobe den Herrn, meine Seele (see No. 52 of this Appendix) "; nothing therefore is lacking but the recitative.

It is probable that the cantata "Singet dem Herrn " was first performed in January, 1724, in the first place from the watermark which differs from those of Nos. 1, 2, and 3. No. 1 is out of the question, because the text was not written by Picander till the New Year of 1729. No. 3, from the watermark, belongs to 1736 (see No. 3, Appendix A to Vol. III.). No. 2 has an eagle for the watermark, but no date can be inferred from this, as it occurs in MSS. of various periods. But a part subsequently added for the violetta has the initial M A, the watermark for 1727—1736. Hence it is not impossible that the work should have been written before 1727 at the same period as No. 5. If so, No. 2 may have been performed so early as 1724, and then No. 5 would belong to 1725—26 or 1727. Still it is more probable that No. 5 belongs to the same brief period as Nos. 2, 3, 4, 11, 25, 29, 30, and 35 of the list in Note 19, as all bear the same watermark. As to No. 4, in the total absence of any original MS. it is impossible to decide to what period it belongs, excepting on internal evidence. The circumstance that in the verse set to a tenor aria allusion is made to a great war then being carried on, in which Saxony itself was not involved, indicates a period after 1723—30, as during those years all Europe was at peace.

28 (p. 389). **Epiphany Cantatas.** Besides " Sie werden aus Saba alle kommen" we have two others for the Epiphany, "Liebster Emanuel" and " Herr, wenn die stolzen Feinde schnauben." This last is in fact the sixth section of the Christmas oratorio, "Lord, when our haughty foes assail us" (Ed. Novello), and the former must be assigned, from the watermark, to a period after 1735 (see No. 3 of Appendix A. of Vol. III.). We here and there find mention (as in Mosewius, Op. cit., p. 21) of a cantata for Epiphany, beginning " Die Könge aus Saba kamen dar," but this is the same cantata, the second movement having been wrongly placed before the first in some copies. The peculiarities noted in this work, as well as the watermark, assign this cantata to the same period as "Christen ätzet," and if the latter was written for Christmas Day, 1723, the former no doubt was composed for Epiphany, 1724.

29 (p. 392). **Cantatas for the Purification.**

1. Der Friede sei mit dir.
2. Erfreute Zeit im neuen Bunde.
3. Ich habe genug.
4. Ich habe Lust.
5. Ich lasse dich nicht.
6. Mit Fried und Freud ich fahr dahin.

No. 5 belongs to the year 1727 (see ante, p. 412). No. 3, as will presently be proved, must have been written in about 1730. No. 6 is of the period subsequent to 1735. It cannot be absolutely proved that, of the first two, it was the second that was performed in 1724. No. 4 is lost, and the only trace of its existence is in Breitkopf's list for Michaelmas, 1761, p. 19, where we find "Bach's, Joh. Seb., Capellm. und Musik-directors in Leipzig cantate : *In Fest. Purificat. Mariae.* Ich habe Lust zu, etc., *à 2 Oboi, 2 Violini, Viola, 4 Voci, Basso ed Organo, à* 1 thl. 4 grs." This statement does not deserve absolute confidence, for a few lines farther on two cantatas are entered under Bach's name, which are certainly not by him, and the publisher, J. G. J. Breitkopf, in his preface, apologises for possible mistakes. Still there is no means of proving that "Ich habe Lust" is not genuine. No. 1 was used for the Purification and for Easter Tuesday. In its present form it is not exactly suited to either day. The first movement, a bass recitative, and the closing chorale " Hier ist das rechte Osterlamm," are connected only with Easter, and more particularly with the Gospel for Easter Tuesday. The aria, on the other hand, and the recitative that follows deal exclusively with the feelings aroused by the Gospel for the Puri-fication. As the aria is the only independent composition in the cantata that is cast in any definite form, it must have been adapted to the earlier date, for the Purification, and only remodelled later for the Easter festival. Still we can hardly suppose that the aria, the recitative, and perhaps some other chorale better suited to the day were at first all it consisted of. This is a question that could only be solved by the discovery of the original MS., which, at present, is not known. The text I take to be Franck's; the music I also ascribe to the Weimar period, and any one who compares it with the first aria in the the cantata, "Komm, du süsse Todesstunde," will certainly share my opinion. In each we find a chorale in one part, allotted to a solo voice, and allied to the emotional character of the piece; in the first case, "Wenn ich einmal soll scheiden," and here "Welt ade! ich bin dein müde"—words which freely reproduce the sentiment of the text of the aria. The combination with the instrumental parts is also identical, many passages are almost exactly alike, and so is the fundamental feeling of the two pieces. If the cantata was written in Weimar we must still hesitate to assume that it could have been performed again before 1724, since Bach would surely have prepared some new piece for the first occurrence of the Purification rather than have repeated a composition so small and unpretending, notwithstanding its depth of feeling. Nor is there anything to hinder our regarding No. 2 as the composition in question; the watermark in fact indicates this very period.

30 (p. 392). **The Cantatas for Easter Day** are five in number:—

1. Christ lag in Todesbanden.
2. Denn du wirst meine Seele.
3. Der Himmel lacht.
4. Ich weiss, dass mein Erlöser lebt.
5. Kommt eilet und laufet.

No. 2 is a work of Bach's youth (see Vol. I., p. 229). He remodelled it, however, for use at Leipzig, but even this was when he was but thirty years old. No. 3 was composed at Weimar, but certainly not for the first Easter of his residence there. No. 4 was also written at Weimar (see Vol. I., p. 501). No. 5 stands in connection with the cantata for the second day of Easter, "Bleib bei uns," and this was also written, as I shall presently prove, in his thirtieth year. Only No. 1 remains, and the watermark assigns this also to the period between 1724—27.

31 (pp. 399 and 404). Of **Whitsuntide Cantatas**, four remain:—

1. Erschallet ihr Lieder.
2. O ewiges Feuer.
3. Wer mich liebet.
4. Wer mich liebet (a longer setting).

No. 2 is re-arranged from a wedding cantata. Even if it were not improbable that Bach should have produced a mere re-arrangement for his first Whitsuntide, it can be shown that No. 2 was written at the same time as Kirnberger's copy of the St. Matthew Passion. It can be determined with tolerable accuracy when Kirnberger's copy was made; here it suffices to note that the St. Matthew Passion was composed in 1729. As regards Nos. 3 and 4, I would refer the reader to Vol. I., pp. 512 and 631. It will there be seen that No. 3 is assigned to 1716 and No. 4 to 1735.

Notwithstanding a date on an old copy of the score of No. 3, it is certain that this cantata was not written in 1731, because the original parts, are on paper bearing the watermark of 1723—27, while the autograph score has a watermark which does not recur on any Leipzig MS. Bach must therefore have had new copies made of the parts early in Leipzig, and of course with a view to a performance. It cannot be proved with any certainty that this was not in 1724. But here, again, it is probably safe to assume that Bach would not come forward with an old work. If, however, this was the case, No. 1 must be assigned to Whitsuntide, 1725; it was certainly composed before 1730. In that year an independent and separate *Rückpositiv* was added to the organ in St. Thomas' (see No. 15 of this Appendix). This was not brought into use in the duet, as we may see from the original parts, till a second performance of the cantata; originally the *cantus firmus* in the duet was given to an instrument, and Bach could certainly not have done this if he had had the *Rückpositiv* at his command when he first composed the work. We farther gather that this mus have been before 1728, since the parts prepared for the revival of the work have the watermark M A, and the paper with this mark was used by Bach after the autumn of 1727. The watermark of the older parts is given in this woodcut, and it is in paper of remarkably

fine and thick quality. The same paper was used in some of the original parts of the Christmas Cantata "Christus ätzet diesen Tag," and in some of the autograph parts of "Wachet betet." This, which was written in Weimar, was often performed in Leipzig between 1723 and 1727, either 1723 or 1725 (see No. 23 of this Appendix). Moreover, the same paper is found in the autograph score, and some of the original parts of the Cantata "Himmelskönig, sei willkommen," which was also composed in Weimar for Palm Sunday, and performed at least twice in Leipzig at the festival of the Annunciation, since there no music was performed on Palm Sunday, as it was in Lent. One performance, to judge from the watermark M A, must have been about 1730, the other between 1723—27 (see No. 19 of this Appendix). But this cantata, of which the text underwent no alterations, could only be used for the Annunciation when this festival fell on Palm Sunday (see ante, p. 271). This happened in 1723 and 1725; Bach, however, was not yet in Leipzig on Palm Sunday, 1723, and thus the first performance of this cantata, "Himmelskönig," must have taken place March 25, 1725. We may therefore limit the possible period of the composition of "Erschallet ihr Lieder" to 1723—25. In 1723 Bach was not yet in a position to perform the Whitsuntide music in the churches of St. Nicholas and St. Thomas, so this cantata, if it was composed then, can only have been intended for the University Church. This hypothesis is contradicted by the fact that it seems to have been composed at the same time as the cantata "Weinen Klagen," for Jubilate Sunday, which falls four weeks before Whitsuntide.

The paper on which they are written is the same; the structure of the text is very similar, and both are undoubtedly by Franck; and in both these cantatas we find double viola parts, as also in the Easter cantata, "Christ lag in Todesbanden," and these would have been of no use at Leipzig. If "Weinen Klagen" and "Erschallet ihr Lieder" were composed in the same year, this cannot have been 1723, since in that year Bach's official work did not begin at the University Church till Whitsuntide, and not till the first Sunday after Trinity as Cantor of St. Thomas'. Hence we must decide on 1724 and 1725.

32 (p. 400). **In the Cantata "O heilges Geist,"** the watermark is the only evidence of the date (see No. 19 of this Appendix), besides the fact of the text being by Franck. Bach made use of his writings in the early time of his residence in Leipzig, but he had not yet entered on his office of Cantor by Trinity Sunday, 1723. The MS. is in the Amalien Bibliothek at Berlin, and in the handwriting of Anna Magdalena Bach.

33 (p. 401). **Cantatas for the Second Sunday after Christmas.** A Sunday after New Year's Day (the second Sunday after Christmas) does not occur every year. During Bach's residence it fell in 1724, 1727, 1728, 1729, 1733, 1734, 1735, 1738, 1739, 1740, 1744, 1745, 1746, 1749, and 1750. We may also throw out of this list 1728, since, in consequence of the death of the Queen Christiana Eberhardine, from September 7, 1727, till Epiphany 1728, "all organ playing, and all other stringed or jovial music, part singing in all the churches, at weddings, baptisms, funerals, in the streets, or by scholars at the doors," &c., were forbidden.

We have a second cantata for the second Sunday after Christmas,

"Ach Gott, wie manches Herzelied" (B.-G., XII.,[2] No. 58). The original parts have the watermark M A, indicating that it was composed either in 1729 or 1733—35. It is not very probable that Bach should have composed a second work in these years for a Sunday which does not regularly recur, and is of no particular importance, and the extensive use of the simple four-part chorale makes it almost certain that "Schau lieber Gott" was an early work, since this mode of treatment is frequent in the early Leipzig period, for instance in "Dazu ist erschienen der Sohn Gottes" (see No. 25 of this Appendix), and in the cantata written for the first Sunday after Epiphany, 1724, "Mein liebster Jesus ist verloren." Irrespective of these considerations, the watermark assigns this cantata to the period between 1723—1727 (see No. 19 of this Appendix), that is either 1724 or 1727. The treatment of the chorale seems akin to that in "Dazu ist erschienen" and "Mein liebster Jesus," and the text has an unmistakable resemblance to this last. In each we find a Bible verse set *Arioso*, with a figured bass in imitation, and a text for an aria, consisting of four trochaic, and two dactylic lines, of four feet each, in a form which is rarely met with in Bach's compositions, though it occurs in the cantata by Franck, "Der Friede sei mit dir" (see No. 29 of this Appendix).

34 (p. 403). "**Mein liebster Jesus ist verloren.**" The original score and parts are in the Berlin Library. The score is imperfect: it contains the whole of the first number, the second only in a fragment, the third minus the text, the fourth in a fragment; the remainder is wanting. In each of the figured bass parts are the words *senza basso*, but there is an autograph figured part for the harpsichord in A major. The harpsichord bass in this works throughout with the continuo of the score, but an octave lower, and is figured even in the closing cadence, and wherever the oboes are silent. It is easy here to see the use made of the harpsichord as an instrument for conducting from (see ante, p. 328). It cannot be meant to be essential to the whole effect, since its natural tendency to give a light and brilliant character to the piece is counteracted by the added weight in the bass; but it was very useful in keeping the performers together, being clearly audible to those who sat near, and yet not so strong as to intrude on the audience. The chords in the figured bass during the rests for the oboes serve the purpose of rendering the progression of the harmony more solid and intelligible to the other players, but they are not essential to the effect on the hearer, because the harmonic progression is perfectly accounted for by the bass. Consequently, indeed, the harpsichord is not mentioned in Breitkopf's list for Michaelmas, 1761, and it is simply styled "Cantata: In Dom. I. Epiph. Mèin liebster Jesus ist, etc., à 2 Oboi, 2 Violini, Viola, 4 Voci, Basso ed Organo." It may be assumed that the same method was followed by Bach in similar solo pieces, as for instance the soprano aria in the Ascension Oratorio (B.-G., II., p. 35).

35 (p. 403). "**Jesus schläft.**" B.-G., XX.,[1] No. 81. The fourth Sunday after Eiphany occurred during Bach's life at Leipzig only in the years 1725, 1728, 1731, 1733, 1736, 1738, 1739, 1741, 1742, 1744, 1747, 1749, and 1750. Hence, as the watermark assigns the cantata to a period between 1723 and 1727 (see No. 19 of this Appendix), it must have been composed in 1726 or 1727, if not indeed in 1724. But 1727 is out of the question, because the Feast of the Purification fell on the fourth Sunday after Epiphany, and we must therefore decide between 1724 and 1726. On the last page of the autograph score there is a fragmentary sketch of the first chorus of the Epiphany cantata " Sie werden aus Saba alle kommen." From this it appears that both the cantatas were composed at about the same time, for, when we consider Bach's free use of music paper, it is incredible that after the lapse of at least two years he would have used a sheet which had been previously used for the first sketch of " Sie Werden aus Saba." Thus, if this work was composed in 1724, " Jesus schläft " must have been also.

36 (p. 407) " **Siehe zu, dass deine Gottesfurcht.**" The chronology is based in the first instance on the watermark (see No. 19 of this Appendix), and on the resemblance of the first subject of this cantata with that for Trinity Sunday, " O heilges Geist." No further data are available, but no one can fail to attribute great importance to this resemblance who has duly observed, again and again, the way in which Bach was never satisfied with one attempt in any new or peculiar form, but could not rest till he had worked out its powers of utterance on all sides, and in a certain sense exhausted it.

37 (p. 407). "**Lobe den Herrn meine Seele.**" The Gospel for the twelfth Sunday after Trinity relates the miraculous healing of one born deaf and dumb ; of course it is not impossible to connect with this event a cantata of thanksgiving for the numberless blessings bestowed by God on man throughout life, but, apart from any other motive, it seems remote enough. When we carefully consider the details of the text we must be convinced that the first purpose of this cantata was not a performance on the twelfth Sunday after Trinity. Nor need we seek far to discover what this main purpose was, for about the same time as this Sunday fell the annual election of the Town Council ; and if we compare it with the words of other " Rathswahl cantatas," as " Preise Jerusalem den Herrn " (B.-G., XXIV., No. 119) and " Wir danken dir Gott " (B.-G., V.,[1] No. 29), their general resemblance shows that the Rathswahl must have determined the choice of the text. Moreover Bach, in order to emphasise its purpose, subsequently had the text remodelled, in part giving it a distinct allusion to the municipal authorities. This alteration, which involved a change in the music, was made about 1730, for the sheets with the new parts inserted among the old ones have the watermark M A (see No. 43 of this Appendix), while the older ones have the watermark of 1723—27 (see the B.-G.

edition for a comparison of the two forms). In bar 16 of the original composition there is a choice of two readings in the text, "Sprich dein kräftig Hephata"—"Speak, the almighty Epphatha." This refers directly to the Gospel for the day, and could be sung so at the Sunday service; but over the word "Hephata" the more general "gnädig Ja" ("Gracious Yea") is inserted. It is easy to detect that this has been written in by Bach himself, after the part had been finished by Anna Magdalena Bach. This variant in the text can have nothing to do with the alterations made in 1730, for those involved the removal of the original recitative and the insertion of another. We may then certainly infer: (1) That the first performance of this cantata in the service on the occasion of the Council election must have been between 1723 and 1727. (2) That the performance for the Sunday must have preceded that for the election; and since, from the first, the cantata was evidently better fitted for the latter than for the former purpose, both performances must be ascribed to the same year, and this must be a year in which the twelfth Sunday after Trinity preceded the election. In 1723 Bach composed another cantata for the election (see ante, p. 362); in 1726 and 1727 the Sunday came after the election. We have to choose between 1724 and 1725. I must decide on 1724, and the reason is at hand; in 1724 the election was on Monday, August 28, the next day after the twelfth Sunday after Trinity, and this would probably suggest to Bach the possibility of composing a piece which might serve for both occasions (compare No. 40 of this Appendix).

38 (p. 411). "Bringet her dem Herrn Ehre seines Namens." (The reader who is interested in comparing Bach's verses with Picander's will find both poems at length in the German edition of this biography, Vol. II., p. 993. Translators). On comparing the two texts it is easy to detect that, irrespective of the Bible text and chorale, the lines by Bach are largely derived from Picander. Though no whole stanza has been borrowed from it many entire lines are repeated almost word for word, and special stress must be laid on the resemblance of their general purport. In both a feeling of rejoicing in the House and Word of God is the ruling sentiment, and the Gospel for the seventeenth Sunday after Trinity strictly speaking does not give rise to this. It is only in one place that the sanctity of the Sabbath is mentioned at all, and there Jesus acts in an opposite sense. It is only by a reference to the original source of the poem that we can understand how it should have occurred to Bach to compose this cantata for this particular Sunday. Picander's verses form the sequel to a satire in rhymed Alexandrines reflecting on the worldly and unworthy use of the Sabbath by the multitude; the poet there exhorts us to keep holy the Sabbath day, and closes with the hymn. Thus, without the antecedent lines by Picander, the cantata text, as used for this Sunday, is unintelligible. There can be no doubt therefore that Bach's and Picander's poems must have been written about the same time (see too the remarks as to

the Michaelmas cantata, p. 408). Accordingly this cantata must have
been composed for September 23, 1725, and is an inseparable companion
piece to the Michaelmas cantata first performed in this year. No
autograph copy exists, but a MS. by Harrer, Bach's successor as
Cantor, is a tolerable substitute; it is in the Berlin Library. The text
of the chorale is not given, and Erk (Choralgesänge No. 13) thinks it
was verse vi. of "Auf meinen lieben Gott." It seems to me that the
last verse of "Wo soll ich fliehen hin" is more suited to the idea of
the composer.

39 (p. 412). **"Herz und Mund und That."** The first four
sheets have the Weimar watermark, the last two M A; the parts on the
other hand have the mark of the period between 1723—27 (see No. 19
of this Appendix). We find the M A paper used throughout for the first
time in the autograph parts of the mourning ode for Queen Christiana
Eberhardine, which was finished October 15, 1727. Hence the new
MS. of "Herz und Mund" must have been written at a transition time,
the summer probably of 1727.

40 (p. 413). **Telemann's Influence in certain Cantatas**
of the early Leipzig period. In No. 27 of this Appendix I have already
spoken of the cantata "Herr Gott dich loben wir," and shown that it
is possible, but not probable, that it should have been composed by
January 1, 1724. Strictly speaking nothing can be inferred from the
watermark beyond the fact that it cannot have been written later than
1736. For the period during which Bach used paper marked M A
extended from 1727 to 1736; but during this time he used various other
kinds of paper, consequently there is nothing to hinder our supposing
that this New Year's cantata was composed later than 1727, and then
only completed in 1736 by the addition of the well-known Violetta part.
My reasons for attributing it to the earlier date are founded on internal
evidence; the imitation of Telemann's style is so conspicuous that it
cannot have been unconscious and accidental, but clearly betrays a
purpose; and this purpose is accounted for by the position, as to
musical taste, in which Bach stood during his first years at Leipzig.
These made a certain reference to the ruling taste desirable, nor was
Bach unwilling, within the limits set by his own character and powers.
By 1730 he himself had become the ruling authority in matters of
musical taste in Leipzig, and I know no example of his having subsequently set so deliberately to work to write in a style not his own.

Even Winterfeld expressed an opinion that Bach had been deeply
influenced by the art of the greatest masters of his time (Ev. Kir. III.,
p. 385). As to the fact I agree with him, but I cannot regard the
instances he adduces as satisfactory evidence. I can find nothing in
the Cantatas "Jesus schläft" and "Halt im Gedächtniss" which
points to the direct influence of the Hamburg masters. Nor is
Winterfeld's suggestion a happy one, that Bach first became intimate
with their music at the time when he wrote these compositions;

it will be seen, when speaking of the Passion music, that even in Weimar Bach had a Passion set by Keiser performed. As regards the cantata "Gedenke Herr," in which Hasse's influence is said to be perceptible (Ev. Kir., III., p. 386), until more reliable evidence is forthcoming I am absolutely incredulous as to its genuineness. Breitkopf's list for the Michaelmas book fair, 1761, in which it figures under Bach's name, is insufficient warranty, as has been said in No. 29 of this Appendix, and so too is the MS. copy (44 in the Joachimsthal Gymnasium at Berlin). The first chorus of the cantata shows a few points of resemblance to the final chorus of Part I. of the St. Matthew Passion; but these are mere similarity, the true spirit of Bach is not in this, still less in either of the other pieces. In the whole work there are scarcely any polyphonous passages, and not one striking combination. Single passages avail not; the whole effect is to me conclusive.

41 (p. 415). **The Shield and Crossed Swords watermark.** The autograph score and the original parts, in the Berlin Library, have the watermark of a shield with crossed swords; this is very frequent in paper of that time, and it occurs in paper used by Bach at the most various periods of his life. The form of the outline varies considerably, however, and where the well-known peculiar Saxon shield is not recognisable no importance is to be attached to the circumstance. The sign occurs in Cöthen MSS., as in the orchestra Partita in B minor (see No. 10 of this Appendix), in portions of the St. John Passion; again in the cantata "Gott, wie dein Name," written for the New Year, 1729, and in the autograph alterations of "Vergnügte Pleissenstadt" written in 1728; in portions of the St. Luke Passion, in the cantatas "Ihr werdet weinen" and "Gott fähret auf" of 1735, and in a report to the Council made by Bach with reference to his dispute with Ernesti, August 12, 1736. This, however, does not exclude the possibility of Bach having used paper with a similar watermark early in his residence at Leipzig, but the evidence at hand, so far, does not allow us to assume that he did so during the first year and a half. The cantatas which have this watermark and no other data as to the time of their composition are:—

1. Gottlob, nun geht das Jahr zu Ende, Sunday after Christmas.
2. Unser Mund sei voll Lachens (see No. 24 of this Appendix).
3. Liebster Jesu, mein Verlangen, first Sunday after Epiphany.

That all three belong to the Leipzig period is beyond a doubt from the character of the writing and of the compositions themselves. No. 1 may, at soonest, have been first performed on December 31, 1724, since in 1723 there was no Sunday after Christmas; No. 2 on December 25, 1724, for reasons given above; No. 3 on January 7, 1725, since "Mein liebster Jesus ist verloren" was written for 1724 (see No. 27 of this Appendix). The fact that the text of "Gottlob, nun geht das Jahr," is by Neumeister forbids our placing it later than 1726, because Bach evidently did not have recourse to his "Fünffach Kirchenandachten" after he had become acquainted with Picander. The same may be said concerning Franck's text "Alles nur nach Gottes Willen," and this was certainly composed in Leipzig at an early date, but not before 1725.

42. (Incorporated in note 49, p. 703).

43 (p. 431). **The original parts of " Liebster Gott, wann werd ich sterben ?"** display in some of the sheets a small shield-shaped outline, in some a C, and in some a device with a scroll above and two hanging sack-shaped tips, which is not in the middle of the page but nearer to the fold down the sheet. This mark only occurs again in the original MS. of the cantata " Ihr, die ihr euch von Christo nennet," of the year 1723 or 1724 (see No. 22 of this Appendix); we must therefore assign " Liebster Gott " to the same date. The original parts in the Thomasschule are in D major instead of E major, and in the first chorus the parts of the two oboi d'amore are given to two violins *concertante*. A comparison with copies of the score—for the original score is lost—proves that E major was. the original key. As the introduction of the oboi d'amore precludes the possibility of its having been written earlier than in Leipzig, while the parts must have been copied out by 1723 or 1724, it is clear that Bach must have made the arrangement—which greatly facilitates the labours of the oboe players —soon after composing the cantata, and probably before it was performed in public.

44. **The watermark M A as marking a period.** I here give a list of cantatas, with secular and occasional music, which constitute this group of MSS., including a motett and a mass. Many have, besides the M A, other watermarks which shall be presently discussed.

1. Ach Gott, wie manches Herzeleid (C major).
2. Der Geist hilft unsrer Schwachheit auf (Motett, 1729).
3. Der Herr ist mein getreuer Hirt.
4. Erhöhtes Fleisch und Blut.
5. Es ist das Heil uns kommen her.
6. Es ist nichts Gesundes an meinem Leibe.
7. Gelobet sei der Herr, mein Gott.
8. Geschwinde, geschwinde (the contest between Phœbus and Pan).
9. Herr Gott, Beherrscher aller Dinge.
10. Ich glaube, lieber Herr.
11. Ich liebe den Höchsten.
12. Ich ruf zu dir, Herr Jesu Christ (1732).
13. In allen meinen Thaten (1734).
14. Jauchzet, frohlocket (Christmas Oratorio, 1734).
15. Jauchzet Gott in allen Landen.
16. Jesu nun sei gepreiset.
17. *Kyrie* and *Gloria* of the B minor Mass (1733). B.-G., VI., p. xv.

18. Lass, Fürstin, lass noch einen Strahl (Mourning ode for Queen Christiana Eberhardine, 1727).
19. Lasst uns sorgen (cantata in honour of the birth of the Crown Prince-Elector, 1733).
20. Nun danket alle Gott.
21. Preise dein Glücke, gesegnetes Sachsen (*Cantata gratulatoria in adventum Regis*, 1734).
22. Schweight stille, plaudert nicht (Coffee Cantata).
23. Schwingt freudig euch empor.
24. Sei Lob und Ehr dem höchsten Gut.
25. Tönet, ihr Pauken (cantata in honour of the Queen, 1733).
26. Wachet auf, ruft uns die Stimme (1731 or 1742).
27. Was frag ich nach der Welt.
28. Was Gott thut, das ist wohlgethan (in G major, a setting of the Hymn).
29. Was soll ich aus dir machen, Ephraim.
30. Wer da glaubet und getauft wird.
31. Wer nur den lieben Gott lässt walten.
32. Wir danken dir Gott (1731).

The oldest of these works is the mourning ode. Bach finished it, as stands attested in his own handwriting, on the autograph score, October 15, 1727. We find the dates noted on others, as they are given above. No. 2 was written for the funeral of Ernesti, who died October 16, 1729. The date of No. 20 is doubtful, because it was written for the twenty-seventh Sunday after Trinity, which occurred only twice during Bach's residence at Leipzig (see ante, p. 459). With regard to No. 8, the text is by Picander, and occurs in Part III. of his poems (Gedichte, p. 501). The preface to the volume is dated February, 1732, and the title to the poem itself states that this *Drama per musica* had already been performed; at p. 564 of the same volume we find the *Caffee cantate*.

It must finally be mentioned that in the Berlin Library a MS. copy of the Partita out of Part II. of the Clavierübung exists which has hitherto been ascribed to Bach himself, but which appears to me to be in the writing of his wife, and which has the watermark M A. According to a MS. note by J. G. Walther, in his own copy of the Lexicon (now in the collection of the Gesellschaft der Musikfreunde of Vienna), Part II. of the Clavierübung came out for the Easter fair, 1735. After the work was printed Bach could of course have had no farther occasion to copy it or to have it copied; this MS. must therefore date before 1735; but since Part II. was certainly not composed till Part I. was finished, not earlier than 1731.

The period when Bach ceased using the paper marked M A was about 1736. On August 13, 15, and 19, 1736, Bach wrote three documents in the matter of his quarrel with Ernesti, and the watermark in the paper is a man on horseback blowing a post horn; but in Bach's musical MS. this watermark occurs but twice so far as is known: in the cantata "Schleicht, spielende Wellen," and in the autograph score of the C minor concerto for two claviers and strings, now in the Berlin Library (B.-G., XXI.,[2] No. 3, and preface, p. IX.). And of the latter MS. only the first eight sheets have this watermark; the last has the letters M A, and it can be seen that this had shortly before been intended by Bach for another purpose, and then laid aside, for it has upon it the sketch of the commencement of a cantata in D major. The trumpet begins:—

This autograph belongs to the period when Bach was ceasing to use the M A paper. No. 28 is to be assigned to this period, and it must at the same time be dated 1736, because it has the same mode of notation for the oboe d'amore as the cantata "Schleicht, spielende Wellen" (see No. 50 below). The most frequently recurring watermark in the last period, beginning in 1736, is a half moon, somewhat differing from that of the period between 1723—27, but the paper is more easily distinguished by the absence of the corresponding watermark on the other half sheet (see Note 3 of Vol. III., on this watermark). By 1737 the M A mark seems to have disappeared; in a few autographs, as in "Wo soll ich fliehen" and in "Jesu nun sei gepreiset," both marks occur.

45 (p. 438). **The date of the Cantata " Wer nur den lieben Gott lässt walten "** is approximately known from the watermark M A (see the foregoing note 44). It is farther restricted by the fact that in 1731 the fifth Sunday after Trinity coincided with St. John the Baptist's day, while another cantata " Siehe ich will viel Fischer aussenden" was written for either 1732 or 1733; this however does not help us greatly. But a close study of the text reveals the probability of its being by Picander. It includes a paraphrase of the fifth verse of a hymn by Neumark, which much resembles a poem by Picander (Part II. of the Gedichte, p. 89, " Bey dem Grabe Herrn C. K. Freyberg, July 6, 1728"), and certain references to verses of the Bible such as he was wont to display his knowledge of the Scriptures in. And by comparing the dates of this funeral poem with that of the performance of the cantata we may infer that this was probably June 27, 1728. Nor can it be regarded as seriously adverse to this conclusion that, of the three continuo parts for this contata, the original MS. of the organ part is on paper with the half moon, which is the watermark of the latest period, beginning in 1735, for this part may very likely have been added at a later date. (The student who is interested in a detailed comparison of the cantata texts is referred to the German original of this work, Vol. II., App. A., Note 34, Page 798.)

46 (pp. 444, 445, 447, 455, and 473). The watermarks here figured occur

in the autograph score, and most of the original parts of the following compositions, ten in all :—

1. Der Herr ist mein Getreuer Hirt.
2. Ehre sei Gott in der Höhe.
3. Geist und Seele sind verwirret.
4. Gott, wie dein Name.
5. Herr Gott Beherrscher aller Dinge.
6. Ich bin vergnügt.
7. Ich habe genug.
8. Ich liebe den Höchsten.
9. Lobe den Herrn, den Mächtigen König.
10. Der Streit zwischen Phöbus und Pan, a secular cantata.

In the original MSS. of Nos. 1, 5, 7, 8, and 10, we find mixed with these watermarks the M A mark (see No. 44 of this Appendix), which of itself indicates certain limits to their date of composition. No. 4 has a text from Picander's cantatas for the year, and was written for January 1, 1729. But in No. 3 an obbligato organ part is introduced, and this cannot have been earlier than 1730 (see No. 15 of this Appendix). With regard to No. 5, the original parts, all marked M A, are written by Ph. Emanuel Bach, and have only a few additions in Seb. Bach's hand, so it must have been composed before 1733, when Emanuel Bach left his father's roof for Frankfort on the Oder. No. 7 underwent a subsequent revisal, and the new parts prepared in consequence have for the most part the watermark of an eagle and for counterpart HR (H I R). These marks, which rarely occur together in Bach's MSS., are found combined in one earlier, in the text of the cantata " Preise dein Glücke, gesegnetes Sachsen," in Bach's own hand, which is added to the autograph score. This was performed October 5, 1734, so No. 7 must have been written earlier. No. 8 has in the autograph score a long passage written by W. Friedemann Bach in the staves for violins and violas, from bar 24 ; and farther on again other portions are in his hand. Now in 1733 Friedemann Bach, who till then had lived with his father, became organist to the Sophienkirche at Dresden. In this year, moreover, all church music was suspended from Estomihi Sunday till the fourth Sunday after Trinity, in consequence of the public mourning, and No. 8 is a Whitsuntide cantata. It must therefore have

been written in 1732 at latest. No. 10 is set to a text written by
Picander; it occurs in Part III. of his poems, p. 501, and the Preface
to this Vol. is dated February 18, 1732. The secular poems (Schertz-
haffte Gedichte, beginning at p. 241), most of which are dated, besides
having titles indicating the occasions for which they were written are,
with few exceptions, arranged in chronological order. But that used
for this cantata, 10, has no date, whence we may conclude that it was
written for no special occasion, but for an ordinary performance by the
Musical Society of which Bach was at that time director. From the
order of the remaining poems and the position this one fills, we may
ascribe it with certainty to the year 1731; and since above it we find
the words "performed in a *Dramatc*," the music must have been composed when Picander's volume was printed, and we may therefore
assign the composition to the summer of that year. Thus we have
determined the church year 1730—31 as being most probably the period
when these ten cantatas were composed, and 1731—32 as its latest
term. It is to be remarked, however, that there are among them two
(Nos. 3 and 9) for the twelfth Sunday after Trinity; they must therefore extend through two church years; but to which each cantata
belongs can only be guessed with more or less probability—in many
cases not even guessed.

With regard to No. 2, the preface to B.-G., XIII.,[1] has an inaccurate
statement. The autograph fragment contains, before the bass recitative "Das Kind ist mein," the last nineteen bars of the alto aria
"O du angenehmer Schatz." This fragment consists of only one
folio sheet, which is marked 7 in the top right hand corner.
Judging from this, the opening chorus must have been of considerable
length, and perhaps introduced by an instrumental symphony; the
closing chorale "Wohlan so will ich mich" is included in Erk's collection, No. 278, but the text is inaccurate, and he does not mention the
source whence he derived it.

The autograph score of No. 4 has the watermark figured above in the
first two sheets only; the two last have the shield with crossed swords.
They are evidently of later date, and contain the two borrowed movements of the cantata "Jesus soll mein erstes Wort" (out of "Der
zufriedengestellte Aeolus," and "Lass uns dass Jahr vollbringen"
(out of "Jesu nun sei gepreiset"). The first is lowered and the
second raised a tone, and both are fair copies, while the recitative that
divides them is, on the other hand, a rough copy. Bach probably
began this cantata towards the end of 1730, left it unfinished, and did
not complete it till after 1736.

47 (p. 446). "**Ich habe meine Zuversicht.**" The Berlin Library
possesses a copy of this cantata, formerly belonging to Professor
Fischhoff, of Vienna, transcribed from the original autograph, but of
which the chief part has been lost; some fragments, including bars
24—67 of the first aria, and the second aria from the last crotchet of

bar 24, with the recitative that follows, and the closing chorale, were in the possession of Professor F. W. Jähn, of Berlin. He, after taking a careful copy, gave them to Petter, a collector of autographs in Vienna. The earlier half of the cantata, which included the beginning of the first aria, Petter parted with to Herr Otto Usteri, of Zurich, who was good enough to send it to me to look at in January, 1870. It is numbered 7 in the top right hand corner. This number cannot refer to the paging, since in that case there would be no more than five pages for the introductory organ concerto, a space too small for the first movement only. If the number refers to the sheets, we must suppose that it was not the first movement only, but the whole concerto that served as the introduction; the number of sheets would suffice for this, but would be much too large for the first movement by itself. This suggestion is confirmed by the note on the title-page of Fischhoff's copy, that the organ concerto served as the *Introitus* to the cantata (the chief subject is added in notes). The first two subjects were used again by Bach for the cantata "Wir müssen durch viel Trübsal," the first forming the instrumental intro-duction, while the principal chorus is worked into the *Adagio*. The upper part is taken down an octave, but is not otherwise altered from the original form of the clavier concerto as it is given B.-G., XVII., p. 275. We may suppose that this older form lay at the root of the re-arrangement for the cantata "Ich habe meine Zuversicht," since there is too much in it which is properly suited only to the clavier. The aria "Unerforschlich ist die Weise" is set in E minor for the voice and violoncello, and in D minor for the organ obbligato; according to a note on the cover of the Fischhoff copy, in the original autograph, the voice part in the violin clef was written an octave too high; and since in this, as well as in the Jähn fragment, the aria is in the alto clef, this plainly indicates that in the autograph score both the alto and violin clefs were given. I believe the reason to have been that E minor in the alto clef being in the same notes as D minor in the violin clef, the singer had only to sing his part an octave lower. We often meet with such two-fold notation in Bach (see No. 20 of this Appendix). It naturally follows that Bach must have had this aria sung sometimes in E minor and sometimes in D minor, and in the latter case would perform the organ part on an instrument tuned to chamber pitch. It cannot be denied that the key of E minor is foreign to the scheme of modulation of the work as a whole; still it flows more smoothly with the movements which immediately precede and follow it than that of D minor; when we consider that D minor has already largely predominated, the composer may have thought a digression into a remote key a desirable variety.

48 (pp. 448, 451, 453, 455, 461, 463). **The Watermarks of 1731 —1733.** To determine the date of "Gott soll allein" certain marks must be collated. A small number of Bach's original MSS. have a

shield-shaped watermark supported on each side by palm branches, and bearing a chevron. The cantatas which have this watermark are the following :—-

1. Ach Gott, wie manches Herzeleid, C major.
2. Es wartet alles auf dich.
3. Gelobet sie der Herr.
4. Gott soll allein mein Herze haben.
5. Ich armer Mensch, ich Sündenkneckt.
6. Ich will den Kreuzstab gerne tragen.
7. Siehe ich will viel Fischer aussenden.
8. Vereinigte Zwietracht der wechselnden Saiten.
9. Vergnügte Ruh, beliebte Seelenlust.
10. Was Gott thut, das ist wohl gethan, B major.
11. Wer weiss, wie nahe mir mein Ende.

Of these, No. 8 may be set aside; it is an occasional secular cantata, written for December 11, 1726, but that this cannot be the date at which this group generally was composed is easily proved. Bach must have accidentally used for it a kind of paper which, though the watermark is the same, is itself quite different.

Nos. 1 and 3 have in some of the parts the M A watermark, which assigns them to a date between 1727 and 1736. In Nos. 4 and 11 we find an organ obbligato; this limits them to the years between 1730—1736, and we are still farther limited as to the organ part for No. 11, which is in Bach's own writing. It has a different watermark from the score :—

These marks occur in only two other cantatas, whence we may refer them to the same period, and that a short one. These are :—

1. Herr deine Augen sehen nach dem Glauben.
2. Wir danken dir Gott, wir danken dir.

And in the first of these they only occur in the paper forming the original wrapper, in which they are very distinct. In the second they occur only in the autograph score, while the M A mark distinguishes the parts ; this cantata has also an organ obbligato, and finally from a note in Bach's own hand we learn that it was written for the Rathswahl service on Monday, August 27, 1731. We may therefore assume that this year is the earliest limit of the period during which these cantatas were composed, and this is confirmed by our finding the same paper used for the Credo of the B minor mass. The next point is to ascertain the latest limit. We shall here find that the cantatas in question, with the exception of No. 8, must have originated within a by no means lengthy period. No. 7 was intended for the fifth Sunday after Trinity, which in 1731 coincided with the festival of St. John, and was merged in it. No. 3 is for Trinity Sunday, and so cannot have been written in 1733, the year of the public mourning. No. 5, again, composed for the twenty-second Sunday after Trinity, cannot have been written in 1733, since in that year it fell on the same day as the Reformation festival. No. 1, on the other hand, being composed for the second Sunday after Christmas cannot have been written in 1732, nor in 1730 or 1731, since there was no second Sunday after Christmas in those years. We must therefore date 1733, and this determines a period of about a year and a half, beginning with the tenth Sunday after Trinity, September 9, 1731, and ending with the second Sunday after Christmas, January 4, 1733.

49 (p. 456). **The autograph score of " In allen Meinen Thaten "** (which is published B.-G., XXII., No. 97) is in the possession of Professor Rudorff of Lichterfelde, near Berlin. It consists of six sheets, and the title on the cover is in the hand of Anna Magdalena Bach. The watermark of the wild man and fir tree is to be seen only in the wrapper and the first two sheets, the others have no watermark. These four contain all the cantata after the opening. Not only is the paper different, the staves have been marked with a narrower ruler, and different ink has been used; but whether these are superficial accidents, or the greater part of the work was written later than the beginning, cannot be determined. It is quite possible that a different composition originally followed the opening chorus; this is too short ever to have formed an independent cantata. An investigation of the original parts preserved in the Thomasschule makes a remodelling of the cantata—the first chorus being retained—seem highly probable. These parts were copied in 1735 at the earliest, the watermark of 1723—27 is visible only in the bass and tenor parts. Bach no doubt used for these some blank sheets of paper remaining from the original MS.; that he was careful in such matters has already been mentioned (Vol. I., p. 643). Before the autograph score of this cantata was known, W. Rust had been of opinion that it was an early work, perhaps of the Weimar period; and he thought himself justified in adhering to this view, although the score bears at the end, in Bach's own hand, the words "*Fine. S. D. Gl.* 1734." He founded it on certain discrepancies between the figuring of the organ part and the harmony of the upper parts. There are two original parts written out for the organ, the older in A flat and the later in G. This last is not here of any consequence, for if in one or two places the figured harmony does not agree with that of the other parts, Bach may have intended to alter it subsequently. But the variations in the other organ part certainly

point to the conclusion that it was prepared for an earlier score than that we now possess, and it suggests some quite different original readings. Those adduced by Rust are but three; and of these, that in bar 8, of p. 218 of the B.-G. edition, does not, in my opinion, argue a different progression in the *obbligato* parts; the collision between the *b′* in the second violins and *b′* flat in the organ part is a passing discord, such as we find in innumerable cases in Bach's works. In bar 5 of the same page there is a real discrepancy, the question being as to the presence or absence of a natural before the *e* flat; the older organ part would require *e′* flat, the latter *e′*, in accordance with the score; but there is nothing to hinder us from supposing that in the subsequent performance, for which he used the second organ part, he added the natural. The third deviation is in bar 1 of p. 193, and in the same passage again, bar 2, p. 201, and here, to render the figured bass at all possible, the first half of the bar must be entirely altered. I consider the passage in the organ bass to have been simply incorrectly copied. It not unfrequently occurs that Bach's organ parts do not accurately correspond to the other parts, for in hastily writing them out he often neglected to refer to the score, trusting to his memory for the harmony, and so making mistakes. Thus, in the first chorus of the Cantata "Halt im Gedächtniss," in bar 72 in the continuo, which is not transposed, we find on F sharp in the bass, the chord $\frac{9}{7}$, while in the organ part, which is transposed, we

have $\frac{7}{4}$. Rust has accepted the former, but in my opinion the latter is

the correct form; comparing bars 51 and 102 it is evident that, when figuring the continuo, Bach had in his head a different scheme of harmony from that which was required by the strings. Or if we assume that the chord for the strings was wrongly copied, bar 2 ought to have an analogous harmony, and then it is the organ part that Bach wrote wrong. There is an error in either case. As to the curious clerical mistakes of which Bach was capable even in notation, we have an instance in the Cantata "Angenehmes Wiederau" (B.-G., V.,[1] p. 404, bar 3), where, in five MS. parts written out by himself for violins and violas, he has set down a wholly inaccurate and ill-sounding phrase, and it is clear that at the moment he had in his mind a bass quite unlike what he had previously written. Still, these discrepancies between the organ part and the original score are few and trifling; it seems to me very bold to derive from them so serious an inference as that the date at the end of the score counts for nothing as regards the date of composition, and refers only to that of the copy or of some special performance; it is too contrary to our experience of Bach's practice.

Nor is the evidence as to style, adduced by Rust, convincing. It is precisely in the first movement that I detect that mature and artistic development which, from all we know of Bach's work in Weimar, he had not as yet attained. As regards the final chorale in some parts and its relationship to the Cantata "Wachet, betet," I must remind the reader that this cantata is known to us only through the re-modelled Leipzig form (see No. 23 of this Appendix), and that a composition similar in every respect occurs at the end of the Cantata "Lobe den Herren." The date in the master's own hand, the internal resemblance of the work with other cantatas of the same period, and the watermark in the paper (the letters M A, see No. 44 of this Appendix) all afford such sufficient grounds for assigning the composition of "In allen meinen Thaten" to the year 1734 that Rust's arguments to the contrary are quite inadequate to disprove it.

50 (p. 463). **In the original parts of the Cantata, "Christus der ist mein Leben"** there is no watermark by which to judge of the date of the composition. But the method of notation used for the *oboi d'amore* leads us to assign it to the year 1732. At three different periods Bach adopted three different and unusual methods of noting music for this instrument, and I entirely agree with W. Rust in regarding these as unerring chronological data; see B.-G., XXIII., p. xvi. It may also be added that during the whole of the Leipzig period Bach used for this instrument the same notation as for the ordinary oboe; as in "Es erhob sich ein Streit," 1725; Trauerode, 1727; St. Matthew Passion, 1729; "Es ist das Heil uns kommen her," about 1731; Christmas Oratorio, 1734; "Freue dich, erlöste Schaar," after 1737; "Du Friedefürst," 1744. From this it is plain that it was only occasionally that Bach was compelled to write for *oboi d'amore* which were a minor third lower than chamber pitch; and we have all the more reason, therefore, for assigning all the compositions which exhibit this peculiarity to a narrow period of time, unless other circumstances prove the contrary. The *Kyrie* and *Gloria* of the B minor Mass were presented to the Elector of Saxony, July 27, 1733; in the *Kyrie* we find the *oboi d'amore* in this low pitch, and noted in the same way as in the Cantata "Christus der ist mein Leben." Both these portions of the Mass were at any rate composed by the spring of 1733. (See the next note.) I have, however, one objection to raise against the views taken by Rust (in the preface just referred to). I cannot understand why, at p. xvii., he refers the re-arrangement only of "Lobe den Herrn meine Seele" to a period between 1733 and 1737, on the ground of the notation of the *oboe d'amore*, since it is identically the same in the first state of the work, and it will be seen, on reference to p. 692, that my researches have led me to a different conclusion. Still, the notation of the *oboe d'amore* supports me in assigning it to 1724, for it is the same as that in the Cantatas "Die Elenden sollen essen" and "Die Himmel erzählen," written in 1723. The use of the C-clef on the first line is intended to facilitate the reading of the score (see No. 20 of this Appendix). It is not possible to determine whether the same

method was followed in the score of " Lobe den Herrn," since it is lost, while of the other cantatas it is the parts that are missing.

51 (p. 463). In this cantata, or **Dialogus between Hope and Fear,** there is no watermark. It must, however, be observed that if it is to be assigned to the early Leipzig period, though the form of it is opposed to this inference, it can hardly have been written before 1730—33, since in 1726—29 there was no twenty-fourth Sunday after Trinity, and in 1727 the general mourning put a stop to all music after the thirteenth Sunday after Trinity; and in 1728, when the twenty-fourth Sunday after Trinity fell on November 7, Bach was so busy with other work that it is not likely that he should have found time for this. The twenty-fourth Sunday after Trinity was again wanting in 1734, 1737, 1740, and 1745. The parts for the *oboi d'amore* have the same pitch and notation as in the Cantata " Christus der ist mein Leben " (see No. 50 of this Appendix), so that we may assign them to nearly the same date ; nor is there any reason to prevent our referring them to the same year, 1733. On the same grounds we may fix the performance of the re-modelled form of the grand Magnificat at Christmas, 1732, and the watermark M A agrees with this (see No. 19 of this Appendix).

52 (p. 469). **The Wedding and Jubilee Cantatas.** " Herr Gott, Beherrscher," cannot have been composed later than 1733, for the reasons given in No. 46 of this Appendix. The Jubilee Cantata " Gott man lobet dich in der Stille" was performed June 26, 1730. The text is like those of the first and third Jubilee Cantatas by Picander. These were first reprinted in Sicul's " Des Leipziger Jahr-Buchs Zu dessen Vierten Bande Dreyzehente Fortsetzung." Leip. 1731, p. 1126, with a note that they were composed (that is, the music for them) by the *Cantor oppidano,* Herr Johann Sebastian Bach. In 1732 Picander himself published them in the third part of his " Gedichte," and on comparison it is apparent that the text of the Rathswahl Cantata is adapted to the same music. This fact has already been pointed out by A. Dörffel, the editor of the music, as regards the second aria (" Heil und Seegen " in the Rathswahl Cantata—" Treu im Gläuben " in the Jubilee Cantata). The designation of *Aria* given to the lines in the printed edition by no means excludes the possibility of their being set by Bach as a chorus ; the word in this use only indicates a text of the *da capo* character. On comparing the two texts with the music belonging to them it is evident, from the adaptation of the music to certain words, that it was intended only for the Rathswahl Cantata ; hence this must be the earlier of the two. The text of the Jubilee Cantata suits the music so badly in some places that we might doubt whether they were meant for each other; but the text of the Wedding Cantata " Herr Gott, Beherrscher," suits equally ill, and yet it was certainly sung to the music (B.-G., XIII.,[1] p. xiv). Indeed, the Rathswahl Cantata, in the form in which it exists for us, cannot be in its first state, but must be a later copy and probably

remodelled; on this point I would refer the reader to Dörffel's careful disquisition in the preface to B.-G., XXIV., p. xxxiv.

Though the text of the Rathswahl Cantata is not to be found in Picander's poems he no doubt wrote it, and in the collected edition of his works, p. 192, we find a Rathswahl text, which, apart from the recitatives and closing chorale, corresponds in every part of its metrical structure with the Jubilee text, proving that the third of the Jubilee cantatas, " Wünschet Jerusalem Glück ! " is nothing else than a Rathswahl Cantata with fresh words. Only an *arioso* corresponding to " Der Höchste steh uns ferner bey " is wanting. But Bach does not seem to have set this *arioso* at all; for in " Nützlichen Nach-richten " for 1741, where the text of this Rathswahl Cantata was first printed, it is also wanting. In such investigations as these the re-currence of similar cases strengthens the argument. Thus, at p. 686, it has been seen that the first Jubilee Cantata, " Singet dem Herrn," is founded on an older composition. Thus, not one of these three works was, strictly speaking, new; the first having been written as a New Year's cantata and the two others as Rathswahl cantatas. And with due reserve we may also.trace out something as to the history of the closing chorale of the first Jubilee Cantata, " Es danke Gott," in place of which we find another in the Christmas music. " Lobe den Herrn meine Seele " was also a Rathswahl Cantata for 1724, and we find at the end of it the chorale in question. It is probable that it was trans-ferred hither from the end of the first Jubilee Cantata; and all the more so because we find it again in " Herr Gott, Beherrscher," and there is no doubt as to the relationship between this and the Jubilee Festival, though it is an indirect one.

53 (p. 474). **Cantata for the Purification,** " Ich habe genug." The remarks in the preface to the B.-G. edition as to the original MS. of this cantata I cannot but regard as inaccurate. The part for mezzo-soprano which is there spoken of must certainly, and indeed evidently, have been originally in the key of E minor, and so, properly, for a soprano voice. Afterwards the signature and the accidentals were carefully altered; the signature being ⸬. This does not indicate E flat minor, as this preface asserts, but C minor. The autograph score, in which the cantata is set in C minor, was begun by Bach with the intention of giving the voice part to a mezzo-soprano or an alto, and the voice part of the first aria was even written in the alto clef. Then the composer changed his mind ; he wrote the rest of the cantata for a bass voice, and wrote at the bottom of the first page this note with reference to the aria :—" The voice part must be transposed into the bass." But the whole cantata is written for a mezzo-soprano voice. From this it is plain that the copy in E minor, for a soprano, must have been the first, and there even exists a complete part for the

flute in E minor (subsequently given to the oboe in C minor). It was then set in C minor for an alto or mezzo-soprano, and finally a bass voice was substituted for the alto. A part of the cantata, worked out for the soprano, occurs in Anna Magdalena's book, which thus betrays its original plan and purpose. In the preface to the B.-G. edition it is not mentioned that the score has the autograph note "*Festo Purificationis Mariae. Cantata.*" This explicit designation is not without its bearing on the character of the work.

54 (p. 508). **The Score of the St. Luke Passion** consists of fourteen sheets of closely written paper, and one sheet which serves as a wrapper; on the first page of the wrapper is the title, and the back half of the sheet forms the last two pages of the score. The title is as follows: "*J. J. Passio D. J. C. secundum Lucam à 4 Voci, 2 Hautb., 2 Violini, Viola e Cont.,*" but does not enumerate all the instruments, since there are also flutes and a bassoon. The score has the appearance of having been written at intervals, and it is on three different kinds of paper. The sheet which serves as the cover and sheets 1, 11, 12, and 14 have the watermarks shown on p. 699. Sheets 2 to 10 have the shield with crossed swords; and sheet 13 has the eagle with the corresponding H I R. This mark indicates the year 1734 (see No. 46 of this Appendix); the post-horn and G A W, the years 1731—32. Hence, the score was written between 1731—34, and, as it was in 1731 that the St. Mark Passion was first performed, it may have been produced in Leipzig in 1732—33 or 1734. It probably was not in 1732, since in that year the Passion music had to be performed in the Church of St. Nicholas, in which Bach must have been much straitened for room. The real history of the score appears to me to have been this: Bach would have begun it towards the end of 1732, with a view to performing the work on Good Friday, 1733. The King-Elector died, however, unexpectedly on February 1, 1733, and there was a general mourning in consequence until the fourth Sunday after Trinity. Bach, therefore, laid the work aside for the time, but took it up again in the course of the year and finished it in the early part of 1734, when it was first performed at St. Thomas' on Good Friday. It is evident, both from the style of the work and from the aspect of the MS., that the score, as we possess it, was a revised copy from some quite early work.

55 (p. 509). **Keiser's St. Mark Passion.** That this copy was made at Weimar is proved by the fine and elegant writing which was characteristic of Bach in his youth, and by the watermarks figured in Vol. I., p. 638, which are an unfailing indication of the Weimar period. These parts are preserved in the Berlin Library, and consist of soprano, alto, tenor, and bass, with 1st and 2nd violins, and 1st and 2nd violas—all single copies—and harpsichord. There are also belonging to them duplicates, and an organ part, which were copied at Leipzig. Bach must, therefore, have performed Keiser's St. Mark

Passion again at Leipzig, and (if we may judge from the watermarks of the organ-part, which are the same as those of the cantatas " Denn du wirst meine Seele," "Gott fähret auf," and " Gott de rHerr ist Sonn," to be discussed in No. 2 of Appendix A. to Vol. III.) this must have been about 1735. In the same library there is a copy of this Passion, which must have been in Bach's possession, for the whole of the words are in his writing, as Chrysander pointed out in his life of Handel. It is dated 1720, which has been subsequently altered to 1729. It is clear that this cannot refer to the time of its composition, which must have been before 1725 at the latest.

56 (p. 522). **The St. John Passion** in the B.-G. edition, Vol. XII.,[1] was edited by W. Rust after a most careful critical study of all the MS. authorities, and his conclusions may be taken as final so far as regards the assigning of the different MSS. to the several phases of remodelling it underwent, and the evidence of at least four performances of the work during Bach's lifetime. With regard to the chronology, however, much remains to be desired, and I will here give the results of my own investigations.

The oldest copy of the score of the St. John Passion no longer exists. The one we possess is a much later copy, and only the first twenty pages are in Bach's writing. The parts copied out for the first performance, on the other hand, still exist, and, with them, some that were added for a second performance, and others for a fourth. It is chiefly from this collection of parts that we are able to judge of the alterations which Bach made by degrees in this work. The question now is when these three different batches of parts were prepared. It will be best to begin with the middle set, which have the same watermarks as the cantatas enumerated at p. 680, and thus belong to the period between 1723—27. But he did not set the first copies of parts altogether aside at the performance for which the second set was made. This we learn, 1st, from finding the "concerto," soprano, tenor, and first violin parts of the old set stitched up with a new leaf on which the opening chorus, composed for the second performance, is written; 2nd, from the old continuo part, in which a sheet has been inserted for the arioso " Betrachte meine Seele " and the aria which follows " Erwäge "—also new compositions. Both the early sheets, the inserted portion, have the watermark M A, and, as has been said, this distinguishes another group of cantatas written between the years 1723—1727 (see ante, p. 696). This second set of parts must, therefore, have been written just about this time, that is to say, in 1727.

As has been said, the chorus " Herr unser Herrscher " is already substituted for the original chorus " O Mensch, bewein dein Sünde." Hence, Rust's hypothesis cannot be correct, that this chorus was expunged from the St. John Passion, and used instead at the end of the first part of the St. Matthew Passion (which was not written till 1729) in order to give it a more dignified close when it was remodelled later—thus assigning the composition to a date after 1729. Why should its position have been changed? It is impossible to suppose that Bach was no longer satisfied with it. If this had been so with some of the arias the reason might have been obvious; but Bach never wrote a more perfect composition than "O Mensch, bewein," nor a piece more overflowing with the genuine sentiment of Passion music. Thus, he must have used it previously for some other purpose, and from its character this can only have been in some other Passion. But then, during Lent and Passion week, concerted music was performed only on one occasion, namely, Vespers on Good Friday; not to omit a single possibility, however, it may be mentioned that on Quinquagesima Sunday, though not properly in Lent, it was usual to introduce some reference to Christ's Passion into the music performed. Still, it is almost impossible that Bach should have used this chorus for the service on that Sunday; 1st, because it was quite contrary to his practice to despoil a great work for a small one; 2nd, because the chorus is constructed on a scale which does not fit into the limits of an ordinary cantata; 3rd, because it is highly improbable that, of five Quinquagesima cantatas which Bach wrote, he should have composed no less than four between 1723 and 1730. We must conclude from all this that, between the writing of the first and second sets of parts of the St. John Passion, Bach must have composed another Passion, a theory which is confirmed by the fact that a text for a Passion exists, written in 1725, by Picander, who had already worked for Bach. Having got so far we can fix the date of the first performance of the St. John Passion with tolerable exactitude.

Bach wrote in all five Passions; the St. Matthew Passion was composed in 1729, the St. Mark in 1731, the St. Luke in Bach's very earliest time, probably during his first years at Weimar. Of course the first Passion music conducted by Bach at Leipzig was his own composition. It cannot have been the St. Luke Passion, since Bach would not have made his first appearance in Leipzig with an immature and youthful work, nor would he under any circumstances have repeated it without retouching it, and it did not in fact undergo this process till after the performance of the St. Mark Passion in 1731 (see ante, p. 708). There remain then only the St. John and the lost Passion music. If this lost work was that performed in 1724—setting aside for the moment its probable identity with that of which Picander wrote the text in 1725—we must assign the St. John Passion to a date prior to the Leipzig period. It cannot have been written for Cöthen, because Bach had not to provide any church music there, and Passion music was not usual in the Protestant churches. It bears at the first glance a stamp of maturity and distinction beyond those of the Weimar time.

We must also give due weight to the connection between the St. John Passion and the cantata "Du wahrer Gott." Now, a multitude of clear indications render it almost certain that this cantata was originally composed for performance at Leipzig on Quinquagesima Sunday, 1723 (see ante, p. 679); it closes with the chorale chorus " Christe, du Lamm Gottes." But when Bach determined to compose another cantata for Quinquagesima Sunday, and set this one aside for a time, he transferred this chorus to the St. John Passion, and I have already endeavoured to prove (see ante, p. 679) that this was in fact what happened, and not as Rust assumes (B.-G., V.,[1] p. xix) that the chorale was adopted into the cantata from the Passion, which therefore must have been finished before the cantata. It was in May, 1723, that Bach moved to Leipzig, and if we insist on holding the vague theory that Bach composed the St. John Passion for some other town—for an installation or some other occasion—no alternative remains but to conclude that the St. John Passion was first performed April 7, 1724. For it is improbable that Bach should have written it for any other place when all his energies were claimed by the worthy performance of his new duties in Leipzig, and we have only two settings of the Passion to choose from—of which the fifth, now lost, was the later—while it is certain that, on the first Good Friday of his residence in Leipzig, Bach would have performed a composition of his own.

Of course, it does not necessarily follow that it must have been composed immediately before its performance ; and an investigation of the oldest copies of the parts proves that it was not. The paper on which they are written has the shield and crossed swords watermark, and though he used such paper in Leipzig he does not seem to have done so within the first year and a half (see ante, p. 695) while there is evidence of his having used such paper in Cöthen (see No. 41 of this Appendix). I consider from this that the St. John Passion was sketched when in Cöthen at the same time as " Du wahrer Gott," and, like that, with a view to his removal to Leipzig. The original form of the text also points to a want of time, and it was one main cause of the subsequent remodelling of the whole work. I have already discussed this in the text, p. 520.

Thus, after the first performance in 1724, there was a second in 1727, this is farther confirmed by the circumstance that, as the Passion music was given in the two churches in alternate years, and had taken place in St. Nicholas', in 1724, the performance in 1727 must have been in St. Thomas'. Between these dates came the lost Passion music which, on Picander's account, I have dated 1725. In 1729 came the St. Matthew Passion, and 1731 the St. Mark. We here see the determined effort made by Bach to secure the performance of his works, which required ample space, in the larger church of St. Thomas. The St. Luke Passion must have been performed in 1734 by reason of the general mourning in 1733, when it was the turn for St. Thomas' again, and we may date the third performance of the St. John Passion 1736. Thus Bach would have performed his four Passions in the order of the four Gospels. It is not possible to determine the date of the fourth performance of the St. John Passion; no certain data can be derived from the watermarks in the paper on which the parts were newly written out; and even the time when the earliest score we possess was written out can only be approximately given—it was after the latest copies of the later parts, and so at any rate towards the end of the master's life.

57 (p. 537; this note will also be referred to in Vol. III.). **The Text of the St. Matthew Passion** is to be found in Part II. of Picander's " Ernst-Scherzhaffte und Satyrische Gedichte," p. 101. The year of its production is not given here, nor is there any date on the autograph score; but the printed text is accompanied by a note to the effect that it was written for music for the church of St. Thomas. Still, as this Part II. of the poems came out at Easter, 1729, and the Passion music in 1728 and 1730 was performed in St. Nicholas', while in 1731 Bach brought out his St. Mark Passion (also at St. Thomas'— the text is in Part III. of the poems, 1732); this is undoubtedly the year of the performance. It is certain that it was not already before the public in 1727, because in that year Picander published Part I. of his poems, and would of course have included it.

The date of the second performance of the work in its extended form can only be approximately discovered. The first state of the score is not an autograph, but in Kirnberger's writing, a copy preserved in the Library of the Joachimsthal Gymnasium at Berlin, and the date of this copy can be approximately ascertained.

Kirnberger, who was born at Saalfeld, in Thuringia, in 1721, left his native town to study music under J. Peter Kellner, of Gräfenrode and in 1738 went to advance his studies first to Sondershausen and then— by the advice of Heinrich Nikolaus Gerber—to Leipzig to learn from Bach. He was his most assiduous and devoted pupil from 1739 to 1741; he then went abroad and only returned in 1751, after Bach's death. Hence 1741 must be the latest date for his copy, and probably 1739 is the earliest. For, even if the St. Matthew score should have come under his ken through the intervention of Kellner or Gerber, is it likely that, as their pupil, he should have been competent to understand it? Is it not more likely that his copying out so extensive a work is evidence of his enthusiasm, and of the close intimacy between him and his master? Certain circumstances contribute an element of certainty to these views. The paper on which Kirnberger wrote is the same as that which Bach often used for his first copies, and is of so unusual a character that we cannot suppose Kirnberger to have met with it accidentally elsewhere. The watermarks here given—

are also found in Bach's score of the cantata "O ewiges Feuer," in the chorus "O Jesu Christ mein's Lebens Licht," and in the autograph of a Latin Christmas hymn constructed on the Gloria of the B minor Mass. Kirnberger may even have written out the score in Bach's own house, if, like some other pupils, he resided there. The St. Matthew Passion could only be performed in St. Thomas' on account of the large scale of the work, and it came to St. Thomas' turn in 1740, so that the revised form of this work cannot have been performed before 1740 at earliest ; this might suggest that Kirnberger had made his copy in the previous year. Still there are certain facts which make it probable that it was not made before 1741. Kirnberger, who went through a complete course of composition, cannot have been introduced to such a work till the end of the course ; moreover, there exists a St. John cantata by J. G. Goldberg, who was also Bach's pupil just at this time ("Durch die herzliche Barmherzigkeit unsers Gottes," score and parts in the Berlin.Library), and the autograph parts are on similar paper to that of Kirnberger's copy. From this the earliest date of the revision would be 1742. On examining the paper and writing of the autograph with other autographs by Bach, we find a resemblance between the original parts and the autograph clean copy of the *Ricercar* in six parts out of the "Musikalisches Opfer," preserved in the Berlin Library. This work was written in 1747, and according to this the revision of the St. Matthew Passion was not made till 1746 or even 1748.

There is a discrepancy in time between these results and a date given by Marpurg (in Legende einiger Musikheiligen, Cöln, 1786, p. 62). Friedemann Bach at Halle was commissioned to compose a serenata in 1749 (see Bach, F., in the index to Marpurg's Legende), and had made use of some airs out of " a certain highly artistic Passion oratorio." When the serenata was performed " there was among the audience a cantor of Saxony, not far from Leipzig, to whom the parodied airs were well known." Through him it came out that the airs were not new at all—" far from it, being at least thirty years old, and taken from the Passion of a certain great master of double counterpoint." Though Sebastian Bach is not named, the whole story leaves no doubt that it was a Passion music by him. But which? This we cannot infer from Marpurg's narrative, but if the date is seriously meant it must have been a work composed before 1719, and this date does not correspond with either of the known five Passions. My opinion is that no importance attaches to the number of "thirty years." It would seem as though Marpurg himself was not clear as to which of the Passions Friedemann had taken such a liberty with, and his saying " at least thirty years " shows that he did not intend to give an exact date.

58 (p. 591). **The Easter Oratorio** exists in three forms. The first we know from the original parts; the second in the autograph score and a few parts belonging to it; the third, again, only from some autograph parts copied out later. The score supplies the most exact data for the chronology. The watermark in the front half sheet is this:—

and in the back half sheet an M surrounded by arabesques. Both these marks recur in the autograph score of the St. John's Cantata " Freue dich, erlöste Schaar." This is a remodelled form of a secular composition "Angenehmes Wiederau," which was performed September 28, 1737. But the watermark in the autograph of the secular work is different, we have there—

But from various experience I find that such a variation, in detail, does not imply a radical difference in the character and manufacture of the paper, and is less important here, as the other watermark, shown above, is exactly the same in both. Another MS. helps to prove that this paper was in use in 1737; namely, a petition addressed by Bach to the King-Elector, October 18, 1737, on the occasion of his quarrel with Ernesti. Hence, we may argue that the St. John's Cantata was written immediately after the secular cantata, and so for June 24, 1738; and consequently, that the score of the Easter Oratorio was written for Easter Day, April 6, 1738. Among the parts which represent the oldest state of the Oratorio, and which have the shield and crossed swords watermark, we find a continuo part, and on the last page of this is the beginning—subsequently crossed out—of the Cantata "Bleib bei uns." This was written for the second day of Easter; thus it is clear that the copyists were employed on it and on the Easter Oratorio at the same time, and perhaps at the same table; whence we may fairly conclude that the two works were composed for the same Easter-tide. The watermark of the Cantata "Bleib bei uns" is a half moon; Bach began using paper of this description in 1735. If, then, the revision of the work, as it stands in the score, was made in 1738, the copying of the older parts and the antecedent composition of the Oratorio must have taken place within the two or three years preceding. It cannot be assigned to 1737, because the revision was no doubt undertaken with a view to a performance, and it can hardly be supposed that Bach would repeat the same music at an interval of only a year. Thus probability points to the year 1736 as that of its composition.

The latest set of parts, finally, in which we have the third state of the Oratorio, are on paper with the watermarks of an eagle and HR (H I R); this paper has, till now, never been found to have been used by Bach excepting in 1734 (see ante, p. 699), and, if this is to be considered as final, any contradictory evidence is, of course, useless. We have here an irreconcilable discrepancy. Still, it may be observed that the same watermark also occurs in one single part-sheet of the Cantata "Gelobet sie der Herr," which must be attributed to the year 1732 (see ante, p. 702), so that it is not an immutable landmark. Thus, as all the strongest probabilities are in favour of the autograph score having been written after 1737, since the paper on which that is written can, on various grounds, be shown to belong to that date, and as it is also probable that the oldest part-copies were not made before 1735—and these two probabilities harmonise as to date—we must found the chronology of the work on them, and assume that, by chance, some old paper was used for the latest part-copies.

59 (p. 595). **On Bach's Motetts.** In the Necrology, p. 168, we find, as No. 4 of the list of Bach's unprinted works, "Einige zweychörige Moteten." Forkel, on the other hand, writes, p. 61, "*Viele* ein-und zweychörige Motetten," and farther on informs us that, of the motetts for double chorus, eight or ten still remained in existence, but in the hands of different possessors; and, at p. 36, he says that

Bach wrote motetts for single, double, and more choirs ("ein- zwey-und mehrchörige"). We must suppose that Forkel was not talking at random, and, therefore, that several more motetts have been lost, or have not come to light. We certainly, at present, know of none for three choirs, for instance; and even if we accept all of those for two, which are known under Bach's name, they fall short of the highest number given by Forkel. But some of these are certainly spurious, or at least doubtful. At any rate, the score published in 1819, by Breitkopf and Härtel, of the Motett "Lob und Ehre" is not genuine, though it afterwards was republished as No. 3 in the new edition of Schicht's collection, after the Motett " " Ich lasse dich nicht " had been rejected as being by Joh. Christoph Bach. The fact that it bears Bach's name in a MS. copy in the Gotthold Library at Königsberg (No. 13569, 2) proves little, since the copies of Bach's motetts in this collection appear to have been made by Schicht.

The Motett "Lob und Ehre" is full of the grossest musical blunders, and it is difficult to imagine how it can so long have passed for Bach's work. In the collection of Herr Hauser (Kammersänger), of Carlsruhe, the same motett is to be found in score and two parts, as a composition by Georg Gottfried Wagner, whom we may more easily suppose to be the author. (Wagner, born in 1698, was a St. Thomas' scholar from 1712—1719; studied theology till 1726, and was still a performer in Bach's choir from 1723—26, then he became Cantor at Plauen. It is easy to understand from this that the work should frequently remind us of Bach, whom Wagner evidently took as his model).

The double chorus motett "Jauchzet dem Herrn alle Welt" is also in part certainly spurious; but it is mentioned in the catalogue of Emanuel Bach's property under the heading of Seb. Bach's com-positions, p. 73, as "*Motetto:* Jauchzet dem Herrn alle Welt. Für 8 Singstimme und Fundament, in 2 Chören. In Partitur." This MS. is now in the Berlin Library; in the right hand bottom corner of the first page is the name J. G. Parlaw (Parlaw seems to have been a musician of Hamburg; the name occurs on MSS. in the Library of the Academy for Singing at Berlin which formerly belonged to Pölchau. Hilgenfeldt says, p. 112, that this motett was edited by J. S. Döring, and published by Kollmann, Leipzig, but I have not seen a copy). The motett is in three subjects, of which the middle one is the chorale chorus out of the cantata "Gottlob, nun geht das Jahr," but with the fifth verse of the hymn instead of the first, so this is in fact Sebastian's work. The third movement, an "Amen, Lob und Ehre und Weisheit und Dank," for double choir, is to be found in Röchlitz's publication "Sammlung vorzüglicher Gesangstücke," Mainz, Schotts Söhne, 1835, Vol. III., p. 66, where it is given as a separate piece by Telemann; and that it is actually by Telemann, and certainly not by Seb. Bach, any one can see who knows the style of the two men. The genuineness of the first must remain doubtful, for though it bears unmistakable traces of Telemann's hand, it has a certain breadth of outline, and that richness of harmony and certainty of part treatment which are peculiar to Bach (see Vol. I., p. 633). I think it probable that it was patched together by Emanuel Bach out of heterogeneous elements; but the title in the catalogue is not decisive, since it was not compiled till after Em. Bach's death.

Sebastian's Bach's compositions have often been tampered with in this way. At the Academy for Singing, in Berlin, there is a Christmas motett in D major for four voices, "Kündlich gross ist das gottselige Geheimniss," with figured bass, and a long instrumental interlude which was probably played originally by violins and bass. Professor A. W. Bach, of Berlin, died 1869, also had a MS. copy of this work. Zelter arranged this for a double chorus, and gave the interlude to a soprano and alto soli above a figured bass, and in a note at the end, dated December 31, 1805, he says this piece is by the great Sebastian Bach, and originally set with instruments. This however is certainly not the case; the smooth flowing style and lack of richness of harmony point to Graun, of whose chorus "Christus hat uns ein Vorbild gelassen" it frequently reminds us; indeed, the venerable musician, Professor Grell, informs me that it was formerly ascribed to Graun. But appended to it are two interludes really by J. Seb. Bach, one from the great Magnificat, "Vom Himmel hoch," transposed into D major, and "Freut euch und jubilirt," set in A major; in the second the continuo has been given to a bass voice.

The motett "Ich lasse dich Nicht" was also lengthened by the addition of a chorale set by J. Seb. Bach (see Vol. I., Appendix A., No. 6).

60 (p. 600). I found the five-part motett "Nun danket alle Gott" in a very inaccurate, but—so far as I know—unique, MS. in a volume in the Gotthold Library at Königsberg (No. 13569), containing also the motetts "Komm Jesu komm" and "Lob und Ehre," all written by the same hand. It may have been copied in about 1800, and probably belonged to Schicht. The title is "3 Motetten | von | J. S. Bach." It is expressly added with regard to the last two that they are by J. Seb. Bach (which I have shown to be incorrect as regards the last, see ante, p. 716), but this is simply called "Motett | Nun danket alle Gott." But the title of the volume proves that it was regarded as Bach's work by the writer of this copy, and from internal evidence it is the one whose genuineness we have least reason to doubt. The final chorale has the same bass, two notes excepted, as Bach's chorale-subject, reprinted by Erk as No. 270 of his collection; but the middle parts move rather more freely in places, though without affecting the harmony, so that they are essentially identical, though the copy according to Erk seems rather more ornate, as if for a different purpose. The MS. no doubt came from Leipzig, as shown by this among other proofs; over the chorale "Gott Vater, dir sei Preis," in the motett "Lob und Ehre," it is noted: "Aus No. 584 Altes Gesb. O Gott du frommer Gott," and this hymn is to be found in the Leipzig Hymn-book, No. 584.

61 (p. 620). **The Cöthen Secular Cantata** is an autograph MS. in upright folio, and on the cover is written, in another but antique writing : " Sechs Bogen starckes Fragment einer eigenhändigen Cantate von Joh. Sebastian Bach auf das Geburtsfest Leopolds, Fürsten zu Anhalt-Cöthen" (six sheets, being part of an autograph cantata by Joh. Seb. Bach for the birthday of Leopold Prince of Anhalt-Cöthen). Below this in a different hand ("Durch Tausch anderer Manuscripte von D. Pölchau, in Berlin erhalten. D. Fst.") [Obtained by exchange of other MSS. from D. Pölchau.]

D. Fst. is Dr. Feurstein, formerly an autograph collector at Pirna, and after his death it was acquired by the father of the present owner. The watermark is the wild man and fir tree (see ante, p. 679), and the writing is evidently that of a mere sketch, hasty, abridged, small, and full of corrections. For the repeats the bars only are marked off and left empty, to be filled up subsequently. The last page is blank, and on the foregoing page is a little addition sum in money, which no doubt relates to some of Bach's pecuniary affairs. The MS. begins with the second half of a tenor aria which closes with an indication of *da capo*. The principal key—as may be gathered from the sacred cantata which was altered from it, " Ein Herz, das seinen Jesum "—was B flat major, and the cantata closes with a four-part air in the same key. Since the fragment which remains is of considerable length, almost exceeding that of an ordinary cantata, the tenor aria, with perhaps an introductory recitative, was probably the first movement and no more than a sheet of the MS. may have been lost. The text (which the curious reader will find at full length in the German edition of this work) is in honour and praise of the Prince and his family, and the second recitative appeals to the " happy land " to contemplate the prudence and enlightenment of one princess and the " crown of virtue " of the other.

The second number was a recitative, and must have begun on the lower staves of the lost sheets, being continued on the first of those remaining. It is a dialogue between alto and tenor soli, no doubt as allegorical personages. The third number is a duet between alto and tenor in E flat major common time. Number 4 is the second recitative, and the next is an alto aria in G minor common time ; then follows another recitative for alto and tenor, and then the finale, which is in the Italian aria form, and consists of 418 bars in 3-8 time. In the second portion of this finale the alto and tenor stand out from the general four-part background in various places in duet, and then retire and mingle with it again. These were in fact the two solo parts of the cantata, as is made clear by their not having precisely the same words ; the alto sings *Gnade*—Mercy—where the tenor has *Segen*—Blessing. The alto and tenor being intended for solo voices, it is evident that the whole work was meant to be sung in single parts, not in chorus. The first words of the text, as well as those of the foregoing recitative, are written under the corresponding words of the altered form.

It is, however, perfectly clear from the character of the text that the statement on the cover, as to the work having been composed for Prince Leopold's birthday, is founded in error. The text, "Bedencke nur, beglücktes Land" (Reflect, O Happy Land!), is a guide to the chronology, for it contains allusions to all the members of the royal family then living. Leopold himself, the reigning prince; his brother, Prince August Ludwig; their youngest sister, Princess Christiana Charlotte (Eleonore Wilhelmine, the elder sister, had married in 1716, Duke Ernst August of Saxe-Weimar); and, finally, the princess. The question is, whom are we to understand by *the princess?* If Prince Leopold's wife is intended, the cantata can only have been written between December 11, 1721, and January 13, 1722, for Leopold was married on the former date, and on the latter, Prince Ernst August, whose wife, however, is not mentioned at all; moreover, it must be the first wife of Prince Leopold who is alluded to, since on September 21, 1722, she had a daughter, who certainly would not have been omitted. From all this we should be inclined to date this cantata somewhere about the beginning of 1722. But, on the other hand, the attributes of "prudence and enlightenment" are far more proper to Gisela Agnes, the prince's mother, than to Leopold's first wife, who died very young, and was eulogised for her gentleness and patience. And if Gisela Agnes is meant by "the princess," as I am convinced is the case, the cantata can only have been written between the Autumn of 1717 and the end of 1721.

62 (p. 631). **The date of the performances of "Schleicht Spielende Wellen"** is founded, 1st, on the allusions in the recitatives; 2nd, on the subsequent alterations in these portions of the text of the recitative, and in the title to the score; 3rd, on the connection between the score and the parts; 4th, on the watermarks in the original MSS. In the text of the bass recitative (see p. 27, &c., of the B.-G. score) we find the following allusions and inferences, which help to fix the chronology: 1st, the words on p. 56, Sop. Rec., "To-day we see the longed-for day, on which our heart's desire, the gracious Augustus was bestowed on us and the world," assure us that the cantata was composed, as the title-page tells us, for the King's birthday; this fixes the day as October 7; 2nd, on p. 27, the Bass Rec. says:—"*My stream, so lately like Cocytus flowing and bearing corpses,*" &c., referring to some recent carnage in Poland, or somewhere on the banks of the Vistula, where King Augustus had remained the master of the field. This only agrees with the year 1734, when the bloody battle of Cracow was fought in April, and the siege of Dantzig was carried on from April till June. In 1733 the enemy had not yet been reduced, and after 1735 peace reigned on the shores of the Vistula; 3rd time, p. 33., Ten. Rec., it appears that the king was in Saxony when the cantata was written—"*Blessed be thou, O Vistula, if only thou respect my wish, and take not my king from me again;*" but on p. 55 we find that his

departure was imminent. "*I* (*the Elbe*) *feel the loss bitterly, but thy* (*the Vistula's*) *advantage over-rules my will.*" In fact, the king started for Poland, November 3, 1734, and did not return till August 7, 1736 (see Mittag, op. cit., pp. 490 and 612) ; 4th, at p. 47, the Sop. Rec.:—"*I am filled with delight* * * *my nymphs rejoice, and at our hero's coming we will dance and play,*" implies that the cantata was performed soon after the king's return to Leipzig, and we know that this was on October 2, 1734.

The alterations made in the text later all refer to the passages here quoted, and in them we can clearly trace the attempt to fit the allusions to somewhat different circumstances. The cantata was no longer intended for a birthday, but for a *fête* or name-day, August 3, and the recitative, on p. 56, had to be altered accordingly ; the king, too, was in Poland, involving a change in the text at p. 33—"*My king is taken from me again.*" In 1736 the king had not returned from Poland—as has been said—by August 3, and later in Bach's life, in 1748, he again spent his name-day in Poland (see Fürstenau, Zur Geschichte der musik und des Theaters am Hofe zu Dresden, II., p. 260), but this year, for reasons presently to be given, is quite out of the question. The title to the autograph score is exactly as follows, and I give it to correct and supplement the preface to the B.-G. edition, XX.[2]: "Drama auf Hohem Geburths —(" Nahmens " written above) Fest Augusti $\frac{3}{3}$ Regis Poloniarum unterthänigst aufgeführet von J. S. Bach." (Misprinted ? *Poloniorum* in the B.-G. ed.)

Rust has already pointed out in this preface that the score is a clean copy and gives the best readings for the parts. I agree in this, and even believe that the progression of the continuo on p. 18 of the score is the better of the two, and ought to have been included in the B.-G. edition. At the same time, the idea that the work is a remodelled form of older compositions with a different text seems to me very doubtful from the highly characteristic style of the first chorus. The watermark in the autograph score is a man on horseback, blowing a horn ; this mark, which we never meet with again in Bach's MSS. of music, recurs in three documents addressed by Bach to the Leipzig Town Council, dated August 13, 15, and 19, 1736 (see ante, p. 697) ; and as the name-day of the king was August 3, and the year 1736 is the only one besides 1748 which agrees with the alterations made in the text, this score must have been written in the summer of 1736. Since the first performance must have been on October 7, 1734, it is probable that Bach copied out the older score, and took the opportunity of making such alterations as he thought desirable, while the parts still existing are transcribed directly from the older score. Nor does the fact that the Cantata still bears the original title ascribing its use to the king's birthday contradict this view ; he may have wished to preserve the remembrance of the first purpose of the work, or it may have been a mere oversight. Several corrections and improvements and the omission, from the score of whole sections of the B minor aria (whereas the parts, on the other hand, have always contained those readings which were ultimately fixed upon) can be accounted for by an attempt, subsequently abandoned, to substitute new readings for the older ones when writing out a fresh score. Still, the part copies lead us to a singular issue. To all appearance, although they undoubtedly contain the older reading, they have been written later than the score we now possess. The watermarks, for instance, are the same as in the autograph score of " Angenehmes Wiederau," which was performed September 28, 1737, and in a petition addressed to the king, October 18, 1737 (in the town archives at Leipzig). Judging from this Bach must have had the parts copied out afresh in 1737, and, for some unknown reason, from the old score. This brings us to the question whether Bach repeated the performance of the Cantata both in 1736 and 1737, and whether for the name-day each time—on which it may be noted that the king was staying in Leipzig from September 29, 1736, for a few days. Bach himself reveals a certain vagueness as to the purpose of the work, since the alterations in the text stand side by side with the older words, so that either one or the other could be used according to circumstances; and the same holds good with regard to the title. The upshot is that the Cantata " Schleicht spielende Wellen " was composed October 7, 1734, and that Bach intended to repeat it August 3, 1736, and that the repetition must have taken place in 1737 at latest—either August 3 or 7—but probably it was in 1736.

63 (p. 473). **The autograph score of the Coffee Cantata** is in the Royal Library at Berlin ; the autograph parts in the Royal Court Library (Hofbibliothek) in Berlin. The watermark is M A (see ante, p. 661). The text first occurs in Part III. of Picander's poems, p. 564, the last piece in the volume ; so that, as the preface is dated February 18, 1732, it must have been written at latest at the beginning of that year, and as the " schertzhafften Gedichte " in this Vol. are arranged in chronological order we can hardly date it much before. It does not, of course, follow that the music was written in the same year, but the watermark shows that it cannot well be of later date than 1736. If Bach intended it for use in his own home circle, the composition of the music probably followed hard on that of the words, for this was the most flourishing period of Bach's family band, while his sons, Wilhelm Friedemann and Philipp Emanuel, were still living at home. It is certain that the words of the last recitative and finale are not by Picander, for if he had added them in obedience to Bach's wish they would have appeared in the collected edition of his works, 1748; but here also the text ends with Lieschen's second aria (p. 1244).

A CATALOG OF SELECTED
DOVER BOOKS
IN ALL FIELDS OF INTEREST

A CATALOG OF SELECTED DOVER
BOOKS IN ALL FIELDS OF INTEREST

CONCERNING THE SPIRITUAL IN ART, Wassily Kandinsky. Pioneering work by father of abstract art. Thoughts on color theory, nature of art. Analysis of earlier masters. 12 illustrations. 80pp. of text. 5⅜ × 8½.
23411-8 Pa. $3.95

ANIMALS: 1,419 Copyright-Free Illustrations of Mammals, Birds, Fish, Insects, etc., Jim Harter (ed.). Clear wood engravings present, in extremely lifelike poses, over 1,000 species of animals. One of the most extensive pictorial sourcebooks of its kind. Captions. Index. 284pp. 9 × 12.
23766-4 Pa. $12.95

CELTIC ART: The Methods of Construction, George Bain. Simple geometric techniques for making Celtic interlacements, spirals, Kells-type initials, animals, humans, etc. Over 500 illustrations. 160pp. 9 × 12. (USO)
22923-8 Pa. $9.95

AN ATLAS OF ANATOMY FOR ARTISTS, Fritz Schider. Most thorough reference work on art anatomy in the world. Hundreds of illustrations, including selections from works by Vesalius, Leonardo, Goya, Ingres, Michelangelo, others. 593 illustrations. 192pp. 7⅛ × 10¼.
20241-0 Pa. $9.95

CELTIC HAND STROKE-BY-STROKE (Irish Half-Uncial from "The Book of Kells"): An Arthur Baker Calligraphy Manual, Arthur Baker. Complete guide to creating each letter of the alphabet in distinctive Celtic manner. Covers hand position, strokes, pens, inks, paper, more. Illustrated. 48pp. 8¼ × 11.
24336-2 Pa. $3.95

EASY ORIGAMI, John Montroll. Charming collection of 32 projects (hat, cup, pelican, piano, swan, many more) specially designed for the novice origami hobbyist. Clearly illustrated easy-to-follow instructions insure that even beginning papercrafters will achieve successful results. 48pp. 8¼ × 11.
27298-2 Pa. $2.95

THE COMPLETE BOOK OF BIRDHOUSE CONSTRUCTION FOR WOOD-WORKERS, Scott D. Campbell. Detailed instructions, illustrations, tables. Also data on bird habitat and instinct patterns. Bibliography. 3 tables. 63 illustrations in 15 figures. 48pp. 5¼ × 8½.
24407-5 Pa. $1.95

BLOOMINGDALE'S ILLUSTRATED 1886 CATALOG: Fashions, Dry Goods and Housewares, Bloomingdale Brothers. Famed merchants' extremely rare catalog depicting about 1,700 products: clothing, housewares, firearms, dry goods, jewelry, more. Invaluable for dating, identifying vintage items. Also, copyright-free graphics for artists, designers. Co-published with Henry Ford Museum & Green-field Village. 160pp. 8¼ × 11.
25780-0 Pa. $9.95

HISTORIC COSTUME IN PICTURES, Braun & Schneider. Over 1,450 costumed figures in clearly detailed engravings—from dawn of civilization to end of 19th century. Captions. Many folk costumes. 256pp. 8⅜ × 11¾.
23150-X Pa. $11.95

STICKLEY CRAFTSMAN FURNITURE CATALOGS, Gustav Stickley and L. & J. G. Stickley. Beautiful, functional furniture in two authentic catalogs from 1910. 594 illustrations, including 277 photos, show settles, rockers, armchairs, reclining chairs, bookcases, desks, tables. 183pp. 6½ × 9¼. 23838-5 Pa. $9.95

AMERICAN LOCOMOTIVES IN HISTORIC PHOTOGRAPHS: 1858 to 1949, Ron Ziel (ed.). A rare collection of 126 meticulously detailed official photographs, called "builder portraits," of American locomotives that majestically chronicle the rise of steam locomotive power in America. Introduction. Detailed captions. xi + 129pp. 9 × 12. 27393-8 Pa. $12.95

AMERICA'S LIGHTHOUSES: An Illustrated History, Francis Ross Holland, Jr. Delightfully written, profusely illustrated fact-filled survey of over 200 American lighthouses since 1716. History, anecdotes, technological advances, more. 240pp. 8 × 10¾. 25576-X Pa. $11.95

TOWARDS A NEW ARCHITECTURE, Le Corbusier. Pioneering manifesto by founder of "International School." Technical and aesthetic theories, views of industry, economics, relation of form to function, "mass-production split" and much more. Profusely illustrated. 320pp. 6⅛ × 9¼. (USO) 25023-7 Pa. $9.95

HOW THE OTHER HALF LIVES, Jacob Riis. Famous journalistic record, exposing poverty and degradation of New York slums around 1900, by major social reformer. 100 striking and influential photographs. 233pp. 10 × 7⅞.
22012-5 Pa $10.95

FRUIT KEY AND TWIG KEY TO TREES AND SHRUBS, William M. Harlow. One of the handiest and most widely used identification aids. Fruit key covers 120 deciduous and evergreen species; twig key 160 deciduous species. Easily used. Over 300 photographs. 126pp. 5⅜ × 8½. 20511-8 Pa. $3.95

COMMON BIRD SONGS, Dr. Donald J. Borror. Songs of 60 most common U.S. birds: robins, sparrows, cardinals, bluejays, finches, more—arranged in order of increasing complexity. Up to 9 variations of songs of each species.
Cassette and manual 99911-4 $8.95

ORCHIDS AS HOUSE PLANTS, Rebecca Tyson Northen. Grow cattleyas and many other kinds of orchids—in a window, in a case, or under artificial light. 63 illustrations. 148pp. 5⅜ × 8½. 23261-1 Pa. $4.95

MONSTER MAZES, Dave Phillips. Masterful mazes at four levels of difficulty. Avoid deadly perils and evil creatures to find magical treasures. Solutions for all 32 exciting illustrated puzzles. 48pp. 8¼ × 11. 26005-4 Pa. $2.95

MOZART'S DON GIOVANNI (DOVER OPERA LIBRETTO SERIES), Wolfgang Amadeus Mozart. Introduced and translated by Ellen H. Bleiler. Standard Italian libretto, with complete English translation. Convenient and thoroughly portable—an ideal companion for reading along with a recording or the performance itself. Introduction. List of characters. Plot summary. 121pp. 5¼ × 8½.
24944-1 Pa. $2.95

TECHNICAL MANUAL AND DICTIONARY OF CLASSICAL BALLET, Gail Grant. Defines, explains, comments on steps, movements, poses and concepts. 15-page pictorial section. Basic book for student, viewer. 127pp. 5⅜ × 8½.
21843-0 Pa. $4.95

BRASS INSTRUMENTS: Their History and Development, Anthony Baines. Authoritative, updated survey of the evolution of trumpets, trombones, bugles, cornets, French horns, tubas and other brass wind instruments. Over 140 illustrations and 48 music examples. Corrected and updated by author. New preface. Bibliography. 320pp. 5⅜ × 8½. 27574-4 Pa. $9.95

HOLLYWOOD GLAMOR PORTRAITS, John Kobal (ed.). 145 photos from 1926–49. Harlow, Gable, Bogart, Bacall; 94 stars in all. Full background on photographers, technical aspects. 160pp. 8⅜ × 11¼. 23352-9 Pa. $11.95

MAX AND MORITZ, Wilhelm Busch. Great humor classic in both German and English. Also 10 other works: "Cat and Mouse," "Plisch and Plumm," etc. 216pp. 5⅜ × 8½. 20181-3 Pa. $5.95

THE RAVEN AND OTHER FAVORITE POEMS, Edgar Allan Poe. Over 40 of the author's most memorable poems: "The Bells," "Ulalume," "Israfel," "To Helen," "The Conqueror Worm," "Eldorado," "Annabel Lee," many more. Alphabetic lists of titles and first lines. 64pp. 5³/₁₆ × 8¼. 26685-0 Pa. $1.00

SEVEN SCIENCE FICTION NOVELS, H. G. Wells. The standard collection of the great novels. Complete, unabridged. First Men in the Moon, Island of Dr. Moreau, War of the Worlds, Food of the Gods, Invisible Man, Time Machine, In the Days of the Comet. Total of 1,015pp. 5⅜ × 8½. (USO) 20264-X Clothbd. $29.95

AMULETS AND SUPERSTITIONS, E. A. Wallis Budge. Comprehensive discourse on origin, powers of amulets in many ancient cultures: Arab, Persian, Babylonian, Assyrian, Egyptian, Gnostic, Hebrew, Phoenician, Syriac, etc. Covers cross, swastika, crucifix, seals, rings, stones, etc. 584pp. 5⅜ × 8½. 23573-4 Pa. $12.95

RUSSIAN STORIES/PYCCKNE PACCKA3bI: A Dual-Language Book, edited by Gleb Struve. Twelve tales by such masters as Chekhov, Tolstoy, Dostoevsky, Pushkin, others. Excellent word-for-word English translations on facing pages, plus teaching and study aids, Russian/English vocabulary, biographical/critical introductions, more. 416pp. 5⅜ × 8½. 26244-8 Pa. $8.95

PHILADELPHIA THEN AND NOW: 60 Sites Photographed in the Past and Present, Kenneth Finkel and Susan Oyama. Rare photographs of City Hall, Logan Square, Independence Hall, Betsy Ross House, other landmarks juxtaposed with contemporary views. Captures changing face of historic city. Introduction. Captions. 128pp. 8¼ × 11. 25790-8 Pa. $9.95

AIA ARCHITECTURAL GUIDE TO NASSAU AND SUFFOLK COUNTIES, LONG ISLAND, The American Institute of Architects, Long Island Chapter, and the Society for the Preservation of Long Island Antiquities. Comprehensive, well-researched and generously illustrated volume brings to life over three centuries of Long Island's great architectural heritage. More than 240 photographs with authoritative, extensively detailed captions. 176pp. 8¼ × 11. 26946-9 Pa. $14.95

NORTH AMERICAN INDIAN LIFE: Customs and Traditions of 23 Tribes, Elsie Clews Parsons (ed.). 27 fictionalized essays by noted anthropologists examine religion, customs, government, additional facets of life among the Winnebago, Crow, Zuni, Eskimo, other tribes. 480pp. 6⅛ × 9¼. 27377-6 Pa. $10.95

PERSPECTIVE FOR ARTISTS, Rex Vicat Cole. Depth, perspective of sky and sea, shadows, much more, not usually covered. 391 diagrams, 81 reproductions of drawings and paintings. 279pp. 5⅜ × 8½. 22487-2 Pa. $6.95

DRAWING THE LIVING FIGURE, Joseph Sheppard. Innovative approach to artistic anatomy focuses on specifics of surface anatomy, rather than muscles and bones. Over 170 drawings of live models in front, back and side views, and in widely varying poses. Accompanying diagrams. 177 illustrations. Introduction. Index. 144pp. 8⅜ × 11¼. 26723-7 Pa. $8.95

GOTHIC AND OLD ENGLISH ALPHABETS: 100 Complete Fonts, Dan X. Solo. Add power, elegance to posters, signs, other graphics with 100 stunning copyright-free alphabets: Blackstone, Dolbey, Germania, 97 more—including many lower-case, numerals, punctuation marks. 104pp. 8⅛ × 11. 24695-7 Pa. $8.95

HOW TO DO BEADWORK, Mary White. Fundamental book on craft from simple projects to five-bead chains and woven works. 106 illustrations. 142pp. 5⅜ × 8. 20697-1 Pa. $4.95

THE BOOK OF WOOD CARVING, Charles Marshall Sayers. Finest book for beginners discusses fundamentals and offers 34 designs. "Absolutely first rate . . . well thought out and well executed."—E. J. Tangerman. 118pp. 7¾ × 10⅜. 23654-4 Pa. $5.95

ILLUSTRATED CATALOG OF CIVIL WAR MILITARY GOODS: Union Army Weapons, Insignia, Uniform Accessories, and Other Equipment, Schuyler, Hartley, and Graham. Rare, profusely illustrated 1846 catalog includes Union Army uniform and dress regulations, arms and ammunition, coats, insignia, flags, swords, rifles, etc. 226 illustrations. 160pp. 9 × 12. 24939-5 Pa. $10.95

WOMEN'S FASHIONS OF THE EARLY 1900s: An Unabridged Republication of "New York Fashions, 1909," National Cloak & Suit Co. Rare catalog of mail-order fashions documents women's and children's clothing styles shortly after the turn of the century. Captions offer full descriptions, prices. Invaluable resource for fashion, costume historians. Approximately 725 illustrations. 128pp. 8⅜ × 11¼. 27276-1 Pa. $11.95

THE 1912 AND 1915 GUSTAV STICKLEY FURNITURE CATALOGS, Gustav Stickley. With over 200 detailed illustrations and descriptions, these two catalogs are essential reading and reference materials and identification guides for Stickley furniture. Captions cite materials, dimensions and prices. 112pp. 6½ × 9¼. 26676-1 Pa. $9.95

EARLY AMERICAN LOCOMOTIVES, John H. White, Jr. Finest locomotive engravings from early 19th century: historical (1804–74), main-line (after 1870), special, foreign, etc. 147 plates. 142pp. 11⅜ × 8¼. 22772-3 Pa. $10.95

THE TALL SHIPS OF TODAY IN PHOTOGRAPHS, Frank O. Braynard. Lavishly illustrated tribute to nearly 100 majestic contemporary sailing vessels: Amerigo Vespucci, Clearwater, Constitution, Eagle, Mayflower, Sea Cloud, Victory, many more. Authoritative captions provide statistics, background on each ship. 190 black-and-white photographs and illustrations. Introduction. 128pp. 8⅞ × 11¼. 27163-3 Pa. $13.95

THE WIT AND HUMOR OF OSCAR WILDE, Alvin Redman (ed.). More than 1,000 ripostes, paradoxes, wisecracks: Work is the curse of the drinking classes; I can resist everything except temptation; etc. 258pp. 5⅜ × 8½. 20602-5 Pa. $5.95

SHAKESPEARE LEXICON AND QUOTATION DICTIONARY, Alexander Schmidt. Full definitions, locations, shades of meaning in every word in plays and poems. More than 50,000 exact quotations. 1,485pp. 6½ × 9¼. 2-vol. set.
Vol. I: 22726-X Pa. $16.95
Vol. 2: 22727-8 Pa. $15.95

SELECTED POEMS, Emily Dickinson. Over 100 best-known, best-loved poems by one of America's foremost poets, reprinted from authoritative early editions. No comparable edition at this price. Index of first lines. 64pp. 5³⁄₁₆ × 8¼.
26466-1 Pa. $1.00

CELEBRATED CASES OF JUDGE DEE (DEE GOONG AN), translated by Robert van Gulik. Authentic 18th-century Chinese detective novel; Dee and associates solve three interlocked cases. Led to van Gulik's own stories with same characters. Extensive introduction. 9 illustrations. 237pp. 5⅜ × 8½.
23337-5 Pa. $6.95

THE MALLEUS MALEFICARUM OF KRAMER AND SPRENGER, translated by Montague Summers. Full text of most important witchhunter's "bible," used by both Catholics and Protestants. 278pp. 6⅝ × 10. 22802-9 Pa. $11.95

SPANISH STORIES/CUENTOS ESPAÑOLES: A Dual-Language Book, Angel Flores (ed.). Unique format offers 13 great stories in Spanish by Cervantes, Borges, others. Faithful English translations on facing pages. 352pp. 5⅜ × 8½.
25399-6 Pa. $8.95

THE CHICAGO WORLD'S FAIR OF 1893: A Photographic Record, Stanley Appelbaum (ed.). 128 rare photos show 200 buildings, Beaux-Arts architecture, Midway, original Ferris Wheel, Edison's kinetoscope, more. Architectural emphasis; full text. 116pp. 8¼ × 11. 23990-X Pa. $9.95

OLD QUEENS, N.Y., IN EARLY PHOTOGRAPHS, Vincent F. Seyfried and William Asadorian. Over 160 rare photographs of Maspeth, Jamaica, Jackson Heights, and other areas. Vintage views of DeWitt Clinton mansion, 1939 World's Fair and more. Captions. 192pp. 8⅞ × 11. 26358-4 Pa. $12.95

CAPTURED BY THE INDIANS: 15 Firsthand Accounts, 1750–1870, Frederick Drimmer. Astounding true historical accounts of grisly torture, bloody conflicts, relentless pursuits, miraculous escapes and more, by people who lived to tell the tale. 384pp. 5⅜ × 8½. 24901-8 Pa. $8.95

THE WORLD'S GREAT SPEECHES, Lewis Copeland and Lawrence W. Lamm (eds.). Vast collection of 278 speeches of Greeks to 1970. Powerful and effective models; unique look at history. 842pp. 5⅜ × 8½. 20468-5 Pa. $14.95

THE BOOK OF THE SWORD, Sir Richard F. Burton. Great Victorian scholar/adventurer's eloquent, erudite history of the "queen of weapons"—from prehistory to early Roman Empire. Evolution and development of early swords, variations (sabre, broadsword, cutlass, scimitar, etc.), much more. 336pp. 6⅛ × 9¼. 25434-8 Pa. $8.95

THE INFLUENCE OF SEA POWER UPON HISTORY, 1660–1783, A. T. Mahan. Influential classic of naval history and tactics still used as text in war colleges. First paperback edition. 4 maps. 24 battle plans. 640pp. 5⅜ × 8½.
25509-3 Pa. $12.95

THE STORY OF THE TITANIC AS TOLD BY ITS SURVIVORS, Jack Winocour (ed.). What it was really like. Panic, despair, shocking inefficiency, and a little heroism. More thrilling than any fictional account. 26 illustrations. 320pp. 5⅜ × 8½.
20610-6 Pa. $8.95

FAIRY AND FOLK TALES OF THE IRISH PEASANTRY, William Butler Yeats (ed.). Treasury of 64 tales from the twilight world of Celtic myth and legend: "The Soul Cages," "The Kildare Pooka," "King O'Toole and his Goose," many more. Introduction and Notes by W. B. Yeats. 352pp. 5⅜ × 8½.
26941-8 Pa. $8.95

BUDDHIST MAHAYANA TEXTS, E. B. Cowell and Others (eds.). Superb, accurate translations of basic documents in Mahayana Buddhism, highly important in history of religions. The Buddha-karita of Asvaghosha, Larger Sukhavativyuha, more. 448pp. 5⅜ × 8½. ,
25552-2 Pa. $9.95

ONE TWO THREE . . . INFINITY: Facts and Speculations of Science, George Gamow. Great physicist's fascinating, readable overview of contemporary science: number theory, relativity, fourth dimension, entropy, genes, atomic structure, much more. 128 illustrations. Index. 352pp. 5⅜ × 8½.
25664-2 Pa. $8.95

ENGINEERING IN HISTORY, Richard Shelton Kirby, et al. Broad, nontechnical survey of history's major technological advances: birth of Greek science, industrial revolution, electricity and applied science, 20th-century automation, much more. 181 illustrations. ". . . excellent . . ."—Isis. Bibliography. vii + 530pp. 5⅜ × 8¼.
26412-2 Pa. $14.95